Jacob's Ladder and the Tree of Life

American University Studies

Series V
Philosophy

Vol. 14

PETER LANG
New York · Bern · Frankfurt am Main · Paris

Jacob's Ladder and the Tree of Life

Concepts of Hierarchy and the Great Chain of Being

edited by
Marion Leathers Kuntz
and
Paul Grimley Kuntz

PETER LANG
New York · Bern · Frankfurt am Main · Paris

Library of Congress Cataloging-in-Publication Data

Jacob's ladder and the tree of life.

(American university studies. Series V, Philosophy ;
vol. 14)
Consists chiefly of papers presented at a program of
the Medieval Institute of Western Michigan University,
Kalamazoo, May 1975.
   Bibliography: p.
   Includes index.
   1. Chain of being (Philosophy)—Congresses.
I. Kuntz, Marion L. (Marion Leathers) II. Kuntz,
Paul Grimley   . III. Series: American
university studies. Series V, Philosophy ; v. 14.
B105.C5J33   1987   111   86-18621
ISBN 0-8204-0233-8
ISSN 0739-6392

CIP-Kurztitelaufnahme der Deutschen Bibliothek

Jacob's ladder and the tree of life : concepts
of hierarchy and the great chain of being / ed.
by Marion L. Kuntz and Paul G. Kuntz. - New York ;
Bern : Frankfurt am Main : Lang, 1987.
   (American university studies ; Ser. 5,
   Philosophy ; Vol. 14)

ISBN 0-8204-0233-8
NE: Kuntz, Marion L. [Hreg.]; American university
studies / 05

Cover illustration:
Charles de Bouelles (Bovillus), *Liber de Intellectu*, 1510.
By permission of the Folger Shakespeare Library,
Washington, D.C.
See also page 312.

© Peter Lang Publishing, Inc., New York 1987

Printed by Weihert-Druck GmbH, Darmstadt (West Germany)

For our esteemed colleagues
Paul Oskar Kristeller
J. Russell Major
Richard Popkin
Gregor Sebba - in memory
Douglas Van Steere
Paul Weiss

TABLE OF CONTENTS

PREFACE

V. HIERARCHY IN THE NINETEENTH AND TWENTIETH CENTURIES AND HIERARCHY REDISCOVERED IN THE EAST BY THE WEST

The Hierarchical Idea of Man and the Cosmos in Emblems

PREFACE

Most of the papers in this series were presented in a program of the Medieval Institute of Western Michigan University. Kalamazoo has proved a welcoming haven for historian of ideas. The time was May, 1975 when we were anticipating publication the very next year, to mark the fortieth anniversary of the publication of Arthur O. Lovejoy's *Great Chain of Being*. We had anticipated early publication in time to mark the decades 1936-1976. But typical difficulties have now forced us to the more conventional, though less Biblical watershed of a fiftieth rather than a fortieth. Perhaps this has proved a happy accident because an interest in the hierarchical structures of the cosmos, persons and their experiences, and societies as well as of sciences, has grown exponentially. We have also written further papers and discovered other pieces of research which fitted the original plan. The publications 1976-1985 amply justify the increasing interest in the issues raised by Lovejoy, and what we still have to learn about our heritage and its destiny excites us to anticipate *The Great Chain of Being After Sixty Years* (1996).

We are grateful to all contributers to our initial and eventual symposium, to our institutions, Georgia State University and Emory University for support, to our secretaries, Carolyn Alexander and Grace Casnel, to our student assistants, Anne Owens and Ivia Cofresi, for assistance in proofreading and indexing. Without the generous help accorded us by Georgia State University in the use of word processor equipment this book would not have come to fruition.

I.

PLATO, ARISTOTLE, ST. AUGUSTINE AND OTHER GREAT THINKERS
WHO FOUNDED AND PERFECTED THE MEDIEVAL WORLD

The Ladder of Thirty Virtues by which the monk may ascend to the welcoming arms of Christ. The highest rung is Faith, Hope and Charity. Many hear the call to perfection, but we see them fall from the steep ascent into the mouth of the beast waiting at the foot of the ladder. From a manuscript of The Heavenly Ladder of John Climacus of Sinai, copied in the year 1081. Garrett Collection of Medieval and Renaissance Manuscripts, Princeton University, and used by permission. The tradition may be studied through John Rupert Martin, The Illustration of the Heavenly Ladder of John Climacus, Princeton, Princeton University Press, 1954.

PAUL G. KUNTZ

A FORMAL PREFACE AND AN INFORMAL CONCLUSION TO
THE GREAT CHAIN OF BEING: THE NECESSITY AND
UNIVERSALITY OF HIERARCHICAL THOUGHT

INTRODUCTION

A. O. Lovejoy's *Great Chain of Being* has, in fifty years since first published in 1936, established itself as a classic in intellectual history and
the masterpiece of the history of ideas movement in the United States. The influence upon scholars in different fields is testimony to its importance. Is
there another work as valuable to students of history and literature, art and
architecture, as well as to theology and philosophy? And the applications of
hierarchy should be made evident by scholars in sociology and political science as well. Our bibliography shows also the concern in logic, mathematics
and natural science.

Lovejoy's appeal is that of splendid historical sweep--from the ancient
Platonists to his own post-Darwinian age. In quick succession he considers the
records of philosophy, theology and literature, but all carefully selected to
show the centrality of the plenitude of the infinite source and the exemplifi-
cation of all possible steps in "unilinear gradation."[1] His work invites development in at least two respects, the one formal and the other informal. Can
the concept of hierarchy be defined other than as "the great chain of being?"
And if so defined, do we find it a living concept beyond the occidental tradition down to the Romantic period? I believe the answer to both questions is
affirmative. At least what appears to me evident is not, as Lovejoy concluded,
that the idea is one to which evolutionary order wrote the epitaph, but that
hierarchical thought is as necessary now as it ever was. That will be the
"Formal Preface." Then comes an "Informal Conclusion" to suggest that hierarchical thought is universal throughout the human race, and has a part in each
tradition.

DEFINING HIERARCHY

It is fairly common to write an article about hierarchy without definition, or to write a book on the great chain of being with a collection of illustrations. Is it not true of all the common ideas of order such as series,
balance, analogy and harmony that these concepts are so common that we may as-

sume agreement about meanings? Is it not then a superfluous scholastic exercise in analysis to arrive at a statement of what is essential and common to
all instances? I have found in Thomas Aquinas a definition of hierarchy that I
would defend as neither too broad nor too narrow, and it amazes me that no one
pauses to admire the logical beauty of this achievement. We find it in Prima
Pars, *Summa Theologica*, as abstracted in the Index of the Leonine Edition:

> Hierarchia est ordo, id est relatio, inter diversos gra-
> dus; non autem ut dicit unum gradum.[2]

I have argued elsewhere in detail that the greatness of medieval thought
is not merely to sum up the past but to point forward to future achievement.
Certainly Thomas is very modern to think of order as a relation, and to recognize the obvious asymmetry of such an ordering relation as above-below or before-after. In general it is the same to say that A is prior to B as that B is
posterior to A. Thus serial order comes in the 19th and 20th centuries to be
defined, in the logic of Whitehead and Russell, as a relation that is asymmetrical, transitive and connected.[3]

If hierarchy is an order, then we must first note the essential characteristics of order. Asymmetry has been defined for two terms, A and B, and
connexity can be stated: either A is prior to B, or B is prior to A, when they
are different terms in an order. Transitivity requires three terms, and Thomas
insists also on at least three grades to have hierarchy. The most lucid way to
make the transition from simple series to hierarchy is to think that if *A* is
greater than *B*, and *B* is greater than *C*, then *A* is greater than *C*. Arithmeti-
cal "greater than" may constitute a simple series as 1, 2, 3, but what more
does "greater than" mean when the "order" is a level (gradus)?

This is much more general than any specific Neo-Platonic vision of the
levels of being. The most recent vigorous defense of the great chain of being,
John N. Findlay's, uses "order" as a definition of hierarchy: "the Three Hypostases ... is a doctrine of *a series* of Principles emerging from one another
...."[4]

We might have a numerical series like 1, 2, 3 in which we could say that
the terms are on the same level. But when we go from arithmetic to algebra,
that is, to *A*, *B*, *C*, we should recognize what hierarchy is about: "non autem
ut dicet unum gradum." "*A*" as *any* number is on a higher level of generality.
Some analyses of hierarchy therefore begin with the conceptualization of mem-

bers of classes, classes, and classes of classes. There are parts of wholes, wholes, and wholes of larger wholes.

Is it equally obvious that wherever we have quantity and quality we have degrees? There is more or less quantitatively and more or less qualitatively. Obviously, with time and space, however we measure these dimensions, we have the ordering relations that may be viewed as an extension of classification in the relation of including-included. Whether we can quantify all qualities and kinds of extension is problematic, so another hierarchical principle is intensity. As with fractions we can always find some quantitative mean, so between any two qualitative degrees, a medium between them. At least when we can construct a linear scale of sound or color, both of which have various dimensions that are continuous.

To give a full account of the kinds of hierarchy demands also that we think of the causal order. There are degrees of power, control or influence that are uppermost in analysis of social institutions.

But "higher than" does not necessarily mean "greater than" in the sense of controlling what is less. "Higher than" may mean "better than" in some value dimension such as more beautiful or morally superior or holier or more completely true. Things are judged to have a higher rank or nobility.

What seems to me so permanently right about medieval philosophy is that in reflecting on order of degree or hierarchy one begins from common sense; for example, St. Anselm and St. Bonaventure begin from the most obvious ranking such as rocks, plants, animals, men. To put it more as they did: some things are, other things are and live, yet other things are and live and think.[5]

We can easily understand the background of thinking on three levels. There is the sky above and the earth below and man finds himself below sky and above earth. Man mediates between the higher and the lower. Man has tendencies in opposite directions, ascending and descending. It is comprehensible that ascending is approaching what is supreme and has all values whereas descending is approaching what is not and has no value. It would make sense to account for the levels from being, but not from nothingness, and in this way the ascent is a return. But if we begin from any extremes, the question is, what is there that is between and which mediates?[6] Even if we considered a dimension horizontally rather than vertically, say the past and future, as does St. Augustine, the structure of experience and language requires the present between past and future.

There must be at least three levels, and a characteristic statement is the higher, the middle, the lower.[7] Sometimes with regard to angels, these are the first hierarchy, the second and the third. But it is not satisfactory to define hierarchy according to its etymology, sacred rule, for this order is earthly as well as heavenly, natural as well as supernatural, human as well as angelic.[8]

St. Thomas comments on the meaning of Jacob's Ladder, a metaphor far more common than the Golden Chain from Homer.[9] Even if he had used the other common picture of degrees, that of the tree of life and of love and of knowledge, it would leave the language open to the rebuke of contemporary analytic philosophy. Is this not merely a semi-artificial language or "the artificialization of natural language?" In this the scholastics in general are said to have followed Aristotle rather than Boethius. If Boethius was excellent in distinguishing nine senses of "in" rather than using some ambiguous verb-like noun like "is," does the topic hierarchy also indicate the similar failure to distinguish different kinds?[10]

If we would follow Lovejoy's account we might be tempted to think that all the kinds of hierarchy were but one vaguely defined chain of being. But this impression fails to recognize the analytic tendency of the medieval scholastic. Some read all the accounts of degrees in Dante, for example, as variations of the metaphysics of light.[11] But others find in Dante a sharp distinction between different principles of degrees: in the relations of church and state, one is higher in dignity, the other in power.[12] We have overemphasized the one ultimate hierarchy, and we have failed to notice the distinctions made. Hence the relevance of analytic questions. These are: how many levels? Is there one relation between levels or several? Is the sequence continuous and of unit links and therefore represented by a chain or line?

One of the most pertinent illustrations of analytic thought is the use of the term *gradus*. In the offices of society the ranking is from noble to vile.

But when Thomas argues from grades or levels in general, he uses this as only one of four kinds, which do not exhaust all the types.

> Invenitur enim in rebus aliquid magis, et minus, et bonum, et verum, et nobile, et sic de aliis hujusmodi.[13]

If we begin from the comparative, in various respects more or less, can we arrive at a highest level, or the superlative? Is there any fixed number of grades beyond three or one principle running through all to account for the kinds?

Thomas' kinds of *gradus*, which would be types of hierarchy, include at least nine, and they vary from the literal steps we climb to the 360° (trecenta sexaginta, qui est numerus graduum caeli, 2 anim. 3_c). He has gone beyond the ecclesiastical and angelic of which Pseudo-Dionysius spoke to, the degrees of life and kinds of life, degrees of family relationship or blood kinship, degrees of closeness or of goodness, degrees of being—and we should add "et sic de aliis hujusmodi."[14] Whether thought is still dominated by the Great Chain of Being or not, we must still use the concept of hierarchical order, that is, of gradation. Thomas used it in many different ways as we do.

Hierarchical thinking is not as easily mocked as the Great Chain of Nothing. "This Scale of Being" observed Dr. Samuel Johnson, "I have demonstrated to be raised by presumptuous Imagination, to rest on Nothing at the Bottom, to lean on Nothing at the Top, and to have Vacuities from step to step through which any Order of Being may Sink into Nihility without any Inconvenience ... to the next Rank above or below it."[15]

But I do not conclude with Lovejoy that this is the "root of the matter" and disposes altogether of "plenitude, continuity, and gradation." Dr. Johnson, to speak only of "grade," ignored the fact that people use the term; the Dictionary takes no note of "grade." There was indeed "degree" and "level," but by 1819 Todd notes it as not yet established. The language recorded in the Oxford English Dictionary is testimony to a necessity of thought.[16] That is, everything cannot be on the same level. Just as St. Thomas listed "gradus" of different sorts, so we might say following the Oxford English Dictionary, that "grade" (or "gradient") is "the amount of inclination to the horizontal; [or] rate of ascent or descent," and just as we must take account of angular measurement, so, also of the "step or stage in a process [or] a step" towards some goal, as in "making the grade." The modern world may not be feudal, but people occupy a rank in a scale, measured no doubt by proficiency. In education we pass through grades, and we judge whether things have such value comparable to the highest grade. There is also degree of intensity by which we judge.

The point I make with regard to "grade" has been argued forcefully in the philosophy of science with regard to the semantics of the term "level." Because of the ambiguity, Mario Bunge finds it necessary to distinguish nine different meanings, as does a lexicon to St. Thomas' usage; yet none of them is dispensable. Contemporary science, without reference to links in a Neo-Platonic chain of being, finds it necessary to discriminate degrees of complexity or levels of organization. In a system called an 'emergent whole' there are integrative levels. Bunge concludes

> Although perhaps none of the nine concepts listed above
> can be dispensed with in contemporary science and ontolo-
> gy, the notion of level ... seems to be particularly use-
> ful in the building of scientifically oriented ontologies
> and outlooks, since it affords a means for a realistic
> and unified categorization of the pieces of material and
> cultural reality, in a way reminiscent of natural or evo-
> lutionary classifications .... Such theories may yield an
> increasingly faithful and rich picture of the universe
> that, to the extent to which it succeeds in combining di-
> versity with unity, it could be called *integrated plural-
> ism*.17

To get from the many meanings of hierarchy, grades, levels to a systematic metaphysics there is required a theory of analogy to show that the many have some common meaning.

AN INFORMAL CONCLUSION

Hierarchy and the other modes of order are necessary because we find such structures in the cosmos, and we live in societies with structures based upon nature, and we create beautiful things following various principles of order. Hierarchy is necessary in thought because all the categories of being indicate how things are ordered and demonstrate degrees in all the dimensions. The problem of modes of order with which A. O. Lovejoy's *Great Chain of Being* confronts us is this: has hierarchical thought been completely supplanted by evolutionary thought? If we deal with hierarchy are we therefore dealing with a peculiar metaphysical pattern that has a past in Western thought, in Plato Aristotle, and Plotinus, for example, but no future?

The Great Chain of Being neglects in the Western tradition the developments of Jewish and Moslem philosophies. If these seem to be also Neo-Platonic in origin and similarly provincial and remote from us, then it becomes necessary to examine philosophies of all the world. Quite independent of Jacob's Ladder and Homer's Golden Chain we find in Hinduism a rich heritage of the

stages by which Atman can ascend to union with Brahma. This is a central theme
in the *Upanishads*, and Hindu systems are rare that do not tell us of the degrees of perfection, even if they emerge, as Buddhism, by denying Atman and
Brahma. Chinese thought although quite reticent about higher beings and the
soul's ascent, is nevertheless always subjecting even the emperor to the man-
date of heaven. And the striving to be a sage along with a deep sense of the
proper ceremony to be observed in relation to those on a higher level, is as
powerful a motive in Confucianism as in any tradition.

The translator of The Great Chain of Being into Arabic, Dr. Fakhry, takes
pride in the fact that Dr. Johnson called hierarchy "the Arabian scale." We
might from reading Philo or Maimonides learn it as "the Jewish scale," and the
same for learning it as "the Hindu scale" or "the Chinese scale."

What is so special about hierarchy is its crucial role in religious aspiration, even when it has ceased, as in the case of Gautama, to have much of a
theology. Hierarchy is capable of being restated in a humanistic way and has
recently been so restated by an American philosopher.[18]

Hierarchy is a mode of ordering society that takes many forms. It need
not be established by inheritance, as we learn in Jefferson's protest against
hereditary rule of landed aristocrats: there may be the rank achieved by the
industrious and virtuous. Some sort of rank seems necessary in order to have
any kind of leadership. In an institutional fashion, the American constitution
has an appeal from lower courts to higher, ending in a supreme court. Legal
order requires a single and final court to resolve conflicts and confusions on
lower levels.

> Starting from individual beauties, the quest for the uni-
> versal beauty must find him [one initiated to the myste-
> ries and grasping the vision] – EVER MOUNTING THE HEAVEN-
> LY LADDER, stepping from rung to rung – that is, from one
> to two, and from two to *every* lovely body, from bodily
> beauty to the beauty of institutions, from institutions
> to learning, and from learning in general to the special
> lore that pertains to nothing but the beautiful itself—
> until at last he comes to know what beauty is.[19]

Hierarchy has a strong aesthetic appeal and in our tradition was given
its classic statement in Plato. Has the ladder of beauty ceased to control our
thought in the aesthetic realm? In a recent examination of the good Gestalt of
works of art Rudolf Arnheim remarks:

> Orderliness comes in degrees; order comes in levels. A
> structure can be more or less ordered at any level of

complexity. The level of ordered complexity is the level of order.[20]

Hierarchy is also found in science because nature requires a distinction between levels; hierarchy is central in religion, in society and in art. We owe much to the ontological realism of James K. Feibleman. He has restated the ancient and medieval ladder in modern terms. In the sciences we study entities with distinct processes and emergent qualities, and between these levels are found cleavages. There is a lower level, the physical atom, out of which emerges the chemical atom, the biological organism, the psychological mind, the anthropological society. "The integrative levels are stepwise phenomena, structures existing one above the other logically ...."[21]

Feibleman is one of many philosophers and scientists who are now contributing, in the light of current research, to the theory of hierarchy. Lovejoy had found Aristotle's theory of "zoological and psychological hierarchies" more intelligible than the Neo-Platonic Chain of Being.

My argument concludes that modern philosophy, however it has rejected and modified the tradition, is far from abandoning concepts of levels or degrees. The structures of being make us recognize the necessity of these concepts. Such hierarchical schemes are universal because they are not only "naturally found," as Feibleman argues, but also have the deepest religious, social and aesthetic appeal. Some concept of the chain of being, therefore, needs to be devised which allows translation into the many philosophies of mankind. Hierarchy offers one of the best hopes for philosophical integration of the traditions of mankind.

NOTES

[1]A. O. Lovejoy, *The Great Chain of Being, A Study of the History of Ideas* (N. Y.: Harper & Brothers, 1960), p. 59. The index refers to this passage as defining the concept. There is an "ontological scale" which is also a "single order of excellence" in which essences are found in existence. Lovejoy admits this is "vague" compared with "the more intelligible conceptions of zoological and psychological hierarchies which Aristotle had suggested." Lovejoy therefore continues to specify the hierarchical universe: "composed of an immense, or--by the strict but seldom rigorously applied logic of the principle of continuity--of an infinite, number of links ranging in hierarchical order from the meagerest kind of existents, which barely escape non-existence, through" every possible grade up to the *ens perfectissimum* kind of creature, between which and the Absolute Being the disparity was assumed to be infinite--every one of them differing from that immediately above and that immediately below it by the 'least possible' degree of difference."

Lovejoy's definition of the "great chain of being," as principles of "plenitude, continuity, and gradation" may have been true enough of the Neo-Platonic tradition. But it will not do to miss the more general definition of hierarchy within this tradition that points forward more than restating the inheritance.

[2]I have preferred this to four others in the *Index Tertius, Res Praecipuae et Doctrinae Memorabiles*, Divi Thomae Aquinatis *Summa Theologica*, Editio Altera Romano, Leonine Ed. (Rome: n.d.,) Vol. VI, p. 191. The specific question is 108, Article 2, in the midst of a discussion of the angels. The problem raised by the Pseudo-Dionysius is of the orders within a hierarchy, that is to say; first, seraphim, cherubim, thrones; second, dominations, virtues, powers; third, principalities, archangels, angels. But Thomas sees the generality of the problem: the same general problems might just as well be raised by order of courts, warriors, laborers "et sic de aliis."

[3]Paul G. Kuntz, "Order," *The New Catholic Encyclopedia* (N. Y.: McGraw-Hill Book Co., 1967), Vol. 10, pp. 720-723.

[4]J. N. Findlay, "The Three Hypostases of Platonism", *The Review of Metaphysics*, Vol. XXVIII, No. 4, June 1975, p. 662.

[5]St. Anselm does not assume "a single degree of dignity" because a horse has a superior nature to wood, and man to horse. He who doubts this "does not deserve the name of man." *Monologium*, Ch. IV. This ad hominem is one aspect of the examination of the diversity of goods and natures: there is an ordering relationship "greater than" that holds between them. What is called the "ontological argument" in the *Proslogium* is in the prior work the problem of that which is greater than anything else and that than which nothing is greater.

The hierarchical relationship is variously defined as "greater than in some respect," natures of various sorts in an order of dignity, dependency or living by sustenance offered by, or inclusion.

Saint Anselm, *Basic Writings* Tr. S. N. Deane, (La Salle, Ill.: Open Court Publishing Co., 1962).

St. Bonaventure puts the matter very plainly: "one sees that some things merely are; others, however, are and live; others finally, are, live, and discern. And the first are lesser things, the second midway, and the third the best." The *Mind's Road to God*, Tr. George Boas, (N. Y.: Liberal Arts Press, 1953), pp. 11-12. This is the mode of rational inquiry, which is one of three, the others being contemplation and faith.

Boas analyzes the metaphysical point of view as springing from Plotinus, if not Philo. "Fundamental to his whole system is that fusion of the three hierarchies of Neo-Platonism: the hierarchy of logical classes, that of values, and that of reality." This is most helpful in thinking of the respects in which there can be levels and one can be said to be "higher than" another, but

I find this completely obscures the discernment of levels of love in Bonaventure. Paul G. Kuntz, "The Hierarchical Vision of St. Bonaventure," read at IX Conference on Medieval and Renaissance Studies, 1974 and published in Acts of the Bonaventure Congress, Rome, 1974.

San Bonaventura Maestro di Vita Francescana e di Sapienza Cristiana, Ed. A. Pompei, (Roma: Pontificia Facoltà Telogica "San Bonaventura," 1976), Vol. II, 233-248.

[6]The problem of hierarchy is sometimes posed as the problem of mediation between opposites that are otherwise unrelated. These are, in Calvin's theology, God and man or heaven and earth. There cannot be successful mediation by introducing angels on a ladder, presumably because these do not partake of the natures to be mediated. So long as there is anything "between," one is still "alienated" from the other. John Calvin, Institutes of the Christian Religion, Tr. John Allen (Philadelphia: Presbyterian Board of Christian Education, 1922), Vol. I, Ch. XIV, esp. XII, pp. 160-161.

If the problem of hierarchy was posed in late Hellenic thought as that of filling the gap between two worlds, then the difference between the Christian Logos and the Neo-Platonic hypostases is that the latter are intermediaries which are below the highest and above the lowest but the former joins both together. C. C. J. Webb analyzes the problem of both Judaism and Neo-Platonism as the bridging between God and man. St. Augustine, Confessions, VII, c. 9, calls our attention to the difference between "light and life of men" and the "Word ... made flesh [Who] dwelt amont us." C. C. J. Webb, History of Philosophy (London: Oxford University Press, 1956), pp. 76-88. One of the conspicuous gaps, then, in Lovejoy's Great Chain of Being in the Christian development is the doctrine of the Logos.

There is another sort of continuity that Lovejoy ignored between the medieval Catholic and the Reformation Protestant. St. Bonaventure is his Itinerarium, The Mind's Ascent to God, op. cit, p. 8 "Christ ... is our ladder" and John Calvin "It is Christ above who joins heaven and earth. He alone is Mediator ... He it is through whom the fullness of all heavenly gifts flows down to us and through whom we on our part may ascend to God .... Therefore, ... we say that the ladder is a symbol of Christ ...." Commentaries, Library of Christian Classics, Tr. and Ed. J. Haroutunian and L. P. Smith (Philadelphia: Westminster, n. d.) p. 147 on Gen. 28:12.

[7]Of many examples, St. Bonaventura "Sapientis est ordinare. Ideo quaedam facit bona, quaedam meliora, quaedam optima." I Sent. 44, 1, 2 ad 3, t. I, 785b. This is the three fold form of the adjective, the positive, the comparative, and the superlative, but the realism of common sense begins with things so characterized.

[8]The article "hierarchia = heilige Vorsterherschaft, heilige Herrschaft: hierarchia est sacer principatus ..." fails to define the concept broadly enough. Ludwig Shütz, Thomas-Lexikon (N. Y.: Frederick Ungar, 1957), p. 356.

[9]Had Lovejoy attended to Jacob's Ladder, he could have found easily a hundred examples, in contrast to the half dozen uses of the Golden Chain. Perhaps he did not care to complicate the derivation of a Neo-Platonic scheme by admitting an Hebraic source. The chain has a number of links that must overlap. But the ladder has discrete sections separated by rungs held in continuous rails. St. Thomas finds it significant that there are two rails, one to signify the descent of angels, the other to signify the ascent of man. Although one ascends and becomes more perfect by contemplation, there is also the descent "to action to care for lower creatures." Summa Theologica II, II, CLXXXI, IV. Hence, it is not as sometimes suggested, that ascending the ladder means leaving lower levels behind.

The Cosmic Tree of the Pseudo-Chrystostom, the tree of salvation and joy, is equated with "the stairway of Jacob." See Henri de Lubac, Catholicism, (New York: New American Library, 1964) pp. 279-280. The passage is from Sermon VI for Holy Week, p. 6. lix, 743-6.

The passage connecting Jacob's Ladder to the Golden Chain has only now been made available to us in the translation, with introduction, annotations and index: Marion Leathers Daniels

Kuntz, *Colloquium of the Seven Concerning Secrets of the Sublime*, Jean Bodin's *Heptaplomeres*, (Princeton, N. J.: Princeton University Press, 1975) p. 32. "Salomon: I think the Homeric chain is nothing other than the ladder represented in the nocturnal vision of Jacob ...."

[10]That failure of medieval philosophy was to use a semi-artificial language, "the artificialization of natural language," following Aristotle, and *not* to follow Boëthius' careful distinctions of meanings ("in" has 9 senses, "is" is ambiguous, etc. resulted in verblike nouns which led to "breakdown of communication." Hence the humanists demand a natural language and Locke condemns the "unintelligible terms" of Schoolmen. Desmond Paul Henry, "Medieval Philosophy," in Paul Edwards, Ed., *Encyclopedia of Philosophy*, (N. Y.: Macmillan, 1967), Vol. 5, 252-258.

[11]A most interesting example of reduction of various hierarchies to one is the analysis of Dante in Joseph A. Mazzeo, *Medieval Cultural Tradition in Dante's Comedy* (Ithaca, N. Y.: Cornell University Press, 1960) "... The hierarchies of being, truth, beauty, perfection, indeed of all value are reduced to the very Primal Light itself, spiritual, uncreated, divine, the vision of which is the vision of all. The doctrines we have considered are the bare bones of the most important part of Dante's universe."

[12]Although in St. Thomas, according to Gilson, there is one hierarchy, "a hierarchy of dignity is at the same time invariably a hierarchy of jurisdiction, whereas, except where God is involved, Dante never regards a hierarchy of dignity as a hierarchy of jurisdiction." We saw above the use of Jacob's Ladder as an image of the parallelism of action and contemplation and their unity. In contrast to the unitative and synthetic is the analytic and dispersive in Dante. "He who contemplates does not govern, he who governs does not contemplate. To each his beatitude." E. Gilson, *Dante and Philosophy*, (N. Y.: Harper, 1963). (N. Y.: Sheed and Ward, 1949), pp. 153, 140.

[13]Although it is said that "the Fourth Way is the least widely accepted of Aquinas' proofs for the existence of God," there is in every way a crucial hierarchical moment. Structure essential to the argument of all the Ways. The First Way rests on the principle that Act is higher than potency, the Second Way that Cause is higher than effect, the Third Way that Necessity is higher than possibility, the Fourth Way that End is higher than means. For debates about "Degrees of Perfection," David Sanford in Paul Edwards, Ed., *The Encyclopedia of Philosophy*, (N. Y.: Macmillan, 1967), Vol. 1, pp. 324-326. Analyzing the hierarchical structure of Thomas' metaphysics: George G. Leckie, Translation of and Preface to St. Thomas Aquinas, *Concerning Being and Essence*, (N. Y.: Appleton-Century Co., 1937), John Goheen, *The Problem of Matter and Form "De Ente et Essentia: of Thomas Aquinas* (Cambridge, Mass.: Harvard University Press, 1940), especially pp. 89-90, et seq.

A most interesting definition of "levels of reality" is from J. F. Ross, "The Fallacious Bases of Two Theistic Parodoxes," mimeographed. "B is of a lower level of reality than A if and only if: B belongs by essence to a class of things such that no member of that class could exist unless: (1) some member of the class of things to which A belongs by essence, actually exists; (2) actually produces the existing members of B's class; and (3) maintains a conserving relationship to those members throughout their existence; (4) and no member of B's class has any property whatever that is not bestowed upon it by some member of some class of things which the members of A's class stand in relations (1), (2), and (3). As this definition stands, it does not preclude an infinite set of levels of reality; nor is there any *a priori* reason to think there is no such set. The relation which a particular thing of lower level has to the particular thing of higher level which produces it is called *metaphysical dependence*. All of the members of the higher class are said to be *ontologically prior* to those of the lower. Thus metaphysical dependence is a relation which obtains between a cause and its effects which are of a lower level of reality."

14

[14]Schütz, *Thomas-Lexikon*, *loc. cit.*, art "gradus" p. 344.

[15]Arthur O. Lovejoy, *The Great Chain of Being*, *loc. cit.*, p. 254.

[16]James H. H. Murray, in *A New English Dictionary*, (Oxford: Clarendon Press, 1901, Vol. IV, pp. 332-333.

[17]Mario Bunge, "Levels: A Semantical Preliminary," *The Review of Metaphysics*, Vol. XIII, No. 3, March 1960, p. 406, reprinted as Ch. 3, "Levels," in *The Myth of Simplicity, Problems of Scientific Methodology*, (Englewood Cliffs, N. J.: Prentice-Hall, 1963), pp. 47-48.

[18]David Norton, *Daimons and Human Destiny*, (Princeton, N. J.: Princeton University Press, 1976).

[19]*Symposium* 211, E. Hamilton & H. Cairns, *Plato: The Collected Dialogues*, (N. Y.: Pantheon, 1963), pp. 562-3 (capitals ours).

[20]Rudolf Arnheim, *Entropy and Art: An Essay on Disorder and Order*, (Berkeley: University of California Press, 1971), p. 51. The author adds that "Order ... is a necessary although not a sufficient condition of aesthetic excellence."

[21]James K. Feibleman, "The Integrative Levels in Nature," in *Focus on Information and Communication*, Barbara Kyle, Ed., (London: ASUB, 1965), p. 28. For many other contributions of this prolific seminal mind see Paul G. Kuntz, "Hierarchy: From Lovejoy's Great Chain of Being to Feibleman's Great Tree of Being," *Studium Generale*, vol. 24, 1971, pp. 678-687, and below, Part V.

DOMINIC J. O'MEARA

THE CHAIN OF BEING IN THE LIGHT

OF RECENT WORK ON PLATONIC HIERARCHIES

Is it really possible to study concepts of "hierarchy" or of a "chain of being" in ancient philosophy? That such a question has a certain legitimacy may be seen from the following considerations. First, one might note that the term "hierarchy" and the phrase "chain of being" do not appear in Plato, Aristotle, or even Plotinus, and are in fact later coinages.[1] That the term for a concept, we might respond, is not to be found at a certain period in the history of thought, does not mean, however, that the concept itself is not in existence at that time. As things exist for which as yet no names are provided, so cannot there be concepts for which there may be found at a particular moment in history no name, or perhaps, on the contrary, several names? This argument assumes a similarity between concepts and things, on the basis of which the relation between concepts and terms for them is thought to be analogous to the relation between things and their names. But are concepts things? And do terms relate to concepts as names do to things? A second consideration might be developed as follows. If the terms identifying concepts are not to be found in certain historical texts, and yet we assume the concepts themselves to exist in these texts, how do we identify and describe them? We must suppose the properties of an unnamed concept to be such that they can serve to indicate it to us. We can only identify such a concept on the basis of a prior understanding of its nature, constituent factors, functions, operations, which will act as signs whereby the presence of the concept in a text can readily be discerned.

Thus, the study of concepts of hierarchy and of a chain of being in philosophical texts predating the coining of these terms must presuppose, to be at all possible, certain positions, explicit or implicit, concerning the nature of concepts, their relation to terms and their functions and operations within thought and its expression. As the concepts in question here (hierarchy and chain of being) can be described in general as concepts of structure, the presuppositions implicit in a study of concepts of hierarchy or of a chain of being in ancient thought will relate specifically to the nature and properties of concepts of structure.

In this essay, I propose to examine briefly the accounts given by Arthur Lovejoy and by some more recent interpreters of concepts of hierarchy and of a chain of being, as these concepts are found primarily in Platonism. In the course of this examination, I shall attempt to indicate in particular how these various accounts presuppose certain positions concerning the nature and properties of concepts of structure. I will then review these accounts thus analyzed with the purpose of initiating a critique of them in the light of some contemporary insights into the nature and properties of concepts of structure.

I

Arthur Lovejoy begins his study of the "Great Chain of Being" in the history of thought with an introductory chapter in which he indicates his general attitude to the nature and properties of concepts, or, in his language, of "conceptions" or "ideas." "Ideas," he finds, are rational and irrational factors in the human mind or "spirit." They include psychological and social tendencies, such as tastes, fashions, habits, susceptibilities, as well as "conceptions" not reducible to psychological or social origins, such as particular propositions "invented" by philosophers in response to specific questions.[2] These "ideas," or better, "unit-ideas," have only a loose relationship with the various possible terms or expressions through which they are indicated. They manifest a certain independency; they have a life of their own. "The most migratory of things," they cross from one area of human intellectual activity—be it philosophy, literature, religion, art, science, or politics—to another. They move from one nation and generation to another.[3] By virtue of their particular affinities for and antagonisms (logical, psychological) to other ideas, they may come together, become agglutinated, or split apart and conflict with each other. Each idea thus has a history of changing relationships with other ideas, a history spanning many areas of thought, many periods and many countries.[4] Undertaking biographies of ideas is all the more important, in Lovejoy's opinion, given their vital role in human thought. Ideas are the primary constitutive recurrent dynamic forces, motives or reasons which give rise to philosophical systems, literary works, etc. In fact a philosophical system, for example, is little more than an unstable aggregate of unit-ideas, a surface appearance of a set of ideas which can equally generate another and divergent system.[5] The study of the "history" of a unit-idea in its manifestations in different areas of human thought will therefore dominate, rather than be dominated by, the specialized study (history of philosophy or history of literature, for example) which considers merely products, in a limited domain, of more fundamental and widespread factors.[6] Lovejoy's discipline of the "history of ideas," in prosecuting this study of the elements constitutive of the true and basic history of the human mind, will contribute to his ultimate philosophical project: reaching an understanding of *homo sapiens* considered in his most characteristic activity.[7]

These general remarks concerning the nature and properties of "ideas" and the study of them, the "history of ideas," are an appropriate introduction to *The Great Chain of Being*, since this work is presented precisely as an example of the practice of the "history of ideas."[8] The conception expressed loosely by the phrase "chain of being" is in fact for Lovejoy not one unit-idea, but the product of an agglutination of three unit-ideas, namely the principle of "plenitude" (first introduced by Plato) and the principles of "continuity" and of "gradation" (first formulated in Aristotle). The history of the conception of a chain of being will accordingly be the history of the origins of these three "ideas" in the minds of Plato and of Aristotle, their fusion into one conception (first totally realized in Neoplatonism) and their influence in various fields in latter times. The unit-idea which Lovejoy expresses by the phrase "principle of plenitude" originates from what he feels was Plato's response in the *Timaeus* to the question: "How many kinds of temporal and imperfect beings must this world contain?" Identifying God's "goodness," as self-sufficiency, with "goodness," meaning generosity, Lovejoy's Plato responds that the divine demiurge could not begrudge the existence of anything, so that all possible kinds must be realized in the world. No genuine potentiality of being can remain unfulfilled.[9] Logically implied, furthermore, in this principle of plenitude is another unit-idea, the principle of continuity formulated by Aristotle. Since, according to the principle of plenitude, all potentialities must be realized, if "there is a theoretical possible between two types, it must be realized."[10] In other words, there must be a continuity from type to type in the plenitude of types in the world. Finally, Aristotle also expresses the principle of gradation when he orders things in a *scala naturae* based on degrees of perfection, or potentiality. (The idea of placing *all* things in a unilinear gradation is however not so much formulated as suggested in Aristotle's works.) These three principles, the ingredients of the conception of a chain of being, are first fully integrated into a general scheme of things in Neoplatonism, in that the Neoplatonists conceive the world as being structured in terms of an immense number of links arranged in *hierarchical* order (gradation), going from the lowest through *every possible* grade to the highest (plenitude), each grade differing by the *least* possible difference (continuity).[11]

We need not follow here the fortunes of this conception of a chain of being, as it travels through later periods and different contexts. I would note, however, that Lovejoy distinguishes the concept of hierarchy (gradation) from the conception of a chain of being. The latter is a complex of which the former is but an element. As for Lovejoy's attitude to the nature and properties of concepts of structure, we have seen that concepts of structure are understood by him in the context of "ideas" in general. Whether as ideas (gradation) or as products of ideas (chain of being), concepts of structure manifest the type of existence characteristic of ideas. Sometimes perhaps originating from a response to a philosophical question (as in the case of the principle of plenitude), ideas rapidly emerge as self-subsistent mental units characterized by properties (properties of logical or psychological implication, affinity, antagonism) responsible for the history of their behavior with respect to other ideas. Through their mutual attractions and repulsions, ideas come to determine thought and its expression in philosophical systems, literary works, and in other areas of human intellectual activity.

II

At a recent international colloquium, Hans Jonas presented a paper on "The Soul in Gnosticism and Plotinus" in which the theme of a Neoplatonic chain of being reappears, but in a very different perspective. Jonas points in this paper to the existence, both in Plotinus and in certain religious movements of Plotinus' time, notably Gnosticism, of a common speculative system, a conception of a vertical chain of being going from the higher to the lower, the lower deriving from the higher, each level being a level in a range of degrees of perfection, divinity and goodness. This chain or hierarchy (Jonas does not distinguish the two) is not static. The vertical order in fact represents the descent of all things in that order. It is a "record of the generation of reality" in a linear movement of becoming, going downwards towards alienation and otherness. If we regard time as the dimension of process and change, the vertical axis of being, as representing a movement of becoming, is primarily, despite its spatial connotations, a "time axis." It represents a "curious metaphysical time of causal *prius* and *posterius*" which can be transformed from a mythological conception of events (in Gnosticism) into a philosophical conception of a timeless movement behind the world (in Plotinus).[12] Having presented this speculative system common to Plotinus and Gnosticism, Jonas describes how the origin and nature of the soul is determined within this system. He finds that soul is a result of a primordial "fall." The reason given by Plotinus for this fall is as mythical as that supplied by the Gnostics: the fall is due to an act of self-will, self-assertion, audacity, apostasy. By quoting *Ennead* III 7, ch. 11 at length, Jonas shows that this act also produced time. In falling, soul temporalized herself. Time in fact is a self-alteration of soul's being and a condition of her creativity.[13]

In considering Jonas' paper, it may be helpful to remember a larger project from which it seems to stem, namely Jonas' existential interpretation of Gnosticism in his *Gnosis und spätantiker Geist*.[14] Indeed the paper I have summarized clearly emphasized subjects close to the heart of existential philosophy. The vertical axis of being, I have noted, is understood as fundamentally a "time axis," time being thought of as the dimension of process and change. Other themes in the paper—the progress to the always other, soul's self-will, audacity, alienation, its self-alteration as a condition of its creativity—also clearly have existential significance. However, to discern more fully the existential approach to the concept of hierarchy implicit in Jonas' account of Plotinus and Gnosticism, it will be useful to examine the concept as it appears in Jonas' own philosophical work, in particular in the collection of essays entitled *The Phenomenon of Life*.[15]

Jonas offers, in *The Phenomenon of Life*, an existential interpretation of biological facts, thus extending existential insight beyond an exclusive interest in man to a concern with the organic realm in general. Life, he finds, "presents itself as an ascending scale in which are placed the sophistications of form, the lure of sense and the spur of desire, the command of limb and power to act, the reflection of consciousness and the reach for truth."[16] Jonas retains from Aristotle's *De anima* the principles of stratification: progressive superposition of levels; dependance of the higher on the lower; retention of all the lower in the higher. However, he orders the scale of life in terms of rising degrees of world perception and of progressive freedom of

action.[17] The way in which life constitutes this scale is described as follows. Life begins with an act of secession from matter, the point of life being its "self-centered individuality, being for itself and in contraposition
to all the rest of the world, with an essential boundary dividing 'inside'
from 'outside.'"[18] The secession from matter is the assumption of a position
of independence from matter and constitutes the first emergence of freedom.
However, this independence (freedom) brings also a dependence on matter (necessity) for the continuance of its being. Life stands in a dialectical relation of "needful freedom" to matter.[19] Corresponding to this dependence inherent in the freedom of life is a potentiality of non-being included in life's
very effort to be. The process of life is always open to interference; in the
straining of its temporality it is always facing an imminent "no-more." Death
is thus a condition of life.[20] However, the antinomies of self-world, freedom-
necessity, being-non-being implicit in the unstable finite and temporal act of
life lead to a self-transcendence of life. Life, driven by want, entertains
horizons beyond its point-identity. It opens itself and relates to the outside
world. This transcendence in terms of openness to a spatial horizon can be
complemented by a self-transcendence in terms of an openness to a horizon of
time, an openness which embraces "the imminence of that future into which organic continuity is each moment about to extend by the satisfaction of that
moment's want."[21]

It is not necessary for our present purposes to go further into this philosophical biology. Despite his reference to formal principles of stratification in Aristotle, it seems that Jonas' approach to concepts of structure is
intelligible primarily in terms of his vision of the acts and processes which
make up the existential drama of life. The structure of life depends on, and
represents, a dynamic history of the striving to be of living things. Concepts
of structure will correspondingly be expressions of concepts of process and
change. Hence, the Plotinian and Gnostic concept of a vertical axis of being
is interpreted by Jonas as a concept of the becoming of things, and as temporality is fundamental to becoming, so will it characterize the axis of being.
As theories of the generation of things may readily be discernable in the
events and processes of Plotinian and Gnostic reality, so will the conception
of that reality as structured emerge, as representing the dimension of these
events and processes.

III

I would like to move now from Lovejoy's theory of "ideas" as applied in his interpretation of the ancient conception of a chain of being, and Jonas' existential interpretation of Plotinian and Gnostic concepts of structure, to some significant developments in modern Platonic scholarship. These developments relate mainly to the reconstruction of a part of the history of Platonism which appears to be lost. Such a loss means that the related material still extant remains in need of much interpretation, but that material can also act as a body of clues permitting some reconstruction of what is lost. If what is lost is thus recovered, we gain not only a fuller view of the past, but also a means for interpreting the surviving material. What is lost is the technical, "oral" philosophy, in its various forms, developed by Plato and by his colleagues and successors in the Academy. The body of related material which has survived, however, and which both lacks a context of intelligibility and also provides traces of that context includes: (i) the more technical and obscure passages in Plato's (especially later) dialogues; (ii) the works of Aristotle and in particular those passages referring to Plato, Speusippus, Xenocrates and other colleagues of Aristotle in the Academy; (iii) scanty references to the historical development of the Academy; and finally (iv) the philosophical systems of the Hellenistic and Roman Imperial period, including Neoplatonism, insofar as they relate to the history of the Academy. Although subject to much debate, the modern attempt to reconstruct the technical philosophy of Plato and his successors is without doubt a most important movement in modern Platonic scholarship, and has proved already very fertile.[22] It has in particular led to a rapprochement between Neoplatonism and Plato, through finding that certain structural concepts characteristic of Neoplatonism go back to Plato's Academy.

The demonstration, on the basis of structural similarities, of the relationship between Neoplatonism and the Academy was given, for example, by Philip Merlan in his book *From Platonism to Neoplatonism*. Merlan finds the following doctrines characteristic of Neoplatonism: a plurality of spheres of being strictly subordinated to one another and representing higher and lower degrees of being; the derivation of each sphere from the sphere superior to it; the culmination of the system in a transcendent source, the One. Then, in an investigation of classifications of the sciences in various Neoplatonic and Aristotelian texts, Merlan establishes the existence already in the Academy of a Neoplatonic-type system of spheres of being, the spheres representing different levels of being, each sphere deriving from the higher and ultimately from two principles, the constituents of an uppermost sphere.[23] Cornelia de Vogel, in an article published in *Mind*, reinforced this parallel between Neoplatonism and the Academy. She noted that the Neoplatonic "four-storied universe" and theory of emanation can be found in the second century A. D. Middle Platonist Albinus, in the Platonizing Gnostic Valentinus, and finally in Plato himself. The Form of the Good of Plato's *Republic*, to be identified with the "One" referred to by Aristotle and Aristoxenus, constitutes in Plato the highest level of reality, from which derives a hierarchically ordered intelligible world, below which appears the level of the mathematical (attested by Aristotle and indicated in the *Republic*), an intermediary level between the intelligible and the sensible. The structure terminates with the so-called "indefinite dyad" situated below sensible reality.[24] The attempt to trace Neoplatonic structures and derivation back in a continuous Platonic tradition to the philosophy of Plato and his Academy has finally acquired considerable strength through the publications of Hans Joachim Krämer and Konrad Gaiser.[25]

If we ask ourselves what the attitude of these historians to concepts of structure might be we may find no immediate and ready answer. A beginning might be made, however, towards meeting the question by noting that the historians' reconstruction of the thought of the Academy is based on scattered texts constituting, it is assumed, a set of clues from which a systematic body of doctrine can be recovered. One may wonder if such a system lies behind the texts, or if in fact the alleged doctrinal system is a principle of organization whereby the scholar, in a more or less arbitrary way, unifies basically heterogeneous material.[26] It therefore seems legitimate to ask (i) on the basis of what principles of organization or system does the historian elaborate his texts into a coherent doctrine? and (ii) are these principles, and the use to which they are put by scholars, given in the texts themselves?

Responding to the second question would clearly lead to a critique of the historical value of the results of recent Platonic scholarship. A few comments with respect to the first question, however, will not lead us beyond the bounds of this paper. Merlan and de Vogel use, as principles of organization, concepts of "spheres" or "stories," fairly vague and schematic concepts no doubt, but which represent, they assume, the actual "system" of a Plato or a Plotinus. More precise and detailed formulations of concepts used as princi-

ples of organization of texts and assumed to be the system underlying the
texts are found in Krämer and Gaiser. In their view, the system of the Academy
is based on a "mathematisierend-analytischen Elementenmetaphysik." Reality is
reducible to, and derives from, the "elements" it presupposes. The model for
this is the mathematical dimensional series, or "Dimensionenfolge," in which
the three-dimensional solid presupposes, as "elemental" to it, the plane which
in turn presupposes the line. The line stands to the plane as an "element"
from which the plane (more complex) is generated.[27] Analogous to the structure
of relations in this mathematical series is the structure of relations in reality as a whole. The first and highest "element," the One, is followed by a
succession of levels of being (ousiai, genē, phuseis), each bringing with it a
"Material increase" and a "categorial novum."[28] Although each level, or stra-
tum, will thus have an identity in itself and be structured internally, it
constitutes a complex presupposing a higher, more simple level, as element,
just as it constitutes an element with respect to the level below it. Thus,
the discontinuities between regions of being, between the intelligible and the
sensible for example, must be viewed in the context of the place of these
levels in a universal progression of reality analogous to, and modeled on, the
progression of the dimensional series.[29] The concept of structure which Krämer
and Gaiser find in the Academy will therefore be primarily mathematical in
character; the idea of hierarchy in Plato is a conception of mathematical progression. Alongside this mathematical approach to structure, however, Krämer
in particular attributes also to Plato the conception of a stratification of
reality. One may wonder how a concept of reality as a superposition of strata
can be consistent with an interpretation of reality in terms of a mathematical
progression, but Krämer finds no conflict between these concepts, stressing
that stratification develops from, and is reducible to, mathematical progression.

IV

In surveying the accounts of ancient concepts of hierarchical structure
provided by Lovejoy, Jonas and others, it has not been my intention to assess
the historical value of these accounts. I have sought rather to bring out the
assumptions these accounts contain concerning the nature of concepts of structure. In Lovejoy, concepts of structure, whether they be the "idea" of gradation or the composite conception of a chain of being, are treated as compar-

able in their nature to other "ideas" and their products. Originating, in some
cases, as answers to questions, they soon form, with other mental phenomena,
rational and irrational, an independant body of units endowed with various
characteristics (logical, psychological) and possessing an individual and com-
munal history. Jonas approaches concepts of structure not so much in terms of
their being units or objects in the mind, as in terms of the specific content
or meaning they may have. Concepts of hierarchical structure, in particular,
express and refer to theories of process and change. Finally, we find in Krämer and Gaiser that the concept of hierarchical structure in Plato is viewed
as being mathematical in content, and also analogical in function: the dimensional series constitutes a system of relationships applicable, outside its
primary sphere of reference, to reality in general. Simplifying things somewhat, we may say that in these various interpreters we have met concepts of
structure considered (i) as objects in the mind, (ii) as having specific contents or meanings, and (iii) as functioning as models.

To speak, as Lovejoy does, of concepts of structure as objects or units
in the mind would seem to make some sense. But surely concepts relate to the
process of conceiving in which they arise. As part of this process, they, in
their indentities, will refer to characteristics both of the cognitive approach of the mind and of that which forms the object of thought. Insofar as a
diversity of cognitive approaches and of objects of thought obtains, it
should be possible to differentiate between concepts, establishing distinctions, for example, between concepts of structure and other concepts. In putting concepts of structure, taken as mental units, on a par not only with
other concepts but also with mental phenomena more psychological or social in
character, Lovejoy does not sufficiently consider, I feel, concepts of structure in relation to the particular cognitive contexts of which they are part.
If he indicates the specific characteristics of certain concepts (referring to
their logical or psychological affinities and antagonisms), he seems to view
those characteristics as attaching to the concepts independently of the thinking mind and the objects of its thought. Hence the mind and its objects recede
into the background, ceding the stage to a drama, the "history of ideas," en-
acted between concepts as embodied in the preferably undistinguished but representative writings of whole generations and nations.[30] I find, therefore,
that although Lovejoy does differentiate between concepts, this differentiation is not made in terms of distinctions between the particular cognitive

contexts to which concepts relate. This seems moreover to be symptomatic of a more general lack of attention to concepts in their relationship to thought and the objects of thought.

More depth may be given to these criticisms by the following considerations. In speaking of "concepts of structure," we use the preposition "of" to indicate not so much the concept as a mental object taken in itself, as that "of" which it is a concept. The "of" qualifies the concept insofar as it points to what the concept signifies, what the "content" or "meaning" of concepts of structure is. Hence Jonas' interpretation of the Plotinian notion of an "axis of being" as signifying a theory of process and change. Concepts of structure can therefore be regarded as having specific content. If however we may speak of concepts in terms of their content, what they are "of," it is clear also that this content is not an object, or objects, in the field of experienced things. The concept of "hierarchy" is not the concept of a particular hierarchy. What then is the content of a concept of structure? It is best described, perhaps, as the result of an ordering activity of the mind in relation to an experienced set of objects or aspects of an object. Related presumably in part to logical principles of ordering implicit in thought and in part to the potentiality for ordering contained in the object or objects, the content of a concept of structure appears as an "interpretation." This interpretation will both reflect cognitive principles of ordering and have reference to realities whose susceptibility to ordering it expresses. The content of the concept of hierarchy, for example, may be understood in terms of a logical process of arranging entities in a scale of priority and posteriority, yet it is not the ordering activity itself but the order as established with respect to entities as potentially thus ordered. In identifying the content of a concept of structure with notions of change and process, Jonas passes over, it seems, this particular and important aspect of the content of concepts of structure.

In discussing the content of concepts of structure, I have distinguished between the mind's activity of ordering, objects as potentially ordered, and the meeting of mind and object in a concept of structure which is both the product of an activity of ordering and a framework for the expression of the order of things susceptible to ordering. As distinguishable from both the mind's ordering activities and the particular objects being grasped as ordered, concepts of structure assume an identity related to, but distinct from,

specific acts of thinking and specific objects. This is not quite the independence given to "unit-ideas" by Lovejoy, but is rather the distinctiveness of a
product of thought which can become an object of thought, insofar as it functions as a medium for further cognitive access to perceived objects. Concepts
of structure thus can function not only as an expression of certain things as
ordered, but also as an order through which other things can be grasped. This
is a common function of concepts of structure in sciences where "models" are
used in the analysis of diverse objects.[31] Gaiser, in particular, seems to approach this perspective on concepts of structure when he represents Plato as
using the mathematical structure of relationships constituted by the dimensional series as a model applicable outside the mathematical sphere.[32] I myself have explored this aspect of concepts of structure in a recent book on
hierarchical structures in Plotinus.[33] However, while pointing to a mathematical series as a model applied by Plato to reality in general, Gaiser does not
view Plato as using the mathematical model as a heuristic method for the interpretation of various aspects of reality. In fact, the mathematical structure *constitutes* reality in Plato and hence is applicable to reality. Whatever
the historical validity of this, it is clear that the possibility of using
concepts of structures as models in the analysis of diverse objects must depend to a degree on the existence in these objects of something corresponding
to these concepts. However, it might be maintained that this correspondence
must remain dynamic, for the reason that concepts of structure, as interpretative orders, relate not only to the order of things, but also to the mind's
approach to these things, an approach which, in its continued activity, might
indicate an ever renewed relation between mind and object.

POSTSCRIPT

In the ten years since the above article was written much has been published having a bearing on various topics treated in the article. I would like
to mention in particular some more recent discussions of Lovejoy: the 1980 issue of the *Journal of the History of Ideas*; N. B. Kvastad, "On Method in the
History of Ideas," *International Logic Review* 9 (1978), 96-110; J. Hintikka,
"Gaps in the Great Chain of Being: an Exercise in the Methodology of the History of Ideas," *Proceedings American Philosophical Association 49 (1975-6)*,
22-38; D. Wilson, Arthur O. Lovejoy and the Quest for Intelligibility, Chapel
Hill, N. C., 1980. On the question of the "oral teaching" of Plato and more

generally on the variety of interpretations of Plato I would like to note two
instructive works by E. N. Tigerstedt, *Interpreting Plato*, Helsinki, 1977 (especially chapter 6) and *The Decline and Fall of the Neoplatonic Interpretation
of Plato*, Helsinki, 1974.

NOTES

[1] Cf. D. O'Meara, *Structures hiérarchiques dans la pensée de Plotin*, Leiden 1975, p. 1; for the "chain" metaphor in Neoplatonic and earlier Greek thought, cf. L. Edelstein, "The Golden Chain of Homer", in *Studies in Intellectual History*, ed. G. Boas, H. Cherniss *et al.*, Baltimore 1953, pp. 48 ff.; P. Lévêque, *Aurea catena Homeri*, Paris 1959. Edelstein suggests (p. 65) that of the Neoplatonists it was Iamblichus in particular (or "the circle around him") who considered the chain a figurative expression "applicable to Plotinus' theory of the Scale of Being". There are important differences between the ideas expressed by the chain metaphor in the texts studied by Edelstein and what is signified by the phrase "chain of being" in 17th and 18th century texts in the light of which, it seems, A. O. Lovejoy finds a "chain of being" in ancient philosophy (cf. *infra* n. 9).

[2] A. O. Lovejoy, *The Great Chain of Being*, Cambridge, Mass. 1936, pp. 7-14; cf. Lovejoy, "The Historiography of Ideas", *Proc. Amer. Philos. Soc.* 78 (1938), p. 538; "Reflections on the History of Ideas", *Journ. Hist. Ideas* 1 (1940), pp. 16 ff.; M. Mandelbaum, "The History of Ideas, Intellectual History and the History of Philosophy", *History and Theory*, Beiheft 5 (1965), p. 35.

[3] *Great Chain of Being*, pp. 4-5, 15-19; *J. H. I.* 1 (1940), p. 4, 23; cf. G. Boas, in *Studies in Intellectual History*, pp. 4-5.

[4] *Great Chain of Being*, pp. 14-15, 22; *J. H. I.* 1 (1940), pp. 22-3; cf. Lovejoy, in *J. H. I.* 2 (1941), pp. 264-5.

[5] *Great Chain of Being*, pp. 3-7; cf. G. Boas, in *J. H. I.* 9 (1948), p. 408.

[6] Cf. Lovejoy, *JHI* 1 (1940), pp. 4-8 (this has of course provoked some critical reaction; cf. *JHI* 9 [1948], p. 442); cf. also *Great Chain of Being*, pp. 16-18, and *Proc. Amer. Philos. Soc.* 78 (1938), pp. 530-7, on the cross-disciplinary character of the history of "ideas".

[7] *Great Chain of Being*, pp. 22-3; cf. *JHI* 1 (1940), pp. 3, 8; M. Mandelbaum, in *J. H. I.* 9 (1948), p. 422; Mandelbaum discusses (pp. 412 ff.) Lovejoy's philosophical positions, some of which are relevant to the theory of a "history of ideas".

[8] *Great Chain of Being*, p. 20; in the following lines I am summarizing the main points of ch. II (pp. 24-66).

[9] Lovejoy bases his interpretation on an identification of the Demiurge of the *Timaeus* with the Form of the Good of the *Republic*. Other debatable parts of his reading of Plato are the question ("How many kinds of temporal and imperfect beings ... ?") and answer ("All possible kinds ...") attributed to Plato, but which will not be found in a careful reading of the relevant texts (*Tim.* 29e-30d). However, Lovejoy has in view mainly what he thinks is "immanent" in Plato (pp. 52-4), what will be "developed" later (pp. 43, 339; on the dangers of this approach, cf. R. Robinson, *Plato's Earlier Dialectic*, Oxford 1953, pp. 1-5: it is an approach which is encouraged by the methodology of the history of ideas; cf. *JHI* 2 [1941], pp. 264-5). Lovejoy is more concerned with the later "influence" of Plato than with Plato himself (pp. 49-50), and it is no coincidence that 17th and 18th century texts are cited in illustration (pp. 49-50; cf. pp. 60-1, 64). It would seem fair to consider *The Great Chain of Being* primarily as a study of 17th and 18th century thought with introductory chapters on Antiquity (ch. II), the Medieval period (ch. III) and the Renaissance (beginning of ch. IV) viewed in the perspective of the main (and later) period studied in the work.

[10]For an alternative view on the Platonic background to the Aristotelian concept of continuity, cf. J. Souilhé, *La notion platonicienne d'intermédiaire dans la philosophie des dialogues*, Paris 1919, pp. 246 ff.; O'Meara, *Structures hiérarchiques*, p. 23 n. 18.

[11]The remarks (*supra* n. 9) on Lovejoy's interpretation of Plato may also be made with respect to his treatment of Plotinus (I may be permitted to refer the reader to my *Structures hiérarchiques* for another approach to Plotinus); where Plotinus resists the interpretative scheme, he is found guilty of quibbling and evasion (*Great Chain of Being*, pp. 63, 65-6).

[12]This is a felicitous expression of the aspect of change characteristic of the unchanging transcendent world of Plotinus; cf. A. H. Armstrong, in *Le Néoplatonisme*, Colloque internat. du C.N.R.S., Paris 1971, pp. 67 ff.; S. Gersh, *Kinesis Akinetos*, Leiden 1973.

[13]H. Jonas, "The Soul in Gnosticism and Plotinus", *Le Néoplatonisme*, pp. 45-53 (reprinted in Jonas, *Philosophical Essays*, Englewood Cliffs 1974).

[14]Vol. I, Göttingen 1934 (3rd ed. 1964); vol. II, 1 Göttingen 1954 (2nd. ed. 1966).

[15]New York 1966.

[16]*Op. cit.* p. 2.

[17]*Loc. cit.*; cf. p. 57; H. Plessner, *Die Stufen des Organischen und der Mensch* 2nd ed., Berlin 1965, pp. VIII-IX, refers to Max Scheler's role in reviving the Aristotelian concept of a hierarchy of living forms (cf. *infra*, n. 21).

[18]Jonas, *op. cit.*, pp. 5 (speaking also of the "audacity" of life), 79; cf. Plessner, *op. cit.*, pp. XX-XXI, 127, 173 ff., on the concept of "Begrenzung".

[19]Jonas, *op. cit.*, pp. 4, 80.

[20]*Op. cit.*, p. 5.

[21]*Op. cit.*, pp. 5, 84-5; for the emergence of higher forms of life, cf. also pp. 103-7, 174, 183-7; cf. Jonas, *Philosophical Essays*, pp. 196 ff.; for other philosophical biologies reflecting a more or less existential influence and exploiting concepts of structure, cf. K. Goldstein, *The Organism*, American ed. Boston 1963, ch. XI; Plessner, *op. cit.*; and of course Max Scheler, *Die Stellung des Menschen im Kosmos*, Darmstadt 1928.

[22]For a survey of this research, cf. J. Wippern (ed.), *Das Problem der ungeschriebene Lehre Platons*, Darmstadt 1972; H. J. Krämer, "Die platonische Akademie und das Problem einer systematischen Interpretation der Philosophie Platons", *Kantstudien* 55 (1964), pp. 69-101 (reprinted in *Das Platonbild*, ed. K. Gaiser, Hildesheim 1969).

[23] *From Platonism to Neoplatonism* 3rd ed., The Hague 1968, pp. 1, 179 ff. (and ch. VII in general), 221 ff.; cf. Merlan, in *The Cambridge History of Later Greek and Early Medieval Philosophy*, ed. A. H. Armstrong, Cambridge 1967, pp. 15 ff.

[24]C. J. de Vogel, "On the Neoplatonic Character of Platonism and the Platonic Character of Neoplatonism", *Mind* N. S. 62 (1953), pp. 47-55; cf. O'Meara, *Structures hiérarchiques*, p. 11 n. 27, and, for the evidence cited by de Vogel, pp. 12-15.

[25]H. J. Krämer, *Areté bei Platon und Aristoteles* 2nd ed., Amsterdam 1967; *Der Ursprung der Geistmetaphysik* 2nd ed., Amsterdam 1967; K. Gaiser, *Platons ungeschriebene*

Lehre, Stuttgart 1968. These scholars do not agree on all points: Merlan, for example, hesitates to attribute the system of the Academy to Plato himself (*From Platonism*, p. 231); cf. also O'Meara, *Structures hiérarchiques*, p. 15 n. 36.

[26]Cf. Krämer, "Die Platonische Akademie ...", p. 82 n. 23.

[27]Krämer, *art. cit.*, pp. 82 ff.; *Aretē*, pp. 423 ff.; *Der Ursprung*, pp. 106 ff., 150 ff.

[28]Krämer, *art. cit.*, pp. 88-9; *Der Ursprung*, pp. 32, 210: Krämer uses the language and concepts of Nicolai Hartmann's stratificational ontology (cf. O'Meara, *Structures hiérarchiques*, pp. 9, 111).

[29]Krämer, *art. cit.*, pp. 88-9; *Aretē*, pp. 540-1; *Der Ursprung*, pp. 150, 210; K. Gaiser, *Platons ungeschriebene Lehre*, pp. 20-6, 107 ff., 169-70, 305, 309 ff.

[30]Cf. Lovejoy, *Great Chain of Being*, p. 19.

[31]Cf. my *Structures hiérarchiques*, p. 114

[32]Cf. *supra* n. 29.

[33]*Structures hiérarchiques*, pp. 105-8, 116-9.

R. F. HATHAWAY

FORMAL AND MATERIAL PRINCIPLES OF HIERARCHY

An elusive general concept that guides much of our thinking and that shaped large areas in our philosophical tradition in various ways at different times is the concept of hierarchy. Is there *one* concept of hierarchy? Doubtless, it would be a serious mistake to think that there is a 'unit idea' of hierarchy readily accessible in the history of ideas.[1] It could be argued that our concept of hierarchy is a congeries of unrelated principles of rank ordering. Yet one can ask whether the concept is at base an empirical one, or *a priori*. The ranking of animal species first hinted at by Aristotle, however rationally elegant a Linnaean taxonomic chart looks, is an empirical ranking.[2] Yet how one interprets empirical data here seems to depend on one's general principles of ranking. Thus morphological features or functions can be treated as emerging from a constant material basis, or as diverging, nature exploring branches from irreducibly dissimilar potentialities.[3] The criteria by which we rank species shifts accordingly as we treat functions as emergent or as divergent.

I shall say nothing in what follows about the sweeping questions about the *a priori* basis, if any, of these general principles of hierarchic ranking, but will confine myself to certain general comments about the place of hierarchy in ancient metaphysics. I shall contend that Aristotle's account of substance (*ousia*) implies that the place of hierarchy in his vision of reality is not primarily between substances (or substance-kinds), as Lovejoy and others believed, but within substance itself. I shall also argue that at the foundation of the concept of hierarchy in Aristotle there are bifurcating, rival principles of hierarchy, and that these are not necessarily complementary. Because Aristotle's account of substance is far from clear to us, I shall merely outline in a programmatic way the sort of interpretation which I have in mind.

1.

The implicit assumption of Aristotle's metaphysics is that reality is hierarchic. We must not confuse this assumption with the view that individuals, living and nonliving, in the world are factually arranged by hierarchic relations, for example, in governments, bureaucracies, families, dominance relations, or, to name the institution that is still connoted by the term 'hier-

archy', the church. It is a remarkable fact about the western family of languages that the term 'hierarchy' came into use so long after principles of
ranking of strikingly analogous types had become an entrenched and evident
feature of empirical reality, and long after philosophers had uncovered principles of ranking with powerful similarities.[4] The fact that 'hierarchy' was
first used in an early medieval context does not confine us to medieval assumptions.[5] The question whether reality is irreducibly hierarchic is not a
question about whether the world appeared to be so for certain cultures at
certain times, or whether the world now appears to be so (as an inductive gen-
eralization). Philosophers have avoided raising the question. The reason for
this may be the modern assumption that the concept of hierarchy is restricted
to pre-modern ideas and institutions. But a more plausible reason may be that
philosophy contains a drive towards simplicity, and many structures are sim-
pler than hierarchy.

Let us note here that although hierarchy has emerged in many significant
ways in recent philosophical discussion, it is by no means the only structure
with very general applications. There is some disagreement about what one may
call a hierarchy. Moments on a temporal continuum do not form a hierarchy (the
'before-after' relations do not generate hierarchy), nor are simple regresses
produced by simply applying the same rule iteratively. Only where iteration
produces entities of clearly distinct types is hierarchy found[6], or where
lines branch into divisions (or unbranch in fusions[7]), in which case something
remains constant while something else changes. The latter can range either
over individuals, or over properties (characters, forms, passive or active
powers, functions, etc.), or over both. Whereas iteration produces one-one hierarchy, line-branching trees tend to produce one-many hierarchy.

The notion of form as *energeia*, as articulated activity or functioning,
lies at the heart of Aristotle's account of substance (*ousia*). One of his major concerns, as Furth and others have correctly emphasized[8], was to provide a
general theory for the science of animals. It is clear that the concept of *energeia* finds its paradigm in the highly articulated functionings of living
things. The term, as Aristotle twice tells us[9], is used in such a way as to
refer to the work (*ergon*) something performs, or to certain changes, which explains why some translate it as 'activity'. *Energeia* is not the 'actualization', that is, the coming into being of some definite substance. It is *not*
facts having to do with the serial emergence of features in the embryo that

show why *energeia* is a structure with hierarchic features. These facts, well known to Aristotle, are merely evidence of such a hierarchic order. It is the concept of *energeia* itself that establishes the presence of one of two rival principles of hierarchy in Aristotle's account of substance, namely, a material hierarchy.

What I mean can be understood as follows. Insofar as I describe a given function of an animal, for instance, perception, under my concept of *energeia*, I will emphasize the 'work' of some underlying thing, for instance, certain perceptual organs such as eyes. The *energeia* (functioning, activity) is the *energeia* 'of' whatever one chooses to pick out as underlying, either the eyes, say, or whatever the eyes are, 'water' of some kind, for instance. The step from *energeia* to what it is the *energeia* 'of' is logically compelling, and leads downwards to a matter conceived as an underlying thing, though not in precisely the same way that a substrate of change underlies. An ontology with nothing but different instances of *energeia*, in this sense of the term, would be logically incomplete.

Aristotle further gives us a rule for generating a series of hierarchically ranked underlying materials.[10] In more familiar terms, for replacing 'proximate' matter with more ultimate or general matter.[11] Because my remarks are merely programmatic, I will merely indicate what Aristole's rule is. He alludes to it at *Metaphysics* Δ 4, 1015a7-10, when he remarks that

> Nature is a first matter, and it is this in two ways: first relative to the same thing, or first in general, for example, as relative to the same things bronze is the first [matter] of bronze works, but in general perhaps [the first matter is] water (*hydōr*), if everything meltable is water (*hydōr*).[12]

If 'M_1' refers to matter that is first relative to the same things[13], and 'M_2' refers to matter that is first in general, then the condition stated in the last clause of Aristotle's remark is

> (1) Everything that is ϕ-able is M_2.
> It is clear that Aristotle assumes here that bronze is meltable. He therefore assumes the following rule for what I will term the equivalence of M_1 and M_2.
>
> (2) If M_1 is ϕ-able, and if everything that is ϕ-able is M_2, then M_1 is equivalent to M_2.[14]

Interpreted in terms of Aristotle's examples, (2) asserts that if everything meltable is water (*hydōr*), and bronze is meltable, then bronze is equivalent to water.

Aristotle's remark thus gives us the following general rule of substitution.

(3) If M_1 is the first matter relative to the same f things, and M_1 and M_2 are equivalent, then M_2 is the first matter in general of those f things.

Since M_2 is not necessarily ultimate, it follows that (3) can be applied for successive substitutions for 'M_1' and 'M_2'. If an animal (or animal kind) is Aristotle's paradigm, then its first matter relative to the same thing will be certain non-uniform parts, e.g., its organs or work-performing units; and its first matter in general will be whatever these are equivalent to, e.g., uniform parts like blood or bone.[15] For the moment, it is necessary merely to note what this entails, namely, the assumption that a non-uniform part in some sense 'is' blood (or bone, or whatever). However, the same rule can again be used with the uniform parts as one's starting point. Blood, bone, etc. have their *energeia*. Nothing prevents us from taking the animal's organs as organized wholes or units, whose first matter relative to them is blood, bone, etc., but whose first matter in general is whatever these are equivalent to, viz., 'water' (*hydōr*) or whatever, and so on down the line to whatever is truly irreducible in Aristotle's physics.[16] If we let 'M_1' stand as the name of some first matter of an f-thing, and let 'M_2' be the name of the f-thing's first matter in general, then if a g-thing is apart of the f-thing (by analysis or observation) that is named by 'M_1', 'M_2' will be the name of the g-thing's 'proximate' matter, which in turn will be equivalent to M_3, *its* first matter in general, and so forth. The rule stated by (3) generates a cardinal hierarchy of descending materials, M_1, M_2, M_3, ... M_n.

Aristotle's analysis uses a material principle of hierarchy, therefore, which is started by his own concpet of the *energeia* of an entity. Insofar as he (tentatively) understands the form of a thing as its *energeia*, his analysis of form surprisingly yields a material principle for ranking. This is what Aristotle means, I suggest, by his doctrine of the 'inherence' of form in matter.

2.

It would be an error to think that this exhausts Aristotle's theory of substance. Contrasting with the material principle of hierarchy just briefly outlined, Aristotle assumes another, different way of understanding the 'form' or *energeia* of an entity. Although *energeia* derives its primary meaning from 'work' or 'change', it has a rival sense, that, namely, of *entelecheia*. The integrated functioning of an animal is more than an activity. We can understand *what* such-and-such a functioning is only with reference to a goal or end (*telos*). *Entelecheia* is how a thing 'holds' (*echein*) in reference to an end.[17] We understand what something is as being 'for the sake of' this. In one sense, if what something is is a set of definite 'powers', then what it is is always logically for the sake of some definite outcomes. We cannot understand what it is to be these powers, without their being powers for these certain outcomes and none other. Yet outcomes in this sense appear only to be *energeia* in its first sense.

The notion of *entelecheia* requires us to think further about how the powers of a thing are focused on certain essential outcomes. In this sense, a functioning unit of some larger integrated unit is a 'part' not merely of some aggregate of activities (some generalized activity), a sum of other activities, but of certain organized or unified actions, which we might call the 'purpose' of the whole entity. To illustrate this, the capacity of the eye of a bee to see can better be understood for what it is, if it is known what it is for the sake of (perhaps food-sharing, or queen-tending, or brood-rearing, which all tell us that the essential function of the bee is the life and survival of the hive), but the same organ, if it is the eye of a man, will be for the sake of a different integrative function, for instance, the getting of knowledge. *Entelecheia* is how a thing holds in reference to an integrative functions.

The functions (and corresponding capacities or powers) of the lowest subunits of the larger organized unit can be arranged in a formal hierarchy, ascending step by step, by considering what the powers of the minimal 'parts' of matter are (the heat of the blood) in the light of what they are for the sake of (movement of the limbs, for instance), and so on upwards to whatever is limiting for the given whole, that is, whatever gives its essential marks. Perception, in this case, will be treated not as compelling a downward analysis or material hierarchy, but as requiring an opposite, upward analysis until it is seen to be 'part' of the 'form'. Aristotle's account here is still functional as well as teleological.

The 'nature' of an entity or substance is both constitutive and integrative. Every substance according to his account is doubly hierarchic. How we say what a thing is generates logically distinct principles of hierarchy. Are formal and material principles *rival* principles of hierarchy? At times, Aristotle seems to argue that every complete account of a substance ought to make dual reference to form and to matter. It may be true that he thought that minute observational analysis would show that the least details of the materials of a thing are in some way linked to an essential function.[18] This suggests that every 'part' or sub-unit of an organized unit has an account that tells us what it is 'for the sake of'. But this implies that just as the presence of organs (feet, eyes, heart, lung) logically differentiates classes (or kinds) of animals, so also must the least sub-units, and in such a way as to be directly linked to the 'form'. The last mentioned condition requires, I suggest, that Aristotle treat every sub-unit as an organized unit, and that this should be logically linked to the 'form' in the way that powers are linked to *energeia*. At times, Aristotle does seem to think that the organized unit we point to when we point to the organ *is* a power.[19] 'Finished' *qua* being a definite power or capacity, every power is necessarily 'for the sake of' some definite *energeia* or functioning. But we cannot identify what the power is by identifying the materials of which the organ is made, unless these also are decomposed into properties that if together yield the right function. If Aristotle's theory of elements yields a list of such irreducible properties, then he might be able to satisfy the stringent condition that *all* matter is in some way linked to form in the requisite manner. If he could, it is perhaps correct then to regard the doubly hierarchic character of substance as a single isomorphic descending and ascending series of ranks.[20]

3.

Thus far I have said nothing about ranking *between* forms, or between substances. In *The Great Chain of Being*, Lovejoy assumed that the ranking or grading principle in Aristotle is a ranking of different substances, rather than a ranking *within* substance itself, as I have argued here.[21] But as Lovejoy himself was aware, Aristotle treats the boundaries between substance (substance-kinds) as systematically elusive. 'Nature', he says, 'passes by so little [a degree] from soul-less things to living things, that in virtue of the continuity their boundary is indistinguishable.'[22] He is doubtless using 'continuity' (*synecheia*) here in a non-technical sense, and even if he is thinking of a perfectly dense continuum, he may be referring only to the difficulty of marking the boundary empirically. Yet this suggests that we can only fix the

boundaries between substances if we first fix the hierarchy internal to substances. If the lowest 'power' differentiating the living from the non-living
(the soul-less) is the nutritive (*threptikē*), there is nonetheless a downward
analysis pointing to whatever materials are needed for the functioning of the
nutritive power in the body of the animal. The boundary between the living and
the non-living is present, paradoxically, within the living substance itself.

If from the standpoint of theory the internal hierarchy is prior, the
'chain of being' is not a chain of species or classes, and Lovejoy's principle
of plenitude must accordingly also be modified.[23] If we lay aside the nagging
doubt about precisely which sort of 'principle of plenitude' is meant, we
might envision a plenitude *internal* to substance. By this we would mean that
every organized unit or substance will contain a doubly well-ordered formal
and material hierarchy without gaps. Let us note also that since the hierarchy
internal to substance is iterative and not branching (i.e., not a 'tree'), we
need not adopt a tree-like (or pyramid-like) picture of hierarchy for Aristotle's metaphysics. Lovejoy's *ens perfectissimum*, on this minimalist picture,
would be the highest integrative functioning possible (and here and there,
actual), whatever else it may signify. 'Plenitude', on this view, means that,
whatever the lower or higher bounds of Aristotle's hierarchy, it has no gaps.
We might pronounce this to be the true ideal of an Aristotelian metaphysics.

One might wonder what Aristotle's idea of the ordering *between* substances
might be. But the question implies that he has just one such ordering relation. His various remarks and hints in this respect suggest that he had, to
the contrary, several different, not always consistent ideas about how species
or substance-kinds might be ordered. His general theory of elements suggests
that he would tend to treat intersubstance hierarchy as divergent (upward
branching), not as emergent (degrees of differentiation of one matter). The
eye of a bee and the eye of a man are *analogous* organized non-uniform parts,
not the same, regardless of their general sameness of function. Each is best
understood as part of the hierarchy internal to its *own* substance. Aristotle's
theory of substance thus would guide empirical biology in making difficult
choices between models, even though he knew nothing about its present Dar-
winian assumptions.

NOTES

[1] Compare Jaakko Hintikka, 'Gaps in the Great Chain of Being: An Exercise in the Methodology of the History of Ideas,' Presidential Address, 50th Annual Meeting of the American Philosophical Assoication, *Proceedings* LXIX (1976-77), pp. 22-38.

[2] Cf. Arthur O. Lovejoy, *The Great Chain of Being: A Study of the History of an Idea*, William James Lectures, 1933 (Cambridge, Mass., 1961), pp. 58-59, who cites Aristotle, *De an.* B3, 414a29-415a13 and *G. A.*, 732a-733b. These passages give us not one, but two different principles for a *scala naturae*, the former based on the 'arrangement in order of succession' of the 'powers' (*dynameis*) of different kinds of souls; the latter based on different types of animal generation, assumed to depend both on the material properties of the bodies of animals (heat, coldness, moistness, dryness), as well as on the formula (*logos*) given in generation by the male parent to certain underlying matter. In addition, Lovejoy argues that for Aristotle the *scala naturae* is a genuine continuum (p. 56). Since a continuum is dense, the segments that mark off different forms are infinite in number, which is inconsistent with the concept of a hierarchy or 'ladder'. Although Lovejoy's basic insight seems sound, he leaves it unclear what generates a hierarchy or 'chain of being'.

[3] Emergent properties yields a Spencerian hierarchy; divergent properties, a Bergsonian hierarchy (a genuine 'tree'). Cf. Werner Stark, *The Social Bond* (New York, 1976), Vol. I, p. 74.

[4] The best known of these is perhaps the 'Tree of Porphyry', or Plato's method of division (*diairesis*), a supposedly straight forward dichotomous division of genera (whether these are high level forms or classes remains an open question). Cf. the papers by Moravscik and Cohen in *Patterns in Plato's Thought*, ed. J. M. E. Moravscik (Reidel, 1973), pp. 158-92. These lead naturally to notions of class membership and class inclusion, which one could argue are underpinned by a principle of hierarchy.

[5] Cf. the author's *Hierarchy and the Definition of Order in the Letters of Pseudo-Dionysius* (The Hague, 1969), p. xxi and *passim*. Medieval thought about hierarchy is supported by Platonic assumptions of a very general type, and it is these assumptions that the term 'hierarchy' connotes, in the medieval context, in addition to its other connotations.

[6] For example, as when one distinguishes between first order rules and seocnd order (procedural) rules (for making, adopting, and applying first order rules); or between knowing that p, and knowing that one knows that p (being certain); or between wanting ϕ, and wanting to want ϕ; or when one requires that 'is a member of' can be iterated only between variables of consecutively ascending types (Russell's theory).

[7] Cf. J. H. Woodger, *The Axiomatic Method in Biology* (Cambridge, 1937), pp. 61-2.

[8] Cf. Montgomery Furth, 'Morphogenesis: Some Elements of Aristotelian Embryology and Some Ontological Ramifications, 'Paper delivered at the meeting of the Society for Ancient Greek Philosophy, New York, 1975; and 'Notes on the Construction of Aristotelian Biological Individuals,' Paper delivered at the Princeton Conference on Aristotle's Biology, Princeton University, 1976. Furth claims that Aristotle's theory of substance is in fact 'preeminently aimed' in this direction.

[9] *Met.* θ3, 1047a-31; θ8, 1050a22-23; W. D. Ross, *Aristotle's Metaphysics* (Oxford, 1958), Vol. II, p. 245, 'Strictly speaking ἐνέργεια means activity or actualizations.' Cf. below.

[10]Aristotle's advanced account in *Met.* θ requires that we think of these as passive or active 'powers'.

[11]I write 'more ultimate', not wanting to close the issue about Aristotle's commitment, if any, to a 'prime' matter.

[12]*Hydōr* and 'water' are not synonyms. This is clear from Aristotle's treatment of *hydōr* at *Meteor.* 5, 382b13-16, and it is even clearer from Plato's account in *Timaeus* 58D5ff., where the two forms of *hydōr* are 'the liquid' (τὸ ὑγρόν) and 'the fusile' (τὸ χυτόν); and instances of the former are *all* forms of water, ice, hoarfrost, snow, as well as juices, saps, wines, pitch, oils, honey, and acid, while instances of the latter are metals like gold and copper, which at 59C2 is called 'one of the bright and solid kinds of *hydōr*'.

[13]'Same' what? Or the 'same' how? Aristotle's example implies that 'same' simply means 'having the same material-name'. Or does he have some notion of count-nouns in mind? His odd remark at *Phys.* A 7, 190b24-25, 'Man and gold and in general, *the matter*, is what gets counted', might indicate this. Ultimately, he appears to have a common sense clue to what gets counted, or what modern philosophers like to call 'material objects', as though we have *one* clear idea of a 'material object'.

[14]Equivalence is evidently a kind of identity, but I shall not consider what sort of identity is implied here.

[15]Aristotle does not distinguish, as a modern biologist would, between cells as unit parts, and constituents of an organism, e.g., parts of cells like cellular secretions, in contrast to extra-cellular fluids, which in turn might have unit-parts. But these modern additions would only strengthen the tendency of Aristotle's own analysis to intercalate *many* ranks of unit-parts between the organism and its ultimate matter (whatever we take it to be).

[16]The first level of composition of matter (stuffs) is clearly said to be certain powers at *P. A.* B1, 646a14, as Furth correctly notes. Cf. *Notes*, p. 1. The hot, cold, moist, and dry are 'the starting points of the natural elements' (*P. A.* B2, 648b8-10). The true elements, or foundations of the elements, are properties (dispositional indicators) of the so-called elements (and again, we must recall the 'water' *refers* to the liquid and the meltable in general, and similarly, the other so-called elements refer to what we might be tempted to call *states* of matter). Cf. *De an.* 432a6 'the forms which are objects of perception ... the states (*hexeis*) and properties (*pathē*) of objects of perception'.

[17]Ross, *op. cit.*, pp. 245-6, argues that since there is no evidence for the word *enteleches* in Aristotle's time, the term must be formed from *enteles*, 'perfect'. Whence the common vague translations, 'completion', 'perfection', and 'actualization'. Since we do not *know* how Aristotle formed the term, a literal, etymological approach is as sound as any other.

[18]As David Balme suggests in 'Form and Species in Aristotle's Biology', Paper delivered at the Princeton Conference on Aristotle's Biology, 1976, p. 10.

[19]*Met.* Z16, 1040b5-8 'It is obvious that of the things estimated to be substances, most are powers, e.g., the parts of animals.' Is *this* what Aristotle means here?

[20]There are many problems about this neat picture. The ascending hierarchy is well-ordered (x is for the sake of y, y is for the sake of z, etc.), and unified by the form, but the descending hierarchy is threatened with partial or total collapse by the notion of equivalence above mentioned. If bronze *is* water (which sort of 'is' of identity?), then nothing prevents the highest level matter from being identical with the lowest level, with obvious consequences for the

explanatory value of matter. Form is prior to matter in an interesting sense. Any analysis of matter as 'power' (*dynamis*) depends on a clear notion of the *activity* relative to which a given 'power' is the 'power'. One can treat a centipede's crawling as an aggregate of micro-processes of its smallest material units, or as a linear movement that is the outcome of the forms of turning movements of its limbs or bodily parts, whose geometry can be analysed independently of the former micro-processes. The form of animal motion is both separable from its lowest material sub-units, and gives unity to these. Thus the theory of form as *energeia* does not guarantee that form inheres in matter down to the finest level of our observations (even with the unaided eye). Moreover, one can conceive of the *same* outcomes (same form), but substituting different matter. Aristotle, moreover, was aware of these problems.

[21]*Great Chain of Being*, p. 59.

[22]*H. A.* 588b4-6, cited by Lovejoy, p. 56. I have retained Lovejoy's term 'indistinguishable'; λανθάνειν might more properly be said to mean 'eludes notice'. If neighboring kinds are truly indistinguishable, we would have a continuum and not a hierarchy. Lovejoy's reference to Ross' view that 'All individual things may be graded according to the degree to which they are infected with potentiality' only leaves us wondering what Ross means by 'infected with potentiality'. If every 'power' is in some way definite, one cannot slide by 'degrees' from one 'power' to another. If the interpretation above is correct, 'potentiality' is for Aristotle not a kind of formless broth or 'oatmeal' (Furth), but an already articulated realm.

[23]Lovejoy in fact traces his principle to Plato's *Timaeus* (*The Great Chain of Being*, p. 52). His contention that 'It is of the nature of an Idea to manifest itself in concrete existence' raises an important question: is there in Plato's theory of form an analogue to the principle of abstraction (for every property there is a set whose members are the objects having the property)? It is not in the *Timaeus*, however, that we can find an answer to this difficult problem.

PAUL G. KUNTZ

"FROM THE ANGEL TO THE WORM:"

AUGUSTINE'S HIERARCHICAL VISION[1]

In *The Great Chain of Being* we hear too little of Augustine's concept of
grades of being, to which we now apply the name "hierarchy."[2] Augustine could
have used the term only if he had lived a century later when the Pseudo-
Dionysius invented it. This inquiry into the hierarchical structure of his
vision is one of a series, beginning with several contemporary thinkers, J. K.
Feibleman and F. Schumacher; one from several Renaissance thinkers, Robert
Bellarmine; two about Medievals, Thomas Aquinas and Bonaventure, and if I continue working backwards, I shall have to take account of Plotinus, Aristotle
and Plato.[3] The present study of Augustine is one of a triad: one called "Homo
Erro to Homo Viator" is an analysis of the spiritual pilgrimage depicted in
the *Confessions*.[4] Another one is the philosophic growth towards an inclusive
completeness of all the meanings of "truth:" "St. Augustine's Quest of Truth:
The Adequacy of a Christian Philosophy."[5] In contrast to the rather more personal and the epistemological, the present paper is metaphysical. Especially
in Augustine, the metaphysics must be personal and concerned with knowledge.
Metaphysics is a kind of mapping of the world, a laying out of all the categories of being. It is the most fundamental kind of ordering, and not primarily an argument, but the structure within which arguments occur. Because vision
is so commonly neglected in considering metaphysics, I have deliberately chosen a poetic title. My point is that "without vision, metaphysics perishes."[6]

The phrase "from the angel to the worm" occurs in the book depicting conversion, Book VIII, and the note is one of joy in the divine order of all
things. There is in creation an ebb and flow, and in wonder man asks

> Is this their allotted measure? Is this all Thou hast as-
> signed to them, whereas from the highest heavens to the
> lowest earth, from the beginning of the world to the end
> of ages, from the angel to the worm, from the first mo-
> tion to the last, Thou settest each in his place, and re-
> alizest each in their season, every good after his kind?
> Woe is me! how high art Thou in the highest, and how deep
> in the deepest! and Thou never departest, and we scarcely
> return to Thee. (*Conf.* VIII. III. 7, p. 139)[7]

If this is what Augustine learned from Victorinus, who is mentioned immediately before and immediately after, it is a Christian Neo-Platonism. The
significance of creation rather than emanation, is that God is present in all

levels, and available immediately throughout the hierarchy. It is an ordering
in time rather than only a timeless order, and it is followed by a summons to
act. The vision requires action: "Up, Lord, and do; stir us up, and recall us;
kindle and draw us; inflame, grow sweet to us; let us now love; *let us run*."
If there are contemplative visions that transcend and exclude action, Augustine's is not of that sort. Augustine's Mary would have responded to Martha's
rebuke: the "good part which [Jesus said] shall not be taken away from [me]"
compels me also to serve and to be "cumbered about much serving." (Luke VIII:
38-42)

But the hierarchical vision is a turning from the many only that waste
away time, and are "wasted by time" and a turning to the One, the SelfSame, in
whose "Simple Essence" are found things we need in time, "*corn, and wine, and
oil*" which presumably Martha served. (*Conf*. IX.IV.10, p. 163)

The vision of the graded whole is one of continuity. The cosmos reflects
the fullness of God. God is the answer to "whence all beings have come," and
God is the answer to "whither man ought and can return." Book IX celebrates
the arrival of his mother Monica to the company of the saints. Her earthly
pilgrimage had carried her to heaven.

> ... We raising up ourselves with a more glowing affection
> towards the "Self-Same," did by degrees pass through all
> things bodily, even the very heaven, whence sun and moon,
> and stars shine upon the earth; yea, we were soaring
> higher yet, by inward musing, and discourse and admiring
> of Thy works; and we came to our own minds, and went be-
> yond them, that we might arrive at that region of never-
> failing plenty .... [This is not to "have been" or "here-
> after to be"] but only "to be" ... and what is like unto
> Thy Word, our Lord, who endureth in Himself without be-
> coming old, and maketh all things new? (*Conf*. IX.V.24,
> pp. 173-4)

But has not the literature on Augustine already taken full account of
Augustine's hierarchical vision? I am not satisfied with Vernon Bourke's
"Three Levels of Reality," which reduces the hierarchy to a three-level ontology: "there are three kinds of natures: divine, psychic and corporeal." The
lowest level, of bodies, is of the "completely mutable; they grow older in
time and are buffeted about in place. Souls are mutable in time but immutable
in place .... "God is at the top, ... wholly immutable ...."[8] Although God is
unchangeable, yet he is all-changing, "ever working, ever at rest." (*Conf*. I.
IV. 4, p. 3)

This analysis is helpful, but not wholly so, because the Augustinian hierarchy is constructed as a kind of map for the pilgrim and the important thing is not the level on which a thing is, but how it is related to what is below and to what is above. In a static hierarchy, it is right to say that the human soul "stands in the middle." But in dynamic terms, which Bourke then introduces in a second paragraph, man's instability is that he may turn "upward or downward." If his will turns up to God, it is *conversio*, if downward, it is *aversio* or *perversio*. As Bourke notes, it is only this dynamic picture that makes the Augustinian hierarchy distinctive.

The hierarchical mapping is presented by Augustine the explorer of the ups and downs of life. He is creating his map as a by product of finding life's way. A geographer of hierarchy does his work in more formal way: his chapters may begin with the One and descend, or begin within the many and ascend. The explorer of the hierarchy is somewhat between extremes, but not exactly sure, since he has no trusted map, and stumbles along, even stumbling upon such guides as Cicero, Ambrose and Victorinus.

Augustinian exploration is venturing into the unknown, and as all exploring, most adequately expressed in the verbs, whether of the form of the first person finding something, or something being above or below something else. I say this because I find ontological analyses, in this case Bourke's version of Augustine, view the subject as a set of answers to the question "What is there?" Then we get a, b, and c as answers. But the more important question is "What is x in relation to y?" Then the answers, when in terms of "higher than" and "lower than," which is the language of grading, gives us the sense of which route to follow. Nouns may name, but verbs and adverbs are needed to relate objects. What is the context of naming the levels from top to bottom, as "from the angel to the worm," the *whats* of creation below God and before reaching the vegetable, tree and grass? Clearly it is to answer the questions of whence came creatures? And this question is always coupled with the question of "how man can return?" The *Whence*? is always given human importance by being linked to *Whither*?

All the creatures speak of the same ultimate origin. A most interesting passage to be read together with ascending the degrees (*gradatim in idipsum*). Augustine's way up is this "Dicebamus ergo, si cui sileat tumultus carnis, sileant phantasiae terrae et aquarum et aëris, sileant et poli ...." "We were saying then, if the tumult of the flesh were hushed, hushed also the images of

earth and waters, and air, hushed also the poles of heaven ...." (*Conf.*
IX.X.25, p. 174) We then get seven levels:

1. Flesh
2. Images of earth and waters and air*
3. Poles of heaven*
4. Soul
5. Dreams and revelations*
6. Tongue and sign*
7. Whatsoever exists only in transition*

It is to be noted that 5 levels are polarities.*

What do they say together when they are silent? "We made not ourselves,
but He made us that abideth forever." The dramatic passage reminds us of the
paradoxical "still voice." (I Kings XIX:12) He alone speaks, not through a, b,
c, d, e, f, g; creation is silent so that Eternal Wisdom itself can speak.

Can these seven be reduced to three? Or, what seems easier, can five levels be reduced to three? Let us take the easier case first.

In the famous formulation of the ultimate peace and order (*De Civ. Dei*,
XIX, 13 pp.) Augustine has

1. Body
2. Irrational soul
3. Body and soul
4. Men obedient to law and man in concord
5. Celestial city

before we get to "the peace of all things is the tranquility of order."
(Bourke, pp. 16-17)

Are there 3, or 5, or 7 levels of being? If there is a continuum, it
makes little difference how many grades we chose to discriminate. If between
any two, say a and b, and b and c, there is an intermediate, then three developes into five. Or if between 0 and 1, we have a, b, c, then these generate
seven.

My argument is that what matters is not the exact number of kinds of beings or substances but the direction which is up or down. Let me support this
argument as one reads the *Confessions* book by book. At the beginning of Book
One there is the statement of the ultimate whence and the ultimate whither.
"Thou madest us for Thyself, and our heart is restless, until it repose in
Thee." (*Conf.* I.I.1, p. 1) Could there be an argument for the identity of the
whence and the whither? The category that would establish this identity is
purpose. The final cause, why there should be a world, is also the end to
which all man's striving should be directed. If man finds himself in a world

in which he is alone endowed with reason and spirit, the apex of creation, and this creation cannot be by chance or explained by secondary causes, within the creation, it is then not irrational or gratuitous to affirm a Creator's mind and will.

My interpretation of the opening pages is that we encounter difficulties of paradox and confusion when we endeavor to define "God," but that in spite of the difficulties of conceptualization, the presence of God can be affirmed because of the dependence of all levels. Each level is dependent, therefore His presence is throughout. Omnipotence and omniscience lead to contradictions with omnibenevolence; yet omnipresence is secure: "if I go down into hell, Thou art there." (*Conf.* I.II.2, p. 2, quoting Ps. 139) This text leads to affirming the relation of finite to infinite: "Thou wholly everywhere, while nothing contains Thee wholly." (*Conf.* I.II.3, p. 2)

Book I concerns the deepest questions of the relations between finite man and infinite God. It is not merely that they are interdefinable; the important point hierarchically is that dynamically the limitations of the finite soul are transcended. Pusey translates "Narrow is the mansion of my soul; enlarge Thou it." (*Conf.* I.V.6, p. 3), but the Latin uses three verbs, to be, to come, to be expanded: "Angusta est domus animae meae: quo venias ad eam, dilatur abs te." But does our knowledge of ourselves begin on this high level? Far from it, we are first unreasoning little animals, who are dependent in every way on elders. (*Conf.* I.VI.7, p. 4) Yet we resist the subordination, and assume a place of master, if we could make slaves of our parents. (*Conf.* I.VI.8, p. 5)

The framework of hierarchy is required to explicate sin. It is a rebellion of the will against the ordered levels of creation and its necessary hierarchy of goods. In the God-man relation, God creates all levels good, and man introduces the confusion through "inordinate affection." God orders all things; therefore, sinful acts which man does must then be ordered. The principle of God's ordering this human disorder is "every inordinate affection should be its own punishment." (*Conf.* I.XII.19, p. 11) We could use this as the principle governing Dante's vision of *Inferno, Purgatorio* and *Paradiso.* The germ of the idea is at the conclusion of *Confessions* Book I. If a child is allowed to prefer false to true, he will, as Augustine, fill his mind with fiction, and ignore mathematics. The consequences of mistaken ranking come to prove the right ordering. "I sought for pleasures, sublimities, truths, so fell headlong into sorrows, confusions, errors." (*Conf.* I.XVIII.31, p. 18)

Can there be an experience supporting the metaphysical assumption of ultimate unity, the common point between one Creator and a Plotinian One? The evidence of this assumption of one highest, the top of the ladder, comes in Book II. Sometimes Augustine characterizes order as having the unity of the center of a circle (*Conf*. pp. 18-19, Pusey's notes). The argument of the *Confessions* is that unification of the self comes from loving "One Good." Contrariwise, to love many things, each ultimate, and unranked, is to fall into confusion. "I lost myself among a multiplicity of things." (*Conf*. II.I.1, p. 19)

The ultimate in the denial of the order of hierarchy is even more to be deplored than the deliberate rejection of unity and preference for multiplicity. This is the rejection of any purpose, and destruction for its own sake. The "gratuitous ... evil" of vandalism, the wasting of a neighbor's pears is the soul turning, not to multiplicity, but beyond, in the negation of the good, to nothing. (*Conf*. II.IV.9, p. 23) In this way Augustine can convey the full depth of the scale of being. It is not sexual sin, Augustine's defiance of his mother's admonition against fornication, and worse, adultery. Augustine makes too much of sexual sin, and his interpreters follow him. After all, God makes male and female, and on the biological level, the attraction and union is a manifestation of good. On this level bodies are lovely and to love. "For there is an attractiveness in beautiful bodies" writes Augustine (*Conf*. III.IV.9, p. 23, cf Bk IV.XII.18, p. 56, "If bodies please thee, praise God on occasion of them, and turn back thy love upon their Maker ....") Even fornication is a kind of imitation of God. (*Conf*. II.VI.14, p. 26)

The drama of hierarchical life is that we learn the importance of rising when we fall. When the creature turns from the Creator, it turns away from its own good, and what follows? Not only confusion but grief (dolor) and self-loathing. (*Conf*. III.I-II.1-4, pp. 29-31) In spite of the arrogance, there is yet the attraction of wisdom, and Cicero's *Hortensius* kindles in Augustine a "burning desire to" re-mount from earthly things to the divine. Yet, lacking humility, Augustine turns to the counterfeit, the image, and thus descends "steps ... to the depths of hell," which is philosophically to be read as nothingness, the complete privation of God (*Conf*. III.IV.7 - III.VII.12, pp. 33-36).

The one at the top is characterized as "Thou Good omnipotent, who so carest for every one of us, as if Thou carest for him only; and so for all, as if

they were but one!" Is there an argument here, to bestow upon the one, purposive, ordering, the principle of judgment, the characteristic of impartial
love? The context is analogical because what Augustine knows directly is his
mother's care for him in spite of his fall. He talks of "wallow[ing] in the
mire of that deep pit," the Manichaean faith (*Conf.* III.XI.18 - III.XII.21,
pp. 42-44).

The *Confessions* prefigures the *Divine Comedy*: that is, the way down gives
us knowledge of the way up, and indeed, the further down, the closer to the
bottom. Then the only further move is up. Book IV is about "stumbling in that
slippery course." (*Conf.* IV.II.2, p. 46) Towards the bottom is the torment we
call "alienation:" "I became a great riddle to myself," in context: "my native
country was a torment to me and my father's house a strange unhappiness."
(*Conf.* IV.IV.9, p. 50) The bottom is the despair produced by death: there is
here no level above change and decay. (*Conf.* IV.VI.11--IV.VII.12, pp. 51-53)

How is it possible to "descend, that ye may ascend?" Even in the mutable
is love. "If bodies please thee, praise God on occasion of them .... (*Conf.*
IV.XII.18, p. 56) The creation provides the way when the flesh is understood
as the way the *logos* of God was incarnated. The meaning of beauty, which he
then did not know, was sacramental. (*Conf.* IV.XII.19 - IV.XII.20, pp. 57-58)

The turning upward is defined more carefully in Book V. The way down is
the way of ignorance that leads to error. The way up is the way of knowledge
that leads to truth. Earlier it was turning to fable that neglected truth.
Here discovering fallacy is turning to validity. The specific fables are the
Manichaean, and their disproof is the turning toward the light. (*Conf.*
V.III.4, pp. 67-68) By identifying God as Truth, the recognition of the Word
within each man can be the discrimination between true and false. The obvious
objection is that the move is sideways, on the same plane, from one fable, the
Manichaean, to another fable, the Christian. Therefore it is necessary to read
the stories of Scripture as expression of truths concealed in figurative language. (*Conf.* V.XIII.23 - V.XIV.24, pp. 82-83)

A still more careful consideration of hierarchy occurs in Books VI - VII.
This is an attempt to answer the question of the ordering of levels, why is
level A higher than level B? While Augustine *believes* that God is "incorruptible, and uninjurable, and unchangeable; ... not knowing whence or how," yet
he says of himself, "I saw plainly and was sure, that that which may be corrupted, must be inferior to that which cannot ...." (*Conf.* VII.I.1, p. 107)

Here is a metaphysical principle of hierarchy. What prepares the way is a moral certainty; a man who is incorruptible, an assessor who will not take a bribe, is better than one "who could prefer gold to honesty." (*Conf*. VI.X.16, p. 98)

The hierarchical vision of Augustine is then not primarily a descriptive ontology in which "higher than" can be said to mean "inclusive of further attributes" or, as commonly, "more complex" but an evaluation. It is the ordering of all things under the Good, and direction of all beings towards the Good. In the midst of the most searching questions about evil, Where? Whence? How? What root? What seed? What being? Why fear what is Not? comes the affirmation "He indeed, the greater and chiefest Good, hath created these lesser goods; still both Creator and created, all are good." (*Conf*. VII.V.7, p. 122) The clarification of this is that although all things are good, because some are corruptible and there are degrees, "not all things [are] equal ...." (*Conf*. VII.XII.18, p. 122)

A most crucial point of the hierarchy is the movement down and the movement up. The incarnation is the self-humbling of God to human level, and the presence of the "Word, the Eternal Truth," makes possible the raising of the lower world to Divinity. The Word, above "the higher parts of Thy Creation, raises up the subdued into Itself ...." (*Conf*. VII.XVIII. 24, p. 126)

The metaphysics of Augustine has sometimes been called a metaphysics of conversion. Augustine does not merely construct a metaphysics of grades, he shows himself descending and then ascending. In this context the crucial passage from Book VIII is the analysis of struggle as the conflict between the binding of his "own iron will" to the lower while the contrary will strove upward. (*Conf*. VIII.V.10, p. 141) "Let them no more say then, when they perceive two conflicting wills in one man, that the conflict is between two substances, from two contrary principles, one good, and the other bad." (*Conf*. VIII.X.24, p. 150)

The crucial hierarchical point about conversion is that it is each person's own bondage of the will that binds him to a lower level. The chain of being is within each person, and not in the cosmos as such. Augustine longs for the devotion of Victorinus.

> Which thing I was sighing for, bound as I was, not with another's irons, but by my own iron will. My will the enemy held, and thence had made a chain for me, and bound me. For of a forward will, was a lust made; and a lust

served, became custom; and custom not resisted, became
necessity. By which links, as it were, joined together
(whence I called it a chain) a hard bondage held me en-
thralled. But that new will which had begun to be in me,
freely to serve Thee, and to wish to enjoy Thee, O God,
the only assured pleasantness, was not yet able to overcome my former wilfulness, strengthened by age. Thus did
my two wills, one new, and the other old, one carnal, the
other spiritual, struggle within me; and by their discord, undid my soul. (*Conf.* VIII.V.10, p. 141)

The liberation of Augustine from bondage is naturally followed by Book
IX, a celebration of Monica's ascent "from the *valley of tears* and singing
that *song of degrees*." (*Conf.* IX.II.2, p. 156)

The hierarchy of Augustine is more than a metaphysics of conversion. The
ascent is not merely from bondage of lust to freedom of the spirit. The natural environment also provides a ladder: earth, sea, air, sun, moon and stars.
Each of them says "I am not He" but "He made us." (*Conf.* X.VI.8, p. 186) The
ascent of the soul within the soul is judged more appropriate. This is the
turn from the visible to the invisible hierarchy. (*Conf.* X.VI.9, 10 – VII.11,
pp. 187-8) "I will pass then beyond this power of my nature also, rising by
degrees unto Him, who made me. And I come to the fields and spacious palaces
of my memory ...." (*Conf.* X.VIII.12, p. 188) The importance of rising by degrees is that it reveals that memory is organized: it is divided into "fields
and spacious palaces." This metaphor is intended as a most serious philosophical observation. When we seek something hidden in memory, then, when it
comes, it comes not alone but with "other things ... readily, in unbroken
order, as they are called for; those in front making way for the following
...." Not only is there the sequence of words, but there are "general heads"
under which qualities are classified, such as colors, and shapes which we have
seen. There are sounds when we have heard, odors which we have smelled. And so
the memory reveals the kinds of qualities: "hard or soft; hot or cold; smooth
or rugged; heavy or light ...." (*Conf.* X.VIII.12-13, pp. 188-189)

Of even more general categoreal level is the causal principle, expressed
"I will do this or that," in the context of possible "action, events, and
hopes." The agent himself is free to consider alternatives in the contemplation of "this or that [to] follow." (*Conf.* X.VIII.14, pp. 189-190)

There is no limit to the self discovered inwardly, and memory is "a large
and boundless chamber." (*Conf.* X.VIII.15, p. 190) Yet all that memory contains
falls under "three kinds of questions, 'whether the thing be? what is it? of

what kind is it?'" The categories that Augustine, scorned when taught from Aristotle's list, reappear inwardly as question types. (*Conf.* X.IX.17, p. 191)

The ascending consciousness is reflective. It is not merely a matter of collecting but of sorting out what is known, and the contrast is between *cogo*, to collect, and *cogito*, to re-collect. The mind that thinks thinks reflectively. (*Conf.* X.XI.18, p. 192) At this level we think not Greek or Latin, but of things in no language. This surely must be what we call the proposition, in contrast to the sentence. (*Conf.* X.XII.19, p. 192) Likewise, at this level we can abstract numbers from their images (*Conf.* X.XV.23, p. 195)

There is always in this search yet another step, and the next step beyond numbers is the recognition of the memory itself in memory. "What am I then, O my God? What nature am I?" (*Conf.* X.XVII.26, pp. 196-97) This I seeks a happy or blessed life, and at that point in ascent, the inward search finds God through the self. "For when I seek Thee, my God, I seek a happy life .... For my body liveth by my soul; and my soul by Thee. How then do I seek a happy life, seeing I have it not, until I can say, where I ought to say it, 'it is enough'?" (*Conf.* X.XX.29, p. 198)

There must then be present to the mind that which will satisfy it. At this point comes "joy in the truth [which] all desire." Earlier God was identified as truth itself. Here is a universal standard, a goal sought by all, which is good and beautiful. It is beyond the level of human thought, and therefore we should call it "transcendent." "... So neither art Thou the mind itself: because Thou art the Lord God of the mind; and all these are changed, but Thou remainest unchangeable over all ...." (*Conf.* X.XXIV. 35, pp. 202-203)

Too often we have read Kierkegaardian discontinuity of stages into the Augustinian hierarchy, particularly when we cease reading with Book VIII or Book IX. Book X gives us Platonic continuity of forms in an exposition that shows the overlap of levels, each lower participating in the next higher. Too much we have stressed what we read in Book X, "I have become a problem to myself ...." (*Conf.* X.XXXIII.50, p. 211) We need also to recognize that Augustine found a solution within himself. "Too late loved I Thee, O Thou Beauty of ancient days, yet ever new! too late I loved Thee! And behold, Thou wert within, and I abroad, and there I searched for Thee; deformed I, plunging amid those fair forms, which Thou hadst made. Thou wert with me, but I was not with Thee." (*Conf.* X.XXVII.38, p. 203)

There is a similarity of structure between the self and God: "In the
Eternal nothing passeth, but the whole is present." (*Conf.* XI.XI.13, p. 233)
In the human soul, "in thee, my mind, ... I measure times." (*Conf.*
XI.XXVII.36, p. 245)

Between God and the human soul is a heaven of forms. Augustine translates
the Creation from Genesis into the comprehensible Platonic language. Matter,
which is "almost nothing" can be only if it has form. Otherwise it is "a nothing something," an "is, is not." (*Conf.* XII.VI.6, p. 252) What is "heaven"
that God created along with earth? "... That spiritual or intellectual creature which always beholds the face of God ...." (*Conf.* XII.XVII.24, p. 261)
The hierarchical scheme is at this point:

1. God
2. Heaven
3. Man with soul
4. Bodies
5. Matter

But hierarchical thought based on continuity and participation must always be expanded to take care of the intermediate cases and process. Augustine
adds that there is not only "corporeal matter, antecedent to its being qualified by any form" but also "spiritual matter, before it underwent any restraint of its unlimited fluidness, or received any light from Wisdom." (*Conf.*
XII.XVIII.25, p. 262)

The five-fold hierarchy must then be expanded to seven. Quickly we shall
recognize the principle of the expansion in the last book.

1. God
2. Forms
3. Spiritual formed
4. Spiritual unformed
5. Material formed
6. Material unformed
7. Nothing (*Conf.* XIII.II.2, p. 277)

What is it for something to be formed? What is it for something to be unformed? A life without form is "turned away from the unchangeable ...." (*Conf.*
XIII.II.3, p. 277, quotation from *de Gen. ad Lit.* I,i,5) What is it to be
turned away from the unchangeable? I believe this is to be disordered, not
properly related to the next highest level, and to the source of all order.

The important question is not "How many levels of being are there? Three
turns into five, and five into seven, and that number has no final adequacy.
Between each of two levels in the seven steps is another, and if it were con-

venient we could go to 13, but a common number, in Bonaventure, for example, is 9.

Augustine was struggling to restate the principle of hierarchical order. He was attentive to the principle of the natural order, whereby physical elements are ordered, and to the principle by which human life is ordered. We have here a cosmology as well as a metaphysics of salvation. The search of the restless spirit was for rest, and the pilgrimage is in a restless world. Augustine's philosophy has God as a supreme principle of unity. In reflecting on "Glory to God in the highest" from the Christmas story in Luke II:14, his thought is of the order of nature.

> The body by its own weight strives towards its own place. Weight makes not downward only, but to his own place. Fire tends upwards, a stone downward. They are urged by their own weight, they seek their own places. Oil poured below water, is raised above the water; water poured on oil, sinks below the oil. They are urged by their own weights to seek their own places. When out of their order, they are restless; restored to order, they are at rest. My weight, is my love; thereby am I bourne, whithersoever I am borne. We are inflamed, by Thy Gift we are kindled; and are carried upwards; we glow inwardly, and go forwards. We *ascend Thy ways that be in our heart*, and sing *a song of degrees* .... (*Conf.* XIII.IX.10, p. 282)

Much as we may question whether there is an identity between the Alpha and Omega, the whence of the world and the whither of man, so we may now question whether there is a strict analogy between the order of nature and the order of the good. "Pondus meum, amor meus" is the kind of unity that we find in Hindu thought where "dharma" is both the nature of a thing and the duty of a person. Augustine fought hard to unify himself. Could it be that we cannot accept his world view because we as persons are only on the bottom rungs of the ascent? Is it possible that should we ascend that we would attain such a vision of all things?

NOTES

[1]The author thanks for their support, the Emory Research Committee, the American Philosophical Society, and the Smithsonian Institution, where he was a Woodrow Wilson Scholar.

[2]In "A Formal Preface and an Informal Conclusion to *The Great Chain of Being*: The Necessity and Universality of Hierarchical Thought," the author uses the writings of St. Thomas Aquinas and contemporary philosophy of science to define "hierarchy."
     In "Jacob's Ladder and the Tree of Life," in conjunction with Dr. Marion Leathers Kuntz, the author attempts a survey of the non-Hellenic sources of the great idea.

[3]"Hierarchy: From Lovejoy's Great Chain of Being to Feibleman's Great Tree of Being," *Studium Generale*, July/August 1971, pp. 678-687.
     "The Metaphysics of Hierarchical Order: The Philosophical Centre of *Small is Beautiful*," *Proceedings of the American Catholic Philosophical Association, Ethical Wisdom East and for West*, Vol. LI, 1977, pp. 36-46.
     "The Hierarchical Vision of St. Roberto Bellarmino," *"De Pétrarche à Descartes*, Vol. XXXVIII, *Acta Conventus Neo-Latini Turoneuris*, Ed. Jean-Claude Margolin (Paris: Librairie Philosophique Vrin, 1980) Vol. II, pp. 960-77.
     "The Hierarchical Vision of St. Bonaventure," *Atti Bonaventura Congresso*, Roma (1974), 1977, Vol. II, pp. 233-248.

[4]"Homo Erro to Homo Viator," *Augustinian Studies* Vol. XI, 1980, pp. 79-89.

[5]"St. Augustine's Quest for Truth: The Adequacy of a Christian Philosophy," was given at the XVI International Conference of Medieval Studies, Kalamazoo, May 1981, and is to appear in *Augustinian Studies*, Vol. XIII, 1982, pp. 1-21.

[6]R. F. Hoernlé in "The Religious Aspect of Bertrand Russell's Philosophy," *Harvard Theological Review*, 1916, Vol. IX, pp. 157-189.

[7]*The Confessions of S. Augustine*, Tr. E. B. Pusey (Oxford: J. H. Parker) 1843.

[8]Vernon J. Bourke, *The Essential Augustine* (New York: New American Library, 1964) pp. 43-66.
     By no means is my disagreement with Bourke total. Indeed I should say that I agree with all of the following except the opening paragraphs which state the three-level ontology: Vernon Bourke, "Augustine of Hippo: The Approach of the Soul to God," *The Spirituality of Western Christendom*, Ed. R. Elder (Kalamazoo, Michigan: Cistercian Publications, 1976) pp. 1-12, 189-191.
     I am deeply in Bourke's debt because I have found no comparable writing on the idea of *gradus* in Augustine. All other references are only incidental to some other topic. Perhaps I have failed to take note of some work which would have made this present paper not worth writing.

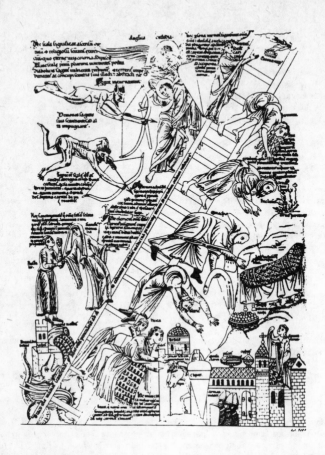

The Ladder of Virtue of Abbess Herrod of Landsberg's <u>Hortus Deliciarum</u>, Alsatian, twelfth century. Rather than thirty rungs of the Byzantine model this ladder is of fifteen only, but the top most remains Faith, Hope, Charity. The climbing figures are ecclesiastical but, not monastic only, and a knight and his lady are at the bottom. Demons attack but armed angels protect the climbers. Those who fall may enjoy mundane pleasures on the hillside rather than fall into the dragon's mouth. Copy reproduced in John Rupert Martin, <u>The Illustration of the Heavenly Ladder, op. cit.</u> pp. 19 and Fig. CXI Strasburg original destroyed in 1870.

KEVIN P. KEANE

ORDO BONITATIS: THE *SUMMA FRATRIS*
ALEXANDRI AND LOVEJOY'S DILEMMA

In the Chapter of *The Great Chain of Being* devoted to medieval thought,[1]
Arthur O. Lovejoy says that medieval thinkers, in elaborating their cosmolog-
ies, confronted a dilemma that has bedeviled Western thought since the time of
Plato: either (1) God is "good" in the sense given that word in Plato's *Timae-*
us,[2] a being essentially generous and creative of being outside himself, in
which case creation is necessary and it is impossible to set any limits to his
productivity in time, extent, or number; or (2) the act of creation is utterly
free and uncaused, in which case a definite limit in time, space, and number
may be consistently assumed for creation, but only at the cost of making creation a fundamentally irrational act and the description of God as good vacu-
ous. The former tradition, described by Lovejoy as "rationalist," is that of
the emanationist school, initiated by Plato, transmitted to the Middle Ages by
Plotinus, Augustine, and especially Pseudo-Dionysius,[4] and represented in the
scholastic period by Abelard, Richard of St. Victor, and the early Franciscans. The latter tradition, called extreme anti-rationalism by Lovejoy, included the Scotists, William of Ockham and his disciples, generally speaking
those thinkers considered nominalists.[5]

Lovejoy eventually closes his study by conceding victory to the anti-
rationalists along with such later thinkers as Voltaire, Dr. Johnson, and especially Alfred North Whitehead, all of whom held, as Lovejoy understands
them, the priority of will over intellect.[6] Along with Whitehead, Lovejoy
tells us, we ought to conclude that the concrete limitation to the number and
diversity of individuals and species, a limit evident to our experience, is
not rationally grounded, that the hypothesis of the world's having an absolute, determinate point of beginning--should it be granted[7]--implies an essential irrationality to the world's existence; in fine, as principle of arbitrary limitation, "God is the ultimate irrationality."[8]

The aim of this paper is surely not to retrace the whole of Lovejoy's
massive historical inquiry nor to dispute his historical findings over the
course of that history. What it does seek to suggest is that Lovejoy failed to
take account of a third systematic approach to this problem, developed from
within the emanationist tradition by a group of early Franciscan scholars at

Paris. These scholars, working under the direction of John of La Rochelle and Alexander of Hales, produced the *Summa Fratris Alexandri*, an important early *summa* (books I-III completed ca. 1245)[10] which concerns itself at length with the divine fecundity, the relationship between that fecundity and the concrete limits to finite existence, and the vexed medieval debate over the necessity and temporality of the created universe.[11] Our contention is that the *Summa's* understanding of Goodness as self-diffusive takes the form of a consistent, coherent, and universally operative logic[12] of the Good which grounds the rationality of creation and of that creation's seemingly arbitrary existence and form. Further, this logic allows us to see creation as rational, and thus somehow "necessary," yet the result of a free, personal decision. In so doing, the *Summa's* logic of self-diffusive goodness transcends voluntarism and rationalism alike, offering a cosmology superior to those of Abelard, Thomas Aquinas, Scotus, and Ockham in its own era, and—at least in some ways—to that of Alfred North Whitehead in our own.

We will begin with a brief sketch of Lovejoy's two traditions, Abelard representing the rationalists and Scotus, Ockham, and Aquinas the anti-rationalists. After a presentation of the *Summa's* teaching on the self-diffusion of the Good within the Trinity and in creation, we will attempt to formulate the *Summa's* logic of the self-diffusive Good in more detail and justify the contention that it provides for the positive insights of the rationalistic and voluntaristic theories but avoids the difficulties intrinsic to both.

RATIONALISM AND ANTI-RATIONALISM

Abelard, with his characteristic clarity, brilliance, and honesty, is an excellent representative of the rationalist position. Although he does note that, absolutely speaking, the created universe does not derive from any necessity in the divine nature,[13] Abelard concludes from the divine goodness that the universe is the best possible, that God's goodness compels him to create things as they are in the most minute detail—he offers the example of the exact timing and form of a rainstorm.[14] Lovejoy quotes him at length, and a part of that quotation is worth repeating here:

> We must enquire whether it was possible for God to make more things or better things than he has in fact made.... Whether we grant this or deny it, we shall fall into many difficulties because of the apparent unsuitability of the conclusions to which either alternative leads us. For if we assume that he could make either more or fewer things

> than he has, ... we shall be saying something exceedingly
> derogatory to his supreme goodness. Goodness, it is evi-
> dent, can produce only what is good; but if there are
> things good which God fails to produce when he might have
> done so or if he refrains from producing some things fit
> to be produced (facienda), who would not infer that he is
> jealous or unjust--especially since it costs him no labor
> to make anything? ... God neither does nor omits to do
> anything except for some rational and supremely good rea-
> son, even though it be hidden from us; .... To such a de-
> gree is God in all that he does mindful of the good, that
> he is said to be induced to make individual things rather
> by the value of the good there is in them than by the
> choice (*libitum*) of his own will 15

Aware that "few or none" of his contemporaries agreed with him,[16] that
his opinion seemed to conflict with many pronouncements by the Fathers and
Doctors, and even with reason itself, Abelard nonetheless held to his conclusion:

> For these reasons or solutions to objections, and in
> spite of everything to the contrary, I assert that God
> can make or omit making only those things which, at any
> time, he does make or omit making, and only in the manner
> or at the time he does it, not in any other manner or
> time. 17

Abelard thus joins a necessitarian optimism to a rigorous rationalism--a
determination to see all of reality as having a "reason," a definite and, in
the final analysis, necessary cause--and the result is an epitome of what
Lovejoy suggests is the tragic destiny of any systematic vision of the God-
world relationship starting out from the Platonic theory of the Good as essentially generous and self-giving.

The harsh reaction of Bernard and others to Abelard's view was a sign of
things to come. While an understanding of God as goodness itself could not but
be attractive to Christian thinkers, when the issue was clearly drawn--and
Abelard had the virtue of doing that--many Christian scholars would feel
obliged to defend the freedom of God, as much a part of the Hebrew and Christian understanding of God as his goodness. So it was that, prompted by the necessitarianism prevalent in the Arabic Aristotelianism and present in Latin
Averroism, Scotus and Ockham (and Thomas Aquinas before them) would embrace
what Lovejoy calls "extreme anti-rationalism" in the defense of that freedom:
the divine will is subject to no coercion whatever, even on the part of the
divine intellect or nature, in the act of creation.

It being impossible and undesirable to dispense with the divine goodness, these thinkers adopted the strategy of turning Aristotle against his own necessitarian disciples by interpreting goodness along strictly Aristotelian lines: the Good is understood as final cause alone and is thus freed from its Neo-Platonic interpretation as efficient cause. Thomas Aquinas, for example, in spite of his willingness to quote the almost universally accepted Neo-Platonic axiom, "the good is self-diffusive",[18] pioneered this line of thought. The goodness of God is seen as purely passive *ad extra*, becoming active only insofar as it is freely taken as goal for imitation by the divine will, which alone is efficient cause of creation: "the good is said to be diffusive of itself in the same way that the end is said to move [things];[19] in no way does the will of God have a cause."[20]

Scotus makes the same point in his *De Primo Principio*:

> Nothing is willed necessarily unless it be a necessary condition for whatever is willed about the end. God loves himself as end, and *whatever he loves about himself as end will remain even if nothing* besides God exists, because what is necessary of itself depends upon no other. Therefore, from the volition of himself, he wills nothing else necessarily. Neither then does he cause necessarily. [21]

Ockham, of course, is even less willing to allow any taint of necessity in his understanding of divine causality.[22] And both Scotus and Ockham agree in opposing any necessitarian optimism,[23] though Scotus seems to imply, in a rather odd passage of the *De Primo Principio*, that a perfect world is not impossible.[24]

So we have Lovejoy's dilemma: Either one sees God as good, and therefore necessarily diffusive, the paradoxical result being a rationalistic necessitarianism, or one chooses an arbitrary voluntarism and pays the price of making the world's existence the whimsical fruit of an irrational act. The *Summa Fratris Alexandri's* authors set out to avoid both these pitfalls, and to their efforts we now turn.

THE SELF-DIFFUSION OF THE GOOD IN THE *SUMMA FRATRIS ALEXANDRI*

As the summists understood it, the Good finds its principal and perfect self-diffusion in the Trinitarian processions, creation being, to borrow an image from St. Bonaventure, a mere "dot" of diffusion compared to the immeasurability of divine generation and spiration.[25] To understand the diffusion of the good in creation, then, it is imperative that we understand the Self-diffusion that is root and reason for this lesser gift.

Along with the Greeks, the *Summa* understands the Father as *fons et origo totius divinitatis*, seeing in the innascible person of the Father, and not in the nature, the ground of divine unity and source of the processions.[26] And it is because this innascible person is the highest good that he is self-diffusive: we might, says the *Summa*, call actual self-diffusion, as opposed to the mere tendency to do so, the *laus boni*, the renown of the good. But if we take two goods, equal in everything save that the one makes gifts of its goodness while the other does not, it is obvious that the generous, giving good would be the more praiseworthy, the "better" of the two. The perfection of goodness (*completa ratio boni*) thus includes self-diffusion. As the *Summa's* tractate on goodness in general puts it, goodness is "the indivision or undividedness of act from potency" (*indivisio actus a potentia*)[26a]--to be in act is to be diffusive. But we are speaking of the highest of goods here, so that any self-diffusion of this highest good must be of the highest order. Now the greatest possible self-diffusion is that which cannot conceivably be bettered (qua maiori excogitari non potest). The highest of possible self-gifts is generation, the gift of one's own nature or substance.[27] In animals and man this gift is always partial and imperfect: the parent can only share his proper nature to the degree he possesses it, and even that partial share can be only imperfectly given. Since the Father is in perfect and absolutely untrammeled possession of the divine nature,[28] he can make total and perfect gift of it to his Son in a generation that, like God, must be eternal.[29]

It ought to be noted that this self-diffusion, like all actions of God as the *Summa* understands them, is personal and belongs to the Father as person (qui habet naturam),[30] one as free possession of a nature. Given this fact, the Good's self-diffusion is free, not a matter of blind and mechanical necessity.[31]

The logic of self-diffusion also leads us to posit the second procession, that of the Spirit. Two arguments are adduced, the one a variant of the argument used to demonstrate the Son's procession, the second an argument based on the concept of diffusive goodness but centering its immediate attention on the incomparable value of mutual charity, an approach borrowed explicitly and verbatim from Richard of St. Victor.

According to the first argument, based on an Aristotelian division of all
possible motion into the natural and the voluntary,[32] there are two and only
two irreducible types of self-diffusion paralleling these two types of motion:
natural and voluntary diffusion. Generation is the most perfect form of diffusion by nature, and so we conclude to the generation of the Son. Self-gift by
way of free, rationally directed love is the highest form of voluntary self-
diffusion, and so we conclude to the production of the Spirit by way of spiration. That both modes of production must be present in God is evident so soon
as we consider that a good diffusing itself in both ways is superior, better,
than one doing so in only one way; since the highest good cannot lack *any*
goodness, there must be diffusion by love, the procession of the Spirit.[33]

The second argument presumes the validity of Richard of St. Victor's argument, based on the excellence of charity, for the generation of the Son.[34]
It being granted that, with the existence of two persons in the Trinity, charity is now possible, it remains that the fullness of charity demands the existence of a third person, a person capable of sharing each person's delight in
the other, a person who can also be loved by the other as he (the third person) loves the other.[35] The *Summa* sums up its argument for the procession of
the Spirit in the following succinct passage:

> According to Richard of St. Victor it must be said that
> just as the greatest charity, which cannot be understood
> not to exist in the highest good, necessarily proves the
> generation of the Son by the Father and is the reason for
> that generation--because it is necessary that love go out
> towards another in order for love to be charity, and
> where there is the highest charity it is necessary that
> there be one person willing good to another, which good
> is the sharing of the lover himself, and this will neces-
> sarily be in the way of a sharing of the whole substance:
> when there is generation--so also the excellence of char-
> ity is the reason for the procession of the Holy Spirit
> ... "the most excellent thing about true charity is to
> will that another be loved just as you yourself are
> loved." Just as long as one person is alone in being
> loved by another, he is alone in possessing the delights
> of charity's most excellent sweetness; likewise the
> other, so long as he does not have a "co-beloved" lacks
> the sharing of the most excellent joy. In order for both
> to be able to share the delights of this kind, it is ne-
> cessary for them to have a "co-beloved," [36] to wit the
> Holy Sprit .... The reason for generating the Son, there-
> fore, is the highest love which is understood to exist in
> the person of the Father; conjoined love (condilectio),
> the highest conjoined love which is understood to exist

in Father and Son is the reason for the procession of the Holy Spirit from them. [37]

It is significant that the *Summa* rejects the argument for the distinction between Son and Spirit based on the difference between intellect and will. This argument, first developed by St. Augustine[38] and adopted by Thomas Aquinas,[39] is considered invalid because acts of understanding and will, having the self as their object, are inward in their dynamic, while the divine processions are outgoing acts of generosity, centrifugal, not centripetal--the God of the *Summa* is not the utterly self-centered God of Aristotle:

> Where generation takes place there is multiplication and a difference between the generator and the generated; by-lin saying that God understands himself I do not assert any difference or multiplication, because God's understanding himself is nothing else than a kind of turning in upon himself; therefore to generate and to understand are not the same thing.[40]

How then are Spirit and Son different? Aside from the fact that the one proceeds by nature, the other by way of will, each has a unique mode of receiving, possessing and giving the divine nature. The Son receives the divine being in such a way that he is like the Father not only in having the same nature (this also belongs to the Spirit) but also in the precise way he proceeds from the Father; he proceeds *secundum principalem modum*,[41] as a principle from a principle, because he shares the Father's personal *proprietas* of producing another from himself. The Son is like the Father in both person and nature, the Spirit in nature alone:

> ... when I speak of the person of the Father, I speak of one having the divine being (*esse*) without having received it from another and from whom another has received that being through generation, still another through procession. When I speak of the person of the Holy Spirit, I speak of one having the same divine being from others.... And thus the being of the Father and the Son and the Holy Spirit is the same, to wit divine being, while their proper modes of personal existence (*proprietates*) are different and unsharable. [42]

The "personalist" emphasis in all this can hardly be overemphasized. It is precisely in their very personality that the three *personae* differ, their mode of origin being identical with their personhood. It is, for instance, because of the way he is person that the Son can be called the Father's Word, not as Aquinas would have it, because of the perfection of his being a Word that he can be called Son (*eo Verbum quo Filius*).[43] And the Father, who has a

certain reality even prescinding from the processions as Innascible Person
(the *Summa* adopts the view that innascibility is not a merely negative property), produces the Son freely because he is a person, *habens naturam*, and in
his goodness, gives that nature to a Son.[44] The Spirit, again, proceeds from
Father and Son in an act of full freedom, his procession being the act of a
clear and determinate loving volition on the part of Father and Son, "like
love arising out of understanding (sicut amor ab intelligentia)."[45] Freedom is
thus present in the Trinity even before it comes into play in creation.[46]

Finally, it is on the basis of personal relationships that the *Summa* defends the *Filioque*: were the Spirit to proceed from the Father and not the
Son, there would be nothing in common between Son and Spirit, and they would
therefore be lacking that *germanitas*, that profound intimacy and relatedness
characteristic of persons in communion.[47]

This same "personal" bias is evident in the *Summa's* approach to creation:
it is the Father who creates, or all three persons, but not the essence.[48] The
Father creates because he is good, and if it is true that he creates through
his will, not by any strict necessity,[49] it is nonetheless his goodness that
moves the Father's will to creating. There is therefore a certain fittingness
and congruity, a necessity of sorts,[50] to the act of creation, so obviously in
harmony with what God is, the self-diffusive Trinity. Although free, then, it
is no arbitrary will that creates, but one moved by its own diffusive goodness.[51]

To sum up the ground we have covered so far: the logic of diffusive goodness offers an attractive, rationally coherent explanation for emanation of
the Trinitarian persons and the fact of created existence, as Lovejoy himself
would admit. The question Lovejoy asks is whether this logic proves far too
much, whether it forces us to posit an utterly unlimited profusion of beings
in creation (exhaustive self-diffusion in extent), an eternal and necessary
creation (exhaustive creation in time), and whether it compels us to think of
this creation as necessarily the best possible. This last, that the world is
the best possible world, seems very doubtful in light of the general experience of evil as not only unnecessary to the nature of things but actually repugnant, obscene. It is to this set of problems, all related to the question
of a limit to diffusion on its various levels, that we must now turn.

THE GOOD AS PRINCIPLE OF ORDER

The question of the relationship between finitude and infinity is closely related to the *Summa's* understanding of what it is to be good. Along with Plato, Aristotle, and the general belief of Western philosophers, the *Summa* considers precise limit or definition to be a positive good.[52] To fail to have a limit is to be disordered, chaotic, beneath the level of being: it is only insofar as the things of our experience, and we ourselves, are this and not that that we and our world of things have any value, any utility or genuine subjectivity. On the other hand, the summists were the convinced inheritors of the Hebrew-Christian tradition's experience of God as transcendent, and they recognized that if God is to be truly absolute, and not be a subordinate reality within an overarching, impersonal cosmic order, he must be infinite in the sense that he is the source of all determination and limit: *divina essentia est infinita, quia non habet finem, sed est finiens omnia.*[53] There are, then, two modes of goodness or *bene esse*: the infinite and the finite. For the infinite being, the divine essence, lack of any limits is positive goodness, goodness that grounds all other, subordinate goods. For the finite being of creation, and for the quasi-finite, quasi-numerable being of the Trinitarian persons, limit and order are positive goods, lack of any limits is evil.

Goodness, then, is not the same thing in relation to the infinite and the finite. This being so, there must be an order to goodness, an *ordo bonitatis,*[54] governing the diffusion of the Good. This order will necessarily dictate a certain arrangement and limit to the Good's self-diffusion, since it would be self-contradictory for Goodness to give rise to the evil of disordered being: the Good is characterized by productivity, to be sure, but productivity of ordered goodness, not chaos.

If we apply this reasoning concretely, we find that there are three levels of being. On the first level, if we may speak so, that of the divine essence, infinity is the proper mode of being and there are no limits of any sort, for this is the reality that gives definition to all else (*finiens omnia*). On the second level, that of the Trinitarian persons,[55] we find a mode of being that might be described as "quasi-finite," for while the persons are infinite in *what* they are, their essence, they are obviously finite insofar as one is not the other as person. The personal order, then, is finite, even on the divine level, though assuredly in a manner different from that of the created personal order. On the third level, that of created being, all is finite and finitude is the positive good of beings.

For the Trinity this means that there can be no infinite emanation of divine *personae*, for such a diffusion would be the worst sort of chaos (*confusio*) and disorder (*inordinatio*).[56] There is a principle of parsimony at work in this. Plurality need not be symptomatic of weakness and imperfection; it can indicate and manifest power and love, and it is required for the mutual personal exchange of love that the *Summa* sees as the inner reason for the processions.[57] Communion and love are the motive for the fact that we can, after a fashion,[58] speak of number in God. On the other hand, any needless duplication of an embodiment of the good, especially when that embodiment is perfect (as in Father, Son, and Spirit), would be a positive imperfection, serving no end whatever; it would be utterly empty of purpose (*supervacuum*). There can be no duplication of either Son or Spirit, because each is a perfect production and with their procession the full tally of possible modes of possession and giving the divine nature (that is, of being divine persons) is complete: *ubi est numero infinitum, non est ordo; si ergo peneretur ibi multitudo ... infinita, non esset ordo in divinis personis.*[59]

Moreover, a production of divine persons to infinity would make impossible that full and intimate love which alone gives rise to the Trinity, for if the number of persons is unlimited, that number is unknown, and it is impossible to love what cannot be known.[60] Number, even at the divine level, requires finitude, as an intrisically finite and ordered reality; wherever number is found, therefore, there must at some point or other be *status*, a "standing" or achievement in fulfillment.[61]

The need for finitude is even more emphatic on the created level, where to be is to be limited in all respects. Therefore:

(1) There can be no creation *ad infinitum*.[62] Such an unlimited diffusion of created goods would serve no purpose, and would only serve to rob the universe of the completion and prefection possible to it. Since the First reality is one whose work is "ordered and perfect," there can be no infinite diffusion in number; instead there is *status*, fulfillment at a specific number.

This does not, however, mean that the diffusion of the good ends. Instead, quantity yields to quality, and there is a reflection of goodness toward its source. Just as the Spirit marks the culmination of processions within the Trinity, so the outermost boundary of the universe, in space, number or whatever, marks the achievement of the creative emanation.

(2) There can be no creation from eternity, in the sense of an unlimited duration to time *ex parte ante*, because far from requiring the existence (*co-existentiam*) of Creatures, God simply cannot communicate his eternity. Given that creation is by definition finite, and given that infinite, positive existence is simple and cannot be "partially" enjoyed (e.g., as to time), temporal duration must be finite, must have a determinate beginning and, at any given moment, a set measure.[63]

(3) It is intrinsically impossible to create a perfect world, perfect in the sense that it could not be improved upon. Any given world-order will be finite and ordered because of its very goodness. But any definite order can be changed and improved upon: like the line that is always patient of further division, the world is always subject to improvement.[64]

The divine freedom is highlighted by all three points: while logic of diffusion does after a fashion require the creation of the universe, it also dictates that there be a specific number of ceatures, a limit to duration, and a specific level of perfection. But given the nature of finite reality, there can be no preset level of perfection, nor a predetermined, "right" number of creatures. The nature of finite reality and its proper perfection therefore require divine freedom: the precise choice must be arbitrary and thus perfectly free. Any given choice of limits consonant with harmony and justice is rational and as perfect an achievement of the diffusive logic of the good as is possible.

THE SCOPE OF THE *ORDO BONITATIS*

In the light of what we have said, it is obvious that the logic of diffusive goodness, expressed in the concrete order of goodness, is impressive as a theoretical achievement: a principle of cosmic origin and order unlimited in its concrete application. For the *Summa* it is Goodness, the *completa ratio boni*, that is the source and principle of the Trinitarian processions, goodness too which moves the Father to create and thus establish a certain but radically arbitrary order of rational limits. For the ultimate ground of rationality is not arbitrary will (as in Scotus, Ockham, and to a lesser extent, Aquinas), nor a mechanically necessary creation (as in Abelard), but a free, personal reality.

Even at the most abstract metaphysical level, goodness is the determining principle: it is the Father, not the divine essence, which is absolutely primordial, the *ens cum actu*; the essence cannot be conceived as metaphysically prior to the Father's person, as it can be in Thomas's Trinitarian theory (i.e., it is because the divine essence is rational and volitional that Father, Son, and Spirit exist for Thomas; for Alexander, it is because the Father is good that Son and Spirit proceed from him).[65] This permits us to say that in view of the Trinitarian structure of God, unity and plurality are equally primordial and intrisically related: the infinite unity of the divine essence makes possible the active life of charity and communion that is the highest *de facto* reality--the community of Father, Son and Spirit.

On the level of causality, abstractly considered, the good is again the regulative principle. As final cause (in a sense much stronger than that finality has for Aquinas), the Good is *causa causarum*, and all the other causes, with the partial exception of material causality insofar as matter is passive, not active, are understood in terms of the good,[66] are in a sense subordinate modes of causal goodness.

The Trinitarian life of Father, Son, and Spirit is governed, by the order of goodness which determines the number, order and relationships of the *personae* just as it gives them rise. The processions are marked by a generous love, which achieves full clarity and freedom in the generation of the Spirit.

The order of goodness dictates that creation be finite, because limitation is being and goodness itself for created reality, and a good Creator cannot create a disorderly, evil world. This world must be freely created because creation from eternity is a self-contradictory idea. Moreover, the precise level of achieved values and the exact number of species and individuals must be contingently determined, for there is, intrinsically, no possibility for a "best" number or a "best" world of creatures. The only requirement is that there be a determination, that number be servant to content, quantity to quality.

We conclude, then, that Lovejoy was needlessly pessimistic in his evaluation of the principle of diffusive goodness and the question of a universally operative principle or rationality for the cosmos. The necessity of specific limits, limits which our experience teaches us must be contingently chosen, does not necessarily entail irrationality for the universe as a whole nor even for its precise, determinate shape in space and time. To the contrary, the au-

thors of the *Summa fratris Alexandri* in developing their logic of diffusive
goodness found such limitation, with its implied and necessary free determination, an intrinsic aspect and the only sufficient condition for created good.
Nothing in the creative ordering of the universe is irrational, nor is anything necessarily determined. Ultimate reality is personal and generous, and rationality is primordially the freedom of love.

NOTES

[1]Arthur O. Lovejoy, *The Great Chain of Being: A Study of the History of an Idea* ("Harper Torchbooks"; New York: Harper & Row, 1960), pp. 67-98. (= GCB)

[2]*Timaeus*, 29D-30C.

[3]GCB, 69-71.

[4]See Pseudo-Dionysius, *De div. nom.*, esp. IV, 1. For an excellent summary of the tradition see Ewert H. Cousins, "The Notion of the Person in the *De Trinitate* of Richard of St. Victor" (unpublished Ph.D. dissertation, Fordham University, 1966).

[5]GCB, 69-70.

[6]GCB, 332-33. It must be noted that Whitehead is in very unusual company indeed; Lovejoy's interpretation of the quoted remarks needs a good deal of nuance and is misleading as it stands.

[7]Whitehead and his school in general would, of course, demur on this point.

[8]A. N. Whitehead, *Science and the Modern World* (New York: Macmillan, Free Press Paperback, 1967), p. 178. Quoted in GCB, p. 333.

[9]The single best source of information on the *Summa Fratris Alexandri* and the school of Alexander of Hales in general, is V. Doucet, *Prolegomena in Librum III necnon in Libros I et II "Summae Fratris Alexandri"* (Quaracchi: Collegium S. Bonaventurae, 1948), pp. 151-234.

[10]For an evaluation of the *Summa's* importance, see E. Gössman, *Sacramentum Mundi* (N.Y.: Herder, 1968-70), s.v. "Scholasticism." Scholars now generally agree that there were two principal redactors, one for Books I and III, called Frater Inquirens after his typical methodological opening, the other, called Frater Considerans by scholars for similar reasons, the redactor of the two parts of Book II. Inquirens is almost certainly John of La Rochelle, while Considerans, identity is unknown to us at this time. See F. M. Henquinet, "Fr. Considerans, l'un des auteurs jumeaux de la Summa Fratris Alexandri primitive," *Recherces de Théologie Ancienne et Médiévale* 15 (1948): 76-96.

[11]Information on the dispute over the *Summa's* composition can be found in great detail in Doucet, *Prolegomena*. It now appears certain that almost all of Bks. I-III existed in their present form before 1245, cf. *Prolegomena*, pp. 369-70.

[12]We are using the term "logic" to mean an inclusive, organizing principle or concept.

[13]Abelard, *Theologia Christiana*, IV (PL 178, 1311b); cf. *Dialogus inter Philosophum, Judaeum et Christianum*, PL 178, 1658b.

[14]*Theologia "Scholarium" (Introductio ad Theologiam)*, 3 (PL 178. 1098).

[15]*Ibid.*, III, PL 178, 1093-1101.

[16]Cf. St. Bernard, Epist. 190, PL 182, 1953-72; Hugh of St. Victor, *De Sacramentis*, I, PL 176, 216b.

[17]*Theol. Christ.*, PL 178, 1157-58.

[18]See Julien Peghaire, "L'axiome 'Bonum est diffusivum sui' dans le néo-platonisme et le thomisme," *Revue de l'Université de Ottawa*, Special section (1932), 13ff.

[19]S. T., I, 5, 4, ad 2; cf. I, 5, 2 resp.

[20]S. T. I. 19. 5. resp. For a full discussion of the question of creation's raison d'être in Thomas and Bonaventure, the heir in this of the summists, see the author's article, "Why Creation? Bonaventure and Thomas Aquinas on God as Creative Good," *The Downside Review* 93 (1975): 100-121.

[21]John Duns Scotus, *De Primo Principio*, trans. and ed. Allan B. Wolter, O. F. M. (Chicago: Franciscan Herald Press, 1966), ch. 4, pp. 90-91.

[22]See F. Copleston, S. J., *A History of Philosophy*, Vol. III, Pt. 1 (Image Books; Garden City, N. Y.: Doubleday & Co., 1953), p. 60.

[23]Scotus, *De Primo Principio*, 4.20.

[24]*De Primo principio* 4.20. See L. Baudry, *Lexique philosophique de G. d'Ockham* (Paris: P. Letheilleux, 1958), s.v. "mundus."

[25]St. Bonaventure, *Itiner. Mentis in Deum*, 5, 2.

[26]*Summa Fratris Alex.* (S), I, 481, sol (684b); 76, ad 4.

[27]For Aristotle's definition of generation, see *Metaph.*, VI, 8.

[28]I, 296, sol. (420a).

[29]S, I, 295, b (414-15).

[30]S.I. 297, sol (424-25); 298, sed contra (429-30). For def. of divine person, S, I, 312, c.

[31]S, I, 295, f (415b); 297, ad 23 (428b), 301, rsp. (434b).

[32]The editors of Alexander's *Glossa* suggest Physics II and Metaph. VI as possible sources. I suspect it is actually Avicenna: "Motus autem causae sunt tres: natura, voluntas et violentia. *Avicennae Metaphysices Compendium*, trans. N. Carame, (Rome, Pont. Inst. of Oriental Studies, 1926), p. 102.

[33]S, I, 304, a (438a).

[34]Richard of St. Victor, *De Trinitate* 3 (PL 196. 915-18).

[35]S, I, 304 (438-40).

[36]Richard, DT, III, 15, PL 196, 927.

[37]S, I, 311, resp (453).

[38]Augustine, *De Trinitate*, X, 11, 17; XIV, 12, 15.

[39]S, T. I, 27, 1, rsp.

[40]S, I, 296, ad opp. b (419b).

[41]S, I, 296, sol. (419-20).

[42]S, I, 312, sol. (456a).

[43]See Th. DeRegnon, *Etudes de Théologie positive sur la sainte Trinité* (Paris: Retaux, 1892), II, p. 368.

[44]S, I, 295. b (414-15).

[45]I, 324, d (476a).

[46]See S, I, 307, 310, *passim*.

[47]S, I, 323, ad 1 (475b), 324, a (475).

[48]S, I, 406, sol. (598-99); I, 297, ad 10 (427a); not the essence, I 297, ad 23 (428b).

[49]S, I, 110 (171-72); cf. II, 18 (28) and II, 18, ad 5 (29).

[50]S, I, 110, ad 1 (172b); II, 18, ad 1 (28b).

[51]I, 110, sol. I-II (179).

[52]See H. P. Owen, "Infinity in Theology and Metaphysics," *Encyclopedia of Philosophy*, IV.

[53]S, I, 34, sol. (56a).

[54]It should be noted that the *Summa* only rarely uses these two words together.

[55]Note that the essence never is considered prior in any sense to the person of the Father. It is properly infinte, but it is always an infinity that is a property of the Father--the essence does not in any sense bring the Father into being.

[56]S, I, 318, sol. (467).

[57]S, I, 317, sol. (465b).

[58]S, I, 313, sol. (459).

[59]S, I, 318, ad 1 (467).

[60] S, I, 219, sol. (469); cf. 318, sol. and ad ob. (467).

[61]S, I, 297, ad 23 (428b); 304, ad 5 (440b); 318, ad 1 (467b); 122, (191-92).

[62]S, I, 122, sol. II (192b). Note that the summists were aware of an important point raised by Lovejoy: if the divine self-diffusion does not exhaust the possibles in creation, then something is held back, the manifestation of the divine goodness is niggardly. This means that creation must be exhaustive of all possibles. But this seems impossible and, in point of fact, not true. Thus creation's limits are irrational, as is its existence--it does not flow logically and as it is from the divine goodness. The summists assert, to the contrary, that perfect diffusion

and gift occurs in the Son's generation; there is thus no aspect of generosity or fecundity which is not realized and creation is not called upon to fulfill an impossible task, that of being the exhaustive recipient of divine generosity. See S. I. 64. ad 5 (97-98), 295. ad 2 (416-17).

[63]S, I, 64, resp. (95); cf. ad 5 (96b).

[64]S, I, 143. resp. & ad obj. Compare the summists' view with that of Peter of Lombard in *I Sent*. 44. 1. 2 (and not 44. 2, the reference in GCB). Lovejoy (p. 73) finds Lombard's argument—that to say the world could not be better is absurd because such an assertion would be tantamount to making the world equal to God. What Lovejoy apparently fails to grasp is that for Peter Lombard, as for the summists after him, to say that the world is perfect is to say that it is infinite, hence divine. To be finite is to be meliorable.

It seems worth noting that astronomers, working within a very different framework from that of the summists of course, are now convinced that the universe is finite both in extension and time, that there was a unique beginning to the universe and that it shall have a unique end. For a popular summary of the current state of the question, see Robert Jastrow, *Until the Sun Dies* (New York: W. W. Norton & Co., 1977), pp. 19-53. Not too much should be made of these developments, however, in discussing the issues at hand; cosmology has always been subject to significant and rapid change, and the picture could change drastically in the next few decades.

[65]S, I, 297, ad 23 (438b).

[66]S, I, 104, resp. (163).

Lull's text to show the point of ascent: "We begin at the imperfect, so that we might ascend to the perfect; and conversely, we may descend from the perfect to the imperfect." God is the threshold of the dwelling place of Wisdom. From S.K. Heninger, Jr., <u>The Cosmographical Glass: Renaissance Diagrams of the Universe</u>, San Marino, California, The Huntington Library, 1977, p. 160. Ramon Lull, <u>De nova logica, De correllativis, Necnon de ascensu descensu intellectus</u>, Valencia, 1512. Many of Lull's tree symbols can be studied in Frances A. Yates, <u>Lull and Bruno, Collected Essays</u>, Vol. I, London, Routledge and Kegan Paul, 1982.

EWERT H. COUSINS

FECUNDITY AND THE TRINITY:

AN APPENDIX TO CHAPTER THREE OF

THE GREAT CHAIN OF BEING

Lovejoy's book *The Great Chain of Being* is a masterful study of the tension between two basic paradigms of God in relation to the world, viewed
throughout the history of Western thought. On the one hand, God is the self-
sufficient Absolute, all-perfect and far removed from the imperfections of the
world. On the other hand, God is the self-diffusive Good, who out of the fecundity of his fullness communicates his perfections in creation.[1] These two
paradigms have provided the basis for another tension: between an other-world-
ly and a this-worldly spirituality. Furthermore, the paradigm of God as self-
diffusive fecundity has served as the ground for complex hierarchies in the
history of Western thought and thus for the book's title *The Great Chain of
Being*.

Lovejoy's book is a remarkable achievement: in identifying these two paradigms of God in Western thought, in surveying them over a vast sweep of history and in bringing to light the philosophical and theological problems tied
up with these paradigms. However, I would like to call attention to a major
omission. Throughout his book, Lovejoy failed to take into account data from
Christian Trinitarian theology. Since Lovejoy took on such a monumental task,
he might easily be excused for omitting material. However, the omission I am
pointing to is crucial in two respects: (1) Christian Trinitarian theology represents a vast amount of speculative thought which plays a crucial role in a
number of the thinkers studied in *The Great Chain of Being*. (2) This speculation adds an entirely new dimension to the problematic of the book. To ignore
this material is not only to give an incomplete historical picture, but it is
to fail to grasp the heart of the very issues which Lovejoy has raised.

This omission is especially glaring in Lovejoy's treatment of the Middle
Ages, for a major tradition of medieval Trinitarian theology was explicitly
concerned with the problematic explored in *The Great Chain of Being*. If this
material is included, I believe it can substantially alter the thrust of the
book. The present paper will attempt to supply this material as an appendix to
Chapter Three of *The Great Chain of Being*, which is entitled "Conflicts in
Medieval Thought."[2] I shall begin with a study of this chapter, indicating how

Lovejoy uses the medieval material to present his problematic. Then I shall show how a major tradition of medieval Trinitarian theology addressed itself to this problematic: namely, by situating the principle of plenitude not in creation but in the Trinity. By this move it completely by-passed the problems which according to Lovejoy ultimately caused the collapse of the "great chain of being."[3]

LOVEJOY ON THE MIDDLE AGES

In exploring the conflicts in medieval thought, Lovejoy draws from Augustine, Pseudo-Dionysius, Abelard, Aquinas and Dante. Against the background of their thought, he sketches the two paradigms of God which he had brought to light in the previous chapter: "The God in whom man was thus to find his own fulfillment was," Lovejoy states, "not one God but two. He was the Idea of the Good, but he was also the idea of Goodness."[4] According to Lovejoy, "no two notions could be more antithetic."[5] As the Idea of the Good, he was the apotheosis of unity, self-sufficiency, perfection and quietude; as the Idea of Goodness, he was the apotheosis of diversity, fecundity, self-transcendence. According to Lovejoy, these two models of God cannot be reconciled, although the medieval mind managed to hold them both simultaneously. Lovejoy writes:

> There was no way in which the flight from the Many to the One, the quest for a perfection defined wholly in terms of contrast with the created world, could be effectually harmonized with the imitation of a Goodness that delights in diversity and manifests itself in the emanation of the Many out of the One.[6]

In citing Abelard, Thomas and Dante, he indicates how they came dangerously close to heresy when they attempted to deal with the divine fecundity. Speaking of Dante, he says: "Dante verged upon a heresy; indeed it was impossible for a medieval writer to make any use of the principle of plenitude without verging upon heresies."[7] According to Lovejoy, the principle of plenitude calls for the actualization of all possibilities. If God is fecund, and not envious, He will share his perfections without holding back. This leads ultimately to the notion that God has created the best possible world. Such a conclusion limits God's freedom in two respects: by making the act of creation necessary and by claiming that this is the only world God could have created. Thus the two different notions of Good are in conflict. If God's self-diffusive Goodness requires him to create out of necessity, then this very necessity negates the perfection of his freedom and transcendence. "Hence it fol-

lowed," according to Lovejoy, "that God's freedom of choice must be maintained
by denying what Dante came so perilously near to asserting, viz., that the actual exercise of the creative potency extends of necessity through the entire
range of possibility."[8] Lovejoy goes on to show how Thomas Aquinas became embroiled in the same issue. Although Thomas struggled valiantly with the problem, he was, according to Lovejoy, ultimately unsuccessful. The latter traces
at some length "the ingenious but futile logical shifts" taken by Thomas to
solve the problem and overcome "the embarrassment which this internal strain
in the traditional doctrine caused him."[9]

The issue then is sharply drawn: How can God actualize his fecundity
without negating his freedom? Are the two paradigms of God, then, contradictory? Does the fecundity of God have to be limited in order to maintain his
absolute perfection? And if so, does that undercut the basis of hierarchy and
shatter the great chain of being?

AN ALTERNATE APPROACH

Lovejoy has raised a crucial problem, which troubled medieval thinkers,
as the evidence he cites so clearly indicates. However, there was a strand of
medieval thought which approached the problematic in a different way. It acknowledged that the central problem of the self-diffusive paradigm of God was
the actualization of the divine fecundity. But it recognized that creation was
not adequate to the task. Consequently, it shifted the principle of plenitude
from creation to the inner life of God, i.e., to the Trinity, thus radically
transforming Lovejoy's problematic. According to this medieval Trinitarian
theology, the divine fecundity is unconditionally actualized in the Trinitarian processions. In himself, God can be both self-sufficient and self-diffusive to the maximum degree. This means that the world is not required to make
God actually self-diffusive, but at the same time, creation is an overflow of
the self-diffusion within the Trinity. Thus God's freedom can be saved and the
gateway opened to a variety of hierarchies. The divine fecundity is free to
express itself in a variety of cosmological schemes and not merely in the rigid chain of being that resulted from situating the principle of plenitude
within the world.

The approach I just described is found in varying degrees of articulation
in the Pseudo-Dionysius, Scotus Erigena, Anselm, Richard of St. Victor, Bonaventure, Eckhart and much of the mystical tradition. I believe that elements

76 EWERT H. COUSINS

of it are present also in Dante. In fact, I believe that it is the dominant strand of medieval Trinitarian theology. It is not found, however, as a central theme in the *Summa Theologiae* of Thomas Aquinas, which may be the reason why Lovejoy and others do not take it into account when dealing with the Middle Ages. To treat this tradition adequately would require a book in itself. The most I can hope to do here is to present some of its highlights and indicate how these affect the problematic of *The Great Chain of Being*. I will now treat successively the Pseudo-Dionysius, Anselm and Bonaventure.

DIONYSIUS AND ANSELM

In the second chapter of *The Divine Names*, Dionysius distinguishes between the undifferentiated and the differentiated aspects of God.[10] The Trinity is the eternal differentiated aspect of God and the mystery of the inner divine emanations or processions. Thus the notion of self-diffusiveness, which Dionysius expressed so eloquently in Chapter 4 of *The Divine Names*, is seen first in the eternal life of the Trinity. The undifferentiated Godhead is fecund in the Father, from whom flow the Son and the Spirit. "The Father," Dionysius states, "is Originating Godhead, while Jesus and the Spirit are (so to speak) Divine Off-shoots of the Paternal Godhead ..."[11] This linking of fecundity with the Father is the strategic move of this tradition of Trinitarian theology. It is characteristic of Greek patristic thought and according to the research of de Régnon constitutes what has been called the Greek model of the Trinity.[12] The Greek patristic tradition looked upon the Father as the source of both the unity of the Godhead and its dynamic processions. As Dionysius says, "The Father alone is the Source of the Super-Essential Godhead."[13]

The Greek model of the Trinity is distinguished from the Latin model, elaborated by Augustine, who grounded the unity of the persons in the single divine nature and their distinction in their mutual relationship.[14] While the Augustinian model appears static, the Greek model is dynamic, with the source of fecundity and dynamism in the Father. In dialogue with Lovejoy's position, we observe that the principle of plenitude in this tradition is lodged in the Father and not in the divine act of creation. True, this fecundity must be actualized, but actualization takes place from all eternity, in the Trinitarian processions—not in creation. Dionysius did not spell out these metaphysical implications; his chief contribution, rather, was to be the bearer of the dy-

namic Greek Trinitarian model to the West. In the more dialectical thought of
Anselm and Bonaventure, the metaphysical implications were brought to light.

The structure of Anselm's *Monologion* closely parallels Lovejoy's exposition of the two paradigms of God in Chapter Two of *The Great Chain of Being*.
In the first section of the *Monologion*, Anselm presents proofs for the exis-
tence and attributes of God as the absolute, self-sufficient, all-perfect
Good.[15] As Anselm says in Chapter Twenty-Eight of the *Monologion*, "That Spirit
[God] alone exists simply, and perfectly, and absolutely; while all other beings are almost non-existent, and hardly exist at all."[16] Having established
the self-sufficient paradigm of God, he turns in the very next chapter to the
Trinity as the fecund, self-expressive aspect of the divinity. After treating
God as the all-perfect Good, Anselm says, "I think it reasonable to examine
this Spirit's expression (*locutio*), through which all things were created."[17]
Anselm claims that there must be an internal expression within the Godhead,
not merely an expression in creation. This internal expression is identical
with the supreme Spirit himself and is his eternal Word. Even if there were no
creation, God would express himself eternally, "Whether, therefore," Anselm
states, "it be thought of in connection with no other existing being, or with
other existing beings, the Word of that Spirit must be coeternal with him."[18]

Like Dionysius, Anselm has placed the principle of fecundity within the
Trinity and in the person of the Father, whom he speaks of as "Spirit" in the
above quotations. It is clear from the movement of Anselm's thought that he
did not see the same radical incompatibility between the two paradigms of God
that Lovejoy saw. For Anselm the all-perfect Absolute is also the self-expressive Goodness, which expresses in a single eternal Word its own likeness and
all it can create. Anselm can accept the compatibility between the two paradigms precisely because he sees them linked within the inner life of God—in
the fecundity of the Father—not in creation, where Lovejoy rightly judged
them to be incompatible.

BONAVENTURE AND THE PRINCIPLE OF PLENITUDE

In the *Monologion* Anselm did not explore directly some of the further
metaphysical implications of this Trinitarian approach to fecundity. However,
throughout his writings he developed a dialectical approach and a specific
theological method which Richard of St. Victor and Bonaventure used for their
own metaphysical clarification of the issue. Anselm's method consisted of a

search for the "necessary reasons" (*rationes necessariae*) of the mysteries of faith.[19] In his *De Trinitate*, Richard of St. Victor applied this method explicitly to the Trinity and showed the inadequacy of creation to meet the demands of divine fecundity.[20] Following in the same direction, Bonaventure achieved a remarkable integration of Dionysius, Anselm and Richard of St. Victor in the Sixth Chapter of the *Itinerarium Mentis in Deum*. There he applies the Anselmian dialectic to the divine fecundity. Taking Dionysius' notion of self-diffusion, he claims that this must be realized within the Trinity since it cannot be realized in creation. He completed his picture with elements from Richard of St. Victor on divine love. Bonaventure's articulation brings this medieval Trinitarian tradition to its full self-consciousness of the central issue of Lovejoy's book.

Bonaventure begins his treatment with the Anselmian dialectic of the *Proslogion*: "Behold, therefore, and observe that the highest good is unqualifiedly that in comparison with which a greater cannot be thought. And this good is such that it cannot rightly be thought of as non-existing, since to be is better than not to be." He then links the Anselmian ascent to the all-perfect Good with the Dionysian notion of self-diffusion: "Good is said to be self-diffusive, and therefore the highest good is most self-diffusive."[21] Bonaventure is uniting Lovejoy's two paradigms of God by subsuming the notion of self-diffusion under the logic of absolute perfection. But notice Bonaventure's turn in the argument. He moves to the Trinity and not to creation. In fact, he uses Anselm's method of *rationes necessariae* to establish that this maximum of self-diffusion can be realized only in the Trinity and not in creation. For Bonaventure claims that the highest self-diffusion must be "actual and intrinsic, substantial and hypostatic, natural and voluntary, free and necessary, unfailing and perfect."[22]

The crucial issue here is the actuality of maximal expression. Like Lovejoy, Bonaventure sees that the diffusion must be actual and that it must be maximal. The self-diffusion cannot be merely potential, and it cannot be less than supreme. This is indeed the principle of plenitude, and Bonaventure comes to grips with its logic directly. But instead of moving in Lovejoy's direction, Bonaventure moves to the Trinity. Only within the Trinity is there an eternal, actual and maximal self-diffusion of the divinity: in the generation of the Son from the Father's fecundity and in the spiration of the Holy Spirit. For as Bonaventure observes, "the diffusion that occurred in time in the creation of the world is no more than a pivot or point in comparison with the immense sweep of the eternal goodness."[23]

Bonaventure explores these themes further in the *Collationes in Hexaemeron*, where he states that the divine diffusion must be ultimate, so that "the one producing gives whatever he can give; but creatures cannot receive whatever God can give."[24] This notion of maximal diffusion is developed in Bonaventure's earlier writings under the notion of the Father's fountain-fulness (*fontalis plenitudo*). Since the Father is the primordial principle in the Trinity, he has the fecundity of primordiality.[25] In the *fontalis plenitudo* of the Father the principle of plenitude is realized in its maximal possible degree. For the Father expresses this plenitude not only in generating the Son but in producing in the Son the *rationes* or archetypes of all he can make. Thus in the Trinity the Father expresses in the Son his perfect Image who is at the same time his expressive Word, through whom creation takes place as the outer expression of the Trinitarian fullness.[26]

What are the implications of this position for hierarchies and the great chain of being? First, the world is freed from having to bear the impossible burden of expressing the fullness of the divine fecundity. On this point Lovejoy was absolutely correct. It is impossible to the world to perform this task. Since for Bonaventure the principle of plenitude is realized absolutely in the Trinity, there can now be a variety of expressions in creation. No world is the best possible world, and yet every possible world is a significant expression of the divine fecundity. Hierarchies are possible and so are their negation. It is not by chance that Bonaventure is a follower of Francis of Assisi, whose characteristic vision is of the coincidence of opposites rather than a hierarchical ladder.[27] Francis could see God in an earthworm and in the sun. His characteristic view was of the highest in the lowest. The joy he took in the variety expressed in creation reflects Bonaventure's joy in the fecundity of the Father.

At least theoretically, this conception of the divine fecundity opens up the possibility of a variety of cosmic schemes, such as those conceived in the successive scientific revolutions and others that might arise in the future. In the light of this transformation of the principle of plenitude, it would be of great interest to explore the later chapters of *The Great Chain of Being* and also enter into dialogue with such thinkers as Hegel, Whitehead and Teilhard de Chardin.[28] But that would take us beyond our appendix to Lovejoy's chapter on "Conflicts in Medieval Thought."

NOTES

[1]Arthur O. Lovejoy, *The Great Chain of Being: A Study of the History of an Idea* (New York: Harper & Row, 1960), pp. 24-66.

[2]*Ibid.*, pp. 67-98.

[3]*Ibid.*, pp. 315-333.

[4]*Ibid.*, p. 82.

[5]*Loc. cit.*

[6]*Ibid.*, p. 84.

[7]*Ibid.*, p. 69.

[8]*Ibid.*, p. 70.

[9]*Ibid.*, p. 73.

[10]Dionysius, *De divinis nominibus*, II, 4.

[11]*Ibid.*, n. 7; translation by C. E. Rolt, *Dionysius the Areopagite: The Divine Names and the Mystical Theology* (London: SPCK, 1940), p. 74.

[12]Théodore de Régnon, *Études de théologie positive sur la Sainte Trinité*, 4 vols. (Paris: Retaux, 1892-1898); Cf. Ewert H. Cousins, "Models and the Future of Theology," *Continuum*, 7 (1969), 88-91.

[13]Dionysius, *De divinis nominibus*, II, 5; Rolt, p. 91.

[14]Augustine, *De Trinitate*, V-VII; cf. Harry Wolfson, *The Philosophy of the Church Fathers*, Vol. I (Cambridge: Harvard University Press, 1964), 350-359.

[15]Anselm, *Monologion*, c. 1-28.

[16]*Ibid.*, c. 28; translation by S. N. Deane, *St. Anselm: Basic Writings* (La Salle, Ill.: Open Court, 1962), p. 87.

[17]*Ibid.*, c. 29; Deane, p. 89.

[18]*Ibid.*, c. 32; Deane, p. 95.

[19]Anselm, *Monologion*, prol.; c. 64; *Epistola de Incarnatione Verbi*, c. 4.

[20]Richard of St. Victor, *De Trinitate*, I, 4-5; III, 2.

[21]Bonaventure, *Itinerarium Mentis in Deum*, c. 6, n. 2; translation by Philotheus Boehner, *Works of Saint Bonaventure*, Vol. II *Saint Bonaventure's Itinerarium Mentis in Deum* (Saint Bonaventure, N. Y.: The Franciscan Institute, 1956), 89.

[22]*Loc. cit.*

82

[23]*Loc. cit.*

[24]Bonaventure, *In Hexaemeron*, XI, n. 11.

[25]Bonaventure, *I Sent.*, d. 2, a. un. q. 2 (I,468-474).

[26]Bonaventure, *In Hexaemeron*, I, n. 16.

[27]Cf. Ewert H. Cousins, "La 'Coincidentia Oppositorum' dans la théologie de Bonaventure," *Études franciscaines*, 18 (Supplement annuel, 1968), 15-31.

[28]For a discussion of Bonaventure's position in relation to Hegel, Whitehead and Teilhard, cf. Ewert H. Cousins, "God as Dynamic in Bonaventure and Contemporary Thought," *Proceedings of the American Catholic Philosophical Association*, 48 (1974), 136-148.

PAUL G. KUNTZ

THE HIERARCHICAL VISION OF ST. BONAVENTURE

To call St. Bonaventure "the Seraphic Doctor" suggests the hierarchical structure present in all his thought: whether he writes about nature, man, or the spiritual world, there are levels and must be levels. Everything there is is ordered, and this means clearly for him that to be is to be higher, or intermediate, or lower.[1] On this central and crucial metaphysical commitment there is no disagreement among his commentators. But as soon as the interpreters characterize the hierarchies, they follow such very diverse lines that they do not even recognize each other sufficiently to disagree explicitly. I should like very swiftly to expound a fundamental divergence between the interpretation of Bonaventure's hierarchy from the history of ideas and that coming from certain Franciscan interpreters. I shall call the first interpretation "Plotinean" because Bonaventura's hierarchical structure is presented as a neo-Platonic rational metaphysics. The second I shall call "Franciscan," for life itself is a journey, and the problem is how we should act so as to arrive at the best destination. My paper is based on the text "Duplex est ordo rerum: unus in universo, alter in finem." I shall argue that the Plotinean history of ideas approach has stressed only the first order, which may be called static, and it is the Franciscan approach which has more adequately presented the dynamic conception, which is suggested by the active participle ordering, because it is ordering man's acts toward an end.[2] My key text here is "Sapientis est ordinare. Ideo quaedam facit bona, quaedam meliora, quaedam optima."[3]

It is strange that that great book *The Great Chain of Being* has no reference to the Seraphic Doctor. Lovejoy stressed the plenitude of being and how appropriate it would have been to cite Bonaventure on the "fontalis plenitudo," the fountain fullness! But let us surmise from Lovejoy's ideological brother, George Boas, what they saw and didn't see in his hierarchical vision. Boas translated the *Itinerarium Mentis in Deum* and published *The Mind's Road to God* in the Library of Liberal Arts in 1953. It is probably best known in this edition:

> The metaphysical point of view of St. Bonaventure can be
> traced back to Plotinus, if not to Plato. Fundamental to
> his whole system is that fusion of the three hierarchies

of Neo-Platonism: the hierarchy of logical classes, that
of values, and that of reality.[4]

Does St. Bonaventure suppose that the universe is like the hierarchy of
classes, the Tree of Porphyry? Does St. Bonaventure suppose that "the more
general a class, the more real and the better?" Was his problem as Boas says
it was, to discover the precise correspondence between the most general and
the most real, the less general and the less real, the least general and the
least real? Does Bonaventure repeat what Boas ascribes to Plotinus, that each
lower step in the emanation from the One is as effect, necessarily lower and a
step toward utter degeneration? I should answer all these questions in the negative.

Boas does not cite texts for these claims He admits that Bonaventure did
not know Plotinus' position, and that Bonaventure's first principle is "the
personal God of *Genesis*" and not the One. It makes a great deal of difference
in the concepts of hierarchy whether the cosmology is one of emanation or of
creation. The crux of Boas' refutation is that a logical order is not a temporal order. In Boas' restatement of the conclusion of *The Great Chain of Being*,
"one simply could not deduce from any taxonomical order a temporal order." The
logical classifications we construct are not, in fact, the way mutations, for
example of the fruit fly, occur.[5] My point in quoting Boas is not to disagree
that there is something essentially different between these two orders, nor to
disagree with this as a difficulty in Plotinus, but to ask critically whether
Bonaventure fell into this trap, as Boas says he did. On the correspondence
between the abstract order of being and the order of goodness, I happen to
think that Boas is right in questioning the traditional assumptions of theology and metaphysics:

> The attribution of goodness and beauty to the hierarchy
> was another logical surd. But from the time of Plato on
> the immutable and the unified were believed to be better
> than the changing and multiple. This could only be an as-
> sumption. But once the assumption was made, one could as-
> sert, that as one went up the hierarchy one proceeded to-
> ward the better. [6]

As to neo-Platonic sources, what Bonaventure cites and uses is the *Mystical Theology* of Dionysius (MRG.p.8,IMD I,1). The importance of texts of the
one we call the Pseudo-Dionysius, but regarded by Bonaventure as the disciple
of St. Paul, is that the conception of hierarchy is Judeo-Christian as well as
Greek. It would be utterly inappropriate in every way for Plotinus to write:

.... He who wishes to ascend to God must, avoiding sin,
which deforms nature, exercise ... natural powers for re-
generating grace, and do this through prayer. He must
strive toward purifying justice, and this in intercourse
.... No one comes to wisdom save through grace, justice,
and knowledge .... Grace is the foundation of the will's
rectitude and of the enlightenment of clear and penetrating reason .... We must strive toward the reflection of
truth and, by our striving, mount step by step until we
come to the high mountain where we shall see the God of
gods in Sion (Ps.83.8).

Since, then we must mount Jacob's ladder before descending it, let us place the first rung of this ascension
in the depths, putting the whole sensible world before us
as a mirror, by which ladder we shall mount up to God,
the Supreme Creator, that we may be true Hebrews crossing
from Egypt to the land promised to our Fathers; let us be
Christians crossing with Christ from this world over to
the Father; let us also be lovers of wisdom .... (MRG
p.10 IMD I,9)

When we call him the "Seraphic Doctor" we must then remember the angels
between heaven and earth, for this Jacob is one who strives to ascend (but
does Bonaventure's Jacob also wrestle against an angel?) Not only is man depicted in dynamic terms but God also. The Creator is the Trinity of Persons.
Father Bougerol, who uses his vast knowledge to show Bonaventure as a development of the Areopagite, concedes the influence of Saint Augustine, Saint Anselm, Richard of Saint-Victor who passed from "la contemplation statique ...
de Denys pour s'elever a une synthèse essentiallement dynamique de la Trinité
de Dieu ...." God the Father is not sheer plenitude. "... Chez Saint Bonaventure la fécondite jaillissante du Père s'ouvre au monde dans le Verbe incarné,
unique médiateur parce que personne médiane de la Trinité."[7]

Whatever the Christ of Denys may have been in a neo-Platonic hierarchiza-
tion of the universe (some light of light?), in Bonaventure the Franciscan he
is a living person in history. If the work of St. Francis was to shift the emphasis toward the incarnate Word, then the implicit philosophy in this theology is even further from Plotinus than from Pseudo-Dionysius.[8]

Father Bougerol stresses the series of acts whereby man ascends: "gradus:
Saint Bonaventure nomme ainsi la série d'actes ou de vertues, en correspondence avec les neuf choeurs des anges, par lesquels, l'ame passe dans la mon-
tée des créatures à Dieu ou dans la descente de Dieu aux créatures."[9]

The hierarchical concept of St. Bonaventure that dominates his thinking,
making it appropriate to call him "the Seraphic Doctor," is the ninefold hier-

archy. If Bonaventure had been as pure a rationalist as Plotinus, the way would have been primarily "illuminative" rather than "perfective," for the latter involves the affections. The ends of the human process of salvation are the repose of peace, the way of purgation expressed in angelic terms as "thrones," the splendor of truth expressed in angelic terms "cherubim" and the "sweetness of love" expressed in angelic terms as "seraphim." This is most clear in "De sex gradibus dilectionis Dei."[10]

No one can deny that there are some very close parallels in Bonaventure to the Neo-Platonic arguments. There are whole passages that parallel Pseudo-Dionysius very closely indeed. But these seem to be borrowings that do not fit the main thrust of the *Itinerarium Mentis in Deum*. It seems to me more fitting to say that sometimes he put the message of Jacob's ladder in the cosmic terms of degrees of forms and of reality. But this was the language then available for interpreting Christian Mysticism. The content that he cites is overwhelmingly Biblical. Hence he was expressing something that can now be restated even if, as Boas argues, all the main points of Neo-Platonic hierarchy have been refuted.

The principle at work in this thinking is teleological, *ordo in finem*, and not primarily taxonomic or classification from individuals to classes of greater and greater generality. It is indeed, in approaching the end, closeness to God. And if God were thought of as being, then the approach to God would be to being as such, but the Seraphic Doctor characterizes his ends in terms we should call those of value, *peace, truth, love*.

Sometimes he classifies the virtues as six rather than three, and when six they are called the six wings of the seraph: zeal for justice, kindness, patience, exemplary life, prudent discernment, devotion to God. Again, the thought is teleological, and the end salvation. It is the love of God that helps carry all the other virtues, without which they would fail to bring man to perfection, for love "teaches all things concerning salvation."

> The sixth and last wing, most necessary, and indispensable for the full development of the other five, consists in a superior's *devotion* to God. As a result of this devotion, zeal will be inflamed, the kindness of compassion infused, patience increased, virtuous example made attractively fragrant, and discernment enlightened. Such devotion is called function of the Spirit: it teaches all things concerning salvation.[11]

One might try to assimilate this teleological thought into some version of the Platonic hierarchy whereby eros leads us to supreme beauty. The best case in Bonaventura could probably be made from the frequent citation of the Areopagite, "bonum et pulchrum idem." There is here a kind of convertibility, such as Boas ascribed to all thinkers in the Platonic and Neo-Platonic tradition.[12]

But then we encounter the identification of God with sacrificial and suffering love Again, whatever there might be that is Platonic, the stress is distinctively Christian. If Greek thought of God led to identifying God with pure act, utter simplicity, absoluteness to the exclusion of suffering, multiplicity, relatedness, then there is something non-Greek in St. Bonaventure:

> The sixth and most abundant shedding of blood was caused
> by the piercing nails .... It is in the depth of passion
> that we should see the depth of the love; in this redness
> of the passion that we should see the fire of the rose of
> love. Who, indeed, has ever suffered such pain and such
> disgrace? God is the One who suffers; yet He who so often
> removed or reduced the pressure of His servants' pains in
> no way eases the pressure of the passion's wine press.
> The One who knew how to spare His own did not spare Him-
> self.[13]

If Christianity leads to ascribing to deity the changing and multiple as well as the changeless and simple, then St. Bonaventure's text shows him, at least in part, to have escaped the dogma about which Boas complained, the unquestioned assumption "that the immutable and the unified were believed to be better than the changing and multiple." (above p. 84) St. Bonaventure writes: "Truest love ... repeatedly sheds his blood."[14]"

So much writing about St. Bonaventure deals with the organization into the three that are respectively top, middle, or bottom, or the six that are three pairs of supreme, intermediate, and inferior, or the six that are six steps or degrees leading to the top of the flight, the seventh, consummation of the efforts of climbing. Much of the exposition of St. Bonaventure on hierarchy, such as Gilson's draws up, with regard to the soul's return (regressus) to God (retour vers Dieu) are "tables de correspondence des deux series entre elles et avec les hiérarchies ecclésiastiques et célestes"[15]

To get behind the artificiality about which Fr. Boehner complains to hierarchical thought itself, we can stress what St. Bonaventure brings to focus in his *Itinerarium*. It is not the schematism but the fact of history that St. Francis of Assisi attained holiness and peace and ecstasy in seraphic love.

Saint Bonaventure's *Itinerarium* is singular if not unique in its use of a concrete case. This is more important than what is quoted from the Areopagite or
St. Bernard.

> Mais ce que Saint Bonaventure doit à Saint François,
> c'est un exemple concret, la preuve par le fait que comme
> la perfection de la pauvreté n'est pas une grâce d'excep-
> tion réservée à des rares privilégiés, la voie de la con-
> templation mystique est ouverte à tous ceux qui savent en
> trouver l'accès.[16]

If what St. Bonaventure is doing is parallel to Giotto's painting of the
legend of St. Francis, then he is not primarily instructing us in how the universe is organized but luring us by the beauty of St. Francis' life and incit-
ing in us the passion to live similarly, and telling us how to achieve such
consummation in ecstatic peace. Gilson puts this very well.

> .... La première condition dont l'example de Saint Fran-
> çois manifeste la nécessité, c'est le désire. Pour at-
> teindre l'intelligence et la sagesse, il faut d'abord en
> avoir soif. Le don d'intelligence, par example, est une
> nourriture solide, comme le pain, dont Saint François
> disait qu' il faut bien des travaux pour l'acquerir. On
> seme le grain, il croît, on le moissonne, on le porte au
> moulin ou le cuit, et nous passons bien des opérations
> intermédiaires ....[17]

St. Bonaventure's language of hierarchy sounds like an extrapolation into
a spiritual realm of the levels of the natural world, as though we go on from
the inanimate, animate and mental levels to another three or six or nine
orders above man. It is not unnatural to suppose man to be intermediate in the
universe, with at least as many levels above him, between man and God, as below him, between man and nothing. How should one read this metaphysical vision? George Boas is an aesthetician as well as historian, and concludes:

> There would be no point in trying to translate it in
> terms of the twentieth century, for the attempt would
> fail .... Similarly one would not attempt to translate
> Dante's cosmology into modern terms nor justify Chartres
> Cathedral in terms of functional architecture .... This
> book is a kind of prose poem, with a dramatic development
> of its own as one rises from step to step toward a mystic
> vision of God. (MRG.p.xxi)

There is a very deep conflict here in the understanding of language. If
it is simple-minded to take St. Bonaventure's indicative sentences to be descriptions of celestial geography, then it may be only an exercise of imagination and make believe. We can enjoy the pictures he paints as a verbal companion piece to Giotto. (MRG.p.v) But this would be a very superficial interpre-

tation at best. If St. Bonaventure is not primarily delighting the senses, then what he is doing might better be put in the imperative mood, which he frequently uses, "Pray ye for the things that are for the peace of Jerusalem (Ps.121,6)." (MRG.p.3) He not only borrows imperatives from scripture, in his own speech he warns, guides and goads the reader: "Bestir yourself then, O man of God, you who previously resisted the pricks of conscience, before you raise your eyes to the rays of wisdom shining in that mirror, lest by chance you fall into the lower pit of shadows from the contemplation of those rays." (MRG. p.5)

In this Prologue he does present a vision from Mt. Alverna, meditating on "ascent of the mind to God," specifically the event there thirty-three years before when St. Francis had the vision of "the winged Seraph in the likeness of the Crucified." It is entirely natural to divide his work into six chapters corresponding to the three pairs of wings.

But St. Bonaventure knows this is a device "so that their contents may be the more easily understood." (MRG. pp.3-5) But then a warning to the reader:

> I ask therefore that one think rather of the intention of the writer than of his work, of the sense of the words rather than the rude speech, of truth rather than beauty, of the exercise of the affections rather than the erudition of the intellect. (MRG. p.5)

What kind of "truth" is that correlated with desire rather than with the "erudition of the intellect?" When he speaks of the hierarchical arrangement of the universe under "the aspect of one inquiring rationally, one sees that some things merely are; others, however, are and live; others, finally, are, live, and discern. And the first are lesser things, the second midway, and the third the best." (MRG. pp.11-12) Here is a kind of Aristotelian classification, still present in scientific thought, and called recently by a noted American philosopher, James K. Feibleman, a "naturally found ontology"[18]. St. Bonaventure builds upon it, in strict continuity of levels, the angelic and the divine.

> Again, one sees that some are only corporeal, others partly corporeal and partly spiritual, from which it follows that some are entirely spiritual and are better and more worthy than either of the others. (MRG. p.12)

My difficulty with Bonaventure's hierarchical vision is whether he has not confused the mode of existence involved in stating "there are fish" and "there are archangels." We have been through a great period of examining God-talk. To read and restate the truth of St. Bonaventure we need to examine his angel-talk.

How does one get from the temporal to the eternal?

> From these visible things, therefore, one mounts to con-
> sidering the power and wisdom and goodness of God as be-
> ing, living, and understanding; purely spiritual and in-
> corruptible and immutable. (MRG. p.12)

The argument requires the premise of symmetry. If man is above the animals, higher than the lower, then by the presumed orderliness of *bona, meliora, optima*, there must be the highest. How does one "see" this? Another kind
of "seeing" from sense perception.

> One sees ... that some are mutable and corruptible, as
> earthy things; others mutable and incorruptible, as ce-
> lestial things, from which it follows that some are im-
> mutable and incorruptible, as the supercelestial things.
> (MRG. p.12)

Should we then conclude that the hierarchical vision of St. Bonaventure
rests upon an untenable and fallacious argument? Father Bettoni, interpreting
St. Bonaventure, would be willing to concede all the strange medieval talk of
the steps on steps, but still to conclude that "it is necessary to acknowledge
once again that the statement (that we can rise step by step to "the mountain
height where the God of gods is seen on Sion") is still valid--*that to know
the truth one must love it and love it strongly.*"[19]

I believe the simple continuity between naturally found hierarchy and the
teleological hierarchy of spiritual aim ignores Bonaventura's own distinction
between the two orders. There must be a connection but it seems that when he
asserted it he ignored "Duplex est ordo rerum: unus in universo, alter in finem (above p.)." In what senses do the creatures below man also exemplify the
hierarchy, or in the dynamic functional language "return to God?"

There are many puzzling problems in reading any scholastic, and much of
the writing about St. Bonaventure is apparently in the hope that when enough
kinds of hierarchy are correlated, and all the distinctions of kinds and degree are observed, the whole intricate whole will be so coherent and all comprehensive that the metaphysical truth will be so evident that the reader will
feel all his questions are somewhere answered and any problems are due to in-
attention to some hidden aspect.

Perhaps the best exposition that analyzes the many metaphors St. Bonaventure uses for hierarchy is Romano Guardini, *Systembildende Elemente in der*

Theologie Bonaventuras, Die Lehre von Lumen Mentis, von der Gradio Entium und der Influentia Sensus et Motus.[20] Guardini tries to show that the model of the ladder expresses what St. Bonaventura assumed throughout his work: the ultimate origin, or cosmic Alpha, is the same as all creatures' (and hence man's) ultimate goal, the teleological Omega. St. Bonaventura once addressed God: "Lord, I come from you and by you I return to you."[21] The principle of hierarchy is then "von Natur jedes Ding, zu seinem Ursprung zurückstrebt".[22] Whether it is weight (pondus) that carries a thing to its physical level, or the psychic lure that draws a lover to his beloved, the law is supposed to cover both in a universe like Dante's where love moves the sun and all the other stars. In a theistic context Love is the ultimate origin and therefore the ultimate aim.

But what if the model is not perfectly adequate? The model of the ladder in expressing the descent (cosmic origin) and the ascent (aim of man) may seem the medium for expressing creation and salvation. But if the universe is a ladder, as St. Bonaventure says, is God the very top, the last stretch after the top rung, or beyond the ladder? If the first, then God is a finite section of the cosmos, and that won't do. If the second, then what connection between the ladder and the creator? How calculate the distance, as we must, between the rungs that we ascend or descend? It might be better to express the metaphor absurdly, a "rungless ladder."[23]

A strictly straight line is not an adequate model for the relation of God to man. It should rather be a circle. For "gratia ... fluit et refluit. Fluit a Deo et facit hominem refluere in Deum ...."[24] A bent line or circle is more appropriate to circulation.

> Die Grundkraft, die diesen 'circulus intelligiblis' beherrscht, ist die Liebe: amor effusivus der göttlichen Gutheit, im Akt der Schöpfung; amor unitivus der Geschöpfe, durch den sie zu ihrem Ursprung zurückstreben.[25]

The circle is better than the line to express St. Bonaventure's meaning. There is not a sharp break, a cut-off, between Creature and creator. What is meant is that one leads into the other without identification of one with the other except in the incarnation.[26]

But the circle itself fails to express the interrelations between creatures. Since there is an organic interrelationship, the model should rather be a network. It is not merely that the less strive upward towards the greater,

but the better care for the less, and all care for themselves, and all together care for the good.[27]

We should not expect any model to be adequate, whether line or circle or
network. The thoughts about such relations as those between God and man
involve parodox. In the history of salvation there is the breaking of the
ladder, Adam's fall (scala fracta) and the repaired ladder through Christ
(scala reparans).[28] God is then both distant and present (summe distans a
creaturis" and "intime praesens est omnibus creaturis")[29] Again, the relationship between levels is one of dignity (praelatio)[30] but also one of service
(ministerium).[31] All these examples, and many others, seem to bear out the
contention of Ewert Cousins that we can make sense of such complexity only as
a *coincidentia oppositorum*.[32]

The parodoxes may arise from the attempt to express qualitative degrees
in quantitative language and symbols. We judge the degrees of love qualitatively, as more or less intense, but there is no measuring such degrees lin-
early or in any other kind of line that can be divided into fixed segments.

What, in the end, is the Seraphic Doctor doing? I believe he is evaluating the degrees of love and recommending the more intense degree of love, and
between the kinds of love recommending altruistic devotion above egocentric
desire: the message of the crucified seraph is that sacrificial love is the
highest, the divine, as presented in Christianity.

The kinds of love are distinguished: either love is self-centered (amor
commodi) or centered in another (as amor amicitiae) and either love is for the
sake of something else (propter aliud) or for its own sake (propter se).[33]
What love is most perfect and the standard by which any love can be judged?
The inferiority of self-centered love lies in the passion to possess something, and the object may be unworthy of the passion, or the degree of intensity. Love centered in another can never be trivial.[34] But here is a norm: "the
depth of the affection itself .... Strength of this desire to be in the company of the beloved or his desire for more and more complete possession."[35]
The love for its own sake that is supreme is the love of God. There can be
here no excess. And therefore for this love there is a second test of intensity: "the extent to which one is willing to suffer in order to maintain union
with the beloved. If the love will not bear the strain of any suffering at all
then it is weak, but if it is maintained in face of much suffering then it is
strong."[36]

Sacrifice may be selfish or unselfish. "The difference between a selfish
and an unselfish sacrifice lies in this, that the selfish lover sacrifices so
as not to lose the beloved, whereas the unselfish lover sacrifices so as not
to offend him."[37]

At no point is St. Bonaventure more Augustinian in his analysis of the
dynamics and standard of human action. Man is primarily will or affective potency.[38] From the above gauges of intensity, the highest love is the love of
God. Nothing is more worthy of love because of his nature, and nothing is to
be loved more, nor is God to be loved for the sake of anything else.[39]

The most serious ordering principles that St. Bonaventure offers are not,
as Boas claimed, logical generality of classes, or the correlation with degrees of value and reality. Rather they take the form of answering the question: what should man love supremely?

> Inordinatio amoris duplicter potest esse, aut quia amatur
> res quae non debet ut quia amatur res amplius quam de-
> beat.
> Amor rectus esse non potest, si aliquid diligat supra
> Deum vel aeque vel aliquid diligat proper se et Deum
> propter aliquid.[40]

There is a problem of correlation of love and knowledge, for it is impossible to love an object without knowing it. "Nullus diligit aliquid nisi prae-
cogitans."[41] But is St. Bonaventure committed to the principle of strict correlation, expressed "quod maior tunc dilectio quia maior cognitio?"[42] It would
seem that he is examining cases and considering the norms applicable.

Both love and knowledge admit of different levels. More perfect than
knowing is knowing that one knows. And to love that one loves is a more profound degree of love than simply to love.

> Sed dilectio est actus completionis et perfectionis, si-
> cut scientia; unde sicut perfecte qui scit se scire, ita
> perfecte qui amat dilectionem. (Sent 1, d.17, p.1, a7,
> q.2, I, 297b)[43]

But the degrees are not strictly correlate. One may know very well without loving with corresponding intensity.

> Conversely, knowledge is not always the more intense of
> the two acts. For it does happen that love will far out-
> strip knowledge .... In its alterocentric form love far
> outruns knowledge ....[44]

According to the norm knowledge and love ought to be of equal intensity.
The only way this is possible is where the "lover" is given an experimental

knowledge of the beloved. The one case that satisfies "quod maior tunc dilectio quia maior cognitio ...." is "de cognitione experimentali."[45]

The position logically leads to the kind of mysticism we find in the *Iti-*
nerarium Mentis in Deum. Where the love is alterocentric and the objects are
all creatures as well as the Creator, on two scores the knowledge must be deficient. The knowing must then go beyond all ordinary cognition by sense and
reason. The consummation

> is not due to the intensity of the knowledge, that is to
> say, the love does not borrow its strength from knowl-
> edge, but the knowledge is raised to the level of the
> love by love itself. Love approaches and embraces the be-
> loved, and in so doing he lays open to view the whole in-
> terior of the soul. In such loving the real individual is
> known in his individuality; it is a knowing that is a
> loving and a loving that is a knowing.[46]

Obviously then one who does not love cannot know in this supreme case of
loving, the love of God. For the non-lover the claim here that the lover knows
must be nonsense. Hence St. Bonaventure's approach cannot be purely rational.
It must be exactly what we found it to be, an urging of this love upon the
reader. He can be approached because by nature he loves something and by nature he is potentially a lover of the best.[47]

If Father Prentice has guided us correctly to St. Bonaventure's *scala*
amoris, then we can see indeed that it might initially seem like a Platonism
or a Neo-Platonism. Everything is ordered as lower, intermediate and higher
and there is a principle that moves everything towards the highest. St. Bonaventure did indeed use the hierarchy of light. God is said to be pure Being,
and all others flow from him in various degrees, such as image, vestige, and
shadow. In this kind of hierarchy a thing is better to the degree that it approaches Being ("omnino melius est esse quam non esse." IMD VI, 1f, V, 310b)[48]

But is there primacy of timeless logic, such as is found in Plotinus? If
so, there would be no place for the seraphim of Isaiah's vision which became
part of the angelic hierarchy of St. Paul. The Areopagite could assimilate one
to the other because both Neo-Platonism and Christianity were ways of salvation that took the hierarchical form. But Plotinus depended on reason for his
analysis of a cosmology of lower levels flowing from the One. St. Bonaventure
made the human search for God central. After the rational cosmology, based on
logic, John Herman Randall, Jr. adds: "This analysis also furnishes Plotinus
with a scale of values ...."[49]

This logical scale is *ipso facto* a scale of value. Value, what is real, Being, is what gives understanding: because Plotinus in his whole analysis starts from the experience of knowing as the basic good, He shares the religion of the Knower, for whom perfection, the highest good, is the source of truth. Hence ... the most consistent illustration of the Greek devotion to the life of theoria.[50]

Plotinus' vision is "thoroughly consistent and true, in the only sense in which a philosophy can be called true: it offers a rational interpretation of man's experience in his world, and a harmonious discrimination of values."[51]

St. Bonaventure would wish to have a philosophy that is "thoroughly consistent" but that did not mean so much to him as to have at its center what he held to be factually true, an event. That God became man was an article of faith in the Christian plan of salvation. But what grounded his faith in factuality was the fact of St. Francis. He had become one with the crucified seraph. The supreme sacrifice attained the supreme love, and he bore the stigmata. Somehow again, according to this Christo-centric philosophy, the nature of God was made so plain that all could see it.

Unless we reject the idea that the philosophy of St. Bonaventure is a version of Plotineanism we cannot make sense of his hierarchical vision which is personal, affective, temporal, not primarily rational, and social in its basis and implications.

Christ ... is our ladder. (MRG 8)

The way is only through the most burning love of the Crucified. (MRG 4)

These stages are implanted in us by nature, deformed by sin, reformed by grace, to be purged by justice, exercised by knowledge, perfected by wisdom. (MRG 9)

[The way is not known without love and is presented by] exercise of the affections rather than the erudition of the intellect. (MRG 5)

The way has become manifest in the Church. (MRG 13)

St. Bonaventure did not write of his hierarchical vision as rationally coherent and therefore true. Rather he says that not to respond to "such great splendor of created things is [to be] blind," and he adds, deaf, dumb, and foolish. (MRG 13)

The refutation of such a claim, if it is coherent, could not be merely logical, as Boas assures us it is. Would it not itself have to be factual:

that this saviour has not in fact saved the world or that this St. Francis did
not attain union with Christ or that the way prescribed does not in fact produce the results predicted?

NOTES

[1]"Every order necessarily has a lowest level, a highest level, and an intermediate level." Alexander Schaefer, *The Position and Function of Man in the Created World According to Bonaventure*, Studies in Sacred Theology No.154, Catholic University of America, Washington, D.C., 1965, p. 41.

[2]I *Sent.* 44, 1, 4, Concl. t.I, p.786-787, cited and interpreted by Etienne Gilson, *La Philosophie de Saint Bonaventure*, 3rd Ed., J. Vrin, Paris, 1953, p. 144-145.

[3]I *Sent.* 44, I, 2, ad 3, t.I, 785b, commented on by Schaefer, *op.cit*, p. 40. It is interesting to note Bonaventure's need of the comparative and superlative to characterize the world.

[4]Saint Bonaventura, *The Mind's Road to God*, Translated, with an Introduction, by George Boas The Liberal Arts Press, N.Y., 1953, pp. ix-x. Hereafter references to this translation will be made in text with the initials "MRG." Sometimes the place in the Latin text is indicated by "IMD."

[5]George Boas, *Rationalism in Greek Philosophy*, Ch. IX, "The Final Capitulation," Johns Hopkins University Press, Baltimore, 1961, p. 477.

[6]*Ibid.*, p. 477.

[7]Jacques-Guy Bougerol, "Saint Bonaventure et le Pseudo Denys l'Areopagite," *Actes du Colloque Saint Bonaventure, Etudes Franciscaines* 18 (Supplement annuel, 1968, p. 118) It is the neglect of the hierarchical concept outside Greek philosophy that has led to a very necessary correction. The basis of the Areopagite's celestical hierarchy is in thronoi, kyriotes, basileiai, theotetes, leitourgiai (Col. I:16), which with angels and archangels, make seven classes. What the Areopagite worked up into nine was worked on by others also. See Robert M. Grant, "Chains of Being in Early Christianity," *Myths and Symbols, Studies in Honor of Mircea Eliade*, Joseph M. Kitagawa and Charles H. Long, Edd., University of Chicago Press, Chicago, Ill., 1969, pp. 279-289. The only contemporary American philosopher who uses the image of Jacob's ladder (Gen. 28:10-15; 32:22-31) is George Santayana, *The Last Puritan*, Scribner's, N.Y., 1936, pp. 313-316.

[8]*Ibid.*

[9]Jacques-Guy Bougerol, *Lexique Saint Bonaventure*, Editions Franciscaines, Paris, 1969, p. 74.

[10]*Opusculum* I, de triplici via, Capitulum II, 4, Opera, Quaracchi, 1.VII, 1898, pp. 10-11. Baron J. deVinck, in *Works, Mystical Opuscula*, St. Anthony Guild Press, Paterson, N.J., 1960, pp. 61-2 notes that the ordering of steps is logical rather than temporal. That is, one does not have to read before prayer, or to pray before contemplating, but there is moral cleansing, rational illumination and spiritual illumination.

[11]*Ibid.* Vol. III, *Opuscula*, Second Series, 1966, p. 187.

[12]Karl Peter, *Die Lehre von der Schonheit nach Bonaventura* (diss Basel), Dietrich-Coelde-Verlag, Werl/Westf., 1964, p.119.

[13]J. de Vinck, *op.cit., Mystical Opuscula*, "On the Sixth and Seventh Sheddings of Blood," p. 199.

[14]*Ibid.* The best exposition of the philosophical importance of suffering as divine is in Charles Hartshorne and William L. Reese, *Philosophers Speak of God*, University of Chicago Press, Chicago, 1953. This is most clear in the section from Baron Friedrich von Hügel on Patri-passionism pp. 152-163. Some Franciscans complain that St. Bonaventure "unlike Francis' histori-cal-view of the journey" has "adopted the radically aristorical world-view of progress, of the soul's progress in ascending to God." Sergius Wroblewski, O.F.M., *Bonaventurian Theology of Prayer*, Franciscan Publishers, Pulaski, Wisconsin, 1967, p. 61. Professor Ewert H. Cousins has ventured various compatible claims that there are aspects of process philosophy in St. Bonaven-ture. It is only his excellent address at the 1974 meeting of the American Catholic Philosophical Association to press various other claims that St. Bonaventure is more radical a critic of the standard orthodox view that Hartshorne has criticized. Hartshorne has devoted much attention to St. Thomas Aquinas because he finds here points with which to disagree. I wonder if he would not find more in St. Bonaventure with which he could agree. See the Summary "God as Dynamic in Bona-ventura and Contemporary Thought," *Thomas and Bonaventure: A Septicentinary Commemo-ration*, ACPA, p. 1. This is one of a most significant series of essays. Two of the others are "Truth in St. Bonaventure," *Proceedings of the American Catholic Philosophical As-sociation*, Vol. XLIII, 1969, pp. 204-210 and "The Coincidentia Oppositorum in the Theology of Bonaventure," *The Cord*, Vol. XX, 1970, pp. 260-269, 307-314.

[15]Etienne Gilson, *op.cit.*, p. 365.

[16]*Ibid.*, p. 67.

[17]*Ibid.*

[18]Paul G. Kuntz, "Hierarchy: From Lovejoy's Great Chain of Being to Feibleman's Great Tree of Being," *Studium Generale*, Vol. 24, 1971, pp. 678-687.

[19]Efrem Bettoni, O.F.M., *Saint Bonaventure*, transl. by Angelus Gambatere, O.F.M., Uni-versity of Notre Dame Press, 1964, p. 110 (underscoring mine) cf. Matthew M. Benedictis, *The Social Thought of St. Bonaventura*, Catholic University of America, Washington, D.C., 1946, p. 44: in the "hierarchically constituted universe God is the central point; in the sphere closest to Him is the purely spiritual creation; in the sphere furthest from Him is the purely material ...; and in the intermediate sphere exists the union of the corporeal and spiritual in the creature man." On distance from God as the principle of hierarchy, there is an acute exposi-tion of the continuity of image-vestige-ombre, the near and distinct, the far and distinct, the far and confused.

E. Gilson, *op.cit.*, p. 204. Several recent articles on St. Bonaventure have attempted to take into account the human pilgrimage expressed in terms of cosmic hierarchy. One is Anthony Nemetz, *"The Itinerarium Mentis in Deum.* The Human Condition," *St. Bonaventura*, 1274-1974, II, *Studia de Vita, Mente, Fontibus et Operibus Sancti Bonaventurae*, Col-legio S. Bonaventura, Grottaferrata, Roma, 1974, pp. 345-359. Another essay is Esther Woo, "Theo-phantic Cosmic Order in Saint Bonaventure," *Franciscan Studies*, Vol. 32, Annual X, 1972, pp. 306-330. Although the author recognizes the priority of the "order to an end" over "the order of parts in the universe," the latter occupies her attention almost to the exclusion of the "order of return," pp. 327-329.

[20]*Studia et Documenta Franciscana*, Cura Fratrum Minorum in Austria, Belgio, Ger-mania, Neerlandia Edita, III, E. J. Brill, Leiden, 1964.

[21]Sister Emma Theresa Healy, *St. Bonaventure's "De Reductione Artium ad Theolo-giam,"* a Commentary with an Introduction and Translation, The Franciscan Institute, St. Bonaven-ture University, Saint Bonaventure, N.Y., 1955, p. 158.

[22]Guardini, *op.cit.*, p. 107.

[23]Charles H. Foster, *The Rungless Ladder: Harriet Beecher Stowe and New England Puritanism*, Duke University Press, Durham, N.C., 1954.

[24]Guardini, *op.cit.*, p. 114.

[25]*Ibid.*, p. 117.

[26]*Ibid.*, p. 116.

[27]*Ibid.*, p. 119, p. 153.

[28]*Ibid.*, p. 166.

[29]*Ibid.*, p. 147, references to I Sent d. 25, a.2q, 2f. 1 (1444a) and I Sent. d. 37 p.1, a. 3 q 1, i.c. (647a).

[30]Guardini, *op.cit.*, pp. 155-156.

[31]*Ibid.*, p. 158-159.

[32]See above footnote 14.

[33]Robert P. Prentice, O.F.M., *The Psychology of Love According to St. Bonaventure*, The Franciscan Institute, St. Bonaventure, N.Y., 1951, pp. 71-76.

[34]*Ibid.*, pp. 88-89.

[35]*Ibid.*, p. 89.

[36]*Ibid.*, p. 89.

[37]*Ibid.*, p. 90.

[38]*Ibid.*, pp. 16-20.

[39]*Ibid.*, p. 78.

[40]*Ibid.*, p. 78,ft.

[41]*Ibid.*, p. 104, fran Sent. 3, d.27, a.2, q.3; III, 608a.

[42]*Ibid.*, Sent. 2, d.29, a.3, q.2; II, 708a.

[43]*Ibid.*, p. 91, Sent. I, d.17, p.1, a.1, q.2; I, 297b.

[44]*Ibid.*, p. 105.

[45]*Ibid.*, p. 105 ft.

[46]*Ibid.*, pp. 105-106.

[47]*Ibid.*, p. 20-23 on synderesis as "pondus spirituale" that draws us to a center.

100

[48] Romano Guardini, *op.cit.*, pp. 93-98.

[49] John Herman Randall, Jr., *Hellenistic Ways of Deliverance and the Making of the Christian Synthesis*, Columbia University Press, N.Y., 1970, p.132. Plotinus' rationalism allows in his "metaphysical ultimates ... no Christian tradition of personality .... They indicate archai, not wills; truth, not thinking." (p. 126ft).

[50] *Ibid.*, p. 133.

[51] *Ibid.*, p. 135.

PAUL G. KUNTZ

FROM THE HIGHEST VIRTUE TO THE LOWEST VICE:
WHAT ARE THE PRINCIPLES OF HIERARCHY
ACCORDING TO MODERN INTERPRETATIONS OF
DANTE'S *DIVINE COMEDY*?

Dante's journey is a descent through ten levels of Inferno, and then an
ascent up the seven-storeyed mountain of Purgatorio into the ten spheres of
Paradiso. How is it that during a period of progressive demythologizing of the
"three-decker" universe the powerful *Divine Comedy* has gained loving readers
and zealous interpreters?[1] I believe what we discover in the poem is the supreme expression of faith in order. Dante expresses the order of the cosmos
coupled with the struggle to find order in the tangled confusion of history.
When this is coupled through the most thorough integration of the Hellenic and
Hebraic wisdom about virtues and vices and told as a story of salvation in a
hundred cantos so beautifully concatenated, the three realms parallel, and
climaxing in a final vision, we find it irresistible. To a lover of order the
favorite lines from Paradiso I are

> E cominciò: "le cose tutte quante
> Hann' ordine tra loro; e questo è forma
> Che l'universo a Dio fa simigliante.
> (Par. I, 103-105)[2]
> And then began: 'All things that he have order
> Among themselves; 'tis this that is the form
> Which makes the universe like unto God.[3]

This is a mother's maxim to a raving child. Of course she is claiming the parent's authority of size, age, and experience, and it is altogether to be expected that the kind of order she insists upon is hierarchy.

> Nell' ordine ch'io dico sono accline
> Tutte nature, per diverse sorti
> Più al principio loro, e men, vicine ....
> (Par. I, 109-111)
> Under this order things of every kind
> Do all incline, each following its lot,
> Nearer or less near to their Principle
> (Bergin, p. 4)

Dante finds a principle in the "gran mar dell' essere," (1. 113) the "great
sea of being" and he places his ethics as well as his cosmology within a metaphysical context.

Since the structure of thought is allegorical, and Dante's polysemous theory of meaning requires four-fold signification, when we read Dante with his interpreters, we would expect many meanings of hierarchical order. Without attempt to connect them closely to the four standard kinds of meaning of medieval hermeneutics, current thought seems to reduce hierarchical principles to seven: light; love and beauty; the divine ladder; jurisdiction of authority; the excessive, violent, the malicious; the degrees of fulfilment; the degrees of causal efficacy and eminence. But it would not be difficult, surveying the interpretations, to produce a different list.

My thesis, in bare outline, is this: No one doubts that Dante used a cosmological geography that is hierarchical: beneath earth's surface there is a pit of Inferno and there rises a mount of Purgatorio, and beyond the spheres is Paradiso. The human hierarchical meaning is that there are levels of vice, the deeper the worse, and rising on levels of purgation through beatitude is replacing vice with virtue, and the journey through temperance, courage, wisdom and justice is fulfilled in faith, hope and charity. There is then a moral hierarchy.

Every interpreter, whether literary critic or historian of philosophy, supplies some principle by which to interpret the cosmological and aretaic hierarchies, and the range includes Platonic and Aristotelian principles of degrees of form and being and chains of movers from the Prime Mover, and these principles related to Christian theologies of light and divine love. More historical are views of church and state organized by degrees of dignity and power. There is also the ethical theory of a moral gradation of the virtues and vices by excess, defect and perversion (e.g., of love).

The hermeneutical problem presented by so many principles may be the problem of reducing the number by eliminating the false ones. But proponents of each new variation do not offer to refute the alternatives. The law of contradiction does not seem to apply; that is if principle 1 (of hierarchy in the *Divine Comedy*) is true, principle 2 is not therefore necessarily false. Therefore, an adequate theory is not to be secured by elimination, but by appropriate combination. Could it be .that each being some aspect of the whole, all need to be interwoven? This would mean that hierarchy in Dante is an analogous principle which may require, as *hierarchia* in Thomas Aquinas, at least nine various definitions. In modern (Wittgensteinian) language, there is a family resemblance between the various meanings.

Dante's principle of polysemous meaning applies not merely to each separate symbol, but to the entire structure of the vision. "Hierarchy" then, as various particular symbols such as "gradus," "arbor," "scala," is a root metaphor that can be expressed in such a symbol of all life as journey, descent and ascent, that includes all the categories. All are analogous in meaning, neither simply univocal nor simply ambiguous.

Wouldn't it be more orderly, and hence truer to Dante's principle, if we could construe the many hierarchies as all one? In one sense of "order," finding unity of the many, this would indeed be more satisfactory.

Let us therefore take the best and strongest thesis; that there is one fundamental hierarchy, that of light. Joseph A. Mazzeo puts it: "the hierarchies of being, truth, beauty, perfection, indeed of all value, are reduced to a hierarchy of light, ascending to the very primal light itself, spiritual, uncreated, divine, the vision of which is the vision of all. The doctrines we have considered are the bare bones of the most important part of Dante's universe."[4] In the philosophical poetry of *Paradiso*, there is "a systematically ordered world of pure thought in terms of images." It is light that makes continuous the two orders of the sensible and the intelligible.

The case for the hierarchy of light as the one and basic hierarchy is strong. Does not the *Divine Comedy* begin in darkness, "where the sun is silent," and end in the final vision of light? Are there not all the degrees in between total absence of light and total presence? God is light, and the source of all light, and all others are creatures which reflect His radiance. The graded intensity of "a ladder of light" leads us back to one source in all the many ways (p. 191). This light is both intellectual, material, and moral—as Plato joined analogically the Good and the sun. This light, St. Augustine added from scripture, is God (pp. 192-3). It is the light that lightened every man, and so within us is the principle of intelligibility (p. 194). If we follow the principle we can "see the whole universe *sub specie lucis*" (p. 195).

The strongest philosophic case is developed by Mazzeo from Albertus Magnus, Grosseteste, and St. Bonaventure. Light is the principle of being: "causa enim prima lumen purum est, super quod non est aliud lumen, propter quod in ipsa idem est esse et quod est."[6] There is continuity of radiation: "ordinem in gradibus entium non facit nisi casus et occubitus a lumine primi entis."[7] "Light is also the measure of nobility in that the divine being is communicated to the lower beings in the form of light so that the more luminous a thing

appears the nobler it is. Indeed, *nobilis* is virtually a transcendental predicate corresponding to *lux*. Light thus not only constitutes a hierarchy of being and causality but a hierarchy of value, of good, 'nobility' and ... of
beauty. From this notion the author of *De intelligentiis* draws the conclusion
that light is the principle of life."[8]

Was Dante one of the metaphysicians of light? Did he reduce "all the positive principles of the universe to light" and use light itself as "the measure (mensura) of the place [all things] occupy in the "hierarchy of gradations?"[9] Is "the whole of reality" really "light in various disguises?"[10] Does
Dante emphasize the Father as source of light ('luminis fontale principium')
and the Son Jesus Christ the chief ray ('per ipsum principalem radium')?[11]

There are passages in the "Convivio" and "The Letter to Can Grande" that
are very similar, but the chief support of the light theory is *Liber de Causis*, with its emphasis on the chain of causes, of which light given and received, is one example.[12] There must be other causes, material and final, to
account for particular agents, such as "the compassionate lady, the perfect
individual of the human species."[13] How does light account for the "divine
virtue" of a particular person, even if her virtue is received as an angel's
from God? Where is an act of will? Does not the effusion of light make the
whole process so much an automatic process that both the Creator and the
creature lose their freedom to act or not to act? Dante and Beatrice are more
than rays of light. And why should we think of the damned in hell as being explained by no more than the degrees of absence of light? Sinners have turned
their backs to the light.

These doubts may have occurred to Mazzeo because he is also the author of
"Dante, the Poet of Love: Dante and the Phaedrus Tradition of Poetic Inspiration."[14] The findings are neatly summarized in "Plato's Eros and Dante's
Amore."[15] The points in common are: 1. "A ladder of love and beauty leads to
an absolute reality." 2. "Love is a dialectical progress through a hierarchy
of various good and beautiful objects, a striving which cannot be satisfied
except in the eternal possession of the Good and Beautiful." The erotic ascent, Dante stresses, begins a process of knowing. 3. "Love is also some kind
of supernatural possession, an inspiration ... which leads to intuitions of
truth ...." Dante adds to Plato that after this moral life man can have direct
knowledge of what he now can only think. 4. "Man is endowed with a sense which
enables him to grasp this beauty at its corporeal level and follow its ascent

up to the highest. This sense is sight and its organ is the eye." Dante adds
to Plato that man "loves because he is not in his proper place. His home is in
heaven. ... God ... implanted within [man's unique soul] a natural desire to
return to Him who created it."[15]. "A beloved person is an individual who initiates *eros* and 'reminds' the lover of that perfect beauty once seen and now
forgotten." Dante adds to Plato that "the beloved is not left behind on the
bottom rung of the ladder, or at the first stage of the process." The love is
of "a particular beloved, a concretely conceived individual ...." this is more
than "the abstract recognition ... that the human body is beautiful."[16]

This *scala amoris* is more satisfactory than the *scala lucis*. The hierarchy of light has more difficulty in accounting for virtue or vice. The scale
of love, which in Dante's case included the courtly love, can account for virtuous love and its opposite. "No matter how fine or understandable, the love
relationship which is final, which becomes an end in itself and is not transcended, can only become meaningless and lead to damnation. We must not forget
that Paolo and Francesca were reading about Lancelot on that fateful day."[17]

The *scala lucis* is without individuality or the sensuality of the body,
though light is grasped by the eyes. The *scala amoris* is "intensely personal."
Dante, like Plato, is a great lover, and love of a particular, like Beatrice,
"initiates the 'journey of the mind to God'" and guides him through Purgatorio
and Paradiso.[18]

When Mazzeo began persuading us that all the hierarchies reduce to light
he began by telling us that the journey is from utter darkness to blinding
light. He could end his persuasion that all the hierarchies reduce to love by
citing the concluding line

> L'Amor che move il sole e l'altre stelle
> (Par. XXXIII, 145)
> "... the Love that moves the sun and all the stars."
> (Bergin, p. 108)[19]

Can the hierarchies of the *Divine Comedy* be reduced to either light or
love? These are the two likeliest ways, in addition to the causal chain, to
find hierarchical order in the great "sea of being." The criticism of all such
conceptions of the cosmic order is that they are reflections of the human ordering of virtues and vices, and that the fundamental basis in Dante is concern for the human good. It is notable that Santayana, because of his naturalistic materialism, defends his preference for Lucretius, *De Rerum Natura* as

close to the truth, yet remains in substantial agreement with Dante on the
moral order.[20]

Hierarchy is best found in the ordering by degree of the virtues and
vices. These have been the subject of exhaustive study by two old classics
hardly matched in this century.[21] The studies of Witte, Wicksteed and Moore
are rich and full.

Dante attempted to harmonize two principles of love. One is eros of the
creature, moving up toward the satisfaction of desire. This is the desire that
is subject to the mean. On either side of the mean, the neighbors, excess or
defect, are vices. The other is agape of the Creator, moving down to rescue
the fallen, and by sacrifice to secure salvation. Here the prudent calculation
of a mean would be a vice, for there is neither limit nor excess. The classical pagan and the specifically Christian seem to merge through Beatrice, who
guides Dante through the purifying fire of Purgatory to the Blessed Virgin
Mary. At this stage the passionate love is transmuted into an intellectual
love of the Form of the Good. The best solution is not to attempt any strictly
linear arrangement that will reconcile the difference between the levels of
Inferno and the levels of *Purgatorio*. The principle of *Inferno* is that the un-
repentant sinner has chosen his mortal sin (or besetting vice) and deserves
the natural punishment as strict justice. The principle of *Purgatorio* is that
souls which repent may expect mercy, and there are provided ways to wash away
the guilt of vice (or sinful acts). The system of justice drawn from Aristotle
and Cicero, when fully detailed, does rank Incontinence as the least heinous,
then Violence or Brutishness, and lowest, Fraud or Malice, and the final sub-
division of twenty-four vices ranks treachery against benefactors as the lowest.[22] The important point is that some vices are more excusable, as lust,
gluttony, avarice and anger, and are less damaging to social order than the
violent and perverse. The worst are those that are calculated, because the responsibility is more deliberately assumed.

The seven deadly sins are familiar teachings of the church, and from a
Christian perspective, they are in increasing difficulty to purge: sloth, anger, envy, pride. The agreement of the pagan and Christian ranking is only
that sins of excess--lust, gluttony and avarice--are on a lower level of *Puga-
torio* as they were on the higher levels of *Inferno*. Can we understand why
sloth (acedia) should be the middle sin in the Christian seven? If the principle of virtue is love that flows from the Creator, then not to care, not to be

zealous to respond to God's love is to cut oneself off from charity. The Christian analysis of sin stresses the motive as well as the act, and therefore anger against one's neighbor, envy of one's neighbor, pride in oneself, are the denial of one's humble status beneath God and as a member of the community.[23]

Because of the failure to reconcile the ranking of sins in *Inferno* and vices in *Purgatorio*, some scholars have abandoned the effort. Much of the specification of sins comes from St. Paul who has no final definitive listing.[24]

A very interesting way to preserve the judgement of "higher" and "lower" without formalization is to follow the allegory of pilgrimage. John Freccero's "Dante's Firm Foot and the Journey Without a Guide." This is in the tradition of the *Confessions* of St. Augustine as a connected literary masterpiece and a rich study of the vices dragging him down to hell and the virtues lifting him up toward God.[25]

Had Dante chosen a non-metaphorical symbol of hierarchy, he could have turned to St. Thomas' succinct definition: "Hierarchia est ordo, id est relatio inter diversos gradus; non autem ut dicit unum gradum." This is so abstract that when specified, Thomas has nine different concrete hierarchies. The definition states wherein all share in an essential order.[26] Dante chose the less abstract and therefore as a poet employed the more concrete and metaphorical.

We are reading a poem, and we need to attend to the concrete images such as the Tree of the Knowledge of Good and Evil, whose fruit Adam tasted, and found no true wisdom. The true fruit is of the tree Christ. Dante speaks as did St. Bernard: "He alone is verily the Tree of Life to them that lay hold on him." The bride says, as Beatrice (Par. XXI), "I sat down under the shadow of him for whom my soul longed, and his fruit is sweet to my taste."[27]

In *The Ladder of Vision* Irma Brandeis states the *itinerarium* finally as the soul's ascent. Dante's hierarchy must also be stated as purgation, illumination and union.

> The pilgrim's voyage in the *Paradiso* is in its simplest
> sense an effortless rising from sphere to sphere of a
> concentric, tensphered universe, with the earth at centre
> and the unmoving Empyrean outmost. It is at the same time
> the travelling of an immaterial path of intellectual
> light, educating him in the relation of human life to
> eternal being, and of human judgement to absolute truth;

leading him finally to a momentary glimpse of the ordering and limiting principle of all existence, the totally
immaterial Goal and Source of all thought and all matter. [28]

Why do we still read Dante's vision? We are not so dogmatic any more
about the "false" science of the pre-Copernican astronomy, the pre-Galilean
theory of motion, and all the other aspects of cosmology. We are not only
children of the revolution in science, but also of thinking about nature.
Dante's world was integral, while ours is fragmented. He could bring man into
close accord with his cosmos. It sets us a challenge; is this impossible for
us? Whether the ranking of virtues and vices is letter-perfect is not so much
the question as is the power of the poem to make us see the nature and consequences of vice (or sin) such as Ugolino's heartlessness. A student of mine
was inspired by Dante to write a canto of her own. She vividly portrays the
rapist and his just deserts. Perhaps the greatest appeal of the life of virtue
is that it is a passionate struggle. There are not merely lists of seven virtues on the asset side to correspond to seven vices (or sins) on the liabili-
ty side. Dante's God is not the moral accountant of the Cosmos. And the hierarchy of virtues? In the last account they are the stages toward the beatific
vision. [29]

NOTES

[1] Rudolf Bultmann, *Entmythologisierung: Eine Auseinandersetzung zwischen Julius Schniewind, Rudolf Bultmann und Karl Barth* (Stuttgart, Evangelisches Verlagswerk, 1949).

[2] Dante Alighieri, *La Divina Commedia*, Ed. C. H. Grandgent (Boston, D. C. Heath, 1913), *Paradiso*, p. 15.

[3] Dante Alighieri, *The Divine Comedy*, Tr. Thomas G. Bergin (Arlington Heights, Ill.: AHM, 1948, 1953, 1954), *Paradise*, p. 4.

[4] Joseph A. Mazzeo, *Medieval Cultural Tradition in Dante's Comedy* (Ithaca, New York: Cornell University Press, 1960), excerpts reprinted in N. F. Cantor and P. L. Klein, *Dante and Machiavelli; Renaissance Thought* (Waltham, Mass.: Blaisdell Publishing Co., 1969), p. 195.

[5] Joseph A. Mazzeo, "Light Metaphysics, Dante's 'Convivio' and the Letter to Can Grande Della Scala," *Traditio*, Vol. XIV, 1958, pp. 191-229.

[6] *Ibid.*, from Albertus Magnus, *De causis et processu universitatis, Opera Omnia*, Ed. Borgnet, Vol. 10, 2.1.25, p. 475b.

[7] *Ibid.*, 1.4.5 (p. 419a). On this theory of analogy of degrees of being see Paul G. Kuntz, "The Analogy of Degrees of Being: A Critique of Cajetan's Analogy of Names," *The New Scholasticism*, Vol. LVI, No. 1, Winter 1982, pp. 51-79, and "De Analogia Graduum Entis: On Cardinal Cajetan's Neglect of Thomistic Hierarchy" in *Acta Conventus Neo-Latini Bononiensis, Proceedings of the Fourth International Congress of Neo-Latin Studies*, Ed. R. J. Schoeck, (Binghamton, New York: Medieval Texts and Studies, 1985), pp. 72-79.

[8] Mazzeo, "Light Metaphysics," *op. cit.*, p. 203.

[9] *Ibid.*, p. 205.

[10] *Ibid.*, p. 206.

[11] *Ibid.*, pp. 208-9, from Bartholomew of Balogna.

[12] *Ibid.*, p. 224, Ep. 10-21.

[13] *Ibid.*, p. 221.

[14] Joseph A. Mazzeo, "Dante, the Poet of Love: Dante and the Phaedrus Tradition of Poetic Inspiration," *Proceedings of the American Philosophical Society*, 99.3 [1955], pp. 133-45.

[15] Joseph A. Mazzeo, "Plato's Eros and Dante's Amore," *Traditio*, Vol. XII (1956), pp. 315-37.

[16] *Ibid.*, pp. 333-35, 330.

[17] *Ibid.*, p. 335.

[18] *Ibid.*, p. 337.

[19]I have written but not published "Entropy, Evil, and God: A Meditation on 'L'Amor che move il sole e l'altre stelle.'"

[20]George Santayana, *Three Philosophical Poets* (Cambridge, Mass.: Harvard University Press, 1910), p. 108.

[21]Karl Witte, "The Ethical Systems of the Inferno and the Purgatorio," in *Essays on Dante*, Tr. and Ed. C. Mabel Lawrence and Philip H. Wicksteed (London: Duckworth, 1898) with Appendix V, pp. 117-52, 434-8.

Edward Moore, "Classification of Sins in the *Inferno* and *Purgatorio*," *Studies in Dante*, Second Series (Oxford: Clarendon Press, 1899), pp. 152-208.

[22]See the summary table from Wicksteed in *The Divine Comedy* (New York: Modern Library, 1932, 1950), pp. 3-5.

Edward Moore, *op. cit.*, shows eleven variant lists of seven deadly sins, from Cassian (d. 448) through St. Gregory (d. 604) down to Dante's time.

[23]A helpful summary is found in *Ibid.*, pp. 189-91.

[24]Karl Vossler, *Mediaeval Culture: An Introduction to Dante and His Times*, Tr. W. C. Lawton (New York: Harcourt Brace, 1929), pp. 224-7. "Paul refrains from constructing a strict system of virtues and sins on an intellectual plan. Political and civic virtues interest him but little for even where he builds up ethical grades, he is chiefly interested in the higher steps that are close to God, rather than in the lower ones that have to do with human relations" (p. 226). Vossler prefers the more objective Platonic thinking about virtues of social existence. This he finds in Dante's *Divine Comedy* (p. 227).

[25]John Freccero, "Dante's Firm Foot and the Journey Without a Guide," *The Harvard Theological Review*, Vol. LII, No. 4, October 1959, p. 245-81.

Paul G. Kuntz, "Augustine: From Homo Erro to Homo Viator," and also "Man the Wayfarer," in *Itinerarium: The Idea of Journey*, Ed. Leonard J. Bowman (Salzburg: Institut für Anglistik und Amerikanistik, 1983), pp. 34-53, 216-34.

Paul G. Kuntz, "The I-Thou Relation and Aretaic Divine Command Ethics: Augustine's Study of the Virtues and Vices in the Confessions," to appear in *Augustinian Studies*.

[26]Paul G. Kuntz, "A Formal Preface and an Informal Conclusion to the Great Chain of Being," *The Modern Schoolman*, Vol. LX, No. 4, May 1983, pp. 273-282.

[27]Sheila Ralphs, *Dante's Journey to the Centre: Some Patterns of His Allegories* (New York: Barnes and Noble, 1973), p. 36.

[28]Irma Brandeis, *The Ladder of Vision: A Study of Dante's Comedy* (Garden City, New York: Doubleday, 1962), p. 213.

[29]The most convincing part of Vossler's *Mediaeval Culture*, loc. cit., is the section "The Mystical Doctrine of the Ladder of the Soul," Vol. I, pp. 309-14.

PAUL G. KUNTZ

THE HIERARCHICAL VISION OF ST. ROBERTO BELLARMINO[1]

INTRODUCTION

Of all his many writings, Bellarmino's *De Ascensione Mentis in Deum* was
the most frequently reprinted in Latin in his own age. Within a year of its
publication, 1615, it had been translated into English, and the number of
translations into each language during the centuries adds testimony to its
widespread appeal. Then and now it is the most easily available of St. Roberto's writings.[2] Yet this text, however frequently disseminated, has not been
used in forming a general estimation of Bellarmino's place as a thinker. It is
rarely recognized as an attempt in the Seventeenth Century to redo the hierarchical vision of the middle ages. Bellarmino shared with St. Bonaventure that
devotion to St. Francis of Assisi[3] expressed in St. Bonaventure's *Itinerarium
Mentis in Deum*, and respect for this classic of 1259 forbade using the same
title in 1615. This specific indebtedness of a Renaissance text to a Medieval
text is clearly an invitation to study the continuity behind the periodiza-
tions and to clarify the exact contrasts between the middle thirteenth century
conception of hierarchy and that of the early seventeenth century.[4]

Bellarmino has been neglected because he was an interpreter of St. Thomas
Aquinas in an age of Humanism, and therefore he has been regarded as a reac-
tionary and an anachronism. He was also a theologian rather than an Erasmian
proponent of simple Christian virtue. Since he was involved in negotiations
with Galileo, those who rightly see the scientific line of progress through
Copernicus, Kepler, and Galileo have regarded him as the enemy of the mathematical conception of space and the mechanical conception of matter in motion.
Since Bellarmino was also by circumstances of the time involved in controversy
with Protestants, and did indeed class Erasmus with the heretics in *Disputa-
tiones de controversiis Christianae fidei*, he seems a dark shadow cast by the
past on the bright emerging modern age. This view of Bellarmino, I shall argue, is as inadequate as it is common.

Three interpreters of Bellarmino in our age are of great help in getting
into this hierarchical vision. These are the Jesuit biographer James Brodrick,
who in *The Life and Work of Blessed Robert Francis Cardinal Bellarmine S. J.
1542-1621* calls attention to his deep response to the beauty of nature. What
moved Bellarmino was the order of the visible world: "Every verse of the

Psalms that declares the wonder of the visible world is drawn out and used as an incentive to the praise, the reverence, and the service of its Maker." (*Ibid.*, Vol. II, p. 381) The second is John Riedl in "Bellarmine and the Dignity of Man."[5] Although man shares with animals bodily appetites, he shares with angels "a certain propensity for a spiritual and intelligible good." This gift of justice is "a golden bond, [making] the inferior part easily subject to the superior and the superior part to God." (*Ibid.*, p. 212) Only the spirit could rebel, not the flesh, and in spite of the fall, with the struggle of the inferior against the superior, there is a natural light leading man to know God and even sinners respond to divine direction. (*Ibid.*, p. 222) The third interpreter is A. O. Lovejoy, who in *The Great Chain of Being* cites the *De Ascensione* as a summary of the medieval hierarchical vision, yet without any mention of the *Itinerarium*.[6]

The Bellarmino who now emerges is then a lover of the beauty of nature, a defender of human dignity because man freely responds to the good, and one who takes the old metaphysics seriously enough to revise it. At least in the last and most serious expression he is enough of a humanist and cognizant of the virtues of Protestantism to stress both the classical heritage and the Hebrew and Greek Bible. His confidence in an intelligible order of nature is so deep that he expresses no disagreement with the new science.

This essay is an attempt, based on the *De Ascensione Mentis* and the kind of interpretation cited above, to correct the one-sided emphasis on Bellarmino the controversialist. There has been too much consensus among the interpreters in agreement with the first line of the article in Bayle's *Dictionary*: "one of the best controversialist writers of his time."[7] If there is first fixed in one's mind the view that his life was spent fighting Protestant theologians, engaging James I and others in political disputes, and as papal representative in condemning Bruno and Galileo, one gains so very negative an impression that there is no place for any other side of this man's work. Yet in *De Ascensione* we find him irenic rather than polemical, humane rather than ascetic and dogmatic, and with such love of nature and its understanding that he is completely without opposition to the new science. Is it not then better to be ignorant of the traditional and secondary literature, provided that one comes to his text with a concern for the problems to which he believes he has solutions? What are the relations between nature, man and God? The one text it might be best to know is that to which the author of *De Ascensione* refers as its model: Bonaventure's *Itinerarium*.[8]

THE STRUCTURE, CONCLUSIONS AND METHOD OF BELLARMINO'S *DE ASCENSIONE*

Method should be discussed first in a 17th Century work, except for two facts: Bellarmino does not explicitly refer to his method until Gradus Decimus, and Bellarmino's critics have ignored it entirely. There are indeed studies of his method in history and theology, but none of his method in philosophy. It is the structure and conclusions that have been severely censured, and so it may be better to say what these are, for in analyzing them, we must consider method and thus gain perspective on the text. Then we can treat more fully the neglected aspect of method in reappraising the structure and conclusions.

It seems in this, as in other cases of metaphysical musing, expressed as a vision, that metaphor is the key to structure. This is of more than literary interest; it reveals the metaphysical type.[9]

The metaphor that serves as model for the *De Ascensione* is that man's life on earth is a pilgrimage. Just as Bonaventure places us first at the foot of Mount Alverna and guides us to the vision of the crucified Seraph, which he shared with St. Francis, so Bellarmino pictures life also as a journey. I believe it significant that it is man, the man reading the book, who must himself erect the ladder. There is again ascent, but the ascent that prefigures our climb is that of the Jews liberated from Babylon who return to Mt. Sion. The journey is accompanied by song, the "graduals" of the Psalter, as once, according to St. Augustine, sung by the pilgrims mounting the fifteen steps of the Temple at Jerusalem.[10]

There are fifteen steps, from "gradus primus" to "gradus decimus quintus," and it would be natural to think of fifteen rungs or fifteen links in a chain. Father Brodrick thinks this way and quickly finds fault. "Blessed Roberto's fifteen steps are not all as evenly disposed, one above another, as the steps of a good ladder ought to be. He found his metaphor too difficult to maintain after he had mounted a little way .... The scheme goes awry. Each step is in itself a compendium of holy wisdom." (*op. cit.*, p. 383)

Bellarmino had Bonaventure's *Itinerarium* before him and knew that his predecessor using this model had used seven as the number of "speculations" that lead us from the wilderness, the vale of tears, to the mount of vision.

Bonaventure often thought of the six preparing us for the highest, as Bellarmino did not, as the six wings of the seraph.[11] As we read Bonaventure, we can
keep Giotto's painting in mind. The stigmata of St. Francis are tied to the
wounds of the Crucified to suggest that Francis is another Christ. Did St. Roberto have as close an analogue in the visual arts? The obvious response of a
man of the 17th Century to the man of the 13th Century is that more approaches
have opened.

Bonaventure devotes two books to the universe and the sensible world:
Bellarmino needs five (III to VII). Bonaventure gets to man's natural powers
and man reformed by grace in his second pair of chapters. Bellarmino deals
with man from the beginning and returns in his eighth step. The seraphic doctor is throughout meditating upon the blessed spirits above human reason; Bellarmino devotes but one step to the angels. Then Bonaventure devotes his last
three chapters to God's unity and trinity and to man passing into divine
peace. Bellarmino devotes his six final steps to God, but he is far more specific about the attributes: we think of God in terms of the four dimensions of
corporeal things, as St. Paul had referred to breadth, length, height and
depth. Similarly, there is God's power, wisdom, practical wisdom, mercy, justice, all considered under the image of the four dimensions.

What is Bellarmino doing and saying? I believe it is this: man finds himself in a great world, and there are correspondences between this macrocosm to
himself, the microcosm. The significance that he finds in considering the
earth, water, air and fire have the significance attached to them in the
Psalms. Here God is the rock, God is the spring of life, God is the inspiring
wind, God is the cleansing fire. When we consider life's dependence upon the
elements we are led to the glory of the whole, sun, moon and stars, and we
find it altogether appropriate to say "the heavens declare the glory of God."
The world is fitting and beautiful in aspects and altogether. To spirit, human
and angelic, the creation is also intelligible. It is not only orderly and
harmonious, but it has also quantitative dimensions. Why can there be the ascent of the mind into God "per scalas rerum creatarum?" Because the world has
four spatial dimensions. Space is intelligible, and nature read as a message
leads us to think of what its author is saying. "*Deus omnia in sapientia fecit*, ut dicit in Psalmis .... Ex artificio admirabili, quod in singulis cerni-
mus, admiramur sapientiam Conditoris, disposuit enim omnia et singula *in mensura et numero et pondere*, ut dicit Sapiens." (XIII) Everything that is has a

certain weight. It is perhaps this thirteenth step which is the most distinctive of all in the *De Ascensione*. If the method of the 17th Century is that of
measuring rather than of the Aristotelian classifying, as Whitehead put it,
then Bellarmino has a most interesting combination of the new with the old.
Measuring reveals not merely regularity of law but the rightness of size and
number for the purpose.[12]

What is so very important in the medieval heritage is the conviction,
based upon experience but *experience reflected upon or considered*: the cosmos
is unendingly orderly and intelligible and beautiful and beneficent:

> Attribuit Deus homini duos oculos, duas aures, duas man-
> us, duos pedes, nasum unum, os unum, pectus unum, caput
> unum, et res pulcherrima et ornatissima apparuit. Inverte
> ordinem, pone alicui homini unum oculum, duos nasos, unam
> auriculam, duo ora, unam manum, et unum pedem, duo pec-
> tora, et duo capita, nihil foedius, nihil inutilius fieri
> poterit. Denique pondus, id est, aestimationem unicuique
> rei Deus attribuit, quam ejus natura requirebat. Porro
> nomine ponderis, sive pretii, qualitates intelligimus,
> quae bonas res pretiosas reddunt ... numerus partium, qui
> necessarius est ... commensuratio, sive apta proportio
> partium: denique qualitates internae, sive externae, ut
> suavitas coloris in externa superficie corporis, et vir-
> tus interna, quae ad actiones varias utilis, vel neces-
> saria est. (III, 296)

Does Bellarmino's scheme "go awry?" Yes, if the question is how many degrees are there and what is the exact relation between them. But Bellarmino is
not concerned with the exact number of links in the chain or rungs in the ladder. In a work so comprehensive of the many ways in which we think hierarchically this is surprising: unless we take a very different approach. Bellarmino
does not have the familiar Aristotelian analysis of the lifeless (the stone),
the living (vegetable and animal) and finally the intelligent (Man) with each
succeeding step including all below but marked by a differentia. Nor does he
here stress either a Platonic or Christian ladder of love, going from sensual
to intellectual or from egotistical to altruistical.

The exact difference in Bellarmino is that we are always, in each of the
fifteen steps, dealing with man in relation to nature. Interpreters who are
interested in the life of prayer and devotion have been embarrassed by this,
and try to ignore the subtitle "per scalas rerum creatarum." In the *Praefatio*
"Scala vero ascensionis in Deum nulla videtur nobis mortalibus patere posse,
quam per opera Dei ...." Others might have been, as St. Paul, caught up into
paradise, but ascending is by reason, and the reasoning of ascent is knowing

the effects and thereby knowing the cause, or knowing the copies and thereby knowing the original.

If there is but one cause and one original, it matters less how many "considerations" there are, so long as each enquirer can find one. Bellarmino provides fifteen, I believe, not because he is counting steps to salvation or perfection, but so that each reader can find some avenue. He makes no attempt to reduce the search for wisdom and man's ultimate goal to an actuarian's ledger that can be balanced by a kind of religious mathematics.[14]

Bellarmino's "ladder" is something whereby man climbs, and so long as man is in process of rising, rather than falling, he is going in the right direction. Any reader of Bonaventure has seen the world arranged according to the ninefold hierarchy of angels from Pseudo-Dionysius and Bonaventurean scholarship has been concerned with how everything must come out in nine boxes to be orderly.[15] Those who say "the scheme goes awry" may well forget the differences between Gothic and Baroque style. In Baroque the fixed number of levels melts into fluidity. If God is above, he also descends. If man is below, he also rises. Is God always above the angels? God becomes man and humbles himself in Christ. Is man always below the angels? Not only in Christ, but in Mary, man is exalted above the angels. Man is at one point in motion, as a pilgrim, much less than angels, but then when he arrives, he shall be made equal with angels.[16]

Father Brodrick is committed to the same theological conclusions as Bellarmino, but disagrees with the structuring of *De Ascensione*. Professor Lovejoy is hostile to these conclusions, but shows no concern with the context of propositions which he finds contradictory. Indeed, Lovejoy uses the text to summarize his chapter "Conflicts in Medieval Thought."[17] *De Ascensione* is "medieval in its philosophy though not in its date," "perhaps the most celebrated modern elaboration of [the cosmological Chain of Being]." This seems but a step from labeling *De Ascenscione* an anachronism or an intellectual fossil. But worse, "it shows plainly the usual incongruity between the importance given to the principle of plenitude in the doctrine of the attributes of deity and the exclusion of it from the theory of the chief good of man."[18]

Although Lovejoy has stressed plenitude he has ignored the Franciscan tradition completely. To find a thinker dealing with "plenitudo" no one is more appropriate than Bonaventure. Why has he been ignored? The reason is that Franciscan and Bonaventurian thought does not fit the construction of Lovejoy:

Medieval thought is a Manichean hatred of matter (Macrobius' reference to "the dregs of being"), hence the "mere existence of imperfect beings" is to be "spurned and transcended." The world is to be despised, hence inquiry into nature (science) and representation of nature (art) are of no value. Hence man should spurn the world and flee to the ultimate one, and aspire to be a higher being. Hence theoretically, there is no reason why matter should be or why creation was created. It would have been better had there been only God. And man has reason therefore only to despise himself. This is packing Lovejoy's thesis into a nutshell.

Is this really what Bellarmino meant, but failed to say clearly enough until Lovejoy took the opportunity to say it for him?

Respondeo dicendum: Bellarmino starts from delight in the beauty of earth. He shows no contempt for matter when he talks of earth, water, air and fire. There may be a few passages that sound Manichean (see 17), but they are very rare and minor. The world has a rich variety of forms and a plenitudinous creation is appropriate to a plenitudinous Creator. Bellarmino delighted in the artistic representation of nature and uses those passages from the Psalter that deal with the variety of living things, and uses such an authority on nature as Galen describing the hand. With this strong use of Biblical writing he shares a strong sense of the reality of the world and never suggests its unreality. Man is indeed not the highest but he is to know higher beings, without trying to become the highest, God. Lovejoy should have known he didn't understand Bellarmino: he admits Bellarmino isn't the ascetic fleeing the world. (see 17)

Although Bellarmino defers to the beginning of X a discussion of the "modum ascensionis" (X, 283), it is used from the first. It is unusual, I believe, to find an author of the Seventeenth Century giving the lineage of his method: St. Paul, St. Bernard of Clairvaux, St. Bonaventure. It would indeed be a significant difference in Bellarmino to have the tradition interpreted as a method. This would explain why Bellarmino so stresses that *we erect a ladder*.

The "method" is nowhere precisely outlined, but from Gradus Primus it seems to have several moments:

1. Everything found in the world is also in man; whatever is in the great world is found also in the little world ("a sui ipsius consideratione ... invenit quasi compendium mundi totius" (VIII, 242).

2. From the great world we may move by analogy of the world to Its Author and clock or houses which man creates: "Architectus, ipse autor ... quomodo qui horologia componunt, aut domos aedificant" (I, 242).

3. We recognize the degrees of lower and higher, and the higher illuminates the lower nature as the archetype makes the copy clear.

4. What is diverse and seemingly contrary on the lower level is harmonious and one on the higher level.

The method then of correspondence between microcosm and macrocosm, analogy of creature and Creator, understanding lower in terms of the higher, and finding an ultimate unified harmony are the ways of thought Bellarmino uses, and uses assiduously. To criticize Bellarmino requires examining whether he has used his method coherently and whether anything is incongruous with these steps.

CONCLUSION

The wisest introduction to *De Ascensione Mentis* was written by the first English translator in 1616

> ... If *Vertue* and *Truth* appear best apparelled, when they are most naked: then are they heere sett forth in their *Hollydaie attyre*. *Diuine* and *Humane* Philosophy also (like the *Sunne* and *Moone* in one *Hemisphere*) shine here both together, and cast their *beames* upon all that are desirous to receaue *Light*, or *Life* from their heate .... *Voces Artis* (of which there are many in this booke) are *strangers* to our language, and cannot be made *Denizens*, but by prescription.

> > It is the sweetest note that man
> >   can sing.
> > When grace tunes natures Key
> >   to sweetest string.[19]

This contemporary grasped the true greatness of *De Ascensione*: it is to counter such a claim as that of John Donne "tis all in peeces, all Cohaerance gone." St. Roberto had been deeply influenced by all the movements that threatened coherence. He knew the disruption of the inherited hierarchical order of the universe and of society—yet he did not reach the conclusion of Donne, so much better known and so widely advertized in our own age of chaos. What St. Roberto said was far more important and profound.[20]

What contemporary editors ignore, Bellarmino's excellent translator knew was the main and valid point: there is no real conflict between theology and philosophy, between traditional faith and the new science, between tradition and scripture, between sense and reason, for they are all based on grasping the underlying order of all things. The controversies in which he had taken a leading part had dealt with the superficialities that fill the histories—the disagreements between Roman Catholics and Protestants, the differences between Aristotelians and the new mathematical physicists, the differences between Platonists and nominalists—none of these conflicts is beyond resolution.

Bellarmino's resolution lies in finding in the contesting and quarrelling partisans the fundamental underlying commitment of their positions. Bellarmino's statement is both deeply Hebraic and deeply Hellenic because he has found just those general statements of order to which Jew and Greek, Protestant and Catholic, traditionalist and modernist must consent. The fundamental commitment of all is to the cosmos.

> And surely it is such a thing to be marvelled, that the stars, moving so speedily and continually, and some performing their course so slowly, and some so swiftly in their several orbs: yet they always keep such measure and proportion together, that from it ariseth a most sweet and pleasing harmony. Whereof God speaketh in the book of Job, when he saith: *who shall declare the* manner of the heavens, and the harmony of heaven who shall make to sleep? (Job xxxviii 37)[21]
> What kind of harmony (concentus) is this? Non est iste concentus vocum, aut sonorum, qui auribus corporis percipiatur, sed concentus proportionum in moribus syderum, qui cordis aure sentitur. (VII-273)

But this is no mere metaphysical vision, for there are observed and empirical regularities. "Si quidem stellae firmamenti, omnes simul eadem velocitate viginti quatuor horis totum coeli ambitum percurrunt ...." (VII, 273)

Having descended to fact, Bellarmino's mind now rises to his vision of ultimate order: "Et quoniam stellae servata proportione, semper in orbem se convertendo non fatigantur, videntur instar virginum honestarum, et saltandi peritarum, in caelo semper choreas jucundissimas agere" (VII, 273: The English has this sentence: "The stars also keep a just measure always in turning round: and therefore they seem to dance continually in heaven, like honest virgins skillful in that art." (*The Ascent of the Mind*, etc., *op. cit.*, p. 137)

The conclusion is not hatred of the world or flight from it, as Lovejoy claimed. "Then shall it come to pass that neither the beauty of heaven will seem great unto thee, nor the things below heaven (which are small, short, and of no value) will be rejected and condemned." (*Ibid.*, p. 138)

The remarkable feature of this synthetic vision is that it uses all the ways of hierarchical thought, all the respects in which anything could be higher or better or greater than another thing. This aspect alone deserves study, along with the unification of these respects. The symbol of the sun suggests one source; the symbol of the ladder one ascent; the symbol of the fruits of the tree, one purpose.

Bellarmino's hierarchical vision is not the same old medieval theology, as Lovejoy claimed. It is not the dreaming of Pseudo-Dionysus that came to be despised by Calvin. Bellarmino took great care to show its Biblical foundation, without losing its basis in reason and Greek philosophy. Bellarmino found a way of restating tradition so that there is no conflict with mathematical science.

NOTES

[1] The present paper is a sequel to "The Hierarchical Vision of St. Bonaventure," *Atti Bonaventura Congresso*, Roma, (1974) 1977, Vol. II, pp. 233-248, which is one of four other articles on hierarchical order. Others are "Hierarchy: From Lovejoy's Great Chain of Being to Feibleman's Great Tree of Being," *Studium Generale*, Vol. 24, 1971, pp. 678-687, and "A Formal Preface to the *Great Chain of Being*: The Necessity and Universality of Hierarchical Thought," XI. Annual Conference on Medieval Studies, Western Michigan University, Kalamazoo, 3 May, 1976, 14 pp., and "The Metaphysics of Hierarchical Order: the Philosophical Centre of *Small is Beautiful*: A Critical Exposition and Appreciation of E. F. Schumacher's Principles of Order," Emory University, 1976, *Proceedings of the American Catholic Philosophical Association*, 1977, Vol. LI, pp. 36-46.

[2] James Brodrick, S. J., *The Life and Works of Blessed Robert Francis Cardinal Bellarmine S. J.*, 1542-1621, P. J. Kennedy and Sons, N. Y., 1928, is the exceptional book that attempts to estimate the importance to this work.

> It had immediate and amazing success. The first translation, made but a
> few months after the appearance of the original Latin, was into English.
> Within four years it had gone into several editions, and was being read
> in Italian, Spanish, Portugese, and French. Then there followed Bohemian,
> Chinese, German, Russian, Polish, Illyrian and other versions. It has
> been translated into German nine different times, and into French as of-
> ten. Fuligatti asserts that an English Protestant divine had made a wide-
> ly popular adaption of the work for his own country, prior to 1644. (Vol.
> II, 388)

The translations listed must be, although Father Brodrick had not traced the second: T. B. Gent. *A Most Learned and Pious Treatise, full of Divine and Humane Philosophy, framing a Ladder, Whereby our Mindes May ascend to God, by the Steppes of his Creatures*, Douay, 1616; and *Jacob's Ladder Consisting of fifteene Degrees of Ascents to the Knowledge of God by the Consideration of His Creatures and Attributes*, London, 1638. The former was reprinted as *The Ascent of the Mind of God By A Ladder of Things Created*, with an introduction by James Brodrick, S. J., Benziger Brothers, N. Y. (Orchard Books, XVI, Burns, Oates & Co., London) 1928. Father Brodrick also comments on the various Engish translations, paying high compliments to that of 1925 by an Anglican nun and approving the Anglican preface, by Dr. P. N. Waggett. Bellarmine "does not give them crutches they might dispense with, but a secret of escape from all worldliness and all despondency. He does not naturalize our prayer. He spiriutalizes our daily walk." (*The Mind's Ascent into God By a Ladder of Created Things Done into English* ... by Monialis, A. R. Mowbray & Co., London, 1925). A facsimile edition of the 1616 translation has been published by the English Recusant Literary Society and published by Scolar Press Ltd., 39 Great Russell St. The shortened title in the catalogues is "Treatise Framing a Ladder Whereby Our Mindes May Ascend to God." This Society also is responsible for *Eglurhad Helaeth-lawn*, Tr. from Italian, 1618; *Of the Seven Wordes Spoken by Christ Upon the Crosse* WITH *How True Christiane Libertie Consisteth in the True Service of God; and Short Catechisme.*

Father Brodrick's interest is in the spirituality of the book, that of the "active contemplative" St. Ignatius (*Ibid.*, p. 389). This is also apparently the Italian career of the book, for *De Ascensione* is discussed among "Gli Scritti Ascetici." Angelo Portaluppi, *San Roberto Bellarmino*, Casoni, Milano, 1945, mentions thirty editions, p. 347f. One went into second edition in 1943; *Elevazione della mente a Dio*, traduzione di mons. L. de Marchi, 2ed, Istituto missionaris, Pia societa s. Paolo, Roma, 1943.

[3]The best interpretation of Bellarmino's continuation of the Franciscan movement is from Father Brodrick's "Introduction."

> No saint in the Calendar gave of his time and his resources with more lavish generosity in the relief of human distress. He literarally beggared himself for the sake of the needy. For them he pawned nearly every article of furniture in his house, his episcopal ring, the very matress of his bed. One of his few purple robes went to make a frock for a poor lady .... After his death, the Pope had to pay for his coffin as there was nothing in his account at the bank. No wonder the Roman populace christened him 'the Father of the poor,' and 'the new Poverello.' (p. x)

[4]The passage that best conveys Bellarmino's reaffirming the central emphasis of Bonaventure on *fontalis plenitudo* is at the end of the fourth step, ex consideratione aquarum ac praecipue fontium "Whatever good thou seest in creatures, know that it flows from God, the fountainhead of all good things, and so with St. Francis learn to taste the primal source of goodness in each created object, as in a little stream that has it for its origin." (*Ibid.*, p. 388 ft.) The Latin reads: "Et quicquid boni in creaturis videris, scito illud a Deo fonte totius bonitatis defluere, ut sic cum B. Francisco discas fontalem bonitatem in singulis creaturis, tamquam in rivulis degustare. De qua lege S. Bonaventuram in vita S. Francesci." (IV, 260)

Earlier in "Gradus Secundus" writes Bellarmino, "Erige nunc, anima mea, oculos mentis ad Deum in quo sunt rationes omnium rerum, et unde tamquam ex fonte infinitae ubertatis manavit illa pene infinita varietas ...." II, 248

[5]John O. Riedl, "Bellarmino and the Dignity of Man" in *Jesuit Thinkers of the Renaissance*, Milwaukee, 1939, pp. 193-226, also "A Bellarmine Bibliography," pp. 242-254. This essay is valuable, apart from its extraordinarily rich documentation, in setting the problem of how human nature was to be estimated, whether as "nothing" or as of high estate, and in what respects low or high. (pp. 193-4) This question is of more breadth than of "revealed theology," even though not making the distinction between theology and philosophy common to those who follow St. Thomas. (p. 204) The difficulty of the question for Platonists, as for Christians, is whether to estimate man in his original or fallen state. Riedl suggests that Adam's habitus can be conceived in Bellarmino as "the subjection of the inferior to the superior." (p. 211) Then the fall is a loss of hierarchical order and salvation is a restoration of order. Then the punishment of sin is not "like the punishment imposed by a judge, St. Thomas says, but rather consequences ... in the same way as the flooding of rivers or of a sea results in damage to the fields in which the force of the waters is great ...."(p. 217)

[6]Arthur O. Lovejoy, *The Great Chain of Being: A Study of the History of an Idea*, Harvard University Press, Cambridge, Mass., 1936 (Eleventh Printing, 1973). The pagination of the chapters, though not of Notes and Index, is identical with Harper Torchbook Edition, N. Y., 1960.

[7]Pierre Bayle, *A General Dictionary: Historical and Critical*, London, 1738, Vol. III, p. 163. Other than controversies we learn of his activities only what Hume remembered from Bayle about Bellarmine, that he would not brush away the insects from his person. The explanation given in the footnote, "that it was not reasonable to disturb those insects, since they know no other paradise, than the liberty of flying and resting, where they pleased." p. 174. Perhaps this extraordinary patience makes more sense in a Franciscan context in which all creatures have dignity and each is to pursue its own purposes rather than the common doctrine that all subhuman creatures exist only for human pleasure. Bellarmine's patience may be more a modern ecological orientation than a continuation of medieval self-torture.

The dominant Catholic interpretation is not much different from Bayle. Xavier-Marie Le Bachelet S. J., "Bellarmin," *Dictionnarie de théologie Catholique*, Vol. II, pp. 560-600 devotes so much time to the controversies that only the praise of St. François de Sales takes the place of analysis of *De Ascensione*. But Bellarmino is "marteau des hérétiques." Not only is he defender of the faith, but a builder of a fortress, an arsenal full of weapons. p. 586A.

Bellarmino as a Papal controversialist was so disliked in England that the English caricatured him in "Grey-beard" jugs. Dr. Waggett is one of the few to point out that the inner life of the man, "liberated in solitude and prayer," was free from the combative spirit which made his work so hated by his enemies. P. N. Waggett, "Preface" to *The Mind's Ascent to God, op. cit.*, p. iii, "All harsher elements must be set down, as was said of the Cardinal by a Pope ... to the troubles of the time and not to the character of the debater." *Ibid.*, p. IV. When one gets into the 17th Century literature about Bellarmino there is frequently found "responsio recusa," "controversia," "disputatio," "defensus," "confutatio," etc.

[8]Seraphici Doctoris Sancti Bonaventurae *Itinerarium Mentis in Deum, Opera Omnia,* Tomus V, Ad Claras Aquas (Quaracchi), Ex Typographia Collegii S. Bonaventurae, MDCCCXCI, pp. 295-316. The most readily available translation is George Boas, Tr., Saint Bonaventura, *The Mind's Road to God,* Liberal Arts Press, N. Y., 1953. Another text on which *De Ascensione* is explicitly based in St. Bernard of Clairvaux, *De Consideratione ad Eugenium Papam* (X, 283). The basis of the method is in the Psalms and in St. Paul: "Certe S. Bernardus eximus contemplator ex his dimensionibus gradus sibi fecit ad cognoscendum Deum, in libris quos scripsit de consideratione ad Eugeniam Papam. Neque ille primus inventor fuit scalarum hujus generis: sed ab Apostolo, qui in tertium coelum ac Paradisum penetravit, hunc modum ascensionis didicit, sic enim loquitur Apostolus in epistola ad Ephesios: Ut possitis comprehendere cum omnibus sanctis, quae sit latitudo, et longitudo et sublimitas et profundum."

[9]Stephen C. Pepper, *World Hypotheses,* University of California Press, Berkeley and Los Angeles, 1942. This is an outgrowth of an article "The Root Metaphor Theory of Metaphysics," *The Journal of Philosophy,* 1953, Vol. XXXII, No. 14, pp. 365-374, reprinted in James L. Jarrett and Sterling M. McMurrin, *Contemporary Philosophy,* H. Holt & Co., New York, 1954, pp. 258-265. Professor Pepper neglected the root metaphor of ladder or chain probably because most hierarchical thinkers are theistic, and Professor Pepper regarded this as unscientific, or at least dubious in its claims to truth. But he later showed he had to be more generous and went beyond his canonical four (formism, mechanism, contextualism and organicism) to add a fifth, using the metaphor of the willed act, to allow the speculative scheme of Alfred North Whitehead. I believe there is ample evidence of Hindu and Buddhist use of the scheme of stages toward the ultimate (whether Brahma or Nirvana) to require a sixth world hypothesis. So regarded, Bellarmino's *De Ascensione* would be a classic of great merit.

[10]The Psalms which bear the description "canticum graduum" are numbered in the Vulgate 119-134. In the KJV they are "Songs of Degrees," CXX-CXXXIV. On six different interpretations of the meaning of "ascents" see W. T. Denison, "Psalms, Book of," James Hastings, *A Dictionary of the Bible,* Scribner's, N. Y., 1902, Vol. IV, pp. 153-154. These include the return from Babylon, the annual festival journey to Jerusalem, the fifteen steps from the women's court to the men's court in the temple, the ladder-like ascent in the structure leading each psalm to a climax, the raising of the voice, or the lifting up of the heart. Whereas the modern historiographic method leads the learned scholar to select the second as most probable, the theory of meaning implicit in St. Roberto lets four meanings stand side by side giving the term "ascent" or "gradual" a special richness. Father Brodrick reports that Bellarmino's Commentary "gave two well-known explanations of the title 'gradual' first that of the Greek writers Theodoretus and Euthymius, who held that the name was an allusion to the 'ascent' of the Jews from Babylon to Jerusalem after the Captivity, and the other, the explanation favoured by St. Augustine, that these psalms were composed to be sung by pilgrims to Jerusalem as they mounted the fifteen steps of the Temple. 'Whatever is to be thought about these opinions,' Bellarmine continues, 'it is quite certain that, whether the ascensions originally referred to the return of the Jews from Babylon to Jerusalem or to the progress of pilgrims up the steps of Solomon's Temple, they were meant to typify

the progress of elect souls who by the steps on the ladder of perfection, and especially the steps of charity, ascend from this valley of tears to the heavenly Jerusalem." *Brodrick, op. cit.*, p. 383, ft.

[11]A very important clue to the connection between the two texts lies in Bonaventura's "speculatio" and Bellarmino's "consideratio." Boas says significantly that "speculatio," which appears over and over again in this work, is used in a variety of ways. St. Bonaventura plays upon its various shades of meaning--*reflection, speculation, consideration*--for he seems haunted by the basic metaphor of the universe's being a sort of mirror (*speculum*) in which God is to be seen. The Italian and French translators have the advantage of those of us who write English, for they have merely to transliterate the Latin word. "What Bonaventura calls *speculatio* is in Bellarmino *consideratio*. Each of the fifteen gradus is a "consideratio," as "Ex consideratione hominis, qui est mundus minor," Gradus I, "Ex consideratione mundi maioris," Gradus II. Bellarmino is not giving any new facts about man and the world, but getting his reader to reflect upon the meaning of man in the world. Clearly the Bonaventurian traces or footprints (*vestigia*) are the author in his work of art. The handiwork shows the living author, not the traces of a mechanic who has abandoned his machine. Boas, *op. cit.*, p. 7 ft.

Speculatio occurs in Boethius *Consol. Phil.*, 4, I; 5, 2 and this usage is translated "speculation" as well as "contemplation." "Consideratio" occurs in Cicero, "Consideratio contemplatioque naturae" Ac. 2, 41, 127, etc. It is noted as "rare; not in Quint." and translated "contemplation, consideration, reflection," C. T. Lewis and C. Short, *A Latin Dictionary*, Clarendon Press, Oxford, 1958.

[12]Father Peter W. Nash S. J., contributed a translation of "The Thirteenth Step" in Anton C. Pegis, *The Wisdom of Catholicism*, Michael Joseph, London, 1950, pp. 564-578. This is particularly good because it links so closely the sense of order with the 17th Century concern for the order of nature to be understood mathematically. But "pondus" has a deeper meaning than physical "weight."

> ... God has bestowed on each thing a weight, that is, the worth that its
> nature requires. By 'weight' or 'value' we mean the qualities that make
> goods valuable; for everything is perfected by the number of its parts;
> (none may be missing), its measure (or proper proportion of the parts),
> and the internal and external qualities, such as the outward and healthy
> glow of the skin and the inner powers that is both necessary and useful
> for any activity. (p. 566)

[13]A simple first reading might lead us to diagram the structure as spirit above matter, or a two step relationship. There are many passages that sound dualistic: "anima vero human proprie spiritus est, non corpus, neque ex materia producitur sed a Deo creatur, de qua re apud Catholicos nulla controversia est." (VIII, 274) But dualism is too simple, for man shares characteristics with animals, and he makes things and acts as do animals, and he understands as do angels. With God as well as angels man shares freedom. Hence it is at the beginning of Gradus Octavus that we find a more comprehensive and systematic statement, and it is a dynamic statement of the direction in which man ought to move

> Pertransivimus hucusque res omnes corporales dum mentis consideratione ex
> rebus creatis ad creatorem ascendere nitimur. Jam vero supra omnium cor-
> porum dignitatem, invenimus animas humanas, quae ad infinum genus spiri-
> tualium substantiarum pertinere nascitur, inter quas, et Deum nihil me-
> dium nobis occurrit, praeter Hierarchias et ordines Angelorum" (VIII,
> 274)

[14]The English translation of 1638 attempts to make of Bellarmino a diagramatic road-map to heaven. The emblematic title page makes of the fifteen steps two ladders with seven rungs each and the leftover fifteenth, "Essentia Dei" is an oval sun surrounded by clouds of glory, up beyond the ladders which have feet on earth and heads in heaven. The arrangement is

Essentia Dei

Omipotentia Dej	Iustitia Dej
Sapientia Theoretica Dej	Sapientia practica Dej
Misericordia	Angeli
Aer	Sol, Luna, Stellae
Ingis	Aqua
Mundus	Terra
Anima Hominis	Homo

The chapter numbers show some difficulties between author and interpreter:

X

XI	XV
XII	XIII
XIV	IX
V	VII
VI	IV
II	III
VIII	I

There are curious points here: earth is above man, and between fire and water no rank difference. Air is on the same level as sun, moon and stars, one level of these latter three. Angels are on the same level as mercy, with justice on a higher level, which is the same level as omnipotence.

[15]Only incidentally does Bellarmino refer to the nine fold order of angels. This is not in IX, on the angels, but in XII.

In yet another distinct way Bellarmino is concerned with movement rather than fixed place. There are the rich and the poor. Bellarmino's concern is that the rich should share wealth with the poor and the poor should be grateful for their advantages. (XIII)

I take Panofsky's analysis of "gothic" style in scholasticism, on the basis of his analysis of Thomas Aquinas, to be satisfactory as far as it goes. "Postulate of clarification for clarifications sake" suggested to me that with regard to "hierarchia" St. Thomas might be the greatest in defining the necessary and sufficient characteristics of all hierarchies. This, I believe, is the case: "Hierarchia est ordo, id est relatio, inter diversos gradus; non autem ut dicit unum gradum." (*Index Tertius, Res Praecipuae et Doctrinae Memorabiles, Divi Thomae Aquinatis, Summa Theologica*, Editio Altera Romana, Leonine Ed., n. d., Rome, Vol. VI, p. 191. My essay "A Formal Preface ..." *op. cit.* pushes the claim that this clarification is unmatched until our own analytic philosophy). Erwin Panofsky, *Gothic Architecture and Scholasticism*, Meridian Books, N. Y. 1957. We cannot expect to find the same formal articulation into parts of wholes and parts of parts, all clearly distinct in such a piece of Baroque thinking as Bellarmino's. My argument is that it has its own distinct style.

The same lack of compartmentalization holds true of Baroque Architecture. No longer does one find a strict definition of each part. Rather the structural and decorative alignments melt into one synthesis. In his perceptive analysis Christian Horberg-Schulz (*Architettura Barocca*, Venezia, 1971) p. 9, ariticulates the problem:

Il diciassettesimo secolo fu caratterizzato da una varietà di tendenze mai sperimentata prima. Il *cosmo*, unificato e organizzato gerarchicamente in epoca medioevale, si era disintegrato durante il Rinascimento, che aveva apportato all'esistenza umana l'elemento innovatore della scelta. "Nel sistema religioso del Medio Evo, cristallizzato dalla Scolastica, ogni fase della realtà riceve una collocazione specifica che ne determina finitamente il valore, in base alla maggiore o minore distanza dalla Causa Suprema. In questo tipo di sistema non c'è posto per il dubbio, e in ogni attività della mente è inerente la consapevolezza della protezione dell'ordine inviolabile che non è più compito del pensiero di creare, ma solo di accogliere". Con l'avvento dell'Umanesimo, comunque, insorse il problema del libero arbitrio, che a Firenze doveva assumere un aspetto e dei fondamenti policito-sociali. Nell'orazaione funebre per Nanni Strozzi (1428), Leonardo Bruni ebbe a dire: "Un'equa libertà esiste per tutti-la speranza di ottenere delle alte cariche è di progredire e uguale per tutti". Ma già cento anni prima i fiorentini erano tanto all'avanguardia da nominare i loro magistrati mediante sorteggio. Il sistema assoluto del Medio Evo veniva così ad essere sostituito da una vita politica attiva basata sui nuovi *studia humanitatis*. Comunque il Rinascimento non aveva abbandonato del tutto l'idea di un universo preordinato. Si può parlare piuttosto di un'interpretazione nuova, basata sulla geometria e sull'armonia musicale, che stabilì una scala di valori diversa, assegnando ad ogni cosa un posto conforme al suo grado di "perfezione". Entro questo schema l'uomo acquistava la libertà di scelta, come venne illustrato da Pico della Mirandola in una famosa parafrasi della creazione: "Prese dunque l'uomo, quest'opera di tipo indefinito, è postolo nel mezzo dell'Universo, così gli parlò: Né determinata sede, né proprio aspetto, ne dono veruno speciale ti abbiamo dato, Adamo, affinché quella sede, quell'aspetto, quei doni che coscientemente tu abbia bramato quelli, di tuo volantà, per tuo sentimento, tu abbia e possegga ... Potrai degenerare in quelle (forme) inferiori che sono brute; potrai, per decisione dell'animo tuo, rigenerarti nelle superiori che sono divine".

Ma il concetto rinascimentale di libertà, integrata in un universo armonioso e significativo, non ebbe lunga durata. Già Erasmo e Lutero dimostrano di dubitare della libertà e della "dignità dell' uomo", e Copernico (1545) rimuove la terra dalla sua posizione centrale nell'universo. Cadono i fondamenti politici della civiltà fiorentina e la divisione nella Chiesa sanziona la disintegrazione di un mondo unificato e assoluto. Nel corso del sedicesimo secolo questa innovazione fu risentita come una frattura paurosa che si ripercosse sull'individuo con un senso di dubbio e di alienazione. Questo atteggiamento si manifestò nell'arte attraverso tutti quei fenomeni che vanno in genere sotto il nome di "Manierismo". Nel tragico mondo di Michelangelo esso appare con singolare intensità:

> "Squarcia'l vel tu, Signor! Rompi quel muro che
> con la sua durezza ne ritarda il sol della tua
> luce al mondo spenta!".

Verso la fine del sedicesimo secolo si possono notare dei mutamenti nell'atteggiamento umano. Il caso di Cartesio è particolarmente illuminante. Avendo scoperto che di tutto si può dubitare egli conclude che il suo dubbio, in quanto *pensiero*, rappresenta l'unica certezza! "Esaminando con attenzione ciò che io ero, e vedendo che potevo si fingere di non avere corpo, e che non esistesse il mondo o altro luogo in cui io fossi, non potevo perciò fingere di non esistere, al contrario, dal fatto stesso che avevo pensato di duvitare della verità delle altre cose, ne conseguiva nel modo più evidente e certo che io esistevo ..." Sulla base di questa certezza egli procede alla strutturazione di un sistema compresivo di "fatti". La grande originalità di Cartesio, e quel che gli permette di sottrarsi alle conclusioni di Montaigne e degli scettici, consiste nel fatto che, invece di considerare gli oggetti del dubbio, egli separa l'atto del dubitare da qualsiasi elemento ad esso estraneo, eliminando così i fondamenti stessi dello scetticismo." (p. 9)

I am indebted to Marion L. Kuntz for the idea drawn from Baroque Architecture and also for this reference.

[16]A fault of many philosophers, for Lovejoy is not unique, is to ignore the theology of the medieval and renaissance thinker. Bellarmino as Bonaventura was committed to God incarnate in Jesus Christ--not simply to God from whom the world flowed or God Creator of heaven and earth. This is clear in the *Itinerarium*: (MRG 8): "Christ is our ladder." And Bellarmino speaks of "two steps of Christ." (IX. 4) The beings are not once for always in the same cosmic rank. In the Christian hierarchy there is the hierarchical absurdity, by Neo-Platonic standards, of the God-man. Divine grace exalting the saints to the highest level below God means that the hierarchical scheme is not one that fits the Neo-Platonic model. (IX. 5)

[17]One of the curious neglects of *The Great Chain of Being* is ignoring what Christianity did with the doctrine of the *logos*. If, as noted above, the Word becomes flesh (ft. 16) then dualism (ft. 13) is inappropriate, at least a doctrine that holds God to be spiritual and creatures to be material, and one so essentially different that they are never combinable into a substantial unity. Bellarmino's incarnational theology has a parallel in hylomorphic substantiality of man. Lovejoy, by leaving out the incarnation, omits the unifying bond between spirit and matter, God and man. There are surely intense tensions between the poles of being.

Lovejoy asserts that Bellarmino's "concern is still with the One, not with the Many" even though he is "no harsh ascetic." I believe Bellarmino is no ascetic because his concern is with what unites and relates Creator and creature. Anton Pegis noted that Lovejoy wrote of medieval philosophy as though it were simply a continuation of Neo-Platonism.

Bellarmino's alleged asceticism or Manicheanism: There are ugly passages about the low estate of man which take the form of refering to his "dirty" origin: menstrous blood (I, 242). But these are in a context of the incarnation: God took on human flesh. If Bellarmino says in one place that man is "omnino nihil," he quickly gets to the divine emptying. Bellarmino is a master of dramatic contrast, and this fits his Baroque style.

[18]Just as the "style" of Bellarmino is distinct, so I feel the method is distinct. What makes this difficult to describe is that it does not fall into the easy trichotomy of modern philosophy, rationalism, empiricism, to which we have added pragmatism.

Something has been missing from "modern" philosophy since Descartes and Locke, in spite of their memorable isolation of procedures that have not yet been fully replaced by other methods. A Study of systems between "medieval" and "modern" can therefore be of extreme importance.

[19]*A Most Learned and Pious Treatise*, etc., *loc. cit.*, "The Translator to the Reader," pp. A 2-3. James Brodrick in his edition of 1928 omits this part of the preface, p. xvi, without noting the elision. Father Brodrick notes that "all attempts to identify the translator have failed." *Ibid.*, p. xi.

[20]Victor Harris, *All Cohaerence Gone*, University of Chicago Press, Chicago, 1949.

[21]Sed illud est omnino admirabile in stellis, quod cum velocissime moveantur, et nunquam a cursu illo incitatissimo cessent, et aliae tardius, aliae celerius currant in orbem, tamen semper

128

modum suum et proportionem cum aliis ita servent, ut inde concentus harmonicus, isque suavissimus oriatur. De hoc concentu loquitur Deus in libro Job, cum dicit: Quis enarrabit caelorum rationem et concentum caeli quis dormire faciet?

BIBLIOGRAPHICAL NOTE

The Latin text most easily consulted is from *Opera Omnia* Ven. Cardinalis Roberti Bellarmini Politiani S. J., ex. Editione Veneta, Pluribus tum Additis tum Correctis. Rerum Edidit Justinus Fevre, Paris 1873, facsimile reproduction Minerva, Frankfurt a.M., 1965. "De Ascensione Mentis in Deum per Scalas Rerum Creatarum" appears in T. VIII, pp. 239-313, and references are to book and the page in this edition. As far as I have checked this text against earlier editions, Antwerp 1615, Paris 1616, Egmond 1626, Douai 1627 the Venice edition of 1746 seem to differ only in punctuation.

The English translations published in 1925 by Monialis and that of 1616 edited in 1928 by Father Brodrick have fuller annotated references and the distinct advantage of books divided into chapters which are listed in a table of contents.

II.

THE HIERARCHICAL STRUCTURE OF MEDIEVAL SOCIETY:
CAROLINGIAN, CISTERCIAN, CASTILIAN, CONCILIAR

Ladders up the Mountain of Purgatory: the virtuous who gain the top level of earthly paradise rise above the level of the negligent, the proud, the envious, the angry, the greedy, the gluttonous. Emblem used by the Dartmouth Dante Institute, 1986.

HELEN DICKINSON BALDWIN
ARCHITECTURAL AND SPATIAL ANALOGIES TO
THEOLOGICAL AND POLITICAL HIERARCHIES:
THE CAROLINGIAN CHURCH

Carolingian architecture was designed to make visually apparent and compelling a hierarchical system of religious and political observances. High
towers rose to mark important sanctuaries, and announced to all both the
placement of church's altars to the Saviour and his saints, and the seat of
secular power. The well-known triple-towered west front of the great Carolingian churches was invented in the eighth century and widely developed in the
ninth. The theme of the triple towers became for centuries a compelling symbol
of royal, political, and religious power.

The motif of towers on important churches was one which reached back into
the early days of Christian church building. But it was the Carolingian kings
who developed towers into monumental structures evocative of a ruler symbolism
drawn from ancient royal architectural motifs. The famous towered westworks,
or west churches, of the late eighth and ninth century great abbeys were a
specifically Carolingian invention and showed a keen recognition in potent
symbolism of the power of royal status, becoming as they did, highly charged
visible symbols of the Carolingian assertion of the invisible concept of supreme secular and spiritual power. This power had been recognized and reli-
giously sanctioned when Pope Stephen II traveled north to the court of Pepin
the Short in 754, and on Christmas day consecrated him king in the royal abbey
church of St. Denis. At the same time the Pope anointed Pepin's sons Carloman
and Charles and forbade the Franks to choose future kings from any other family line. The event marked a new era for western Europe. Henceforward the
Frankish kings, as the most powerful rulers of the West and as the anointed of
God, took it as their right not only to govern politically but to take an au-
thoritarian and protective role in church affairs. Although the Popes could
never be comfortable with the royal assertion of spiritual authority, and an
ultimate result was the shattering Eleventh Century Investiture Controversy,
in 754 tangible Frankish protection was too sorely needed for the Papacy to
protest.

Pepin's death in 768 and the short reign of his son Carloman over the divided kingdom left Charlemagne from 731 to 814 as the sole inheritor and im-

plementor of the new order. His genius for orderly administration, his determination to extend his Christian rule over a wide territory and his concept of
himself as a new Constantine led to Charlemagne's well-known efforts to regu-
larize the church so as to make it the unifying bond among his diverse peoples
with himself as supreme guide and arbiter. While issuing a multitude of regu-
latory capitularies, it is clear that Charlemagne's mind was also occupied
with the problem of establishing visible monuments of his political and spiritual power. Given a Christian state, ruled by a king who saw in the orthodox
Christian religion the security and foundation of his kingdom and who was so
anointed by the Pope himself as to consider himself the chosen of God, Charlemagne's logical choice was to build magnificent churches. Monumental
churches would in themselves represent the sheer power of the ruler. For only
he could command the wealth and craftsmen, the forests and quarries, the
transportation and organized labor necessary for their realization. By the
erection of noteworthy churches Charlemagne would also be following the lead
of Constantine who had laid out the first great Christian basilicas. But
Charlemagne's choice of just what kind of churches to build was both shrewd
and imaginative. In monasteries he saw a new field for church building which
he could form to his own purposes and which was suited to his rural and rather
frontier society. Though Charlemagne did not neglect the cathedrals of what
were then the comparatively lifeless cities, he chose for special attention
certain often obscure monastery churches. He saw that monasteries represented
a kind of power vacuum, but that their potential was great. Monks had evange-
lized Western Europe, and everywhere there were monasteries varying greatly in
their degrees of fame or obscurity, prosperity or poverty, learning or ignorance, orthodoxy or irregularity. Between the lavish wealth of St. Denis with
its apse encased in silver, and the poor, unworldly monks of St. Riquier at
Centula, there were great differences. But monasteries as a whole were much
respected and shared a rural foundation suited to a land-based society. And
due to the lack of effective administrative cohesiveness from the church,
there was the opportunity to build in a new way without serious interference
from the bishops of the cathedral cities. So it was at certain carefully chosen abbeys that Charlemagne built entirely novel, monumental, and influential
state churches which incorporated time-honored, especially Roman, architectural symbols which visibly expressed the supremacy of the king, both spiritual and temporal.

The distinctive sign of Charlemagne's new abbey churches was the construction of a triple-towered western addition to the traditional basilica, today most commonly known as a westwork. The west church façade was made up of a new synthesis of ancient symbols of the ruler, taken primarily from ancient city gates at which rulers were ritualistically received in elaborate and splendid ceremonies. The main architectual features of the great gates were forms traditionally expressive of the earthly and heavenly authority of the ruler, and were symbolic of his supremacy whether or not he was present. Often represented on Roman imperial coinage, the royal gate motif was a clear ideogram for the power of the Caesar.

One of the few surviving actual gates is the great Roman Porta Nigra at Trier, Constantine's northern capital. There are clearly seen the main elements of ruler symbolism: a pair of flanking towers, a triple entranceway and above an arcaded room of appearances, in this case of double level. These were the features of imperial symbolism which Charlemagne took over for the entrances of his great abbey churches where the ceremonies of welcome had much in common with the ancient Roman city gate rituals.

One of the greatest of Charlemagne's transformed abbeys was the new monumental monastery of St. Riquier at Centula. Though destroyed in the eleventh century it is known today by seventeenth century copies of a drawing made before its destruction. Founded in the mid-seventh century by a local saint, St. Riquier was both isolated and poor. Though endowed with lands for its support, in the words of its chronicle its monks followed a quite unworldly course, caring little for fine buildings or efficient management of their holdings.[1] Located in northern France near the Somme river, in the diocese of Amiens, it was in the heart of Charlemagne's ancestral lands. When he chose this monastery for transformation into a state establishment he must have done so not only out of respect for the piety of its founder, but more importantly because it would provide him his power base in the midst of the lands which were most closely his own. Its monks could have been in no position to offer resistance to the drastic transformation of their abbey. Charlemagne's first step, taken in 789, was to appoint a new abbot, one Angilbert, who was not from the monastic community, but was one of Charlemagne's closest friends and advisors at court. Angilbert was a distinguished Frank, well-educated and well-traveled, a diplomat on whom Charlemagne depended for many delicate missions. Though justification for his appointment was written into the abbey chronicle as being

Angilbert's sincere wish to take up the religious life, it is clear that this was far from the case.[2] Angilbert continued after his abbatial appointment to act as Charlemagne's close advisor, to live with his daughter, and along with the immense job of overseeing the construction of the new church, he continued to engage in public business. Indeed the building of the new church of St. Riquier was itself public business, entirely financed by Charlemagne and under his own close control. No effort or expense was spared to build as magnificent a structure as possible, and the great church was dedicated, a bare ten years after its foundation, on New Year's Day of 799. Built on a heroic and lavish scale, in plan it extended some two hundred fifty feet, its towers rose one hundred eighty feet into the sky (as high as some Gothic spires), and its marble columns, bases, and mouldings were brought from Italy. It totally eclipsed any church previously built in northern Europe by its height, richness, and bravura, and proclaimed to all the power and glory of the king. Encompassing a visual vocabulary which was drawn from the architectural richness of the varied Christian tradition, its west entrance was dominated by the new arrangement of the architectural vocabulary of gateway ruler symbols.

The distinguishing sign of Charlemagne's new abbey churches, both at St. Riquier and elsewhere, was the unification under one roof of two entirely distinct churches. What appears as a large double transept church was in both concept and liturgical practice actually two independently consecrated churches. To the east rose the triple towers of the basilica dedicated to St. Riquier whose oak coffin was now encased entirely in gold. To the west rose a parallel group of triple towers which marked the centrally organized west church dedicated, typically, to the Saviour. Between the two sanctuaries was the short nave of the Riquier church. The west church was the entrance church and was dominated by its huge central tower with a several-staged spire of wood ad which represented a monumental amplification of the heavenly canopy traditionally held over a ruler's head. Beside it were the flanking towers which were taken over from the ancient gateway motif, now raised to new heights, and in between was a narrow porch with the traditional triple entranceway. The Saviour church was two-storied and paralleled the arcaded room of appearances above a city gateway, inventively turned to the interior where Charlemagne made his appearance from the dominating second story platform of the Saviour church to the worshipping throng in the Riquier church below. These forms of the Carolingian west churches re-created on a monumental scale the ancient symbols of kingly, even god-like authority. The entire structure made apparent the union of local and universal Christianity under the supremacy of the Saviour, and just as clearly the alliance with the Saviour of his earthly ruler who took his high, commanding place in the upper sanctuary. It was to St. Riquier that Charlemagne came to celebrate Easter of 800, but even when he was not present, the awe-inspiring forms of the Saviour church proclaimed his rule, and it was in the Saviour church that the most striking and important liturgies of the year took place. In a hierarchical system of liturgical observances it was the Saviour church which was preeminent. There were celebrated at Christmas and Easter Angilbert's own account of the abbey liturgies tells that it was so arranged that on these occasions all the worshippers would receive communion in the Saviour church.[3] Communion was served first to the important persons present in the upper sanctuary, and then the priests descended the stairs and served to all below in the crypt of the Saviour church. In this crypt was a reliquary which held a vast number of relics of the Saviour including a portion of the Holy Sepulchre. Designed as a central church, the Saviour church at the abbey of St. Riquier must be understood as a *martyrium*, and therefore analogous to the greatest *martyrium* of all, the Holy Sepulchre itself. That the symbolic parallelism was purposeful and understood in Carolingian times is shown by a ninth century ivory of the sleeping soldiers of the Resurrection in which the tomb of Christ is shown as a triple-towered west church structure. Such symbolic associations carried the message of the Saviour-like nature of the ruler.

The Saviour church at St. Riquier transformed the recognized symbols of the royal gateway, the towers, the triple entrance, the room of appearances, into a monumental assertion of Charlemagne's heavenly authority. Just as the Saviour stood at the apex of the heavenly hierarchies in Carolingian thinking, so Charlemagne and his successors stood at the apex of the earthly hierarchy, and the west church became the recognized symbol of a united spiritual and secular government just as during the later Middle Ages the castle stood for the ruling power. Charlemagne's realm was one in which the king, like the Caesars, was a divine person comparable to the Son of God and with supreme authority.[4] His society was one in which by a hierarchical system of vassalage oaths he sought to create, as Robert Folz puts it, a great chain of loyalties with himself holding one end.[5]

The developed Carolingian view of the king as supreme and the chosen of
God was dramatically shown in the presentation page of the Vivian Bible of
846. There the finished manuscript is being presented to the young Charles the
Bald, grandson of Charlemagne. The king is seated above the center of the picture and distinguished from the circling courtiers and clerics by his centrality, by his elevated throne and by his size. Were he to stand up he would be
gigantic. The presentation is significantly taking place not in any specific
locale, though the whole is framed by a heavenly, church-like arch, but in a
generalized exterior setting in which the king's throne and the feet of his
nearest attendants are placed in the clouds. Though the artist stopped short
of representing Charles as in heaven, since above him is the veil which traditionally separated heaven and earth, still he is literally well above the
earth and as close to heaven as possible. And directly above the king, emerging from the center of the arch of heaven, is the hand of God, clearly pointing to the king as his chosen earthly ruler. The hierarchically supreme position of the king and his singular position as the chosen of God could hardly
be more explicitly or dramatically portrayed.

It was this supreme position which the west churches dedicated to the
Saviour made evident to all. For it was by means of comprehensible forms that
the ideas governing the state could achieve convincing reality. The impact of
the west church façade of St. Riquier was powerful for the ideas it expressed
and important in the history of architecture, which Conant has called "the
earliest really imposing and boldly articulated façade in church architecture."[6] The form both through and beyond Carolingian times had a long and tenacious history, especially in the Rhineland where the Investiture Controversy
was so long and bitter. For there can be little doubt that the theme marked
the king's earthly supremacy over all, including the Pope. Significantly, the
triple-towered west church theme was never used in Italy save in one instance:
the abbey of Farfa outside Rome, where the Carolingian emperors habitually
stayed before making a ceremonial entrance into the holy city.

At Charlemagne's Palatine Chapel at Aachen, built at the same time as St.
Riquier, the whole hierarchical arrangement can be clearly shown despite the
reworking of the church in Gothic and later times. There too is a triple-towered westwork and a west church sanctuary on the upper level dedicated to the
Saviour, the altar of the church below being dedicated to the Virgin. Placed
on his throne at a height which effectively separated him from ordinary wor-

shippers below, Charlemagne's supremacy was clear. That he saw himself as hierarchically placed just between heaven and earth is shown by his throne's placement at a dominating, regal, and distant height; above him only the golden mosaics of the heavenly splendors described in the fourth chapter of Revelation. There, just as the throne of the Lord was placed on high, so was that of Charlemagne high on earth. And the architectural richness of the church was carefully designed to make the upper level the more glorious. The great pillars of the ground floor are of stone, but those of the second story are of polished marble between gilded bronze railings. The whole was, as Fichtenau puts it, a reflection of the great cosmic order of government.[7]

The great churches built by Charlemagne have rarely survived due both to natural disasters and to what could be called Gothic urban renewal, but it is clear that their construction formed a major part of Charlemagne's plans from his early days as king. The first west church to be built was actually begun by his father, Pepin the Short, at the ancient royal abbey of St. Denis. The excavations at the west end of this notable church have been problematical in interpretation, but it does appear that an experimental west church with towers was begun here by Pepin and completed by Charlemagne in 775. At the same time the church of St. Nazarius at Lorsch appears also to have had an early western tower complex, and Charlemagne was present at its consecration in 774. In 782 Benedict of Aniane, the mentor of Charlemagne's son Louis the Pious, built a magnificent church with a west church complex, reportedly on the advice of Charlemagne.

At Fulda a new and huge double church completed in 819 was dedicated to Boniface and the Saviour. There the monks found the building program so burdensome that in 812 they begged Charlemagne for relief from the "enormous superfluous building" which they said made "the brethern unduly tired and the serfs ruined."[8] St. Wandrille at Fontanella was built in 833 on the model of St. Riquier, St. Nicasius at Reims in 862, and a west church at Frankfurt was finished in 876. The ninth century abbey church of Corvey on the Weser still stands, and there much of the usual arrangement can be seen. Though since altered, it originally had the typical triple tower complex, and inside is still the second story sanctuary with its arcaded openings into the basilica.

That certain cathedrals did have west churches of the Saviour, although less frequently than did abbeys, is an indication of the Carolingian establishment of royal authority over the Frankish church. The new Reims cathedral

begun in 817 by Archbishop Ebbo was built on the model of St. Riquier and interestingly enough, its west church was specifically torn down in 976. The cathedral at Hildesheim had a west church in 872 and so did Minden cathedral as
late as 952. Even in the twelfth century the royal west church still carried
the symbolism of imperial supremacy. Frederick the First, who instituted the
canonization and cult of Charlemagne, built a grandoise triple-towered west
church at the venerable royal church of St. Servaas in Maastrict in 1180. Its
upper sanctuary was known to all as the *Kaiserzaal*.

There are a great number of churches still standing which carry the triple tower west front theme, though their impact as symbolic of the hierarchical system of Carolingian government is not always recognized. The twelfth
century church of Marmoutier has still its three towers, as has also the
twelfth century abbey of Maria Laach. The monastery of Freckenhorst founded in
851 carries still on its present twelfth century church the Carolingian west
front theme. The church of St. John the Evangelist in Liège was built on the
model of the Palatine Chapel at the turn of the eleventh century and though
entirely remodelled in the eighteenth century, significantly the old triple
west towers were left intact. They appear today exceedingly archaic since they
are attached to the more modern building, but their very existence is a telling spokesman for the tenacious power of the theme. A similiar late re-model-
ling of an abbey church in St. Trond left the old west towers also, the central one having the staged wooden spire which is reminiscent of those of St.
Riquier.

Many other examples exist, for throughout what is now northern France,
Germany and Belgium, the symbolic potency of the theme held for many generations. Once recognized as such, the surviving structures speak tellingly of
the innovative concept of the union of political and spiritual affairs in
Carolingian government through the architectural forms that went far beyond
simple utilitarian and aesthetic purposes. For an age accustomed to the expressive content of visual symbolism, the Carolingian west churches carried
the message of the supremacy of the ruler.

NOTES

[1] Hariulf, *Chronicon Centulense, ou Chronique de L'Abbaye de Saint-Riquier*, Traduction par Le Marquis Le Ver, Publiée et Annoté par Ernest Prarond. Abbeville: Imprimerie Fourdrinier et Cie, 1899, pp. 61-62.

[2] *Ibid.*, p. 62.

[3] Carol Heitz, *Recherches sur les Rapports entre Architecture et Liturgie à l'Epoque carolingienne*. Paris: S.E.V.P.E.N., 1963, p. 27.

[4] E. Baldwin Smith, *Architectural Symbolism of Imperial Rome and the Middle Ages*. Princeton Monographs in Art and Archaeology, XXX. Princeton: Princeton University Press, 1956, p. 81.

[5] Robert Folz, "Charlemagne and his Empire," *Essays on the Reconstruction of Medieval History*. Ed. by Vaclav Mudroch and G. S. Course. Montreal: McGill-Queen's University Press, 1974, p. 92.

[6] Kenneth John Conant, *Carolingian and Romanesque Architecture, 800-1200*. The Pelican History of Art. Ed. by Nikolaus Pvesner. Baltimore: Penguin Books, 1959, p. 12.

[7] Heinrich Fichtenau, *The Carolingian Empire, The Age of Charlemagne*. Trans. by Peter Munz. Harper Torchbooks. New York: Harper & Row, 1964, p. 55.

[8] Richard Krautheimer, "The Carolingian Revival of Early Christian Architecture," *Modern Perspectives in Western Art History*. Ed. by W. Eugene Kleinbauer. New York: Holt, Rinehart and Winston, Inc., 1971, p. 335.

The majority of the material for this paper has been drawn from E. Baldwin Smith's book, *Architectural Symbolism of Imperial Rome and the Middle Ages*, note 4 above, and from: Helen D. Baldwin, *The Carolingian Abbey Churches of St. Riquier at Centula*. Unpublished Master's thesis, Vanderbilt University, 1970.

SLIDE LIST

1. Porta Nigra, Trier.

2. Engraving of St. Riquier, by Petau, 1612.

3. Reconstruction of St. Riquier facade by Effmann.

4. Reconstruction view of St. Riquier by R. and H. Baldwin.

5. Ninth century ivory of the Resurrection.

6. Presentation page of the Vivian Bible, 846.

7. Facade of the Palatine Chapel, Aachen.

8. Interior of the Palatine Chapel, Aachen.

9. Charlemagne's throne in the Palatine Chapel, Aachen.

10. Schematic drawing of the Palatine Chapel, Aachen.

11. Drawing of 1699 of the mosaics of the Palatine Chapel, Aachen.

12. Corvey on the Weser, reconstruction view.

13. Corvey interior, to the west.

14. Twelfth century chruch of Marmoutier.

15. Twelfth century abbey of Maria Laach.

16. Monastery of Freckenhorst.

17. Church of St. John the Evangelist, Liège.

18. Abbey at St. Trond.

JOHN R. SOMMERFELDT

EPISTEMOLOGICAL AND SOCIAL HIERARCHIES:
A POTENTIAL RECONCILIATION OF SOME INCONSISTENCIES
IN BERNARD'S THOUGHT

Saint Bernard's *Sermon to the Clergy of Paris* (usually called *On Conversion*) has often been taken as a monastic assault on the clerical status and the intellectual life associated with it.[1] Geoffrey of Auxerre has reported to us that, as a result of Bernard's sermon, he and two of his colleagues "... were converted from vain studies to the cultivation of true wisdom, renounced the world, and joined the family of God."[2] That family dwelt at Clairvaux.

But Bernard's sermon, which has seemed to some to be a most powerful statement of monastic intolerance and mystical obscurantism, was not a criticism of the clerical office or the education in dialectics necessary for that office. His sermon was rather an indictment of those who held, or hoped to hold, the office of unworthy reasons. The sermon was an attempt to convert the clergy, to be sure, not to a monastic vocation, but to a way of life which would make them capable of filling--and finding fulfillment in--their own office.[3]

However, the sermon on conversion to the clerics of Paris does contain a passage which could be interpreted as an effort to recruit monks; in one empassioned sequence, Bernard urged his audience to fly to "the cities of refuge."[4] I have pointed out elsewhere[5] that I believe this passage to be an extension of the principle Bernard proposed in his letter to Thurstan, archbishop of York. Thurstan was to abandon his pastoral charge only if he had sinned gravely or had the permission of the pope.[6] Bernard believed a life of service in the world and the intellectual preparation for it were commendable. But both were dangerous, and this points to a hierarchical evaluation of the social classes and their attendant epistemologies by Bernard.

If life in the monastery were less dangerous than life in the world and were, indeed, a more efficacious remedy for the sinner, then perhaps there was a hierarchy associated with Bernard's sociological and epistemological concepts. Bernard's attitude is clear, especially in his view of other monastic orders. Bernard did, of course, enthusiastically approve of much contemporary, non-Cistercian monastic life;[7] however, he qualified that approval. In his *Apology* he answered his own question on life at Cluny in this way:

> If you should ask me why I did not choose [Cluny] from
> the start when I thought thus [so highly] of it, I reply,
> because of what the Apostle once said: "All is licit, but
> not all is expedient." Surely not because the Order
> [Cluny] is not holy and just, but because "I am a thing
> of flesh, sold into the slavery of sin," and I recognized
> the weakness of my soul for which a stronger medicine was
> necessary.[8]

Not only was Cistercian medicine stronger, its stricter life was a way of greater perfection.

This justified, for Bernard, the shifting of a monk's obedience from one house to another which we call *transitus*.[9] Bernard wrote the Black monks of Flay who complained at his receiving one of their number:

> If one of my [monks] should come to you for the gift of
> greater perfection and out of the desire for a more aus-
> tere life, I should not only not complain if you should
> consider his request, but I would beg you to do so ....[10]

There is no doubt that Bernard considered the monastic institutions of his day to be arranged in an hierarchy culminating in Cîteaux and her daughter houses because of the greater austerity of Cistercian life of which he spoke to his monks at Clairvaux:

> Does any of you seek a more austere life? I tell you that
> this is the most strict [life], and, if you wish to be
> candid, it above all corresponds as much as possible to
> the first school of the Savior. Or perhaps you dare de-
> scend even in thought to an easier life? Oh, if you only
> knew how much you owe and to how many! You would see how
> what you do should be accounted as nothing when compared
> with what you ought to do.[11]

The superior monastic life at Clairvaux and her sister abbeys meant that *transitus* was possible in only one direction, toward, not away from, the Order of Cîteaux. He wrote to an abbot of a monastery in York:

> Perhaps it would be best for me to send you ... to one
> more learned than I and one whose authority is more re-
> vered and holier. Pope Saint Gregory says in his book *On
> Pastoral Care*: "Whoever has chosen the greater good makes
> the lesser good which he might have chosen unlawful." And
> then to prove this he adds the words of the Gospel, say-
> ing: "No one who has put his hand to the plow and then
> looks back is fit for the kingdom of heaven." And from
> this he concludes: "Whoever, therefore, has undertaken
> the greater work shall be guilty of looking back, if he
> leaves the greater good to turn back to the lesser." Thus
> he says in his third homily on Ezechiel: "There are those
> who do the things which they know to be good indeed, and,
> while doing this, consider better things and then change

their minds. And the good which they have begun, they do;
but from the greater which they had considered, they fall
away. Such persons may seem to be just in human eyes, but
in God's eyes they have fallen away.[12]

Bernard's citation from Gregory and attendant argument not only condemned
the transfer of monks from a stricter life to one less austere, it could also
explain why his letters to young men living in the world after their promise
to become monks were so insistent on their embracing the contemplative life of
the cloister.[13]

Bernard not only had definite opinions on the relations between monastic
orders, he also explicated a theoretical foundation for the relationship between the various states of life: monastic, clerical, and lay.[14] He wrote to a
brother of one of his monks: "I wish you to be a friend of the poor, but I
would rather have you imitate them. The former is the stage of the proficient,
the latter of the perfect."[15] Thus, although the states of life were all good,
there was an ethical factor which established them in a hierarchical relationship.

I would argue that Bernard applied the same value hierarchy to the epistemological methods appropriate to the various states of life: contemplation
for the monk, reason for the cleric, and a sort of common-sense training and
method for the layman.[16] Bernard pointed out in his thirty-sixth *Sermon on the
Song of Songs* that the knowledge associated with the lay and clerical states
of life, however useful, was not essential to the ultimate goal of life:

But it seems to me that I ought first to inquire whether
all ignorance is culpable. I do not think it is, since we
shall not be condemned for every kind of ignorance, and
there are many, indeed innumerable, things the ignorance
of which is no obstacle to our salvation. For example, if
you do not know the mechanical arts, either that of the
carpenter or the mason or any other arts of this sort
which men practice for the sake of this life, how would
that impede your salvation? Even without those arts which
are called liberal--the study and exercise of which are
considered more noble and useful--how many men have been
saved, pleasing [God] by their virtues and their actions?
How many does the Apostle enumerate in his *Letter to the
Hebrews* who became dear [to God] not by their knowledge
of letters but by their pure conscience and their sincere
faith. All pleased God in their life--by the merit of
their life not by their knowledge. Peter and Andrew and
the sons of Zebedee and all the other disciples were not
chosen from the school of rhetoric or philosophy, and yet
the Savior worked through them for salvation on this
earth.[17]

Thus, some knowledge was unessential, even though useful. The value of knowledge acquired, and thus the means by which it was acquired, was related to the efficacy of that knowledge in the pursuit of salvation:

> However, what is this, "to be wise to sobriety": to ob-
> serve most carefully what we ought to know first and
> foremost. For the "time is short." Now every sort of
> knowledge which is founded on Truth is good in itself;
> but you who hurry to work out your own salvation with
> fear and trembling in the short time available should
> take care to know, first and foremost, that which you
> sense to be most intimately connected with salvation. Do
> not doctors decide which medicine to administer at meals,
> which before, and which after, in what order and amount?
> Now it is certain that all food is good, because created
> by God; however, you can easily make it bad for yourself
> by not observing due measure and order [in eating].
> Therefore, that which I have said of food, understand as
> so with knowledge.[18]

Bernard had no doubt that the contemplative epistemology he associated with the monastic way of life was at the summit of the hierarchy of means to truth:

> He is a great man who busily spends his use of the senses
> as if they were the resources of society, thus providing
> for his own and the salvation of many. And he is no less
> a man who has made for himself steps to the invisible by
> philosophizing. The latter way [philosophy] is sweeter,
> the former [use of the senses] more useful; the latter
> happier, the former stronger. But he is greatest of all
> who, spurning the very use of things and senses as much
> as human frailty permits, has accustomed himself to soar
> occasionally to contemplation of the most sublime, not by
> ascending steps but by sudden ecstasies. I think the rap-
> tures of Paul belonged to this last sort--raptures, not
> ascents--for he himself relates that he was swept up
> rather than ascending himself.[19]

There is a problem implicit in this passage: although the superiority of contemplation is established, the role of reason and the senses seem inverted. There are, most likely, three reasons for this. First, in the passage Bernard described the epistemology *and* the life of the layman but only the epistemology of the cleric. It is also quite probable that, in describing the uses of the senses in one's own and other's salvation, Bernard was also referring to the *means of action* of the secular clergy in their role in society: to preach, teach, and make relevant the truths of Christianity to their age.[20] This would mean that "the senses" in this passage represent both the means to truth of the laity and the mode of action of both laity and clergy. Viewed in this way, the senses can understandably be described as more profitable than reason. In

addition, the respect which Bernard thought laymen should show to their teachers, the clergy,[21] surely shows that the clergy and their attendent epistemological method were superior to the laity and their common-sense means to
truth. Finally, in a passage in his treatise *On Loving God*, Bernard did place
reason above sense-experience:

> And would that they wished to attain to an intellectual
> grasp of all things and not an experiential knowledge of
> them! This they could do easily and not in vain. For the
> mind is more speedy and more penetrating than the bodily
> senses. And it is given for this that it should go before
> sense perception in everything and that the senses should
> never dare to touch what the mind, preceding them, should
> not prove useful.[22]

This passage reverses the prior one on the relationship between sense-
experience and reason. Indeed, it seems to go too far and limit the efficacy
of the senses drastically. However, the limitation stems, I believe, not from
the epistemological inadequacy of sense data, but rather from its inefficacy
in moral questions. Bernard seems to have meant that one should not allow the
senses free play without determining the moral effect of the object sensed.
Thus, in this respect, Bernard adhered to a consistent epistemological hierarchy.

Despite my statement earlier in this paper that there was no doubt in
Bernard's mind about the superiority of the contemplative life, there are a
number of passages in his works which require explanation before the statement
can go unchallenged. For example, in his ninth *Sermon on the Song of Songs*,
Bernard wrote: "Although Rachel [the contemplative life] is more beautiful,
Lia [active life] is more fruitful. Therefore, let no one crave the kiss of
contemplation too much, for the breasts of preaching are better."[23] Not only
did Bernard here seem to declare the superiority of the active to the contemplative life, in his twelfth *Sermon on the Song of Songs* he actually made an
apology for having chosen the part of the monk:

> Sometimes when I ... am seated at the feet of Jesus de-
> serving and offering the sacrifice of an afflicted spirit
> at the thought of my sins, or surely when standing, how-
> ever rarely, at [his] head and exulting in the memory of
> his gifts, I have heard, "Why this waste?"--caused surely
> because I have lived for myself alone and not, as people
> might say, as I could, for the benefit of many. And [the
> voices] say: "For this could have been sold for much and
> given to the poor." But it would not be a good sale for
> me if I should gain even the whole world and damn myself
> and suffer loss .... Let those who accuse me hear the

Lord excusing me and responding for me; he asks "Why do
you trouble this woman?" That is, "You look on the face
and therefore judge by the face. He is not a man, as you
suppose, who is able to stretch forth his hand to difficult things; he is a woman. Would you lay a yoke upon him
which I see he is incapable of bearing? He is doing good
work in me. Let him remain in the good until he is strong
enough for better. If he ever changes from a woman to a
man, and a perfect man, he will be able to undertake the
work of perfection."[24]

Bernard was aware of the disparity between his various analyses of the relative merits of states of life; indeed, he found the same seeming disparity in
the Scriptures:

What do you think, my brothers, about what is said about
her who chose the best part? What shall we make of the
argument which we use against her [Mary] when we find her
disposed to regard as iniquity Martha's bustling solici-
tude: "Better is the iniquity of a man than a woman doing
good"? And what about: "Whoever is greater among you, let
him be your minister"?[25]

Bernard did not offer a complete solution in the sermon I have quoted,[26]
but an investigation of the circumstances of his various appraisals of states
of life explains, I believe, their seeming opposition.

For example, when Bernard referred to the contemplative life as being for
those too weak for the active,[27] his audience was undoubtedly monastic. He
wished to disabuse monks of the notion that the active life was sinful, and
his rather extreme statement must be taken as a case of rhetorical overempha-
sis. Indeed, in the same place, he continued:

My brothers, let us revere bishops and venerate their labors; if we think about those labors, we should never desire their honors. Let us acknowledge that we are inferi-
or men and not desire to support the burdens of men with
our feeble, womanly shoulders. We should not scrutinize
them, but honor them. It would be inhuman to find fault
with them whose burdens we have fled, just as it would be
impertinent for a woman spinning at home to rebuke her
man when he returns from battle. I say, if he in his
cloister should observe one working among the people occasionally behaving with too much freedom or too little
circumspection, for example, in eating, sleeping, laugh-
ing, anger, or judgment, let him not hasten to condemn,
but remember the words of Scripture: "Better is the iniquity of a man than a woman doing good." For you do well
in watching yourself closely; but he who cares for many
does the better and more manly thing. And if this cannot
be done without some iniquity, that is, without some un-
evenness of life or conversation, remember that love cov-

> ers a multitude of sins. I say these things against the
> germ of temptation with which the devil often tries to
> incite monks to envy the glory of bishops or judge them
> for their failings.[28]

Bernard was, of course, trying to share with his fellow monks some of the em-
pathy and understanding he felt for the clergy burdened with life in the
world. He was also trying to extinguish any smoldering desires for the flames
of episcopal "glory" which his monks may have been nourishing.

In his third *Sermon on the Assumption*, Bernard performed a similar service of instruction for those engaged in active labors who murmured against
contemplatives:

> But he is a man of the flesh and surely does not perceive
> the Spirit of God, if he reproaches the idle soul for her
> want of activity. Let him know that this is the best part
> which lasts forever. Does not the soul somehow seem art-
> less which, deeply experienced in divine contemplation,
> enters that condition where this is the most important
> work, the sole endeavor, its very life?[29]

Here the "best part" is restored to the contemplative life. In both cases his
pedagogical purpose justified for Bernard a certain rhetorical overstatement.
It is quite probable that Bernard considered the active life superior when the
needs of one's neighbor were considered, while the contemplative life was superior when considered from the point of view of intrinsic worth.

To buttress my argument that Bernard viewed the contemplative life and
means to truth as the pinnacle of his social and epistemological hierarchies,
it is only necessary to examine the great bulk of his declarations on this
subject. Bernard asserted the superiority of monastic to scholastic education:
"But [God] is more fittingly sought in deep prayer than in disputation and
more easily found."[30]

Geoffrey of Auxerre and William of St. Thierry tell us that Bernard was
himself faced with the choice of education in the classroom or the cloister. I
quote Geoffrey:

> They [his brothers] urged him to the study of letters in
> as much as they hoped to be able to detain him [in the
> world] most easily in this way. This seemed right to him
> and the day was set, his brothers providing what was nec-
> essary for his trip so that he might set out for Germany.
> However, hurrying to the appointed place and day he sud-
> denly began to ponder and be confused by the image of his
> mother, and he felt the hope which she had had for him
> was being frustrated ....[31]

Bernard's choice of Cîteaux indicates his early views on the relative efficacy
of the two educational systems.

This view remained Bernard's throughout his life. In his treatise *On
Grace and Free Will*, Bernard declared that contemplation was superior to other
modes of knowing because through it one attained a state most closely approxi-
mating eternal life:

> It should be said that they who are sometimes rapt in the
> Spirit by overwhelming contemplation are able to taste a
> little the sweetness of heavenly happiness, free from
> misery as often as they are enraptured. It cannot be de-
> nied that they enjoy the freedom of union even in this
> life on those rare rapturous occasions. They have chosen
> the best part with Mary, and it shall not be taken away
> from them. They who hold now what cannot be taken away
> from them surely experience that which is to come. But
> that which is to come is happiness, and happiness and
> misery cannot exist at the same time. Therefore, as often
> as they share happiness in the Spirit, they will not feel
> misery. Thus, only contemplatives enjoy true freedom of
> union in this life ....[32]

Contemplation was not only a foretaste of the joys of the next life, the contemplative life was most precious because it was totally oriented toward God
and was the most direct route to him:

> To aim at something other than God for the sake of God is
> not the repose of Mary, but the activity of Martha. But
> never let it be said that I attribute deformity to this.
> Nor would I affirm the attainment of perfect beauty, for
> it is "care and trouble about many things" and sprinkles
> the soul with a layer of the dust of earthly occupations.
> This dust can be washed away easily, at least in the hour
> of a holy death by pure intention and the testimony of a
> good conscience before God. Therefore, to seek God alone
> for himself alone, this clearly is to exhibit absolute
> beauty in both cheeks. And this is proper and special to
> the spouse who by the merits of her singular prerogative
> can hear [her Bridegroom] say: "Your cheeks are as beau-
> tiful as the turtle dove's."[33]

The contemplative life was thus superior to the active life because the proper
activity of the contemplative was also his goal, union with God. The life of
the monk was best because in it one's end and one's means to that end were one
and the same.

The monastery was the ideal environment for this all-absorbing attention
to God. The education of the monk[34] was specifically oriented toward preparing
him for contemplation, and distractions from contemplation were not so press-

ing in the monastery. Bernard once wrote to a young man who had shown reluc-
tance to fulfill his promise to come to Clairvaux:

> Dearest son, if you would prepare your interior ear for
> the voice of your God, which is sweeter than honey or the
> honey-comb, flee exterior cares that, with your internal
> sense free and unimpeded, you can say with Samuel:
> "Speak, Lord, for your servant hears." This voice does
> not sound in the market place nor is it heard in public.
> It is a secret council, secretly sought and secretly
> heard.[35]

I hope I have shown that much of Bernard's apparently contradictory views
in social theory and epistemology were consistent when viewed from the hierarchical perspective I have described, and which I believe was Bernard's own.
Praise of the active life, patronage of scholars,[36] and a high regard for the
method and goals of the schools[37] were not inconsistent with Bernard's mysticism. The layman, the cleric, and the monk, with their attendant means to the
truth, were all prized by Bernard. But the contemplative life of the monk was
best, because most efficacious.[38]

NOTES

[1]See, for example, Hayden V. White, "The Gregorian Ideal and Saint Bernard of Clairvaux," *Journal of the History of Ideas*, 21 (1960), 321-48.

[2]Geoffery of Auxerre, *Vita prima, liber quartus*, II, 10; *Patrologia Latina* [PL] 185:327.

[3]See my "The Intellectual Life According to Saint Bernard," *Cîteaux: Commentarii Cisterciensis*, 25 (1974), 249-56.

[4]*Sermo de conversione ad clericos*, 21, 37; PL 182:855; Op. S. Bern. 4:113. Op. S. Bern. refers to the definitive edition of Bernard's works: *Opera* (edd. Jean Leclercq *et al.*; Romae, 1957-).

[5]"The Intellectual Life ...," p. 255.

[6]*Epistola* [Ep] 319, 1-2; PL 182:524.

[7]See my "The Social Theory of Bernard of Clairvaux," in *Studies in Medieval Cistercian History* (*Cistercian Studies*, 13; Spencer, Massachusetts, 1971), pp. 37-38.

[8]*Apologia ad Guillelmum abbatem*, IV, 7; PL 182:930 Op. S. Bern. 3:87.

[9]See the article, on *transitus* in the twelfth century by Douglass Roby, "Philip of Harvengt's Contribution to the Question of Passage from One Religious Order to Another," *Analecta Praemonstratensia*, XLIX (1973), 69-100. On Bernard, see pp. 74-80.

[10]Ep 68, 3; PL 182:178; Op. S. Bern. 7:167.

[11]*Sermones de diversis*, 22, 5; PL 183:597; Op. S. Bern. 6/1:173.

[12]Ep 94, 1, PL 182:227; Op. S. Bern. 7:243-44.

[13]Ep 108, 2; PL 182:249-50; Op. S. Bern. 7:277-79. Ep 412, 2; PL 182:621. See "The Intellectual Life ...," pp. 251-52.

[14]See "The Social Theory ...," pp. 39-48.

[15]Ep 103, 1; PL 182:237; Op. S. Bern. 7:259.

[16]See my "Epistemology, Education, and Social Theory in the Thought of Bernard of Clairvaux," in *Bernard of Clairvaux: Studies Commemorating the Eighth Centenary of His Canonization* (*Cistercian Studies*, 28; Kalamazoo, Michigan, 1977).

[17]*Sermones super Cantica Canticorum* [SC] 36, 1; PL 183:967; Op. S. Bern. 2:3-4.

[18]SC 36, 2; PL 183:968; Op. S. Bern. 2:5

[19]*De consideratione* [Csi] V, ii, 3; PL 182:789; Op. S. Bern. 3:468-69.

[20]"Epistemology, Education, and Social Theory ...."

[21]*Ibid.*

[22] *De diligendo Deo*, 20; PL 182:968; Op. S. Bern. 3:136.

[23] SC, 9, 8; PL 183:818; Op. S. Bern. 1:47.

[24] SC 12, 8; PL 183:831-32; Op. S. Bern. 1:65-66.

[25] *Sermones in Assumptione Beatae Mariae* [Asspt] 3, 3; PL 183:422; Op. S. Bern. 5:240.

[26] Indeed, in another part of Asspt 3, 3 (PL 183:423; Op. S. Bern. 5:240), Bernard seems to have described the mixed life as best. I shall deal with this in another paper.

[27] See above.

[28] SC 12, 9; PL 183:832; Op. S. Bern. 1:66.

[29] Asspt 3, 3; PL 183:423; Op. S. Bern. 5:240-41.

[30] Csi V, xiv, 32; PL 182:808; Op. S. Bern. 3:493.

[31] Geoffrey of Auxerre, *Fragmenta de vita et miraculis s. Bernardi*, 10, in *Analecta Bollandiana*, L (1932), 93-94. See also William of St. Thierry, *Vita prima, liber primus*, III, 9; PL 185:231-32.

[32] *De gratia et libero arbitrio*, V, 15; PL 182:1009-1010; Op. S. Bern. 3:177.

[33] SC 40, 3; PL 183:983; Op. S. Bern. 2:26.

[34] See my "The Educational Theory of St. Bernard: The Role of Humility and Love," *Benedictine Review*, XX (1965), 25-32, 46-48.

[35] Ep 107, 13; PL 182:248; Op. S. Bern. 7:275-76.

[36] See my "Bernard of Clairvaux and Scholasticism," *Papers of the Michigan Academy of Science, Arts, and Letters*, XLVIII (1963), 266-68.

[37] *Ibid.*, pp. 268-75.

[38] See my "The Epistemological Value of Mysticism in the Thought of Bernard of Clairvaux," in *Studies in Medieval Culture* [I] (Kalamazoo, Michigan, 1964), 48-58.

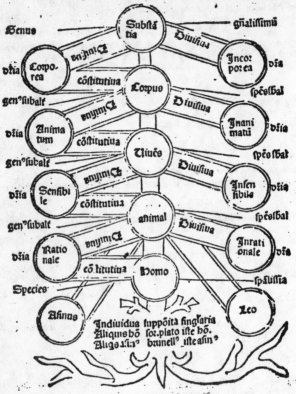

Logica magistri Pauli pergulensis. In the introduction to this text the author wrote that "transcendentals are six in numbers, namely: Being, Thingness, One, Good, True and Things. These are called transcendentals because they include all things in themselves and are verified from all things." By permission of the Biblioteca del Museo Correr e Civico, Venezia, collocamento Cicogna G, 102.

LINA L. COFRESÍ

HIERARCHICAL THOUGHT IN THE SPANISH MIDDLE AGES: RAMÓN LULL AND DON JUAN MANUEL

Hierarchical thought was one of the constants of medieval philosophy, and Medieval Spain was not excepted from this trend. Two of the most important manifestations of hierarchical thought in Spain are the theological and religious writings of the Majorcan Ramón Lull and the social and political theory of the Castilian noble Don Juan Manuel.

The mystic Ramón Lull (1232-1315) was born in Majorcaa few years after the acquisition of this island by the king James I of Aragón. He grew up among the culturally mixed inhabitants of his native island and was therefore conversant with the Moorish and Jewish cultures, so much so that all his evangelical effort and the main goal of his life was to bring the Moors, whose faith he considered an incomplete revelation of the true nature of God, to accept the Christian faith. Lull's work is vast and all enveloping. A great part of it is written in Arabic and many more of his books are written in Catalonian. Perhaps he used the common languages in the wake of the current reaffirmation of the Romance languages in preference to the Latin tongue favored by older scholars, or perhaps simply as an effort to reach the masses of people not schooled in that language. But it is undeniable that Lull took into consideration his readers, many of whom were common people unable to follow the erudite's language. Also for their sake he cultivated all the genres, striving thus to ease the reader's comprehension into the complicated dogmas and teachings of the Church. It is in this manner that Lull acquired importance in the literary history of Spanish. Although his work is always didactic[1], his literary merit has made him a pivotal figure in the Medieval Catalonian literature.

Lull's work had, as an ultimate goal, the conversion of the infidels to the Christian Faith through persuasion and reasoning. To achieve this he strove to render the Christian conception of the universe and the Christian theological thought clear, indisputable, and, above all, intelligible. According to him it was possible to attain the knowledge of God and the universe through study and the help of faith. His *Ars generalis* describes a method to acquire this knowledge. But, as Lull himself declares, the *Ars generalis* presents insurmountable difficulties to those who did not have a strong intellectual background[2], and in order to help them attain the coveted knowledge of

God and of the order of the universe he wrote a simplification of his method, the *Liber de ascensu et descensu intellectus* (Montpellier, 1304).

This book is then a "popularization" of the theory of knowledge expounded in the *Ars generalis* and is governed by the idea of the hierarchical organization of the world and the hierarchical nature of knowledge. This theory is not only central to the work but also indispensable for acquiring a thorough comprehension of the universe as God's creation.

The *Liber de ascensu et descensu intellectus* is divided in a way that is symptomatic of the theory it presents. It has ten principal sections. The first one covers the ladders of knowledge. From the second to the ninth sections the components of the universe are presented in ascending order. These are: (2) the stone, (3) the flame, (4) the plant, (5) the beast, (6) man, (7) heaven, (8) angel, (9) God. The tenth section is a table of contents, composed by Lull himself in order to give the readers better access to the different treatises of the book.[3]

This organization of the book in hierarchical ladders is of utmost importance to the understanding of the Lullian work, since it is through these ladders that one reaches the ultimate knowledge. Thus he proposes three different ladders for this book. The first one is composed of the elements of the universe themselves, as I have just listed them. Through these eight elements hierarchically arranged in an ascending order the reader perceived the arrangement of the universe.[4] The second ladder is formed by the steps that the reader's knowledge has to take in order to understand fully each one of the elements of the first ladder; that is to say, the reasoning required to attain a thorough comprehension of the creation. These steps are twelve in number: 1) act, 2) passion, 3) action, 4) nature, 5) accident, 6) substance, 7) simplicity, 8) composition, 9) individuality, 10) species, 11) gender, 12) being.[5] Through this ladder the reader analyzes each one of the element of the first ladder, arriving, once all the results are added, at a full understanding of the universe. However, this comprehension is not instantaneous but gradual and hierarchically organized. There are five ascending steps to surmount: 1) the sensitive, 2) the imaginative, 3) the doubtful, 4) the credible and 5) the intelligible.[6] This ladder constitutes the third part of the *Liber de ascensu et descensu intellectus* and reveals the ascending process of the human comprehension, which goes from sensual experience to intellectual understanding.

As is evident, the three ladders are inextricably interrelated by their mutual dependency for the full understanding of the book. Their hierarchical nature reflects the Lullian idea of the orderly and ascending constitution of the universe. Thus, human knowledge is capable of ascending the ladder of creation to attain, in a gradual manner, the ultimate comprehension of God and to delve into His beauty. But at the same time man can also descend these ladders to disobedience and sin. Perhaps it is because of this that Lull places man at the height of the earthly creation. There he is endowed with all the substances of the lesser levels, that is to say, the five Lullian natures (which are the elemental, vegetative, sensitive, imaginative, and rational). Of these five natures the first four correspond to the first four levels of creation preceding man. But the fifth one, the rational nature, is proper to him. This rational capacity enables man to comprehend his function within the hierarchical scheme of creation, which is to love and praise God above all things.[7] This rationality which constitutes free will and is not present in the lower levels of creation, where adoration of the Creator is an integral part of the nature of the created, separates man from the others. Thus man alone in these earthly forms of creation has the power to choose, a power characteristic also of the higher echelons of the universe. But this capacity of choice is not perfect in man, and that is the reason he can be evil instead of good. In contrast this possibility never exists for beings in the upper realms since their perfection always drives them to choose the right way. Thus man is in an intermediate position between the stone and God, mirroring both ends of the ladder of creation and forming in that way a microcosmos ordered in the same way as the larger creation of which he is a part[8] and designed to glorify it.

The ultimate motivation of the hierarchical formation of the world and its zenith is God. Placed by Lull in the ninth step of his ladder, knowledge of God is the most difficult for man to grasp. And this is so because His nature is neither perceptible through the senses nor through the intellect. To overcome this difficulty Lull depends on the words of the prophet Isaiah, "if you do not believe, you will not understand"[9] bridging thus one of the largest disputes of the Middle Ages concerning the divine knowledge. In this manner Lull does not agree with those especially in the Moslem world who deny the possibility of the rational knowledge of God or those who thought that rationality was the only way to reach the divinity. For Lull the ascent to the ultimate grade of the ladder of knowledge was governed by the faith that illumi-

nates man's mind which was not only attainable but desirable in order to fulfill one's place in creation. In this way Lull explains his conception of the
universe as a hierarchically ordered unity in which every form and substance
finds its perfect expression in God, from whence it came, and yearns to return
in order to unify itself again with its Creator. This is also the ultimate
message of the *Liber de ascensu et descensu intellectus*: that all men should
strive towards God through knowledge and faith.

Lull's hierarchical thought is not unique in the late Middle Ages in
Spain. The work of Don Juan Manuel, nephew of Alfonso X, the Wise, also expresses an idea of the hierarchically orderd world of human society. Younger
than Ramón Lull (Escalona, 1282–Córdoba, 1348), Don Juan Manuel had many
points of difference with the Majorcan theologian. In the first place his personality bordered on the scholastic, contrasting with the mystical exuberance
of Lull. He was attached to the teachings of the Dominican order while Lull
was a lay member of the Franciscan order. More importantly, the bulk of Don
Juan Manuel's work was more inclined to the socio-political vein than to the
philosophico-theological interests cultivated by Lull.

But there were also points in common between the two thinkers. Like Lull,
Don Juan Manuel strives to teach the common man, and he also uses the vernacular as his expressive vehicle. His work is also frequently an effort to popu-
larize his ideas, which were mainly about Christian morals and the concept of
the divine organization of society. Like Lull Don Juan Manuel has also earned
great importance in the literary history of Spain, especially through his collection of exempla titled *El Conde Lucanor*. There are two other works, however, which show not only his value as a thinker, but also the influence of
Lull in his work. Marcelino Menéndez Pelayo ascertains that in Don Juan Manuel's *Book of the Knight and the Apprentice-Knight* Lull's influence was quite
strong,[10] this book being molded after the *Book of the Order of the Knighthood*
by Lull. But it is difficult to estimate exactly how much Don Juan was influenced, since the chapters III to XVII of his book are missing.

The other book which was clearly affected by Lull's work is the *Book of
the Estates*, a manual of government that faithfully portrays the Spanish society of the XIV century and its organization. In the manner of the *Blanquerna*
of Lull the society in Don Juan Manuel's book is contrasted with the ideal society conceived by the author thus showing where it needs improvement in order
to follow God's design. In both Lull's and Don Juan Manuel's books the didac-

tic material is enveloped in a faintly anecdotic situation. But Don Juan Manuel follows the inspiration of *Barlaam and Josafat* and not Lull's model. Besides, in Lull the depiction of society is only a lively background for the
moral tale of Blanquerna's life, while in Don Juan Manuel the fictional dimension of the plot takes a second place to the all important depiction of society.

The hierarchical organization that Don Juan Manuel expounds in his work
is not new. His work, as that of Adalbert of Laon, divides society into three
main groups: the orators, the warriors, and the tillers. The world and society
are presented as a well organized, hierarchically ordered structure where each
class has a well defined array of duties and rights, all designed to render a
better service to God. Don Juan Manuel, in the positive way of Aquinas, con-
cieved society as a body whose function was to serve and exalt the Creator.
Thus we recognize Lull's idea that everything comes from God and yearns to return to him.

In this theocentric social scheme it was only logical that the orators or
clerics would occupy the highest level of the social ladder. This was so since
they were the continuators of Christ's work and the mediators between God and
man. They were the dispensers of the sacraments and also the keepers of the
divine law. One of their main duties was also the conversion of the infidels,
in addition to the care of the faithful.[11]

The next step below was occupied by the warriors, the emperor and his
knights. Their functions, as those of the orators, were also tripartite. They
had to defend the faith, the community, and the inhabitants of the realm. The
defense of the faith included evangelization of the infidels, but not in the
same degree as the orators.[12] Don Juan Manuel's division of society differs
here from the older molds. This second category reflects the changing political reality of XIV century Castile broadened to include the wealthy soldiers
of the Reconquest,[13] those new "hijosdalgo" enriched by the war against the
Moors. At the same time the broadening of this category exemplifies Don Juan's
ideas that nobility was gained by works rather than by lineage or blood.

In this scheme of society the two upper levels had the duty to maintain
the faith, within and without the realm, and both had to perform their duty
according to their capacity, with the book and with the sword. Both states
were considered to be "the hands of God" through which His designs were carried out. It is because of this divine mission that the knight's investiture

was almost equivalent to the priest's ordination and both were governed by a
rigid standard of conduct. This idea of Don Juan Manuel's was shared by Lull
as indicated by the title of Lull's book: *The Order of the Knighthood*. This
also explains the quasi religious regard for chivalry in both authors. It
should also be noted that in both writers a knight's death in battle was a
form of martyrdom and granted direct access to heaven, a faith that echoes the
similar recompense attained by the Moslem warriors when killed in battle
against the infidels. Perhaps the mixed cultural formation of Lull and Don
Juan Manuel influenced them in postulating this idea.

The lowest of the three estates in Don Juan Manuel's hierarchically ordered society was that of the tillers. This low state can be equated to the
lower steps of the Lullian universe. Both were the vast but passive element on
which the other rested, and they were farthest away from the direct presence
of God. As was the case with the second state, this one is also broadened in
Don Juan Manuel's book to admit not only its traditional elements but also two
new ones: the merchants and the villains. Those groups constituted the emerging bourgeoisie of XIV Century Spain, which had never before been considered
in a work of this nature. The lowest estate did not have any active social
function, but it had to be guided and protected by the other two since its
lack of intellectual preparation could lead its members to error or
damnation.[14]

Even if his work separated rigidly the different classes, Don Juan Manuel
never considered men to be essentially different. He mentioned time and again
the egalitarian power of death that erases all differences and presents men as
they are to the Creator.[15]

The hierarchical order of Don Juan Manuel's society scheme thus corresponds to the medieval idea of the universe. It goes from the lowest to the
loftiest, from the worker to the cleric, the farmer to the mystic. And this is
the basic function of the book, to enable the reader to know his own place
within society in order to serve better his Creator and fulfill his given
function. In this Don Juan Manuel's goal also coincides with that of Lull:
both strive to form a better man and a better society for God's service. Thus
Don Juan Manuel and Ramón Lull join perfectly the philosophical scheme of the
Middle Ages in their conception of God and the Universe.

NOTES

[1] Marcelino Menéndez Pelayo, *Orígenes de la novela* 4 vols. (Madrid: Consejo Superior de Investigaciones Científicas, 1961) I: 117.

[2] Ramón Lull, *Libro del ascenso y descenso del entendimiento* (Madrid: Imprenta La Rafa, 1928), p. 1.

[3] *Ibid.*, pp. 2-3.

[4] *Ibid.*, p. 2.

[5] *Ibid.*

[6] *Ibid.*, pp. 2-3.

[7] *Ibid.*, pp. 85.

[8] Francisco Rico, *El pequeño mundo del hombre* (Madrid: Castalia, 1970), p. 80.

[9] Lull, *Ascenso*, p. 152.

[10] Menéndez Pelayo, *Orígenes*, p. 138.

[11] Juan Manuel, *Libro de los Estados* en Biblioteca de Autores Españoles LI, *Escritores en prosa anteriores al siglo XV* (Madrid: Editorial Atlas, 1952), Chap. LXX.

[12] Luciana De Stéfano "La sociedad estamental en las obras de Don Juan Manuel" *Nueva Revista de Filología Hispánica* 16 (1962): 329-354.

[13] Don Juan Manuel, Estados, Chap. XCII.

[14] *Ibid.*, Chap. XCVIII.

[15] *Ibid.*, Chap. XII.

JONATHAN BECK

A CRITICAL MOMENT IN THE HISTORY OF "HIERARCHY":
SECULAR LITERATURE IN FRANCE IN THE AGE OF THE
SCHISM AND THE CONCILIAR MOVEMENT (1378-1435)

As with all general principles by which man structures and interprets his
experience, the notion of hierarchy, as brilliantly elaborated by Lovejoy in
the *Great Chain of Being*, runs the risk of acceding to the status of an historiographical formula subject to overgeneralization. By neglecting the other
side of the question--manifestations in Western culture of non-and anti-hierarchical tendencies of the profoundest historical import--historians of ideas
less discerning and less rigorous than Lovejoy could easily turn the "Great
Chain of Being" into another of the misleading tags plaguing the history of
ideas (the middle ages as the "Great Age of Faith," preceding a putative "Re-
discovery" of classical antiquity in that mythical construct of 19th-century
Romantic historiography known as "The Renaissance").[1] Although manifestations
and corollaries of the principle of hierarchy are, as Lovejoy himself has
shown, everywhere visible in the history of ideas, this is not the whole picture. My purpose here is to present some of the evidence from French secular
literature of the late 14th and 15th centuries which shows the principle of
hierarchy in its classic formulation to have fared very badly indeed in this
period of social, political and ecclesiastical upheaval, particularly in the
spheres of ecclesiastical and temporal politics.

The texts under consideration deal with a single problem--disorder--stem-
ming however from two quite different sources: the Great Schism and the Conciliar Movement on the one hand, the Hundred Years War on the other. What this
literature reflects most vividly is the fragmentation and polarization of society into adversary factions. The Schism and the Conciliar Movement divided
Christendom into Clementines and Urbanists, Conciliarists, Papalists, Curial--
ists, Gallicans, Hussites and others, while in France, civil war had further
split the society into Armagnacs and Burgundians, the latter allied with the
English against the French. In all the texts under consideration, the essential concern of the authors is the urgent need to restore peace and unity to
the divided Church and State--to put back together, that is, the severed links
in the political hierarchies. And, in the case of the Conciliar Movement, the
attempt was made to join together those severed links in an entirely new way.

In my remarks on the breakdown of "hierarchy" in Church and State, the term is to be understood to apply to political hierarchy both in theory and in practice--in principle and in fact. The dominant historical *fact* in this period is indeed the denial of hierarchy: the Schism and the Conciliar Movement in the Church; in the state, the corruption and treason in the French administration, the popular revolts in Paris and insurrections in the provinces. Challenges to the *principle* of hierarchy accompany these de facto denials of hierarchy, in the writings of conciliarist theoreticians, and in the works of contemporary secular moralists and poets.[2] The crisis in hierarchy which occurred in the fifteenth century was, therefore, a breakdown not only of the theory of the Great Chain of Being, but also of the exercise of power in the great chains of political command.

It may be supposed that these breakdowns were momentary aberrations, since by the end of the fifteenth century papal and royal authority were once again established more firmly than ever before. But this would be to neglect the profound impact Conciliarism had on secular political thought,[3] and to neglect the fact that the Great Councils of the fifteenth century--Constance and Basel--constitute the first successful application on a large scale of parliamentary self-government based on principles of popular sovereignty, representation, accountability and constitutionalism.[4] Although it was necessary to depose four popes to prove the point, in doing so the Conciliar Movement established, for the first time in Western political theory and fact, an orderly and effective legal procedure and mechanism for challenging and controlling a towering hierarchical institution.[5] Here then is an example of an anti-hierarchy 'backlash' of the profoundest significance for Western civilization; for had the Conciliar Movement not put an end to the Great Schism, the Schism could well have put an end to the Catholic Church of Rome. Moreover, without the reformist tendencies and doctrines fostered and clarified by the conciliarist reformers, there could have been no Protestant Reformation.

When the people of France in the fifteenth century looked about them for order in their religious and political institutions, what did they see? What they say they saw, according to the bulk of their literary and historiographical testimony, was only chaos and breakdown--corruption, greed, anarchy at all levels of the various hierarchies. The main source of chaos in the Church was of course the Schism, which began in 1378 when a disputed election left Christendom with two supreme pontiffs. In itself a flagrant *de facto* denial of hi-

erarchy, the very idea of a body (even a mystical body) with two heads was
fundamentally repugnant to the medieval mind—it was not only a juridical im-
possibility, but an unthinkable monstrosity in the allegorizing and anthropo-
morphizing minds of medieval canonists and theologians (Gerson for example
speaks with horror of the detestable "monstrum biceps"). And it was not only
the theologians and ecclesiologists who viewed with consternation this crisis
in the Christian hierarchy; for *any* fifteenth century Christian, whatever his
station in life, the question of which pope was indeed the *real* pope was of
crucial and immediate importance, for it was thought that the wrong decision
could entail eternal damnation. Propagandists on both sides warned that salvation could not possibly belong to the heretical followers of a false pope.

Small wonder, then, if disorder and anarchy pervaded the ecclesiastical
hierarchy from top to bottom—at the bottom, indeed (as it was argued), *because* order at the top had broken down. The corruption of the lower clergy, as
described in the perennial and somewhat ritualistic condemnations of their im-
morality, disobedience, simony, greed and general lawlessness, was seen as the
inevitable effect of disorder at the top. The schismatic popes, each claiming
to have been legitimately and canonically elected and above all human jurisdiction, scandalized the Christian world by refusing resolutely and repeatedly
to step down, and continued to do so until finally deposed by general councils. Lawlessness and intransigence at the top of the hierarchy, no less in
the fifteenth century than in the twenth century, fostered corruption and dis-
regard for law and order at all levels.

Things were no better in the temporal sphere; the same corruption and anarchy prevailed in the royal administration. And, as in the Church, the self-
serving abuses of power by tax-collectors, judges and administrators at all
levels of the secular hierarchy were considered the necessary consequences of
the disorder and power vacuum at the top—in the royal family, that is, where
partisan factions contending for power during the king's intermittent spells
of insanity opened the way to the most divisive and contentious period in the
French monarchy in the Middle Ages.

Thus with schismatic popes and a mad king whose brother and uncles, ruling in his stead during his periods of insanity, did more damage sane than
Charles VI ever did at his most demented, under such conditions of social division and disorder, the undermining of hierarchy in Church and State had as
its result in the literature of the period a veritable outpouring of invective

and vituperative condemnation of the universal disarray present in all levels
of a society and Church which, according to a commonly-used metaphor (although
timeworn, it was particularly appropriate to the age) seemed to have been
"turned upside down." But, on the positive side, there came as well an endless
flow of exhortations directed to the various orders in the hierarchies to renounce their abuses, reform their ways, and, by reinstating morality, equity
and obedience, to return to a state of order, stability, and unity--and, above
all, peace.

The most vivid expressions of these crises may be seen in the moralistic
and satiric writings of the time. Interestingly enough, nearly all of them employed the principle of hierarchy itself as a mimetic convention and compositional technique. For in any moralistic and/or satiric presentation of contemporary society, it was a matter of course for the author to begin his description at the top of the social ladder, following the conventional tripartite division of society--*clergé, chevalerie*, and the *"tiers état"*--and then
to describe in descending order, with meticulous attention to rank, the proper
duties (and lack of attention to them) of each of the internal divisions of
the three estates. These compositions, which constitute a whole separate genre
in medieval French literature, are called *"états du monde"* (social conditions
of "estates of the world").[6] The hierarchical *états du monde* descriptions had
been used, even from the beginning (twelfth century in he vernacular) as a vehicle for satire, recriminations and exhortations to renounce vice and abuses
and return to virtue and the orderly exercise of one's proper duties in society. However, in the fifteenth century the conventional tirades denouncing
vice and corruption take on a more urgent tone and a more topical intent, due
to the pressures of the Schism and the Hundred Years War.

This development can be seen quite clearly in the works of Eustache Deschamps, the most prolific of French poets of the period.[7] In his earlier
works, Deschamps uses the *états du monde* framework to remind his contemporaries, in the most conventional of terms, of their proper duties in society.[8]
Similarly the tone is more moralistic than polemical in poems such as "The
Suffering of the People and of the Church" (II, 83-84), and "On the Division
of the Church" (V, 230-32), where he attributes the evils of the Schism and
the suffering of the French people to the vices of the three estates. But in
later works he becomes more outspoken. In the poems entitled "Against the
Vices of the Cardinals" (III, 115-18) and "Against Clerical Abuses" (VII; 29-

31, 74-75, 75-77), the satire is much more aggressive. Finally, provoked by
the worsening division of the Church, Deschamps attacks head-on, in the *Miroir
du mariage*, what he perceives to be the cause of the Schism: the simony, nepo-
tism, fraud, greed, venality, ignorance and hypocrisy which he attributes to
all levels of the ecclesiastical hierarchy, rebuking with particular acrimony
the higher clergy, whom he accuses of fomenting discord in the Church in an
attempt to gain more power and profit for themselves.[9]

But, vigorous as the criticism was, up to this point Deschamps had limited himself to generalities. As the crisis worsens, he becomes more specific
and writes a series of six polemical poems against the antipope Peter de Luna
(Benedict XIII), the most tenacious of the schismatic popes.[10] Benedict, having promised to put an end to the Schism when he succeeded Clement VII in
1394, on the contrary made matters worse by refusing to abdicate when called
upon to do so by the council of Pisa. France expressed its displeasure with
Benedict by the unprecedented "subtraction of obedience," which lasted five
years (1398-1403), during which time Peter, having barricaded himself in the
papal palace at Avignon during a four-month siege by royal troops (1398), was
finally taken prisoner and held in captivity for four years. It is difficult
to conceive of a more striking image of ecclesiastical hierarchy in crisis
than this one of the successor of St. Peter behind bars.

Benedict had acquired a notorious reputation in France as an ambitious
and conniving schemer. In the eyes of our poet, he seemed the very incarnation
of Ecclesiastical Corruption and abuse of power. In his poems stigmatizing
Benedict's perpetuation of the Schism, Deschamps treats the crisis of hierarchy in the Church as a catastrophe of cosmic proportions: the very harmony of
the universe has been disrupted by the lunacy of Peter de Luna's pretension to
the seat of St. Peter. Obviously Deschamps, never one to shun an easy pun,
made the most of the pope's name as a source of polemical jibes: Peter de
Luna, known in France as Pierre de la Lune, is thus shown to be responsible,
following the principles of medieval astrology, for the "lunar" deviations
which have thrown the earth and all its institutions into utter turmoil—witness the Schism and the war in France. In the "Balade sur le division et cisme
de l'Eglise, qui est au jour d'un moult troubleé par la lune," Deschamps begins with an apostrophe to Mercury, Mars, Jupiter and Venus, before coming to
the real subject of the piece: the seventh planet: "cold and wicked ... full
of every vice and sin ... simony and ambition, ... by infernal covetousness

determined to throw the world into desolation," all of which, says the re-
frain: "Puis que je voy vouloir regner la lune"—all because of the preten-
tions of Pierre de la Lune. The same treatment and the same astronomical metaphors of natural order and hierarchy upset by lunar deviations recur in two
latin poems by Deschamps on the same subject, and which apparently had wide
diffusion. In his *History of the Papacy*, Creighton mentions certain defamatory
and scurrilous satires which circulated at the councils of Pisa and Constance
(some of which were even affixed to cathedral doors):

> There were many such pamphlets, and much coarse wit was
> mingled with theological discussion. In one, which issued
> from the University of Paris, Peter de Luna is reminded
> of the moon in a clear sky; as it is, he is eclipsed by
> clouds of vanity. [11]

The theme of hierarchy overturned, used to criticize disruptive forces in the
Church and the monarchy was, although topical, certainly widely employed.

In the 1390's Deschamps changes his approach to the crisis in hierarchy,
and substitutes for the moral exhortations and satire of his previous writings
a concrete proposal for a political and legal remedy to the Schism: the convo-
cation of a general council by which a new pope would be elected to replace
the two rival pontiffs. [12] This he does in the *Balade qui parle sur l'estat de
Religion"* (V,276-78), addressed directly to the political powers capable of
acting decisively to help end the Schism: emperors, kings, dukes, counts,
etc.—and, more importantly as it turned out—to the University of Paris, from
whose ranks were to come the most powerful and articulate spokesmen of the
Conciliar Movement—Nicolas de Clémenges, Pierre d'Ailly, and the famous Chancellor of the University of Paris, Jean Gerson. Having progressed from the
conventional satire of the *états du monde* to personal polemic against a specific schismatic pope, and finally to a concrete proposal for a conciliar solution to the Schism, Eustache Deschamps provides an accurate reflection of
the general movement of public opinion in France, which responded more and
more vigorously to the crisis in the Church hierarchy as the Schism widened
and the partisan factions prepared for battle in a general council.

A young contemporary of Deschamps, Christine de Pisan (famous as the
first feminist poet in French literature), also saw the Schism as an intolerable scandal, a "pestilential and contagious venomous plant," she says in a
vigorous but grotesque mixed-metaphor, "growing at the instigation of the De-
vil in the very lap of the Holy Church." [13] She too sees no remedy other than

recourse to the decision of a general council, following, in this opinion, not only Eustache Deschamps, but also the king, Charles V, whose deathbed declaration of adherence to any eventual decisions of a general council she recounts in her biography of him.[14]

Christine's most vigorous condemnation of the wickedness and corruption of the crumbling ecclesiastical hierarchy occurs in her *Livre de la mutacion de Fortune*[13]--the *Book of Fortune's Reversal*, *"mutacion"* implying here the idea of overturning, of hierarchy upside down. This appears quite clearly in her description of the "castle of Fortune" (The goddess *Fortuna*), where she describes in a vertical depiction all the "degrees" in the ecclesiastical hierarchy (*"degrez"* = steps in a stairway or rungs in a ladder). The most interesting and original feature here however is that in Christine's portrayal, increasing elevation in the hierarchy is made to correspond with increase in corruption and moral degeneration: the highest are the worst! Writing in 1402 when the effects of the Schism were becoming more disruptive each year, she describes the inverted hierarchy as follows: entering the castle of Fortune, she saw a series of elevated seats, each higher than the last. "At the very summit," she says, "where our Saviour had seated St. Peter," she saw "two powerful men, sitting quite cramped--and in evident discomfort," she adds, "since the chair was designed for only one, and yet in fact two are seated there. Still in all, despite their discomfort both are so insistent upon keeping the seat, that neither will hear of leaving it, nor of abasing himself to a lower chair." She goes on to detail the troubles and suffering which have arisen from the disputed chair, descending rung by rung the ecclesiastical hierarchy in a vehement attack on the vices, ambition, sins, malice, sacrilege, simony (these are her words) of the subalterns, their fraudulence, trickery, deceit, repine, even murders. (This is an allusion to Bartholomew Prignano [Urban VI, 1378-89] who was reputed to have taken excessively harsh reprisals against those of his cardinals who had plotted against him, five of whom, in particular, disappeared mysteriously in 1386 and were rumored to have been put to death at the pope's behest.[15]) Finally, having reached the bottom of the heap, Christine states very clearly the causal link which unites all the members of the great chain of ecclesiastical command: marvelling that such men could have become the supreme rulers of Christendom, she concludes, with respect to the subalterns: "It is no great suprise if the members are misshapen and distorted when the high head itself is so wicked and corrupt" (she uses the term *infect*, lit. "filthy"). "And so if the body underneath is worthless," she repeats, "it should come as no great surprise"--observations which have become familiar to us in recent times.

The use of the allegory of head and members which we have just seen in Christine de Pisan is of course a traditional image of hierarchy in medieval political symbolism, and is particularly prevalent in theology and theoretical ecclesiology: the Church is the *Corpus mysticum*, the pope is the head, the clergy and the faithful are the limbs. The same image is applied to the state. Gerson for example writes in 1409 that a secular state is nothing other then a "corps misticque civil,"[16] an allegory found as well in the *Policraticus* of John of Salisbury, and as far back as Aristotle--whence the expression "body politic" still in use today in English. Now, during the period of hierarchy in crisis, the allegory of head and limbs naturally presents itself to the imagination of secular writers not only as a symbol of hierarchy, but also to provide a structural compositional technique, as when the Church, or France itself, is personified (invariably as a woman) as suffering from troubles in the head and limbs, e.g. in Eustache Deschamps' poem, "Comment le chief se plaint moult durement de ses membres, c'est assavoir l'Eglise" (V, 219-20; How the head bewails most vehemently its limbs, i.e., the Church). This metaphor recurs repeatedly in the literature of the period, especially in the literature of the Conciliar Movement.[17] Here the image of the chain never appears, it is always the body which metaphorically represents the Church. Undoubtedly this is because in a vertical chain of being, each successively higher link is more excellent than the last; and in a chain of command, each successively higher link has more authority than the last. But in a *body*, power is to be found not only at the top, but also diffused throughout the limbs. The exercise of power is thus necessarily a cooperative and *corporative* activity.

Those familiar with Church History will have recognized here the classic formulation of what is known as the "conciliar thesis"--the intrinsically anti-hierarchical and basically populist idea that power/ (or "*auctoritas*") in the Church resides in the Church as a whole, which, represented by the general council, is superior to the pope in matters concerning extirpation of heresy (and intransigent in a schismatic pope was defined as a form of heresy), in matters of faith and doctrine, in the reform of the Church *in capite et in membris*, and in all matters pertaining thereto. But how could the lower judge the highest? Canon law said that an inferior could not so much as accuse a su-

perior, much less judge him, and all were inferior to the pope. These arguments, which formed the basis of the papalist counter-offensive against the
conciliarists, assumed the ecclesiastical hierarchy to be still intact, which
it was not—this in fact was the source of the whole problem; had there been
no Schism, the Conciliar Movement would never have arisen. But the theologians
and canonists of the Conciliar Movement approached the problem of hierarchy
from a different direction, recurring to a principle which we should call,
with Lovejoy, "otherworldly": the notion of the Church as the *universitas fi-
delium*, that mystical totality of all the faithful, of which the pope himself
was but a part, and superior to which he could surely not pretend to be. Coupled with this "otherworldly" definition of the Church was the eminently mundane observation that the Church was not only a mystical body but also a
sprawling international institution (or "multinational corporation" as it
would be called today), having to deal in the purely terrestrial sphere with
its everyday administrative affairs, and therefore subject to the same administrative principles of civil law which applied to the definition and regula-
tion of any other corporation. By reminding their colleagues, the theologians,
that the Church was not only a *corpus mysticum* but also a *corporatio*, the
canon lawyers brought to the formulation of conciliarist doctrine the weighty
principles and precedents of more than a thousand years of legal tradition
from ecclesiastical and civil jurisprudence.

Because of the profound significance and impact of the Conciliar Movement
and its radical redefinition of ecclesiological hierarchy, it would be useful,
now that the "conciliar thesis" has been defined, to summarize the major steps
in the conciliarist redefinition of hierarchy. In the early period (Pisa and
Constance), it was necessary first to establish the basic 'thesis' itself—
that the pope, though head of the Church, was not its sovereign—so that the
business at hand (ending the Schism) could be dealt with in a legal and orderly way. That is, before the pope(s) could be subjected to the general council,
it had to be established that the council could and did in fact "represent"
the universal Church, and that the "universal Church" was in fact the ultimate
source of ecclesiastical sovereignty. How this was accomplished has been set
forth in expert detail by Brian Tierney in the *Foundations of the Conciliar
Theory*; it will suffice here to recall that the truly remarkable feat achieved
in this new definition of hierarchy was that it was accomplished not by in-
venting new political theory, but by the ingenious recombination of princi-

ples, doctrines and precedents *already existing and well-established* in Canon
and corporate law--a *tour de force* of creative synthesis which attests to the
immense sophistication and resourcefulness of some of the finest legal minds
in the "middle ages."

Having been successful in ending the Schism by the deposition at Constance of Benedict XIII and John XXIII, the conciliarists at Basel (1431-49)
sought to extend their prerogatives. Black notes that at Basel, the council
was defined no longer (as at Constance) as "an emergency weapon with 'occasional' power in time of papal heresy or schism; [it now became] the normal
vehicle of the Church's supreme authority and the regular ecclesiastical superior of all. Papal theory had indeed been turned on its head"[18]--or, in
terms of our discussion, the notion of ecclesiastical hierarchy had been turned upside down. No longer was hierarchy seen to create and define society; for
the conciliarists, it is society which creates its own hierarchy as an expression of the common will of all its members. The council, meeting at fixed in-
tervals, was the institutionalization of this theory of ecclesiastical constitutionalism.

This view of conciliarism as the denial or the radical reformulation of
political hierarchy in its classic form is not just my interpretation; such
also was precisely the way the papacy perceived conciliarism, and the way the
popes wanted the kings to perceive it. Eugene IV--to take merely one example
from the arsenal of papal and papalist counter-propaganda--when faced with the
prospect of deposition by the council of Basel in 1436, addressed a *Tract of
Self-Defense* to all Christian rulers, warning them that the Conciliar Movement
in the Church contained pernicious seeds of subversion that could easily
spread from the ecclesiastical monarchy to the secular ones:

> Eugene [compared] Conciliarism to Hussitism, because it
> "superiors." ... Since, he argued, Basle was placing pow-
> er "in the hands of the people," and trying to replace
> "monarchy" in the church with "the rule of the people and
> democracy," it was [also] a potential threat to all rul-
> ers: "This is fatal for the whole estate of Catholic
> princes" [he argue], "for in exactly the same way their
> own peoples, by assembling together, could claim power
> over *them*. This would *turn upside down at once the epis-
> copal order and the Christian polity*-which is both un-
> speakable and insufferable." [19](my emphasis)

Similarly, three years later, Eugene wrote to Alfonso V of Aragon, claiming
that the council of Basel "*disrupted the whole earthly hierarchy*" by giving

power to a "tumultuous mob."[20] This was more than simply a series of accusations of subversion by each side against the other; what was at issue in fact was the definition and localization of sovereignty itself.[21]

There were of course flaws in the conciliar theses, and the Conciliar Movement eventually consumed itself in the excesses of its reforming fury and petered out at the end of the 1440's as the council of Basel drew to a close. But during those 40 years from the inauguration of the council of Pisa to the dissolution of the council of Basel, four popes were deposed by three general councils.[22] The deposition of a pope had *never* occurred before; but then again, never before in the history of the Church had there been a crisis of hierarchy as potentially destructive as the Great Schism of 1378. We have seen in Eustache Deschamps and Christine de Pisan striking examples of the repercussions in fifteenth century. French secular literature of this crisis, and the appeal to an anti-hierarchical institution, the general council, to end the Schism. There were other such works, by lesser writers, most of them anonymous. Noël Valois has published some of them in his monumental study of *La France et le Grand Schisme d'Occident* and elsewhere, others he describes in summary.[23] The significance of the literature of the Schism and the Conciliar Movement is that it shows, with a force and immediacy that historiography cannot match, how widely and profoundly the crisis in hierarchy was felt in fifteenth century France.

As for the civil and English wars (the "Hundred Years War"), their historical causes include the corruption, division and weakness of the French monarchy, particularly under Charles VI, and the attempts by the English to profit from the disarray in the tottering political hierarchy in France, in order to make good, by force of arms and by opportune alliances, Edward III's claims to the French throne. Here too, political hierarchy in crisis spawned an abundant literature of moralistic appeals to the various social classes to cease their discord and disobedience and unite against the common enemy of the homeland. And here too we find again Eustache Deschamps, writing against the English and the Flemish, against the war in general and against particular aspects of it: merciless mercenaries; factious princes; the decline of the French knighthood; the misery of the common people burdened by war taxes and plundered by roving bands of soldiers from both sides; the devastation of the countryside, the churches, the cites; and so on.[24] And here too we find the same metaphors of hierarchy upside down: France is personified repeatedly as a

mother ravaged by her violent and rebellious children,[25] or as a wife ravished
by two brutish adversaries (the same image, rather graphic by our standards,
also appears—and is developed in lurid detail—with respect to the Schism:
the Church laments being possessed, against natural and human law, at the same
time by two husbands; this allegory of the bigamy and rape of the Church occurs both in Eustache Deschamps and Christine de Pisan[26]). And here too we
find again the allegory of head and members. Christine writes an entire book,
the *Book of the Body Politic* or *Livre du corps de Policie*, characteristically
divided into three parts and addressed to the three estates, in which she outlines their respective civic duties and reproaches them for not fulfilling
these duties. She is not afraid to criticize openly the king and the princes
for failing to preserve the social hierarchy and maintain order, nor does she
hesitate to criticize the clergy for their crimes and abuses. Similarly in the
Avision-Christine and the *Lamentacion sur les maulx de la guerre civile* she
takes to task the divisive regents (the king's brother and uncles) for their
misrule during the periods of Charles' dementia. All of this literature—polemical and didactic, feverish and violent while filled at the same time with
high moral and patriotic spirit—all of it was provoked by and responds to the
same situation: the crumbling political hierarchy in the period from roughly
1400 to 1435. Few of these works are literary masterpieces, although Alain
Chartier's *Quadriloque invectif* is often ranked in that category; the majority
however are obscure indeed. And yet it is in the most obscure that are, at
times, to be found the most vivid and *significant* indications of how grave the
crisis really was. One example will suffice, and with this I shall conclude.

The obscure work in question is the anonymous *Complainte du povre commun
ou des povres laboureurs de France*, which dates from between 1410 and 1420.[27]
The author addresses himself to the king, prelates, princes, lawyers, bourgeois, merchants, soldiers—in short, he says, "to all those who live off of
us, the working class." He recounts the poverty and misery of the peasants and
their exploitation by the rich landowners. Then—and this is truly remarkable—he disputes the validity of the hierarchical social organization itself,
saying that it is based on force, and goes against reason. Having enumerated
what he considers to be the crimes of the rich against the poor, he antici-
pates his adversaries' response and points out that their extortions are impossible to justify by saying simply, "This is our established right." "By
reason," he replies, "could that scarcely be justified .... And how dare you

say and think such things as you tell us? That our poverty and suffering are punishments for our sins, and that you have nothing to do with it!" Finally, he resorts to open threats of violence, warning that "one of these days, if you do not take care, you may well see with your own eyes your property burned to the ground!" And he does not stop here; he goes on to threaten the king himself: "Now," he says, "*think* about this! You wouldn't be the first who, by failing to rule according to reason, mercy and justice, would have found himself chased into exile." P. S. Lewis, an historian of the political literature of the Hundred Years War, notes that such threats were not uncommon during this most difficult period in the French monarchy, and that in 1440, the Bishop of Beauvais, Jean Juvénal des Ursins, "threatened the king with the sedition of the lower orders if conditions were not improved for them."[28]

And so it went: one pope in jail, four popes deposed; in the royal family two princes of the blood assassinated each by the partisans of the other (Louis d'Orléans, 1407; Jean sans peur of Burgundy, 1419); in the countryside, peasant rebellions (*Jacquerie* in the North, 1358; *Tuchinat* in the South, 1360); in Paris, bourgeois revolt (Etienne Marcel, 1358) and popular insurrection (the Cabochian uprising, 1413); and everywhere civil war from 1407 to 1435;[29] the king of France incapacited by insanity, his regents corrupt and divisive, his successor threatened with sedition. Clearly the principle of hierarchy in the Church and in the monarchy in France in the first half of the 15th century was in trouble, and the great chains of command would not be reforged with their former solidity until the resurgence of papal supremacy after mid-century, and the ascension of the great architect of French unification and recovery in the later 15th century, Louis XI.

NOTES

[1]The inadequacy of the "Great Age of Faith" tag has long been recognized, while the formulation of a more nuanced and accurate redefinition of the Renaissance is still going on among historians of ideas—among historians of historiography in particular. For the hisory of the idea of Renaissance, and especially the French Renaissance, see Franco Simone, *Il Rinascimento francese* (Turin: Società Editrice Internazionale, 1961, 1965).

[2]For the Schism, see Noël Valois, *La France et le Grand Schisme d'Occident*, '4 vols. (Paris, 1896-1902; repr. Georg Olms, Hildesheim, 1967). For the origins, early developments and evolution of the theological and juridic principles of Conciliarism: Brian Tierney, *Foundations of the Conciliar Theory* (Cambridge U.P., 1955, 1958). For the specifically political aspects of the Conciliar Movement (esp. Basel)—the popularizing or 'democratizing' principles and analogies it provided for theoreticians of secular monarchy, the horror it inspired among papal and royal absolutists, who saw in Conciliarism the utter negation of monarchy (= Hierarchy = Order)—see Antony Black, *Monarchy and Community: Political Ideas in the Later Conciliar Controversy, 1430-1450* (Cambridge U.P., 1970).

[3]Black refers to F. Oakley's study of "direct influences of Conciliarism on sixteenth- and seventeenth-century thinkers" (Black, p. 8); points out, for the 18th c., if not the direct influence of John of Segovia on Locke and Rousseau, nevertheless some striking coincidences in their respective formulations of the principle of representation (texts pp. 27-28); and sees in John of Segovia

> the first thinker to formulate ... the concept of trust as the basis of society and governemnt .... In its monarchical form, it would turn up again in Thomas Eliot (1601), in Bodin and in Hegel .... While such ideas were to find new application in America, and to be developed more fully by Locke and Rousseau, their basic pattern [Segovia's formulation] would change little (pp. 51-52).

P. Ourliac touches on this point in concluding his study of what he calls the "Sociologie du Concile de Bale" (*Rev. d'hist. ecclésiastique*, LVI (1961), 32), in mentioning a few instances of "l'influence souvent insoupçonnée des idées et des pratiques bâloises dans la 'crise de le conscience européenne.'"

[4]This, indeed, is Black's thesis in *Monarchy and Community*. "What Marsiglio had already said of the small state, Conciliarism applied to a larger community; the notorious weakness of 'medieval' constitutionalism, namely the lack of *sanctions enforceable by a legal process, without recourse to arms*, seems to have been overcome [by the councils of Constance and Basel]" (p. 41, my emphasis). I emphasize the council's power of deposition, for this in fact (and it is always the fact of power and not theory which prevails), was responsible for the success of the conciliar episode in the history of the Church. A pope simply could not send an army against a general council, leaving questions of right and wrong to be decided afterwards, as do secular princes. The Church having been defined as the universal corporation of the faithful, the pope was defined as its chief administrator; the council legislates, the pope executes. "In this, as in other things," concludes Black, Basle seems to have been the first to have applied the model of the *universitas* to goverrment on a large scale; and in doing so, it drew implications which could have pointed the way for constitutionalism in the national or territorial state" (p. 44).

[5]"It was surely Conciliarism that mediated between the medieval and the modern conceptions of popular goverrment. For it took up the ideology of the commune and transplanted it onto the large scale. Though parliamentary movements had similar aspirations, these were hardly, at least

until the English Revolution, so explicitly worked out in theory or in practice. In the short term, Conciliarism established within the church--for two decades--first the practice of constitutionalism, involving the full accountability of the ruler, and secondly the theory of popular sovereignty. In the long term, it anticipated, whatever its actual influence, the aspirations of later parliamentarianism, which followed a similar pattern, with the theory of democracy supporting constitutionalism in practice (Black, p. 134)."

[6]Socio-literary historical summaries of the *estats du monde* tradition in N. Regalado, *Poetic Patterns in Rutebeuf* (New Haven: Yale U. P., 1970), ch. 1-3 (esp. pp. 20-28) and in A. Serper, *Rutebeuf: poète Satirique* (Paris: Klincksieck, 1969), ch. 1, "Le Courant satirique et moral avant 1250." Texts (selections and analytical summaries) in Ch.-V. Langlois, *La Vie en France au moyen âge d'après des moralistes du temps* (Paris, 1926; repr. Slatkine, 1970).

[7]The critical edition of the *Oeuvres complètes d'Eustache Deschamps* runs to 10 vols. (eds. Q. de Saint-Hilaire and Gaston Raynaud, Paris, 1878-1903). All references are to this edition. Deschamps spent most of his life at the French court, in the service of Charles V (d. 1380), and of his two sons, Charles VI and Louis d'Orléans. The Duke of Burgandy, Philippe le Hardi, was also among his patrons. He was thus in a position to be closely acquainted not only with the entire cast of characters, but also with the political (and other) intrigues of the royal family. Not only a well-informed observer of the political events of his time, Deschamps was also a most outspoken one, as G. Raynaud notes:

> A chaque événement de sa vie, à chaque acte politique ou privé auquel il
> assiste, le poète, soit guidé par une raison personelle, soit obéissant
> au désir plus noble de s'ériger en moraliste désintéressé, ne ménage les
> dures vérités, ni aux grands personnages, ni aux corps constitués les
> plus puissants (XI, 288).

For Deschamps' political writings, see A. Dickmann, *E.D. als Schilderer der Sitten seiner Zeit* (Bochum-Langendreer, 1935).

[8]E.g., the *Lay des douze estas du monde* (II, 226-35) and the *Dictié* on the same subject (VIII, 142-45).

[9]Contre les prelas d'au jour d'uy qui sont trop curiaux et mondains sanz servir Dieu et l'Eglise," "Comment les sains prelas du temps passé n'aquistrent pas paradis par faire ainsi que les prelas de maintenant," and "Comment les prelas d'au jour d'ui en leur vie desordonnee veulent estre appellez tressains" (ch. 48-50; IX, 154-74).

[10]V, 165-67; VI, 281, 282; X, iv, v, vi.

[11]M. Creighton, *A History of the Papacy from the Great Schism to the Sack of Rome* (London, 1897; repr. AMS Press, 1969), I, 230. The text in question is preserved in the *Amplissima Collectio* of Martène and Durand (references in Creighton, loc. cit.).

[12]This of course is precisely what was to happen from 1409-1417 at the council of Pisa and Constance. But Deschamps died in 1406, three years before the council of Pisa began, and his poems proposing a conciliar solution to the Schism date from the 1390's. He was thus one of the first secular writers in France to urge appeal to the council as the only viable solution to the anarchy in the Church.

[13]*Le Livre des fais et bonnes meurs du sage roy Charles V*, ed. S. Solente (Paris, 1936-40), II, 155-56. Mme. Solente has taken the trouble to indicate in her critical edi-

tions of Christine's *Livre des fais* (I, 155n5) and *Livre de la mutacion de Fortune* (Paris, 1959; II, 333-34) all the passages in Christine's writings where she alludes to the Schism.

[14]*Livre des fais*, ch. LXI and LXII. For a more nuanced and objective view (Christine was less a biographer than an apologist for Charles V), see N. Valois, "Le Rôle de Charles V au début du Grand Schisme," *Annuaire-Bulletin de la Soc. de l'Hist. de France*, XXIV (1887), 225-55) (repr. and further developed in Valois' *La France et le Grand Schisme* [supra n. 1], I, 2 and 6).

[15]Valois, *La France et le Grand Schisme* I, 68-69; II, 113-18.

[16]*Tractatus de unitate ecclesiastica* (1409) in *Joannis Gersonii opera omnia*, ed. L. E. DuPin (Antwerp. 1706), II, 114d. The treatise is repr. in the new ed. of Father P. Glorieux, *Oeuv. compl. de Jean Gerson* (Paris, 1960-), VI, 272ff.

[17]But as early (at least) as the council of Vienne (1311) one finds the formula calling for a reform of the Church *in capite et in membris*.

[18]Black, p. 22

[19]*Ibid.*, p. 88.

[20]Quoted by Black, p. 93.

[21]When Eugene accused the Council of subverting authority, the Council replied that it was Eugene who was subverting authority; when Eugene specified that the Council was subverting monarchical authority in both Church and State, the Council replied that Church and State could not logically be compared in their organization, since the "universal church, legitimately assembled in the name of Christ" (the formulaic preamble with which all decrees, communiqués and official documents of the Council of Basle begin) had special divine authority given by revelation and was not to be compared to a secular association which had no such authority. As it turned out, Eugene was in fact deposed by the council of Basle in 1439.

[22]Gregory XII (Pisa, 1409); Benedict XIII (Pisa, 1409 and again, definitively, at Constance, 1415); Eugene IV (Basel, 1439).

[23]E.g., two anon. poems from 1381 by a Parisian cleric in favor of Urban VI and a conciliar solution to the Schism (an *Apologia super generali consilio* and a *Lamentatio ecclesiae*, I, 377-94); and two rejoinders: a "Poème en quatrains sur le Grand Schisme," also by an Urbanist, also in favor of a council (ed. P. Meyer and N. Valois in *Romania*, XXIV (1895), 197-218), and a "Poème de circonstance composé par un clerc de l'Université de Paris," by a supporter of Clement, and opposed to a council (ed. Valois in *Annuaire-Bulletin de la Soc. de l'Hist. de France*, XXI (1894), 211-38; the *Complainte de l'Eglise* (c. 1394) by Jean Petit, inventory of the evils of the Schism and an appeal to the secular powers to bring about its resolution (II, 408-410); the *Somnium super materia scismatis* (1394) of Honoré Bonet, addressed to Charles VI and urging him to take diplomatic measures in seeking an end to the Schism (II, 418-19).

[24]See Dickmann (op. cit. supra, n. 7). For contemporary accounts of the ravages of the Hundred Years War in France, P. Denifle, *La Désolation des églises, monastères et hôpitaux en France pendant la guerre de Cent Ans*, 2 vols. (Paris, 1897-99), and R. Boutruche, "The Devastation of Rural Areas during the Hundred Years War and the Agricultural Recovery of France," in P. S. Lewis ed., *The Recovery of France in the Fifteenth Century* (Lon-

don, 1971). Boutruche surveys the devastation and depopulation of France in the 14th and 15th cc. acording to contemporary accounts, from Petrarch (1360) to Thomas Basin (1461) and J. Fortescue (1465).

[25]E. g., in Eustache Deschamps, *La dolente et piteuse complainte de l'Eglise moult desolée au jour d'ui* (VII, 293-311) where one sees

> La povre mere tresdolente, desolee et desconfortee, de laquelle les en-
> trailles sont tranchees et divisees en deux parties pour le pechié et
> abhominacion de ses enfans forlignans de la voye de justice, meurs et
> condicions de leur Pere pardurable (p. 293);

in *L'Avision-Christine* of Christine de Pisan (1405-1406, ed. Sister Mary Louise Towner, Washington: Catholic U. P., 1932) where an allegorical France "se plaint de ses enfants":

> Quelle plus grant perplexité puet venir ou cuer de mere que veoir yre et
> contens naistre et continuer jusques au point d'armes de guerre prendre
> et saisir par assemblees entre ses propres enfans legittimes et de loy-
> aulx peres, et a tant monter leur felonnie qu'ilz n'ayent regart a la
> desolacion de leur pouvere mere, qui, comme piteuse de sa porteure, se
> fiche entre .ii. pour departir leurs batailles? etc. (pp. 85-86);

and, finally, in an anon. political morality play from 1434 written by a French conciliarist (*Le Concil de Basle*, ed. Jonathan Beck, Turin: Giapichelli, in press) wherein another allegorical "Eglise" and an allegorical France attribute in mournful monologues their respective woes, due to the Schism and the Hundred Years War, to their "children" (vv. 502-503; 513-19).

[26]First, in a poem by Deschamps "Sur la division de l'Eglise":

> Saincte Eglise qui moult se puet doloir Quant .ii. espoux l'ont si
> violemment Prinse, et un seul la deust sainctement, Ou nom de Dieu,
> gouverner comme amie ... (V, 231);

Then again in Deschamps' prose *Complainte de l'Eglise*:

> Moy, povre Eglise, presentement desolee, suis envahie de deux soy disans
> mes espoux, qui par force et violence veulent mon unité couvoiteusement
> tranchier en deux et efforcer ma voulenté par le default de vous, mes
> enfans [cf. n. 24 supra] et ministres, qui deussiez garder et deffendre
> vostre povre mere (VII, 304);

and still again in Deschamps:

> Et que la trancheure du cisme qui si detestablement m'a voulu et veult
> faire adultere, cesse du tout, me face et rende la verité, vraie mere de
> la foy catholique, si que ne soye adultere clamee et que mon voile ainsi
> trenchié et divisié ne puist engendrer a aucune heresie ou crime de foy
> par les voulentez tenans a chascune des deux parties, moy voulans occup-
> er, prandre et ravir en maniere de proye (VII, 307).

Christine de Pisan uses the same image in the *Avision-Christine*; this time it is France, not the Church, who is speaking:

... Car pour moy ravir et embler, s'assembloient diverses provinces et
gens estranges qui a grant ost dessolerent ma terre, bruslerent mes vil-
les et mes manoirs, faisoient de mes gens grand essart, et toute me pil-
loient! Et en tres grant quantité de foiz pareillement ay esté en peril
d'estre perdue, ravie, prise a force et du tout deshonnouree ... (p. 81).

The frequency with which this allegory of the brutal invasion and violation of the homeland (and
of the Church) appears in the literature of the Schism and the Hundred Years War may be more
readily understood when one considers that it is after all, a reflection of contemporary reality,
as described e.g. by the Bishop of Beauvais, Jean Juvénal des Ursins, in his account of rape and
plunder in his bishopric by English and French troops:

Et ne prennent pas seulement hommes, mais femmes et filles, et les em-
prisonnent et aucunesfois en font par force leur plaisir en la presence
des maris, peres ou freres ... etc. (in Denifle, I, 498-99).

[27]Ed. L. Douët-D'Arcq in the *Chronique d'Enguerran de Monstrelet* (Paris, 1857-62),
VI, 176-90. The work, not by Monstrelet, was inserted in the first printed ed. of his *Chronique*
by the 16th c. printer Antoine Vérard.

[28]"Jean Juvénal des Ursins and the Common Literary Attitude Toward Tyranny in Fifteenth-Century France," *Medium Aevum*, XXXIV (1965), 110-11.

[29]1407 is the date of the assassination of the king's son, Louis d'Orléans, by the Burgundians. 1435 is the date of the Treaty of Arras, concluded between Charles VII and the Duke of Burgundy, Philippe le Bon. This treaty (brought about, incidentally, by one of the peace-making em-
bassies sent to France by the council of Basle [see Beck, *Le Concil de Basle*, ed. cit. supra.
n. 24, pp. 4-5]), by which Burgundy renounced his alliance with the English and made amends with
the king of France, marks the end of the civil war and the beginning of the end of the Hundred
Years War. Paris was recaptured from the English in the following year, and although the definitive expulsion of the English (from Guyenne) was not achieved until 1453, the tide had turned,
unity had been restored, and the remainder of the war consisted merely in "mopping up."

III.

MYSTICAL HIERARCHY: JEWISH AND CHRISTIAN

DAVID R. BLUMENTHAL

LOVEJOY'S *GREAT CHAIN OF BEING* AND THE MEDIEVAL JEWISH TRADITION

Within the circle of Jewish symbolism, the fortieth anniversary is a most fitting time for crystallizing major insights because, according to tradition, Noah left the Ark after forty days, Moses returned from God after forty days, the poeple left the desert after forty years, and the seed of the Messianic dynasty was sown after King David's forty-year rule over Jerusalem. I do not think that Professor Lovejoy (or Professor James in whose honor the lectures originated) intended *The Great Chain of Being*, or its fortieth anniversary echo, to have eschatological import. Yet the impact of the book and the evaluation of it now in process have certainly been turning points in the intellectual history of the twentieth century. And it is fitting that so many should gather to honor and to appraise this work at this symbolic juncture of its existence. In this essay, I shall recapitulate Lovejoy's main theses, illustrate them from the Judaic tradition, and suggest a critical retrospective view of Lovejoy's undertaking from the point of view of that tradition.

RECAPITULATION

Lovejoy, in his attempt to articulate what he called "the primary and persistent or recurrent dynamic unit" of the thought and the culture of an era (p. 7),[1] set forth two main principles according to which the Western concept of the world could be organized. The first was the principle of the continuous, hierarchical *plenum*. This was well summarized as follows (p. 59):

> The result was the conception of the plan and structure of the world which, through the Middle Ages and down to the late eighteenth century, many philosophers, most men of science, and, indeed, most educated men, were to accept without question—the conception of the universe as a "Great Chain of Being," composed of an immense, or—by the strict but seldom rigorously applied logic of the principle of continuity—of an infinite, number of links ranging in hierarchical order from the meagerest kind of existents, which barely escape nonexistence, through "every possible" grade up to the *ens perfectissimum*—or, in a somewhat more orthodox version, to the highest possible kind of creature, between which and the Absolute Being the disparity was assumed to be infinite—every one of them differing from that immediately above and that

immediately below it by the "least possible" degree of
difference.

The second main principle set forth by Lovejoy was the principle of the
dialectic tension between the self-sufficient good and the self-extending
good, the latter being called "goodness." This, too, was well summarized as
follows (p. 49):

> The concept of Self-Sufficing Perfection, by a bold logi-
> cal inversion, was--without losing any of its original
> implications--converted into the concept of a Self-Trans-
> cending Fecundity. A timeless and incorporeal One became
> the logical ground as well as the dynamic source of the
> existence of a temporal and material and extremely multi-
> ple and variegated universe.

This second principle, the principle of dialectic tension, had a very important corollary which Lovejoy also clearly articulated: namely, that, in the
context of the divine, there is a certain theological dualism and that, given
this dualism, a self-sufficient God requires a different kind of piety than a
self-extending God. This, too, was lucidly summarized as follows (pp. 315-6):[2]

> The two were, indeed, identified as one being with two
> aspects. But the ideas corresponding to the 'aspects'
> were ideas of two antithetic kinds of being. The one was
> the Absolute of otherworldliness-self-sufficient, out of
> time, alien to the categories of ordinary human thought
> and experience, needing no world of lesser beings to sup-
> plement or enhance his own eternal self-contained perfec-
> tion. The other was a God who emphatically was not self-
> sufficient nor, in any philosophical sense, 'absolute':
> one whose essential nature required the existence of oth-
> er beings, and not of one kind of these only, but of all
> kinds which could find a place in the descending scale of
> the possibilities of reality--a God whose prime attribute
> was generativeness, whose manifestation was to be found
> in the diversity of creatures and therefore in the tempo-
> ral order and the manifold spectacle of nature's proces-
> ses ....
>   With this theological dualism--since the idea of God
> was taken to be also the definition of the highest good--
> there ran, as we have likewise seen, a dualism of values,
> the one otherworldly (though often in a half-hearted
> way), the other this-worldly. If the good for man was the
> contemplation or the imitation of God, this required, on
> the one hand, a transcendence and suppression of the
> merely 'natural' interests and desires, a withdrawal of
> the soul from 'the world' the better to prepare it for
> the beatific vision of the divine perfection; and it re-
> quired, on the other hand, a piety towards the God of
> things as they are, an adoring delight in the sensible
> universe in all its variety, an endeavor on man's part to

know and understand it ever more fully, and a conscious
participation in the divine activity of creation.

ILLUSTRATION FROM THE JUDAIC TRADITION

A study of the Judaic materials for the Talmudic and Medieval periods--
i.e., for that continuous culture called "Rabbinic Judaism"[3]--confirms Lovejoy's hypothesis that these two principles and the corollary, were "primary
and persistent or recurrent dynamic units" of thought (p. 7).

The principle of the continuous, hierachical *plenum*--the Great Chain of
Being--unfolded first in the Talmudic period.[4] In this literature, God was
conceived as a King, seated in His Throne room, hidden behind the protective
screen of the wings of His chief archangels. Between this divine realm and the
mundane world of the rabbi-mystic was the *plenum* which was filled with the
seven heavenly palaces, each of which had guards. These guards were the lowest
form of heavenly being, and they were outranked by the higher angels, the
heavenly "Beasts and Wheels," the archangels, and by the Divine Names. These
Names, when inscribed on seals and shown to the guards, neutralized the power
of even the most ferocious guards, thus asuring the rabbi-mystic safe passage
through the *plenum*. The following brief citation from the "Chapters on the Ascent" illustrates dramatically the hierachical, continuous nature of this *plenum* and its powers:[5]

> Ishmsel said: When you come and stand at the gate of the
> first palace, take two seals, one in each hand--[the
> seals] of Tootrusea-YHVH, Lord of Israel, and of Surya,
> the Angel of the Presence. Show the seal of Tootrusea-
> YHVH, Lord of Israel, to those who stand on the right and
> [the seal] of Surya to those on the left. Then, Bahbiel--
> the angel who is in charge of the gate of the first pal-
> ace, is appointed over the palace [itself], and who
> stands on the right--and Tofhiel--the angel who stands to
> the left of the threshold--grab you [the initiate], give
> you peace and send you forth with radiance to Tagriel,
> the angel who is in charge of the gate of the second pal-
> ace and who stands to the right of its threshold and to
> Metpiel who stands with him to the left of its threshold.
> Show them, then, two seals--one of Adriharon-YHVH,
> Lord of Israel, and one to Ouzia, the Angel of the Pre-
> sence. Show the one of Adriharon to the [guards] standing
> on the right and the one of Ouzia, the Angel of the Pre-
> sence, show to those [guards] standing on on the left.
> Immediately, they grab you--one on your right and one on
> your left--as they accompany you, hand you over, give you
> peace and send you forth with radiance to Shevooriel, the
> angel who is in charge of the gate to the third palace

> and who stands on its right threshold and Retzutziel, the
> angel who stands with him on its left threshold.

This conception of the *plenum* had, and still has, a definite allure and attraction. It generates what Lovejoy called (p. 11) "the pathos of the esoteric" and even the modern reader has a sense of being seduced by a world of powers beyond his own. As Lovejoy commented somewhat sarcastically (p. 11), "How exciting and how welcome is the sense of initiation into hidden mysteries!" This world-view, however, modeled as it was on the pattern of a royal court with its careful pecking order of courtiers, had no systematic philosophic or metaphysical roots. It was not a closely-knit ontological chain of being. It was not even a hierarchy, except in the political sense of the word. And, in the course of time, it passed from the stage of history and was supplanted by a new and more elegant conception of the Great Chain of Being.

The principle of the continuous, hierarchical *plenum* unfolded for the second time in the realm of medieval Jewish philosophy. There it found its most authoritative expression in Maimonides who envisioned the Great Chain of Being as two parallel chains--a spiritual one and a material one.[6] The spiritual continuum was composed of the Ten Intelligences, the intellect of man, and the soul, i.e., the principle of movement and existence in each lower being, while the material continuum was composed of the nine supernal spheres, the four elements, and the sublunar bodies compounded of those elements. Along the spiritual chain flowed the divine emanation which was, at once, ontological and intellectualist. Being ontologically fructifying, it conveyed existence, as a predicate, to all spiritual and material beings and, being intellectualist in quality, it provided the means of communication between God and man. Insofar as the direction of this flow was from God to man, Maimonides called it revelation, prophecy, and providence. Insofar as the direction of the communication was from man to God, Maimonides called it study and prayer, i.e., man's communication formed itself into a pattern of illuminationist piety.[7] The following brief citations, from the *Guide of the Perplexed* illustrate clearly the double hierarchy and its application to the concept of Providence:[8]

> ... it follows necessarily that the deity, may He be ex
> alted, has brought into existence the first Intelligence,
> who is the mover of the first sphere in the way that we
> have explained. Again the Intelligence that causes the
> second sphere to move has as its cause and principle the
> first Intelligence, and so on, so that the Intelligence

that causes the sphere that is contiguous with us to move
is the cause and principle of the Active Intellect. With
the latter the separate Intelligences come to an end,
just as bodies begin similarly with the highest sphere
and come to an end with the elements and what is composed
of them ....

The Providence of God, may He be exalted, is constantly watching over those who have obtained this emanation,
which is permitted to everyone who makes efforts with a
view to obtaining it. If a man's thought is free from
distraction, if he apprehends Him, may He be exalted, in
the right way and rejoices in what he apprehends that individual can never be afflicted with evil of any kind.
For he is with God and God is with him. When however, he
abandons Him, may He be exalted, and is thus separated
from God and God separated from him, he becomes in consequence of this a target for every evil that may happen
to befall him. For the thing that necessarily brings
about providence and deliverance from the sea of chance
consists in that intellectual emanation.

This second conception of the *plenum* was far more elegant than the first-
-so much so that Maimonides, in an act of considerable courage, declared the
Talmudic *plenum* to be only a metaphor in need of philosophic esoteric reinter-
pretation which he, then, supplied.[9] The new world-view provided a better hierarchical and more continuous *plenum*. It allowed for an even flow of being
through the supernal and sublunar realms. And, because of its intellectualist
quality, the new *plenum* could account for a very broad range of religious phenomena, including several distinct types of intellectualist mysticism.[10] However, the medieval Jewish philosophic conception of the Great Chain of Being
removed God, the source of the Chain, to the outermost recesses of the human
effort to understand Him. Philosophy clothed God in negative attributes and
wrapped around Him the mantle of hypostatic emanations and supernal spheres.
Where was He Himself? How could one reach out and engage Him, not just touch
or "taste" Him mystically? Where was the personal aspect of God? These were
the questions men began to ask. And, in the course of time, the philosophic
world-view, too, passed from the stage of history and it was supplanted by a
new, more *engagé* conception of the Great Chain of Being.

The principle of the continuous, hierarchical *plenum* unfolded, then, for
the third time in the realm of medieval Jewish theosophy. There it found its
most authoritative expression in the *Zohar*.[11] In this conception of the Great
Chain of Being, Jewish thought tried to account for the links within the personhood of God, that is an attempt was made to account for the primal unfold-

ing of the divine within the divine—an unfolding which preceded the development of extradeical reality. In accomplishing this, the *Zohar* presupposed an
unknowable, ineffable core within the Divine. From this core, there flowed
forth aspects of God such as His Wisdom, His Understanding, His Grace, His
Power, His Transcendent Beauty, His Majesty, and so on. These aspects are called *Sefirot* and all of them were understood to be intradeical. Only when these
Sefirot had completed their unfolding, did the rest of reality begin to come
into being. This latter extradeical reality was according to the *Zohar*, composed of angels on the pattern of the rabbinic conception and, then, of the
lower, masterial beings of this world.

It was almost inevitable in the milieu of the Middle Ages that someone
would try to harmonize these three Chains of Being: the Talmudic Chain of angels, the philosophic Chain of Intelligences, and the Zoharic Chain of Sefirot, thereby complexifying the whole *plenum* one more degree. And so it happened. Judah al-Botini, a refugee from the Portuguese Inquisition, deftly Maimonides' Intelligences between the Zoharic Sefirot and the Talmudic angels thus
expanding and rendering more complete the Great Chain of Being:[12]

> Indeed, our holy rabbis, peace be upon them, the proph-
> ets, the sons of the prophets, the Tana'im, and the
> 'Amora'im, who had in their hands the true Tradition from
> Moses, our Rabbi, peace be upon him, together with the
> wise men of the Kabbala of recent generations and even
> the ancient wise men of research of the nations [of the
> world] who inclined toward the wisdom of the Sages of
> Israel in [these] matters—all agree that the worlds
> which encompass all created beings are three [in number]:
> the world of the separated Intelligences with its ten
> steps and hosts; second, the world of the spheres with
> its ten heavens, the stars, the constellations, and their
> hosts; [and] third, the world of the lower beings with
> its four elements; inanimate, vegetable, living, and hu-
> man beings and their progeny. And the Master of all rules
> over all of them as David, King of Israel, peace be upon
> him, said, ... But, all those whose wisdom has been ex-
> alted [and who have] seen the luminescent and the non-
> luminescent glass agree that, between the Cause of the
> causes, may His Name be praised, and the world of the se-
> parated Intelligences, there is an intelligent, spiritu-
> al, simple existent being [which is] subtler than the
> subtlest, very much exalted above the world of the sepa-
> rated Intelligences as light is exalted above darkness.
> This intelligent existent being was emanated from the *Ein
> Sof* (the Infinite), may He be praised, from the depths of
> the hiddenness of the Tetragrammaton, and they called
> this intelligent, spiritual being "the world of the Ema-

nation" .... And the wise men of the Kabbala, the author
of *Sefer Yesira* which is ascribed to Abraham, our father,
peace be upon him, at their head, have agreed that this
intelligent existent being is the ten holy, spiritual
steps from which the levels of the angels and the separated Intelligences are emanated and the kabbalists (*ha-
mekubbālīm*) call these ten holy steps "the ten *sefirot*"
... indicating that they are ten [in number], holy, "se-
firotic," pure, luminescent, and the subtlest of the subtle; [that] their radiance, "sefirocity," subtlety, and
intelligence is greater than [that of] the "Holy Beasts"
which are the highest of the ten ranks of the angels;
[and that] they are inmeasurably above [these] Holy
Beasts."

As Lovejoy points out, however, the Great Chain always contains room for
one more sub-division, and just such a thing occurred in sixteenth Safed, producing the fourth unfolding of the principle of the continuous, hierarchical
plenum within Jewish tradition. In Safed, Rabbi Isaac Luria[13] expanded the Zoharic view of the *plenum* and taught that, in the beginning, there was God--on-
ly God--and He occupied all space. He, then, contracted part of His being--
created a hole within Himself as it were--and, into this empty space, He
caused His aspects, the Sefirot, to penetrate. In the process of acquiring
form, these Sefirot shattered, generating fragmented primal matter on the one
hand and loose sparks of the divine on the other. Slowly, a second intradeical
plenum evolved and, even more slowly it generated an extradeical *plenum* of angels. Luria also taught, however, that the universe thus produced was only the
highest of the universes and that, actually, there were four such universes.
Only at the last stage of the fourth universe, the physical world, as we know
it, came into being.

The logic of the continuity of the Great Chain as well as the logic of
harmonization led once more to an expansion, this time of the Lurianic view
such that it would include the philosophic Intelligences.[14] This last expansion yielded a Great Chain of Being that: began, intradeically, with the space
generated by the contraction of the divine; proceeded to the generation of the
Sefirot; then proceeded to the generation of the extradeical, yet supernal,
four universes comprising Intelligences and angels; and finally, proceeded to
the generation of physical reality as we know it. With this, the principle of
the continuous, hierarchical *plenum* reached its fullest expression. With this,
the complexification of the Great Chain of Being within Jewish tradition
reached its ultimate.

Before proceeding to comment upon Lovejoy's second principle and its corollary, it is instructive to note that Lovejoy, himself, characterized the entire attempt to articulate a Great Chain of Being as "the history of a failure" (p. 329). His grounds for this were, in summary briefly: that this world
of time and change is not logically reducible to a world of atemporality and
immutability; that in any case a qualitative continuum is a contradiction; and
that the laws of nature as we know them seem to have an idiosyncratic quality
to them. In all of these objections, he was anticipated by Maimonides who,
Lovejoy to the contrary notwithstanding, used them to indicate the reasonable-
ness of *creatio ex nihilo*.[15]

The second principle of Lovejoy--the principle of the dialectic tension
between the self-sufficient good and the self-extending good--needs no special
illustration. Every page of medieval Judaism is replete with the tension of
that dialectic. Similarly, the corollary of the second principle--that the
self-sufficient God requires a different type of piety than the self-extending
God--requires no special illustration, for the conflicting models of piety--
the mildly ascetic, socially withdrawn model and the rabbinic, activist model-
-are also visible everywhere in medieval Jewish pietism.

One fascinating footnote should, however, be added to Lovejoy. In articulating this corollary of the different types of piety, Lovejoy wrote (p. 84):

> The one program demanded a withdrawal from all "attach-
> ment to creatures" and culminated in the ecstatic con-
> templation of the indivisible Divine Essence; the other,
> if it had been formulated, would have summoned men to
> participate, in some finite measure, in the creative pas-
> sion of God, to collaborate consciously in the processes
> by which the diversity of things, the fullness of the
> universe, is achieved. It would have found the beatific
> vision in the disinterested joy of beholding the splendor
> of the creation or of curiously tracing out the detail of
> its infinite variety; it would have placed the active
> life above the contemplative; and it would, perhaps, have
> conceived of the activity of the creative artist, who at
> once loves, imitates, and augments the "orderly various-
> ness" of the sensible world, as the mode of human life
> most like the divine.

Now, approximately this type of piety did develop in the *Zohar*[16] and in
later Jewish mysticism for, according to those systems of thought, the divine
energy (or light) was radiated along the Great Chain but, when it reached man,
it was reflected, it was turned around. The energy, then, returned along the
Chain, all the way back into God, i.e., into the intradeical realm of the Sef-

irot. There, if the reflection had been directed by good deeds and proper meditation, it stimulated the unification of the divine with itself. This unification, in turn, produced a yet more intense flow of energy downward which was
the creative blessing. Man, thus, did, as Lovejoy would have had it, "participate, in some finite measure, in the creative passion of God." He did "collab-
orate consciously in the process by which the diversity of things, the fullness of the universe, is achieved." Furthermore, consistent with the logic of
this corollary the *Zohar* taught that, if the reflection of the divine energy
had been misdirected by evil deeds and improper meditation, disorder was generated along the whole Chain of Being, intradeically and extradeically.

CRITICAL RETROSPECT

Lovejoy's *Great Chain of Being* is a significant contribution to the history of ideas. His principles organize a vast body of data spread over vast
periods of time in very different religious traditions. However, in reflecting
upon the Judaic materials, it seems to me that Lovejoy failed to articulate
two other main principles which also organize the data clearly.

The first major principle overlooked by Lovejoy, perhaps because he
started with the Greek philosophic tradition, is the principle of the dialectic tension between God's transcendence and His accessibility. This dialectic
is central, indeed definitive, to all Biblical and post-Biblical religious
tradition. One could even say that the basic mystery of Western religion lies
in this tension between God's complete otherness on the one hand and His read-
iness to communicate (prophecy and revelation) and be communicated with (prayer and piety) on the other hand. Indeed, one could write a history of ideas
tracing this dialectic tension, showing how the expression of God's transcendence and accessibility varied from one cultural context to another. This
principle seems to have eluded Lovejoy.

The second major principle overlooked by Lovejoy, again perhaps because
he approached the data from the point of view of philosophy, is the principle
of a harmonizing exegesis. This principle, far more than the philosophic principle of critical analysis, motivated and continues to motivate almost everyone who writes within a religious tradition.[17] Indeed, one could write a history of ideas tracing the harmonization process and showing how the process
remained the same while the material to be integrated varied from one cultural
context to another. This, too seems to have eluded Lovejoy.

These reservations notwithstanding, *The Great Chain of Being* has been, and will continue to be, an important conceptualization of what he called "one of the most grandiose enterprises of the human intellect" (p. 329).

NOTES

[1]This paper was originally presented at the meeting of the International Conference of Medieval Studies at Kalamazoo, on the fortieth anniversary of *The Great Chain of Being*, 1936-1976. The symbolism of forty as a number so significant in Jodark thought was preserved in this publication ten years later. All references to Lovejoy's *The Great Chain of Being* are taken from the first Harper Torchbook edition (1960) and are included in the text of the paper in parentheses.

[2]Cf. also the following (p. 82-3):

> But the God in whom man was thus to find his own fulfillment was, as has been pointed out, not one God but two. He was the Idea of the Good, but he was also the Idea of Goodness; and though the second attribute was nominally deduced dialectically from the first, no two notions could be more antithetic. The one was an apotheosis of unity, self-sufficiency, and quietude, the other of diversity, self transcendence, and fecundity .... The one God was the goal of the 'way up,' of that ascending process by which the finite soul, truning from all created things, took its way back to the immutable Perfection in which alone it could find rest. The other God was the source and the informing energy of that descending process by which being flows through all the levels of possibility down to the very lowest.

[3]On this, cf. J. Neusner, *Understanding Rabbinic Judaism* (New York: Ktav Publishing, 1974) 1-26.

[4]For the Merkabah literature, cf. G. Scholem, *Major Trends in Jewish Mysticism*, 3rd rev. ed. (New York: Schocken Press, 1941; reprinted many times); idem., *Jewish Gnosticism, Merkabah Mysticism*, and *Talmudic Tradition* (Jewish Theological Seminary, N. Y.: 1965); M. Smith, "Observations on *Hekhalot Rabbati*," in *Biblical and Other Studies*, ed. A. Altmann (Cambridge, Mass.: Harvard University, 1963) 142-60; and my forthcoming translation of, and commentary to, the Sefer Yesira and "The chapters on Ascent" of the *Pirqei Heikhalot* in *Understanding Jewish Mysticism* (New York: Ktav Publishing, 1978).

[5]From my translatin mentioned above.

[6]For the Maimonidean literature, cf. A. Hyman, "Maimonides," *Encyclopedia Judaica*, 2nd ed., 11: 768-77; J. Guttmann, *Philosophies of Judaism*, transl. D. Silverman (New York: Holt, Reinhart & Winston, 1964) 152-82; and, more directly, Maimonides' *Guide of the Perplexed*, I: 72; II: 4; etc.; and his *Mishne Torah*, "Hilkhot Yesodei ha-Torah."

[7]On this, cf. D. Blumenthal, "Maimonides' Intellectualist Mysticism and the Superiority of the Prophecy of Moses," *Studies in Medieval Culture*, vol. 10; and idem., "An Illustration of the Concept of 'Philosophic Mysticism' from Fifteenth Century Yemen," soon to be published.

[8]*Guide*, II: 4 and III: 51 respectively. I have modified slightly the translation of S. Pines (Chicago: University of Chicago, 1963) 258 and 265-6.

[9]Cf. above note 6 and *Guide*, "Introduction" and elsewhere where he redefines "Ma'aseh Bereshit" as physics and "Ma'aseh Merkabah" as metaphysics.

[10]In addition to the articles cited in note 7, cf. *Me'or ha-'Afeilah*, ed., Y. Qafih (Jerusalem: Mossad Harav Kook, 1955) passim and my translation of, and commentary to, Judah al-Botini's "Chapter on Ecstasy" in *Understanding Jewish Mysticism*.

[11]For the Zohar, cf. G. Scholem, *Major Trends*, ch. 6 and the forthcoming book by I. Tishby.

[12]Al-Botini's work is still not available in translation. Cf. the work of Joseph ibn Waqqar in G. Vajda, *Recherches sur la philosophie et la kabbale dans la pensée juive der moyen age* (Paris: Mouton, 1962) part two, for a parallel though slightly more complex system.

[13]On the Lurianic Kabbala, cf. Scholem, *Major Trends*, ch. 7 and idem., *On the Kabbalah and its Symbolism* (New York: Schocken, 1965).

[14]This is probably the point of view of Shneur Zalman in *Igereth Hakodesh*, ch. 20, English transl., J. Schochet (New York: Kehot, 1968) pp. 183ff., esp. no. 30).

[15]Cf. Maimonides' *Guide*, II: 22-24.

[16]Cf., above, n. 11. These matters are very complex and the interested reader must follow them further.

[17]Much of the work the late H. A. Wolfson was devoted to just this type of history of ideas.

RICHARD SCHNEIDER

MEISTER ECKHART'S REFLECTIONS ON
THE RELATION BETWEEN THE SUPERIOR AND THE INFERIOR

Neoplatonism as exemplified by Proclus, the author of the *Liber de causis*, and other writers had a great influence on Eckhart. He placed himself formally within the Neoplatonic tradition when he described creation as a "fall from the One". Creation is God's external word, outside of himself inasmuch as He is one; but within Himself, inasmuch as He is being. The Neoplatonic influence also comes to the fore in other notions. In his discussion of the relation between God and creatures, Eckhart compared God to an infinite intellectual sphere and to the soul in its relation to the body. He saw the relationship between God and creatures as a dynamic one, not merely in the way a cause is related dynamically to its effects, but he preferred to say that God, inasmuch as He is being, flows into things, penetrates them as a soul informs its body, and unifies their partition and division by his unity. Creatures participate in God's being and unity, and thus exist. Eckhart's inclination to think within the framework of the Neoplatonic tradition is also apparent in his interpretation of the notion of participation literally as grasping a part (*partem capere*),[1] not as receiving God's effect in the created perfection of the act of existing.[2]

These characteristics of Eckhart's metaphysics are closely related to his notion of being. He conceived and treated being like an essence. The starting point of his metaphysical considerations[3] was not this or that individual act of existing as it is grasped in judgment. Rather, Eckhart took the timeless and abstract notion, *esse commune*,[4] and identified it with God in the principle, Being is God (*esse est Deus*). As a consequence of this identification he emphasized that outside of being or outside of God there is nothing. There is, accordingly, only one being (*esse*) which makes essences exist. The transcendental perfections of unity, goodness and truth, which are convertible with being, are also identical with God. Because being is taken on the level of essence, it receives the unity and absolute indivisibility of an essence. Creatures, in order to exist and to be one, have to "take part of" God's being and unity. But since there is no "part" of an essence, Eckhart can maintain that, *qua* part, their being is not God; but *qua* being, their being is the whole God.[5]

It is accordingly within the Neoplatonic framework that Eckhart could stress both God's most intimate relationship to creatures and his transcendence to them. As the soul is totally within and outside of its body, so is God (inasmuch as he is identical with the transcendental perfections) within and outside of creatures. God is in things in His entirety insofar as they are one and being; but He is totally outside of, and thus distinct from them, inasmuch as they are multiple or divided into parts. God is like an infinite sphere whose center is everywhere, and whose circumference is nowhere.

These metaphysical interpretations of God's relationship to creatures push the notion of efficient causality into the background. This observation is further verified by Eckhart's interpretation of efficient causality as a making outside (*extra facere*).[6] He was more concerned with emphasizing that the creation of things is their being made "outside of" God as the one, in contrast to the formal welling-up (*ebullitio formalis*) of the Son and Spirit within the one. The effecting (*efficere*) of creation is a fall from unity rather than a giving or causing of a perfection. This shift in the meaning of efficient causality may have had its source in Eckhart's zeal to maintain that all transcendental perfection is on the part of God and that there is none on the part of creatures. In the preceding considerations numerous texts have been studied in which Eckhart did not leave room for any caused intermediate perfection of being between God and the essences of creatures. This question of the transcendental perfections of creatures will have to be studied more closely. Do creatures really have any transcendental perfection of being, unity, truth and goodness? The texts studied up to now gave a negative answer to this question. However, since Eckhart nevertheless spoke in other texts,[7] of an efficient causing of being and called God the cause of the being of creatures,[8] does he not contradict the texts analyzed above? Is there, then, still room for perfections on the part of creatures? In other words, is there, for Eckhart, an analogy of transcendental perfections in the Thomistic sense of analogy?

An analysis of those texts which refer to God as an essential cause and speak of his effects in creatures is therefore indicated. The notions of cause and effect flow from a metaphysical line of thought which tries to do full justice to the revealed notion of the creation of the world out of nothing. The most outstanding representative of this kind of metaphysical thinking is Thomas. As has been seen,[9] Eckhart acknowledged the greatness of the famous

teacher of his order. But it has also been noticed[10] that he gave the Thomistic terms a different meaning. When he said, in accordance with Thomas, that
being is the act of all things and even of forms, he meant something quite
different from Thomas. Being, according to Thomas, is created being (*esse
creatum*), whereas for Eckhart, it is God himself. God, insofar as he is identical with being, is the act of forms. The function which, in Thomas' metaphysics, is assigned to created being is here taken over by God himself. Thus
the relation between God and creatures becomes most intimately dynamic. God
penetrates creatures as a form informs matter; he flows into the essences of
things. Creatures immediately grasp a part of God's being. The relation is on
the level of formal participation, which, as the preceding discussion showed,
is mainly within the Neoplatonic framework.

It becomes important then to determine the role which the existential
philosophy of Thomas played in Eckhart's thought. If Eckhart had both the
cause-effect interpretation of God's relation to creatures as well as the formal participation interpretation, then one may ask whether he succeeded in
reconciling them. One may ask whether he was able to bring both the Neoplatonic and the Thomistic existential lines of thought into harmony, or whether he
emphasized the one over the other, or whether he re-interpreted the one in
terms of the other.

A discussion of those texts which indicated the Neoplatonic influence in
Eckhart's metaphysics, led to the peculiar discovery that, within the Neoplatonic framework of thinking, he did not distinguish between God and the transcendental perfections of creatures. Some attention will now be devoted to
those texts in which Eckhart presented God as the cause of the being of creatures. This subject will be introduced with an exposition of Eckhart's teaching on the relationship between the superior and the inferior, since he explicitly said that the cause is to its effect as the superior to its inferior.[11] God is superior to all created things, and, as such, is the highest
and foremost essential cause of all things.[12] God is related to all things as
a superior to its inferiors.[13] An analysis of the general characteristics of
the relationship between the superior and the inferiors, accordingly, are of
value in understanding Eckhart's notions of cause and effect as applied to the
relationship between God and creatures.

The notions of the superior and inferior have their roots in a Neoplatonic line of thought with a Pseudo-Dionysian coloring. Pseudo-Denis emphasized

194

RICHARD SCHNEIDER

that the universe is made up of a hierarchy of gradations in which the inferior touches with its highest part on the lowest part of its superior[14] and in
which all hierarchies participate to a different degree in the divine unity,
being, life and intelligence.[15]

In his comparison of the relation between cause and effect to the Pseudo-
Dionysian notions of the superior and the inferior, Eckhart revealed his
inclination to interpret the notions of cause and effect within this peculiar
Neoplatonic framework. That the notions of the superior and inferior and their
relations to one another play an important role in Eckhart's thought is indicated by the fact that in his *Opus propositionum* he devoted a special treatise
to these notions.[16] Unfortunately, this treatise is not extant[17] so that
Eckhart's doctrine on this must be reconstructed from the passages in his
writings which deal with the subject.

Looking at the superior and the inferior in themselves rather than at the
relation between them, Eckhart made the observation that the superior is always prior and perfect; while the inferiors as such are in need (*egena*), bare
(*nuda*), passive, unformed (*informia*), void (*inania*) and empty (*vacua*). The
inferiors are imperfect, and as such they are indigent. The inferior is perfected by the superior.[18] In his commentary on the *Gospel of John*[19] Eckhart
emphasized that the way superiors perfect inferiors depends on whether they
are analogically or univocally related. Superiors and inferiors are analogical
to one another when they have nothing in common as to matter or genus; they
are univocal when they correspond in matter, genus and species.[20] When the
superior and the inferiors are analogical they are related in such a way that
the inferiors have everything merely through the generosity of the superior.
Whatever is in the inferior is proper to the superior; it follows upon the
very nature of the superior: (*Ipsum passionum totum quod habet de mera gratia
superioris habet, utpote consequens ipsam naturam superioris ut proprium*).[21]
Consequently, whatever the inferior "has" from the superior does not inhere in
it when the superior is absent. Eckhart saw an example of this in the relation
of light (*lumen*) to the medium.[22] But he did not elaborate this example here,
probably because he had already discussed it in one of the preceding passages
of his commentary on the *Gospel of John*.[23] This example will be studied after
the presentation of the characteristics of the relation between univocal superior and its inferiors.

When the superior or active being and the inferior or passive being correspond in matter, genus and species, they are univocal. In this case the
inferior has what it receives through the generosity of the superior, but the
inferior has it through no mere generosity. The inferior, while it is being
perfected, also is active and the superior is passive or receptive even while
it is active. The inferior is not passive in its entirety (*se toto*) nor does
it lack all actuality. The inferior receives the similitude and form of the
superior through the grace of the superior, but it merits it by its own nature, because it is of the same specific nature as the superior. Eckhart illustrated this relation with the example of fire which causes heat in wood.[24]

It is not difficult to recognize that the analogical relation is more appropriate than the univocal to describe the relationship between God and creatures. The analogical is the only relation in which the superior and the inferior have nothing in common as to matter, species or genus. Since contrasting
sometimes clarifies, it will be of value for the understanding of the relationship between God and creatures to point out the difference between the two
relations.

In the analogical relation, the inferior has everything (*totum quod
habet*) through the generosity (*de mera gratia*) of the superior; whereas in the
univocal relation the inferior by its own nature merits the similitude and
form of the superior. When the superior and inferior are univocal, the inferior receives (*recipit*) the similitude and form of the superior; there is a
giving of a perfection; the giving is gratuitous (*de gratia quidem*) but also
merited by the inferior, since both the superior and inferior are of the same
specific nature. When the superior and inferiors are analogical, there is no
question of "receiving a perfection"; everything which the inferior receives
follows upon the nature of the superior. Whatever the inferior "has" is the
property of the nature of the superior.[25] This is why the superior has to be
present in the inferior. It has to be in the inferior with its nature, because
it is the nature which carries along (*consequens*) all that the inferior "has".
As soon as the nature of the superior is absent, all that the inferior "has"
is also absent. Here Eckhart used the term, nature of the superior (*natura
superioris*), in order to emphasize that he was considering the superior from
the viewpoint of its activity. Nature is the essence of a thing insofar as it
is considered as active.[26] In the univocal relation it seems that Eckhart
wanted to stress the handing on or causing of a perfection. In the analogical

relation, on the other hand, he seems to have emphasized the presence of the
superior in the inferior. The difference is seen more clearly in the two
examples which he used to clarify these relations.

Eckhart illustrated the relation between a univocal superior and inferior, by fire.[27] Fire causes (*agit*) heat in wood, thereby assimilating the
wood to itself with respect to heat. That the wood is hot is not due to the
wood; it is gratuitous (*de gratia*). But the action of fire in generating
(*generans*) heat, does not as such (that is, as generating heat) end with the
heat nor with the heating of the wood, but it directs the gift (*gratia*) of
heat toward the generation of the substantial form of fire, which is a higher
perfection than heat. Thus the fire gives to the wood the gift of being heated
and of amenability to the substantial form of fire, so that the wood may be
capable of receiving the substantial form of fire. Accordingly, the heating of
the wood is intended by the generating fire only by accident; the heating
takes place accidentally or through the accidents of the fire. The wood
receives the gift of the form of fire (*lignum recipit gratiam formae ignis*)
for the sake of its being assimilated to fire, which, in a process of becoming, disposes it for the form of the fire. Accordingly, whatever the inferior
receives from the superior, it receives not merely as a gift, but also out of
merit.

This example does not seem to be satisfying for several reasons. The
superior is fire; but it is difficult to determine what the inferior is. As
Eckhart said, the superior and the inferior have the same matter, genus and
species.[28] It is difficult to understand how the superior and the inferior can
have the same matter, yet be distinct from each other. In another place[29]
Eckhart was more exact when he stressed that the superior and the inferior
agree in form, but are distinct in matter.

If the superior and the inferior are said to be of the same species, then
wood cannot be the inferior, because it is a different specific nature than
fire.[30] Yet Eckhart seemed to think of wood as the inferior because it
receives the form of fire. It is also hard to understand what Eckhart meant
when he emphasized that, to some extent, the inferior merits the similitude
and form of the superior, because it is of the same specific nature as the
superior: (*Meretur tamen ex natura sua, eo quod sit eiusdem naturae in specie
cum agente*).[31] Moreover, the example is of no help to us in knowing whether
the perfection caused in the inferior remains in it when the superior is not

present to it; yet Eckhart made it a criterion of distinction in his general remarks on the relation between analogical superior and inferiors. It becomes necessary, therefore, to look for an answer to the question in other pertinent passages of Eckhart's writings.

In his second commentary on *Genesis*[32] he discussed at length the relation between univocal superiors and inferiors and set down some characteristics of it:

First, he pointed out that the activity of the univocal superior is limited, because both the superior and inferior are material.[33]

Second, the superior is also receptive in its activity.[34]

Third, the natural activity which belongs to the inferior becomes more forceful; and that which belongs to the superior wanes and finally ceases.[35]

Fourth, the superior assimilates the inferior to itself during the process so that the inferior becomes active like the superior.[36]

Fifth, the superior which is univocal with its inferior is of the same species as the inferior, and has the same name. For example, fire is from fire and what is white is so from whiteness. A univocal superior communicates to its inferior all that the superior has; even the activity of the superior is taken over by the inferior. Consequently, the inferior also receives the name of the superior which denominates its specific nature. To the wood, accordingly, which is converted into fire belongs the name and the nature of fire, since the wood in flame proceeds from, and is formed and taken over by, the power of fire.[37]

Sixth, the univocal superior is not the cause of the species nor does its activity extend over the whole species. Fire is not a cause with respect to all wood, turning all wood into fire, because then it would be a cause itself. But fire is only the cause of this fire by converting this particular kind of matter to fire. Fire is thus only a particular cause.[38]

Seventh, in contrast to an analogical superior and inferior, the effect of a univocal superior retains the specific form and the name of the superior. For example, the form of fire caused in matter inheres in it even if the original fire dies out.[39]

Eighth, the specific form of the superior is caused in the inferior, so that it inheres in the inferior independently of the superior; its specific activity is handed on as a remaining quality. Fire, for example, not only heats the piece of wood, but it converts it into fire so that it falls heir to

the characteristic activity of fire, that is, it can itself heat other things.
Fire, in heating its medium, first heats the part which is closest to it. This
part of the medium heats the next and so on until the whole of the medium is
heated. This progress of heating the medium accordingly takes place by
stages.[40]

From these eight considerations the identity of the inferior becomes
clear. The inferior is actually the wood, but only inasmuch as it is already
transformed by the superior. When the wood has received the form of fire,
there is sameness in species between the inferior and the superior.[41]

These considerations also indicate a key point of importance for the
understanding of the relation betwen a univocal superior and inferior. In the
univocal relation, a gradual transference of a perfection from the superior to
the inferior occurs. The substantial form of the superior is caused in the
inferior as an inhering perfection (*habet radicem in medio*). That which was
proper to the superior becomes the property of the inferior; the inferior does
not lose the perfection when the superior is absent or ceases to exist.[42] The
perfection becomes the property of the inferior so that the inferior receives
all that which follows upon this perfection. Along with the perfection, the
inferior receives the activity which is proper to the perfection and thereby
gains a new name. Because both the superior and the inferior are material,
their activity is restricted to the limits of their individual matter. The
causality of the superior is not extended over the whole species of the inferior.

Eckhart explained the relation of an analogical superior to its inferiors
through the illustration of light in the medium. He gave the illustration in
his commentary on the *Gospel of John*.[43] He had just completed his general remarks on the relation of the analogical superior to its inferiors. He then
stated that the best illustration of this relation was that of light to its
medium. For light he used the word, *lumen*.[44] He actually discussed the example
much earlier in his commentary, in connection with his remarks on John's words
in the prologue to his *Gospel: Lux in tenebris lucet, et tenebrae eam non comprehenderunt*. Here he used both *lux* and *lumen* for light. Eckhart perhaps
intended to distinguish between them.[45] We shall therefore consistently translate *lux* with "light"; *lumen*, with "shining".[46]

Light illumines the medium, Eckhart said, but it does not strike roots
into it. The whole medium receives the shining immediately from the luminous

body; not first in the east and then in the west, nor the west from the east, but both east and west at once and immediately from the luminous body. Light does not strike roots and therefore does not inhere in the medium. The medium does not become heir of the shining. The luminous body does not make the medium heir of its action which is to illuminate. The luminous body communicates its shining to the medium as if only lending it to the medium in passing, so that it is illumined and may be called an illumined medium. But it does not communicate its shining in such a manner that the shining would become an inhering quality of the medium, and the light would remain and adhere and actively illumine when the luminous body is absent.

From this example one can see the most obvious difference between the analogical and univocal relation. In the univocal relation the perfection is caused in the inferior in such a way that the inferior has the perfection even if the superior is absent. The inferior becomes the heir of the perfection and consequently also of the activity of the superior. This perfection does not always have to be a substantial form; it might be just a quality like heat.[47] However, when the superior and inferior are analogical, the superior itself has to be present in the inferior so that the inferior may "have" the perfection of the superior. The inferior is not heir of the perfection, nor can it of itself cause such a perfection in others. The perfection is in all the parts of the inferior at the same time and immediately. When the superior is in the inferior, the perfection is immediately present. As soon as the superior is distant from the inferior, the perfection is also absent. These differences were easily established in the two examples.

It is difficult to determine, however, in the example of light, what exactly is the superior, and what is the perfection which the inferior borrows from the superior. The problem becomes even more confusing in Eckhart's talk of a luminous body which he distinguished from light and the shining, and which renders the light and the shining interchangeable. We recall the observation above[48] that after the discussion of the general characteristics of the relation between the analogical inferior and superior, Eckhart spoke of the relation between the shining (*lumen*) and the medium as suitable to illustrate the relation.

In his sermons and lectures on the book of *Ecclesiasticus*,[49] Eckhart clearly distinguished between the shining and the form of the sun. The shining is an active quality (*qualitas activa*) which follows upon the form of the sun.

The shining has nothing in common with the medium, that is, the inferior. Consequently, the form of the sun, and the quality which follows this form, namely the shining, does not strike roots, nor in any way inhere in the inferior. As soon as the sun is gone, the shining immediately passes with the sun from the inferior. The form of the sun is distinct from the quality which flows from it. The quality is not given to the inferior as a gift, but is simply present to it together with the form of the sun. There is no shining caused in the inferior which would be a perfection belonging to it, and which would be distinct from the superior, even if it were caused continuously by the superior.[50] This shining remains, for Eckhart, a quality of the superior, and the form of the sun is distinct from its active quality.

When the example is made to illustrate the relationship between God and creatures, however, a distinction between the form of God and His quality cannot be made. God is absolutely one in His relationship to creatures, and He is absolutely one in His being.[51] Accordingly, when Eckhart applied to God's relationship to creatures both his insights into the relationship between analogical superior and inferior, and his example of light in the medium he failed to distinguish between light (*lux*), which is identified with God,[52] and the shining (*lumen*).

Because God is the highest among beings,[53] He is simply and absolutely the full and true light (*est lux simpliciter et absolute plena*).[54] In contrast to God, all creatures are in themselves darkness (*tenebrae*).[55] Light stands for God and everything divine and perfect.[56] Darkness stands for everything created.[57] God is the superior, and creatures are the inferiors. Immediately after Eckhart distinguished between the luminous body, light and the shining, he dropped the notion of the luminous body completely; thereafter, light signified the superior. It remains to be seen whether Eckhart considered light (*lux*) and the shining (*lumen*) as two distinct realities.

Divine perfection, which is light, shines in darkness, but the darkness does not comprehend it. Creatures, Eckhart commented, do not actively illuminate. They do not become heirs of God's activity such as creating or ruling.[58] That the darkness does not comprehend the light, means that creatures are darkness in contrast to the Son, the second Person of the Trinity who is heir of the light, and light of light. Creatures are not son, nor heir of the shining, which is the illuminating and creating.[59]

This text does not permit us to make a clear distinction between light (*lux*) and shining (*lumen*). Nor does the text in which Eckhart applied the relation between light (*lux*) and darkness (*tenebrae*), to the relation between God and creatures on the level of the transcendental perfection of being.

In the second text[60] Eckhart said that nothing which has light or the activity of shining (*lucere*) from somewhere else is the true light (*lux vera*); in itself and of itself it is darkness, just as everything which is moved is of itself moved and not a mover. Everything which is not the first, has light and the activity of shining from the first. Augustine expressed the same idea in the ninth book of his *Confessions: Lux divina una est, et alia non est*.[61] John in his *Gospel* also expressed it in the words, *quae illuminat omnem hominem venientem in hunc mundum*.[62]

God illumines all things, Eckhart said in amplification. Although not all things are illumined equally and in the same way,[63] they are nevertheless illumined; not to be illumined by God is not to be (*est non esse*). His shining is being (*lumen suum est esse*).[64] In Job's statement, *quare data est misero lux*,[65] *lux* stands for being (*esse*), that is, light is being (*lux est esse*). Moreover, in the words of *Genesis*, light was made (*facta est lux*) before any distinct things were made, since being is light (*esse lux est*). Light is prior and common to all that is distinct, and remains indistinct in itself. In *Job* it is written, *super quem non surgit lumen illius?*[66] Light illumines either everything and all things, or no thing and nothing. Light, which is being (*lux enim, quae est esse*), is immediately present to all things before they are distinguished. Just so, the soul illumines all parts of its body with and through its being (*suo esse et per esse*), because it is immediately present to the matter before all distinction. Every distinction is through form. An evaluation of Eckhart's argument will now be made.

At the beginning of this passage Eckhart distinguished between that which is first, and all the rest which are second. All those which are not the first or God, have light or the activity of shining[67] from the first. They are in themselves darkness, whereas only the first is true light; there is no other light but the first. Eckhart did not distinguish here between *lux vera* and *lux creata*; he spoke only of light (*lux*) on the side of the first, and of darkness (*tenebrae*) on the side of creatures.

Augustine's statement which Eckhart quoted from the *Confessions, Lux divina una est, et alia non est*, is further evidence that Eckhart meant to say

there is one light only, and this one light is divine. The only light is the
first being; everything else is in itself darkness. Accordingly, it is this
light which must illumine the darkness. The only light which darkness "has" is
the divine light. Expressing the same idea in terms of being, we can say that
creatures exist because they are illumined by the divine light (*lux*), or the
shining (*lumen*). The divine light, or the shining, is their existence. Light
(*lux*) does not seem to be different from shining (*lumen*). Eckhart said of
both, that they are being (*esse*).[68] He said of light what he had said of the
being which is identified with God. Whether named light or being, it is prior
to and common to all things that are distinct, and yet remains indistinct in
itself.[69] To explain the way in which being is immediately present to all
things, Eckhart used the now familiar example of the soul's relation to its
body.[70]

The result of these observations is, then, that God as the superior
enlightens creatures which are the inferiors by His very presence in them.
Creatures "shine", that is, exist, only because God is in them. Creatures do
not have their own shining. They themselves are darkness, and as creatures
remain darkness. All the shining which creatures "have" is the shining of the
light of God.

The relationship again is one of immanence and participation, rather than
of efficient causality. God as light is present in darkness, and darkness
shines only because it participates in the light or being of God. The doctrine
is in agreement with Eckhart's other ways of expressing the relationship between God and creatures. Elsewhere in the writings of Eckhart we find support
for the doctrine, expressed in terms of superior and inferiors.

It is essential to the superior, Eckhart said, to flow into its inferiors
with its properties.[71] This is to be taken literally; the superior descends
into the inferiors with its properties[72] of unity and non-division.[73] The
superior, however, is not affected by the inferior.[74] The superior assimilates
the inferior to itself. God assimilates creatures to Himself inasumuch as He
is being.[75] The inferior is characterized by poverty, privation, emptiness and
darkness.[76] Its assimilation to the superior is its total perfection.[77]
Against the background of the total context, this means that creatures are assimilated to God, because God as being is in them, and they participate in His
being. When the assimilation is expressed in terms of being, the superior is
non-distinct from its inferior; but inasmuch as the inferior is finite or

falls into multiplicity, it is radically other than the superior;[78] creatures
are radically other than God, thus again, although the superior communicates
itself to the inferiors, in that it plunges itself totally into the inferiors,[79] it is totally within and outside of them; God is not confused with
creatures.[80]

Eckhart's interpretation of God's relationship to creatures in terms of
the relationship of superior to inferiors shows again that the notions of
cause and effect have the peculiar Eckhartian meaning of the immanence and
transcendence of God as being, and of the participation of creatures in the
being which is identified with God. His interpretation of causality, namely,
that the effect is placed within the cause, is found in this context. Eckhart
considered the inferior as placed (*locatum*) in the superior.[81] In the essential order the superior always includes (*includit*) in its lowest part all its
inferiors. God, inasmuch as He is being, includes all creatures.[82] Although
the superior contains (*comprehendit*) the inferiors, the inferiors in no way
contain the superior.[83]

NOTES

[1] See the author's unpublished dissertation, *Eckhart's Doctrine of the Transcendental Perfections in God and Creatures*, University of Toronto, 1965.

[2] Cf. chapter 8, note 42 in dissertation, for Thomas' interpretation of the notion of participation in terms of efficient causality.

[3] Cf. Eckhart's prologues to his *Opus tripartitum* and to the *Opus propositionum*. For example, *Prol. gen.* n.12 LW I pp.156,15-158,4; *Prol. op. prop.* n.1 LW I p.166,2.

[4] *In Gen.* I LW I n.160 p. 308,11.3-4: Esse autem tempori non subiacet. Cf. *Prol. gen.* n.9 LW I p.154,3.

[5] See above, note 1.

[6] *Ibid.*, chapter 3.

[7] Cf. *In Joh.* n.326 LW III p.274,8-10; *Sermo* XXV,1 n.252 LW IV p.231,3-5.

[8] Cf. *In Sap.* ch.VIII, #1 ed. Théry IV p.2745,13-14.

[9] Cf. Bange's and Karrer's attempts to make Eckhart a faithful pupil of St. Thomas. (chapter 1, p.4 of dissertation).

[10] *Ibid.*

[11] Cf. *In Joh.* n.91 LW III p. 79,1-2: Causa enim et effectus naturaliter se mutuo respiciunt ut superius et inferius. Cf. *ibid.*, n.219 p.184,12-17; n.21 p. 18,3-4; *Prol. gen.* 10 LW I pp. 154-16-155,1; *In Eccl.* n.38 LW II p. 265,8-10; *In Gen.* I n.32 LW I p. 210,2-4.

[12] Cf. *In Joh.* n.195 LW III p. 163,8-11: Omnis causa essentialis, omne superius et omne divinum, in quantum huiusmodi, est incognitum latens et absconditum, praecipue deus, supremum et prima causa essentialis omnium.

[13] Cf. *ibid.*, n.181, pp.149,14-150,4; *In Gen.* I n.61 LW I p.228,3-6. Cf. also chapter 6 of dissertation.

[14] Cf. Pseudo-Denis, *De divinis nominibus* c.4 no.2; FG 3, 696; *ibid.*, c.7 no. 3 FG 3,869 D-872 B.

[15] Cf. R. Roques, "La notion de hiérarchie selon le Pseude-Denys," *Archives* 17 (1949) pp. 183-322 and 18 (1950-51) pp. 5-44. "Entre les trois hiérarchies célestes, par example, il ne semble pas y avoir de fossés infranchissables: toutes participent quoique à des digrés divers, à l'unité, à l'être, à la vie et à l'intelligence divines." Cf. *ibid.*, p.211. That participation in being is first; cf. *De divinis nominibus* c.5 no.5 FG 3,820.

[16] Cf. *Prol. gen.* n.4 LW I p.150,10; *In Eccl.* n.13 LW II p.243,3-5; *In Gen.* I n.25 p.204,15-16.

[17] Cf. LW I p.150, footnote 3.

[18] Cf. *In Exod.* n.262 LW II p.212,5-6: Semper enim superius prius est et per consequens "dives per se." Inferius autem, in quantum inferius, egenum est et nudum, mendicans; *In Gen.* I

n.32 LW I p.210,2-4: Inferiora autem passiva sunt, informia et nuda, quod est inane et vacuum.
Cf. *In Eccl.* n.38 LW II p.265,12-13.

Cf. *In Joh.* n.180 LW III pp. 148,16-149,1: Primum est quod universaliter superius hoc ipso
quod superius est, plenum est, et que amplius superius, eo amplius plenum est.

Ibid., n.181 pp.149,9-150,3: Secundo notandum quod omne, quod habet inferius aut recipit a
superiori, semper hoc habet de gratia superioris. Agens enim semper praestantius est inferiori,
et ut ait *philosophus* et *Augustinus*. Iterum etiam de ratione et proprietate passivi est esse
nudum et egenum, de ratione vero et proprietate activi est esse actu et dives.

Ex his duobus sic conclude: superius plenum est et sibi proprium est influere et esse causam
eorum quae post ipsum et sub ipso sunt; sed deus verbum supremum est omnium; ergo de plentitudine
eius accipiunt universa et de gratia.

[19]*In Joh.* n.182 LW III p.150,5-6: Tertio notandum quod inferius accipere id quod habet a
superiori et de gratia ipsius, differenter se habet in analogicis et in univocis.

[20]*Ibid.*, p.150,6-7: In analogicis enim, ubi activum et passivum non communicant in materia
sive in genere...; *ibid.*, pp.150,12-151,1: In univocis autem activum et passivum in materia conveniunt et genere et specie.

[21]*Ibid.*, p. 150,8-9. This corresponds to what Eckhart said in another place. See dissertation, chapter 5c, p.774 and notes. Only God is properly the transcendental perfections. God's
presence to creatures, inasmuch as He is identical with the transcendental perfections, is their
transcendental perfection. The transcendental perfections of *esse, unum, verum* and *bonum* are
property of God's nature. They follow upon or go along with this nature. They remain property of
God. There is no room for the giving of a perfection through a kind of efficient causality. The
only notion applicable here is that of participation implying the distinctions between God and
creatures as shown above. (Cf. chapter 8, pp.117ff of dissertation).

[22]*Ibid.*, p.150,6-11: In analogicis enim, ubi activum et passivum non communicant in materia
sive in genera, ipsum passivum totum quod habet de mera gratia superioris habet, utpote consequens ipsam naturam superioris proprium. Propter quod non haeret nec inhaere, passivo absente
superiori activo, ut patet de lumine in medio.

[23]*Ibid.*, n.70 pp. 58,11-59,10.

[24]*In Joh.* n.182 LW III pp.150,12-151,6: In univocis autem activum et passivum in materia
conveniunt et genere et specie: inferius id quod recipit habet quidem de gratia superioris, sed
non de mera gratia. Ratio est, quia in talibus passivum patiendo agit et activum agendo patitur.
Item etiam non est se toto passivum nec carens omni actu: ipsum inferius recipit similitudinem et
formam activi de gratia quidem superioris, meretur tamen ex natura sua, eo quod sit eiusdem naturae in specie cum agente.

[25]See note 21 above.

[26]Cf. Aristotle, *Metaphysics* v. 1014b16-20; *Physics* ii, 192b 20-23. St. Thomas, *De
ente et essentia* cap. 1: Tamen natura nomen hoc modo sumpte videtur significare essentiam rei
secundum quod habet ordinem ad propriam operationem rei, cum nulla res propria operatione desti-
tuatur. (Ed. Roland-Gosselin, O.P. in *Bibliothèque Thomiste* VIII (Paris, J. Vrin, 1948) p.4,
lin.10-13. Eckhart must have had this meaning of *natura* in mind.

[27]*In Joh.* n.182 LW III pp.151,6-152,2: Exempli gratia: ignis agit in lignis calorem et
ipsa assimilat sibimet in calore, et hoc quidem de gratia est quod sint calida. Generans tamen
ignis, in quantum generans, non sistit in calore sive calefactione ligni, sed hanc gratiam ordi-
nat ad generationem formae substantialis, quae est maior perfectio, et sic *gratiam* calefactio-

nis et assimilationis dat *pro gratia* specificae informationis, ut scilicet calefaciendo et assimilando formae substantialis lignum sit capax. Unde calefactio ab igne generante non est intenta nisi per accidens. Propter quod alteratio calefactionis fit per accidens sive per accidentia generantis. Et hoc est quod hic dicitur quod *de plenitudine* superioris recipit omne suum inferius, et *gratiam pro gratia*. Verum est tamen quod etiam e converso lignum recipit *gratiam* formae ignis *pro gratia* assimilatione dispositive et in fiendo. Sic ergo in univocis inferius receipit a superiori non solum ex gratia, sed etiam ex merito.

[28]*In Joh.* n.182 LW III pp.150,12-151,1 quoted in note 20 above.

[29]*In Gen.* II n.123 LW II p.588,6-7: Activum et passivum maxime in univocis duo sunt sive distincta propter materiam, unum autem per formam, ut ait *philosophus* et *commentator* eius. Cf. Aristotle, *Metaphysics* viii, 6,1045a14-20. 23-25; b 4.

[30]Cf. Thomas, *In Sent.* I d.8 q.1 a.2.

[31]*In Joh.* n.182 LW III p.151,5-6.

[32]*In Gen.* II nn.116-127 LW I pp.582,9-591,13.

[33]*Ibid.*, n.116 p.582,9-11: Primo, quod omne activum permixtum habet ratione materiae suae aliquid passibilitatis et per consequens aliquid diminutionis et oppressionis virtutis activae et sic soporatur eius actio.

[34]*Ibid.*, n.117 p.583,1: Item secundo: omne agens tale consequenter agendo patitur.

[35]*Ibid.*, lin.5-7: Item tertio, quod actio naturalis, quamvis in fine intendatur et sit fortior ex parte passivi, ex parte tamen activi lassatur et remittitur. Et hoc tertium sequitur ex secundo, quia scilicet agendo patitur.

[36]*Ibid.*, lin.8-9: Adhuc quarto: passivum assimilatur suo activo in agendo, et activum sibi assimilat passivum, ut ipsum faciat agens.

[37]*Ibid.*, n.118 p. 584,1-11: Quinto: activum naturale et univocum communicat suo passivo in specie et nomine, puta ignis ab igne, album ab albedine et speciem habet et nomen specie, nec ab aliquo prorsus alio sortitur nomen et naturam albi quippiam nisi ab albedine et ipsa sola, adeo ut nec deus posset facere album sine albedine. Et hoc est quod hic dicitur: *adduxit eam ad Adam, dixitque Adam: hoc nunc os ex ossibus meis et caro de carne mea*, quia activum tale passivo tali communicat quidquid sui est et quale ipsum est, actionem scilicet, rem passam a passivo suo, et per consequens nomen suum expressivum et denominans ipsam naturam, quod quid est speciei. Et hoc est quod sequitur hic: *vocabitur virgo, quoniam de viro* sumpta est. Eo enim ligno converso in ignem nomen et natura ignis competit, quia de virtute ignis procedit et formatur et sumitur. This does not agree, however, with *Sermo* xxIV,2 n.247 LW IV p.226,4-5; cf. *In Gen.* I n.159 LW I p.307,5-8.

[37]*Ibid.*, n.119 pp.584,12-858,4: Ex quo patet sexto, quod agens univocum non est causa speciei nec agens super totam speciem. Ignis enim non est causa ligno, ut fiat ignis - iam enim esset causa sui ipsius, cum sit ignis - sed est tantum causa huius ignis per transmutationem huius materiae et huius passivi sub specie, particularis scilicet.

[39]*Ibid.*, n.120 p.585,10-12: Rursus septimo proprium est agentis univoci quod effectus eius manet in specie et nomine sui activi absente suo activo. Secus in analogis, cuius et rationem supra signavi, ubi dicitur: 'creavit deus caelum et terram.'

Ibid., p. 586,2-3: Adhaeret enim et haeret forma ignis materiae ignis generati corrupto igne generati corrupto igne generante.

[40]*Ibid.*, n.122 p.587,6-13: Octavo sciendum quod agens naturale univocum qualitatem suam activam, qua agit, puta ignis calorem, communicat suo passivo non solum in transitu et in fieri, ut est passio, sed communicat ipsam, ut haereat et sit passibilis qualitas. Unde non solum facit passivum esse tale, ut scilicet sit calidum, sed facit ipsum esse calefaciens et heredem actionis suae. Juxta quod signanter advertendum quod in calefactione medii, puta aeris, pars ultima calefit a parte media et illa a parte prima. Et propter hoc calefactio totius medii non fit subito nec in instanti, sed in tempore et successive.

[41]Cf. *ibid.*, n.118 p.584,1-3: Activum naturale et univocum communicat suo passivo in specie et nomine, puta ignis ab igne, album ab albedine et speciem habet et nomen speciei.

[42]Cf. *In Eccl.* n.46 LW II 274,15-275,10.

[43]*In Joh.* n.70 LW III pp.58,11-59,10: Verba ista supra tripliciter sunt exposita. Nunc autem advertendum est quod lux medium quidem illuminat, sed radices non mitti. Propter quod totum medium lumen recipit immediate a corpore luminoso, non prius oriens quam occidens, nec occidens ab oriente, sed utrumque simul, et iterum utrumque immediate a corpore luminoso. Et ratio est, quia radicem non mittit in oriente nec in aliqua parte medii. Propter quod non haeret lux in medio nec fit heres luminis, nec corpus luminosum facit medium heredem suae actionis, quae est illuminare. Communicat quidem ipsi medio quasi mutuo et in transitu per modum passionis et transeuntis et fieri, ut sit et dicatur illuminatum, non autem communicat ipsi medio lumen suum per modum radicati et haerentis passibilis qualitatis, ut scilicet lux maneat et haereat et illuminet active, absente corpore luminoso.

[44]Cf. p.158 above and note 22.

[45]Robert Grosseteste, the first Chancellor of Oxford University between 1215-21 and bishop of Lincoln from 1235 to his death in 1253, also made a distinction between *lux* and *lumen* in his philosophical writings. *Lux* is the first corporeal form which expands itself spherically from one point. [Formam primam corporalem, quam quidam corporeitatem vocant, lucem esse arbitror. *De luce seu de inchoatione formarum*, ed. Clemens Baeumker in *Beiträge* BD. 9 (1912) p.51,lin.10-11.]

    Lux is the first form in prime matter. *Lux*, the form of corporeity has to multiply itself and diffuse itself into each part of matter and thereby extend matter. It cannot break itself loose from matter because it is not separable from matter, nor can matter itself free itself from matter, nor can matter itself free itself from form. (Cf. *ibid.*, p.52,17-31.) *Lux* extends matter spherically to the outermost sphere in which matter has reached the limits of its rarefaction. This outermost sphere is the first body. It is called firmament. The firmament is constituted only of prime matter and the first form (*lux*), (*Ibid.*, p.54, lin.18-30). When *lux* has thus formed the firmament it reflects back to the center of the universe as *lumen*. (*Ibid.*, lin.31-35).

    The *lumen* which proceeds from the firmament to the center is a spiritual body (Et sic procedit a corpore primo lumen, quod est corpus spirituale, sive mavis dicere spiritus corporalis. *Ibid.*, p.55, lin.2-3). *Lumen* is refracted from every part of the firmament to the center of the universe. It constitutes the descending order of the 13 spheres and the four elements. (*Ibid.*, pp.55-58).

    For an English translation of Grosseteste's *De luce* see Robert Grosseteste, *On Light*, transl. and intro. by Clare G. Riedl (Milwaukee, 1942).

[46]The German translation recognizes such a difference when it translates *lux* with "Licht" and *lumen* with "das Leuchten." "Das Licht" emphasizes more the substance of light, whereas "das

Leuchten" is the gerund of the verb "leuchten" and as such expresses more the activity of the light. The English equivalent would be "the shining." These two expression "das Licht" and "das Leuchten" are not simply convertible. One can say, for example, "das Leuchten des Lichts," but one cannot meaningfully say "das Licht des Leuchtens." The same seems to be true in English. One can say "the shining of the light," but it is not correct to say "the light of the shining." The Latin words *lux* and *lumen* have different etymological roots: *lux, lucis* is derived from the Greek adjective *leukôs* and the Latin word *lumen, luminis* goes back to the verb *luceo*. Both expressions, however, seem to have been used indifferently. [Cf. *lumen* and *lux* in *Ausführliches Lateinisch - deutsche* Handwörterbuch, ausgearbeitet von Karl Ernst Georges. 2 vols. (Hannover-Leipzig, 1913)].

[47]Cf. *In Joh.* n.71 LW III pp.59,11-60,7: Secus omnino de calore simul generato cum lumine in medio. Hic enim radicem mittit in medio. Item haeret et manet absente corpore luminoso. Adhuc tertio: posterius fit in occidente quam in oriente, successive et in tempore, non subito nec in instanti. Rursus quarto: calefit non solum pars post partem, sed etiam per partem et a parte. Et propter hoc quinto non quaelibet pars calefit immediate a corpore luminoso. Et hic est sexto quod medium recipit calorem non solum per modum fieri et transeuntis et passionis et mutui et hospitis, ut dicatur et sit calefactum, sed per modum haerentis et heredis filii, cuius est hereditas, ut dicatur et sit calefaciens, heres actionis calefacientis, quae est calefacere activie.

[48]See p.158 and note 22.

[49]N.46 LW II pp.274,14-275,10: Exemplum autem manifestum et ratio dictorum est in luce et calore in medio. Calor enim forma ignis quam consequitur habet radicem in medio, quod est aer, propter convenientiam et identitatem materiae hic inde. Propter quod aere calefacto iam habet radicem et figitur ipsa forma ignis et inchoatur quasi ignis. Secus de lumine, cum sit qualitas activa consequens formam solis aut orbis aut caeli, quod cum elementis nullam habet materiae convenientiam. Propter quod forma solis et sua qualitas formam consequens, lumen scilicet, non mittit radicem nec aliquo modo inchoatur in ipso medio. Hic est quod abscendente sole manet calor iam radicatus et utcumque inchoatus in aere; secus de lumine quod subito abscedit et deserit aerem, utpote non habens radicem nec in minimo formae, quam consequitur, nisi in sola siti, appetitu scilicet.

[50]According to Thomas, for example, who also used the analogy of light in its medium for God's causing of being in creatures, there is a clear distinction between the light and the shining; for example: Respondeo dicendum, quod ista quatuor differunt, lux, lumen, radius et splendor. Lux enim dicitur secundum est in aliquo corpore lucido in actu, a quo alia illuminantur, ut in sole. Lumen autem dicitur secundum quod est receptum in corpore diaphano illuminato. (*In Sen.* II d.13 q.1 a.3, ed. Mandonnet, O.P. vol.II p.332.)

The *lumen* is in a real sense received by the medium.

The *lumen* plays an intermediate role. The air becomes shining by participating in the shining which is from the sun. It does not participate in the nature of the sun: Sic autem se habet omnis creatura ad Deum sicut aer ad solem illuminantem. Sicut enim sol est lucens per suam naturam aer autem fit luminosus participando lumen a solo non tamen participando naturam solis ita solus Deus est ens per essentiam suam, quia eius essentia est suum esse, omnis autem creatura est ens participative, non quod sua essentia sit eius esse. (*ST* I 104,1 resp.)

On this history of the notion of light in philosophy, see Clemens Baeumker, *Witelo...*, pp. 357-437; and Josef Koch, "Über sie Lichtsymbolik im Bereich der Philosophie und der Mystik des Mittelalter," in *Studium Generale* Heft 11, (Berlin, 1960) pp.653-70.

[51]Cf. chapter 2 in dissertation.

[52]Cf. *In Joh.* n.72 LW III p.69,8-13: Non sic de lumine in medio, ut dictum est supra. Et hoc est quod hic dicitur: *lux in tenebris lucet, et tenebrae eam non comprehender-*

unt. *Lux* ... et omne quod divinium et perfectio est. Tenebrae omne quod creatum est, ut dictum est supra. *Lux* ergo, perfectio divina, *lucet in tenebris,* sed *tenebrae eam non comprehenderunt,* ut sint proprie illuminantia active, heredes actionis dei, quae est creatio, gubernatio, et huiusmodi.

[53]*In Joh.* n.87 LW III p.75,9-15: Quarto notandum quod generaliter superius ordine essentiali lux est ut sic, inferius autem e converso ut sic semper tenebra est, ut supra dictum est. Ergo deus, utpote supremum in entibus, est lux simpliciter et absolute plena et vera, utpote nulli inferior et superior omnibus, et consequenter *lux vera*, 'et tenebrae in eo non sunt ullae.' Joh. 1 Secus de omni creato habente superius, deum scilicet. Propter quod dictum est supra: 'lux in tenebris lucet,' deus scilicet in creaturis.

[54]God is the true light also according to the testimony of Scripture which says that there is no darkness in him. *Ibid.*, n.87 p.75,3-6: "Secundo notandum quod verum dicitur unumquodque ex dubous: primo, si attingat formam substantialem illius naturae; secundo, si nihil alieni admixtum habeat. Quorum utrumque est in deo, Joh. 1: deus lux est, et tenebrae in eo non sunt ullae.'

[55]*In Joh.* n.21 LW III p.18,3-9: Vel aliter: universaliter principium lux est sui principiati, et superius sui inferioris. E converso principiatum et inferius hoc ipso quod inferius et posterius, utpote habens esse ab alio, in se ipso tenebrae sunt privationis vel negationis: privationis quidem in corporalibus corruptibilibus, negationis in spiritualibus. Hoc est ergo quod dicitur: *lux in tenebris lucet.* Sed quia inferius nunquam adaequat suum superius, sequitur: *et tenebrae eam non comprehenderunt.*
Note that in contrast to *lux* which is singular and which indicates one (*superius*), *tenebrae* is plural and expresses multiplicity, even if one would talk of only one inferior (*inferius*). The English expressions "light" and "darkness" do not render this distinction. For the notion that creatures are darkness, cf. LW III p.60, note 2.

[56]Robert Grosseteste does not identify *lux* with God. Cf. note 45 above.

[57]*In Joh.* n.72 LW III p.60,8-13, quoted in note 52 above.

[58]Cf. chapter 2 in dissertation; also *In Sap.* ch.VII, #8 ed. Théry vol.III pp.441,3-442, 15. See also LW III p.60 note 3: According to the editors of the LW Meister Eckhart attacked (e.g., in Predigt LXXXII 263,3-8) Dietrich of Briberg's opinion in this matter. Cf. E. Krebs, *Meister Dietrich* in *Beiträge* V,5-6 (1906) pp.75 and 218.

[59]*In Joh.* n.73 LW III p.61,1-5: Ex praemissis manifeste patet, qualiter deus semel loquitur, sed duo audiuntur, in Psalmo; Iob 33: 'semel loquitur deus, seundo id ipsum non repetit,' quia una actione generat filium, qui est heres, lux de luce, et creat creaturam, quae est tenebra, creata, facta, non filius nec heres luminis, illuminationis et creationis.

[60]*Ibid.*, n.151 pp.124,11-125,12: Sequitur decimum principale: *erat lus vera, quae illuminat ommem hominem venientem in hunc mundum.* Notandum quod nihil habens lucem sive lucere aliunde est vera lux, quin immo in se et ex se tenebra est, sicut omne movens motum ex se ipso motum, non movens; omne autem secundum et lucem et lucere habet a primo. *Augustinus* Confessionum 1. X haec dicens ait: "lux divina una est, et alia non est." Et hoc est quod sequitur: *quae illuminat ommem hominem venientem in hunc mundum.* Aut enim ommem et etiam omnia, - quamvis non omnia aequaliter illuminentur nec eodem modo, omnes tamen et omnia illuminantur; ab ipso enim non illuminari est non esse, lumen suum est esse, Iob 3: 'quare data est misero lux?' 'Lux,' id est esse; ad litteram lucem vocat esse. Hinc est quod ante omnia distincta primo 'facta est lux,' Gen. 1, eo quod esse lux est, prior et communis et omnibus distinctis indistincta in se, Iob 25: 'super quem non surgit lumen illius?' Illuminat ergo omnes et omnia vel nullum et nihil; lux enim, quae est esse, adest omnibus immediate, antequam distinguantur. Sic anima

omnes partes sui corporis suo esse et per esse illuminati; adest enim materiae immediate ante omnem distinctionem. Distinctio enim omnis per formam est.

[61]*Confessiones* X c.33 n.52, CSEL XXXXIII p.265,21. The words "et alia non est" are found only in a few editions. (Cf. LW III p.124, note 6.)

[62]Joh. 1,9.

[63]With respect to the "more or less" as a device to distinguish where there is non-distinction, cf. ch. 2, pp.12ff. above.

[64]Here the German translation is inconsistent and writes "Licht." (LW III p.125.)

[65]Job 3,20.

[66]Job, 25,3.

[67]Eckhart used "sive" instead of "et." This seems to indicate that he did not distinguish between the substance of light and the activity of this substance, i.e., shining. Cf. *In Joh.* n.74 LW III pp.61,13-62,2: Septimo: *lux in tenebris lucet, et tenebrae eam non comprehenderunt,* quia principium denominat suum principiatum, non e converso. Et hoc est quod manifeste dicitur: *lux in tenebris lucet.* Dicitur enim medium illuminatum a lumine sive luce, sed lux non dicitur illuminata nec participans lumine.

[68]A few lines later (*In Joh.* n.152 LW III p.125,15) he said *lumen esse est.*

[69]Cf. chapter 6; see also *In Joh.* n.93 LW III p.80,1-10: Adhuc autem tertio sic dico: deus, lux vera et mera, vel omnes illuminat vel nullum; non autem nullum, ergo omnem. Consequentia patet: omnes enim aequaliter, uniformiter et immediate respicit et ipsis adest, et primo omnium adest.

Exemplum et ratio dicit patet in anima, quae ut forma substantialis corporis immediate adest singulis membris se tota, et propter hoc dat esse et vivere omnibus membris. Secus autem de aliis perfectionibus quas non communicat singulis membris, puta videre, audire, loqui et similia. Vivere autem et esse cum sit lux, constat quod anima illuminat per suam essentiam, qua forma et lux quaedam est, omnem partem corporis et omne veniens sub hanc formam et in hoc corpus, in hunc mundum corporis animati.

[71]*In Joh.* n. 318 LW III p.265,10-11: Ratio est, quia superius ex sui natura et proprietate influit et se ipsum communicat suo inferiori et ipsi soli. Cf. *In Ex.* n.187 LW II pp.160,15-161, 1: Sicut enim superioris est naturaliter influere in sola sibi inferiora, sic inferioris est recipere a solo sibi superiori.

Cf. also *Sermo* XX n.206 LW IV pp.191,12-192,2; *In Eccl.* n.38 LW II p.265,12-13. *In Joh.* n.181 LW III pp.149,14-150,4. *In Sap.* ed. Théry vol.III p.399,1-27.

[72]*Prol. gen.* n.10 LW I pp.154,15-16: Priora et superiora afficiunt inferiora et posteriora et in ipsa descendunt cum suius proprietatibus et ipsa sibi assimilant, utpote causa causatum et agens passum. Cf. chapter 6, note 9.

[73]*Prol. gen.* n.10 LW I p.155, 1-3: De ratione enim primi et superioris, cum sit "dives per se," est influere et afficere inferiora suis proprietatibus inter quas est unitas et indivisio. Cf. to this, *In Joh.* n.267 LW III p.222, 8-11.

[74]*Prol. gen.* n.10 LW I p.154,13-16: Secundo est praenotandum quod universaliter priora et superiora nihil prorsus accipiunt a posterioribus, sed nec ab aliquo afficiuntur quod sit in il-

lis; sed e converso priora et superiora afficiunt inferiora et posteriora et in ipsa descendunt cum suis proprietatibus et ipsa sibi assimulant.

[75]*In Sap.* n.23 LW II p.344,3-4: In esse enim solo proprie creatura assimilatur deo, suae causae.

In Ex. n.115 LW II p.111,5-8: Rursus nihil tam simile quam deus et creatura. Quid enim tam simile alteri quam id, quod se toto habet esse et accipit esse ex ipso ordine et respectu ad alterum, cuius totum esse est ab altero deductum et exemplatum?

[76]Cf. *In Joh.* n.21 LW III p.18,3-9; *ibid.*, n.532 at the end; *In Gen.* I n.33 LW I p.211, 4-6: Adhuc autem *terra inanis*, non caelum, quia superiora, caeli scilicet, dant et influunt ex abundantia suae perfectionis, terra autem materialia mendicant paupertate, privatione inania sunt, vacua et tenebrosa.

[77]Cf. *In Eccl.* n.30 LW II p.257,4-5: Notandum quod tota perfectio secundorum est assimilatio superiorum.

[78]*Sermo* X n.105 LW IV p.100,7-10: Sexto, quia superius semper est indistinctum a suo inferiori, inferius autem e converso semper est distinctum, tupote finitum. Indistinctum autem ignorat nec admittit numerum. Note that Eckhart is talking here about God inasmuch as He is infinite and *esse*. Cf. chapter 5, note 5, in the dissertation, and the considerations on Eckhart's notion of participation; *ibid.*, chapter 8.

[79]*In Joh.* n.264 LW III p.218,13-14: Superiora naturaliter se communicant et transfundunt se totis suis inferioribus. Cf. *ibid.*, n.365 and *Proc. Col.* I n.83.

[80]*In Gen.* I n.61 LW I p.228,3-6: Quinto fertur *super aquas*, quia non permiscetur rebus creatis, in quibus est non immersus, sed totus intus, totus foris, utpote superior. *Ferebatur*, inquit, *super aquas*. Omne enim superius ordine essentiali totum inest et totum est extra suum inferius quodlibet. *Ordo essentialis* or *causa essentialis* is equivalent to the relationship of analogical extremes, which as we now know is attributed to that of God to creatures; cf. the following chapter (11).

[81]*In Gen.* I 49 p.220,1-221,1; see to this chapter 4.

[82]*In Ex.* n.167 LW II p.146,9-12: Maior apparet ex natura superioris essentialis, quod sempter includit etiam in suo infimo omne inferius se toto. Sic enim omne tempus et eius differentia includitur aequaliter in nunc aeternitatis, non minus praeteritum et futurum quam praesens. Note that the major of this syllogism is part of the proof that God is properly called *esse*. (Cf. *ibid.*, n.166, p.146,3-8).

[83]Cf. *In Joh.* nn.139-140 LW III p.118,2-9: Infimum vero superiorum comprehendit naturaliter suprema et per consequens omnia inferiorum. Et hoc est quod hic sequitur: *et vita erat lux hominum.*

Quamvis autem suprema comprehendant sui infimo omne quod inferiorum est, tamen e converso inferiora nequaquam comprehendunt superiora. Et hoc est octavum quod hic sequitur: *et lux in tenebris lucet*, ipsa scilicet penetrando et comprehendendo, *et tenebrae eam non comprehenderunt*, id est inferiora. Omne enim inferius luce tenebrae est luci comparatum.

St. Thomas in discussing similar relationships between the superior and the inferior used terms which do not express the strong notion of containing or comprehending. He rather employed terms like *contingere:* Natura superior in sui infimo contingit naturam inferiorem in sui supremo (*CG* II c.91; cf. *ibid.*, c.68); *attingere:* Animal rationale constitutuitur ex hoc quod natura corpoea attingit in suo supremo naturam substantiarum separatarum in suo infimo (*De spirit. creat.* a.2; cf. *ST* 78,2); *tangere:* Inferius in sui supremo tangit superius in suo

infimo. (*De verit*. q.16, a.1); *affinitatem habere:* Nam semper summum inferioris affinitatem habet cum ultimo superioris. (*ST* 108,6.)

Cf. C. Fabro, *Participation et Causalité selon S. Thomas d'Aquin* in *Claire Cardinal Mercier*, 1954 (Louvain, Paris, 1961) p. 445: *"Tangere, contingere, attingere*, sont des expression métaphoriques, qu'un Aristotélicien, comme saint Thomas, ne pouvait employer que parce qu'il pénétrait à fond ces problèmes ardus qui forment les limites du panthéisme et du créationisme."

AGNES HOUSSEAU

UNITY AND THE KABBALISTIC HIERARCHY IN GIORDANO BRUNO

One must not assume, *a priori*, that Giordano Bruno was a Kabbalist. Rather one must analyze his works to establish whether or not this is in fact true. This paper will examine this issue by considering six of the Nolan's Italian dialogues which carry forward the views (expressed earlier by Bruno in his *De Umbris Idearum*) that contraries necessarily exist and that their resolution consists in unity.

The processes of emanation and concentration are common to the philosophy and thought of both Bruno (as seen in his Italian dialogues) and that of the Kabbalists. The concept of hierarchy connotes scale, order and harmony to Bruno and to the Kabbalists. This hierarchy also recalls the triad of truth. Bruno's Truth-Cause, Truth-Reflection, Truth-Knowledge can be compared to the Kabbalistic triad of Kether-Hocmah-Binah. Although Bruno does not explicitly follow Hebrew terminology in every dialogue, his usage is harmonious with that of the Kabbalists. Bruno evinces his mysticism in his cosmology, his search for the One, in using with all the mystics the language of Love. The Kabbalah indicates an identical procedure.

Of the forty books by Giordano Bruno, known and published in their entirety or in part, the majority are written in Latin, the remainder in Italian. Giordano Bruno published in London, from 1583 to 1586, six Italian dialogues: *La Cena delle Ceneri, De la Causa, Principio e Uno, De l'Infinito, Universo e Mondi, Lo Spaccio della Bestia Trionfante, La Cabala del Cavallo Pegaseo, De Gli Eroici Furori.*

I will examine these Italian dialogues with special attention to the theme of Unity and the Kabbalistic Hierarchy; however, we must be suspicious of hasty interpretations which make Kabbalists of all the writers, philosophers and poets of the Middle Ages and the Renaissance. One notes that Renaissance Kabbalistic texts are not reserved to the Hebrew people, as they seemed to have been in the Middle Ages; we see the Kabbalah had great influence in the Christian world. We can cite Scotus Eriugena, Marsilio Ficino, Pico della Mirandola, whose Hebraic knowledge is well known. Our problem is to ascertain in what proportions and limits Bruno's philosophy is connected with the Kabbalah. It is certain that the concepts of Unity, Infinite, and Harmony are already common to Bruno and the Kabbalah. Does Giordano Bruno express them in the same way as the Kabbalah or differently?

The Italian dialogues follow a most important work, published in Paris in 1582, *De Umbris Idearum*, where Bruno expresses the ideas of the existence and the necessity of contraries and unity as a resolution of contraries. He says: "The first unity, the light, the life, the understanding, contains every species, all perfections, all virtues, all the multiplicity, every degree of things; and the things in nature are different, opposite and diverse, but in unity are identical, concordant and one." Are they different aspects of one and the same vision? Is this vision one of unity, emanation, universal harmony, equilibirum of opposites? Yes, certainly, and I want to stress *esotericism*. Bruno does not write anything by chance, but always with the idea of unity, of the symbol, of metaphysical poetry. He underscores three ideas:

a) His personality is that of a pioneer. He says in *La Cena delle Ceneri*, that "he does not see through Copernicus' eyes or through Ptolemy's eyes, but through his own eyes".

b) He underlines the idea that ordinary things are understood by ordinary people, and the godlike, heroic men are those who tend to become divine; they are able to submit to the mystery and secrets of the nature: the mystery of Binary in *La Cena delle Ceneri*, of Truth in *Lo Spaccio delle Bestia Trionfante*, the comprehension of the Soul of the world and the Universe, the One Infinite in *De la Causa, Principio e Uno* and in *De l'Infinito, Universo e Mondi*, and the Unity of Substance in *La Cabala del Cavallo Pegaseo*.

c) He upholds the idea of the single and immanent divinity which is in man, in which every living being participates.

The kabbalistic texts are not presented in a systematic form, and it is useless to look for specific references from texts of the Kabbalah in these texts of Bruno. However, it is interesting and useful to consider two notions of unity and hierarchy, i.e., order, as Bruno expounds them in his Italian dialogues. Then one can compare the ideas which Bruno shares with the Kabbalists.

In *La Cena delle Ceneri* – the first dialogue – Bruno celebrates the *mystery of the number TWO, the Binary*, and quotes 25 examples of two-headed pairs: the finite and the infinite, the even and the odd, the male and the female, the superior and the inferior, the hot and the cold.... In *De Causa,*

Principio e Uno, he returns to the opposition and antithesis which exist between the masculine and the feminine:

- Body   is   masculine,   Soul   is   feminine
- Chaos   "   Organization   "
- Wandering   "   Truth   "
- Default   "   Perfection   "

He emphasizes the Binary again, when he enumerates in *De Gli Eroici Furori* (Part I - Dialogue 2), the different kinds of oppositions:

- oppositions of feelings : love-hate.
- oppositions of power   : the power which pursues the object which flees.
- oppositions of movement : to go up and down.

Bruno also differentiates the superior world and the inferior world, the upper and lower waters, the man and the animal, the good and the bad. But for Bruno "all things are made of opposites: fatigue makes us want rest, separation makes us feel happy when reunited." (*Spaccio* - dialogue 2).

The opposites of day-night, masculine-feminine, good-bad are necessary contrarieties, since life is not an equilibrium between successive opposites, but rather a harmony between simultaneous contraries. Bruno does not speak of contradictions but of the combination of different aspects: the duality is unity. "If we reflect, we see that corruption is only generation, and generation is only corruption, love is hate, hate is love.... In substance and at the root, it is the same thing, love, hate, friendship and discord..." (*De Causa* - dialogue 5).

If we study kabbalistic texts like the *Zohar* and the *Sepher Yetsira*, we again find the Binary, symbol of generation, of universal balance, which is represented by Alpha and Omega, the beginning and the end. The Binary is also Solomon's seal (Mogen David) where the two reversed triangles are seen one on the other, as the man sees himself in God and God in Man. In the *Zohar* the distinction is made between the lower hill and the upper hill, that is, between human nature and intelligence, as a reminder of the union of two natures, of which Elohenous is the root. Giordano Bruno evokes this picture, on many occasions, saying that "everything is in everything," and we must understand that everything is the Single One, but not under the same mode" (in *De Causa, Principio e Uno* - dialogue I). Thus, for the Kabbalah, and for Giordano Bruno, there is no hierarchy between the Intelligence, the Soul, the Substance, the Intelligible World, Nature, because there is no deep incompatibil-

ity. The supreme Intelligence and eternal Principle is the Whole and contains
everything that can be. Matter is indivisible, eternal and contains all dimensions in power and can take every shape. As Bruno says, "One is the absolute
possibility; one is the act; one is the shape or the soul; one the substance
or one the body, one the thing, one the being, one the maximum and the supreme". (in *De Causa, Principio e Uno - dialogue 5*).

Opposites do not destroy each other but live together, supported by only
one substance in the process of Emanation, by which, from the One we descend
to the sensitive and multiple world animated in all its parts. Emanation is
symbolized by the forever springing water from its inexhaustible source. Emanation is related to Concentration, symbolized by Light - Fire or Sun - concentrated in the Infinite, then distributed again by an intolerable radiance
for the limited man.

Hierarchy does not mean a world which climbs step by step, or descends,
when we jump from one sphere to another sphere; it makes no substantial distinction between a world and a superior being, and a world and inferior beings. In Bruno, as in the Kabbalah, hierarchy is a scale and an order and harmony. Bruno affirms the existence of "a single scale by which Nature goes down
to the production of things, and Intelligence goes up to their knowledge:" Nature and Intelligence coming from the Unity and going to the Unity both con-
fonded in it.

The Sephirotic Order in Bruno's writings reflects the influence of the
Kabbalah. Water, spring, river, sea, veil, mirror, scale are so many Sephirotic expressions, constituting a system of Emanation, of Concentration, of Creation. In the *Cabala of Pegasus*, Giordano Bruno enumerates the Ten Sephiroth,
in Hebrew and then in Italian, according to the Sephirotic hierarchy (disposition to the center, the right, the left): Kether, Hokhmah, Binah, Hesed, Gevurah, Tepheret, Hod, Netsah Iesod, Malkhuth. Then, he sets up their connection
with the orders of intelligences, the angels, the spheres, the ten motors, the
four Princes of the four elements, all of which are ways to be of the Single
Substance. So the Sephirotic system - quite like those of Hermes, of Magic, of
Alchemy, of Astrology - brings back the whole diversity in Unity, itself
developed in an order. For Bruno, this is the way to introduce the Ass, dis-
closure of the Second Sephirah = Hokhmah = Binary = Wisdom. The Sephirotic
system is also the reminder of a *triad of the Truth*: Truth-Cause, Truth-
Reflection, Truth-Knowledge, which we can compare to the triad Kether-Hokhmah-

Binah. Bruno composes other triads in *Lo Spaccio della Bestia Trionfante*; he says "the true, the being, the good are one and a single truth". Each Sephirah is the expression of the Infinite and a receptacle of all the other Sephiroth.

Although Bruno does not explicitly follow Hebrew terminology in every dialogue, he always comes back to a harmony of the same type. In this he abandons and surpasses the conceptions of Plato, Plotinus and Ficino, because there is no degradation, no superiority, no inferiority, according to whether we examine God or the One, the Intelligence, the Soul, Matter. It is a Multiple Unity. As Emile Namer reminds us "there is only one God; What we call the Intelligence, the Soul, the Substance, are human concepts, logical distinctions. It is our way to understand reality by degrees, but not the degrees of this reality."

Bruno built a system of thought where every point, every element, and every idea are aspects of the one and the same reality. Indeed, it is obvious that such a conception of Unity shares ideas common to Platonism, Neoplatonism, hermeticism, Christianity.... Bruno is antidogmatic as we must never forget. It is responsible for the visible contradictions, paradoxes which we can uncover. Bruno does not see God in the order of creation and of Nature. For him, as in the Kabbalah, there is no revelation, because the divinity, as he says so often, is in us, and we cannot consider and understand it better than in ourselves. The solution to the Immanence—Transcendence quarrel would be found in an oriental conception of the One, who, without being anthropomorphic or necessarily a creator, supports at the same time, the creation and the being, at the same time Man and God.

Finally Bruno evinces his mysticism in his cosmology, his search for the One, in using, with all the mystics, the language of Love. The Kabbalah shows an identical step. This mystical Unity, in Bruno, is presented in two aspects: 1) *The Infinite* inaccessible to the human intellect. In the Kabbalah, the three degrees of En-Soph are the three supreme lights that no human eyes have ever seen.
2) *A Human World* which shares the concepts of Nature, Substance, Cosmos, Love that men can understand.

These two aspects constitute the One. One must recall Solomon's words about Unity and Hierarchy to which Giordano Bruno grants a real importance:

> Quid est quod est? Ipsum quot fuit
> Quid est quot fuit? Ipsum quod est
> Nihil sub sole novum.

Notes

[1] *De Umbris Idearum* 6 Concetus 13 N.

[2] *La Cena delle Ceneri* - Dialogue I: "Al che rispose il Nolano, che lui non vedea per gli occhi di Copernico, nè di Ptolemo, ma per i proprii, quanto al giudizio e la determinazione;..."

[3] *De gli Eroici Furori* - Dialogue II (First Part): "appresso tutte le cose constano de contrarii;... anzi dico e noto di più, che se non fusse l'amor nelle cose non sarrebe la delettazione, atteso che la fatica fa che troviamo delettazione nel riposo; la separazione è causa che troviamo piacere nella congiuzione;..."

[4] *De Causa, Principio e Uno* - Dialogue 5 -: "Certo (se ben misurano) veggiamo che la corrozione non è altro che une generazione, e la generazione non è altro che una corrozione; l'amore è un odio, l'odio è un amore, al fine... In sustanza dunque e radice, è una medesima cosa amore e odio, amicizia e lite."

[5] *Ibid.* -: "Pero intendete tutto essere in tutto, ma non totalmente e omnomodamente in ciascuno. Pero intendete come ogni cosa è una, ma non unimodamente."

[6] *Ibid.* -: "Una, dico è la possibilità assoluta, uno l'atto, una la forma o anima, una la materia o corpo, una la cosa, unolo ente, uno il massimo ed ottimo..."

[7] *Ibid.* -: "Prima dunque voglio che notiate essere una e medesima scala per la quale la natura descende alla produzion de de le cose, e l'intelletto ascende alla cognizion di quelle; e che l'uno e l'altra da l'unità procede all'unità, passando per la moltitudine di mezzi."

[8] *Lo Spaccio della bestia trionfante* - Dialgoue 2 -: "Sopra tutte le cose, o Saulino, è situata la verità: perchè questa è la unità che soprasiede al tutto, è la bontà che è preeminente ad ogni cosa; perchè uno è lo ente, buono è vero; medesimo e vero, ente e buono."
Also in *De Minimo* -I-4-: "Totum, infinitum, verum, omne, bonum, unum."
Also, in *De Causa, Principio e Uno* - Dialogue 5 -: "Medesima cosa a fatto è la sofia, la verita, la unita".

[9] Emile Namer: *Les aspects de Dieu dans la philosophie de Giordano Bruno*, Paris, Alcan 1926.

[10] *De Umbris Idearum* - II-I -
   Sigillus Sigillorum -II-I -
   De Causa, Principio e Uno - Dialogue II and Dialogue 5.
   Processo Veneto June 2, 1592.

IV.

HIERARCHICAL THOUGHT IN RENAISSANCE ENGLAND, NETHERLANDS,
AND FRANCE, SIR JOHN FORTESCUE, ERASMUS, BODIN, SHAKESPEARE, DESCARTES

אהיה
אהיה ?
יהוה
יהוה

יה ?

אל ?

אלהים ?
להים

יהוה ?
יהוה

יהוה ?
אלהים
צבאות
צבאות

אל שרי ?

ארץ ?

יתקרש שמך מעערב לכפם הארץ

SCALA JACOB.

This Sefirot tree or Tree of Divine Names is the work of Guillaume Postel. This Sefirot tree may be a unique reference to the Sefirot tree as Jacob's Ladder. The ten names of God form the tree; under the tree is written "May your name be blessed from the West to the ends of the earth." This important representation follows a manuscript in Postel's hand entitled Resolutionum Diuinarum Expositio... and is found in The British Library, Sloane ms. 1411 (old shelfmark 2957) fol. 295.

WINIFRED GLEESON KEANEY
SIR JOHN FORTESCUE AND THE POLITICS OF THE CHAIN OF BEING

The notion of the chain of being, as articulated by A. O. Lovejoy and others,[1] is a synthesis of the extraordinarily complex philosophical rationalization by which mankind has attempted to shape a tenable world view. As articulated by Lovejoy, the conception of the chain is perhaps a paradigm of man's efforts to make sense of his life, to account for the awful disparity between the infinite good which is essentially spiritual and the finite inadequacy of the mutable world.

There is some irony in the analogy of the chain, as there is by extension, in our application of that analogy. The physical, interlocked connectedness of a chain makes it an apt metaphoric vehicle to convey the conception of a world of created abundance ranked neatly in an ascending or descending order. But the reductiveness necessarily embodied in metaphor is less paradoxical than the denotative and connotative implications which we must sense in the choice of the chain as vehicle. A chain, through its etymological history, has described the means by which we bind, fetter, restrain and confine. The word comes to English, through Old French, from Latin, where it means *fetter* (*catena*). In all languages, the term has suggested a restriction of freedom, and although as men we have prided ourselves on our position in the alignment of the chain, we must acknowledge that we deserve that position at the expense of freedom of others who link up below us.

The irony is doubled here; in a minor way, the simple metaphoric reductiveness is appalling, and our mortal limitations are exemplified if the best we can do with the profound metaphysical speculations of the greatest of philosophers is to figure their doctrine as a chain. In a more significant way, we demonstrate that perhaps we deserve the tangible limits of our link, for we have used that doctrine, which was shaped to enable us to understand our position relative to the immortal, to define and to elevate our position relative to the mortal. The result is a systematic subordination -- of rock under plant, of plant under beast, of beast under man. Such ranking is in accord with natural law; it has provided us with a scheme of order, which seems a crucial element in mortal existence. Natural law prescribes the ranks, and order prevails within the links as well as between them; thus we apply the restrictive, hierarchical discriminations to our own species. We have always

been able to structure arguments which claim one man's superiority to a less
fortunate fellow man. We should find it ironic that these arguments find cred-
ibility and authority in natural law, which dictates an all-pervasive order
codified in a chain of being.

Although some scholars have questioned the literary, social and economic
consequences of the notion of such a chain,[2] I do not intend to do precisely
that here. It is rather my intention to examine a phenomenon which I find
interesting and somewhat paradoxical: the conversion of the philosophical conception to a pragmatic social weapon. The chain, designed to allow us to accept our finite existence on a relative scale, can become a useful tool in the
real world of human relationships. I shall examine the realization of this potential in a seminal instance in England, in the writings of Sir John Fortescue, a late medieval jurist who was inextricably involved in York-Lancastrian
politics and who wrote again and again on the succession question. I suggest
that Fortescue was a transitional figure, a medieval man who could think (and
write) like a man of the Renaissance, that he had a firm hold on the notion of
order arranged on a chain of being, and that his grasp of this was central to
his political beliefs, actions and writings. He has been called the first of
the modern constitutionalists in England, and I suggest that we can learn
something about what constitutes "modernness" in his thinking by examining his
notion of order as he translates it from a theoretical ideal to a fact of
experiential reality. Educated in the classical and medieval theoretical convictions, he nonetheless experienced and acknowledged the contradictions in
social actuality. His political lifetime was one of compromises, and his prose
works are various attempts to induce concessions from individuals, families or
social groups. His transitional status is thus a significant one, for he applies the methodology of compromise in an attempt to bring about very basic
changes not only in thought but also in social, political activity and structure. There is something of a modern empiricism in his technique, and it is
discernible in his working out of the paradox of the politically functional
chain of being.

Fortescue was a prominent figure in English government between 1430 and
1461. Named Chief Justice of the King's Bench in 1442 by Henry VI, he pros-
pered, both politically and financially as an influential advisor. He was in
the Lancastrian forces at Towton, Ryton and Brancepeth in March and June of
1461, and he fled to Scotland with Margaret of Anjou and Prince Edward when

Edward IV of York claimed the English throne in that year. For ten years Fortescue remained one of Margaret's supporters in exile, first in Scotland and
then in France; when she returned to England in 1471 he accompanied her, and
in May of that year he was taken prisoner by the Yorkists at Tewkesbury. During his exile he had written a number of tracts asserting the legitimacy of
the Lancastrian claim to the throne and disclaiming the Yorkist succession.
After his capture in 1471 he petitioned Edward IV for pardon; Edward withheld
pardon on the condition that Fortescue write a refutation of all his former
arguments against the Yorkist claim. Fortescue complied, and in October of
1473, after he had completed "The Declaracion Upon Certayn Wrytinges"[3] his
petition for restoration to royal favor was granted.[4]

The works which preceded and followed the "Declaracion" are varied in
form and content. The tracts he wrote while in exile in Scotland between 1461
and 1463 are: *De Titulo Edwardi Comitis Marchiae*; *Of the Title of the House of
York*; *Defensio Juris Domus Lancastriae*; *A Defense of the House of Lancaster,
Otherwise Called, A Replication to the Claim of the Duke of York* (the last two
being essentially the same, written in the two languages). His constitutional
works include *De Natura Legis Naturae* (1461-1463), examining the nature of law
and its place in government; *De Laudibus Legum Angliae* (1468-1470), written in
exile for the edification of Price Edward of Lancaster, in preparation for his
tenure as king of England; and *The Governance of England* (1470-1476), a treatise on government and law.[5]

These works, all written after he had abandoned his legal career, embody
a logical sorting out of the complex interrelationship of kingship, subjects,
money, law, and succession. There seems to be no doubt that Fortescue's experiences during the turbulent political years from 1435 to 1461 prompted the
analytical probing of his writing. That the inconsistent abruptness of the
passing back and forth of the crown was detrimental to the country was obvious, especially to a man like Fortescue, who had a sure knowledge of the concept of order as represented in a balanced chain of being. What was not obvious was the formula to end this dangerous game of "musical kings," and it is
this formula that Fortescue searches for in his writings and finally proposes
in his last work, *The Governance of England*.

It has been noted that Fortescue is a transitional figure in constitutional history. He is the earliest of the English legal writers to seek to
bring about specific changes in the social conditions around him. He is like

other medieval constitutionalists in that his conceptions originate in literary sources, both classical and contemporary, but he was not limited to the
realm of theory as were other political commentators of his time. Especially
in *De Natura* and *The Governance*, he offers practical suggestions for reform,
and those suggestions have their genesis in his deductive observations of the
political scene. It is thus his method which distinguishes him from his contemporaries: it seems characteristic of him to be inclined to consider both
the theoretical ideal and experiential reality. Harold Dexter Hazeltine, in
his "General Preface" to Chrimes' edition of *De Laudibus*, observes: "the ideas
which Fortescue founded upon feudal and common law appear to have come for the
most part from his own study as legal practitioner and judge. Fortescue was in
fact the first of medieval writers to base political theories on observation
and practice."[6] Arthur Ferguson notes that "Fortescue's place in the history
of political consciousness may best be appreciated if it is recognized that
his grasp of political reality had far outrun the conceptual equipment he had
inherited.... In his attitude toward the issues ... he demonstrated an ability
we like to think of as modern: to translate even the most abstract principles
into concrete terms, and to keep his mind, even when exploring theory, at the
level of observable conditions."[7] Fortescue could apply his learning to his
life; his writings testify to his tendency to acknowledge and to attempt to
rectify the wrongs in his world.

　　Like other writers of the time, he wrote in three languages, his legal
cases in French and his later writings in either English or Latin; in some
instances he wrote one work twice to leave it in two languages. He seemed to
have had some notion of durability. Although all significant commentary on
Fortescue until now has been restricted to his contributions to constitutionalism in England, he merits consideration from another perspective, one we
might call literary. He wrote English prose in a century which is considered
crucial in the development of that mode, and his work is comparable to much of
the prose literature of that period. Like other writers seeking to correct or
reform, he shapes his suggestions in various generic modes.[8] As he is transitional between Medieval political commentators and Renaissance political commentators, he is also transitional between Medieval literary reformers and
Renaissance literary reformers. The Medieval writers, in their impulse to
teach and correct, aim their maxims and their gentle lessons at the inner man.
In the sermons, the *Ancrene Riwle*, *Handlying Synne*, the *Pearl*, the *Wycliffite*

Bible, the Miracle and Mystery Cycles, and in the writings of the mystics, the motive, expressed in relative degrees of overtness, is to shape man's inner vision of himself. Man's task was to define and accept his place in the scheme of things, however untenable that scheme might be. Even the mystics, who affirm a potential ability and achievement for the individual, and whose beliefs would evolve ultimately to result in the Reformation, confine their affirmation to life within.

Fortescue's literary adaptations of his vision for reform transcend those of his contemporaries, for he directs his attention straight to the scheme by which things work. He has still a concern for the inner man, and he believes in the limits of man, but he moves forward to deal with the structure without. He does not leave behind him the ethics of behavior, for he is very much aware of the physical chaos a corrupt and malicious man can wreak; but he looks to the social structure, to the physical scheme, and he strives to make it less susceptible to those who do wrong and more tenable for those who do right. In this sense he is a forerunner of the Oxford Reformers of the Renaissance. He seeks to improve the quality of life for man by suggesting adjustments and improvements not merely in man's attitudes, but in the social structure in which man must survive. Although he is chronologically a Medieval man, he shares in what we might call a Renaissance vision.

Integral to such a vision and apparently a key to Fortescue's transitional status is his dependence on a universally applicable system of order. The conception of order as hierarchy is an implicit assumption underlying all of his writing, and if he is the first of the modern constitutionalists in that he uses theoretical considerations to bring about real changes in the social strata, then he is also the first of the modern thinkers in England to assert the real political function of the chain of being. Those assertions are most perceptible in two of his works, *De Natura* and *The Governance of England.*

Fortescue outlines the delineations of universal order so precisely in *De Natura* that E. M. W. Tillyard quotes from that work to clarify for modern readers the idea of order as a chain:

> In this order hot things are in harmony with cold, dry
> with moist, heavy with light, high with low. In this or-
> der angel is set over angel, rank upon rank in the king-
> dom of heaven; man is set over man; beast over beast,
> bird over bird, and fish over fish, on the earth in the
> air and in the sea: so that there is no worm that crawls
> upon the ground, no bird that flies on high, no fish that

swims in the depth, which the chain of this order does
not bind in most harmonious concord. Hell alone, inhab-
ited by none but sinners asserts its claim to escape the
embraces of this order.... God created as many different
kinds of things as he did creatures, so that there is no
creature which does not differ in some respect from all
other creatures and by which it is in some respect superior or inferior to all the rest. So that from the highest angel down to the lowest of his kind there is absolutely not found an angel that has not a superior and an
inferior; nor from any man down to the meanest worm is
there any creature which is not in some respect superior
to one creature and inferior to another. So that there is
nothing which the bond of order does not embrace.[9]

De Natura[10] is Fortescue's examination of the applicability of the law of
nature to the principles of government. A polemical work serving as a justification of the Lancastrian claim to the throne, it is the earliest of his writings in which he yokes theoretical analysis and the observation of existing
conditions.[11] Thus his claim on transitional status is first certified in the
work which most explicitly articulates the notion of order signified as a
chain of being. Here he makes royal succession subservient to that order which
is regulated by the law of nature. He makes credible the Lancastrian claim by
invalidating the Yorkist claim, which was based on descent through Philippa,
daughter of Lionel, the second son of Edward III.[12]

In his lengthy disquisition on the place of natural law in the scheme of
things mortal and immortal, Fortescue is not entirely consistent, but he does
at some point subordinate all else to the law of nature. He is at times errat-
ic on the relationship between natural and Divine law, saying in one place
that the Old and New Testament and Divine law are only a fulfillment of natural law, then claiming later that the law of nature is the daughter of Divine
law, the former emanating from the latter: "like light from light, springing
from the Divine law, it becomes one with the Divine law." (p.241) He seems to
be aware of his attempts at compromise, and he uses Aquinas to buttress his
thesis: "it [natural law] is nothing else than a participation of eternal law
in a rational creature." Fortescue is more exact about some things: the human
race, from the time when it went out of Paradise, has been governed by the law
of nature; that law can have no other operation than to dispose man to virtue
(p. 243). It is under natural law that the power of kings took its beginning,
and by its authority and force all just kings have reigned; thus that law,
regulating order, which is the disposition of equal and unequal things whereby

each is assigned its proper place, is the measure by which the question of right succession must be determined.

The second part of the work is a dramatization of Fortescue's use of a conception of order to manipulate political position. The philosophical assertions of the first part yield to application as Fortescue pursues his denial of the claim of York by denying a woman's right to inherit or to transmit the royal title. His pragmatism is somewhat muted here by abstraction: he posits a fictional setting and characters, frames his argument in a debate, and utilizes a mode which is descriptive and narrative rather than expository. The situation is a dispute over the throne of Assyria and Greater Asia; the characters are the three claimants to that throne: the deceased king's brother, daughter, and grandson. The three suitors present their cases before a Justice who deliberates and then renders the decision that only the brother has a natural right to the throne. Although the daughter and grandson claim divine and civil law as support for their respective claims, the law of nature prevails. The daughter cannot rule, since she is a woman, and the grandson, being descended through the woman, cannot rule. A woman can neither have nor transmit the title.

With somewhat ingenuous logic Fortescue elucidates the reasoning behind this verdict through his narrative. The duties of the royal public office are rigorous ones, for which a king must have strength of body and character. Nature always provides the fitting instruments to accomplish appropriate tasks, and a woman, being frail of hands, arms, feet and legs ("the bones and sinews in which strength resides are smaller, weaker and of less virtue in woman than in man." p. 257) is obviously not endowed with the instruments which would make her fit to rule. Conversely, woman is larger than man in her belly, posterior and breasts. It is apparent that nature, who has supplied for every living creature the members adapted to the work for which she designed it, intended women to bear and nurse children and not to rule kingdoms. Fortescue seems to enjoy making this point; he uses Aristotle and Aquinas for support, and is enthusiastic in his analogies. He seems not content with a simple denigration of the physical capacities of women; he apparently feels obliged to demonstrate a naturally complete ineptness: "a woman is a mulcted man (*mas occasionatus*). That hence, as she is deficient in her physical framework, so she is in her reason." (p. 257). Emphatically he reiterates the correctness of nature in apportioning the "appliances" suited to each creature's

purpose. Man must recognize this propriety; women's whole duty is of a "house-
hold and domestic nature only." The analogies sustain his relentless clarification: "An artificer is not so inconsiderate as to cleave wood with a mat-
tock, nor a sailor so careless as to entrust the oar to the hands of one with
palsy." "Who ever hunts hares with cats?" (p. 257). His logic must have violated even some fifteenth-century sensibilities, but the sheer weight of the
argument carries the obvious moral: blunt mattocks, palsied hands, silly cats,
and women are quite naturally lower in the chain and lacking in the keenness
and sureness which are essentially kingly.

The next step seems relatively simple: since one cannot pass on to another a right greater than he himself has, a woman cannot function, instrumental-
ly, as transmitter of a title. The subject is debated at length, and the argument of natural law's prohibition of female rule is buttressed variously,[13]
but essentially woman's subordination to man, analogous to the subordination
outlined along the length of the chain of being, is established and affirmed
in accord with the visible evidence of the law of nature. The lesson and the
formula exemplified in *De Natura* have a real political significance. The orderly relegation of woman to a housewifely niche in the scheme of being serves
to illustrate that the Yorkist claim to the English throne through Phillippa
is in violation of the natural law and therefore invalid.[14]

Fortescue's construct of hierarchical order is used to assert political
order in another work, his treatise on kingship and law, *The Governance of
England*.[15] Written between 1470 and 1476, *The Governance* incorporates and reflects Fortescue's years of involvement in the internecine struggles for succession. During those years it must have become apparent to him that one of
the constants in the assortment of variables of those struggles was the need
for the king, whatever his family ancestry, to be strong. Stability in the
realm depends on the stability of the king, and a king who is not strong is
susceptible, even if he makes no mistakes. *The Governance of England* is an attempt to ensure strength and independence to the royal office; Fortescue proposes to enable a king to rule efficaciously by reforming the structure in
which he rules. Thus Fortescue distinguishes himself from his contemporaries,
both in his apprehension of reality and with his constructive suggestions for
real change in the system of things to delimit the potential for error in man.

The Governance is different from his earlier works in that it seems more
measured in tone, more reasonably persuasive than didactic, more subtle in ad-

vocating political adjustments. Implicit in the thesis, method, and conclusions is Fortescue's notion of order as hierarchical apportionment. Although he does not delineate the alignment of the chain as he did in *De Natura*, he assumes its universal omnipresence. To reinforce his thesis, he cites the negative examples of disorder, such as the tyranny of the French king,[16] the impoverishment of the French commons,[17] and the dangerous spectre of "over mighty" subjects.[18] He supports the persuasive appeal of his thesis with Biblical theory, historical precedent, philosophical premise, and contemporary example, finally convincing us that the only tenable way of life is that which provides for a perpetuation of a stable, self-sufficient royal line.

The work opens with the distinction between *dominium regale* (absolute monarchy) and *dominium politicum et regale* (limited monarchy).[19] The latter, which is preferable, depends on a reciprocal balance between the people's assent to be governed and the maintenance of a king who is adequately equipped to govern them justly. Fortescue illustrates the benefits which the people will derive from assuring such adequate equipment to the king. The weal of the people, in fact, depends on the implementation of the suggested reforms, which include a general resumption of lands, a control over the distribution of the king's offices and benefices, and a scheme for the reorganization of the Privy Council. What Fortescue formulates here is a plan in which the rights of the subjects are protected as a consequence of strengthening the executive.

Although such a process seems paradoxical, it reflects the tenacity of its author's grasp on the notion of hierarchical order. Subjects are naturally subordinate to their ruler, and the reinforcement of the correspondent natural rights of both superior and inferior can only confer a symmetrical, but relative, good on both. Throughout his work Fortescue sustains the conviction that things do belong in their designated places. The "harmonious concord" of the chain, manifested in a universal interaction among the elements of being, becomes a political mutual reciprocity between subjects and king. Central to the argument in *The Governance* is wealth, and it is wealth which becomes a pivot for the negotiations of subject and king toward a stable realm. Power is nullified by poverty, just as individual well-being is jeopardized by poverty. The word *poor*, in all its grammatical variations, looms large in *The Governance of England*. The argument is designed to provide more money for the king, thereby assuring him power and independence, without consequently causing poverty either to the common people or to those who must yield so that the king can be financially secure. The logic proceeds by means of threat and reassurance: a poor king will inevitably behave tyrannically; subjects made poor will certainly revolt. A king's power and his freedom are grounded in the wealth of his coffers.[20] Since the well-being of the people is contingent upon the preservation of royal power and freedom, it is their business to see to the shoring up of that wealth. In Fortescue's theory, the rights of private property are invested in the absolute law of nature,[21] and the orderly inequities of the chain on which that law can be figured are brought to bear on the real political/economic situation. The people must yield to provide for the weal of the king.[22]

Being an astute political observer, and having defined the monarchy in England as a limited one in which the responsibilities of a king to his subjects are clearly defined,[23] Fortescue does not advocate royal usurpation of private wealth. He advises instead a system of reforms and a Council which would control the distribution of public wealth, provide for the resumption of royal lands, and function to prevent any one subject from amassing a fortune which might excel the king's. The association between property and power is one more manifestation of Fortescue's adherence to the natural system of order, for property, as regulated by natural law, sustains power, which is distributed by nature in an orderly system of graduated subordination. Government, if it were made to conform to the natural scheme, would maintain its own delicate balance. Acknowledging the intrinsic weaknesses of man, Fortescue proposes in *The Governance* to arrange the mechanics of governing so as to allow the least possible room and a minimum of incentive for self-serving human action. He institutionalizes the chain of being in a political system, which preserves hierarchy and which embodies a set of checks and balances to ensure the perpetuation of order.

Fortescue's tendency to apply the theoretical to the real and to use that application to effect change in the social instrument of English government marks him as an innovative thinker. Integral to his methodology is his apprehension of the chain of being as functional, as an efficient measure by which to arrange political hierarchies. It is interesting to note here that the etymology holds true, that for Fortescue the chain does indeed bind and restrict: woman's place is in the home, and she is strictly confined to that secondary status; the people of a realm are truly subject to their king, and their access to both power and wealth is systematically limited. The chain of being of the law of nature guarantees the appropriate freedoms by restraining freedom; thus the analogy of the chain, which seems theoretically incongruous, proves to be realistically apt.

Although the incongruity remains, in that social subordination is justified in terms of a philosophical conception which was intended to enable man to accept his finite existence in a cosmic scheme, the realism is also ineluctable. Convinced of the necessity of a theoretical paradigm for governance, Fortescue nonetheless found himself on the battlefield, in exile, and finally imprisoned and charged. His preoccupation with the real problems of life and politics is understandable. Arthur Ferguson has suggested that it is time to take our evaluation of Fortescue from the narrow realm of legal studies and to place it in the context of the history of ideas, broadly considered.[24] I think that Ferguson is right, and that we should perhaps consider that Fortescue's work represents an important stage in English social, political thought. Modern scholars have found his constitutional work to be transitional, and a study of his prose style would reveal that he made progressive contributions to the development of English prose; in both cases, it is his method which marks him as a thinker who could espouse a modern world view from a medieval perspective. The preceding descriptions of *De Natura* and *The Governance* serve to demonstrate his application of that method. What follows is an examination of the thinking which seem to lie behind his tendency to convert theory to action.

Using the assymetrical apportionment of the chain, Fortescue gives us a social contract exemplified. In order to achieve peace, which is the "unity of human society," and love, which is the "bond of peace," man must make trade-offs. Fortescue grounds the sovereignty of the king firmly in the law of nature, and he delineates man's responsibilities of deference to right succession and right rule. He balances this insistence with abundant evidence of the weal that will accrue to a people who insure power to their king, and he waxes hortative in conclusion. "For every man of the land shall by this foundation every day be the merrier, the surer, fare the better in his body and all his goods, as every wise man may now well conceive.... For this shall be a collage in which shall sing and pray for evermore all the men of England spiritual and temporal."[25]

This admirable compromise is not what makes Fortescue noteworthy; more singular is the means by which he achieves it. He yokes two facets of life

which have confounded Englishmen, perhaps all men, from the beginning of time:
the imperfections of mortal beings and the intricacies of the polity of the
king. The former, apparent by thematic weight in the literature and philosophy
of England, is also the dilemma which prompted the formalizing of the notion
of a chain of being. The latter was, of course, a determining factor in the
scale of English history, and it colors the literature of England from its
earliest days. The monarchic institution has roots in native tradition;
neither history nor tribal custom records a form of government other than
kingship for any of the states established in England by Germanic invaders.[26]
The English have always had to deal with the perplexities of regal authority.
With only some modifications, the king has continuously been at the center of
a societal cult, sustaining that stance by means of his function as a link between the realms of the mortal and the immortal: making sacrifices for victory
and plenty in a pagan society, and leading his people to conversion in a
Christianized one. Fortescue's sometimes lamentable compromises derive from
his ability to weigh in one hand man's imperfections, and in the other the
social nature of kingship, and then to bring his hands together, measuring the
extent to which each must yield in order to constitute a functional instrument. The yielding effects the trade-offs, and Fortescue is more sophisticated
than his medieval counterparts in that he demands concessions not only from
individuals but also from the system.

In the popular argument of *The Governance*, wealth is the lever for balance between king and people, but in theory, it is law which can dictate and
regulate the reciprocal relationship. He calls for *dominium politicum et regale*, a rule in which the people give their consent to the laws by which they
are governed. In a very strict sense, then, Fortescue is not a proponent of
the divine right of kingship as literally defined. His work can be read as an
impulse toward the advocacy of a royal office which procures its power from
the people. The impulse is only initial, however, and at times it seems tenta-
tive enough to be inconsistent and even self-thwarting. For example, he is am-
bivalent on the relationship between natural, civil, and Divine law; and although he provides an adequate construct for checks on the excesses of power
among the people, the law and even his reformed council seem not to include a
mechanism to protect the people against a willful king. His admission in *De
Natura* that only divine vengeance could be counted on to punish, and therefore
to restrain, the king, mitigates the republicanism of his system. Still, he

apparently views the law and the reformed council as vehicles for guarding the citizen's liberties, and it is clear throughout his work that he seeks to make life more prosperous for the people by stabilizing the government to which they are subject.

We could expect Fortescue to have an explicit awareness of the intrinsic imperfections of mortals. As a medieval thinker, as a court figure between 1430 and 1461, and as a Lancastrian supporter in years of York/Lancastrian tumult, he would have been thoroughly trained and experienced in the limitations and transgressions of rationality when men come together. It seems significant that this perception led him not to despair but to venture constructive external means to circumscribe these imperfections. For him, the need for a cooperative human compromise originates in the original human compromise. If man were perfect, then the complex, hierarchical social system would be extraneous, but man's first refusal to make a singular concession promulgated the necessity of a lifetime of concessions for the species. This is Fortescue's thinking, as we read it in *De Natura*,[27] and this explains precisely why the theoretical notion of order must suffer pragmatic, political distortion, functioning to restrict individual freedom in a post-lapsarian world. Man's susceptibility to governance, by the law of nature and by its affiliates, civil and human laws, has its genesis at the end of *Genesis* III. Having told us that the human race has been so governed since the time when it went out of Paradise,[28] Fortescue has apparently also told us why it has been so governed. Human deficiencies find circumscription in the law, which functions "with no other operation than to lead man to virtue."[29]

And so, Fortescue, understanding both man's defects and the needs of the social system of governance, interprets them not as mutually exclusive phenomenon but as correlatives which necessarily serve as foils one to the other. Thus he applies the philosophical idea of order to the mechanical construct of government in the hopes of ensuring a complementary stability for all. He was not the last to gain political ground with the metaphorical chain; he has had prominent successors in the perpetuators of Tudor absolutism in the sixteenth century.[30] And in spite of occasional inconsistencies in his motives and logic, he had an understanding of the need to bring the ideal and the real together, demanding concessions from each. It is here that we find his real significance; his work exemplifies a method which bridges historical space between the medieval theoretical world view and a modern empirical world view.

He is the earliest of the English constitutional writers to make this link, which is objectified in his use of the chain of being to achieve pragmatic social reform.

NOTES

[1]Arthur O. Lovejoy, *The Great Chain of Being* (1936; rev. New York: Harper & Row, 1960). See also E. M. W. Tillyard, *The Elizabethan World Picture* (New York: Random House, 1943); S. K. Heninger, Jr., *Touches of Sweet Harmony: Pythagorean Cosmology and Renaissance Poetics* (San Marino, Calif.: Huntingdon Library, 1974); C. S. Lewis, *The Discarded Image* (Cambridge: The University Press, 1964).

[2]Wilbur Sanders, *The Dramatist and the Received Idea* (Cambridge: The University Press, 1968), pp. 143-157; also Michael Manheim, *The Weak King Dilemma in the Shakespearean History Play* (Syracuse, N.Y.: Syracuse University Press, 1973).

[3]The only edition in which this "Declaration" appears is *The Works of Sir John Fortescue*, ed. Thomas [Fortescue] Lord Clermont (London: Ellis and White [printed for private distribution], 1869, 1880).

[4]Biographical material here is drawn from the following: Thomas Lord Clermont, *A History of the Family of Fortescue in All its Branches* (London: Ellis and White, 1880); James Gairnder, "Sir John Fortescue," in the *Dictionary of National Biography*, ed. Leslie Stephen and Sidney Lee (London: Smith Elder, 1885-1901); Edward Foss, *The Judges of England* (London: Longman, Brown, Green and Longmans, 1848-64); Charles Plummer, "Introduction" to *The Governance of England* (London: Oxford University Press, 1885); Percy Henry Winfield, *The Chief Sources of English Legal History* (Cambridge: Harvard University Press, 1925).

[5]All are in *The Works of Sir John Fortescue*; two of the works have been published separately since Lord Clermont's edition: *De Laudibus Legum Anglie*, ed. S. B. Chrimes (Cambridge: The University Press, 1949), and *The Governance of England*, ed. Charles Plummer (London: Oxford University Press, 1885).

[6]Harold Dexter Hazeltine, "General Preface" to *De Laudibus*, ed. S. B. Chrimes, p. xlv.

[7]Arthur B. Ferguson, "Fortescue and the Renaissance: A Study in Transition," *Studies in the Renaissance*, 6 (1959), 193, 184. See also, by the same author, *The Articulate Citizen of the English Renaissance* (Durham, N.C.: Duke University Press, 1965).

[8]For example, *The Governance* is an expository treatise; *De Natura* is shaped as a fictional debate, *De Laudibus* as a dialogue; the last is also within the tradition of the "Mirror for Princes" discourse.

[9]*The Elizabethan World Picture*, pp. 26-7; c.f. *The Works of Sir John Fortescue*, pp. 322-323. Fortescue's probable sources for this conception are numerous. We know that he was familiar with the work of Augustine through *De Civitate Dei* and through excerpts in the *Compendium Morale* by Roger Waltham; he knew the *Summa Theologica* and selections from Aristotle and Boethius at least through another compendium, the *Auctoritates Aristotelis*; see Plummer, pp. 98-100, 169-74. At this point in *De Natura*, Fortescue cites "The Philosopher" [Aristotle], *De Coelo et Mundo*, iij, and *Metaphysics*, xi, and Augustine: 1. *De Civitate Dei*, xv.

[10]*The Works of Sir John Fortescue*, pp. 188-331. English translation by the Right Honourable Chichester Fortescue. On *De Natura*, see Paul E. Gill, "Sir John Fortescue, Chief Justice of the King's Bench, Polemicist on the Succession Problem, Governmental Reformer, and Political Theorist." Ph.D. Diss., Penn. State Univ., 1968; Paul E. Gill, "Politics and Propaganda in Fifteenth-Century England: The Polemical Writings of Sir John Fortescue," *Speculum*, 46 (1971), 333-347; Edgar Lacy, "Sir John Fortescue and the Law of Nature," Ph.D. Diss., Univ. of

Illinois, Urbana, 1940; Veikko Litzen, *A War of Roses and Lilies: The Theme of Succession in Sir John Fortescue's Works* (Helsinki: Academia Scientiarum Fennica, 1971).

[11]Plummer, "Introduction," *The Governance of England*, p. 82.

[12]Information on York-Lancastrian history is taken from: Paul Murray Kendall, *The Yorkist Age* (New York: W. W. Norton & Co., 1962); J. R. Lander, *Conflict and Stability in Fifteenth-Century England* (London: Hutchinson Univ. Library, 1969); J. R. Lander, *The Wars of the Roses* (New York: G. Putnam's Sons, 1966).

[13]The brother claims, for instance, that Civil law forbids a woman to be a judge or magistrate, or to succeed her father in an administrative position which carries personal rank or dignity; he also points out that Scripture, and therefore divine law, places woman under the dominion of man.

[14]Such reasoning, if reversed, would also be disastrous to the Lancastrian claim, which is by descent through Blanche of Lancaster. Fortescue declines to include this piece of information, however.

[15]In addition to the editions cited above in note 6, *The Governance* is reprinted in *Complaint and Reform in England*, ed. W. H. Dunham and S. Pargellus (New York: Oxford University Press, 1938), pp. 51-82. The constitutional theory advanced in *The Governance* has drawn a good deal of attention. See S. B. Chrimes, "Sir John Fortescue and His Theory of Dominium," *T. R. H. S.*, Fourth Series, 17 (1934), 117-147; Felix Gilbert, "Sir John Fortescue's *Dominium Regale et Politicum*," *Medievalia et Humanistica*, 2 (1944), 88-97; R. W. K. Hinton, "English Constitutional Theories from Sir John Fortescue to Sir John Eliot," *E. H. R.*, 75 (1960), 410-425; C. H. McIlwain, *The Growth of Political Thought in the West* (London, 1932), pp. 354-63; C. A. J. Skeel, "The Influence of the Writing of Sir John Fortescue," *T. R. H. S.*, Fourth Series, 10 (1916), 77-114. Because of its early position in the development of English prose, *The Governance* is referred to often in studies of that genre. The constitutional content seems to distract attention from style, however, and analysis is therefore minimal. See H. S. Bennett, *Chaucer and the Fifteenth Century* (1947) rpt. New York: Oxford University Press, 1961), pp. 193ff.; Raymond W. Chambers, "On the Continuity of English Prose from Alfred to More and His School," in *Life of Sir Thomas More*, ed. Elsie Vaughan Hitchcock, EETS, OS No. 186 (London: Oxford University Press, 1932), pp. xlv-clxxiv; P. J. C. Field, *Romance and Chronicle: A Study of Malory's Prose Style* (Bloomington, Indiana: Indiana University Press, 1971), p. 21; Ian Gordon, *The Movement of English Prose* (Bloomington: University of Indiana Press, 1966); Alice Greenwood, "English Prose in the Fifteenth Century," in the *Cambridge History of English Literature* (New York: G. Putnam's, 1908), pp. 337ff.

[16]*The Governance of England*, ed. Plummer, p. 114.

[17]*Ibid.*

[18]*The Governance of England*, ed. Plummer, p. 128.

[19]*The Governance of England*, ed. Plummer, p. 109. Much of the discussion on this work has been centered on the meaning of these two terms. They differ essentially in their relationship to the law. In an absolute monarchy, the King rules by laws which he made himself; in the limited monarchy, the King rules only by laws to which the people give their assent. A representative exchange about the terms is that between Charles Plummer and C. H. McIlwain. Plummer finds the connotation of *politicum* to be "republican"; McIlwain disagrees, claiming that for Fortescue, the king has neither superior nor peer in government; thus the term *politicum* carries the meaning of "constitutional." This kind of controversy about the definition of *politicum* under-

lies the attempts to discern "modernity" in *The Governance.* If Fortescue did mean "repbuli-can," then he was about a century and a half ahead of his time, and his work is truly modern. Plummer, therefore, sees the work as a modern one; McIlwain does not. See C. H. McIlwain, *Constitutionalism Ancient and Modern* (Ithaca, New York: Cornell University Press, 1940), p. 91. The debate about "modernity" here is relative to content; my thesis about Fortescue's modernity is relative to his methodology.

[20]Chapters VI and VII of *The Governance* are devoted to estimations of the king's ordinary and extraordinary charges, respectively, pp. 120-26.

[21]Max A. Shepard, "The Theory of Sir John Fortescue," in *Essays in History and Political Theory in Honor of Charles H. McIlwain,* ed. Carl Wittke (Cambridge: Harvard University Press, 1936), pp. 300-01.

[22]Chapter VII of *The Governance* is entitled: "YFF THE KYNGES LIVELODE SUFFICE NOT, HIS SUBGETTES AUGHT TO MAKE HIT SUFFICIENT," p. 126.

[23]The king's duties, defined in Chapter IV, are: to defend his realm against their outward enemies by the sword, and to defend his people against inward wrongdoers by justice. The source Fortescue cites for his definition is the first Book of Kings (*The Governance,* ed. Plummer, p. 116).

[24]Ferguson, "Fortescue and the Renaissance: A Study in Transition," p. 177.

[25]*The Governance of England,* ed. Plummer, p. 155.

[26]William A. Chaney, *The Cult of Kingship in Anglo-Saxon England* (Manchester: University of Manchester Press, 1970), p. 7.

[27]See on *De Natura* and law of nature.

[28]*De Natura,* p. 243.

[29]*Ibid.*

[30]George Buchanan, *De Jure Regni apud Scotos* [1579], tr. C. F. Arrowood (Austin, Texas: University of Texas Press, 1949), pp. 46-47; J. F. Danby, *Shakespeare's Doctrine of Nature* (London: Oxford University Press, 1949), pp. 51-2; Charles Merbury, *A Briefe Discourse of Royall Monarchie* (London, 1581), p. 43; Irving Ribner, *The English History Play* (Princeton: Princeton University Press, 1957), p. 314.

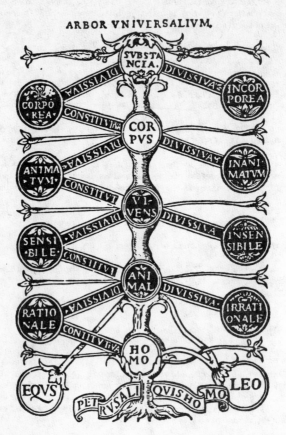

The Tree of Universals from an early logic text published in the new world. From Alfonso Avera Cruce, <u>Dialectica, Resolutio cum textu Aristotelis</u>, Mexico, 1554. A copy is found in the History of Logic Collection, Humanities Research Center, The University of Texas at Austin, and it is used as an emblem of the Graduate Department of Philosophy.

MARGO TODD

ERASMUS, THE GREAT CHAIN OF BEING, AND THE PURITAN REVOLUTION

Ten years ago, Michael Walzer published a somewhat misguided but nonetheless brilliant book called *The Revolution of the Saints*. In it, he argued that "the thrust of puritan doctrine ... was clear enough: it pointed to the overthrow of the traditional order."[1] The book began to draw critical fire immediately, and the shooting is not over yet. Perhaps one measure of the book's brilliance is the fact that a decade after its publication, Patrick Collinson has devoted thirty-eight pages of his analysis of *The Religion of Protestants* in Elizabethan and Jacobean England to criticism of Walzer's work.[2] Collinson has followed the lead of earlier critics in denying to the preachers the exilic anomie with which Walzer endowed them, and he insists on the socially conservative *intent* of their preaching. But even Collinson is forced to acknowledge that the "manifest, if latent, destiny" of puritan doctrine seems indeed to have been the overthrow of traditional order. For when all is said and done, he--and we--are still faced with the fact of the Civil War, with the willingness of those godly gentlemen who sat in the Long Parliament to try and to execute the natural leaders of the traditional social order. How, then, shall we explain the political conscience of radical puritanism? Where shall we find its ideological foundations?

Walzer traced the roots of seventeenth century radicalism to intellectual developments of the previous century. Specifically, he attributed to the Calvinist theology of sixteenth century puritans the demise of the medieval theory of human society as an extension of the cosmological Great Chain of Being. The Chain of Being, a notion derived initially from Neoplatonic theory, conceives of the universe as a hierarchy of essence and degrees, a harmonious order which is by its very nature unalterable. The medieval ordering of the cosmos divides aetherial from aerial beings, and aerial from terrestrial, placing each in its proper sphere. In parallel fashion, it separates reason from appetite, soul from body, king from commons, and fills the space in between with a hierarchical arrangement of intermediaries. What is important is that not only the arrangement itself, but the precise position of each element within it is part of the nature of the cosmos; that is, it is determined not by any action or behavioral merit of the element, but by the natural essence with which it has been endowed.[3]

What this means at the level of human society is that the essential in-
equality of persons is ensconced in a rigid hierarchy of birth in which movement of an individual out of his allotted social space is necessarily regarded
as his attempt to flout the authority of the Forger of the Great Chain; it is
a challenge to the natural order of the universe.[4] Virtue is regarded as in-
bred, not inculcated; hence hereditary aristocracy is a precise reflection of
the cosmic order within the sphere of human relations.

Walzer finds Protestant theology diametrically opposed to the central
tenet of the medieval schema—that degree in the static, hierarchical order of
the universe is a matter of being, rather than behavior. The Protestant emphasis on direct communication between the individual and God, and on the need
for godly behavior as the saint's proper response to his election, is seen as
militating against hierarchy itself, and especially against a static hierarchy
of birth.[5] The arbitrary God of the Calvinists, according to Walzer, establishes his own omnipotence by leveling the cosmos and destroying the intermediary powers of angels, saints, bishops, and kings. Degree in the Kingdom of
the Elect depends on behavior, rather than on being, and from this principle
puritans would conclude that status in the commonwealth ought to be based on
godly action, rather than on birth.

The argument that the Great Chain of Being was thus undermined by sixteenth century intellectual developments is a compelling one. Indeed, this is
one of the few portions of Walzer's argument which critics have not directly
attacked. But Walzer's focus is narrow. If we broaden our vision of the intellectual milieu in which puritanism grew, we find within our scope many intellectual forces other than Protestant theology. Among the most significant of
these in terms of its formative influence on the puritan political conscience
was Christian humanism, best exemplified in the works of Erasmus.

Erasmus' writings are ubiquitous in puritan book inventories and commonplace books.[6] They find a prominent place in the tutorial curriculula of Ox-
bridge colleges in the Elizabethan and early Stuart period.[7] And they are
among the books which puritan parents bought for their children.[8] Puritan
émigrés made Erasmus' *Colloquies* required reading in New England grammar
schools.[9] And both the published sermons and the sermon notebooks of puritans
cite Erasmus in marginal notes on social and political as well as exegetical
issues.[10] Erasmus' view of the Chain of Being, then, is crucial for our understanding of puritan social thought. And those of his works most often read by

puritans--the *Colloquies*, the *Adages*, and the *Institutio principis christiani*
--have a great deal to say about the medieval view of cosmological and social
order. What was Erasmus' view of the Great Chain of Being? The examination of
his works which follows will demonstrate that the initial challenge to the
Great Chain of Being came in the sixteenth century not from Protestant theology, but from Christian humanism. In fact, the social thought of Erasmus will
reveal him to have been not only an opponent of the medieval scheme, but also
the creator of a radically new social design based on that allegedly Protestant principle that behavior, rather than birth, should determine status.

The Erasmus of the *Colloquies* and *Adages* stands out as a staunch, often
bitter opponent of the most basic elements of the medieval social order. The
notion of an aristocracy of birth was repugnant to him, and he bestowed some
of his most caustic social commentary on what he regarded as one of the most
unfortunate outcomes of it--hereditary monarchy. Just as he denied the necessity for intermediaries between men and God,[11] so he rejected the links of the
Great Chain of Being which correspond in human society to the celestial hierarchy. And his rejection incorporated a very basic critique of the medieval/
Neoplatonic model of the cosmos: it insisted that degree is not properly a
matter of being, or natural essence. Degree in society should correspond
rather to virtue, and virtue, in Erasmus' experience, seemed all too often to
bear an inverse relationship to exalted birth. In early modern Europe as Erasmus perceived it, the aristocracy was seldom composed of the *aristos*.

This thesis is perhaps most forcefully argued in Erasmus' lengthy commentary on the adage *Scarabeus aquilam quaerit*, which first appeared in the 1515
edition of the popular *Adagiorum Chiliades*.[12] Here the natural hierarchy of
the animal kingdom, presided over by the eagle and the lion, is presented as
the precise counterpart to the domination of the human social and political
order by king and nobles. Erasmus' conclusions are devastating to the honor
and prestige accorded to royalty and nobility as such. According to the traditional conception, the inherent nobility of the eagle won it its royal title,
and the status of the beetle (popularly thought to dwell and feed on dung) was
likewise determined by its natural position in the Chain of Being, its inherent lowliness. But Erasmus saw the irony of this order:

> The eagle alone has seemed suitable in the eyes of the
> wise men to represent the symbol of a king--the eagle,
> neither beautiful, nor songful, nor good to eat, but car-
> nivorous, greedy, predatory, ravaging, warring, solitary,

> hated of all, a universal pest, the creature who can do
> the most harm and would like to do even more than it can.
>
> It is exactly on the same grounds that the lion is ap-
> pointed king of the animals--when there is no other great
> beast which is fiercer or more noisome.... Obviously it
> must be a royal creature, just like the eagle.[13]

Other animals, even the lowliest, are by contrast positive contributors to the
common weal: dogs watch over men's possessions, oxen till the soil, mules
carry heavy loads. And it is the occupant of the humblest position of all in
the animal realm, the beetle, which receives the highest praise from Erasmus
for its diligence, reliability, and ingenuity: "What valour of spirit the
beetle has! What mental power, worthy of heroes!"[14]

A more complete inversion of the traditional hierarchy can hardly be
imagined. If kings are universal pests, and the least of commoners heroes,
what must Erasmus' readers conclude about their own social order? Elsewhere,
Erasmus was even more blatant in his castigation of those born to prominence.
In the *Institutio principis Christiani*, Erasmus compared the hereditary succession of his own time with barbarian practices of old and argued that "kings
who have the inclination of brigands and pirates should be put in the same
class with them. For it is the character, not the title, that marks the
king."[15] In the adage *Civitas non Civitas* Erasmus' republican sentiments
emerge; acknowledging, however, that monarchy was an unavoidable evil in his
own day, he argued for elective rather than hereditary kings.[16] He called it
absurd to regard birth in determining who should rule, given the evidence of
history and observation that even if kings in the present system are not found
to be downright evil, they create mischief in their realms by their lack of
understanding: "You merely have to turn over the chronicles of the ancients
and the moderns," said Erasmus, "and you will find that in several centuries
there have been barely one or two princes who did not by sheer stupidity bring
disaster to human affairs."[17] Folly obviously maintains her empire even over
emperors.[18]

Erasmus did not restrict his criticism to the summit of the nobility.
Having noted in another adage the obscure, poverty-stricken social origins of
Jesus and the Apostles, "lowest of the low, the objects of everyone's scorn",
he contrasted those who receive honor as nobly-born:

> You would find in no one less real nobility than in those
> Thrasos with their long pedigrees and collars of gold and
> grand titles, who brag of their noble blood; and no one

> is further from true courage than those who pass for val-
> iant and invincible just because they are rash and quar-
> relsome. There is no one more abject and enslaved than
> those who think themselves next to the gods, as they say,
> and masters of all.

"Noble birth," he concluded, "is simply laughable, an empty name."[19] If society were scaled according to true virtue, the present nobility would surely
occupy the lowest position, since they are in practice the deliberate destroy-
ers of the common good. In his commentary on *Ut fici oculis incumbunt*, he portrayed the great lords of the realm as "insatiable in their greed, most corrupt in their appetites, most malignant in their cruelty, inhuman in their
despotism—real enemies of the public weal, and highway robbers ... who fatten
on public misfortune."[20] They are no less despicable in their personal conduct. In the colloquy *De rebus ac vocabulis*, Erasmus defined a knight as one
who has possessed himself by inheritance or by purchase of a title, and who
"never does a good deed, ... dresses like a dandy, wears rings on his fingers,
whores bravely, dices constantly, plays cards, spends his life in drinking and
having a good time...."[21] (One is reminded of puritan criticism of Charles I's
courtiers a century later.) How absurd it is to bestow honor and power on such
an unworthy class; nonetheless, Erasmus observed such absurdity in daily practice. In his view, if preference must be given, it should go to the common-
born; one who glories in his ancestry is in fact "far from virtue, the only
true fount of nobility."[22]

There are obviously strong egalitarian elements in Erasmus' writings. He
reversed the social order not only in the case of kings and commoners, but
also in regard to masters and servants, old and young.[23] His disdain for the
Great Chain of Being is nowhere as supremely evident as in his bold assertion
in the *Institutio* that "Nature created all men equal, and slavery was imposed
on nature."[24]

This should not be construed to imply, however, that Erasmus was completely anti-hierarchical or in any sense of the word democratic in his social
outlook. He was, after all, an early modern man, and he shared the concern of
his contemporaries with the ever-present threat of social chaos should degree
be abolished. He was particularly affected by the German Peasants' Revolt,
which inspired in him a horror of anarchy: "The peasants raise dangerous riots
and are not swayed from their purpose by so many massacres. The commons are
bent on anarchy;... the whole earth is pregnant with I know not what calam-

ity."[25] Accordingly, princes are to be endured "lest anarchy--on the whole a worse evil--takes the place of tyranny. The experience of public events has often proved--and the recent peasants' revolt in Germany shows us--that the harshness of princes is of some degree more tolerable than the confusion of anarchy."[26] His critique of the Anabaptists also revolves around the radicals' disdain for rulers and order: they "go about to disturb the whole world with horrible confusion."[27]

Presumably as result of his fear of that "horrible confusion" of anarchy, Erasmus proposed an alternative social order which does incorporate hierarchy. But in Erasmus' scheme, it is not being or birth which determines status in the hierarchy; rather, it is behavior--active evidence of virtue.[28] Equality at birth simply allows for the potential of wisdom, moral uprightness, and ruling ability in a given individual, irrespective of class or condition of birth. It is an allowance not particularly surprising to discover in the theory of a man ever-conscious of his own base birth.

How, then, shall we explain Erasmus' apparent contempt for the "common sort"? Very amply, Erasmus re-defined the term. For him, the appelation "common" or "vulgar" was related not to social class, but to level of understanding and moral uprightness. The "stupid generality of men" are those who "blunder into wrong judgments because they judge everything from the evidence of the bodily senses."[29] The "common people" include all those who are fooled by the false opinions of astrologers and other superstition mongers; yet Erasmus did not fail to point out that even kings and emperors are susceptible to this folly.[30] To value gems, gold, royal purple, the pomp of heralds, and an exalted genealogy is one characteristic of the "base, vile, and unbecoming" thought of the vulgar. But Erasmus found this trait typical of the opinions of the princely estate. "How ridiculous it is," he exclaimed, for one possessed of these superficial benefits to regard himself as "so far superior to all because of them, and yet in light of real goodness of spirit to be found inferior to many born from the very dregs of society."[31] Erasmus would have concurred heartily with Archbishop Cranmer's judgment that the children of the poor are often more gifted than gentlemen's sons.[32] When Erasmus did use the term "common" in its more usual sense of low social estate, he was as often as not alluding to the wisdom of simple folk.[33]

Given, then, that the combination of birth, wealth, and honor corresponds neither to understanding nor to virtue, it is not a proper criterion for the designation of a ruler or ruling class. Rather, wisdom, learning, and moral excellence--possibilities at any social level--should be the sole considerations. It is noteworthy that when discussing the problem of who should rule, Erasmus established the pattern which Walzer tells us the puritans followed: he rejected the traditional literary image of society as an organism in favor of the more flexible image of the ship. This image allows choice of a captain on the basis of merit, not birth (or *essential* headship, as in the organic metaphor):

> In navigation the wheel is not given to him who surpasses his fellow in birth, wealth, or appearance, but rather to him who excels in his skill as a navigator, in his alertness, and in his dependability. Just so the rule of a state: most naturally the power should be entrusted to him who excels all in the requisite of kingly qualities of wisdom, justice, moderation, foresight, and zeal for the public welfare.[34]

In the Erasmian order, "there is no real honor except that which springs from virtue and good deeds."[35]

One other aspect of the Chain of Being which was discarded by Erasmus deserves mention. The medieval conceptualization of the cosmos was static; in fact, change has been called the "perennial bugbear of the Great Chain". Change is the ultimate threat to a model in which the social order, like the cosmological, is a *given*, a matter of being.[36] A positive view of the possibility of change within the social order was thus one of the most significant innovations of Christian humanist social theory. Sixteenth Century humanists were well aware of changes taking place within their own world. Such circumstances as the increasing numbers and influence of the mercantile elements of society, rising popular disillusionment with old authorities (especially religious authorities), the apparent rise in the numbers of poor and vagabonds-- all were duly noted by Erasmus and set forth as evidence that the cosmos is not, in fact, a static entity. In Richard Taverner's 1539 translation of the *Adages*, his sense of flux is expressed clearly: "There is an alteration of all things ... in men's things nothing is perpetual, nothing stable, but all pass and repass even like to the ebbing and flowing of the ocean sea."[37] New problems arise; new solutions are required. And it was Erasmus' hope that with the spread of the new learning, humankind would be enabled to construct a new, rational, humane social order in the changing world.

For Erasmus, war, ignorance, crime, and poverty are among the social evils which result not merely from individual moral failure, but from a static rather than a progressive view of human society.[38] In his reckoning, these evils both can and must be changed. Change may be in and of itself good; stagnation always spells defeat. The enemy on whom he declared his own war, therefore, was custom, the ultimate barrier to social change, the guardian of all that is archaic. It is custom, he said, which allows the proliferation of holy days which results in idleness and its attendant evils, gluttony, drunkenness, and lechery: "and why should it be an offense against religion to change the custom, for the very same reason for which our ancestors established it?"[39] (It was precisely this line of reasoning which puritans followed when, during the Interregnum, they abolished holy days, including Christmas.) It is custom, according to Erasmus, which prevents bad laws from being amended.[40] Custom, the real ruler of early modern society, is "the fiercest tyrant of them all",[41] a tyrant who must be overthrown for a truly rational and godly society to be constructed. In the area of political theory, the radical implications of this view of change are apparent in Erasmus' warning to the ungodly prince: "no one can have the same rights over men, free by nature, as over herds of cattle. This very right which you hold, was given you by popular consent. Unless I am mistaken, the hand which gave can take it away."[42] The Long Parliament would do just that.

English puritans, I have suggested, grew up with Erasmus. They learned their Latin grammar from the *Colloquies* and *Adages*; surely it is reasonable to suppose that they picked up much of their social and political thought at the same time. When the time came for political change, for action against the "natural" rulers of church and society in the 1640s, those rebels and regicides anxious to legitimate their radical activity had only to look to their commonplace books for an apologetic for action. When William Bright argued from the mutability of the world that "custom is an idiot, and whosoever dependeth wholly upon him, without the discourse of reason, will ... become a slave", he wrote in an Erasmian tradition. He concluded, as Erasmus had, that change is essential for social progress.[43] The preacher Thomas Gataker echoed Erasmus when he warned nobles not to rely on their birth to give them status in God's kingdom, but to look to their actions, since "it is with men as with counters: howsoever while the account lasteth one standeth for a penny and another for a pound, yet are they all counters alike before and after the account, when they are together in the bag." Rulers who neglect the common good in their pride of birth "are more dangerous to Crown and State, I say not than idle vagrants, or than whoremasters and adulterers, or than thieves and murderers, ... but even than popish traitors and conspirators."[44] When Lords Saye and Sele and Brooke were considering emigration to New England, the official response from the puritan registracy there would have delighted Erasmus. The puritans of Massachusetts warned their lordships that exalted birth was no guarantee of political status in the godly commonwealth: should their progeny not be endowed with virtue and ability to rule, "We should expose them rather to reproach and prejudice and the commonwealth with them, than exalt them to honour, if we should call them forth, when God doth not, to public authority."[45] Oliver Cromwell's preference for "a plain russet-coated captain that knows what he fights for, and loves what he knows" to "that which you call a gentleman and is nothing else" is reminiscent of Erasmus' valuation of the beetle.[46] Christopher Feake's location of "an enmity against Christ" in aristocracy and monarchy *per se* is another version of the same."[47]

Nor were puritans always unaware of either the origins or the implications of their social theory. Simonds D'Ewes opined that while Erasmus had doubtless left some of his more dangerous principles out of his published works, a few remained that could be construed to call for "dethroning kings and princes". Still, he purchased the *Adages* for his children, and while he insisted that "I have ever maintained obedience to the registrate in all lawful things," he added the standard humanist/puritan qualification, "and that the conscience ought not to be enforced."[48] D'Ewes was fearful of disorder, as Erasmus had been, but he was convinced that a truly godly order would be achieved not by demanding absolute obedience to traditional authorities, but by informing and exhorting individual conscience to take responsibility for virtuous behavior, and by demanding a reform of the larger social order to exalt godly citizenship, rather than exalted birth. Ultimately the lines were drawn between reformist conscience and constituted authority by the requirements of king and bishops. In 1640 the critique of established authority implicit in the humanist reformism of puritanism forced the "hotter sort of Protestants" into a choice which many would have preferred to avoid. But however reluctant they may have been earlier to admit the implications of their opposition to the Great Chain of Being, those who opted to fight for Parliament found that they had readily available a theoretical basis for their action in the Erasmian challenge to existing structures of authority.

NOTES

[1] Michael Walzer, *The Revolution of the Saints* (New York, 1972), p. 118.

[2] Patrick Collinson, *The Religion of Protestants* (Oxford, 1982), pp.150-188.

[3] Arthur O. Lovejoy, *The Great Chain of Being* (Cambridge, Massachusetts, 1936), pp. 52-66 *et passim*. Lovejoy's is the classic study of the genesis of this idea.

[4] "In the words of a later adherent of the theory of the Great Chain of Being, "Take but degree away, untune that string/ And hark! What discord follows!" (Shakespeare, *Troilus and Cressida*, I.iii).

[5] Walzer, pp.151-171.The preachers, according to Walzer, wanted to build a new, disciplined social order, and in fact did develop "a radically new way of talking about the political and social worlds," a "new description of God and the cosmos, of men and his earthly sojourn" in the context of the "new freedom from custom and personal connection" of their changing world (pp.149, 150, 148).

[6] Among countless examples are the commonplace books of Sir Simonds D'Ewes, British Library MS Harl. 186 (1622-1646), and John Rogers, Bodl. MS Rawl. D.273, pp. 118-135, 343.

[7] An example of tutorial directives including works of Erasmus is Emmanuel College I.2.27. MS commonplace books of university students which give prominent place to Erasmus include Trinity, Cambridge MSS R.16.7-10, R.16.14-15, R.16.17-18; CUL MS Add. 6160; CUL MS Add. 6857 f. 17 *et passim*; Bodl. MS Rawl. D.1423, f. 41.

[8] e.g., Andrew G. Watson, *The Library of Sir Simonds D'Ewes* (London, 1966), pp. 101, 117 139, 177 180, 190 196, 309, *et passim*.

[9] S. E. Morrison, *The Intellectual Life of Colonial New England* (Cornell, 1936), p. 106.

[10] Examples from puritan theological and sermon notebooks include BL MS Harl. 3230 (Arthur Hildersham), ff. 114 *et passim*; Bodl. MS Rawl. D.273, pp. 265-266 (John Rogers' notes on a sermon of Laurence Humphrey's); Bodl. MS Sancroft 25 (Emmanuel College, 1629), pp. 121-124. An example of the published puritan sermons with marginal references to Erasmus is William Gouge, *Of Domesticall Duties* (London, 1622).

[11] *The Colloquies of Erasmus* (tr. Craig R. Thompson, Chicago, 1965), p. 38; *Enchiridion militis Christiani* in *The Essential Erasmus* tr. John P. Dolan, New York, 1964), p. 43; *Liber de Sarcienda Ecclesiae Concordia* in Dolan, pp. 369, 380; *The Praise of Folly* (tr. Hoyt Hopewell Hudson, Princeton, 1941), pp. 56-57. In the *Institutio principis Christiani* (tr. L. K. Born, New York, 1936), p. 196 he argued against a mediating position for the stars.

[12] *The 'Adages' of Erasmus* (ed. M. M. Phillips, Cambridge, 1964), pp. 244-263.

[13] *Ibid.*, p. 245.

[14] *Ibid.*, p. 249.

[15] *Institutio*, p. 169; cf. p. 248.

[16]*Ut fici oculis incumbunt*, *Adages*, p. 359. Contrast, as an example of the medieval view, the opinion of Aegidius Romanus, a pupil of St. Thomas, that hereditary monarchy is the best form of government in *On the Governance of Princes* (1287) (noted by L. K. Born, *Institutio*, p. 118). In any case, Erasmus dedicated works to both varieties of monarchs. In a letter of 1504 to Jean Desmarez, he gave an apology for his 1503 *Panegyricus* for Prince Philip: such a composition "consists in presenting princes with a pattern of goodness, in such a way as to reform bad rulers, improve the good, educate the boorish, reprove the erring, arouse the indolent, and cause even the hopelessly vicious to feel some inward stirrings of shame.... How much better to improve matters by compliments rather than abuse. And what method of exhortation is more effective ... than to credit people with possessing already in large measure the attractive qualities they urge them to cultivate?" *The Correspondence of Erasmus* (tr. R. A. B. Mynors and D. F. S. Thompson, Toronto, 1975), II, no. 180 p. 81.

[17]*Aut fatuum aut regem nasci oportere* (1515), *Adages*, p. 216. Note that the beetle in *Scarabeus aquilam quaerit* is credited with "no common brains" (p. 249).

[18]*Folly*, p. 13; cf. *Meliores naucisci aves*, *Adages*, p. 23, in which he argues that kings are as susceptible as "the vulgar" to superstition.

[19]*Sileni Alcibiadis*, *Adages*, pp. 273-274, 278.

[20]*Adages*, pp. 258-259.

[21]*Colloquies*, p. 388. See also *Folly*, p. 95, and the colloquies *Ementita nobilitas* and *Coniugium impar*, pp. 424-432 and 401-412 in Thompson's edition.

[22]*Folly*, p. 38; cf. p. 59.

[23]*Ne bos quidem pereat*, *Adages*, pp. 379, 375-376. Erasmus paints the older generation as opponents of truth and progress in an adage written when he was himself nearly sixty years old. In the same adage, conscientious maidservants are instructed to warn, help, and correct their mistresses.

[24]*Institutio*, p. 177. The adage *Festina lente* urges masters to treat their servants like men, not beasts of burden, on this basis (*Adages*, p. 184).

[25]*Puerpera*, *Coll.*, pp. 269-270.

[26]*Ut fici oculis incumbunt*, *Adages*, p. 359, cf. p. 378.

[27]Richard Taverner's translation, *Proverbes or adagies with newe addicions gathered out of the Chiliades of Erasmus* (London, 1539), fol. liii.

[28]Clarence Miller, "Some Medieval Elements and Structural Unity in Erasmus' *The Praise of Folly*" *Renaissance Quarterly*, vol. 27 (1974), finds in Erasmus' hierarchical concepts evidence of "medievalism"; however whereas medieval social critics sought restoration of a diseased social organism to health, Erasmus insisted on replacing it with a more workable entity in which different criteria for status are employed, republicanism is preferable to monarchy, etc. Social reform for Erasmus requires reversion not to a medieval Golden Age, but to a classical scheme worked out in a Christian context.

[29]*Sileni Alcibiadis*, *Adages*, p. 276 cf. *That chyldren oughte to be taught ...*, a treatise by Erasmus included in Richard Sherry's *A Treatise of Schemes and Tropes* (London, 1550), fol. Giii; *Apophthegmes* (tr. Nicolas Udall, 1542), fol. 21.

[30]*Institutio,* p. 196 cf. *Adages,* p. 23; *Folly,* p. 13.

[31]*Institutio,* pp. 145-150 in *Apophthegmes,* fol. 47, he deems a beggar superior to an ignorant or unwise man.

[32]Noted by J. H. Hexter, "The Education of the Aristocracy in the Renaissance" in *Reappraisals in History,* p. 53.

[33]e.g., *Festina lente, Adages,* p. 188, notes that "the common people" are in agreement with Quintilian in regard to certain child-rearing practices.

[34]*Institutio,* p. 140 cf. pp. 203-204; *Apophthegmes,* fol. 6.

[35]*Institutio,* p. 198; cf. p. 224; *Enchiridion,* pp. 87-88.

[36]Lovejoy, pp. 329-331; hence Langland's conviction that evil will result from any change in the social order (*Piers Ploumen,* C. vi, 65-81). cf. Arthur Ferguson, *The Articulate Citizen and the English Renaissance* (Durham, N.C., 1965), pp. 42-69, on Langland and Gower.

[37]*Proverbes,* fol. xxiv; cf. *Formulae, Coll.,* pp. 581-582. Ferguson has argued that it is this "new historical consciousness, marked in varying degrees by new sensitivity to the implications of social change" which marked humanist thought in sixteenth century England: *Clio Unbound: Perceptions of the Social and Cultural past in Renaissance England* (Durham, N.C., 1979), pp. x, 179.

[38]Robert P. Adams, "Designs by More and Erasmus for a New Social Order," *Studies in Philology,* LXII (1945), pp. 131-146. On Erasmus' pacifism, see the adages *Dulce bellum inexpertis, Sparta nactus es, hanc orna,* and *Sileni Alcibiadis* in *Adages,* pp. 269-353; the colloquy *Charon, (Coll.,* pp. 388-394); and the *Querela pacis* (1517). A facsimile of the 1559 English translation of the latter, *The Complaint of Peace,* by Thomas Paynell, is available with an introduction by William James Hirten (New York, 1946).

[39]*Ignavis semper feriae sunt, Adages,* p. 268; cf. *Liber de Sarcienda Ecclesiae Concordia,* Dolan, p. 385.

[40]*Institutio,* p. 229.

[41]*Convivium profanum, Coll.,* p. 600 cf. *Franciscani, Coll.,* p. 214: "There is nothing too ridiculous for custom to sanction"; *Abbatis et eruditae, Coll.,* p. 221: "Why tell me of custom, the mistress of every vice?" *Puerpera* and *Synodus grammaticorum (Coll.,* pp. 270, 272, 398) express very similar sentiments.

[42]*Aut fatuum, Adages,* pp. 219-220.

[43]CUL, MS Add. 6160 (1640), p. 21; cf. fol. 135, deriding "grey-headed errours".

[44]Thomas Gataker, *Certaine Sermons* (London, 1637), p. 103; cf. pp. 73, 87-89, 90 and 110.

[45]quoted by Lawrence Stone, *The Crisis of the Aristocracy* (Oxford, abridged edn., 1967), p. 348.

[46]Cromwell is quoted by J. H. Hexter, *Reappraisals,* p. 115.

[47]Quoted in T. Edwards, *Gangraena* (London, 1646), pp. 147-148.

[48]D'Ewes, *Autobiography* (ed. J. O. Halliwell, London, 1845), Vol. II, pp. 64-65, 113; cf. Watson, *Library of D'Ewes*, pp. 101, 139.

The Tree of Being with Man holding onto the roots. This French version may be compared with earlier representations of substance with the opposite attributes of different categories of the levels. This emblem is used by the Philosophy Department of Syracuse University.

MARION LEATHERS KUNTZ

PYTHAGOREAN COSMOLOGY AND ITS IDENTIFICATION

IN BODIN'S *COLLOQUIUM HEPTAPLOMERES*

The influence of Pythagoras was felt "throughout the classical period most notably in the Academy of Plato and in the Roman circle of Neoplatonists around Plotinus, cross-pollinated with Stoics and Peripatetics, scattered seed as far abroad as the Hermeticists and the Cabalists and the Syrian syncretists and St. Augustine, and came to full bloom in the Renaissance."[1] The essential tenets of Pythagoreanism, namely, an ordered cosmos, the chain of being, God and the cosmos, man as microcosm, nature as a paradigmn for discovery of the eternal law, the primacy of numbers, harmony in music and in nature, secrets of the universe hidden from the uninitiate, unity in multiplicity, appear throughout the *Colloquium Heptaplomeres*. Jean Bodin used many ideas of Pythagoras as a framework upon which he developed the themes of his dialogue, the *Colloquium Heptaplomeres de rerum sublimium arcanis abditis*. From his ideas about harmony and order he developed concepts of a chain of being which is not only vertical but also horizontal.[2]

Since the Pythagoreanism in Bodin's *Colloquium* becomes, as it were, the leitmotif of this fascinating dialogue of the late sixteenth century, the object of this study will be to investigate the nature of the Pythagoreanism in the *Colloquium* and discern why Bodin chose Pythagoreanism as his major philosophic orientation. In the *Colloquium* the citations from Plato and Aristotle are also numerous. Bodin frequently cites passages from the *Metaphysics*[3] which detail Pythagorean concepts of harmony and number theory and also from the *De Caelo*[4] where Aristotle posits the Pythagorean belief that "the center (of the cosmos) is occupied by fire, and that the earth is one of the stars, and creates night and day as it travels in a circle about the center" (II. 12.293 a21-293a23). Of the multiple influences of Platonism which occur in Bodin's *Colloquium*, the references to the *Timaeus* far outnumber all others, and Bodin cites Timaeus Locrensis himself in a discussion of the quaternity.[5] Bodin also introduces Numa Pompilius, the second Roman king after Romulus, as one who upheld lofty moral principles and who followed the laws of nature and was imbued with Pythagorean decrees.[6] In addition, Bodin refers to Heraclides of Heraclea,[7] a noted Pythagorean, and also makes use of Diogenes Laertius, Porphyry, and Iamblichus, all of whom were admirers of Pythagoras. References to Pythagoreans occur in all six books of the *Colloquium*. The theme of harmony is a central concept of Pythagoras and his school and is also the central theme of the *Colloquium*. Why Bodin extended the theme of harmony beyond its usual Pythagorean interpretations and why Bodin employs horizontal as well as a vertical chain of being, will be the foci of this paper.

The setting of Bodin's dialogue is the home of Paul Coronaeus at Venice; the learned men whom Coronaeus had gathered there resemble those men around Pythagoras "who were encouraged to search into the principles of things, not just to accept a statement without analysis."[8] Paul Coronaeus was a Renaissance man, "who was very eagerly investigating in every nook and cranny of the city, all the monuments of antiquity and had joined with the most scholarly men in an intimate society, so that his home was considered a shrine of the Muses and virtues. And although he was very slight in stature and too weak to endure stormy seas and distant sojourns, he had an incredible desire to understand the language, inclinations, activities, customs, and virtues of different peoples."[9] Bodin's description of Coronaeus makes him a kindred spirit of Pythagoras. As friendship was emphasized by the Pythagoreans and the "things of friends are common," so the friendship of the seven scholars in Coronaeus' home is detailed at the beginning of the dialogue:

> Although they were exceptionally well trained in the disciplines of the liberal arts, nevertheless each seemed to surpass the others in his unique knowledge. Moreover, while living together in Coronaeus' house, they had easy access to anything new or worthy of note anywhere in the world by means of letters from friends whom they had made a point of acquiring at Rome, Constantinople, Augsburg, Seville, Antwerp, and Paris.

> They lived not merely with sophistication of discourse and charming manners, but with such innocence and integrity that no one so much resembled himself as all resembled all. For they were not motivated by wrangling or jealousy but by a desire to learn; consequently they were displaying all their reflections and endeavours in true dignity.[10]

These friends in their Venetian "shrine of the Muses and Virtues" held discourse on all subjects in which Renaissance men engaged, but their conversations most often centered on the natural world and the nature of true religion. In describing the aims of Pythagoras and his friends, Professor Heninger aptly states:

Experience of the deity was the ultimate aim of the Pythagorean sect, and therefore it became the fountainhead
of a continuing strain of mysticism in Western thought.
But because this experience was to be gained through
study of nature the sect was also the progenitor of systematic physical sciences. In the Pythagorean scheme,
religion and science not only coexisted, but were mutually dependent.[11]

In like manner Coronaeus' home contained a laboratory for the study of
nature. There were instruments "for music or for all sorts of mathematical
arts," but most unusual was the *pantotheca*, a cupboard built of olive wood
which contained 1296 small compartments which were slanted for easy viewing.[12]
This *pantotheca*, as its name implies, housed "the universe, its goods and
materials. To begin with he [Coronaeus] had prepared likenesses of sixty fixed
stars, then the replicas of planets, comets, and similar phenomena, elements,
bodies, stones, metals, fossils, plants, living things of every sort, which he
could secure each in its own class."[13] If a form of plant or animal could not
be secured, "each was marked in its box by a drawing or a description or according to its own classification.... Moreover, he had complete plants or the
roots displayed separately on rather large charts so that each box contained a
particle of plant and animal life and in this arrangement: the last was connected to the first, the middle to the beginning and the end, and all to all
in its appropriate class."[14] All the intermediate stages in a genus were represented so that the inner relationships could be immediately ascertained. For
example, "... between the earth and stones he had placed clay and chalk, between water and diamonds, crystal, between stones and metals, flint and mar-
casite, between stones and springs, coral...."[15]

Coronaeus knew his microcosm by heart, and, like Pythagoras, his prodigi-
ous memory enabled him to remember all that he had heard; "he had developed
the sharpest critical faculty by listening, discussing, and contemplating."[16]
Many of the conversations among the seven friends in Coronaeus' home stemmed
from inquiries into the nature of things, which were stimulated by study of
the *pantotheca*. Study of the natural world was frequently interrupted by discussion of events which seemed to happen outside the natural order such as
stories about talking dogs, magic mirrors, men who fly with bird-like swift-
ness, elephants who walk on ropes, pregnancies which result from copulation
with demons, to name only a few. Toralba, the natural philosopher in the dialogue, states that he "tried to investigate nature itself and its hidden

causes,"[17] but he found he had the same experience that voyagers have. "When
they are as far as possible from land, they lose the use of the leads because
of the depth of the sea."[18] Toralba acknowleges that "as I study the nature of
elements, fossils, metals, plants, animate and celestial bodies, and finally
delve more deeply into the remarkable power of angels and demons, reason seems
to leave me completely."[19] Yet Toralba insists that when natural reason cannot
furnish the causes of all things, one must not assume that these causes result
from necessity, for this would remove free will from God. He cogently argues
that it is very foolish to say that the first cause is the producer and pre-
server of all things and yet bind this first cause by necessity while admitting free will for men.

Salomon, who represents the Jewish position in the *Colloquium*, agrees
that fate or Kodesh is that in which "the holy of holies is contained, that is
God, receiving all things within himself and encompassing all things with free
will."[20] The Catholic Coronaeus asks how the first cause is immutable if the
series of progression of lower causes is changed; or contrarily, if the progression of lower causes is immutable, then the world exists from necessity.
Toralba points out quickly that the Lawgiver of nature is freed from His own
laws by Himself alone.[21]

It is at this point in the dialogue that the chain of being is articulated specifically; the *aurea catena* is equated to the *scala Iacobis*. Bodin's
Colloquium may be unique in placing Jacob's ladder and the golden chain as
equivalents in hierarchical ordering. The idea of the chain of being is introduced into the discussion by the skeptic Senamus, who has maintained that the
power of nature is necessary. If it is not, he asks: "What then will happen to
Plato who, in accordance with the opinion of Homer, represents a golden chain
let down by Jupiter from heaven. Must we not grant that the series of natural
causes is inviolable and completely unchangeable?"[22]

At this point Toralba replies: "In my opinion Homer explains himself sufficiently when he recognized that those lower gods can be drawn upward by the
higher, but the Supreme Deity cannot be drawn down by the lower."[23]

It is the Jew Salomon who joins the idea of the chain to Jacob's ladder
when he says: "I think the Homeric chain is nothing other than the ladder represented in the nocturnal vision of Jacob the Patriarch; God was at the top of
the ladder, and angels descended from the top of heaven to the earth and then
ascended again to heaven."[24]

From a Pythagorean investigation into the nature of things, Bodin directs his speakers toward the consideration of necessity or will in the creation of cosmos. Then by introducing the golden chain and Jacob's ladder as equivalences, Bodin places God as first cause of the progressive cycle, unchanging as First Principle yet allowing change in the lower orders as the movement of the angels up and down the ladder implies. In addition, by linking Jacob's ladder and the chain of being Bodin reveals a cosmos created by unchanging God from His will; at the same time God's will, which is free, emanated to the lower orders as indicated by angels descending or ascending the ladder. By combining the metaphors of the golden chain and Jacob's ladder Bodin posited creation and emanation while keeping God unchanged and free.

Toralba and Salomon agree that the secrets of the highest matters and the hidden treasures of nature are concealed in the divine laws. In these divine laws numbers have great significance, both in the abstract realm and in the sensory realm. Salomon indicates that the Hebrews have ten names which are granted to God[25] and the contemplation of their numerical equivalents reveals many secrets of sublime things. The number ten, as Toralba relates, is especially important, for in this number the divine and natural laws are comingled. As Toralba explains, "those ten headings of the decalogue correspond to the ten celestial orbs in the proper order of nature. The first head is granted to God himself as the supreme author of universal nature...."[26] In like manner he links each heading of the decalogue to a heavenly orb in a significant relationship. The relational aspects of the fourth commandment are especially interesting. "The fourth heading about the holiness of the Sabbath is related to the orb of Saturn to whom also the seventh day of Saturn is vowed, just as the day of the Hebrews' Sabbath."[27] Bodin has Toralba explain all ten headings and their associative qualities with the celestial orbs. To the Pythagoreans the number ten represented the limit of the universe.[28] The number four, the key number for Cabalists as well as Pythagoreans, is constantly represented by Bodin as the Holy Tetragrammaton, the number which represents God Himself. He has Salomon say:

> It would be much more likely to contrive a quaternity
> from the same Tetragrammaton than a trinity, as did
> Basilides the evangelist, whose opinion the Noëtians and
> Lombard himself ... seem to follow, as Abbot Joachim
> wrote, because in addition to three persons, they substi-
> tuted a fourth which they call "power." The Pythagoreans
> seem to have held this opinion. They had been accustomed

to swear to a holy quaternity. Timaeus Locrensis indicated that by means of a tetragonal pyramid this quaternity held many thousands of worlds together.[29]

Bodin even details the story of Apollo's charge to double his cubical altar.
He says that Nicholas of Cusa tried to accomplish this, and Orontius boasted
he had attained it and from this proved a quadrature of the circle.[30] Bodin,
in relating the story about Apollo's command to double his cubical altar,
makes reference to the geometer demon who had proposed a task which no one
"could attain ... by proof but only by physical reasoning."[31] As Professor
Heninger states:

> This image of God as geometer translates the deity as
> *anima mundi* from the noncorporeal world of intellect to
> the extended world of physical objects. We detect here
> the two dominant concepts of deity in the Pythagorean
> tradition .... One postulates the deity as an all pervas-
> ive spirit that infuses the universe but is known only
> indirectly through its effects, a pantheistic numen ...
> which leads to mysticism. The other, in strong contrast,
> postulates the deity as a workman setting about a con-
> crete task, ordering the world according to mathematic
> measure, building with the tangible forms of regular
> solids.[32]

The quaternity represented for Bodin as well as for the Pythagoreans the
reconciliation of opposites, that is, *concordia discors*. In a discussion of
musical harmonies *concordia discors* is cogently stated by Coronaeus who, after
hearing a hymn sung by young choir boys whom he summoned each evening, remarks
that the sweetest harmony occurs when the highest tone is blended with the
lowest. He also asks his friends "why is it that harmonies in unison, in which
no tone is opposite, are not pleasing to the trained ear."[33] Curtius, who represents the Calvinist position in the dialogue, agrees with Coronaeus but disagrees with the Lutheran Fridericus who has indicated that many believe that
harmony is more pleasing when the ratios of numbers correspond. He answers
Coronaeus' question by emphasizing the reconciliation of opposites: "Even that
keenest sweetness of harmony which we have heard most eagerly just now would
not have been so pleasing unless the musician had contrived some dissonant or
harsh note for our sensitive ears, since the pleasure is not perceived without
a pain that precedes it and produces boredom when continued too long."[34] To
strengthen his statement Curtius then recites a poem about the contrariety of
all things. In this poem Bodin pinpoints his concept of the harmony that per-

vades the natural order, a harmony based on multiplicity within unity, that
is, a *concordia discors*:

Creator of the world three times greatest of all,

Three times best parent of heaven,

Who tempers the changes of the world,

Giving proper weight to all things,

And who measures each thing from His own ladle

In number, ratio, time

Who with eternal chain joins with remarkable wisdom two things

   opposite in every way, preparing protection for each,

Who, moderating melody with different sounds and

   voices yet most satisfying to sensitive ears,

   heals sickness, has mingled cold with heat and moisture

   with dryness,

The rough with the smooth, sweetness with pain,

   shadows with light, quiet with motion,

   tribulation with prosperity

Who directs the fixed courses of the heavenly

   stars from east to west,

West to east with contrary revolutions

Who joins hatred with agreement,

A friend to hateful enemies.

This greatest harmony of the universe

   though discordant contains our safety.[35]

The natural philosopher Toralba points out that opposites, which are very
apparent in all nature, "when united by the interpolation of certain middle
links present a remarkable harmony of the whole which otherwise would perish
completely if this whole world were fire and moisture."[36]

This harmony of nature which is based on multiplicity is precisely the
same *concordia discors* which one discovers among the seven savants gathered at
the home of Coronaeus. Each of the seven had a different religious or philosophic position – whether Catholic, Jew, Mohammedan, Lutheran, Calvinist,
skeptic, or natural philosopher – yet, as Bodin states, they lived together
"with such innocence and integrity that no one so much resembled himself as
all resembled all."[37] Here on the human level is an example of *concordia discors*. Early in the dialogue Bodin posits the "all in all" theme by describing

the intimate gathering of the seven who differed in their interests as well as in their views on most subjects, especially the question of religion. Just as in nature, their opposite positions were very apparent, yet there was a middle link which provided the remarkable harmony among the seven, namely, the belief in God. As the dialogue unfolds Bodin never allows one position to triumph. Rather, the various opinions are carefully articulated, and one sees, after much searching, that each participant in the dialogue at some time agrees with one or the other, so that as the reader takes an overview he recognizes that all do resemble all. For example, Curtius the Calvinist disagrees strongly with Catholic Coronaeus about statues or the "worship of idols," as he says, yet they agree on the Messiahship of Jesus. While Coronaeus and Salomon the Jew never agree on the interpretation of Messiah, they do agree on rites and symbols, and so on throughout the dialogue.

In the *Colloquium Heptaplomeres* Bodin has used the harmony of nature, that is *concordia discors*, as an exemplar for harmony among men, and with this precept he extended the Pythagorean concept of harmony as he applied it as a construct for religious toleration. Men who live in harmony, with nature as the model, must of necessity be tolerant of each other.

Bodin chose Pythagorean cosmology as the philosophic orientation of his *Colloquium* because the manifold representations of harmony and the constant reiteration of a harmonious cosmos by the Pythagoreans provided Bodin the analogue from which he developed his theory of religious toleration. At the end of the dialogue the participants did not change their religious opinions, and they held no more conversations about religion. No more were needed. Each man in the dialogue probably saw his own position as related to another, although Bodin never stated this explicitly. He did say, however, that "henceforth, they nourished their piety in remarkable harmony and their integrity of life in common pursuits and intimacy."[38] A blending of opposites was surely apparent in Coronaeus' home just as in a Pythagorean cosmos.

Finally, one must consider the type of ordering which Bodin demonstrates in the *Colloquium*. As stated above, Bodin uses Homer's golden chain and also Jacob's ladder as a paradigm for his discussions of creation and an emanation. In addition to this vertical or hierarchical ordering Bodin also reveals a horizontal ordering. Since he is never explicit on this point, the horizontal ordering is more difficult to ascertain; it is perhaps one of the secrets of the sublime which the title of the dialogue indicates.[39] Yet horizontal order-

ing is as essential to Bodin's theme of harmony and a basis for religious toleration as is the vertical ordering which he made explicit.[40]

With two systems of ordering Bodin has also followed Pythagoras. "The
Timaean scheme of creation, in order to account for variety, devolves actually
into a hierarchy of categories of existence. This hierarchy provides for variety on a vertical scale.... But what is equally important, though less often
recognized, there is also in the Timaean scheme express provision for variety
on a horizontal scale. At each level of creation, within each link of the
chain, there also is diversity. This articulation of the scheme is necessary
to account for differences within each category for the different kinds of
stones and of plants and of animals and of angels."[41]

The horizontal ordering of the *Colloquium* is grounded in the relationship
of the seven speakers. No opinion of any participant is posited as higher than
or better than another. Since no position is allowed to triumph, the ordering
is not vertical in this case but horizontal. The horizontal ordering may be
viewed as a see-saw in balance. In the *Colloquium* it is the Catholic Coronaeus
who maintains the balance. He is essential to the horizontal ordering or balance. The balance is delicate and Coronaeus is the key, since he is more like
each of the others than any other one is like to another. In certain respects
he shares views which are harmonious with the non-Christians, the Christians,
and even the pagans. It is also important to point out that the dialogue has
its setting in the home of the Catholic Coronaeus. The atmosphere in this
shrine of the Muses allowed the harmonious blending of opposites where no
voice reigned supreme. The *pantotheca* also provides a horizontal system or
chain of interrelationships as well as a vertical ladder. The objects in the
pantotheca can be viewed and studied horizontally as well as vertically. This
dual system of ordering is made explicit by Bodin when he states that Coronaeus walks back and forth in front of the *pantotheca*. His vision would naturally follow an horizontal and vertical direction. Two types of ordering which
Bodin used in his *Colloquium*, vertical and horizontal, also represent a contrariety of opposites, when viewed as necessary constructs for a conception of
order. Vertical and horizontal ordering also have an epistemological basis.
Knowledge is gained from higher and lower but also from the relationship of
equals in various classes.

In conclusion, to develop the theme of harmony and to extend this theme
to religious toleration, Bodin used a vertical as well as horizontal ordering.

The vertical ordering represented by the *pantotheca*, the microcosm of the world of nature, demonstrates the multiplicity in the chain of being, while the horizontal ordering, represented by the seven men in the dialogue, demonstrates the unity of a common pattern inherent in the statement, "no one resembled himself so much as all resembled all."[42]

In Bodin's *Colloquium* the vertical and horizontal orders intersect in the home of Coronaeus which is indeed a microcosm. The scholars study the cosmos and its attendant hierarchy, and the *pantotheca* with its 1296 little cupboards is their laboratory. As they discuss the nature of the cosmos, and ultimately the nature of God and true religion, the reader understands that as men they are part of the hierarchical system of the cosmos. Yet to each link in the chain of being, multiple in variety, and to each other, multiple in beliefs, they relate horizontally because their common pattern is God. Bodin has used the Pythagorean "all in all" theme in a most original manner to present his plea for harmony and religious toleration at a time when sixteenth century Europe was bloodied by religious strife similar to that in our world today.

NOTES

[1]S. K. Heninger, *Touches of Sweet Harmony, Pythagorean Cosmology and Renaissance Poetics*, (San Marino, 1974), p. 16.

[2]The only complete edition in Latin is Jean Bodin, *Colloquium heptaplomeres de rerum sublimium arcanis abditis*, ed. Ludovicus Noack (Schwerin: 1857). Abridged editions are *Das Heptaplomeres des Jean Bodin, Zur Geschichte der Kultur und Literatur im Jahrhundert der Reformation*, ed. E. Guhrauer (Berlin: 1841) and *Le colloque de Jean Bodin des secrets cachez des choses sublimes*, ed. Roger Chauviré (Paris; 1914). For the complete text in English see Jean Bodin, *Colloquium of the Seven About Secrets of the Sublime*, Translation with Introduction, Annotations, and Critical Readings by Marion Leathers Daniels Kuntz (Princeton: Princeton Unversity Press, 1975); all citations to the *Colloquium* found in this paper are from this work which will be hereafter referred to as Kuntz, *Colloquium of the Seven*. See also the early Seventeenth Century translation, *Le Colloque ...*, ed. François Rigolot (Genève, 1985: Librairie Droz).

On Pythagoras see Ernst Bindel, *Pythagoras* (Stuttgart: 1962) and Karl Kerenyi, *Pythagoras und Orpheus* (Zürich: 1950). By far the most important book to date on Pythagoras and Pythagoreanism is S. K. Heninger, Jr., *Touches of Sweet Harmony, Pythagorean Cosmology and Renaissance Poetics* (San Marino: 1974); an excellent bibliography is also included.

Of general interest to the topic are Don Cameron Allen, *Mysteriously Meant* (Baltimore: 1970) and *The Harmonious Vision* (Baltimore, 1968); Frances Yates, *The Rosicrucian Enlightenment* (London: 1972).

See also Stillman Drake, "Renaissance Science and Music," *Journal of the History of Ideas* 31 (1970), 483-500; Abraham C. Keller, "Zilsel, the Artisans, and the Ideas of Progress in the Renaissance," *Journal of the History of Ideas* 11 (1950), 235-40; Pierre Mesnard, "Jean Bodin à la recherche des secrets de la nature," in *Umanesimo e esoterismo* (1960), 221-34; Walter J. Ong, "System, Space, and Intellect in Renaissance Symbolism," *Bibliothèque d'humanisme et renaissance* 18 (1956), 222-39; Ernst Benz, "Der Toleranz-Gedanke in der Religionswissenchaft (Über den Heptaplomeres des Jean Bodin), *Deutsche Vierteljahresschrift* 12 (1934), 540-71; Marion Daniels Kuntz, "Harmony and the *Heptaplomeres* of Jean Bodin," *Journal of the History of Philosophy* 12 (1974), 31-40.

[3]In the *Colloquium* ten citations from the *Metaphysics* occur. See Kuntz, *Colloquium of the Seven*, pp. 28, 29, 30, 32, 38, 54, 62, 75, 110, 146.

[4]References to *De Caelo* occur twice. See Kuntz, *Colloquium of the Seven*. pp. 37, 120.

[5]See, *Colloquium of the Seven*, pp. 46, 88, 112, 118, 120, 164, 244, 329, for references to the *Timaeus* and p. 373 for reference to Timaeus Locrensis.

[6]In a lengthy discussion of religious practices Salomon the Jew states that "Plutarch was wrong when he wrote that those who were about to worship should sit down, because this was not practiced by the Latins and was foreign to Pythagorean decrees with which Numa is said to have been imbued." (Kuntz, *Colloquium of the Seven*, p. 218). See also pp. 184, 313.

[7]Heraclides, called Ponticus, was an Academic philosopher and writer (390-310 B.C.). He was left in charge of the school during Plato's third Sicilian journey. Important for his molecular theory and his astronomical discoveries, he even hypothesized that the sun is in the center of the universe and the earth revolves around it.

[8]See Heninger, *Touches of Sweet Harmony*, p. 23.

[9]See Kuntz, *Colloquium of the Seven*, p. 3.

[10]*Ibid.*, p. 4.

[11]Heninger, *Touches of Sweet Harmony*, p. 22.

[12]Kuntz, *Colloquium of the Seven*, pp. 4-5.

[13]*Ibid.*, p. 4.

[14]*Ibid.*, pp. 4-5.

[15]*Ibid.*, p. 5.

[16]*Ibid.*

[17]*Ibid.*, p. 26.

[18]*Ibid.*

[19]*Ibid.*

[20]*Ibid.*, p. 29.

[21]*Ibid.*, pp. 30-31.

[22]*Ibid.*, p. 32.

[23]*Ibid.*

[24]*Ibid.*

[25]*Ibid.*, p. 325.

[26]*Ibid.*, p. 190.

[27]*Ibid.*

[28]See Heninger, *Touches of Sweet Harmony*, pp. 71-145.

[29]Kuntz, *Colloquium of the Seven*, pp. 372-73.

[30]*Ibid.*, p. 179, note 370.

[31]*Ibid.*, p. 179.

[32]Heninger, *Touches of Sweet Harmony*, p. 209.

[33]Kuntz, *Colloquium of the Seven*, p. 144.

[34]*Ibid.*, p. 147.

[35]*Ibid.*

[36]*Ibid.*, p. 146.

[37]*Ibid.*, p. 4.

[38]*Ibid.*, p. 471.

[39]The Latin title is *Colloquium Heptaplomeres de rerum sublimium arcanis abditis.*

[40]The *pantotheca* in Coronaeus' home contained all the elements of the world arranged in a vertical pattern. However, in addition to the study of the contents viewed from top to bottom one could comprehend the relationship of the different genera by moving the eyes in a horizontal fashion.

[41]Heninger, *Touches of Sweet Harmony*, p. 328

[42]Kuntz, *Colloquium of the Seven*, p. 4

266

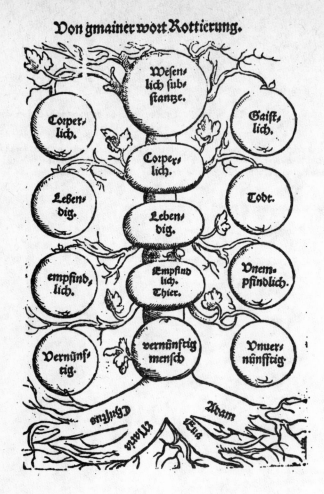

A German Jesuit emblem of the tradition of the Tree of Porphyry common in logic texts. From Ortholph Fuchsperger, Augsburg, 1533. This is used on the cover of Joseph S. Freedman, <u>Deutsche Schulphilosophie im Reformationszeitalter</u> (1500-1650), Münster, MAKS Publikationen, 1985. The curious title connotes the general terms by which the order of creation can be conceived by rank and file. The oak tree is rooted in Adam and Eve, Christ and Mary, signifying the fall of man and human regeneration; once again the meaning of ladder is descent and ascent.

RAYMOND V. UTTERBACK

**THE NATURAL ORDER: DOCTRINES OF HIERARCHY AND CORRESPONDENCE
IN A GENERATION OF SHAKESPEARE CRITICISM**

The subject considered here is what literary scholars and critics have
done in the last 35 or 40 years to relate Shakespeare's plays to the complex
of ideas associated with the great chain of being. While no one seems to have
insisted that the immense range of Shakespeare's dramatic art, extending from
clowns to kings and from farce to high tragedy, somehow exhibits the principle
of plentitude, most critics now take for granted the importance of Shakespeare's references to the principle of degree governing man's social relationships and to the principle of correspondences by which man's place in
nature is defined. Hardin Craig, in *The Enchanted Glass* (1935), and Arthur O.
Lovejoy, in *The Great Chain of Being* (1936), helped make it possible for later
Shakespeareans to say, as C. A. Patrides did in a work on Milton, that "the
Renaissance belief in cosmic order has been made so abundantly clear by a host
of scholars that we have no need to dwell on it...."[1] Lovejoy mentions Milton
frequently, and he cites Alexander Pope just as often, but he is not concerned
to illustrate the manifestations of the ideas he so grandly traces in Renaissance English literature. Such major figures as Colet, Sir Thomas More, Elyot,
Ascham, Sidney, Greville, Hooker, Spenser, Marlowe, or Shakespeare are not
treated, though there is a passing allusion to Hamlet wherein the prince of
Denmark typifies the man who is virtually overwhelmed by acute awareness of
the complexity of the universe.[2] In the wake of Lovejoy's opus, however, the
task of articulating and illustrating the place of the chain of being in
Shakespeare's plays was readily embraced, so that by 1944 E. M. W. Tillyard
could remark, with some exaggeration, "The doctrine of the chain of being was
ignored by readers of Elizabethan literature till Lovejoy wrote his book on
it; now, our eyes being open, we find it all over the place."[3]

The cosmic reverberations of Ulysses' speech on degree (*Troilus and Cressida*) are now ubiquitously cited, as the Archbishop's fable of the bees in
their well-ordered state (*Henry V*) and Menenius' fable of the belly and the
members of the body (*Coriolanus*) could also be. Yet in his various passages
reflecting the Elizabethan conception of the world order Shakespeare makes
quite different dramatic points. The interrelation of individual life and the
body politic produces Brutus's apt comparison of his troubled consciousness as

he considers assassinating Caesar: the conflict of his faculties resembles the
plight of a kingdom suffering rebellion (*Julius Caesar*, II.i.61-69). The nature of Pericles's refined ecstasy is revealed by his hearing the music of the
spheres; this is no mere romantic sentimentalism, but a profound symbol and
vision of an ultimately harmonious and beneficent world order (*Pericles*, V.i.
228-237). Earthly events are often accompanied by reactions in the heavens, as
the unnatural storms preceding Caesar's assassination and accompanying King
Duncan's attest--or the gloomy dawn ending the tragedy of *Romeo and Juliet*, or
the storm during which Lear's wits begin to turn. The same interrelatedness of
man with the cosmos also serves Shakespeare for comedy when Glendower boasts
of the comets and earthquakes accompanying his birth. Hotspur replies that the
earthquake would have occurred even if the cat were only having kittens and
explaining earthquakes as the result of a kind of gaseous colic suffered by
old beldame earth. The very absence of a suitable cosmic manifestation is an
occasion for comment by Shakespeare's characters. When he hears of Antony's
death, Octavius Caesar laments,

> The breaking of so great a thing should make
> A greater crack: the round world
> Should have shook lions into civil streets,
> And citizens to their dens: the death of Antony
> Is not a single doom; in the name lay
> A moiety of the world.   (*Antony and Cleopatra*,
>   V.i.14-19)[4]

The whole series of degrees seems to have been mapped in Shakespeare criticism by now, from the highest to the lowest. The very blocks and stones with
which Marullus identifies the Roman mob have been duly noted in a standard
reference work as illustrative of the lowest degree on the scale of being.[5]
Marullus, in fact, in his rhetorical hyperbole creates an imaginary degree
lower than the lowest degree on the scale of being, calling these deserters of
Pompey's memory, "you worse than senseless things" (*Julius Caesar*, I.i.40).
Yet Hotspur's reference to diseased nature, his "scientific" explanation of
earthquakes, and the very absence of cosmic repercussions at Antony's death--
or Desdemona's (*Othello*, V.ii. 99-101)--are forceful reminders that all is not
well with the doctrine of hierarchical order in Shakespeare's plays. The
destructive influence of the Fall of man upon the original perfection of the
sublunary world is frequently evident, so that the lack of the ideal order or
the expected correspondence is more important than its presence at countless
moments. Ulysses's focal speech on degree (*Troilus and Cressida*, I.iii.75-137)

consists primarily of an inventory of the ill effects ensuing when hierarchy
is *not* observed in society. Nor could a grander appeal be made to the doctrine
of the social hierarchy as a reflection of the God-given cosmic order than
that which the Bishop of Carlisle courageously sounds when the nobility of
England prepare to depose King Richard II:

> Would God that any in this noble presence
> Were enough noble to be upright judge
> Of noble Richard! then true noblesse would
> Learn him forbearance from so foul a wrong.
> What subject can give sentence on his king?
> And who sits here that is not Richard's subject?
> (*Richard II*, IV.i.117-122)

What case could be more open and shut, what imperative more obvious? Yet the
events that follow epitomize the fate of the ideal of order in nearly all the
history plays and tragedies: the Earl of Northumberland silences the Bishop,
sardonically declaring, "Well have you argued, sir; and, for your pains, / Of
capital treason we arrest you here." (IV.i.150-151). An assertive human power
giving no rationale of its own rejects by force and will the argument and the
ethic based on hierarchy. On such an action hangs many a Shakespearean tale.

W. C. Curry's *Shakespeare's Philosophical Patterns* (1937) had largely
been written by the time Lovejoy's book appeared, but it manifested a parallel
interest in Shakespeare's conceptual system. In what Frank Kermode has called
"one of the permanent modern Shakespearian achievements,"[7] Curry found not one
system, but the flexible use of various sets of ideas. Augustinian and Thomistic Christian conceptions of the angelic-demonic hierarchy, and of the proper
hierarchy of reason, will, and passion were seen to form the philosophical
groundwork of *Macbeth*. But in *The Tempest* Curry found Neo-platonic emanation-
ism and the theurgical refinement of the soul through successively higher
planes of being. His judgment that *Macbeth* exhibits medieval scholasticism
while *The Tempest* represents "an altogether different world, which is dominated by classical myth and integrated by a purely pagan philosophy," no doubt
overstates the dichotomy and undervalues Christian elements of *The Tempest*.
But his work clearly illustrates the fruitfulness of investigating the world
order as conceived in Shakespeare's plays and something of the range to be en-
compassed.

Three scholars who appropriated the chain of being for Shakespeare criticism must be singled out—Theodore Spencer, E. M. W. Tillyard, and Lily Bess
Campbell. In *Shakespeare and the Nature of Man* (1942) Spencer outlines the

hierarchical conception of the world order under the category of "the optimistic theory," and distinguishes the three principal realms between which analogies were ubiquitously drawn: the heavens; the earth, its elements, and its vegetable and animal inhabitants; and human society. But he gives a second chapter to the Renaissance conflicts over the traditional frame of ideas, including the Copernican challenge to the cosmological order, Montaigne's challenge to man's place in the natural order and to the powers of man's mind, and Machiavelli's challenge to the traditional concept of the political order. Like all drama rooted in the beliefs of its time, Spencer declares, Shakespeare's histories and tragedies exhibit a threefold pattern affirmative of order, not unlike the morality plays: "an existing order is violated, the consequent conflict and turmoil are portrayed, and order is restored by the destruction of the force or forces that originally violated it."[8] Richard III illustrates the pattern splendidly, and its protagonist manifests the characteristic quality of Shakespeare's villains: "order and society are nothing to him;... [he refuses] to be a part of the order of nature and ... [refuses] to see the interconnections between the various spheres of Nature's activity."[9] But Spencer finds the life of Shakespeare's plays not in their use of traditional ideas, but in their embodiment of conflicts of ideas. Hence he emphasizes throughout all his analyses of the plays the opposition between appearance and reality. Spencer comes close to saying that in *Richard II* the traditional ideas of the king's exalted position, with which Richard identifies himself, are shown to be actually out of touch with reality. In *Hamlet* an even greater disparity between what is said and what ought to be is the basis of the hero's suffering, and the greatness of the play lies in its mastery of conflict between the ideas of man's glory and his misery. Hamlet himself undergoes a profound spiritual development. At the end, Spencer notes, "he is no longer *in* the tumult, but above it; he is no longer 'passion's slave,' but a man who sees himself as a part of the order of things, even though his final view of that order, exhausted, resigned, and in a way exalted, is very different from the youthful rosy picture his Renaissance theoretical education had given him."[10]

Spencer distinguishes three periods and styles in Shakespeare's handling of ideas of the world order, and many subsequent critics have confirmed, modified, or rejected such a scheme. In the early plays the traditional beliefs appear as part of the background; in the great tragedies after the turn of the

century they form part of each protagonist's consciousness, a consciousness
split by its encounter with hostile ideas and experiences; in later plays from
Antony and Cleopatra to *The Tempest* they are part of the texture of the poetic
universe, an enlargement and glorification of characters and events.[11] *Timon
of Athens* and *Coriolanus* prove to be exceptions to the scheme, however. In
evaluating the latter Spencer makes the doctrine of correspondences a kind of
critical touchstone: "Perhaps [the total conflict between Coriolanus and soci-
ety] should make *Coriolanus* the most tragic of all the plays, but in fact it
does not. For *Coriolanus* lacks reverberations. Nothing that happens to the
hero is reflected in external nature.... The play has no cosmology, and the
gods who are referred to by the various characters are mentioned, we feel, for
the sake of local color, not because they are a part of a vision of things, as
they are in *King Lear*."[12]

In explaining Shakespeare's use of the world order Spencer displayed a
comprehensiveness of vision that acutely perceives the role of conflicts of
ideas in the plays. Miss Campbell and Prof. Tillyard tended to regard the
plays as systematic expressions of unquestioned convictions. Miss Campbell's
earlier volume on the tragedies, *Shakespeare's Tragic Heroes: Slaves of Passion* (1930), treats each tragic hero as guilty of failure to respect the hierarchical relationship in which reason stands higher than passion. In her article (in 1947) entitled "Bradley Revisited: Forty Years After," she summarizes:
"Shakespearean tragedy made concrete Elizabethan moral teaching, and that
teaching was centered about the conflict of passion and reason in man's soul.
When passion rather than reason controls his will, man errs or sins,"[13] bringing about turmoil of soul, disintegration, loss of the will to live, disillu-
sion, despair, and doom. The audience can only pity the tragedies' ruined
heroes. This is to read the tragedies as moralities indeed. In 1945 she completed a study of Shakepeare's history plays, independently from Tillyard's
simultaneous similar effort. Believing that a poet "can be understood only
against the background of his own time" and, quite unlike Curry, that "the
plot is bound to express the author's philosophy," she concludes that Shakespeare's plots clearly express his fundamental conception of universal law.[14]
However, Miss Campbell's emphasis is not on the doctrines of hierarchy, correspondence, or even political obedience, but on the lessons of sin and divine
vengeance, and she traces in the histories, with the support of Hall, Grafton,
Richard Crompton, and Sir Walter Raleigh, a dynastic pattern in which the ill-

doing or usurpation of one king is punished in the loss of the throne by the third heir in his line.[15] For her the Shakespeare of the history plays is a teacher of politics applying to issues of current importance, such as the succession, the accepted political philosophy of the Tudors, which of course included the king as the necessary and proper head of the social hierarchy.[16]

Professor Tillyard, in *The Elizabethan World Picture* (1943) and his immediately subsequent book, *Shakespeare's History Plays* (1944), acknowledges his indebtedness to Lovejoy and expounds three prevailing Renaissance images of the universe's gradation and unity—the chain, the corresponding planes, and a dance to harmonious music. He, too, emphasizes the influence of the morality plays and a dramatic pattern wherein nature's order, distorted by crime, is providentially restored through disaster and suffering.[17] Shakespeare's plays stand out from others of the period:

> although most of the writers of these [other Chronicle
> plays] must have known the theory of degree and the hier-
> archical conception of the universe, they seem little
> interested in them. They are mainly practical playwrights
> writing for a popular audience, with small inclination to
> philosophy. The portion of the hierarchy that interests
> them is the social one, but that interest takes the form
> of preaching by example that a sensible man sticks to his
> position in society; it makes no suggestion that by so
> doing a man was taking his own part in the great cosmic
> harmony.[18]

By contrast, the very opening of *Henry VI, Part I,* where comets are bade to scourge the stars that brought about King Henry V's death, evokes the system of corresponding planes. These inauspicious stars Tillyard interprets as "the counterpart in the heavens of the English nobility who have already fallen into discord. The universe, in fact, was so much of a unity that the skies had to re-enact the things that happened in the human polity."[19] It is somewhat odd that Tillyard does not pursue the astrological counterpart of this doctrine—that events on earth respond to the movements of the stars in the heavens. The correspondence is evident enough, but the scientific question of effectual causation is not plumbed; Tillyard would no doubt accept M. M. Reese's formulation of relationships that Renaissance thinkers found in varying degrees vague, profound, reassuring, or troubling: "disorder in the heavens produces a reflexive disorder in the sublunary world, the commonwealth and the soul of man; disorder in any one of these is the cause of disorder in all the others...."[20] Since drama's concern is action and morality, not fatalism, the dramatic facts are human decisions or mistakes and their consequences; even a play with inauspicious stars, like *Romeo and Juliet*, must have its initiative on the plane of human action, though that action always takes place within a framework of cosmic law.

Tillyard also employs the doctrine of correspondences as a critical touchstone and so argues that *Henry V* manifests a falling off of Shakespeare's artistry: "Even the battle of Agincourt evokes no correspondences in the heavens or elsewhere."[21] Tillyard's preoccupation with the hierarchical world has, however, led him to omit a whole range of other correspondences, as Robert Ornstein, one of Tillyard's most vigorous recent critics has pointed out: "[this play's] perspective is large enough to suggest a connection between Agincourt, Cressy, the Norman conquest of England, the campaigns of Caesar and Pompey, and the famous victories of Alexander."[22] The mythological and historical frames of reference supply as fertile a source of images and allusions as the great cosmic scheme of things.

The critical task of verifying, qualifying, or extending the survey of the Shakespearean world order has been approached by a host of subsequent critics—Wilbur Sanders called Tillyard the patriarch of a tribe.[23] Edwin Muir in 1947 extended Spencer's sense of the conflict of ideas in Shakespeare when, in a challenging essay, he pointed out that *King Lear* is the only Shakespearean play to dramatize two opposing views of society; Lear's suffering is compounded by his bewilderment at dealing with creatures whose notions make the nature of things incomprehensible to him.[24] Goneril, Regan, and Edmund exist for the shallow present; they have obliterated all the traditional relationships between men, between past and present, between man and the cosmos. "Having no memory they have no responsibility, and no need therefore to treat their father differently from any other troublesome old man. This may simply be another way of saying that they are evil, for it may be that evil consists in a hiatus in the soul ... a lack of one of the essential threads which bind experience into a coherent whole and give it a consistent meaning."[25] In 1949 John F. Danby developed the implications of the two doctrines of nature—Hooker and Hobbes are his representatives—throughout an entire book on *King Lear* with references to most of the Shakespearean canon.[26] And in 1950 H. B. Parkes laid great stress on the divided consciousness of the Elizabethan age in which the medieval belief in the world's rational order was losing all conviction and for which the Newtonian reformulation lay far ahead.[27] The disharmony between

the traditional view and that which saw nature as a battleground between amor-
al and destructive forces is to him the central theme of Elizabethan and Jacobean literature; while Shakespeare's earlier plays accept the unresolved contradictions, the tragic idea that nature is evil dominates plays of the first
Jacobean decade such as *Hamlet* and *King Lear*.[28] But in *Macbeth* Shakespeare
transcended this conception, founding the tragedy on the view that evil is unnatural; this conviction, Parkes says, is what leads to the vision of life in
the last plays, but it was a vision not accessible to Shakespeare's contemporaries.[29] One should at least remark, however, that the Ghost in *Hamlet* considers murder most unnatural. Not much later Clifford Leech makes a complementary comment about the transitional *2 Henry IV*, which ends with the rejection
of Falstaff. Though the traditional order is in the play, it has disturbing
manifestations, as when Prince John dignifies his treachery as a providential
judgment. Shakespeare "hints at a state of dubiety concerning basic assumptions in the great historical scheme. He shows us the new king adhering to
political order, yet makes us half-doubt whether that order is worth its
price, whether in fact it is of the deepest importance to men."[30]

In 1953 Virgil Whitaker completed a systematic study, *Shakespeare's Use
of Learning*, which had begun in an attempt to review Tillyard's book on the
history plays. Whitaker identifies four stages in the development of Shakespeare's thought and concludes that the plays which significantly use theological and philosophical ideas of the world order are those in the great tragic
period after the turn of the century, from *Hamlet* and *Measure for Measure* to
Macbeth.[31] Whitaker even denies that the young Shakespeare, even in the
scenes of Cade's rebellion (*2 Henry VI*) or of the father who has killed his
son (*3 Henry VI*), conceived of civil disorder as a violation of universal order, thus directly contradicting Tillyard's conclusions about the same epi-
sodes and opening the door for all sorts of questions about the validity of
Tillyard's emphases and conclusions.[32] M. M. Reese, in another book of 1953,
pointed out how the world picture was an obstacle as well as a framework for
Renaissance poetic activity: "It had systematized thought altogether too effectively, and it left the writer with nothing to do but argue by analogy and
reproduce the generalized formulae ... which he found increasingly difficult
to harmonize with the observation of his senses."[33] Shakespeare uses the system more freely than his contemporaries and more comprehensively, and he does
not make his characters and plays manifestations of a pre-determined set of

beliefs. Some freedom resulted from the fact that only in its general outlines, not its details, was the hierarchical conception of the world either
comprehensive or agreed upon by Shakespeare's contemporaries, and further,
some classical ideas were imperfectly attached to the system. Reese objects to
rigid formulations of Shakespeare's positions and gently but firmly puts Campbell and Tillyard in their places: "it is unnecessary to suppose that only
passions spin [Shakespeare's] tragic plots or that his histories merely exemplify the high importance of keeping order in the community. These themes ...
should never be regarded as the sole meaning of the play...."[34] Many more
strident voices have taken up this chorus, that attention to the world picture
in Shakespeare limits the critical field of vision drastically, to the great
harm of that comprehensive appreciation and understanding which is or ought to
be the goal of criticism. Wilbur Sanders complains that in *The Cease of Majesty*, Reese's later book on the history plays, even Reese fails to "push his
criticism of Tillyard far enough to liberate himself from the ethical claus-
trophobia of *Shakespeare's History Plays*."[35] Thus, instead of expanding the
range of modern understanding of Shakespeare, an emphasis upon the world order
is perceived as imposing objectionable limitations on critical activity. On
the other hand, the world order may be invoked in order to correct some other
over-emphasis, such as a pessimistic interpretation of *Hamlet* based on the
imagery of disease, rottenness, and corruption in the play. W. Moelwyn Merchant asserts "it is a grave critical loss to concentrate our attention exclusively on the diseased, the disjointed and tragic [in *Hamlet*], ignoring the
frame of orthodoxy in which they are set."[36] The traditional intellectual
background must be known to establish "the necessary vocabulary of reference
within which a valid critical evaluation may be made."[37] To do this truly,
however, one must match the full range of ideas Shakespeare drew upon. Particularly after he had made the acquaintance of Plutarch, Reese points out,
Shakespeare pursued lines of thought alien to the medieval mind; he used the
world-picture freely, when and how he needed it—"and he needed it a good
deal, for its alternating conception of man as sometimes an angel and sometimes a beast was particularly well adapted to a poetic interpretation of
life."[38]

   Some of Tillyard's conclusions have been confirmed and some modified
without greatly departing from the core of his work. James Winny agrees that
the Elizabethan treatment of the hierarchical world simplified the elaborate

medieval correspondences: "interest seems to have moved from the details of
the design to the simple fact of its existence."[39] Winny also points out, however, that the immutable hierarchies are not the main dramatic business, which
is concerned with activity, with the liberty of creatures to seek their places
in the broad design, impelled by their faculties and will.[40] Irving Ribner
declares that Tillyard was incorrect in saying that the orthodox doctrine of
the social order allowed rebellion against a tyrant, but Ribner certainly
agreed that the justification of such a rebellion is implicit in *Richard III*
and *Macbeth*; Shakespeare must have proceeded on the belief that a tyrant is
not entitled to the rights of a lawful king.[41] David Bevington considers, as
Tillyard did not, that chronicle plays such as *Jack Straw* (c. 1587-91) and
Woodstock (c. 1591-94) were more dominated by the concepts of hierarchy, order, and degree than Shakespeare's history plays, but he confirms Tillyard's
view that Shakespeare endorsed the idea of the social hierarchy as the only
viable defense against social disintegration.[42] On the other hand, Henry Ansgar Kelly has shaken the very foundations of the Tillyard and Campbell providential view of the history plays. Against Tillyard, he reinforces Ribner's
insistence that there are two separate tetralogies, and rejects the idea that
Shakespeare thought the Wars of the Roses were connected with God's punishment
of England for the nation's rejection of order in deposing Richard II. Such a
notion "was so uncommon as to be found in none of the chronicle accounts or
plays of the fifteeenth and sixteenth centuries," Kelly notes, leaving Tillyard's theory about the nation's heinous sin against hierarchical order an *ex
post facto* imaginative construction and sending critics back to Shakespeare's
plays to reassess just what ideas are actually there between Acts I and V.[43]

Much criticism has turned to larger aspects of the traditional world
view, such as providence or natural law. Harold S. Wilson advocated the proposition that Shakespeare's tragedies belong in two categories, each with its
own conception of the world.[44] While four plays, *Romeo and Juliet*, *Hamlet*,
Othello, and *Macbeth*, rely on a providential and Christian world order discerned by the audience but often unrecognized by the characters, four others,
all set in the classical past, belong to the order of nature alone--they are
Julius Caesar, *Troilus and Cressida*, *Coriolanus* and *Timon of Athens*. Two
others, *Antony and Cleopatra* and *King Lear*, seek to harmonize the natural order and the providential one through the value of love. J. L. Simmons pursues
this distinction in a recent book on the Roman plays which adds the English

history plays under the Christian category, while George C. Herndl in *The High Design* (1970) treats the earlier Elizabethan tragic vision as intimately related to natural law understood as a corollary of Degree and Order, and traces the decline of such belief and the alteration of the spirit of later tragedy.[45]

One should take note of the way some critics, such as Douglas Bush, Wilbur Sanders, and Herbert Howarth, regard the elaboration of the world order in Shakespeare as either critically irrelevant or perverse. Bush accepts Lovejoy's judgment that the chain of being concept was a failure; but works like *Hamlet* and *King Lear* are not failures and have survived because they belong to a different enterprise of the mind, "and what is striking about them is that their outcome is so incomplete and inconclusive."[46] Howarth declares, "there were times when [Shakespeare] thought, felt, and dramatized attitudes which owe nothing to the 'world-picture'; and, what is distinctly to the point ... these attitudes sometimes energize his highest work."[47] Howarth is particularly upset at the misuse of the world order and the distortions and misinterpretations fostered by it. When Cornwall's servant opposes him as he is tearing out Gloucester's eyes, "the students write that he deserves Regan's stab in the back," for a man low on the scale of being has lifted his hand against a Duke.[48] That this judgment, despite its hierarchical logic, is totally out of touch with the play surely requires no defense, though it elicits much comment about literary pedagogy. Sanders offers further illustrations of how attention to the orthodox social hierarchy can blind one to the far deeper concerns of plays like *Richard III*.[49]

It would be quite appropriate to conclude by mentioning several recent critics who find the traditional ideas important in understanding Shakespeare, but who at once point out that other ideas, even the opposite ones, are just as firmly present in the same plays. In *The Problem of Order* (1962) Ernest E. Talbert shows how in *Richard II* successive lines of the same speech reflect opposite theoretical attitudes and are also double-edged. Shakespeare's artistry is one which allows antithetical meanings to exist concurrently and thereby "fuses the antithetical attitudes heretofore juxtaposed...."[50] Shakespeare's concern is artistic, not to construct theories or self-consistent systems: "drawing upon conflicting images, conflicting meanings of one image or symbol, and conflicting speeches and actions, Shakespeare intensifies his play-world ... and fuses their contraries ... into 'one thing entire' though

equivocal."[51] Marion Bodwell Smith insists that we must not forget Shakespeare's attitude toward conventional statements of all kinds is "consistently
inconsistent"; he uses the conventions of his age when it suits him to do so,
questions, modifies or rejects them when it does not.[52] The expression of conventional ideas, especially in sententious language, even becomes a Shakespearean convention for indicating insincerity--witness Polonius, Claudius,
and the wily Greek Ulysses, whose speech on Degree is uttered for the express
purpose of undermining the principle of Degree. Shakespeare is consistently
interested in the problem of establishing some line between opposites in a
world of conflicting values; the questions are raised in the early histories
as well as explicitly in the tragedies, and conventional notions of order are
questioned more often and more powerfully in the later plays than in the early
ones.[53] In a similar vein, J. L. Simmons gracefully indicates the sources of
the difficulties in interpreting the tragedy of *Julius Caesar*: "the medieval
view of Caesar as one of the Nine Worthies and the Renaissance view of him as
a proud and aspiring tyrant are both structurally incorporated into the play,
not only in the direct representation of Caesar but also in the indirect and
divergent representations made of him by the other characters."[54]

To conceptualize Shakespeare's artistry Norman Rabkin appropriates the
term "complementarity" from physics, indicating by it Shakespeare's characteristic way of seeing and presenting the ambivalences and dichotomies of reality; Rabkin finds in Shakespeare not the expression of accepted ideas about the
natural order, but a richness of vision that ranges far beyond.[55] Citing Theodore Spencer on the conflicts of ideas in Shakespeare's time, Bernard McElroy
completes a full circle, for in *Shakespeare's Mature Tragedies* he argues much
more extensively than Parkes that the great tragedies fully incorporate and
depend on the tensions between two diametrically opposed world views. These
permeate Shakespeare's characterizations, themes, and tragic structures, and
often bring about surprising inversions. To illustrate from *Hamlet*, it is the
villain, Claudius, who has a solid belief in the orthodox moral universe of
medieval Christianity; it is Hamlet who questions the very existence of that
order and wonders if there is any purpose in the universe. The plays are not,
of course, debating matches about philosophy. But it is the tension between
the traditional concept of the hierarchical world order wherein man had his
appointed place and duty, and the challenges to it that give Shakespeare's
dramatic art its power and its comprehensiveness.[56]

Having gone through a period of appropriating and elaborating the influence of traditional ideas of hierarchy, correspondence, natural law, order, and degree, Shakespeare criticism has also curbed the enthusiasm for regarding such ideas as the key to the interpretation of the plays. The contemporary reader is warned of their misuse and encouraged to discover no formal elaboration or dramatization of a coherent system, but conflicts and struggles between opposed ideas, conceptions of man, and systems of the universe. Shakespearean drama embraces all sides of the intellectual conflicts of the late Renaissance and is not confined within the traditional pattern of hierarchical order.

NOTES

[1]C. A. Patrides, *Milton and the Christian Tradition* (Oxford: Clarendon Press, 1966), p. 56.

[2]Arthur O. Lovejoy, *The Great Chain of Being: A Study of the History of an Idea* (New York: Harper and Brothers, 1960; first pub. 1936), p.7.

[3]E. M. W. Tillyard, *Shakespeare's History Plays* (London: Chatto and Windus, 1944; repr. 1969), p. 18.

[4]Quotations from Shakespeare's plays are taken from *The Complete Works of Shakespeare*, rev. ed., ed. Hardin Craig and David Bevington (Glenview, Ill.: Scott, Foresman and Co., 1973).

[5]W. R. Elton, "Shakespeare and the Thought of his Age," *A New Companion to Shakespeare Studies*, ed. Kenneth Muir and S. Schoenbaum (Cambridge: Cambridge University Press, 1971), p. 182.

[6]"Shakespeare's Learning," *Shakespeare, Spenser, Donne: Renaissance Essays* (New York: Viking Press, 1971), p. 185.

[7]Walter Clyde Curry, *Shakespeare's Philosophical Patterns* (Baton Rouge, La.: Louisiana State University Press, 1937; 2nd ed. 1959), pp. 195, 199. Cf. pp. 69-73, 110-111, 182. Robert Grams Hunter, *Shakespeare and the Comedy of Forgiveness* (New York and London: Columbia University Press, 1965), pp. 227-241, illustrates the importance of Christian elements in *The Tempest*.

[8]Theodore Spencer, *Shakespeare and the Nature of Man* (New York: Macmillan, 1961; first pub. 1942), p. 73; cf. pp. 201-202.

[9]*Ibid.*, p. 72.

[10]*Ibid.*, p. 108.

[11]*Ibid.*, p. 166. Spencer also formulates the three stages of Shakespeare's career as a period of experiment and adaptation, a period of tragic vision, and a period of affirmation (p. 222).

[12]*Ibid.*, p. 178.

[13]Lily B. Campbell, *Shakespeare's Tragic Heroes: Slaves of Passion* (New York: Barnes and Noble, 1963), Appendix A, pp. 250-251.

[14]Lily B. Campbell, *Shakespeare's "Histories": Mirrors of Elizabethan Policy* (London, Methuen, 1968; first pub. 1947), pp. 6,7.

[15]*Ibid.*, pp. 122-125.

[16]*Ibid.*, p. 125.

[17]Tillyard, p. 321.

[18]*Ibid.*, p. 104.

[19]*Ibid.*, p. 150.

[20]*Shakespeare, His World and His Work* (New York: St. Martin's Press, 1953), p. 459. D. C. Allen in *The Star-crossed Renaissance: The Quarrel about Astronomy and its Influence in England* (Durham, N.C.: Duke University Publications, 1941), pp. 165-167, 184-186, argues that Shakespeare, like most of his contemporaries, generally credits man's subjection to the stars' skyey influences.

[21]Tillyard, p. 312.

[22]Robert Ornstein, *A Kingdom for a Stage: The Achievement of Shakespeare's History Plays* (Cambridge, Mass.: Harvard University Press, 1972), p. 225.

[23]Wilbur Sanders, *The Dramatist and the Received Idea: Studies in the Plays of Marlowe and Shakespeare* (Cambridge: Cambridge University Press, 1968), p. 361, note 3.

[24]Edwin Muir, *The Politics of "King Lear,"* (Glasgow: Jackson, Son and Co., 1947), pp. 7, 10.

[25]*Ibid.*, p.17.

[26]John F. Danby, *Shakespeare's Doctrine of Nature: A Study of "King Lear"* (London: Faber and Faber, 1949).

[27]H. B. Parkes, "Nature's Diverse Laws: The Double Vision of the Elizabethans," *Sewanee Review* 58 (1950), 402-403.

[28]*Ibid.*, pp. 404, 410.

[29]*Ibid.*, p. 415.

[30]Clifford Leech, "The Unity of *2 Henry IV*," *Shakespeare Survey 6* (1953), p.17.

[31]Virgil K. Whitaker, *Shakespeare's Use of Learning: An Inquiry into the Growth of his Mind and Art* (San Marino, Calif.: The Huntington Library, 1953), p. 10. The four stages are: (1) the early period in which Shakespeare drew upon the rhetorical methods and classical authors of the grammar school; (2) the plays from 1595-1600 in which numerous contemporary writings are used and a much wider range of Latin and Greek authors appears; (3) the plays after the turn of the century which show a deepening theological and philosophical range and a systematic working out of the nature and consequences of moral choices; (4) the last plays, offering ease and mastery in treatment of the same philosophical ideas.

[32]Whitaker, pp. 76, 76n. Tillyard's views are found on pp. 152-154 of *Shakespeare's History Plays*.

[33]Reese, p. 463.

[34]*Ibid.*, pp. 464, 465.

[35]Sanders, p. 361, note 3. Reese's book on the history plays, *The Cease of Majesty*, appeared in 1961.

[36]W. Moelwyn Merchant, "Shakespeare's Theology," *Review of English Literature*, 5 (1964), 81.

[37] *Ibid.*, p. 84.

[38] Reese, *Shakespeare, His World and His Work*, pp. 467, 468.

[39] James Winny, "Introduction," *The Frame of Order: An Outline of Elizabethan Belief taken from Treatises of the Late Sixteenth Century*, ed. James Winny (London: George Allen and Unwin, 1957), p. 15.

[40] *Ibid.*, p. 23.

[41] Irving Ribner, *The English History Play in the Age of Shakespeare*, rev. ed. (London: Methuen, 1965), p. 117.

[42] David Bevington, *Tudor Drama and Politics: A Critical Approach to Topical Meaning* (Cambridge, Mass.: Harvard University Press, 1968), pp. 237, 251, 241; cf. p. 232.

[43] Henry Ansgar Kelly, *Divine Providence in the England of Shakespeare's Histories* (Cambridge, Mass.: Harvard University Press, 1970), p. 289.

[44] Harold S. Wilson, *On the Design of Shakespearian Tragedy* (Toronto: University of Toronto Press, 1957), pp. 214-215.

[45] J. L. Simmons, *Shakespeare's Pagan World: The Roman Tragedies* (Charlottesville, Va.: The University Press of Virginia, 1973); George C. Herndl, *The High Design: English Renaissance Tragedy and the Natural Law* (Lexington, Ky.: The University Press of Kentucky, 1970), pp. 27-28, 89, 160-161.

[46] Douglas Bush, *Shakespeare and the Natural Condition* (Cambridge, Mass.: Harvard University Press, 1956), pp. 6-7.

[47] Herbert Howarth, "Put Away the World Picture," in *The Tiger's Heart: Eight Essays on Shakespeare* (New York: Oxford University Press, 1970), p. 175.

[48] *Ibid.*, p. 171.

[49] Sanders, pp. 79ff.

[50] Ernest W. Talbert, *The Problem of Order: Elizabethan Political Commonplaces and an Example of Shakespeare's Art* (Chapel Hill, N.C.: University of North Carolina Press, 1962), p. 171.

[51] *Ibid.*, p. 199.

[52] Marion Bodwell Smith, *Dualities in Shakespeare* (Toronto: University of Toronto Press, 1966), p. 26.

[53] *Ibid.*, pp. 27-30.

[54] Norman Rabkin, *Shakespeare and the Common Understanding* (New York: The Free Press, 1967), pp. 30-31.

[55] *Ibid.*, p. 31.

[56] Bernard McElroy, *Shakespeare's Mature Tragedies* (Princeton, N.J.: Princeton University Press, 1973), pp. 8-13.

JAMES CONROY DOIG
DENIAL OF HIERARCHY:
CONSEQUENCES FOR SCOTUS AND DESCARTES

In *The Great Chain of Being*, Professor Arthur Lovejoy amply demonstrated the importance of the notion of hierarchy by showing how the acceptance of that notion can have numerous ramifications in a philosopher's view of reality. What this paper proposes is that the study of the denial of hierarchy can also illustrate that notion's significance.

The denial of hierarchy has two aspects, for it is simultaneously a denial of the plenitude of created being and a denial of the ladder or chain of being. As a denial of the plenitude of created being, it refuses to admit that the extent and abundance of creation are as great as the possibility of existence and commensurate with the productive capacity of the source of creation. As a denial of the chain of being, it refuses to accept reality as arranged in an order of descending perfection with each level sharing in what is above it and containing what is below it.[1] When a philosopher works within the context of such refusals, he is forced into several basic positions, three of which this paper will examine:

    1) some degree of arbitrariness must be admitted as
        integral to God's creative activity;

    2) the meaning of an individual created thing must be
        explained otherwise than as a single, limited expres-
        sion of a unique aspect of the divine essence; and

    3) the human mind, if it is to achieve knowledge of the
        creator, must be capable of understanding more than
        the meaning found in our world.

It is these three consequences of the denial of hierarchy that I propose to trace in the thought of Duns Scotus and Descartes. By examining the positions to which they were logically led by excluding hierarchy from their thought, we will have one more illustration of the importance of Professor Lovejoy's insight.

As mentioned, the first consequence of the denial of hierarchy is the need to admit some degree of arbitrariness into the explanation of God's creative activity. Thus we find Scotus explaining that in the act of creation God assigned to each thing its own nature; for example, to fire, God assigned the power of heating, although he could just as well have given fire the power of

cooling.[2] A doctrine such as this most assuredly sidesteps all trace of a Neo-
Platonic hierarchical universe: here Scotus has turned his back on any explanation of the universe as the necessary diffusion or overflowing of divine
goodness.[3]

It is instructive to note the background of Scotus' view that fire could
have had the property of cooling had God so desired. Scotus presents his
theory of creation in terms of several moments of divine activity. By speaking
of these distinct "moments", Scotus can be understood as attempting to distinguish a logical order of priority and posteriority among the propositions we
affirm of divine creative activity. These propositions, beginning with the
most basic or logically prior, are as follows:

1) God knows his own essence;

2) God produces an infinite number of ideas expressing
   the infinite imitable perfections of his essence; (it
   is in this moment that the ideas of "fire", of "hot",
   and of "cold" are produced;)

3) God knows he has produced these ideas and knows the
   infinite number of possible combinations of the meanings expressed in these ideas; (it is in this third
   moment that God knows the combinations of "hot fire"
   and "cold fire";)

4) God chooses to create one of the infinite number of
   possible orders of beings; (here God chooses the order in which "hot fire" occurs;) and

5) God brings into being the one possible order he has
   chosen.[4]

Since these five propositions are supposed true of God, Scotus must face the
issue of whether there is a distinct reality in God answering to each of these
propositions. As is well known, the notions of "formal distinction" and "formality" are introduced in this context: in God, the knowledge of his own essence is formally distinct from, or is a formality distinct from, the production of the divine ideas, and so forth.[5]

This approach to God in terms of moments has clearly introduced some
degree of arbitrariness into the discussion of divine creative activity. Not
only is God free in choosing to create, but he is free in choosing the eternal
nature of a reality such as fire: fire could have been cold; it is a merely a
de facto situation that according to its nature fire is hot. Such a view has
been deliberately chosen by Scotus in the attempt to safeguard the transcen-

dency of God which to his mind earlier theories did not sufficiently ground. For example, Scotus understood Aquinas to hold that God knows the essence of creatures in knowing his own essence. For Scotus, such a theory debases God for it makes him necessarily related to possible creatures.[6]

Having denied hierarchy in rejecting all necessary relation of God to creation, Scotus must face the issue of how individual creatures express or imitate God. Here the second consequence of the denial of hierarchy is at work. As noted, that denial makes it impossible to see each creature as a stage in a great chain of being, contained in the stage immediately above it and containing all the stages below it. But what then is a creature for Scotus? Simply this: each creature is an imitation of definite combination of divine ideas which in turn is part of that one pattern of creation God has chosen to produce. Perhaps only God knows how many ideas he combined to get the pattern for a being such as Socrates. But one thing seems certain: among the original ideas God produced in the second moment were the ideas of "material being", of "sentient being", of "rational being". So certain is this, that Scotus does not hesitate to say that God could have created material things that would imitate only the idea of "material being": in other words, God could have created material being which had no form whatsoever. Of course, God has not created such a universe. Rather, he has created a universe where form is what is received by matter and where matter is what receives form. For Scotus, this means that matter must be considered to be a being in act, an actual being logically prior to the reception of substantial form.

Such a theory means that Scotus must redefine the Aristotelian notion of "substantial unity". For Aristotle, a substance had its basic unity through the action of one substantial form perfecting purely potential matter: all the essential perfection, all the essential meaning of an existing substance came from its one substantial form, and thus its substantial unity was assured. For Scotus on the other hand, substantial unity is had insofar as the several distinct entities in a being are ordered by nature to constitute one being.[8] Clearly an individual substance is no longer explained as a single meaning expressing its degree of imitation of the divine source for there is meaning not only of the form but of the matter as well.

Having adopted such an approach, it would seem logical for Scotus to have adopted the doctrine of the plurality of forms. Since an individual such as Socrates has matter which expresses one divine idea and a rational form ex-

pressing another, why not maintain that he has also as separate forms the form
of corporeity, the form of living being, the form of sentient being, and so
on? There has been some dispute over whether Scotus did hold such a doctrine.[9]
Whether or not he did, material things, through their matter and their specific form, express a plurality of divine ideas. However, if Scotus did accept
the plurality of forms in a substance, the second consequence of the denial of
hierarchy is even more evident: an individual being is not seen as a single,
unified expression of one aspect of God.

When we turn now to the third consequence of the denial of hierarchy, we
come to a still more complex issue, that of the possibility of knowing God:
how is the human mind to know God, and most basically, how is it to know that
God exists if it cannot climb up some ladder of being?[10]

When Scotus spells out the details of the theory of knowledge which fits
within his non-hierarchical context, he proceeds to modify a very widely held
Aristotelian view which being logically related in Aquinas to the acceptance
of hierarchy, describes human intellection in terms of the possession of a
concept through which one is intentionally related to the quiddity "shining
forth in the phantasm". For Scotus too, the concept in the intellect is said
to be in relation to the "object shining forth in the phantasm".[11] However, in
Aquinas' exposition of this Aristotelian tradition, the proper object of the
human intellect is said to be the quiddity of the material thing.[12] Such an
approach is well and good for Aquinas, since the concrete quiddity, or the being as actually existing, is a participation of the divine being. Thus,
Aquinas can reach God by discovering divine traces in the reality of individuals. Aquinas develops this position by explaining that for Aristotle "being"
is at the heart of any substantial concept, for in each and every substantial
concept we truly get to the particular reality or the being of the individual
known through the concept. To comprehend the concept "being as such", we reflect on the way we use the concept of "being" to know individual objects.[13]
Scotus, having denied a hierarchical universe, will never reach God if he accepts this interpretation of the intellect's relation to the phantasm.[14]
Scotus has turned away from the view of existing material individuals as a
ladder to climb to God. Thus, we find him explicitly rejecting not only
Aquinas' notion of the proper object of the intellect, but as well this Aristotelian approach to the discovery of the concept of "being". The intellect,
he will say, can never find "being as such" by emphasizing the being of the

object present in the phantasm. The intellect can certainly find *this* being or *that* being in the phantasm, but never being as such.[15] Yet the intellect must comprehend the concept of "being as such" if it is to prove God. Scotus' only recourse is to turn away from the "object shining forth in the phantasm" and to turn inward to intelligence itself. Thus, in a unique variation of Augustinianism, Scotus will rise from self to God. In germ, this variation of Augustinianism is contained in Scotus' theory that the proper object of the human intellect is being in all its indeterminateness.[16]

The phantasm, Scotus insists, serves only as the cause which moves the agent intellect to produce in the possible intellect the concepts which express the quiddity of the individual being.[17] Among the concepts produced will be the concept of "being" which will be understood in terms of the quiddity of the particular phantasm involved. It is through a reflection on this concept of "being" that the intellect is able to comprehend its concept of "being as such" and thus to have the foundation to rise to God. It is precisely through considering the concept of "being" produced in the possible intellect that the human intelligence is capable of knowing more than the meaning found in our world, for here the intelligence understands spiritual or nonmaterial being. In Scotus' terms, the intellect must be elevated "to considering truths as they shine forth in themselves, not only as they shine forth in the phantasm".[18] The contrast between Scotus and Aquinas comes then to this: Aquinas understands the concept of "being" by seeing how it is used to understand the quiddity in the phantasm; Scotus, however, turns away from the use of "being" to understand the quiddity in the phantasm and examines the meaning of "being" itself.

The full scope of what Scotus has done can be seen if we recall the Avicennian notion of the three-fold way of considering essence, a notion underlying the approach of Aquinas. For Avicenna, we can consider an essence first, as existing in an individual, and second, as existing in the intellect. But a third consideration is had when we examine the essence without paying attention to its existence; here, we examine the essence in itself. Of course, one cannot examine nonexistent essence, and so one can ask which existing essence it is that we examine when we consider only the essence in itself, that is to say, its meaning, and ignore its existence. To this query, Avicenna would have answered that we examine essence in itself by examining how the essence existing in the intellect is the mind's means of knowing the essence existing in

the individual. In other words, to examine *meaning* is to consider how through
it man knows the individual thing. (It was this sort of examination that
Aquinas carried through to discover the meaning of "being".) On the other
hand, when we examine the essence as *existing* in the mind, we do not examine
meaning, but according to Avicenna, we rather carry through a metaphysical
consideration of the spiritual form through which the intellect is in act.[19]

To this three-fold Avicennian consideration, Scotus by implication is
adding a fourth. Man can, he seems to imply, first examine essence as existing
in the individual thing (here we examine the "common" or specific nature contracted to an individual by the principle of "thisness"); second, we can examine essence existing as the spiritual quality through which the intellect is
in act (here what is examined is the "common nature" freed from the determination to an individual by "thisness", but examined as a spiritual quality and
not as a meaning); third, we can examine essence as the meaning we know about
the individual (in this case, we examine the common meaning freed from "thisness" and so universal, although it is considered as the meaning we have about
the species expressed in the phantasm); and fourth, we can examine essence as
a spiritual or nonmaterial meaning (here we consider the "common nature"
understood as a meaning freed from "thisness" and so understood as in itself a
universal, nonmaterial meaning). Meanings, this fourth consideration implies,
have a *cognitive being*, which is a being or a reality in the intellect distinct from the essence existing as the form through which the intellect is in
act.[20] It is through reflection on such spiritual or nonmaterial meanings that
the intelligence is able to understand the concept of "being" univocal to God
and creatures.[21] At this point all Scotus need do is construct the idea of a
possible infinite being in order to reach God, for the infinite being is possible only if it exists.[22] We have here the third consequence of the denial of
hierarchy mentioned earlier: the human mind, if it is to achieve knowledge of
the Creator, must be capable of understanding more than the meaning found in
our world. For Scotus, since the intellect has as its proper object being in
all its indeterminateness, the intellect does surpass the meaning found in our
world; this notion of being in all its indeterminateness is reached because
the intelligence is capable of examining existent meanings, cognitive beings.[23]

If we turn now to Descartes, we find in him the same three consequences
of the denial of hierarchy noted in Scotus. Descartes' fundamental opposition

to a hierarchical conception is evident. Writing in the Sixth Response, Descartes declares: "... because he (God) determined to make the things that are actually in the world, for this reason they are, as it is written in Genesis, 'very good', that is, the reason for their goodness depends upon the fact that he willed to make them".[24]

The Sixth Response of Descartes is crucial to the issue of this paper, for there Descartes elaborates his insistence on the transcendence of God by explaining his view on the so-called "eternal truths". In brief, that view is the following. In God, there is no room for even the slightest distinction of reason between intelligence and will. Consequently, we cannot say that God created things according to the divine essence as comprehended by His intellect, for that would make the divine intelligence both distinct from and prior to the free choice to create. We must, on the contrary, insist on the total identity of God's intellect and will and power; thus we must emphasize that God's free, eternal choice to create is simultaneously a free, eternal choice of the eternal truths which govern His creation.[25] From our point of view these truths are necessary; for example, to use, 2 + 1 = 3, and (another of Descartes' examples) mountains are inseparable from valleys.[26] For us to conceive the opposite of these two propositions is impossible. From God's point of view however, the truth of 2 + 1 = 3, and the connection of mountains with valleys, are contingent, for He has freely chosen these to be the eternal truths governing His creation.[27]

Does Descartes mean that God could have made the sum of 2 and 1 equal to some number other than 3? or does he mean that mountains could be created without valleys? To this question Descartes answered in effect: I do not dare say He could; but yet I do not dare say He couldn't; I just know that the world is the way God has freely made it, and consequently the truth of things is every bit as dependent on God's choice as the existence of things is.[28]

With such an explanation of creation, Descartes has effectively, logically, barred himself from explaining individual beings as limited expressions or imitations of the divine being. Here we have the second consequence of the denial of hierarchy. As is well known, for Descartes individual material beings have only the characteristic of extension, for that is the only characteristic needed to explain our experience of sensing material things.[29] Consequently, when we study the material universe, we will explain it in terms only of figure, of extension, and of motion.[30]

The connection between the sole property of material substance, namely extension, and the liberty of God is an interesting one. In terms of the chronological development of his system, it appears that Descartes first decided that the physical study of material things emphasized measurement. His question then became one of justifying the necessity of scientific statements in terms of measurement. Did such statements have the character of eternal and necessary truths? They did, if in God's eyes, material things were eternally mathematical in character. [31] God must then have chosen for material things the sole characteristic of extension. This doctrine in turn necessitates that all eternal truths are chosen to be such by God.

We have then the logical connection between Descartes' explanation of material things, his view of God's freedom in creation, and his denial of hierarchy. It matters not which came to his mind first. In his own eyes they are all of a piece, each inseparably united to the other.

But what of the third consequence listed as pertaining to the denial of hierarchy? How does Descartes extend the power of the human mind so that it is capable of understanding more than the meaning found in the world? How does he ground man's ability to surpass the extended universe and his own geometrical knowledge of it and to achieve knowledge of his Creator?

The answer to this question is as well known as any aspect of Descartes' work. God has provided man with the idea of "perfect", an idea which, once recognized, leads us to God as its sole possible cause.[32] However, I believe it valuable to reflect for a moment on Descartes' theory that the idea of "perfect" has not only formal reality but also objective or representational reality.

What is the "formal reality" of the idea of "perfect"? Descartes meant that the idea is a mode of thought.[33] As is clear from his correspondence, this emphasis on the idea as a mode of thought is simply Descartes' way of adopting the traditional medieval theory of the mind's tendency toward an object through an idea.[34] If Descartes had said no more than this about the idea of "perfect", he would have been referring only to the mind's tendency toward God as "the perfect" and to material things as "the not perfect". But such a tendency would not have enabled Descartes to prove the existence of God. Statements about the mind's tendencies do not constitute a proof that the objects tended toward are real.

Yet Descartes does go further, for he attributes an "objective reality" to the idea of "perfect". It is in this doctrine of the objective reality of ideas that Descartes expands the power of human intelligence to the degree that man can rise to knowledge of God's existence. By the doctrine of objective reality, Descartes parallels the Scotist notion of the cognitive being of ideas. Thus Descartes fills human intelligence with existing meanings, meanings whose reality is totally independent of man's intentional relationship to extra-mental things. In other words, by insisting on objective reality, and he did this in the face of objections from a scholastic correspondent, Descartes fills human consciousness with existent meanings which can be understood in abstraction from all reference of those meanings to anything whatsoever.[35]

The philosophies of Descartes and Scotus provide then a striking example of the importance of the notion of hierarchy. Because neither philosopher viewed the universe as a hierarchy of being, each must explain creation in such a way that created essences are founded on a free choice of God. As well, when they turn to the issue of the meaning found in creatures, each must note that whatever that meaning is, it is definitely something other than a single, unitary expression of some aspect of the divine essence. Finally, when they explained the way man rises to knowledge of God, both had to attribute to human intelligence a power to withdraw not only from involvement with the world, but even from involvement with the very reality of intelligence; thus they attributed to intelligence the power to contemplate meanings not only as knowledge of things and as forms of intellectual activity, but as cognitive realities in their own right.

The presence of hierarchy is a crucial aspect of a philosophy. However, as Scotus and Descartes illustrate, the rejection of hierarchy is equally crucial.

NOTES

[1]For the basis of this formulation, see: A. O. Lovejoy, *The Great Chain of Being. A Study of the History of an Idea*, Harvard University Press, Cambridge, 1966, pp. 52 and 58.

[2]*Op. ox.*, lib. IV, d. 46, q. 1, n. 9 (T. X, p. 252). (With few exceptions, references to Scotus are to the Lyons, 1639 edition, as reprinted photographically by Olms, Hildesheim, 1968; the exceptions are to the critical edition of the Scotus Commission, Rome.) Cf. E. Bettoni, *Duns Scotus: The Basic Principles of His Philosophy*, Catholic University Press, Washington, D.C., 1961, pp. 158-159.

[3]The transcedence of God appears also in discussions of our knowledge, e.g.: *Ord.*, lib. I, d. 3, pars 1, q. 1-2, n. 57 (T. III, p. 59, Scotus Comm.) Note A. Wolter's gloss on this text: "All relationships between God and creatures are contingent and dependent upon the divine will, the ultimate source of all contingency". *Duns Scotus. Philosophical Writings*, Bobbs-Merrill, N.Y., 1962, p. 183.

[4]*Op. ox.*, lib. I, d. 35, q. unica, nn. 10-12 (T. V.2, pp. 1251-1252); *Ibid.*, n. 15 (T. V.2, p. 1255); *Report. Paris.*, lib. I, d. 36, q. 2, nn. 34-35 (T. XI.1, p. 206); *Op. ox.*, lib. I, d. 3, q. 4, nn. 18-20 (T. V.1, pp. 489-490). Bettoni, *Op. cit.*, lib. I, p. 155; E. Gilson, *Jean Duns Scot. Introduction à ses positions fondamentales*, Vrin, Paris 1952, pp. 281-282.

[5]*Op. ox.*, lib. I, d. 2, q. 7, nn. 41-45 (T. V.I, p. 351-352 & 355-356); *Ibid.*, d. 8, q. 4, n. 18 (T. V.2, p. 766). See M. Grajewski, *The Formal Distinction of Duns Scotus*, Catholic University Press, 1944, pp. 187-197.

[6]*Op. ox.*, lib. I, d. 35, q. unica, nn. 5 & 7 (T. V.2, pp. 1246-1247 and p. 1249).

[7]*Ibid.*, lib. II, d. 12, q. 1, nn. 14-15 (T. VI.2, p. 673); *Quaes. Subt. in Meta.*, lib. VII, q. 5 (T. XII, p. 680). For further texts, see: Gilson, *Op. cit.*, pp. 440-444; Bettoni, *Op. cit.*, pp. 47-50.

[8]*Op. ox.*, lib. II, d. 12, q. 1, nn. 14-15 (T. VI.2, p. 673); *Quaes. Subt. in Meta.*, lib. VII, q. 13 (T. XII, p. 698).

[9]E.G., Bettoni, *Op. cit.*, p. 50; Gilson, *Op. cit.*, p. 467. The difficulty in deciding what Scotus held is exemplified by *Quaes. Subt. in Meta.*, where lib. VII, q. 20 implies there is no plurality of forms and lib. V, qq. 4 & 10 imply there is a plurality of forms.

[10]Note the rejection of the "negative approach" to knowing God and the approach through participation: *Ord.*, lib. I, d. 3, pars 1, q. 1-2, nn. 10-12, 15, 25, 41ff, & 106 (T. III, pp. 4-6, 7, 16-17, 27ff, & 67 respectively, Scotus Comm.).

[11]*Ibid.*, n. 35 (T. III, pp. 21-24, Scotus Comm.); *Op. ox.*, lib. I, d. 3., q. 8, n. 19 (T. V.1, p. 538).

[12]For Scotus' understanding of Aquinas, see: *Ord.*, lib. I, d. 3, pars 1, q. 3, nn. 110-112 (T. III, pp. 69-70, Scotus Comm.); *Op. ox.*, lib. I, d. 3, q. 6, n. 27 (T. V.1, p. 548).

[13]Cf. the discussion of Aquinas' exposition of the *Metaphysics* in my *Aquinas on Metaphysics. A historico-doctrinal study of the Commentary on the Metaphysics*, Nijhoff, The Hague, 1972, pp. 247-275.

[14]*Ord.*, lib. I, d. 3, pars 1, q. 3, nn. 113-114, 116-122, & 137 (T. III, pp. 70-71, 72-75, & 85 respectively, Scotus Comm.). Scotus met this Aristotelian view frequently, e.g. in Avicenna: *Op. ox.*, lib. I, d. 3, q. 6, nn. 25 & 27 (T. V.1, pp. 542 & 548).

[15]A basic text in this regard is *Op. ox.*, lib. I, d. 3, q. 6. E.g., in *Ibid.*, n. 9 (T. V.1, p. 528) Scotus explains that metaphysics is a "habit" distinct from less universal "habits", and so metaphysics can have its act of intellection about the most universal without acts of intellection of less universal things being simultaenously had; then, having noted that metaphysics can have this act of intellection if the most universal thing is present to the intellect as a universal, he concludes: "Sed si praecise intelligeretur obiectum in phantasmate, nunquam esset maius universale praesens, nisi in minus universali, quia nunquam nisi in singulari phantasiabili: ergo est praesens in specie intelligibili existente in intellectu". This contrast between understanding the most universal ("being") and understanding it in the less universal (the species in the phantasm) should be compared to the earlier discussion in *Ibid.*, q. 4, n. 22 (p. 491). In this text Scotus is contrasting the wise man who understands "whole" in itself with the majority of men who understand "whole" in wood or in stone; he writes that the wise man "... debet intelligi elevando intellectum, ad considerandum veritates, ut relucent in se, non tantum ut relucent in phantasmate". See also: *Ibid.*, q. 6, n. 28 (p. 548).

[16]*Op. ox.*, *Prolog.*, q. 1, n. 13 (T. V.1, p. 11); *Quaes. Subt. in Meta.*, lib. IV, q. 1 (T. XII, p. 574ff).

[17]*Ord.*, lib. I, d. 3, pars 1, q. 1-2, nn. 35 & 63 (T. III, pp. 21-24 & 44-45, Scotus Comm.); *Op. ox.*, lib. I, d. 3, q. 6, n. 17 (T. V.1, p. 529).

[18]*Ibid.*, q. 4, n. 22 (T. V.1, p. 491) quoted in footnote 16. The mechanism of this "elevation" and "consideration of truths shining forth in themselves" seems to be spoken of in the following text; the context is Scotus' answer to the objection that God cannot be known because we have no phantasm of him apprehended by the senses: "... potest enim intellectus abstrahere omnem obiectum inclusum in obiecto primo movente, et considerare illud abstractum non considerando illud a quod abstrahit - et considerando istud abstractum, sic considerat commune sensibili et insensibili, quia in illo consideratur insensibile in universale, sicut et sensibile - et potest considerare illud abstractum et aliud abstractum, in quo sit proprium alteri, scilicet insensibili; sed sensus non est abstractivus, et ideo in omni actu - tam primo quam secundo - requirit obiectum aliquod proprium movens, quomodo non se habet phantasm ad intellectum". *Ord.*, lib. I, d. 3, pars 1, q. 1-2, n. 63 (T. III, pp. 44-45, Scotus Comm.). Elsewhere, Scotus explains that we know we have "being in all its indeterminateness" as the object of our intellect, and not just being in the phantisable object, because we experience our act directed toward the former: *Op. ox.*, *Prolog.*, q. 1, n. 13 (T. V.1, p. 11).

[19]Cf. Avicenna, *Logyce*, Pars I, fol. 2r, col. B (Venetiis, Junctas, 1508; reprinted photographically by Bibl. S.J., Louvain, 1961); *Philosophia prima*, Tract. V, c. 1, fol. 86v, A (Venetiis....Louvain, 1961).

[20]Cf. the texts of footnotes 16 & 19. Also important in underlying the cognitive being of meaning is Scotus disagreement with Aristotle's view that knowledge is a reference to a knowable thing (cf. *Meta.*, Δ 15, 1021a29-31; Scotus writes about this text as follows: "Quod scientia non refertur ad scibile, probatio: scientia per se est in genere Qualitatis. Sed tale non dependet secundum se. Contrarium ponitur a Philosopho in litera". *Quaes. Subt. in Meta.*, lib. V, q. 13 (T. XII, p. 647). If "scientia" - in the context, an act of knowing, is a quality, then not only is the species a quality, but the object present in and by the species is a quality. Elsewhere, the object (meaning) present in the species is said to be "ens diminutum habens esse in intellectu, ut cognitum in cognoscente". *Op. ox.*, lib. I, d. 35, q. unica, n. 8 (T. V.2, p. 1249).

[21]*Ord.*, lib. I, d. 3, pars 1-2, nn. 26-55 (T. III, pp. 18-38, Scotus Comm.).

[22]*Op. ox.*, lib. I, d. 2, q. 2, n. 16 (T. V.1, p. 249).

[23]Gilson writes: "The kind of being considered by the metaphysician is neither a particular physical reality, nor a universal taken in its logical generality; it is the intelligible reality which the very *nature* of being as being is". *History of Christian Philosophy in the Middle Ages*, Random House, N.Y., 1955, p. 456. Speaking of the charge that for Scotus man has an innate idea of God, Bettoni writes: "... if man arrives at knowledge of God..., it is not because of what he sees in things, but because of the innate tendency of his intellect to know not just one particular being, but being without qualification.... Thus we are not only allowed to speak of a certain innatism of the idea of being but ... we must do so. This type of innatism may be best described as 'virtual innatism'". *Op. cit.*, p. 44.

[24]*Resp. 6*, in *Oeuvres de Descartes* (edit. Adam & Tannery), Cerf, Paris, 1897-1913, Vol. VIII, pp. 434-435. (All references to Descartes are to the edition of Adam & Tannery.)

[25]*Resp. 6*, Vol. VII, pp. 431-435; *Resp. 2*, Vol. VII, p. 141. Letter to Mersenne, June 3, 1630, Vol. I, pp. 152-153.

[26]*Resp. 6*, Vol. VII, p. 435.

[27]Letter to Arnauld, July 29, 1648, Vol. V, pp. 223-224.

[28]*Resp. 6*, Vol. VII, p. 435. *Resp. 5*, Vol. VII, pp. 378-380. On the issue of God's freedom in creating eternal truths, see: H. Gouhier, *La pensée métaphysique de Descartes*, Vrin, Paris, 1962, pp. 232-257, esp. p. 249.

[29]*Medit. VI*, Vol. VII, pp. 79-80. *Regula XII*, Vol. X, pp. 412-413. *Resp. 6*, Vol. VII, pp. 435-436. *Resp. 3*, Vol. VII, p. 176.

[30]*Regula XII*, Vol. X, pp. 418-420. *Resp. 1*, Vol. VII, pp. 120-121. On the question of the scientific study of the material world, see: B. O'Neil, *Epistemological Direct Realism in Descartes' Philosophy*, University of New Mexico Press, (Albuquerque) 1974, chs. 1-2.

[31]Note the discussion of the atheist's certainty: *Resp. 6*, Vol. VII, p. 427. *Resp. 2*, Vol. VII, p. 140. Letter to Mersenne, April 15, 1630, Vol. I, pp. 144-146.

[32]*Medit. III*, Vol. VII, pp. 44-51. *Resp. 1*, Vol. VII, pp. 102-105. *Resp. 2*, Vol. VII, pp. 131-132.

[33]*Medit. III*, Vol. VII, p. 40. In the *Preface* to the *Meditations*, Descartes refers to this aspect of an idea as "the operation of the intellect"; Vol. VIII, p. 8.

[34]See Caterus' objection: *Primae objectiones*, Vol. VII, p. 92; and Descartes' answer: *Resp. 1*, Vol. VII, pp. 102-103.

[35]Descartes writes: "... but if one asks what is the idea of 'sun', and if one answers that it is the thing thought insofar as it is objectively in the understanding, no one will understand that it is the sun itself insofar as the external denomination is in it. 'To be objectively in the understanding' does not mean to terminate its operation in the fashion of an object, but to be in the understanding in the way that objects are ordinarily there; in such a way that the idea of sun is the sun existing in the understanding, not in truth formally, as it is in the sky, but objectively, that is to say, in the manner in which objects ordinarily exist in the understand-

ing: even though that fashion of being is truly more imperfect than that by which things exist in the understanding; but nonetheless it is not a pure nothing...." *Resp. 1*, Vol. VII, pp. 102-103 (my trans.) Elsewhere Descartes writes of modes of thought: "... in me esse sum certus". *Medit. III*, Vol. VII, pp. 34-35.

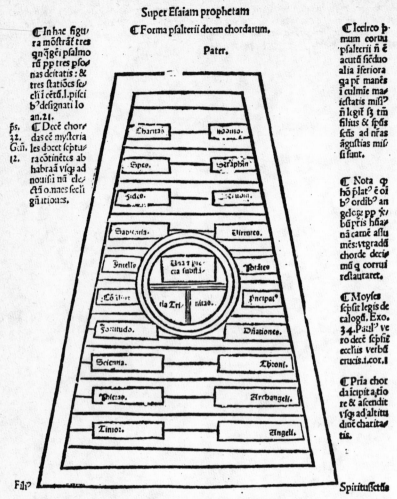

Super Esaiam prophetam

Forma psalterii decem chordarum.

Pater.

In hac figura mõstrãt tres qñ q̃ gẽi psalmorũ pp tres psonas deitatis: & tres statiões seculi i cẽtũ.l.pisci b̃²designati loan.21.

ps. Decẽ chor-
32. das cẽ mysteria
Gñ. les docet septu-
12. ra cõtinẽtes ab habraã vsq̃ ad nouissi nũ ele-ctũ o.mnes seculi gñ.itiones.

Charitas.

Bõnitas.

Spes.

Seraphin.

Fides.

Cherubin.

Sapiẽtia.

Virtutes.

Intelle-

Vna 7 pro-
cia substi-

tia Trinitas.

Potestates.

Cõ.ilium

Principatus.

Fortitudo.

Dñationes.

Scientia.

Throni.

Pietas.

Archangeli.

Timor.

Angeli.

Filius

Spiritussanctus

Iccirco p̃-mum coruũ psalterii ñ ẽ acutũ siẽduo alia iseriora qa p̃ manẽs i culmie maiestatis miss² ñ legit sz tm filius & sp̃us sctus ad nras ãgustias missi sunt.

Nota q̃ hõ plat² ẽ oi b² ordib² angelo̧ pp x̃ bũpris hũaña carnẽ assu mẽs: vt gradũ chorde deci-mũ q̃ corrui restauraret.

Moyses scpsit legis decalogũ. Exo. 34. Paul² vero decẽ scpsiẽ ecclius verbũ crucis.1.cor.1

Pria chor da iicipit a.tio re & ascendit vsq̃ ad altitu dinẽ charita-tis.

Luc. Nota q̃ duo mittunt ab vno filius,s.& spũssanctus a patre:& vnus mittitur a duobus idẽ vi-
18. delicet spũs. Vñ in symbolo Q ui a p̃re filioq̃; pcedit qd greçi nõ recipiũt dũ nõ itelligunt: illũ
Jo.14 cẽcũ imitãtes:q̃ stans secus viam clamabat: Kyrieleison.1.dñe miserere. Nõ enim in via veritati̧s
Ti.1 quẽ christus est ambulant:sed secus aberrãt, Cõfitent ingt se nosse deum factis cutem negant.

This ladder of virtues corresponding to ranks of angels in the form of a lyre of ten strings is taken from <u>Interpretatio praeclara abbatis Ioachim in Hieremiam Prophetiam....Impressum Venetiis per Bernardinum Benalium</u> 1525 and found in the Biblioteca nazionale di San Marco, Venezia, Rari Veneti 364. Ladderlike trees and treelike ladders can be studied in Marjorie Reeves and Beatrice Hirsch-Reich, <u>The "Figurae" of Joachim of Fiore</u>, Oxford, Clarendon Press, 1972.

V.

HIERARCHY IN THE NINETEENTH AND TWENTIETH CENTURIES
AND HIERARCHY REDISCOVERED IN THE EAST BY THE WEST

Thomas Heywood, <u>The Hierarchie of the blessed Angells</u>, 1635, shows the ladder leading the Elect to divine salvation, while for lack of steps to heaven, the "Rejects" fall into the mouth of hell. Used by permission of Special Collections, Woodruff Research Library, Emory University.

LEWIS S. FORD

THE LAST LINK IN *THE GREAT CHAIN OF BEING*

In the final chapter of his celebrated study, Lovejoy offers one of the
most exciting interpretations of Schelling available in English. It rescues
Schelling from the dreary fate of being one of the transitional figures on the
way during the triumphal march from Kant to Hegel, and places him within that
context which displays particular strengths of his thought which the conventional approach had ignored. Lovejoy and Schelling are concerned with the same
problem: how to give ultimate significance to the world if God is to be regarded as completely self-sufficient.

Lovejoy isolates two conflicting strands in Western speculation concerning God and his creation. The first identifies God's perfection with his self-
sufficiency and immutability, while the second seeks to give the world a positive evaluation by declaring it to be a spontaneous manifestation of divine
goodness. But what is the logic of such a spontaneous manifestation? Would
this divine goodness be just as perfect if it never manifested itself? If so,
then why was the world created? On the other hand, if we explain the creation
on the grounds that God's goodness would otherwise lack fulfillment, then we
endanger his self-sufficient perfection. All the major thinkers (Plato, Aristotle, Plotinus, Thomas Aquinas, Leibniz) have insisted upon divine self-
sufficiency, but Lovejoy is able to point out elements in their affirmation of
the created order which lead to difficulties. Lovejoy evidently believes that
the conflict between these two strands of speculation is irresolvable unless
the identification of divine perfection with self-sufficiency is rejected.
Schelling was willing to make this rejection by revising the concept of divine
perfection to include dynamic self-transformation as well as self-manifesta-
tion within a created order.

Here we are considering Schelling's later philosophy. The nature and date
of Schelling's "shift" has been variously estimated, but Horst Fuhrmans has
persuasively argued that it should be placed in 1806, when Schelling came in
contact with Franz von Baader, who encouraged him to delve deeper into the
theological and cosmological ramifications of Jacob Boehme's thought.[1] At
first, this "shift" was gradual, for as Lovejoy notes:

> In much of his philosophizing between 1800 and 1812...,
> he has still two Gods and therefore two religions--the
> religion of a time-transcending and eternally complete

Absolute, an 'Identity of Identities,' the One of Neopla-
tonism--and the religion of a struggling, temporally
limited, gradually self-realizing World-Spirit or Life-
Force.[2]

This is true, for Schelling's enthusiasm for Boehme did introduce conflicting
elements which were not immediately resolved. The essay on human freedom boldly emphasized God.'s participation in becoming, even declaring that God was
involved both in suffering and in the vicissitudes of fate, though vestiges of
the Neoplatonic absolute are also apparent. "The two theologies still subsist
side by side; but one of them is a survival, the other is an innovating idea
which is on the point of destroying the former."[3] At this point Lovejoy goes
on to argue that it was Schelling's controversy with Jacobi in 1812 which provided the necessary catalyst, resolving the conflict in favor of a purely evolutionary theism.

We wish to challenge this historical reconstruction on three counts: (1)
Jacobi's book *Von den Göttlichen Dingen und ihrer Offenbarung*, was not primarily intended as an attack on Schelling, still less as a criticism of his
emerging theory of evolutionary theism. (2) Schelling's violent response simply reflected the position he was already developing privately prior to the
provocation from Jacobi. (3) Finally, Schelling never espoused a purely evolutionary doctrine with respect to God. Let us first look at the circumstances
which gave rise to Jacobi's book.[4]

I.

In the course of 1797 Jacobi accepted a commission to write an announce-
ment-review for the *Hamburger Correspondenten* of the sixth volume of Matthias
Claudius' collected writings. He knows Claudius well, having earlier entrusted
his two sons to him for their education – an unobtrusive way to help support a
struggling author. Jacobi deeply sympathized with his pietistic leanings,
though Claudius never used his religious convictions as a philosophical club
wielded against his opponents, the way Jacobi was wont to do. The volume was a
potpourri of epigrams, satirical essays, poems, essays on raising children and
on immortality, but Jacobi was particularly attracted by a dialogue on religion, entitled "Rencontre," in which both proponents and opponents of religion
despair of proving their point rationally but appeal to the certainty of their
inner feeling. Jacobi wanted to use Claudius' views on faith as a springboard
for developing his own position, but the review grew to unmanageable propor-

tions. The book itself appeared in January, 1798,[5] but Jacobi's review was de-
layed some thirteen years. First he got embroiled in the atheism dispute which
led to Fichte's dismissal from Jena, then he decided to expand the second part
to include general observations "concerning religious realism and idealism."
This greatly expanded review of Claudius was finally offered to the public on
October 5, 1811,[6] by the title *Von den Göttlichen Dingen und ihrer Offenbarung.*[7] This was the book that precipitated the Schelling-Jacobi controversy.

Schelling already had a personal animosity against Jacobi, and was pre-
disposed against the work. On November 12, 1811, he wrote his friend Karl J.
H. Windischmann:

> President Jacobi's *On Divine Things and Their Revelation*
> will appear shortly, if it has not already. It is hard to
> see how the divine things found opportunity to engage
> this man, who is so fully and yet so undivinely employed.
> They certainly did not seek him out in the antechambers
> or in the dining halls of the great. This man (who knows
> how to deceive the world so well) has an amazing arro-
> gance, joined with such an absence of compassion and
> courage that it takes six years' observation to really
> appreciate. No doubt the world will once more be preached
> the reprobate doctrine of know-nothing, with pious con-
> demnations of the godlessness of our pantheism and
> atheism. I hope he will be attacked on many fronts. The
> damage he has caused and continues to cause is unbeliev-
> able.[8]

It is not at all obvious that Jacobi reciprocated Schelling's feelings.
Schelling complained of his underhanded tactics, his hypocritical gestures of
friendship, his devious device of letting his disciples make the attack for
him, but all this may simply indicate that Schelling had no tangible evidence
of Jacobi's ill will. We do know that Jacobi took Schelling's attack very
hard, suffering a relapse and resigning the presidency, and that Schelling's
friend Georgii in Stuttgart found Schelling's reaction all out of proportion
to the cause. Jacobi's book, at any rate, cannot be reasonably construed as a
concentrated attack upon Schelling, even indirectly. For the most part he is
concerned with other things, particularly with his own supposed extension of
Kantian principles, and many of his comments appear to be merely asides.[9]

Schelling is never mentioned by name, but his position is criticized in
Von den göttlichen Dingen along with Fichte's. Jacobi discusses the two daugh-
ters of Kant's critical philosophy, the first being Fichte's *Wissenschafts-
lehre.* The second daughter, he found, "completely removed the distinction between natural and moral philosophy (the distinction between necessity and

freedom) which the first had permitted to remain, and without further ado declared that there was nothing beyond nature, which alone existed."[10] Thirty pages later, he concludes that this doctrine of "naturalism" may have its scientific justification, but it must be clearly distinguished from theology, lest any be deceived. "It must never desire to speak of God and divine things, of freedom, of moral good and evil, of true ethics; for according to its innermost convictions these things do not exist, and whatever it says about them could not be truthfully intended. Whoever should do so would be lying."[11]

Schelling's hypersensitivity to this criticism is borne out by the subtitle of his reply, which speaks of Jacobi's "accusation of a purposely deceitful and lying atheism." Ever since 1803 he had been at work trying to develop the implications of his thought for morality and religion, and now Jacobi was rejecting the whole enterprise out of hand. Jacobi did reject it, but his critique is neither very malicious nor penetrating. It lacks the devastating quality of Hegel's remark that the philosophy of identity resembled "the night in which all cows are black."[12] The generic quality of Jacobi's objections must be noted; they are basically old ones he had already raised against Spinoza. Schelling was too reliant upon the power of discursive reason. His attempt to apply the dialectical categories derived from the study of nature to divine things was impermissible, since our knowledge of higher things must be dependent upon a totally different source. The monistic character of the philosophy of identity might well remove the possibility of a personal encounter between creature and Creator. In this monism Jacobi sees the strongest similarity between Schelling and Spinoza, and his accusation of atheism might be simply a transfer of his judgment upon Spinoza. These criticisms moreover, particularly the charge of monism, are more appropriately directed at the early Schelling (1795-1806) who had not yet encountered Boehme's dynamic dualism.

II.

There is nothing to indicate, as Lovejoy suggests, that Jacobi's critique was occasioned by the radical turn of Schelling's thought after 1806. After discussing the strands of evolutionary theism in the essay on human freedom,[13] Lovejoy devotes a paragraph to "Schelling's friend and disciple, the naturalist Oken," who practically identifies God with the temporal evolutionary process culminating in man. While Lorenz Oken may have been a student of Schelling's, Schelling did not accept his views. By implication, at least, Lovejoy lumps the two men together and adds: "These early manifestations of an approximation to radical evolutionism in theology were not permitted to pass unchallenged... F. H. Jacobi published in 1812 an essay, *Von den göttlichen Dingen und ihrer Offenbarung*, which was chiefly devoted to a vehement and (as Schelling afterwards described it) tearful attack upon this new way of thinking."[14] It may have seemed so to Schelling, but his is hardly an objective account of Jacobi's book. Lovejoy's remarks imply that Jacobi's polemic was a direct response to the recent appearance of Schelling's essay *On Human Freedom* (1809) and Oken's *Lehrbuch der Naturphilosophie* (1810), but there is no evidence that Jacobi had yet read either work. *Von den göttlichen Dingen* never mentions Oken, either directly or indirectly, and we can be sure Jacobi would not have hesitated to reject Oken's views with vehemence, had he known them. Neither the essay *On Human Freedom* nor the earlier anticipatory essay *Philosophie und Religion* (1804) is referred to. Several years later, to be sure, Jacobi offered a detailed critique of *On Human Freedom*, but only after the dispute with Schelling had thrust the work upon him.[15]

Jacobi need not have known Schelling's post-1806 thought at all to write his critique, except in the vague way of hearing that the Schelling whom he knew from the earlier writings on *Naturphilosophie* and *Identitätsphilosophie* was now dealing with topics such as God, providence, and human freedom, topics which, as a "naturalist," he had no right to deal with. The imprecision of Jacobi's references makes it difficult to trace his sources,[16] but apparently he knew of only two essays written by Schelling after 1802 when he wrote *Von den göttlichen Dingen*: an 1806 review of Fichte's latest book[17] and the well-known oration *On the Relation of the Creative Arts to Nature* (1807) which Jacobi doubtless heard in his capacity as President of the Academy of Sciences.[18] In his reply, Schelling even wondered whether Jacobi had used this academic oration as the primary source for his knowledge of Schelling's system.[19] Jacobi is also chided for ignoring the objective demonstration of divine personality in the essay *On Human Freedom*.[20] Schelling's heavy reliance on his own *Presentation of My System of Philosophy* (1801) in correcting Jacobi's misunderstandings indicates his implicit awareness that Jacobi's critique was directed against these earlier writings.

Lovejoy, however, has two very impressive quotations from Jacobi's essay apparently indicating that an attack was made upon the emerging concept of divine evolution in Schelling's thought:

> There can be only two principal classes of philosophers:
> those who regard the most perfect (*Vollkommnere*) as de-
> rived from, as gradually developed out of, the less per-
> fect, and those who affirm that the most perfect being
> was first, and that all things have their source in him;
> that the first principle of all things was a moral being,
> an intelligence willing and acting with wisdom--a Cre-
> ator--God.[21]

Jacobi, Lovejoy implies, is here contrasting an evolutionary concept of God
with the orthodox view. He then argues that Jacobi rejects this evolutionary
concept because it contravenes formal logic by permitting the superior to be
reduced by the inferior. For "always and necessarily a *Beweisgrund* (premise)
must be above that which is to be proved by means of it; it is from the
Beweisgrund that truth and certitude are imparted to those things which are
demonstrated by means of it; from it they borrow their reality."[22] In their
original contexts, however, neither quotation refers to Schelling. Schelling
manipulates both quotations in his reply with scant regard for context, and
this may have misled Lovejoy as to the nature of Jacobi's criticism.

The first quotation occurs as part of a summary commentary on a passage
from Aristotle. The contrast between naturalism and theism, Jacobi felt, is
reflected in the problem of priority between intelligence and nature. Aristotle had reflected on this problem when he sought to clarify the relation between the good and the primordial nature.[23] Does the primordial nature contain
what is truly good, or does the good arise at some later stage? Aristotle's
contemporaries chose the latter alternative, as did the ancient poets who regarded Zeus rather than Chaos or Oceanos as the supreme god. These are the
philosophers, Jacobi summarizes, who regard the more perfect as derived from
or as gradually developing out of the less perfect.

The principle of formal logic Jacobi invokes in the second quotation is
found toward the end of his discussion of Kant. He had already demonstrated to
his own satisfaction that the dialectic of Kant's principles must result in an
absolute monism such as Schelling's philosophy of identity,[24] even though this
monistic tendency is entirely foreign to Kant's intent.[25] Kant had weakened
his dualism between reason and understanding by denying reason's capacity as
an independent source of knowledge. The postulates of practical reason, Jacobi
feels, should rather be considered immediate and intuitive deliverances of the
faculty of pure reason. The attempt to deduce such postulates is inherently

absurd, since they are the highest deliverances of reason, and their deduction
would require the necessary existence of more superior principles. It is in
this context that Jacobi states his principle that the premise must be superior to the conclusion deduced from it. The existence of God, if it were deduced rather than known intuitively, would require the existence of a causal
ground having a superior reality to God.[26]

Whatever else it may be, *Von den göttlichen Dingen* cannot be construed as
a polemic against Schelling's evolutionary theism.

III.

Schelling's reply, the *Schrift gegen Jacobi*,[27] is all that Lovejoy says
it is. It is a biting, slashing attack with no other purpose than to demolish
Jacobi. Schelling treats *Von den göttlichen Dingen* as if it were a single-
minded critique of the evolutionary theism which he was then beginning to
espouse and proceeds to defend himself accordingly. He retracts nothing but
develops the logic of explicative theism, pushing it further than ever before
in his published writings. God is seen in terms of a temporal process with two
extremes, an absolute beginning in *Deus implicitus*, in whom all perfections
exist potentially, but none actually, and an ultimate culmination in *Deus ex-
plicitus*, a final synthesis containing all the divine perfections as actualized together with the conserved values of the created order. The created
world is involved in this divine process, not as its vehicle, to be sure, but
as its principal product. He attacks Jacobi's concept of God, the God of
"ordinary theism," as incapable of explaining creation. If God is eternally
perfect, "ready-made once for all," then He would have no reason for the creation of anything outside of Himself. Since God would then be incapable of
achieving any higher degree of perfection, He could only fall to a lower one
through this act. Furthermore, all that we encounter in nature undergoes
transformation, whether it be the growth of the individual or the evolution of
the species. Any theology which excludes such evolutinary process gives us "a
God who is alien to nature and a nature that is devoid of God – ein unnatü-
ralicher Gott und eine gottlose Natur."[28]

Schelling even goes so far as to devise a logical counter thesis to
Jacobi's claim that the principal premise, the *Beweisgrund*, must be superior
to that which is to be proved: "Always and necessarily that from which development proceeds (*der Entwicklungsgrund*) is lower than that which is developed;

the former raises the latter above itself and subjects itself to it, inasmuch as it serves as the matter, the organ, the condition, for the other's development."[29]

Lovejoy then concludes: "It is--as has too little been noted by historians--in this introduction of a radical evolutionism into metaphysics and theology, and in the attempt to revise even the principles of logic to make them harmonize with an evolutional conception of reality, that the historical significance of Schelling chiefly consists."[30] This remark reveals both the strength and the weakness of Lovejoy's interpretation. Lovejoy has seen, more clearly than any other English commentator, that evolutionary or explicative theism forms the core of Schelling's real contribution to philosophy. On the other hand, he has posed the alternatives too sharply, regarding any attempts at mediation as inconsistent compromises: either God must be eternally complete or he must be perpetually evolving. Schelling emerges from Lovejoy's pages as the champion of a straight theistic evolutionism, since this alternative needs its champion. This is justified insofar as the *Schrift gegen Jacobi* does portray God almost exclusively in terms of a temporal process. Yet by implication, at least, Lovejoy must present this work as truly representative of the mature Schelling. From this it is only a short step to the conclusion that the *Schrift gegen Jacobi* represents the crystallization of these characteristic themes for the first time, under the catalytic influence of Jacobi's polemic.

From his letters we know that Schelling himself did not attach such importance to the *Schrift gegen Jacobi*. He was preoccupied with the personal dimensions of the conflict, justifying himself on the grounds that it was better to bring it out into the open. We get the impression that he was simply restating a position already formulated, though perhaps not as yet published. There was hardly time for a carefully thought-out presentation, as Schelling wrote the entire polemic--215 pages worth--in the space of two months.[31] On November 12, 1811, Schelling had not yet seen Jacobi's book,[32] while by February 25th of the next year he can report that his reply had been published "a month ago."[33] Nor was it the occasion for inaugurating a new epoch in his thought. He was already hard at work on his magnum opus, *The Ages of the World*, and this polemical undertaking simply marked a brief interruption.

The Ages of the World was an enormously ambitious undertaking which Schelling was never able to complete, despite the fact that he spent the bet-

ter part of ten years working on the project. It essays nothing less than to
describe the whole of time and eternity in terms of its three "ages," the
Past, the Present, and the Future. The entire world-process from its creation
to its consummation is contained within the Present. In the epoch of the Past,
Schelling purports to solve that ancient riddle that vexed Augustine and Calvin: "What was God doing before the creation of the world?" Using a dialectic
of dipolar tension, he describes the steady evolution of God out of the initial "absolute indifference" into a fully self-conscious being endowed with complete freedom of will and therefore capable of deciding either for or against
the creation of the world. Of the three epochs, only the second is unambigu-
ously temporal, for the first epoch, the Past, seen from a different perspective, seeks to describe God according to His essential and eternal nature,
while the Future (never written) was to portray the final synthesis of the
world-process seen from its eternal aspect as integrated within the divine
life. The entire structure depends upon an exceedingly intricate theory of
time which Schelling never succeeded in making clear. It is a moot point
whether the theory is intelligible.[34] But what Schelling was after was clear
enough: a concept of eternity rich enough to conserve the traditional values
of simplicity and perfection while including within itself the entire temporal
process as a subordinate diversity.

In other words, Schelling is not the champion of the purely temporal evolutionism that Lovejoy seeks. Schelling rejects the traditional notion of God
as internally complete and self-sufficient, but he does not reject God's eternal simplicity. The task is rather to reinterpret the concept of simplicity so
that it becomes inclusive rather than exclusive, and to discover a meaning for
eternity which can include temporal process.

These thoughts both precede and follow the *Schrift gegen Jacobi*. In 1810,
mainly at the instigation of Georgii, Schelling gave a series of private lectures to a small circle of admirers in Stuttgart. These Stuttgart Lectures,[35]
first published posthumously, give a good concise systematic account of Schelling's position just prior to *The Ages of the World*. The theme of explicative
theism is prominently displayed. He even goes so far as to say: "Really the
whole process of world creation, which continues as the life-process in nature
and in history, is nothing but the process of God becoming completely conscious, completely personalized."[36] Nonetheless he recognizes that "eternal

being" must be present in God as well as "eternal becoming," even though the two aspects are not yet well integrated with one another.[37]

Why, then, is there so little hint of Schelling's acceptance of the eternal dimension in the *Schrift gegen Jacobi*? I think the answer lies in matters of purpose and strategy. This polemic was intentionally one-sided, designed to destroy the argument that temporal process had no place within the divine nature. Schelling emphatically thought that it did, and he set out to show how. He also believed that this temporal process was included within the divine eternity, but this additional step required argumentation which went beyond the scope of the polemic. At the very least it required a brief presentation of Schelling's new theory of time, a thing he was then hardly able to do, being just in the throes of its initial formulation. Had he simply remarked that God was also simple, eternal, etc., these remarks would naturally be understood by his opponents in their traditional, "exclusive" meanings. At best he would be misunderstood; at worst he would be charged with gross inconsistency. Since the polemic was simply designed to demolish Jacobi, Schelling felt under no obligation to present all the facets of his understanding of God, and chose to concentrate on those aspects he conceived to be under direct attack.

One of Schelling's remarks to Georgii late in the year 1812 well illustrates the attitude with which he approached the *Schrift gegen Jacobi*:

> It was also to be expected that they would all pounce upon the apparent affirmation of divine explication and development, and accuse me of heresy. I have to put up with that, since I can only clarify that point with reference to the total context of my position. I happen to believe that we must understand it literally: 'I am he who was, he who is, and he who will be' (although in these three periods the *same* eternal God). But this is an offence to our enlightened theologians.[38]

NOTES

[1] *Schellings Philosophie der Weltalter* (Düsseldorf: L. Schwann, 1954).

[2] *The Great Chain of Being* (Cambridge: Harvard University Press, 1936), p. 317.

[3] *Ibid.*, p. 320.

[4] This essay is an adaptation of "The Controversy Between Schelling and Jacobi," *Journal of the History of Philosophy* 3 (1965), 75-89, which is more extensive with respect to background and documentation, including citation of the original German sources here translated.

Since then, the two principal works of this controversy, Jacobi's *Von den göttlichen Dingen und ihrer Offenbarung*, and Schelling's *Schrift gegen Jacobi* have been made conveniently accessible to us in a photomechanical reproduction edited by Wilhelm Weischedel, *Streit um die Göttlichen Dinge* (Darmstadt: Wissenschaftliche Buchgesellschaft, 1967). In his 90-page introductory essay, Weischedel sees Jacobi's book as more of an intentional polemic against Schelling than I do, and cites important evidence for this. The crucial point to my mind, however, is that any such critique was directed against the early Schelling, and not against the position Schelling was struggling to formulate after 1806.

[5] *Asmus omnia sua secum portans, oder Sämmtliche Werke des Wandsbecker-Bothen*, VI. Theil. (Hamburg: Friedrich Perthes, 1798). Claudius' pen-name "Asmus" is thought to be a shortened form of Erasmus. The second pen-name is taken from the local paper he had edited in Wandsbeck near Hamburg. The Latin title alludes to Simonides' remark after his shipwreck: "Omnia mea mecum porto."

[6] Not 1812, as Lovejoy reports, p. 321. Schelling's reply was published in 1812.

[7] (Leipzig: Gerhard Fleischer dem Jüngern, 1811), 222 pp.

[8] G. L. Plitt, ed., *Aus Schellings Leben, In Briefen, Zweiter band*, 1803-1820 (Leipzig: S. Hirzel, 1870), p. 270.

[9] See, for instance, the brief mention of Schelling's "Alleinheitslehre" on p. 127 of *Von den göttlichen Dingen*, or the description of the "Naturphilosophie" on p. 139. Schelling quotes the latter passage inaccurately in his reply, and it is not clear whether Jacobi actually intended any criticism. *Sämmtliche Werke*, Erste Abtheilung, VII. Band (Stuttgard und Augsburg: J. G. Cotta, 1856), p. 26. (Hereafter cited as *S.W.* I:8.)

[10] *Von den göttlichen Dingen*, pp. 117f.

[11] *Ibid.*, pp. 154f.

[12] Hegel, *The Phenomenology of Mind* trans. J. B. Baillie (London: George Allen & Unwin, 1931), p. 79.

[13] Lovejoy, pp. 318-320.

[14] Lovejoy, p. 321.

[15] *Werke, Zweyter Band*, pp. 77-93.

[16] Jacobi frequently alludes to Naturalismus, Identitätsphilsophie, System der absoluten Identitat, Alleinheitslehre, Naturlehre, Naturphilosophie, etc., but gives only one specific ref-

erence to Schelling's works. On page 118, he refers to the *Philosophische Briefe über Dogmaticismus und Kriticismus* which appeared in 1795.

[17]This review of J. G. Fichte's *Uber das Wesen des Gelehrten und seine Erschein-ung im Gebiete der Freyheit* appeared in the *Jenaische Allgemeine Literatur-Zeitung* for June 26-27, 1806 (Nr. 151-152, cols. 585-598).

[18]*Uber das Verhältniss der bildenden Künste zu der Natur.* Reprinted in *S.W.* I:7 pp. 289-329. Jacobi, pp. 156-160, discusses the idea of productivity as developed in this oration, and on p. 157 quotes a brief passage without mentioning its source. Schelling supplies the reference to *S.W.* I:7, p. 293 in his reply.

[19]*S.W.* I.8, p. 29.

[20]*Ibid.*, p. 36.

[21]Lovejoy, p. 321, quoting Jacobi, pp. 149f. Schelling quotes this same passage in his reply, *S.W.* I:8, p. 62, omitting an unessential phrase and altering the punctuation somewhat. It is evident from Lovejoy's literal translation that he followed Schelling's looser citation rather than the original text.

[22]Lovejoy, p. 321, quoting Jacobi, p. 136 (=*S.W.* I:8, p. 57).

[23]*Von den göttlichen Dingen*, pp. 148f. Jacobi quotes from the Metaphysics, N.4, 1091a29-b10.

[24]*Ibid.*, p. 124 for summary.

[25]*Ibid.*, p. 126.

[26]*Ibid.*, pp. 132-137.

[27]*F. W. Schelling's Denkmal der Schrift von den göttlichen Dingen etc. des Herrn Friedrich Heinrich Jacobi und der ihm in derselben gemachten Beschuldig-ung eines absichtlich täuschenden, Lüge redenden Atheismus* (Tübingen: J. G. Cotta, 1812). Reprinted in *S.W.* I:8, pp. 19-136.

[28]Lovejoy, p. 323, quoting *S.W.* I:8, p. 70.

[29]Lovejoy, p. 325, quoting *S.W.* I:8, p. 59.

[30]Lovejoy, p. 325.

[31]Letter to Windischmann, Feb. 27, 1812 (Plitt, p. 294).

[32]See footnote 8 above.

[33]Letter to Wagner, Feb. 25, 1812 (Plitt, p. 294).

[34]Fuhrmans has not made this a central topic in his investigation of the Weltalter, but see Wolfgang Wieland, *Schellings Lehre von der Zeit* (Heidelberg: Carl Winter, 1956).

[35]*Stuttgarter Privatvorlesungen.* Published in *S.W.* I:7, pp. 309-484.

[36]*S.W.* I:7, p. 433.

[37]*S.W.* I:7, p. 432.

[38]Letter to Georgii, Dec. 8, 1812 (Plitt, p. 333).

312

The way up from the level of what is (a stone) to the level of what lives (a tree) to the level of what senses (a horse) to the level of what thinks (a man). The way down from man who studies (virtue), to the man who admires himself and his adornment (luxury), to the man who eats and drinks to excess (gluttony), to the man who is "stoned" (caring for nothing). Charles de Bouelles (Bovillus), Liber de Intellectu, 1510. By permission of the Folger Shakespeare Library, Washington, D.C.

R. BAINE HARRIS

DEAN INGE'S HIERARCHICAL CONCEPT OF BEING

Although not a professional philosopher, William Ralph Inge (1860-1954) advocated a modified version of the Great Chain of Being doctrine. The author of over fifty books and an equal number of scholarly articles, he served as Dean of St. Paul's Cathedral for twenty-three years until his retirement in 1934, and remained well known until his death at the age of ninety-four. Trained as a classicist, he found no contemporary philosophy suitable for his own needs and deliberately went back to the thought of Plotinus for his philosophical inspiration. His own philosophy is a form of Christian Platonism and may be regarded as a modernized version of the major views of Plotinus with heavy emendations in favor of New Testament themes.

Inge's doctrine of being is to be found in the second volume of his *The Philosophy of Plotinus*, first published in 1918, in his *The Platonic Tradition in English Religious Thought* (1926), in his *God and the Astronomers* (1933), and in his *Mysticism in Religion* (1947). George Santayana wrote his *Platonism and the Spiritual Life* (1927) in response to Inge's *The Platonic Tradition in English Religious Thought*, agreeing in the main with his characterization of the worth of Platonism, but denying one of Inge's main theses in the book, namely, that a concept of being can be grounded in a concept of value.[1]

As a frontispiece to his major work on Plotinus, Inge chose the following quotation from the modern Quaker, Isaac Pennington:

> All truth is Shadow except the last. But every Truth is Substance in its own place, though it be but a Shadow in another place. And the Shadow is a true Shadow, as the Substance is a true Substance.[2]

In an article in the *Hibbert Journal* in 1936 he provides a longer version of the same quotation, namely:

> All truth is shadow except the last, except the utmost; yet every truth is true in its kind. It is substance in its own place, though it be but a shadow in another place, for it is but a shadow from an intenser substance; and the shadow is a true shadow, as the substance is a true substance.[3]

This quotation may serve as a general guide to Inge's own ontology, for he clearly held that there are degrees of reality, truth, and substance, and that the existence of things in the natural order must be related to some ultimate being whose being is not dependent upon the existence of things in the natural

order. The remainder of this paper will be devoted to setting forth his idea
of being with special reference to his view of how the various types of being
are related to each other.

Inge distinguishes between essence and existence but regards their difference as only a matter of degree. For him "reality" is higher existence and
"existence" is assumed to be a lower reality,[4] yet he does not posit two
worlds, one of substance and one of shadow. He does not set an unreal natural
order in opposition to a real supernatural order. "The visible world," he
writes, "is no deceiving phantom; it is the creation and copy of a higher
sphere of existence."[5] The two worlds are numerically one so that the higher
order is actually in the same location as the lower order. "The phenomenal
world contains ... all there is in the eternal world...," he writes, "but in
the world of space and time the absolute values ... are split up and partially
disintegrated by the conditions of existence below."[6]

Reality, according to Inge, is constituted by the laws that make up the
content of the mind of God.[7] These laws are to be identified with the eternal
values and are to be regarded as existents as well as ideals. They are both
powers and creative values.[8] Inge explains:

> The highest forms in which Reality can be known by
> Spirits, who are themselves the roof and crown of things
> are *Goodness*, *Truth*, and *Beauty*, manifesting themselves
> in the myriad products of creative activity. Things truly
> *are* in proportion as they 'participate' in Goodness,
> Truth, and Beauty. These attributes of Reality, which so
> far as can be known, constitute its entire essence; that
> is to say, they belong to a sphere of supra-temporal and
> supra-spatial existence, which obeys laws of its own, and
> of which the world of common experience is a pale copy.[9]

Within nature and within human experience, Goodness, Truth, and Beauty add an
eternal dimension to human experience. They "are not inactive thoughts" or
static first principles.[10] They are the objective representatives of God as
Spirit.[11]

One of Inge's most fundamental assumptions is that value and reality are
ultimately identical. To be is to have value and the cardinal values have objective existence. Our world of existence, our world of process and becoming,
is built up out of our own valuations of existence. As Inge explains it,
"Existence is itself a value, and an ingredient in every valuation; that which
has no existence has no value."[12] We contribute something to the existence of
the world by our act of knowing it for the world is "demonstrably a mental

construction, and like all mental constructions it is based on a valuation of
existence."[13] As such, reality is "neither mental nor material, but a realm in
which thought and thing, fact and value, are inseparable, neither having any
existence without its correlative."[14] The bare apprehension of existence is
not a value judgment but certain valuations are necessary in the construction
of our own conceptual framework within which we can judge things to have
degrees of existence or degrees of reality. Valuation is necessary for existence to have meaning, since "... we cannot understand existence without arranging our experience of things in an order which is frankly valuational or
axiological."[15]

Once valuations of existence occur, however, a scale of values is produced and this will provoke the question of whether there are comparable levels
of existence matching the levels in the scale of values. On this point Inge
frankly admits that an ontology built upon values and valuation has great difficulty in explaining gradations of existence in any other way except on the
basis of our own valuation of our own experience.[16] Inge writes:

> Judgements of value give us an essentially *graduated*
> world; while judgements of existence are not so easily
> graduated .... The Platonist believes that he has the
> witness of the Spirit to the eternal reality as well as
> to the validity of his ideals.... His ontology therefore
> compels him to identify Reality with achieved perfection;
> and this involves the difficulty of postulating degrees
> of existence corresponding with degrees of value....
> There is, in point of fact, no gradation given to us in
> the physical world; gradation is entirely the work of our
> value-judgements interpreting phenomena.[17]

He concludes that "there could be no greater error than to leave the two
worlds, or the two 'judgements,' that of existence and that of value, contrasted with each other, or treated as unrelated in our experience."[18] But the
belief that existence and value are identified on their various levels can
only be asserted as an act of faith.[19]

Our knowledge of reality, according to Inge, is not restricted to any one
realm or discipline or way of knowing. Scientific knowledge is no more or less
valid than any other form of knowledge. Each judgment of reality may be true
and real in its own realm while at the same time being less true and less real
in another, since a reality in one existence may be a shadow of reality in
another.

In the strictest sense, things do not have degrees of existence. They either exist or do not exist. The importance of their existence is to be seen or judged in the light of some other existing thing that has a higher valuation. Thus various valuations may cause us to question the ultimate existential status of any given object. Its real status in the ranking of existence is determined by the value that God, not we, give to it. This is why he refers to reality as a "kingdom of values." In a kingdom all ranks are determined by the king, and this is precisely the point he wishes to convey about the status of the various degrees of being.

For every level of being there is a level of knowing. Knowledge gained through logical and psychological operations may be adequate for scientific purposes, but not for metaphysical judgments. All forms of knowing, including scientific knowledge, must begin with faith, since all valuation must begin with an act of faith. The second level of knowing, and the one we usually identify with "knowing," is the development of connections or relations between all the items, entities, and events that we experience. The third and highest level of knowing is love, a supra-relational form of knowledge that occurs when the "mind in love" rises above the level of *Nous* into a higher synthesis to effect a harmony of feeling, intellect, and will, and thus form a complete unification of the personality. Such an achievement does nothing to solve scientific problems or to eliminate the need for metaphysics, but it is the basis of religious knowledge.

What then, can we conclude about Inge's ontology in relation to the idea of a chain of being? Essentially, it is that Inge did advocate that there are levels of reality, levels of value, and levels of existence. These levels are determined in their actuality by God and not by us, although we must have opinions about them based on our own valuations of our experience. The levels are determined by God as is the status of the specific individuals within each level, but the actuality of each individual can remain only a mystery to us.

Apparently, Inge did not take the notion of a linkage between the levels very seriously and did not advocate that a lower level is held in its place by its connection with whatever is above and below it. Furthermore, it is our conjecture that he would have regarded such a position as a degeneration of the Neoplatonic position and more appropriate to a strictly materialistic ontology of individuals. Rather, he saw a thing to be what it is in terms of its worth to God, and what it is in relation to other things as not as important as its inherent worth, namely, its eternal value.

It is clear that Inge was nearer to the Neoplatonism of Plotinus than to that of Proclus and the later Neoplatonists. He regarded the ideas of the *One*, the *Nous*, the *Psyche*, and *Hyle* as only general levels and essentially rough descriptions of levels of being and not as rigid classification devices containing clearly defined subdivisions. In short, he believed in levels of being, but not in levels connected or held in place by each other.

NOTES

[1]George Santayana, *Platonism and the Spiritual Life* (New York, Charles Scribners, 1927). See especially pp. 2-8, 87-91.

[2]*The Philosophy of Plotinus*, Vol. I., p. viii.

[3]W. R. Inge, "More Gleaning From a Notebook," *The Hibbert Journal 35* (1936-37), p. 184.

[4]*The Philosophy of Plotinus*, Vol I., p. 132.

[5]W. R. Inge, "What is the Future of the Universe?" *Discovery* (May, 1934) p. 134.

[6]W. R. Inge, "Conclusion," in *Science, Religion, and Reality*, Joseph Needham, ed., (London: The Sheldon Press, 1926), p. 363.

[7]W. R. Inge, "Ruskin and Plato," in *Ruskin the Prophet*, J. Howard Whitehouse, ed. (London: George Allen and Unwin, Ltd., 1920), p. 30.

[8]W. R. Inge, *Personal Idealism and Mysticism* (New York: Longmans, Green, and Co., 1907), p. 148.

[9]*The Philosophy of Plotinus*, Vol. II, p. 74.

[10]W. R. Inge, *Science and Ultimate Truth* (London: Longmans, Green and Co., Ltd., 1926), p. 28.

[11]*Ibid.*

[12]W. R. Inge, "Survival and Immortality," *The Hibbert Journal 15* (July, 1917), p. 589.

[13]W. R. Inge, *Outspoken Essays*, Second Series, (London: Longmans, Green and Co., 1922), p. 19.

[14]W. R. Inge, "Philosophy and Religion," *op. cit.*, p. 195.

[15]W. R. Inge, *God and the Astronomers* (London: Longmans, Green and Co., 1933), p. 185.

[16]*Ibid.*

[17]*The Philosophy of Plotinus*, Vol. II., pp. 78-80.

[18]*Outspoken Essays*, First Series, p. 271.

[19]*Ibid.*

MARION AND PAUL KUNTZ
THE SYMBOL OF THE TREE INTERPRETED IN THE
CONTEXT OF OTHER SYMBOLS OF HIERARCHICAL ORDER,
THE GREAT CHAIN OF BEING AND JACOB'S LADDER

Of all great symbols, the tree is the most universally widespread. By that we mean it is the most readily documented from various tribal cultures and great religious traditions. The evidence for this is various encyclopedia articles in volumes dealing with symbols. *Encyclopaedia of Religion and Ethics* has nineteen columns.[1] Although J. C. Cooper's *Illustrated Encyclopaedia of Traditional Symbols* is only 200 pages long, eight columns are devoted to the many kinds of symbolic trees.[2] Gerhart B. Ladner's exemplary article "Medieval and Modern Understanding of Symbolism: A Comparison" is 48 pages long with 165 footnotes.[3] There is such a wealth of material, one is tempted to lament that one can scarcely see the tree for the forest. Are we confronted with a forest of different tree symbols? What of the essential tree? Perhaps the wealth of illustration and elaboration both ethnographic and theoretical springs from a love of trees.[4]

In *Microcosmos Hypochondriacus*, under God symbolized by the tetragrammaton, and the heavenly orbs, there stands in earth's center the Tree of Life, *Arbor Vitae*.[5] Cooper's "Introduction," after using this 17th Century engraving expresses his general appreciation of the way symbols join together opposites as "complementary and compensating characteristics: the union is a sacred marriage."[6] Is there an essential meaning in most or even all symbolic trees of "the unity of life"?[7] Cooper states his interpretation boldly: "As the Tree of Life, axial, unifying and either evergreen or perpetually renewed, stands at the centre of Paradise and the spring at its roots gives rise to the Rivers of Life, so man's thoughts and aspiration, embodied in the myth and symbol, centre on unity and life."[8] The Cosmic Tree of the Scandinavians, Yggdrasil, is used to illustrate the worlds, the underworld, the world of men and the realm of the gods, all three united into one. Beneath this Mighty Ash the gods met in council. "Its roots were in the depth of the underworld, its trunk passed vertically through the waves, the earth and the world of men,... the branches were the heavens end overshadowed Valhalla."[9]

Yggdrasil is a mythical symbol of the origin of cosmic process, the struggle of opposites and their reconciliation--what a pity Hegel did not ex-

press himself sometimes as putting the metaphor of the world as a tree into
dialectical propositions! One interpretation conveys stages of struggle and a
final resolution: "From the root rose the fountain Hvergelmir, the source of
the rivers, the earthly timestream. The root was constantly attacked by Nid-
hogg, the Dread Biter, representing the malevolent forces of the universe.
Odin's charger browsed on the leaves, and in the boughs the eagle and the serpent, as light and darkness, were in perpetual conflict. The squirrel, a
mischief-maker, constantly created strife between the two powers. The four
stags in the branches, as the four winds, also browsed on the leaves which
were always renewed and the foliage was always green. The solar cock, as vigi-
lance, was sometimes depicted on the branches. Odin sacrificed himself and
hung for nine nights from Yggdrasil; a rejuvenation sacrifice symbol."[10]

If the tree is a root metaphor for an organicist world hypothesis,[11] happily the Vedas and Upanishads are rich in such expressions. Whereas with
Yggdrasil the roots are in the underworld, and as we say roots go down, what
is the meaning of roots growing up to heaven? What are we to think of the up-
side-down tree?

Surely the best known cosmic tree with "root above and branches below" is
The Tree of Life, the Cosmic Tree of Chapter 15, "The *Yoga* of the Supreme Person," in the *Bhagavad-Gita*. Because the leaves of the *asvattham*, peepal tree,
"are the Vedas" an explanation is needed. Says Radhakrishnan: "According to
ancient belief, the Vedic sacrificial cult is said to sustain the world and so
the hymns are said to be the leaves which keep the tree with its trunk and
branches alive."[12]

For those who attend to higher life, their roots are in the Supreme
Spirit: but for us ordinary folk, we are rooted in the active life. The contrast suggested is between those rooted-up and those rooted-down. For us, our
"firm-rooted *asvattham* [must be cut] with the strong word of non-attachment."
The result of attachment, through the senses, is that we are caught in "dualities of pleasure and pain. The good of non-attachment is to be liberated for
union with" the Supreme Self, "the imperishable snd Undying Lord."[13]

"Higher" and "lower" are characteristic spatial metaphors used for soul
and body in the hierarchical thought of India as of the West. Ananda Coomaraswamy cautions us against thinking spatially of "the 'up' or 'down' of the
roots and branches:" "this is not a question of local direction." The point is
not of physical space, for substance is omnipresent, signified by "Waters,"

and Self is omnipresent. What then is meant by "upward growth"?[14]

The famous *Katha Upanishad*, which inspired Emerson's "Brahma," ends with "The world-tree rooted in Brahma."[15] "Its root is above, its branches below—This eternal fig-tree! That (root) indeed is the pure." Brahma is the Immortal, and on it the worlds rest, "and no one soever goes beyond it." All the gods, fire (*Agni*), sun (*Surya*), wind (*Vayu*), *Indra* and Death (*Mriyu*) the fifth are aspects of Life. The wise man ascends by steps from the senses to the mind, from mind to true being (*sattva*), and through the Great Self to the Unmanifest, to Person (*Purusha*). "Knowing (this) a man is liberated, and goes to immortality."

The wise life is one of ascent, as it were, climbing the branches. Of what use is the cosmic Tree? It serves as a ladder to heaven.

Although the Hindu tradition initially seems strikingly different from our Hebrew heritage, both of them compare man to a tree. Psalm I: the righteous "shall be like a tree planted by the river of water, that bringeth forth his fruit in his season; his leaf also shall not wither..." (KJV, Ps. 1:3). But adds Job, in a passage used at funerals, what if he is cut down? "For there is hope of a tree, if it be cut down, that it will sprout again, and that the tender branch thereof will not cease." What hope is there if man, cut down, has no roots (Job 14:7 & f)? The sage Yajnavalkya quite similarly, although hair is as leaves, skin as bark, blood as sap, marrow as pith, bones as wood, asks also about the difference, "From what root does he grow up?"[16] The question is asked again and the answer: "Brahma is knowledge, is bliss, the final goal of the giver of offerings, of him, too, who stands still and knows It."[17] The Biblical question, "If a man die, shall he live again?" "Thou shalt call, and I will answer thee: thou wilt have a desire to the work of thine hands" (Job 14:14-15). Different as is the Creator from Brahma, thought of man as a tree cut down turns to the metaphysical ultimate. We are reminded of the maxim of a late medieval preacher: "*Praedicare est arborisare*."[18]

Either reincarnation or resurrection is a mystery. The respects in which man is like a tree, leads to the respect in which they are unlike, and the apophatic, in contrast to the metonymic-synedochic, is also a symbol of the divine. Here Gerhart Ladner's rhetorical analysis is invaluable.[19]

Interpreting our medieval heritage requires attending to the root metaphors that control the thought of this, as of any development of civilization. What the world is said to be like is the metaphysical kernel. Lovejoy was right in choosing his metaphor in *The Great Chain of Being.*[20] But he was wrong in studying only one metaphor for hierarchical order. We are now in position to amplify the picture by studying Jacob's Ladder and the Tree of Life. Lovejoy sought out cases of the golden chain, and by talking of it constantly in his interpretation makes it appear that our medieval ancestors used it frequently. However, there are more references from Hebraic heritage than from the Hellenic. Even the philosophers who were most deeply indebted to Plato, Aristotle, the Stoics and Plotinus, were still dominated by the Biblical picture of the world and man's way to return to God. The key is from the *Colloquium Heptaplomeres*, of Jean Bodin, where he has Jewish interlocutor, Salomon, say: "I think the Homeric chain is nothing other than the ladder represented in the nocturnal vision of Jacob...."[21]

Our western tradition of tree symbolism may seem to be like the ancient Norse cosmic tree, and the tree here is part of the myth of the cosmos. And surely the medieval tradition is hierarchical in the sense of providing a ladder of ascent towards God, and the Mystical tree joins earth and heaven. Man and God are one Jesus Christ. The symbolic expression of union is "Christ is the Tree of Life" (KJV, Rev. 2:7, 22:14). As far as we have explored the sermons and other expressions of piety, Christ is called the Tree; some preachers say that "Christ is our Ladder."[22] This comes as naturally to Luther and Calvin, when they preached on the story of Jacob, as it did to St. Bonaventura, who loved to elaborate symbols, particularly of the tree.

Western man interprets himself as Adam who disobeyed the divine injunction. He followed Eve in eating of the "fruit of the tree of the knowledge of good and evil" (KJV, Gen. 2:16-17, 3:2-24). Other than Neo-Orthodox Protestant theologians, few now take seriously the Fall of Man. Probably our revolt against puritan excess has here cut us off from the Augustinian-Medieval tradition. A great exception in our world is Martin Buber who ponders the question of whether the tree meant, when Adam and Eve ate of its fruit, sexuality: they do discover that they are naked, and ashamed before each other and God. But this is only one condition of man's sinful nature. The other is becoming "as one of us," as the Lord God says, "know[ing] good and evil."[23]

One cosmic tree, which we shall call the old Tree of Life, is fine for the symbol of a cosmic whole. One tree is sufficient for the descent and ascent. But two trees are better for telling a story of before and after the fall, that is, when the downside slope is the point. John Bunyan's *Exposition of Genesis* is picturesque. "The 'tree of the knowledge of good and evil' was a type of the law,... had not Adam eaten thereof, he had enjoyed for ever his first blessedness." But Adam and we "have touched, that is broken the boughs and fruit of this tree, and thereby now for ever, by the law, no man can stand just before God."[24]

In contrast to eating the bitter fruit of sin is partaking of the fruit of the Tree of Life whose leaves are "for the healing of the nations" (Rev. 22:2). This Tree of Life is salvation and regeneration after the fall of eating the forbidden fruit. It is of great interest to note that sometimes one tree turns into the other. When a symbol of virtue, it is the tree of life, but vice turns it into the tree of the knowledge of good and evil. So wrote Philo.[25] But in Augustine "Christ [is] the tree of the knowledge of good and evil."[26]

The symbolism of St. Augustine begins then with the Biblical reading of Christ as the Tree of Life. The old Adam, through whom all fell, ate of the tree of the knowledge of good and evil, and disobeyed God; the new Adam, through obedience to the death on the cross becomes the Tree of Life through whom all can be saved. Thus sacred history cannot be told without the two trees. The second tree is the cross. Jesus was nailed to a tree and died upon the tree. The tree of the dying saviour becomes the new Tree of Life.

Christ "alone is verily the Tree of Life to them that lay hold on him." So wrote St. Bernard.[27] The metaphor can be elaborated into allegory. Perhaps the best illustration is from Jacopone da Todi (1230-1306). In his book *Arbore de ierarchia simile a l'angelica: fondata sopra la fede, speranza e caritate*, the "fear of the fiend" brought Jacopone to the foot of the Tree of Divine Love.[28] "... He gazed up its towering bole to the majestic branches, they seemed inaccessible; but a little bough called humility hung down to the ground, and by this he began his ascent."[29] The branches are rungs, such as poverty, by which he climbs. Holy poverty is used by St. Francis to sum up the virtues that overcome the vices and thus make us capable of knowing eternity. The tree is a cross and also a ladder of ascent; sometimes Jesus is pictured nailed to a tree, and sometimes the branches are a ladder.[30]

Symbols do not operate in isolation from each other. Just as Salomon in the *Colloquium Heptaplomeres* interpreted Homer's golden chain as the Greek way of signifying Jacob's ladder, so we find the interpreters deliberately shifting from one metaphor to another, with the suggestion that there is no essen-

tial difference. The differences are in our diverse modes of expression. One
of the illustrations to support the *Colloquium Heptaplomeres* is from Reuchlin's De Cabala, sev de symbolica receptione. Reuchlin also equates Homer's
golden chain to Jacob's ladder.[31]

This is not an unknown phenomenon. It has been given a name: "metaphoric
fusion," or it could be called "a kaleidoscopic transformation of symbols."[32]
Surely the most successful demonstration of the power of a metaphor to shape
theology, philosophy, literature and the arts is Lovejoy's *Great Chain of Being*. Yet all the combing of cultural expressions between Plotinus and Darwin
yielded only half a dozen examples. The truth is that it was quite rare (one
Latin, one French, one German, several English). Although Milton used the
chain of Bk. II of *Paradise Lost*, in Bk. III he used Jacob's Ladder. Both
"stretch from Heaven to the Zenith of the universe, and ... both are gold."[33]
Jacob's Ladder occurs in all the great Greek and Latin Fathers: Origen, St.
Gregory of Nyssa, St. John Chrysostom, St. John Climacus, St. Augustine of
Hippo, St. Benedict of Nursia. To ignore Jacob's Ladder, as the Tree of Life,
is to pass over the Hebraic and Biblical element in Western culture, and to
pay attention only to the Hellenic. One of the most important truths about our
medieval heritage is that the thought is composite. When Origen, to use but
one example, considers the angels, this makes pertinent "rational natures" of
genera and species. When Celsus offers Plato's ascent of the soul through the
planets, Origen thinks also of Moses, "our most ancient prophet." In a dream
Jacob saw the angels ascending and descending.[34]

The golden chain is Zeus' but above the Ladder is the Lord God of Abraham, Isaac, and Jacob. The symbol is then connected not only with "the gate of
heaven," but with the promise to Jacob of "the land whereon thou liest" (KJV,
Gen. 28:13-17). This is important because in history it is the active virtues
that are exercized. St. Augustine thinks of the rise of the people of God from
Adam's fall.[35] To reinforce the complementarity of the active and the contemplative virtues, St. Thomas Aquinas recalls the balance between the two rails
of the ladder:

> unus angelus docet alium, purgando, illuminando, et per-
> ficiendo; et secundum hoc habent aliquid de vita activa,
> quamdiu mundus durat, ex hoc quod administratione inferi-
> oris creaturae intendunt: quod significatur per hoc, quod
> Jacob vidit angelos in scala ascendentes (quod pertinet
> ad contemplationem, et descendentes, quod pertinet ad
> actionem....[36]

The Midrash of Genesis and Exodus is particularly emphatic about the active life. The ascent of Jacob's ladder signifies the climb to Mount Zion, even Moses' ascent of Mount Sinai. Since the ladder "symbolizes Sinai" who can the angels descending be but Moses and Aaron?[37] The extension of meaning from the lawgiver and leader to the whole people is natural, and the Lord God speaks to his children, "Be thou not afraid, for just as I will never fall from My greatness, so neither thou nor thy children will ever descend from their greatness."[40] How does the Lord guide his people? The angels descending are God's messengers or prophets. The meaning of the ladder is to encourage virtue and discourage vice. When Israel is righteous, she "will rise higher and higher; but when they suffer a decline, then will their messengers share in their downfall."[41]

The ladder of thirty rungs, the guiding metaphor of St. John Climacus, is a holy ladder. Some time after ladders were drawn for his manuscripts, Christ was added on the uppermost rung.[42] As all who mount the rungs on so tall and steep a ladder knew, it is dangerous. The virtues are difficult habits to acquire and the easy and natural way is vice. So the monks are pictured falling off "into the mouth of a dragon lurking in the cave below."[43] The alternative to perfection of heaven is the damnation of hell. Thus devils plague the climbers, while the angels guide them and "the Virgin stands in the merciful role of the one who intercedes."[44]

The full moral significance was best realized in the "Ladder of Virtue" of the Alsatian Herrade de Landsberg. It is not the thirty-rung ladder for monks, but a fifteen-rung ladder used as an allegory for the way of people of all the various walks of life. However, "the ecclesiastical calling still predominates. At the bottom are a knight and his lady, and above them a nun, a cleric, a monk, a recluse, and a hermit. Nearly all of these topple from the rungs, not directly into the dragon's mouth, but ... to the enjoyment of mundane pleasures displayed on the hillside at the right. Near the top a figure receives the crown of life: this is charity, the topmost rung of which is Faith, Hope, and Charity--'and the greatest of these is charity.'"[45]

Ascending the ladder has the dangers of disastrous fall. The risk of fall becomes a remarkable warning against pride. The picture of this chief vice that appears most effective is a twelfth century picture book. Lucifer covets the throne of God, and counts himself victorious. Pride leads to his fall, and throne and all come crashing down. "He still looks very beautiful but right at the bottom of the picture he has reached hell and is chained at its mouth." Then he is ugly and no longer "Lucifer" but "Satan."[46]

Not only angels fall. Man's pride also leads him to attempt to scale heaven. The portrayal of Babel includes the ladder of great plans that do not have God's blessing. "Jacob's ladder was the way [by contrast] which really led from earth to heaven."[47] Probably a monk drew the picture and was thinking of the Rule of St. Benedict which was read every day in the monastery. We must, says the Rule, make our lives like a ladder going up to God.[48]

Those who make their lives like Christ, the ladder, have the satisfaction of conquering the evil one. The ladder of SS. Marco e Marcelliano, in the chapel dedicated to these martyrs, crush the dragon on whose body the ladders rest.[49] In Tintoretto's painting, *La Crocifissione*, in the Scuola di San Rocco, Venice, the artist painted Christ on the cross upon which leans a ladder. The cross and ladder become one symbol in Christ whose figure in the painting appears to be resting on the top rung of the ladder. The cross seems to fade away under the arms of Christ, but the ladder is clearly visible. Tintoretto has made the central focus of his great canvas 'Christ crucified is the ladder.' The ladder of ascent is offered by Christ to mankind. Jacob's ladder becomes fused with the crucified Christ who is the ladder. Tintoretto in the Cinquecento has illustrated this symbol in an unforgettable painting.

By contrast to the chain, as a symbol of degrees by which we ascend, the ladder is many times more significant. Part of the vitality of a symbol is its ability to change with circumstance. The "abiding helpfulness [of the ladder symbol] is attested by the popularity of Longfellow's poem *The Ladder of Saint Augustine*.[50] The inspiration comes from Sermo III, *De Ascensione*, with a clear moral note of conquering our vices "De vitiis nostris scalam nobis facimus, si vitia ipsa calcamus." The Augustinian idea survives also in J. M. Neale, who comments on trials, sorrows and temptations: "What are they but the ladder/ Set up to heaven on earth?"[51]

Thus we have shown the development of the idea of our sorrowful life as a ladder that makes it altogether natural to identify the ladder with the cross. "The combination of ladder with cross is noteworthy."[52]

The Tree of also Life combines with Jacob's ladder. After all, Christ is the Tree of Life, and Christ is the ladder. Both are symbols of the incarnation and, through the cross, of salvation. God became man that man could become God. Perhaps the most eloquent celebration of the joy expressed in pic-

turing life in these combined and reinforcing symbols is from a sermon once
attributed to St. Chrisostom.

> This Tree is my eternal salvation. It is my nourishment
> and my banquet. Amidst its roots I cast my own roots
> deep: beneath its boughs I grow and expand, revelling in
> its sigh as in the wind itself. Flying from the burning
> heat, I have pitched my tent in its shadow, and have
> found a resting-place of dewy freshness. I flower with
> its flowers; its fruits bring perfect Joy--fruits which
> have been preserved for me since time's beginning, and
> which now I freely eat. This Tree is a food, sweet food,
> for my hunger, and a fountain for my thirst; it is a
> clothing for my nakedness; its leaves are the breath of
> life. Away with the fig-tree, from this time on! If I
> fear God, this is my protection; if I stumble, this is my
> support; it is the prize for which I fight and the reward
> of my victory. This is my straitened path, my narrow way;
> this is the stairway of Jacob....[53]

The tree that is most daringly developed is the Sefiroth Tree. The metaphor conveys the idea of all life as one. According to the *Zohar* the branches
are "separated in appearance and communicate ... one with another, being ramifications of a single tree."[54] As the souls are leaves, branches, and trunk,
many, yet emanations from the Holy One, yet also grafted in God.[55] The Tree of
Life and the Tree of Knowledge are one, and the attributes of God are "ten
degrees or stages." It is a scale, and how is this Jacob's Ladder? The use of
names of God is to enable the mystic to ascend toward union.[56]

The more familiar Sefiroth is a mystical Tree of God springing from an
unknowable root, yet whose branches, the attributes, can be distinguished. The
hidden Root of all Roots is *En-Sof*, and the sap runs into every branch, or the
attributes. The ten are "supreme crown (*Kether Elyon*), wisdom (*Hokhmah*), intelligence (*Binah*), love (*Hesed*), power (*Gevurah*), compassion (*Rahamim*), en-
durance (*Netsah*), majesty (*Hod*), foundation (*Yesod*), kingdom (*Malkhuth*)."[57]

Guillaume Postel (1510-1581) formed a tree from the ten Hebrew names of
God. He named this Tree *scala Jacob*.[58] The Divine Names which comprise the
Tree of Life are: (1) *Ehyeh*, (2) *Jah*, (3) *YHWH Elohim*, (4) *El*, (5) *Jah Elohim*,
(6) *Yehovah*, (7) *Yhwh Sava*, (8) *Elohim Sabaot*, (9) *El Shaddai*, and (10)
Adonai. These names are to be identified with the attributes of God revealed
in the Sefiroth tree. It is evident that Postel identifies the Tree of Divine
Names with the Sefiroth tree and by labeling his tree Jacob's ladder, he indicates that the true ascent to God, as in Jacob's dream, is through an understanding of His names and the attributes of the Sefiroth.

Postel numbered his scala with the same ordering as that of the Sefiroth tree; the *scala Jacob* represents the emanations of deity as does the tree of the ten Sefiroth. In each tree the numbers one, six, nine, and ten form the trunk, while the branches are numbered two, three, four, five, seven, and eight. The names of God *ey-yeh*, *Jehovah* or *JHWH*, *el-shadai* and *adonai* which are numbered one, six, nine and ten respectively and form the trunk correspond to *Kether Elyon*, the "supreme crown" of God, *Rahamin*, the "compassion" of God, *Yesod*, the "basis" of all active forces in God, and *Malkhuth*, the "kingdom" of God or the *Shekhinah*, since all bear the same numerical equivalents. These divine names and the corresponding Sefiroth which form the trunk represent the central core from which the other names and manifestations emerge. The trunk and the branches form one tree, and each does not exist independently of the other. The tree of Divine Names illustrates the *omnia in omnibus* theme so dear to Postel and the Kabbalists. By making the tree of divine names an analogue to Jacob's ladder Postel indicates that God's relation to His creation is a structure of descent and ascent.

He enlarges upon the metaphor of the tree in *Le prime nove del altro mondo*, demonstrating by this symbol, the unity of form and matter and of the male-female principles. He also uses trinitarian language in speaking of the tree or trees. The paradox of this enhanced metaphor is that the trees have two separate root systems both planted by God; however, the trees become one by the wedding of their branches, and the life of one tree flows into the life of the other. Hence two trees become one. This union provides life for man and is analogous to that of the Sabbath.

Much remains to analyze the logic of symbols, and here the observations of Ladner are invaluable: ambivalence, antithesis, analogy, metonymy. Surely we have seen in the ladder as in the tree the transformation of these symbols. We have left unexplored the notion that the symbol as a sacrament participates in what it symbolizes. The symbols of the holy, the cross, the tree, the ladder, become themselves holy. They have a meaning denied to Homer's Golden Chain. Perhaps Lovejoy eschewed the cross, the tree and the ladder as symbols of hierarchy to reinforce his picture of a secular age in which the levels are all accounted for by naturalistic evolution.

Ladner ends his exploration with a contrast between the richness of medieval and the poverty of modern art. All symbols we have examined lead to the same conclusion. Ladner ends with the Tree of the Philosophy of Love of Ramon

Lull and the remarkable Missal of an Archbishop of Salzburg. There are "two trees in one--it is a combination of the paradisiac Tree of Knowledge and of Life. The tree has grown a death's head because of Adam's and Eve's transgression, but the evil consequences--sin and death--represented on one side have been redeemed on the other by the sacrifice of the new Adam, Christ on the Cross, while the new Eve, Maria-Ecclesia, distributes the eucharistic host which grow on the tree alongside and really in lieu of the withered apples."[59]

His example of a modern rendering of the tree is Gauguin's "D'où Venons Nous? Que Sommes Nous? Où Allons Nous?" "The central figure plucks a fruit from the tree," but it is invisible.[60] Is it one of the trees of paradise? We are not told. The destiny from childhood to old age is a beautiful but melancholy acceptance of life and death, presided over by an enigmatic idol. Although the modern painter asks the questions, he gives no answers. The medieval painter has a reconciliation of life and death, and the kinds of meaning we have explored in the cross, the ladder, the tree. He had answers.

The picture Ladner chose as his modern contrast is altogether rich and profoundly significant and positive in affirming life and knowledge, when contrasted to bleak horror of Max Ernst's "L'Arbre de Vie." The 9 1/2 feet tall painting is from 1928. It has the title but has no tree. There is only a dark and light blue winged monster, double headed, with three sets of wings. There is a snake with the head of a long-beaked bird, bright red stenciled crabs, and some floating enigmatic organic forms. All hover over a vaguely discernible barren terrain.

Here is going beyond the rational realm, and in unconscious thought there is a portrayal of a nightmare. What is called "Tree of Life" is a bitter joke. There is no tree. There is a kind of blot into which we may read our fears but not our hopes. Ernst's bitter joke is not singular. René Magritte has "Tree." The 1960 drawing is only a stump. There is an axe held by several of the stump's roots. Has the tree cut itself down?[61]

Need we wonder why Jung and his followers, for whom the tree is the symbol of the growth of the Self, return to the symbol of Christ crucified on the tree? The modern world has provided no adequate symbols to replace those of our medieval heritage.[62] Perhaps since we ended with the tree cut down, we should recall the verse of *Job*: "For there is hope of a tree, if it be cut down, that it will sprout again, and that the tender branch thereof will not cease" (KJV, Job 14:7).

NOTES

[1]Thomas Barns, "Trees and Plants," James Hastings, *Encyclopaedia of Religion and Ethics*, Vol 12, p. 448.

[2]J. C. Cooper, *Illustrated Encyclopaedia of Traditional Symbols* (London: Thames and Hudson, 1978).

[3]Gerhart B. Ladner, "Medieval and Modern Understanding of Symbolism: A Comparison," *Speculum*, Vol. LIV, No. 2, April 1979 pp. 223-256.

[4]We hesitate to mention awe of trees, because we might be confused with a tree worshipper. One of the most fascinating reports is W. Crooke, *The Popular Religion and Folklore of Northern India* (Delhi: Munshiram Manoharlal, 1968: The Second Edition was 1896), Vol. I, Ch. II, "Tree and Serpent Worship," esp. pp. 83-121.
The most readily available compilation is of course J. G. Frazer, *The Golden Bough, The Magic Art*, Vol. II, Ch. lX, "The Worship of Trees," and Ch. X, "Relics of Tree-Worship in Modern Europe", pp. 7-96.

[5]Cooper does not identify *Microcosmos Hypochondriacus* further.

[6]Cooper, *op. cit.*, p. 8.

[7]Barns, *op. cit.*, p. 448.

[8]Cooper, *op. cit.*, p. 8.

[9]*Ibid.*, p. 196. A very popular book composed of the scriptures called *The Tree of Life. Selections*, ed. by Ruth Smith (N.Y.: Viking Press, 1942) has selections from *The Prose Edda* by Snorri Sturlson, Tr. from the Icelandic by Arthur Gilchrest Brodeur (N.Y.: The American Scandinavian Foundation (N.Y.: The American Scandinavian Foundation, 1923). The pages on the Wonderful Ash Yggdrasill are in *The Tree of Life*, pp. 54-55.

[10]Cooper, p. 196.

[11]Stephen C. Pepper, *World Hypotheses: A Study in Evidence* (Berkeley: University of California Press, 1942) works out a theory of "Root Metaphors," Ch. V, pp. 84-114. Particularly pertinent to this study is Maxim I, "A World Hypothesis is Determined by Its Root Metaphor," and Maxim IV, "Concepts Which Have Lost Contact with Their Root Metaphors Are Empty Abstractions."
There are also important essays: "The Root Metaphor Theory of Metaphysics," *The Journal of Philosophy*, Vol. 32, July 4, 1935, pp. 365-74, and "Metaphor in Philosophy," *Dictionary of the History of Ideas* (N.Y.: Scribners, 1973), Vol. III, pp. 196-201, recently reprinted by Arthur Efron and John Herold, Eds., *Paunch*, January 1980, No. 53-54, pp. 54-63.
I regret deeply that Pepper was hardly acquainted with medieval concepts of analogy, and omitted from his account of "Formism" medieval concepts of a hierarchy of forms. He was, however, open to the suggestion I made to him that he was rediscovering an ancient truth, that there is no literal or univocal characterization of the whole of being. "Being has many senses" and every category that refers to all the orders must be only more or less true. Along with sameness between the orders there is always difference.

[12]S. Radhakrishnan, *A Source Book in Indian Philosophy* (Princeton, N.J.: Princeton University Press, 1957), pp. 150-51.

[13]*Ibid.*, pp. 151-52.

[14]Ananda K. Coomaraswamy, *Elements of Buddhist Iconography* (Cambridge, Mass.: Harvard University Press, 1935), pp. 63-4. The brilliant success of this art historian in explicating the meanings of the Tree of Life, Earth-Lotus, and World Wheel is that he keeps all three in the context of both Hindu and Western Medievel Metaphysics. The study of the many meanings of the wheel in Hinduism and Buddhism has aided our interpretation of these other symbols presented together in this essay.

[15]Robert Ernest Hume, *The Thirteen Principal Upanishads* (London: Oxford University Press, 1921), *Katha Upanishad*, VI, pp. 358-61. This translation is used by S. Radhakrishnan, *op. cit.*, pp. 49-50.

[16]Hume, *op. cit.*, Brihad-Āranyaka Upanishad 3.9.28, p. 126; other references to the tree analogy are indexed.

[17]*Ibid.*

[18]Ladner, *op. cit.*, p. 252, from Mauritius of Leyden (Saec. XV). As I write I feel myself closer to trees, even becoming a tree. There is a Latin verb "arboresco" meaning "in arborem crescere." Roberti Stephani *Thesaurus Linguae Latinae* (Basileae: E & J. R. Thurnisiorum, MDCCXL), Vol. 1, p. 241.

[19]Ladner, *op. cit.*, p. 254, ft. 159, dependent on E. H. Gombrich, "Icones symbolicae" in *Symbolic Images: Studies in the Art of the Renaissance*, 2 (N.Y.: Oxford, 1978), pp. 123 ff, 130 f about tree schemata, and 151 ff about "two contrasting ways in which God speaks to man in symbols: either representing like through like or like through unlike. The result is either Beauty or Mystery. Both these qualities are or can be a token of the Divine."

[20]Arthur O. Lovejoy, *The Great Chain of Being* (N.Y.: Harper, 1960, originally Harvard University Press, 1936). In criticism of Lovejoy's thesis there have been published Paul G. Kuntz, "Hierarchy: From Lovejoy's Great Chain of Being to Feibleman's Great Tree of Being," *Studium Generale*, Vol. 24, 1971, pp. 678-87, and half a dozen others on St. Augustine, St. Bonaventura, Dante, Cardinal Cajetan, Cardinal Bellarmino, Fritz Schumacher. The latest is "A Formal Preface and an Informal Conclusion to the Great Chain of Being," *The Modern Schoolman*, Vol. LX, No. 4, May 1983, pp. 273-82.

[21]Marion Leathers Kuntz, *Colloquium of the Seven about Secrets of the Sublime* (Princeton, N.J.: Princeton University Press, 1975), p. 32.

[22]The problem of hierarchy is sometimes posed as the problem of mediation between opposites that are otherwise unrelated. These are, in Calvin's theology, God and man or heaven and earth. There cannot be successful mediation by introducing angels on a ladder, presumably because these do not partake of the natures to be mediated. So long as there is anything "between," one is still "alienated" from the other.
John Calvin, *Institutes of the Christian Religion*, Tr. John Allen (Philadelphia: Presbyterian Board of Christian Education, 1922), Vol. I, Ch. XIV, especially XII, pp. 160-61.
If the problem of hierarchy was posed in late Hellenic thought as that of filling the gap between two worlds, then the difference between the Christian logos and the Neo-Platonic hypostases is that the latter are intermediaries which are below the highest and above the lowest but the former joins both together. C. C. J. Webb analyzes the problem of both Judaism and Neoplatonism as the bridging between God and man. Saint Augustine, *Confessions*, VII, c. 9, calls our attention to the difference between "light and life of men" and the "Word ... made flesh [who] dwelt among us." C. C. J. Webb, *History of Philosophy* (London: Oxford University Press, 1956), pp. 76-88. One of the conspicuous gaps, then, in Lovejoy's *Great Chain of Being* in the Christian development is the doctrine of the logos.

There is another sort of continuity that Lovejoy ignored between the medievel Catholic and the Reformation Protestant. St. Bonaventure in his *Itinerarium, The Mind's Ascent to God, op. cit.*, p. 8, "Christ ... is our ladder" and John Calvin, "It is Christ above who joins heaven and earth. He alone is Mediator.... He it is through whom the fullness of all heavenly gifts flows down to us and through whom we on our part may ascend to God.... Therefore,... we say that the ladder is a symbol of Christ...." *Commentaries, Library of Christian Classics,* Tr. and Ed. J. Haroutunian and L. P. Smith (Philadelphia: Westminster, n.d.), p. 147 on Gen. 28:12.

[23] Martin Buber, *Bilder von Gut und Böse* (Heidelberg: Lambert Schneider, 1964). "'Erkenntnis von Gut und Böse' bedeutet nichts anderes als: Erkenntnis der Gegensätze, ..." "Gott kennt die Gegensätze des Seins, die seinem Schöpfungsakt enstammen....", pp. 1617). Man now has the misfortune to know disorder as well as order, and one of the momentous consequences in history is symbolized in the next chapter by Cain's murder of his brother Abel.

The interpretation of "the knowledge of good and evil" as the distinction of "things contrary in their nature" goes back at least to Philo, *Works,* Younge Tr., Vol. 1, pp. 46, 66-7.

[24] This quotation is found in G. A. Gaskill, *Dictionary of all Scriptures and Myths* (N.Y.: Julian Press, 1960), p. 768. There is 16th and 17th literture on the tree of the knowledge of good and evil. Several sources deserve to be examined:

Sebastian Franck (1499-1542) *The forbidden fruit, Or, A treatise of the tree of knowledge of good & evil, of which Adam at the first, & as yet all mankind doe eate death. Moreover, how at this day it is forbidden to every one as well as to Adam.... Lastly, here is shewed what is the tree of life....* By August: Eluthenius, I. E. Eleatherius? pseud. Translated out of Latine into English, London 1640, Tr. of De Arbore scientiae boni et mali.

Christian Chemnitz engaged in two disputations about the trees. The earlier yielded *Disputatio theologica de arbore vitae prima, qualis est de ejus nomine et causa efficiente ...* (Jena, 1657). The second, *Disputatio theologica de arbore scientiae boni et mali* (Jena, 1683).

Campegius Vitringa, *Disputatio theologica de Arbore scientiae boni & mali* (Franeker, 1693).

[25] Philo, *op. cit.*

[26] Augustine, *City of God*, cited in Gaskill, p. 767.

[27] St. Bernard, *Sermons on the Song of Songs, On the Love of God,* Tr. by a Religious of C.S.M.V. (Oxford: Mowbray, 1952) and (N.Y.: Morehouse-Gorham Co.), pp. 151-2.

[28] Jacopone da Todi's book, Ed. G. Ferri, (Rome, 1910).

[29] Evelyn Underhill, *Jacopone da Todi, Poet and Mystic, A Spiritual Biography* (London: J. M. Dent & Lons, London, 1919), pp. 245-6. Underhill is interpreting *Lauda* LXXXIX, "Un arbore e da Dio plantata."

[30] One of the most arresting combinations of the tree-cross-ladder is at the Accademia in Florence. It is The Tree of The Cross by Pacino di Buonaguide (active *ca.* 1303-20). The arms branch, six on either side, each hung with four medallions, which are therefore 48. In the text of Goffredo Rosati's "Symbolism and Allegory," *Encyclopedia of World Art* (N.Y.: McGraw-Hill, 1967), Vol. XIII, Plate 343, he goes without break from illustrations of the ladder of paradise to the tree of the cross (col. 813).

[31]See *Johannis Revchlini Phorcensis De Cabala, sev de symbolica receptione* (Francofvrti: 1612, Impensis Claudii Marnii haeredum, Ioannis & Andreae Marnii & Consort.) p. 714, section D:

> Ad illud bonum quod Deus nominatur non plane a nobis poterit ob nostrae conditionis fragilitatem, nisi gradibus atque scalis ascendi, quae quidem ut vos loqui consueuistis instar Homericae catenae, vt vero Iudaei nos secundum diuina eloquia dicimus, certe ad speciem scalae Jacob patris nostri de supercoelestibus porriguntur in terram, tanquam restis quaedam aut funis aurea coelitus ad nos directa, veluti linea visualis varias penetrans naturas.

[32]Leo Spitzer, *Classical and Christian Ideas of World Harmony: Prolegomena to An Interpretation of the Word 'Stimmung'*, Ed. A. G. Hatcher (Baltimore: Johns Hopkins Press, 1963).

[33]Harry F. Robins' comment on Don Cameron Allen, "Two Notes on Paradise Lost," *Modern Language Notes*, Vol. LXVII, pp. 360-61, *Ibid.*, Vol. LXIX, 1954, p. 76.

[34]Origen, *On First Principles*, Introduction by Henri du Lubac (Glocester, Mass.: Peter Smith, 1973; originally London: S.P.C.K., 1936), pp. 43-44. Origen *Contra Celsum*, vi.21.

[35]Sancti Aurelii Augustini Hipponensis Episcopi *Operum* Tomus Quartus, Parisiis, 1681, col. 1365.

[36]*Summa Theologiae*, Secunda Secundae Partis, Leone XIII Ed., Editio Altera Romana, n.d., CLXXXI, IV.

[37]*Midrash Rabbah, Genesis*, Tr. Rabbi H. Freedman (London: Soncino Press, 1939), Vol. II, pp. 634 & 625.

[40]*Midrash Rabbah, Exodus*, Tr. Rabbi S. M. Lehrman (London: Soncino Press, 1939), Vol. III, pp. 411-12.

[41]*Ibid.*, p. 483.

[42]John Rupert Martin, *The Illustrations of the Heavenly Ladder of John Climacus* (Princeton, N.J.: Princeton University Press, 1954), p. 10.

[43]*Ibid.*, p. 11.

[44]*Ibid.*, pp. 14-18.

[45]*Ibid.*, p. 19.

[46]Nicolette Gray (Mary Binyon), *Jacob's Ladder: A Bible Picture Book from Anglo-Saxon and 12C. England MSS* (London: Faber and Faber, 1949), pp. 16-18.

[47]*Ibid.*, p. 28.

[48]*Ibid.*, pp. 36-7.

[49]George Kaftal, *Saints in Italian Art: Iconography of the Saints in Central and Southern Italian Schools of Painting* (Florence: Sansoni, 1965), p. 750. The chapel

is in the Catacombs of Donitilla, the fresco from the second half of the fourth century.

[50]A. B. Cook, *Zeus: A Study in Ancient Religion* (N.Y.: Biblo and Tannen, 1965; originally Cambridge 1914-1940), Vol. II, Pt. 1, p. 140.

[51]H. W. Longfellow, *Poems* (London: Cambridge Edition, 1895), p. 186f.

[52]A. B. Cook, *op. cit.*, p. 139, ft. 3. The Latin sequence; "haec est scala peccatorum," "tu nos hinc per modum scalae / ducas ad coelestia," "haec est scala novae legis," etc. J. Kehrin, *Lateinische Sequenzen des Mittelalters* (Mainz, 1873), no. 60, p. 67.

[53]The Pseudo-Chrysostom, Sermon VI for Holy Week, *Patrologia Graeca*, IX, 743-6, in Henri de Lubac, *Catholicism* (NY: Longmans, Green & Co., 1950), p. 279.

[54]A. E. Waite, *The Holy Kabbalah* (New Hyde Park, N.Y.: University Books, n.d.), p. 271.

[55]*Ibid.*, p. 589.

[56]Arthur Edward Waite, *A New Encyclopedia of Freemasonry (Ars Magna Latomorum) and of Cognate Instituted Mysteries: their Rites, Literature and History*, New and Rev. Ed. (N.Y.: Weathervane Books, 1970), p. 409. The Tree of Life is discussed in the article "Jacob's Ladder," pp. 408-10. It ends in protest against trying to assimilate the Norse Yggdrasil or Persian or Brahminical trees to Jacob's ladder. Such Analogies "belong to the shallowest institutes of comparison; if such methods continue, Jack and the Beanstalk will be brought into the medly later...", p. 410.

[57]Gershom Scholem, *Major Trends in Jewish Mysticism* (N.Y.: Schocken Books, 1954, 1974), pp. 244-5.

[58]See The British Library, Sloane ms. 1411, fol. 295. Also note Marion Leathers Kuntz, *Guillaume Postel: Prophet of the Restitution of All Things: His Life and Thought* (The Hague: Martinus Nijhoff, 1981).

[59]Ladner, *op. cit.*, p. 255.

[60]*Ibid.*, pp. 255-6.

[61]Max Ernst's "L'Arbre de Vie" has recently been purchased by the High Museum of Art in Atlanta and exhibited with other Surrealists. Catherine Fox, "'Tree of Life' bears Surrealist fruit at High," *The Atlanta Journal and The Atlanta Constitution*, 5 Feb. 1984, p. 3H.

[62]Karl Gustav Jung, *Man and His Symbols* (Garden City, N.Y.: Doubleday, 1964), pp. 80-1. Jung's colleague M. L. von Franz worked out the analogy between the growth of the self and the growth of a mountain pine (pp. 162-4).

PAUL GRIMLEY KUNTZ

FEIBLEMAN'S GREAT TREE OF BEING

A major claim of Feibleman's *Ontology* is that nature, investigated by the
natural sciences, is hierarchical. "The fields investigated by physics, chemistry, biology, psychology, and anthropology" are "entities processes and
laws" in *levels*.[1] That nature is hierarchical or, more precisely, a structure
of *Integrative Levels*, is for Feibleman a metaphysical, or as he prefers to
say, an *ontological truth*. He prefers to say "ontological" rather than "metaphysical" because of the association of the latter with idealistic speculation
about the transcendental One or a spiritual Absolute. He is a metaphysician in
the tradition of Aristotle (without a Prime Mover) and Bertrand Russell, deeply in agreement that there is similarity subsisting between white things as
well as existing white things and that these realms of essence and existence
are in dynamic and teleological process.

The main outlines of the system have been sketched sympathetically by
Hungtington Cairns in *The Two-Story World*,[2] and Andrew J. Reck, "A Mansion of
Philosophy."[3] Feibleman's system has been dealt with generally yet it is imperative to consider "Naturally-occurring Ontologies" as a modern theory of
hierarchy. This theme unites the two foci of Feibleman's work, on the content
of the natural sciences and on the content of the study of culture. It is in
this content that the philosopher finds ontology, not only in methodology of
the sciences or in speculation that transcends them. If Feibleman is right,
nearly everybody doing philosophy today is wrong. The positivistic tradition
focused on logic, the analytic tradition on language, the phenomenalistic tradition on consciousness, the existentialistic tradition on human anxiety, the
Thomistic tradition on being as such, the idealistic tradition on mind, people
influenced by aesthetics and Santayana on alternative realms, methods or metaphors of metaphysical thought. If Feibleman has allies, it is with Aristotelians, Peircians, Whiteheadians, but have any of them in the present generation
considered seriously what is left of "the great chain of being?"

The general idea of hierarchy is much neglected except by Feibleman. Most
of the writing in *The New Catholic Encyclopedia* deals with how the church is
ordered, the "ecclesiastical hierarchy" over against what the Pseudo-Dionysius
called "the celestial hierarchy." One would have expected an article about
"degrees," or "gradation" or "levels of being."[4] Feibleman more than any other

American philosopher makes up for this neglect. His thought developed through
three decades; budding in the 1940's, flowering in the 1950's and bearing
fruit in the 1960's. In reflecting on his contribution one can agree with
Cairns and Reck that he is a unique, important and exciting American philosopher.

Feibleman's "great chain of being" is not Lovejoy's "great chain of being;" that is to say, in several important respects, Feibleman breaks with
traditional metaphysics. He agrees with Lovejoy's rejection of the tradition
insofar as it was necessitarian: he wants a world in process, with real, not
merely apparent change and chance. He further agrees with Lovejoy that such a
doctrine of "absolute rationality of the cosmos is unbelievable" because "it
conflicts ... with one immense fact, besides many particular facts, in the
natural order--the fact that existence as we experience it is temporal."[5] But
here Feibleman parts company with Lovejoy.[6] The world of time and change is
real, but not the only real. There is not only existence, there is essence.
Now Feibleman finds the principles of "plenitude, continuity, and gradation"
true of the realm of essence if not of the realm of existence.[7] Feibleman, in
Lovejoy's view, must have been suffering from the metaphysical disease of
believing in "two antithetic kinds of being," which creates the problems of a
static eternal one and a changing apparent many, or the necessary rational order and the many haphazard or chance events.[8] Probably Lovejoy, who ceased to
bother with such riddles, viewed Feibleman as one not sufficiently cured of
metaphysical pathos, and Lovejoy did not, to my knowledge, bother to reply to
the criticism of 1946. But since Feibleman's essences are possibilities over
against actualities and Lovejoy allowed these, he could also be diagnosed as a
fellow sufferer. Feibleman rejects Lovejoy's efforts, so typical of 20th Century anti-metaphysics, to explain away systematic philosophy. Since such an
hypothesis as the great chain of being is "unbelievable," it must be explained
away as a result of a "craving of our reason for continuity everywhere."[9] The
metaphysical quest, asserted Feibleman, is a sign of health, not of sickness.
The ontological craving, such as motivates Feibleman, is in his view (and in
psychiatry he is no amateur) like the craving

> which the thirsty have for water,... the hungry ... for
> food,... the cold and exposed have for shelter. [If it
> is] no mere idle fancy but represents a real and objec-
> tive set of conditions ... it were ridiculous to deem
> [it] entirely mental. The 'certain persistent craving,'
> which as Lovejoy admits has obsessed philosophers as far

back as we can trace them, must stand for some real human
need; some need, moreover, which is capable of being satisfied by something corresponding to it in the objective
world. It is not a primitive and useless appendage which,
like our tails, were better lost.[10]

Feibleman has not considered other anti-metaphysical attacks upon the concept
of hierarchy, such as those of George Boas, whose critique has been more radical and acute than that of his colleague Lovejoy.

Feibleman's concept of levels is far more strikingly logical than historical. How are there parts of wholes, or how are things organized? If I understand Feibleman, when he says that "if anything has being then it has an ontology"[11] means that, for example, a thing like an apple, "is not composed in
any haphazard combination but in a definite set of relations between these."[12]
In this example of his, the skin encloses the meat and the meat encloses the
seeds. We would not have an organized whole if the parts could be interchang-
ed. One rule of organization is stated as a necessary truth "In every organization there must be a serial relation."[13]

Feibleman thinking of serial order is clearly a development of the logic
of relations invented by such modern logicians as Peirce and Russell. Relations holding between parts are either transitive or intransitive, connected
or non-connected, symmetrical or asymmetrical, etc. A serial order is a relation that is transitive, connected, and asymmetrical. And one sort of series
is familiar to us in the theory of types, where we have such levels as individuals, classes of individuals, and classes of classes. We build up from the
basic parts to more complex wholes.

There is a way in which an apple is made up of discrete parts, ordered by
the relationship of enclosing-enclosed. But what of a quality like the redness
of an apple? Here we have not a discrete, but a continuous series. There is no
fixed number of parts or degrees, but continuity, since "between any two
values there is a value."[14] There is here no "ontological fault" as between
skin and meat, and between meat and seed. There is no relation "next successor
of" in a continuous series. "Plenitude," which is being full in *degree*, nevertheless allows gradation. Gradation makes possible the conditions of comparative rank in the scale of order. This means that the values, which are continuous and full, are arranged in an order which permits some to be higher than
others in the scale.[15]

Can we then agree with Feibleman's contention that "there are in the material world naturally-occurring ontologies, just as there are naturally-occurring metals: the gold which is found on or near the earth's surface, for instance?"[16] We *find* each story or level he talks about: apples on the level of existence and redness on the level of essence. But do we *find* the discrete series of existence and the continuous series of essence? Do we simply pick up an ontology as we do an apple or a nugget of gold? To arrive at a conception of two levels, the existent actual and the essential possible, requires abstractive and analytical thought, definition, hypothesis, testing, confrontation of antithetical interpretations in a dialectical search for truths among errors. Feibleman seems largely correct in what he says, but neglectful of our process of arriving at truth.

There is a puzzle about levels perplexing to any child, who later finds it called a philosophic problem. Becoming acquainted with a watch the parent instructs the child that a day has twenty-four hours, two revolutions of twelve, each hour has sixty minutes, each minute has sixty seconds, and that there is an hour hand, a minute hand, a second hand. Why stop there? asks the child. How many parts has a second? Why not divide a second into sixty? And are not subseconds themselves divisible, and why ever stop? The child may be silenced with the dogma that the second is the least unit of time, but not satisfied, and still continue to wonder about these parts of time and how they were divided into parts. What comes between the parts?

The central problem of hierarchical order seems correctly stated by Feibleman: if we have a continuous series or gradation, as of a quality, without faults or voids or discrete separable parts, how can there be discovered any natural division between levels? That which is contrasted to the discrete is *said* to be discrete after all. Essence is "an undivided one in which there are and are not parts but only one whole. The whole, however, has planes of cleavage with render it susceptible to division into parts in only a certain fashion."[17]

Perhaps there is the naturally-found ontology of day and night, certainly present in the ancient cosmology of Genesis I, according to which the Creator separated light from darkness. But did not man impose upon day and night the ordering levels of hour, minute and second? Isn't it arbitrary to have level 0, seconds, level 1, minutes, level 2, hour, level 3, day, level 4, week? We might, in addition to day and night, call the month a naturally-occurring

unit, and of course the year, but the whole doctrine of naturally-occurring
ontologies seems to be as suspect as believing that the Lord God of Creation
fixed the seventh day as a naturally-occurring holy day or day of rest by
ceasing from His six days of ordering chaos.

Should we say *there are* "planes of cleavage" or that we cleave the conti-
nuities? I think there is good reason to say that we do not experience separable units of time but have conceived it quantitatively, and in Bergson's language, spatially. I am not yet satisfied by Feibleman's statement that "there
is no conflict between the axial postulates of continuity and gradation; the
series of value is a graded series, graded by the distinction lent by emergent
properties...."[18]

Feibleman had made perfectly plain that he was not defending the chain of
being that Lovejoy had found the dominant organizing principle of European
thought from Plato into the Nineteenth Century. Feibleman's hierarchical order
is not a doctrine of all degrees derived from or grounded in or created by
some absolute One, the Absolute or Deity, nor is the deduction of all lower
degrees from the highest, nor the doctrine that the middle level, usually man
or man's soul, is the midpoint or node, between Being and Nothing, and required to complete the fullness of existence.

About the time of *Ontology*'s publication (1951) Feibleman was beginning
his more positive theory of integrative levels, and in 1954 he published an
article "Theory of Integrative Levels."[19] Now we have a much amplified version
of this--growing from twelve basic truths about the naturally-occuring hierarchical order to eighteen such basic truths. An adequate critique of Feibleman's theory would require much intimate knowledge of the sciences, indeed of
all the sciences, both natural and social, their interrelations, and indeed of
the fields these sciences investigate. Aristotles and Leibnizes are in scarce
supply.

Apart from the detail, with which scientists will disagree because of inadequate, second-hand, or obsolete information, can we agree that Feibleman
has a basis for his version of the great chain of being in discoverable relations between *atoms*, *molecules*, *organisms*, *minds*, and *societies*? There is implicit in the division between the levels of study, say between physics and
chemistry, that, interpreted realistically, there is a structure: "there are
cleavage planes in nature, natural joints, which are to be found rather than
made."[20]

There is then, according to Feibleman, a correspondence between the conceived hierarchy of the sciences, their entities, processes and laws, and the
real hierarchy of nature. That answers one question raised in Feibleman's *Ontology*.

Another question is the relation between the levels. Are there only the
relations of human judgment, such as that molecules are more complex than
atoms, and that atoms are more simple than molecules? Feibleman has answered
that with a firm no, there is a real relation of emergence from lower to
higher levels. The emergent quality from atoms, by process of cause-to-effect
on the physical level is energy. The emergent quality from molecules, by process of combination-rearrangement, is valency.

Two other questions were about the models we employ in thinking about
hierarchies. The first is: is it only the linear model of a series, with one
predecessor and one successor, as in a chain (defined as beginning with a link
without predecessor and ending with a link without succesor) or may there be a
branching, with more than one predecessor or successor? The latter, according
to Feibleman. "We have been regarding the integrative levels as a simple linear series of increasing complexities. But ... we must complicate the picture
if we are to be faithful to the facts of the situation. Since Comte it has
been customary to refer to the integrative levels on analogy to arboreal
branching, a method of further dividing and subdividing."[21] So we may talk now
not about *the great chain of being* but *the great tree of being*.

The other question about models was the relation between the order of
society and the order of nature. That we employ social models, conceiving what
is on the model of a kingdom or empire, is evident not merely from words like
the "kingdom of nature," but ascribing its creation to a king, said to lay
down laws, to rule and reign, to execute judgment, as in a familiar Biblical
metaphor. Certainly we hold suspect the ninefold steps between the Father of
Lights and man: Seraphim, Cherubim, Thrones, Dominions, Powers, Authorities,
Principalities, Archangels and Angels. The Celestial Hierarchy of Pseudo-
Dionysius is mystical poetry expressing metaphorically the steps "by which the
knowledge of God may be found."[22] But Feibleman does not doubt, although metaphors are still used for the hierarchy of nature, that the sciences are giving
us the true structure. In society there is an implicit hierarchy of institutions. In the 6th Century when Pseudo-Dionysius is supposed to have lived, the
church was becoming the dominant institution. Its conception of reality pre-

vailed. God was not merely real but being itself. We are told by ecclesiastical authors that the justification for social hierarchy, the headship of Pope
and Emperor was that the divinely appointed cosmos was hierarchically ordered.
Now that the church is weak compared with business, the state, and science, we
would infer that other ontologies are dominant. The highest institution
"governs the others, it dictates the theory of reality for the entire culture;
and it sets the standards of value accordingly."[23] But if this is one that ontologies are naturally-occurring, doesn't this render suspect any claim that
there is a naturally-occurring ontology in the realistic sense? Earlier we saw
how an apple could be said to have an ontology, that is a structure. But also
"cultures have ontologies," that is, structures. But insofar as "cultures have
ontologies" means that people of these cultures have beliefs about reality,
and there is no one true culture, we have beliefs in many systems, but how is
one absolute system there to be found? So why should we not say that Feibleman's great tree of being is the product of the 20th Century business world,
supported by sciences and technology, using the arts and philosophy in minor
ways, but only in a very minor way still continuous with Hellenic-Hebraic
Christian hierarchical culture?

Feibleman's "laws of the levels" seem convincing. Particularly if a
critic dismisses the older hierarchy of angels and reduces all these symbols
to the metaphysics of a medieval imagination, yet does not modern science re-
instate a new hierarchy in basis of fact. Atoms are not merely imagined although not found directly as gold nuggets. The sciences are more subtle and
not an appeal to naive common sense. As says the late Norwood Russell Hanson:
you don't lift a stone and say, lo! the positron.[24]

Feibleman cannot directly show us the naturally-occurring ontology of
levels except in the sense of pointing out the sky above, then mountains, the
plains, the ocean. Sky, earth, and water we find. But that the empyrean is
above and the earth rests upon "water beneath the earth," the naturally-
occurring ontology of Genesis, is a matter of judgment. If judgment enters in,
then there are concepts abstracted from the richness of perceived nature. In
the serial ordering of heavens higher than earth, and waters deeper than
plains and mountains, there is a principle of judgment. It seems mistaken to
say that one "finds" a principle in the way one finds gold. Feibleman seems
too hasty in dismissing all of Heidegger. There might be truth in distinguishing man from nature. At any rate Feibleman's refutation of Heidegger is too

hasty. It is doubly fallacious. Consider the argument: "If man does feel
alienated, it is because of his refusal to recognize that the distinction so
popular with German philosophers, between man and the world is not viable,
since man is a name for a part of the world." Consider a parallel: "The distinction between an arm and a man, so popular with some American ontologists,
is not viable since arm is a name for a part of a man." Why should we not distinguish between a part of anything and the whole of which the part is a part?
If we do not we can talk only about the undifferentiated, and then we cannot
relate anything definitely, and we cannot use categories. I fear then we
should not be thinking at all. Feibleman on Heidegger involves a deeper fallacy. "To say that man was 'thrown into the world' suggests that he had been
somewhere else. But where else and under what conditions?" This is funny, but
it is not dissimilar to asking Feibleman "To say that there is a realm of essences suggests that along with the realms of Louisiana and the moon, etc.,
there is another country. Please tell me how large it is and how we get
there." This is unfair by Feibleman's standards, and so is his question about
Geworfenheit. And he knows that it is a metaphorical way of talking about
man's despair and alienation.

Feibleman is too zealous a realist in his defense of his great tree of
being. He is unmindful of the incoherence of resting ontology on culture, and
ignoring the threat of cultural relativism. Yet his questioning of Lovejoy's
conclusion is unique and valuable. He has constructed a positive reaffirmation
of hierarchy. Moreover he has asked the right questions. Must all possibilities be actualized? Is "destiny" sufficient, being not as real as existence or
essence, to account for actualization? What is the status of value hierarchies
in the system? Is there any parallelism of value orderings, such that the more
true, the more beautiful, the morally better, the more unified and the richer
in being? Is there an apex of the great tree of being that is most real? If
these questions seem antiquarian, not merely historical, but dead and irrelevant history, let us conclude by asking questions about the top level, according to Feibleman. The top level is a society, whose process is contact-and-
adaptation, from which emerges an ethos.[25] Because Feibleman is thinking of
human societies, he takes anthropology to be the characteristic science of the
top level. He has only a biology of organisms. But biologists now study populations of any living thing in their environments as systems. A standard text-
book talks of levels of organization: "Molecular ... through the increasing

complexity of cells, tissues, organs, organisms, populations, and communities, to that of *ecosystems*."[26] The organism must be stated in context of its external environment—coordinate with knowedge of internal structure, as the DNA molecule.

> For a full and comprehensive view of the nature of living things and of their relationships in universal order, the biologist needs a panoramic point of view. Even as he contemplates a system as commonplace a a pond, he is mindful of the chemistry of water; of the biochemistry of plant and animal cells in the pond in terms of photosynthesis and release of energy from foodstuffs; of the physical laws of energy transformations and transfer, and of light and heat; of the growth and reproduction of the organisms inhabiting the pond; of the inevitable change through time that the aquatic system undergoes; and many other phenomena that are related to the pond, its existence and ultimate end. A biologist considering a single living cell also thinks in terms of the chemical and physical processes taking place, of the structures involved, and of the environment in which the cell structures and the whole cell exist.[27]

Where has Feibleman's hierarchy a place for the ecosystem? The ecologist's level has emerged in science after most of Feibleman's great tree of being was formulated. If we take the scientific picture of levels of organization, we must continually be revising our philosophies to keep up with scientific progress.

Feibleman's defense of the great tree of being should be kept up to date and improved. The holistic method of his philosophy of culture could be used, as by ecologists, of nature as an ecosystem. There are naturally-found-ontologists, and one of them is organicism. It is therefore most significant that by logical analysis thought transcends the mechanical model of a chain, and replaces it with the organic model of the tree. The naturally-found hierarchy aims to state how nature developes and to replace the conceptual orders we force upon nature.

We are now considering culture as a composition of different and differing beliefs, and the institution of philosophy, I think we may agree that Feibleman makes explicit the implicit commitments of society and provides speculative alternatives to what we take for granted. It seems somewhat odd to characterize the culture level by beliefs. The oddity is that "belief" is probably, following the early Bertrand Russell, considered only on the level of mind. ("Believing", said Russell once, "is the most mental thing we do.")

The theory of culture is in trouble because it is considered holistically, whereas the rest of the levels are considered atomistically. Feibleman built up from parts, atoms, molecules, cells, etc., and considered how the "bit-parts" are related. But the parts of a culture are what I have called in contrast "aspect-parts." Feibleman has changed methods without warning us and we may be shocked to see the words "the smallest human isolate is a culture and not an individual." (cf. "organismalism" of W. E. Ritter)

I conclude in hearty agreement with Feibleman that there are ontologies found in the sciences. We can find biologists using patterns of order and showing us how to analyze the natural order, and it is valuable to know intimately the content of the sciences. I disagree that ontologies are found in nature as is a nugget of gold or an apple. We must abstract, use principles of judgment, construct systems using logic. All this belongs to the intentional world of man as does meaning, of which language is one type. Therefore I see the ecosystem of man, including now control over the environment, as being essentially of a different and higher order than the ecosystems of other animals. I would be willing to agree with Feilbeman's naturalism if the fish and oysters of the Altamaha River system studied the featherless bipids of the Atlanta Piedmont hills. But as of now it is only man who devises theories of ecology. Other animals only live as populations in environments.

NOTES

[1]James K. Feibleman, "Theory of Integrative Levels," *British Journal for the Philosophy of Sciences*, Vol.V., No. 17, 1954, p. 59.

[2]Huntington Cairns, *The Two-Story World*, Holt, Rinehart and Winston, New York, 1966, "Introduction," pp. 3-17.

[3]Andrew J. Reck, "A Mansion of Philosophy," *The Southern Review*, N.S., Vol. III, No. 4, Autumn 1967, pp. 1020-23.

[4]Paul Edwards, ed., *Encyclopedia of Philosophy*, Free Press and Macmillan, N.Y., 1966 has no general article "Hierarchy" but "Organismic Biology," 5 columns, and "Theory of Types," 9 columns, otherwise the topic is of merely historical concern, articles "Marsilio Ficeno," Al-Farahbi ("Islamic Philosophy"), and "Pseudo-Dionysius."

[5]Arthur O. Lovejoy, *The Great Chain of Being*, Harvard University Press, Cambridge, 1936, p. 329.

[6]James K. Feibleman, "Lovejoy's Revolt Against Realism," Ch. IV., *The Revival of Realism: Critical Studies in Contemporary Philosophy*, University of North Carolina Press, 1946, pp. 99-136.

[7]*Ibid.*, p. 102.

[8]*Ibid.*, pp. 315-27.

[9]Arthur O. Lovejoy, *op. cit.*, pp. 329, 327.

[10]James K. Feibleman, *The Revival of Realism, loc. cit.*, p. 135.

[11]James K. Feibleman, "Naturally-Occurring Ontologies," *Dialectica*, Vol. 23, No. 2, 1969, p. 136.

[12]James K. Feibleman and J. W. Friend, "The Structure and Function of Organization," *The Philosophical Review*, Vol. LIV, 1945, p. 20.

[13]*Ibid.*, pp. 21, 23.

[14]James K. Feibleman, *Ontology*, Johns Hopkins Press, Baltimore, p. 207.

[15]*Ibid.*, p. 208.

[16]James K. Feibleman, "Naturally-Occurring Ontologies," *loc. cit.*, p. 136.

[17]James K. Feibleman, *Ontology, loc. cit.*, p. 208.

[18]*Ibid.*, p. 251.

[19]James K. Feibleman, "Theory of Integrative Levels," *loc. cit.*, pp. 59-66.

[20]James K. Feibleman, "The Integrative Levels in Nature," *Focus on Information and Communication*, Barbara Kyle, ed., ASLIB, London, 1965, p. 27.

[21] *Ibid.*, p. 39.

[22] E. F. Osborn, "Pseudo-Dionysius," *Encyclopedia of Philosophy*, Paul Edwards, ed., Free Press and Macmillan, New York, 1951, Vol. 6, p. 510.

[23] James K. Feibleman, *The Institutions of Society*, George Allen and Unwin, London, 1956, pp. 159-166, and pp. 228ff.

[24] Norwood Russell Hanson, *The Concept of the Positron*, Cambridge University Press, New York, 1963, *ad fin.*

[25] James K. Feibleman, "The Integrative Levels in Nature," *loc. cit.*, p.28.

[26] R. B. Platt and George K. Reid, *Bioscience*, Reinhold Publishing Co., New York, 1967, p. 4.

[27] *Ibid.*, pp. 4-5.

PAUL GRIMLEY KUNTZ

ANAÏS NIN'S QUEST FOR ORDER: BALANCE, HARMONY AND HIERARCHY

Anaïs Nin has a very distinctive quest for order that deserves serious hearing as a philosophy of the human self. Every interpreter of a labyrinthine writer owes his reader a thread that will guide him to the center, so that the apparently disorderly will become meaningful and all the parts will find a place in the total pattern. In as reflective a person as Nin, it is necessary first to state a few questions to which many passages of the Diary and many novelettes are answers. How can one become a creative human being? How can the self escape defeating division? How can opposites be harmonized? How can the self bridge the gap between subject and object, and all the other opposites between which one may seem exclusive of the other? How can the fragmented self attain unity of the parts? How can the self emerge by stages to higher levels? How can man find the love that yields the highest joy? These questions seem to define Anaïs Nin's quest for order and the meanings of order, which is a most ambiguous term that can be clarified by thinking of balance, harmony, and hierarchy. Anaïs Nin has often resolved conflict by saying both—and rather than either—or, and by balance I mean what she meant by saying that she built bridges and found opposites together (NF 76). Of course harmony is one of her favorite principles, but can she ever harmonize order and disorder? My endeavor will be to show how coherent her philosophy of the self is: the fullness of life requires the logical and objective as well as the emotional and subjective, the commonly considered "orderly" is deficient without the inclusion of the mysterious depths of motivation. The quest for order is not easily satisfied, and the self must progress from order to order to find the finally satisfying integration. Because the self ascends by degrees, and may finally reach a higher level, we are required to think not merely of a sequence or series but of hierarchical order. This last principle dominates two recent interpretations of the meaning of Anaïs Nin.[1]

Both in the Diary and in her novelettes Nin presents disorder as a problem for any self, and one that is particularly fascinating because her father, Joaquin Nin, or the father of *Winter of Artifice*, has a solution which seems no solution at all to the daughter. Anyone has observed disorder, but only Nin immediately thinks of people being wasted, discarded, thrown away.

> I look at the dead flowers floating ... Punctured rubber
> dolls bobbing up and down like foetuses. Boxes full of
> wilted vegetables, bottles with broken tops. Dead cats.
> Corks. Bread that looks like entrails. These things haunt
> me. The debris. *When I watch people it is as if at the*
> *same time I saw the discarded parts of themselves.* And so
> I can't see their motions except as *acts which lead them*
> *faster and faster to the waste, the end, to the river*
> *where it will be thrown out.* (WA 123 emphasis mine)

Is the direction of life from order to disorder? Has temporal process but
one direction, and will the process come, as Christian theology predicts, to
the world's destruction, or as some modern physics say, to the heat death by
entropic dissipation of usable energy? Joaquin, or the father, lived a philosophy of order to stave off the inevitable.

> This siesta he always took with religious care, as if the
> preservation of his life depended on it. At bottom he
> felt life to be a danger, a process not of growth but of
> deterioration. To love too deeply, to talk too much, to
> laugh too much, *was wasting of one's energy.*
> Life was an enemy to him, and every sign of its wear and
> tear gave him anxiety. He could not bear a crack in the
> ceiling, a bit of paint worn away, a stairway worn
> threadbare, a faded spot on the wallpaper. (WA 101 empha-
> sis mine)

Thus sprang that anxiety for the morrow, against which Christ counselled,
and a false philosophy of order. From the *Winter of Artifice* is a systematic
condemnation of imposing formal order upon fluid life. Anaïs expresses the
profound judgment that not all order is good and not all disorder is bad.

> *You give the command for stillness, and life stops like a*
> *clock that has fallen. You draw geometric lines around*
> *liquid forms, and what you extract from the chaos is al-*
> *ready crystallized. As soon as I leave you everything*
> *fixed falls into waves, tides; is transformed into water*
> *and waves. I hear my heart beating again with disorder. I*
> *hear the music of my gestures, and my feet begin to run*
> *as music runs and leaps. Music does not climb stairways.*
> *Music runs and I run with it....* (WA 100)

Good order, in this analysis, is vital, organic, the order of flowing
process, which Bergson called durée, rather than the mechanical order representing time in the regular ticking of a clock with hands that sweep the
circle unrelated to events and feeling. But once again Anaïs applies the contrast to people, and in a distinctively Christian way:

> She sought out the failures because he didn't like those
> who stuttered, those who stumbled; she sought out the
> ugly because he turned his face away; she sought out the

weak because they irritated him. She sought out chaos because he insisted on logic. She traveled to the other end
of life.... (WA 102)

So Anaïs' good order not only tolerates those exceptions to good bourgeois order, but actually turns compassionately to the "black, soiled corners
of the world," to the people in the burlesque theatre, the people who push
vegetable carts. (WA 103)

Her father has a superficial view of order:

We are punctual, a stressed, marked characteristic. We
need order around us, in the house, in the life, although
we live by irresistible impulse, as if the order in the
closets, in our papers, in our books, in our photographs,
in our souvenirs, in our clothes, could preserve us from
chaos in our feelings, loves in our work. (DI 207)

Anaïs had faith, which her father lacked, and this took the form of faith
in order in spite of the terrible disruptions of 1934.

Doom! Historical and political. Pessimism. Suicides. The
concrete anxieties of men losing power and money. That I
learned at the school! I saw the headlines, I saw families broken apart by economic dramas. I saw the exodus of
Americans, the changes and havocs brought on by world
conditions. Individual lives shaken, poisoned, altered.... The struggle and instability of it all. (DI 331-2)

In spite of the flood of despair Anaïs "continued to build [her] individual life as if it were a Noah's Ark for the drowning." Thus is added to the
Christian motifs of avoiding anxiety for things of the morrow, compassion for
the poor, the search, with "desperate stubbornness," for salvation of the individual.

I used "faith" advisedly because Anaïs' philosophy of order could make
sense only if it presupposes some principle of order that can transform loss
into gain, disorder into order. If the world were only the temporal process of
material elements arranged and rearranged, there would be no rational solution
other than her father's.

The evidence that Anaïs Nin's philosophy is based on God, the eternal and
infinite over against nature, and one with whom man can be united by love and
find joy in spite of sorrow, fulfillment in spite of tragic loss, is the account she gives of her stillborn daughter. "Symbolic motherhood bring[s] more
hope into the world." The natural is not the only realm, and although she rejects the Catholic picture and practice of the supernatural, there is still
God (DI 346-7). "I melted into God. No image, I felt space, gold, purity, ec-

stasy, immensity, a profound ineluctable communion. I wept with joy.... I knew
that I needed no dogmas to communicate with Him, but to live, to love, and to
suffer. I needed ... no priest to communicate with Him.... Through flesh and
blood and love, I was made whole...."

What could be more profoundly Catholic and Christian than the profession
that human self is truly gained only in relationship to God, but prepared in
love of man?

> But from that moment on, I felt my [full] connection
> [with God] which gives me an immense joy and a sense of
> the greatness of life, eternity. I was born. I was born
> woman. To love God and to love man, supremely and sepa-
> rately. Not to confuse them. I was born to great qui-
> etude, a super-human joy, above and beyond all human sor-
> rows, transcending pain and tragedy. This joy which I
> found in love of man, in creation, was completed by com-
> munion with God (DI 348).

Anaïs tells us of her rebellion against "a God who had not granted my
prayers (the return of my father), who performed no miracles, who left me
fatherless and in a strange country...." (DI 71). However God is still there
and a miracle still happened (DI 348) ("The doctor came, examined me, could
not believe his eyes," etc.) This is but one of many ambiguities in her writing about Catholicism. Others are worth analyzing (Cf. DII 92-3; 182-3) but
there must be hidden in the unpublished works many passages that would help us
understand how order comes out of disorder.[2]

Although the term "order" (and of course the synonyms of "disorder,"
which includes "chaos," "helterskelter," "debris" in Nin's langugage; and
Henry Miller also uses "helterskelter") are vague, there are specific ordering
relations that occur so frequently that they acquire precision in her meaning.
Anaïs applies them to the self in relation to its many characteristics and to
other selves in ways that define what she sought to be, a creative self. They
are also significantly principles that govern a moral world.[3]

BALANCE

In the splendid conclusion of *Winter of Artifice* order is restored in the
relationship between daughter and father. She feels "a strange joy." Here is
defined one of the deep rooted meanings of order, found in Anaximander, that
injustice must be balanced with punishment.[4] In this case the cold father who
rejected his child is himself rejected.

> And this suffering, which in reality she made no effort
> to inflict since she kept her secret, gave her joy. It
> made her feel that she was *balancing in herself* all the
> injustice of life, that she was *restoring in her own soul
> a kind of symmetry to the events of life. It was the ful-
> fillment of a spiritual symmetry. A sorrow here, a sorrow
> there. Abandon yesterday, abandon today. Betrayal today,
> betrayal tomorrow. Two equally poised columns. A decep-
> tion here, a deception there, like twin colonnades: a
> love for today, a love for tomorrow;.... Mystical geome-
> try. The arithmetic of the unconscious which impelled
> this balancing of events.* (WA 105-6 emphasis mine)

Anaïs Nin gives symmetry or balance a cosmic status by ascribing to it
necessity. One might say "law" or "principle" of balance because it seems to
rule or govern events. Is this only a feeling, only something of the soul,
only subjective? The answer has to be no:

> Great forces had impelled her towards symmetry and bal-
> ance, had impelled her to desert her father in order to
> close the fatal circle of desertion. She had forced the
> hourglass of pain to turn. They had pursued each other.
> They had tried to possess each other. They had been
> slaves of a pattern, and not of love. Their love had long
> ago been replaced by other loves which gave life. All
> those parts of the self which had been tied up in a
> tangle of misery and frustration had been loosened imper-
> ceptibly by life, by creation. But the feelings they had
> begun with twenty years back, he of guilt and she of
> love, had been *like railroad tracks on which they had
> been launched at full speed by their obsessions.* (WA 118
> emphasis mine)

Destiny, which is necessary, thus is said to rule over myth, which may be
chosen or rejected.

The problem of the right ordering of feeling and thought, of the right
ordering of persons is a universally human problem. It is therefore a mistake
to interpret Anaïs Nin as a writer of "feminine perception and fancy." There
is no necessity that a female protest against the artificial and mechanical
ordering of life. We have all encountered meticulous housekeepers and strict
school marms at war with untidy and spontaneous young males. It is indeed a
healthy correction of the ungenerous denigration of old maids and their fussi-
ness to have such a delightful satire of male stuffiness and correctness as
that of Joaquin Nin in the Diary and the father in *Winter of Artifice.*

Although most of the earlier interpretation, as that of Edmund Wilson,
Lawrence Durrell, and Henry Miller emphasized "feminine" and thus laid basis
for the "feminist" reading, we have recently seen an attempt to attain bal-

ance. Evelyn J. Hinz puts it: "While other women are concerned with merely demanding a voice, Nin is aware of the need to establish the quality of that
voice. She wants woman to speak *not as a mere equal or duplicate of man but as
his complement*." (MG 3). Male and female traits, so-called, are both needed
for full humanity. If she has been wronged, as she has been, by a male critic
who condemns women as "small, subjective, and personal," Nin does not respond
by "declaration of war between the sexes." (*Ibid.*, 96)

The right ordering between the sexes, between opposite tendencies found
in culture, is that these opposites are found together, belong together, are
meaningless apart. The principle is called polarity because north and south
depend upon each other for meaning and polarists such as Coleridge and Emerson
point out that knowing requires subject and object as speech and logic require
affirmation and negation and electricity requires positive and negative. Anaïs
Nin is clearly in this great Romantic tradition. "In a true relationship there
is no taking sides, no feminine claims in opposition to masculine claims, no
reproaches at all. There is an effort to confront together what interferes
with genuine fusions." (NF 76).

To enlist Anaïs Nin in a war of any one polar opposite against another is
then to suppose her breaking rather than building bridges (*Ibid.*) An important
example of this is in her early study of D. H. Lawrence's "*Androgynous writing*. The intuitional quality in Lawrence resulted in a curious power in his
writing which might be described as androgynous. He had a complete realization
of the feelings of women. In fact, very often he wrote *as a woman* would
write." (DHL 57).

One could go through Nin's writings and show that she reconciled every
great opposition, that for all the either-ors of the makers of war she was the
peacemaker with her both-and.

HARMONY

Who can ignore the deepest need for harmony? Anaïs expresses her poignant
need of harmony with her father: "*Can we live in rhythm, my father? Can we
feel in rhythm, my father? Can we think in rhythm, my father? Rhythm-rhythm-
rhythm.*" (WA 88).

One of the deepest frustrations of life is the failure to find harmonious
sociality. The daughter dances, but "her father could not dance." The daughter
gives herself to the Spanish music and she carries the audience with her,

their senses drawn "into her spinning and whirling." But her father hides his
face. The father was critical and so shamed by his daughter he would have
stopped her. What is disharmony? When one is in delerium, the other walls himself off, "cold, formal, and conventional."

Music is important because through it the many become one. Here is another metaphysical principle:

> Music melts all the separate parts of our bodies togeth-
> er. Every rusty fragment, every scattered piece could be
> melted into one rhythm. A note was a whole, and it was in
> motion, ascending or descending, swelling in fullness or
> thrown away, thrown out in the air, but always moving.
> (WA 99)

Harmony, since the time of Pythagoras, has been applied to the starry
heaven, to society and the state, to the body and soul, as well as to music
because of the simple mathematical ratios. Anaïs is deeply Pythagorean in her
expression of music in everything:

> As soon as she left her father she heard music again. It
> was falling from the trees, pouring from throats, twinkl-
> ing from the street lamps, sliding down the gutter. It
> was her faith in the world which danced again. It was the
> expectation of miracles which made every misery sound
> like part of a symphony. Not separateness but oneness was
> music. (WA 99)

Harmony is not merely finding the oneness between two persons, it is the
intense identification discovered between all persons. Harmony covers so many
kinds of relationships that Nin often qualifies the relation:

> Someday I'll be locked up for love insanity. "She loved
> too much." This could be on my tombstone. What I feel
> intensely and always respond to is the aloneness of
> others, their needs. Which love makes the great close-
> ness, the fraternal, the friendship, the passion, the in-
> tellectual harmony, the tender one, devotion, the lover,
> the brother, the husband, the father, the son, the
> friend? So many kinds of fusions! What is it that annihi-
> lates the loneliness? The understanding of Rank, devo-
> tions, ardor, creative harmony?
>
> Break and shatter loneliness forever! (Quoted in R.
> Zaller, p. 50)

HIERARCHY

The importance of hierarchy is best expressed in Nin's title, *Ladders to
Fire*. Whereas the above patterns of order, balance and harmony, require only
two terms, and are symmetrical ("symmetry" is in her language synonymous with

"balance"), an hierarchical relationship requires at least three terms, and
relates the lower level to the middle as the middle is related to the higher.

Anaïs' imagination uses the elevator of the modern New York skyscraper.
She is not consciously modernizing Dante's Paradiso, Purgatorio and Inferno,
but she has succeeded in showing and discerning links of the great chain of
being. The human situation, with persons constantly rising and falling evokes
one of her most remarkable passages:

> *Levels and levels.* It is as if I were in *an elevator,*
> *shooting up and down,* hundreds of floors, hundreds of
> lives. *Up to heaven,* terraces and planetariums, gardens,
> fountains, clouds the sun. *The wind whistles down the*
> *shafts....* Red lights! Down! Down! (D II 34)

Anaïs then catalogues miseries, from "a man who limps" to "a girl trembl-
ing with fear of man." The purpose, as in Dante's scheme is to raise up the
low: "Free the slaves of incubi, of ghosts and anguish. Listen to their cry-
ing."

> *White lights! Going up!* Playing at being God, *but a god*
> *not tired of listening,* all the while wondering how the
> other god can watch people suffer. Music, the solace.
> *Through music we* rise in swift noiseless elevators to the
> heavens, breaking through the roof. (D II 35)

It is important to notice that there is no fixed highest human level, but
openness to a transcendent and divine level. There is no explicit principle
here of why some rise to joy and others fall into misery.

Happily two perceptive readers of Nin have worked out a hierarchy of
stages of love.

> We may briefly trace this erotic development from the
> complete auto-eroticism of Sabrina, in *House of Incest,*
> through the ritualistic sexuality of *A Spy in the House*
> *of Love,* to its final transformation into compassion in
> *Seduction of the Minotaur.* Each of these works represent
> a specific stage in the growth of love and each has its
> own kind of danger or reward: the consequence of auto-
> cratic narcissism, if carried to its ultimate conclusion,
> is madness; unbridled sexuality or passion leads to
> homeopathic guilt; and finally compassion results in that
> 'miraculous openness of love' and fulfillment of one's
> being. (R. Zaller, p. 109).

This is an important principle of levels discerned by the philosopher
Orville Clark. The lower levels are inadequate and only the highest level can
be maintained. "Compassion is the only key which fits everyone." (D I 52) This
needs to be interpreted. Perhaps the principle is that the lowest love is love

of oneself for the sake of pleasure, that the higher love is love of others
for the sake of pleasure, that the highest stage is love of others for their
own sake, a willingness to suffer for them and with them.

Another way of putting this also has three stages, beginning with self-
love or pure Narcissism and ending with caritas or love of others which is un-
calculating and generous. But Anna Balakian discerns a middle stage of detachment. The movement can be of ascent rather than of descent and the "ladder
[is] intended for climbing upward even if there is danger of fire at the top."
(R. Zaller, p. 121)

Miss Balakian recognizes the Christian character of this scheme of salvation. It is a "modern Christ," wishing his skin peeled off so he could be receptive of all sensory reality: "If only we could all escape from this house
of incest, where we only love ourselves in the other, if only I could save you
all from yourselves, said the modern Christ." (R. Zaller, p. 119)

CONCLUSION

In her way of probing the depths of experience and expressing her thought
in symbols is there another contemporary writer who rivals Anaïs Nin? Her philosophy of the self could be restated with arguments and illuminated by contrast to great positions of the past. As it stands, as yet revealed only in
fragments, it seems to me to succeed in revealing that "deeper structure" for
which she longed (R. Zaller X). I have tried to clarify what this might be,
using balance, harmony and hierarchy.

She is a Romantic and organicist critic of the mechanistic theories of
order exemplified in her father, and much more needs to be said of alternatives to these two. In her sensitive consideration of the alienation of modern
man she has not made clear exactly why she stresses some Catholic and Christian ideas. I believe, and have suggested, that some are broadly humanitarian,
fit experience, and are part of the heritage of mankind generally.[5] Specifically I believe she could be "the nun" in her fellow feeling and desire to
help people in need but "not a nun" because she was no cloistered ascetic (D
II 183). We need to give her more credit as a thinker who knew the "chill
curse" of hatred of the sensuous, guilt because of sexuality, and for having
rejected body-mind dualism. We need then to be careful in noting not only the
oppression and superstition against which she rebelled but also her continua-

tion of feeling and practice of care, caritas or Christian love (agape). If
the latter is what Christianity is about, there is only reaffirmation[6].

Anaïs Nin has given us suggestions of a new order that can include
aspects formerly ruled out as disorderly, as the bourgeois rejected the bohe-
mian, the rich rejected the poor, etc. Nin's new order is a reconciliation of
opposites, and a redemptive order. In spite of all the contrariety of humanity, Nin would recognize all as belonging together harmoniously.

Because she included disorder with order she devised a way of writing
that is open. Her Diary, wrote Henry Miller, is "the unfinished symphony which
achieves consummation because each line is pregnant with soul struggle." Contrary to the first impression, there is "nothing chaotic about the work." (R.
Zaller 13). Like a "shipwrecked sailor thrown up on a desert island, from the
flotsam and jetsam of her wrecked life the author struggles to create anew."
Miller is thinking only of materials, and this misses the purposive drive to
answer questions about the self. She was concerned therefore to discover as
well as to recollect. Hence her "descent into ... the night of primordial
chaos...." Did she *create* "a pattern into which the helterskelter of passing
events fit and makes a significance? (*Ibid* 15-16). Rather she presents balance, harmony and hierarchy in the order of life in the world and not imposed
as an artificial order.

NOTES

[1]Orville Clark, "Anaïs Nin: Studies in the New Erotology," Robert Zaller, Ed., *A Casebook Anaïs Nin*, New American Library, N.Y., 1974, 109-110, traces the growth of love from auto-tic narcissism through unbridled sexuality to fulfillment in compassion. Anna Balakian, "The tic Reality of Anaïs Nin," *Ibid*, discerns similarly three stages of love. The progression e, also from self-love, is through detachment (rather than passion), but arrives finally at on, which in this version is the conjugation of the subjective and the objective. From my dies in medieval Christian philosophies of the self, springing from St. Augustine, one can ily place Anais Nin in this tradition. It is altogether Augustinian that "the images of de-nt..., the spirals of downward movement are replaced by a ladder intended for climbing upward n if there is the danger of fire at the top." (*Ibid.*, 121) The present author expounds the *ala amoris* as the central ordering principle of medieval Christian, particularly Franciscan ught, in "The Hierarchical Vision of St. Bonaventure," in *San Bonaventura Maestro di ta Francescana e di Sapienza Cristiana*, A. Pompei, Ed., Pontifica Facolta Teologica n Bonaventura", Roma, 1976, II, 233-248. If it is objected that Anaïs Nin rejected the Church, is altogether relevant to raise the case that another Spanish Catholic, George Santayana, may e also ceased to commune, but not have ceased to think in categories that are frequently those the Gospel transmuted through a philosophy dominated by patterns of order such as hierarchy or e great chain of being." Among a sequence of studies of Santayana by the present author the t recent is "'The Thread of Salvation in this Labyrinth of Folly:' Santayana's Philosophy Ex-ssed in the Indian Concepts of Karma and Brahma," *Philosophy in the Life of A Nation*, entennial Symposium of Philosophy, City University of New York, N.Y., 1976, pp. 140-144.

[2]The present author found the philosopher Whitehead struggling with the problem and Anaïs t have known this because D. H. Lawrence quotes a concluding passage from *Religion in the king* in *Lady Chatterly's Lover*. Whitehead's struggle towards a solution is recounted in om Disorder to Order or From Order to Disorder?", The Society for the Study of Process Philos-y, Dickinson College, Carlisle, Pa., 1976.

[3]The richness of any of these three principles of order, balance, harmony, or hierarchy, has n developed most lucidly by my wife, Marion Leathers Kuntz, "Harmony and the *Heptoplomeres* Jean Bodin," *Journal of the History of Philosophy*, Vol. XII, No. 1, 1974, pp. 31-41. further examples of Renaissance thought dominated by concepts of polar opposites (form-ter, male-female, etc.) and hierarchy (Jacob's ladder equated with Homer's Golden Chain of s) see Marion Leathers Kuntz, *Colloquium of the Seven about Secrets of the Sub-me*, Translation with Introduction, Annotations, and Critical Readings, Princeton University ss, 1975. The present author owes most to her inspiration.

[4]"The fragment from Anaximander conceives the generation and destruction of things, through ch they pay penalty and retribution to one another, as happening "according to the order of e (Kata ten tou chronou taxin)." Few writers have so connected order with time as clearly alleling this pre-Socratic Ionian insight. Paul G. Kuntz, *The Concept of Order*, Univer-y of Washington Press, Seattle, 1968, p. 442.

[5]In "Hume's Metaphysics: A New Theory of Order," *Religious Studies* (London) Vol. 12, 6, pp. 401-428, I argue that Hume never doubted some principle of order in the cosmos. More-r, since that is what various traditions mean by "God," that such belief is universal in man-d, and a natural belief. He had "system" as he said, and it can be discerned by attending to t he said of balance, harmony and hierarchy.

[6]One of the subtlest analyses of Nin's revision of Christianity comes from Richard R. Cent-'s "Emotional Algebra: The Symbolic Level of *The Diary of Anaïs Nin*, 1944-1947:"

Nin's Catholic background (she once wanted to be a nun) gives her an arsenal of traditional symbols which she playfully uses to tell a pagan
story. The overcoming of guilt is a constant theme: she says Henry Miller
is seeking 'atonement'.... During the time covered in *Diary* IV, Nin is
writing a novel called *This Hunger*, which reminds us of *man's dual-*
ity: his physical and spiritual hunger, Nin seeks to re-
create the Garden of Eden, and unite these warring oppo-
sites. In a marvelous image at the end, she dresses up a friend as a
nun from the waist up, with a cross on her breast,' but in transparent
chiffon below the waist so that 'her legs could be seen in silhouette.'
By reuniting body and soul Nin takes one more step towards paradise. At a
party ... the guests tried to determine if Nin was a *'mystic' or*
'sensual' and decided correctly that she was a combination
of both. Nin specifically says ... that body and soul 'were rent asunder
by Christianity.' (R. Zaller, pp. 170-171, emphasis mine).

Centing is one of many who have made explicit the polarity in Nin's life and thought. Polarity
can be found in such a Christian philosopher as St. Thomas Aquinas, who taught that the soul is
the form of the body, and that all created substances are composite. Had Nin known more of the
history of problems with which she struggled, such as action and contemplation, she might have
been delighted with the theory that they complement and supplement each other as do the contributions of Mary and Martha. Indeed, the symbolism of Jacob's Ladder in St. Thomas is that one rail
of the ladder is action, the other contemplation. The rungs cannot hold without rails on two
sides.

BIBLIOGRAPHY

Primary

The Diary of Anaïs Nin, The Swallow Press and Harcourt, Brace & World, N.Y., 1966, 1967,
etc. indicated by D I, D II, etc.

D. H. Lawrence: An Unprofessional Study, with an Introduction by Harry T.
Moore, The Swallow Press, Chicago, 1964, indicated by DHL.

Ladders to Fire, The Swallow Press, Chicago, 1959, indicated by LF.

The Novel of the Future, The Macmillan Co., N.Y., 1968, indicated by NF.

Winter of Artifice, Alan Swallow, Denver, 1945, 1946, 1948, indicated by WA.

Secondary

Evelyn J. Hinz, *The Mirror and the Garden: Realism and Reality in the Writings of*
Anaïs Nin, The Ohio State University Libraries, 1971, referred to by MG.

Robert Zaller, Ed., *A Casebook on Anaïs Nin*, New American Library, N.Y., 1974, indicated by
R. Zaller.

PAUL GRIMLEY KUNTZ

THE METAPHYSICS OF HIERARCHICAL ORDER:

THE PHILOSOPHICAL CENTER OF "SMALL IS BEAUTIFUL"

Reviewers have so far not noticed that *Small is Beautiful* is, among other
things, a philosophical book. The central "vital idea" of Classical-Christian
culture which Schumacher defends is that man "could create order where there
is disorder. That [conviction, so prominent in the Dark Ages] would 'educate'
him, in the sense of leading him out of the darkness of his metaphysical confusion" (pp. 95-6).[1]

The clearest aspect of Schumacher's philosophy is his defense of metaphysics. His meaning of "classical" includes the belief that man inhabits a
cosmos, and traditional philosophy since the Greeks created an "orderly system
of ideas" of "the world as a comprehensive order within which a place is assigned to him" (p. 85). This is Greek philosophy on its theistic side blended
with the Hebrew idea of God the Creator, who formed man in His own image. That
is the "Christian" element. The cosmos into which man is put is to an extent
lawful and predictable, but also subject to chance. Thus man's high calling is
to use the opportunities of freedom to be, in his own unique way, creative
(pp. 224-9).

Man's life has been rendered meaningless, according to this interpretation, by the loss of the traditional concepts of order. Schumacher refers to
several forms of philosophy that define "order" in a negative way. One maintains that the world is a "chaos," that is, "a mass of unrelated phenomena,"
(p. 84) and evidently to be unrelated is also to be meaningless. Another form
ascribes interrelationships as are found in the world to pure chance—"order"
here apparently meaning design. Again, the meaninglessness of life is conveyed
through the complaints of Kierkegaard and the despair of Bertrand Russell (pp.
85-6). But the nineteenth century which by a denial of objective metaphysical
order often left only sheer mechanical order of nature did promote the idea of
evolution, "that higher forms continually develop out of lower forms." In this
regard Schumacher's analysis is particularly good on the presuppositions of
"educated" people today:

1.   There is the idea of evolution—that higher forms continually develop
      out of lower forms, as a kind of natural and automatic process. The

last hundred years or so have seen the systematic application of this idea to all aspects of reality without exception.

2. There is the idea of competition, natural selection and the survival of the fittest, which purports to explain the natural and automatic process of evolution and development.

3. There is the idea that all the higher manifestations of human life, such as religion, philosophy, art, etc.--what Marx calls "the phantasmagorias in the brains of men"--are nothing but "necessary supplements of the material life process," a superstructure erected to disguise and promote economic interests, the whole of human history being the history of class struggles.

4. In competition, one might think, with the Marxist interpretation of all higher manifestations of human life, there is, fourthly, the Freudian interpretation which reduces them to the dark stirrings of a subconscious mind and explains them mainly as the results of unfulfilled incest-wishes during childhood and early adolescence.

5. There is the general idea of relativism, denying all absolutes, dissolving all norms and standards, leading to the total undermining of the idea of truth in pragmatism, and affecting even mathematics, which has been defined by Bertrand Russell as "the subject in which we never know what we are talking about, or whether what we say is true."

6. Finally there is the triumphant idea of positivism, that valid knowledge can be attained only through the methods of the natural sciences and hence that no knowledge is genuine unless it is based on generally observable facts. Positivism, in other words, is solely interested in "know-how" and denies the possibility of objective knowledge about meaning mnd purpose of any kind (pp. 88-9).

What is valuable about this statement is that it attacks several contradictions of the modern world view:

First, it seems to be that philosophy in the name of science has rejected metaphysics, while actually it is a metaphysics, but "a bad, vicious, life-destroying type" (p. 92).

Second, while placing the highest value on knowledge, it ends denying that we know anything and that anything has value--turning out to be a "blind and unreasonable faith" (p. 93).

Third, the evolutionary order is based on a distinction between "higher" and "lower." Yet "higher manifestations ... are [said to be] nothing but" the lower, or are reduced to the lower (p. 88). Hence the very definition of evolutionary order becomes absurd. Such a *reductio ad absurdum* of the modern world view offers then, two alternatives: live absurdly or recover our ancient and medieval orientation, which like the oriental view, is metaphysical.

The claim to know that one metaphysical system is false and another true is indeed difficult to make. This can be no judgment of any particular science because the sciences are said to deal only with "the world of facts." There is another approach, that of "metaphysical awareness," which gives us what is "true to reality" (p. 94). Schumacher spends no time defending this other kind of knowledge, and leaves us almost without a clue as to whether it be Pascal's "reason of the heart," or Polyani's "personal knowledge," or Hegel's "reason," or Whitehead's "intuition." A philosopher might have discoursed at length, but he could hardly have been more clear in stating that an adequate metaphysics must be coherent and applicable. Tested logically, it must be without contradictions and provide the framework within which, in principle, all problems can be solved. In short, an adequate metaphysics must be complete and leave nothing out. No professional metaphysician could be more eloquent than Schumacher in stressing that metaphysics, that is, good metaphysics, is the basis of civilization and education. "Education cannot help us so long as it accords no place to metaphysics" (p. 93).

As the ancient philosophies declined, Greco-Roman civilization declined. This is offered from R. G. Collingwood as historical knowledge, and Schumacher's parallelism is that as modern philosophy declines, so modern civilization declines. As Christian philosophy rescued civilization in the Dark Ages, so apparently will a philosophy that is in parts of the world Christian, in other parts Hindu, and in other parts Buddhist. The roles to be played by Judaism mnd Islam are not clear, and the relationship between the world religions is beyond the scope of this work. But we are left in no doubt that the good metaphysics like Gandhi's is one of "soul" and "living faith in the God of Love" (p. 39).

Schumacher does find "certain basic truths about man and his world" in the Christian Gospel restating the beatitudes thus: "We are poor, not demigods; We have plenty to be sorrowful about, and are not emerging into a golden age; We need a gentle approach, a non-violent spirit, and *small is beauti-*

ful..." (p. 157, emphasis added). This is the moral faith he professes as an alternative to materialism (p. 147). But the ethics is not, as in Schweitzer's reconstruction, divorced from metaphysics but rather conjoined with metaphysics.

Schumacher defines his ideal as that of the "whole man," one who is in touch with his center, and this center, like the sun whose rays emanate everywhere, is "an orderly system of ideas about himself and the world which can regulate the direction of his various strivings" (pp. 94-5). Possessing these most basic convictions man can "create order where there is disorder" (p. 96).

We have already seen that the order Schumacher refers to is a way of relating things and thereby giving them meaning; order also does not spring from chance but is purposeful and presumably intended by a cosmic orderer. Causal relations are not mere predictable mechanical regularities but aims at goals. Man has multiform capacities, and among these is the grasp on the underlying order which is a moral order.

Schumacher's philosophy is a revival of what Lovejoy called *The Great Chain of Being*. Whereas Lovejoy concluded that the concept died in the eighteenth century and was replaced by the concept of evolutionary order, Schumacher's reading of history is that although hierarchical order was almost killed in the nineteenth century, we have now discovered that we cannot live without it.

> Hierarchical order is an indispensable instrument of understanding. Without the recognition of 'Levels of Being' or 'Grades of Significance' we cannot make the world intelligible to ourselves nor have we the slightest possibility to define our own position, the position of man, in the scheme of the universe. It is only when we can see the world as a ladder, and when we can see man's position on the ladder, that we can recognize a meaningful task for man's life on earth. Maybe it is man's task—or simply, if you like, man's happiness—to attain a higher degree of realization of his potentialities, a higher level of being or 'grade of significance' than that which comes to him 'naturally': we cannot even study this possibility except by recognizing the existence of a hierarchical structure.

This hierarchy is an ontological hierarchy, and it is not mythical man who has imagined and imposed it, but rather philosophical man who has discovered the level of being in reality. Aristotle is invoked to clarify the priority of being to knowing, which is indeed what is called "realism," and the author seems to continue a kind of Christian Aristotelianism, frequently referring to St. Thomas Aquinas (p. 97, etc.). It is a Christian Aristotelianism that combines with it, as did St. Thomas following St. Augustine, the distinctive Platonic stress on "beauty, goodness, and truth," but coupled with love that marks the level beyond man. This is "the power of love" and may be identical with love itself or what is elsewhere called "the God of Love," but the lay philosopher is not concerned with whether universals are really real apart from the real actualities that exemplify these universals.

This theory of hierarchy is not concerned with how many levels there are, or with what the relation "higher than" means in its ordering. It may presuppose the familiar medieval steps: rocks that are, plants that live, animals that sense, and men that understand, and that each successive level includes the lower levels, such that "higher than" means "more inclusive than," with each kind of differentia specifying a level.

Schumacher has a mission much more interesting than historical or systematic philosophy. He defends the necessity of hierarchical thought because, on a given lower level, there are no solutions in terms of that level alone. "The true problems of living--in politics, economics, education, marriage, etc.-- are always problems of overcoming or reconciling opposites. They are divergent problems and have no solution in the ordinary sense of the word. They demand of man not merely the employment of his reasoning powers but the commitment of his whole personality." Among the non-solutions to which Schumacher must be referring are the economics of production and consumption which misses the human dimensions of work and enjoyment, or perhaps the attempts of high energy technology to impose its engineers on the rural poor of the Third World, etc.

This is hardly the same kind of speculative metaphysics as that of Pseudo-Dionysius with its ninefold hierarchy of angels. There is a higher world in the sense of the ideals which draw man towards his fulfillment. Man is inwardly driven towards this higher world, but although Schumacher despises nineteenth century ideas, in one respect, his reconstruction of metaphysics is precisely that of those liberals like Albrecht Ritschl who took theology to be an orientation towards value. The hierarchical scale is a value scale where enjoyment takes precedence over consumption and creative work over production. Should anyone doubt that such hierarchical thought was present in the nineteenth century he may consult Nietzsche's strong sense of regarding the noble far superior to the base, and observe its influence (of this kind of value hierarchicalism) as systematically worked out in Nikolai Hartmann.

The above critique of the weaknesses of the evolutionary model of order ignores the possibility of non-reductive analysis for there might very well be the emergence of higher levels that cannot be explained fully in the categories of the lower levels. It is puzzling that Schumacher fails to show the possibility of combining an evolutionary order with an hierarchical one, which is precisely what Teilhard de Chardin accomplished (p. 303. Schumacher participated in a conference of the Teilhard Centre for the Future of Man and must be acquainted with *The Phenomenon of Man*).

An explanation of this puzzle about hierarchical thought might be that ecological thought has turned against the common definition of "higher than" in terms of "more powerful than." So John Black criticizes the modern Cartesian conception of man's high estate. In *The Dominion of Man* he rejects the conception that only man, because of his intelligence and freedom, has dignity, and that in his power over the lower animals there are no limits of moral restraint. Clearly the "higher" status of man must be shown by his responsibility to and concern for lower forms. The meaning Schumacher draws from the first and second chapters of Genesis is this:

> Man, the highest of his creatures, was given dominion;
> not the right to tyrannise, to ruin and exterminate. It
> is no use talking about the dignity of man without ac-
> cepting that *noblesse oblige*. For man to put himself into
> a wrongful relationship with animals, particularly those
> long domesticated by him, has always, in all traditions,
> been considered a horrible and infinitely dangerous thing
> to do. (p. 108)

What is clear here is trust in the ancient traditions and distrust of modernity. The reason for that rejection of modernity is clear also; it is reductionistic: that animals are *"nothing but* utilities" and man is *"nothing but* a naked ape or even an accidental collection of atoms" (*Ibid.*). The author documents in a general way the hierarchical responsibility of the higher for the lower, presumably on the ground that animals, even without intelligence to the human degree, have life and sentience and are, therefore, close to us. Whatever difference exists should intensify rather than diminish our concern. Schumacher might well have quoted St. Francis of Assisi or Albert Schweitzer, but perhaps they are too obvious and perhaps too extreme, hence he shrewdly refers to *The Proverbs* of Solomon and quotes St. Thomas Aquinas. But the effective statement is Buddhist: "It is because man is so much higher than the animals that he can and must observe towards animals the very greatest care, feel for them the very greatest compassion, be good to them in every way he can."[2]

Medieval thinkers made the distinction between the hierarchy of power and that of ministry. It is the distinction between the master-slave hierarchy and that between the minister and the ministered-to. In the latter tradition the pope was called the servant of the servants of God (*servus servorum Dei*). The Franciscan interpretation of hierarchy clearly exalts the most humble, and the greatest love is suffering love.

The common modern bourgeois liberal thinks that if he rejects feudalism and the hierarchy of class and power and wealth, then the only conceivable alternative is egalitarianism. Liberal philosophers like John Dewey have poured contempt on the whole ideal of hierarchy as ensuring leisure for the idle rich and misery for the slaving poor. But in Schumacher's new order all enjoy work, and not to work is the greatest social curse. There are, however, degrees of freedom and creativity and those who demonstrate the maximum degree, although a tiny minority, must bear the heaviest burdens of social innovation (p. 231).

The "new order," as I called it, is clearly not the structure in which freedom is reserved for those in the top echelons of an organization. For Schumacher, just as much as for an egalitarian, the bureaucratic model is "degrading." "From the factory dead matter goes out improved, whereas men there are corrupted and degraded" (p. 150). Perhaps this is what seems to the author of the Introduction, Theodore Roszak, to belong to the tradition of "anarchism" (p. 4). There is indeed a protest against orderliness: "orderliness, as such, is static and lifeless; so there must be plenty of elbow room and scope for breaking through the established order, to do the things never done before, never anticipated by the guardians of orderliness, the new, unpredicted and unpredictable outcome of a man's creative idea."

If it is "anarchism," then it is not the exaltation of sheer freedom from all structure, but rather the bipolar model espoused by Alfred N. Whitehead and continued by his successor in this tradition, Charles Hartshorne, that is, to defend only that order which is balanced by change and creativity. This metaphysics applied to economic structure and tested in the experience of the Coal Board of Great Britain comes with particular eloquence and pragmatic warrant:

> ... Any organisation has to strive continuously for the orderliness of *order* and the disorderliness of creative *freedom*.... The specific danger inherent in large-scale

> organisation is that its natural bias and tendency favour
> order, at the expense of creative freedom. (p. 243)

The larger the organization the more the tendency towards centralization
and the power of the executive and accountant grow. But this is deadening and
stifling if not balanced by decentralization and if encouragement be not given
to "the man of creative freedom [who] is the *entrepreneur*" (*Ibid.*). The intelligence of the administrator must be balanced by the intuition of the entrepreneur (*Ibid.*).

The old model of hierarchical organization is the pyramid. Schumacher has
a new metaphor that stresses the far more dynamic and organic structure in
which the activity of each agent participates in the movement of the whole:

> The structure of the organisation can then be symbolised
> by a man holding a large number of balloons in his hand.
> Each of the balloons has its own buoyancy and lift, and
> the man himself does not lord it over the balloons, but
> stands beneath them, yet holding all the strings firmly
> in his hand. Every balloon is not only an administrative
> but also an *entrepreneurial* unit. (p. 245)

This new model will look untidy compared with the "clear-cut logic of a mono-
lith." Schumacher scorns the latter as "a Christmas tree with a star at the
top and a lot of nuts and other useful things underneath" (*Ibid.*).

One might suppose that since Schumacher professes Christianity and defends tradition that his concept of hierarchy is the Neo-Platonic model of the
dependence of all lower levels on the higher and ultimately on the One, whence
all has come, as rays from the sun. Schumacher does use the metaphor of finding a center, but the theology of the dominant tradition of the omnipotent and
ommiscient Creator is not and could not be his central belief. Only a few
clues to the revised doctrine of non-omnipotence and non-omniscience are
present in this work. One of the best passages contains these maxims:

> Neither the soft method of government by exhortation nor
> the tough method of government by instruction meets the
> requirements of the case. What is required is something
> in between, a *middle axiom*, an order from above which is
> yet not quite an order. (pp. 251-2)

Schumacher puts the notion of the ideal government in both a theological and a
metaphysical context (pp. 224-5, 250). In the theological context, that of
Creator in the model of Judaism, Islam, and Christianity,

> He reasoned with Himself...: 'If I make everything pre-
> dictable, these human beings, whom I have endowed with
> pretty good brains, will undoubtedly learn to predict
> everything, and they will thereupon have no motive to do

anything at all, because they will recognise that the future is totally determined and cannot be influenced by any human action. On the other hand if I make everything unpredictable, they will gradually discover that there is no rational basis for any decision whatsoever and, as in the first case, they will thereupon have no motive to do anything at all. Neither scheme would make sense. I must therefore create a mixture of the two. They will then, amongst many other things, have the very important task of finding out which is which. (pp. 224-5)

The same deliberate pattern of both-and rather than either-or marks the philosophical statement of the same idea. It might seem a contradiction to have the idea of order-disorder, "the-one-and-the-other-at-the-same-time" (p. 243). "... All real human problems arise from the antinomy of order and freedom. Antinomy means a contradiction between two laws; a conflict of authority; opposition between laws or principles that appear to be founded equally in reason" (p. 250). Apparently this is the most Kantian statement from Schumacher, followed immediately by the most Hegelian expression. Despite his blanket rejection, this is pointed out as yet another example of his thought remaining in nineteenth century patterns, even though the *coincidentia oppositorum* has deep roots in Nicholas of Cusa and Chinese thoughts of yang-yin.

Excellent! This is real life, full of antinomies and bigger than logic. Without order, planning, predictability, central control, accountancy, instructions to the underlings, obedience, discipline--without these, nothing fruitful can happen, because everything disintegrates. And yet--without the magnanimity of disorder, the happy abandon, the entrepreneurship venturing into the unknown and incalculable, without the risk and the gamble, the creative imagination, rushing in where bureaucratic angels fear to tread--without this, life is a mockery and a disgrace. (pp. 250-1)

However we may draw up our exclusive categories, reality is not so simple. Schumacher the metaphysician opposes the actual examples of combining freedom with planning in ways that give the lie to ideological concepts. (p. 284) Although this system of fundamental ideas is not offered as empirically verified, apparently the alternatives, exclusive determinism or exclusive indeterminism, could find counter-instances which disconfirm them. While there may always be theory other than the speculative and practical alternative, a person may still have enough certainty to affirm one system as relatively more adequate and more practical. What Schumacher is doing, on his own terms, is stating "certain ascertainable metaphysical laws" (p. 223).

A positivist might well have held his peace until this late point in the book and in my estimation of its coherence, here he might challenge the author with the question: What do you think are examples of such fundamental laws belonging to no particular empirical science? I believe there are several which are stated more or less explicitly, and that they are more general principles of order than that of hierarchy. These are:

1. that whatever is, has order;
2. that there are opposites such as order and disorder, and these do not rule one another out as contradictory;
3. that there are degrees of predictability and unpredictability and this situation permits creative freedom;
4. that existence and value depend upon the right balance between opposites;
5. that excess spells loss of value and, if carried too far or too long, recovery of the pendular opposite is impossible and the creature perishes.

1. Schumacher could argue that the presupposition of every science and indeed of all scholarship or inquiry is that whatever we study has some pattern, and in some cases falls into lawlike regularity. Thus, far from displacing metaphysics, every science depends upon and confirms metaphysics. This principle also is a principle of value and action, and only metaphysics can do justice to these areas because science's claim to factual objectivity and purely theoretical status has excluded value and action.

2. That there are opposites together is amply evidenced above with regard to the antinomy of freedom and order in human organizations, but this is true also of personality, and should be true also of animals, if we deny a sharp dualism or break between levels in the hierarchy where we find human on one "level" and animal on another "level": the model should be an inclined slope rather than stairs or a ladder.

3. In regard to the degrees of predictability and unpredictability, it seems to me that Schumacher has failed to acheive coherence with the rest of his system. He has failed because, in spite of his doctrine of opposites--the principle of bipolarity--he has adopted the stance of exclusive polarity. Thus, he says not both active and passive, but either active ("within my control") or passive ("outside my control"). Moreover, rather than using the present to mediate between the past and the future, he has set up the two

modes of time as a strict and unmediated dualism. Also, are happenings exclusively "acts" and "events"? In the interest of preserving for man acts in the future, which are within human control, Schumacher follows the common "free will" stance of limiting freedom to man and handing over the sub-human to predictable lawfulness. Hence, he has continued the dualism of limiting individuality to the human and relegating the whole of the sub-human to the non-individual or the typical. Here Schumacher restates commonsense modern philosophy which is as untenable as the nineteenth century system he is out to refute (pp. 226-31).

4. The system could be developed on the psychological and aesthetic side. It is too one-sided in being social-political-economic and ethical. But the principle is exemplified well in Schumacher's own appeal to the heart as well as to the head. It could be developed with illustrations from the arts to show that unity without variety is boring but variety without unity is confusing. Value depends, as the system often claims, on the correct balance.

5. The profundity of *Small is Beautiful* is to be based, as all ecological thought, on the maintenance of balance. The practical thrust is to point out the harm of emphasis on capital-intensive and labor-economical technology, which for underdeveloped economies is destructive rather than constructive. Few are the economists who see in their observations a metaphysical principle. But life depends on the right balance, and capital and labor is but one illustration. "... Spurious solutions, by way of a clever formula, are always being put forward; but they never work for long, because they invariably neglect one of the two opposites and thus lose the very quality of human life" (p. 99). There are countless other examples: the right balance between work and leisure (pp. 148-9), between industry and agriculture (p. 111), between looking forward and looking backward" (p. 155), the right size between too big ("giantism") and too small ("dwarfism") (p. 159, etc.). The ancient principle of Greek philosophy, nothing too much, runs through the wisdom of *Small is Beautiful*. "Neither of those extremes is desirable, and a middle way has to be found" (p. 184).

Small is Beautiful is a most promising sketch of a philosophy; it prepared the way for *A Guide for the Perplexed*[3] which carries further this reaffirmation of the Great Chain of Being in our post-modern age.

370

NOTES

The author expresses deep thanks to Emory University for allowing a year's leave of absence and to the Woodrow Wilson International Center for Scholars at the Smithsonian Institution where he conducted research, 1970-71. The author expresses deep thanks to the Emory Research Committee and to the American Philosophical Society of Philadelphia.

[1] All references by page in text are to E. F. Schumacher's *Small is Beautiful* (New York: Harper and Row, 1974).

[2] From H. Fielding Hall, *The Soul of a People* (London: Macmillan and Co., 1920).

[3] E. F. Schumacher, *A Guide for the Perplexed* (New York: Harper and Row, 1979).

JOHN BORELLI

VIJÑĀNABHIKSU: INDIAN THOUGHT AND
THE GREAT CHAIN OF BEING

INTRODUCTION

India provides a microcosm for the history of ideas. During her grand and multifarious scholastic age, a wealth of thought systems were constructed, key ideas were debated exhaustively, and certain hermeneutical stances in regard to her sacred literature were reiterated in higher syntheses through a complex network of interpretive influences and personal relationships. Specifically, the most significant Indian contribution to the history of ideas is the triple classification, which emerged during this period, of her various schools of thought. These are three large metaphysical models for describing the relationship between God and the world: identity, difference, and difference-in-identity.[1]

The two subjects of this relationship may vary, but the general idea is that what is ultimate, be it God, *nirvāna*, or Brahman, and what is related to ordinary experience, the world as a whole, the individual person experiencing, or a simple fact of experience, are completely identical, completely different, or in some way both identical and different. So too, the descriptions of the relationship may be formulated in other ways. For example, for some the tripartite division may be expressed better as unity, difference, and unity and difference.[2] Even so, such a threefold classification is a way to read the development of Indian schools of thought, and I see nothing presently to contradict it.

Throughout *The Great Chain of Being*, Arthur Lovejoy refers to the specific body of Hindu Scriptures known as the *Upanisads* and to a general philosophical and theological interpretation of those texts associated with the Vedānta theologian Śaṅkara. That position is called "Nondual Vedānta" and represents an excellent example of the identity metaphysical framework. Lovejoy also calls attention to Buddhism, which in its classical and scholastic Indian forms espoused ultimately an identity doctrine. What I hope will be clear at the conclusion of this paper is that Nondual Vedānta, which teaches that everything of our experience is absorbed into a featureless identity with Brahman, and that the Buddhist denial of everything of this world as illusory

do not include the most significant, much less the major, statements on the
individual's relationship to the world as a whole and to what is ultimate.

My purpose in writing about *The Great Chain of Being* after fifty years is
twofold: 1) to address those remarks by Lovejoy on Vedānta and Buddhism and 2)
to make a case for India. What is apparent to me from reading Lovejoy is that
he confused the teachings of Hinduism and Buddhism, like the Nondualists who
were accused of being secret Buddhists by other Vedānta theologians,[3] but the
mistake was not entirely Lovejoy's fault.

Fifty years ago, a second phase of American and Indian cultural and
intellectual relations was drawing to a close. In the first phase, from Emerson's time to the end of the nineteenth century, American scholars knew about
India from the precious little available in translation. From the late nineteenth century to the end of World War II Indological Studies underwent a
growth phase, and Indian teachers, leaders, and intellectuals visited America.
The kind of Hinduism which was taught by them was a reformed Hinduism. A re-
vivalist form of Nondual Vedānta, for some unknown reason, became the philosophical framework for the reform doctrines. Hence it is understandable that
Lovejoy, like nearly all Americans up to his time who knew anything about
India, believed that Nondual Vedānta was and had always been the Hindu philosophical and theological statement.

In any case, what was expounded by the overwhelming majority of Vedānta
theologians was *not* an identity doctrine of everything with Brahman and an
associated doctrine that everything belonging to the experience of this world
is ultimately illusory. Most Vedānta theologians, interpreting the *Upaniṣads*
which contain two sets of statements in this regard, one teaching that Brahman
and the soul are identical and another set proclaiming the two distinct, formulated theological positions on the model of difference-in-identity. Vijñānabhikṣu, as a late Vedānta theologian (fl. ca. 1575), is important to the
discussion for two reasons: 1) he resumed the central doctrines of the *Vedānta
Sūtras* and 2) he synthesized his Vedānta theology with other Indian schools.
In his commentary on the *Vedānta Sūtras*, also known as the *Brahma Sūtras*,
Vijñānabhikṣu reiterated the teachings of identity as nonseparation, eternal
difference, temporary separation, and the part doctrine, to name only a few.
As an ecumenical theologian, he incorporated the methaphysical scheme of dualistic Sāṅkhya, based on the emanations from two first principles, matter and
spirit, and the spiritual methods of Yoga, which trace the return of the Sāṅk-

hya principles back to the isolation of spirit. All three schools, Vedānta,
Sāṅkhya, and Yoga, in their principal doctrines contain no idea of illusion.
To paraphrase Lovejoy, they seem to have this world on their hands as an unac-
countable mystery, a thing unsatisfying, unintelligible, and evil, which seemingly ought not to be, yet somehow undeniably is.[4]

Had Lovejoy been aware of the principal orientation in the Vedānta tradition, the theologians of which interpreted the whole of Hindu Scriptures,
including the *Upaniṣads*, then perhaps he would have had further insight into
that "extraordinary triumph of self-contradiction" at the heart of the conception of the chain of being. Difference-in-Identity Vedānta was in part the
expression of the coincidence of opposites, and hence in comparison with Lovejoy's topic it represents a similar syncretism: "The notion of the *coincidentia oppositorum*, of the meeting of extremes in the Absolute, was an essential part of nearly all medieval theology, as it had been of Neoplatonism;
..."[5] In fact, a third position, advocated by Vedānta and situated between one
pole of absolutist kinds of world denying schools and another pole of those
systems which admit of a profound and abiding polarity at the heart of reality, is the only genuine coincidence of opposites.

LOVEJOY ON VEDĀNTA AND BUDDHISM

Most of Lovejoy's references to Vedānta and Buddhism are to provide
extreme examples of what he terms "otherworldliness"--"the belief that both
the genuinely 'real' and the truly good are radically antithetic in their essential characteristics to anything to be found in man's natural life, in the
ordinary course of human experience, however normal, however intelligent, and
however fortunate."[6] The terms "otherworldliness" and "this-worldliness" are
problematic. I do not quarrel with the suggestion that otherworldliness, in
one form or another, was the dominant official philosophy of classical medieval Europe and India, nor do I wish to contest here the several motives,
which Lovejoy lists, anyone of which can give rise to a limited otherworldly
ontology or a combination of all of them is an integral otherworldliness. What
I will address is this statement:

> But any otherworldliness, whether integral or limited,
> can, it would seem, make nothing of the fact that there
> is a 'this world' to be escaped from; least of all can it
> justify or explain the being of such a world, or that of
> any particular feature or aspect of empirical existence

which it negates. Its natural recourse, therefore, is, as
in the Vedānta, to the device of illusionism.[7]

I will grant that this is true in regard to Buddhism and that there are
some passages in the *Upaniṣads* which support such a view. The major synthesis
which initiates Vedānta as a major Indian school was Bādarāyaṇa's *Brahma
Sūtras*. These nearly 500 short aphorisms were meant to be summaries of the
principal doctrines of the whole of Scripture. From Swāmī Vivekānanda's first
trip to America in 1892 to the present, we have been under a heavy barrage of
a kind of Hinduism that is based extensively on the Nondualist interpretation
of Bādarāyaṇa's aphorisms, but the *Brahma Sūtras* is a summary of not just the
nondual Scriptures. It was not until Surendranath Dasgupta had written and
published the third volume of his *A History of Indian Philosophy* that European
and American scholars were given less of a religious and more of an historical
and academic analysis of Indian thought.

Writing in 1933, Dasgupta asserted: "It seems to me pretty certain, as I
shall show elsewhere, that Bādarāyaṇa's philosophy was some kind of Bhedā-
bhedavāda or a theory of transcendence and immanence of Brahman."[8] *Bhedābheda*
is the Sanskrit term I translate as "Difference-in-Identity," over and against
Advaita or Nondualism which is a pure identity position, and *vāda* means theory
or school. This promise of further elucidation was made in his book *Indian
Idealism*, and in 1940 he wrote this in the third volume of his history: "...it
may be believed that the views of the Vedānta, as found in the Purāṇas and the
Bhagavad-gītā, present, at least in a general manner, the oldest outlook of
the philosophy of the Upaniṣads and the *Brahma-sūtra*."[9]

Very few scholars of Hinduism have attempted lengthy descriptions of
Difference-in-Identity. Dasgupta is one of the scarce exceptions, and in his
chapter on Vijñānabhikṣu in that famous third volume he included this definition:

> Bhikṣu's philosophy is a type of *bhedā-bheda* which has
> shown itself in various forms in Bharprapañca, Bhāskara,
> Rāmānuja, Nimbārka, and others. The general viewpoint of
> this *bhedā-bheda* philosophy is that it believes in the
> reality of the universe as well as its spirituality, the
> distinctness of the individual souls as well as in their
> being centers of the manifestation of God, moral freedom
> and responsibility as well as a spiritual determinism, a
> personal God as well as an impersonal reality, the ulti-
> mate spirit in which matter and pre-matter are dissolved
> into spirituality, an immanent teleology pervading
> through matter and souls both in their origin and mutual

intercourse as well as in the holiness of the divine
will, omnipotence and omniscience in the superior value
of knowledge as well as of love, in the compulsoriness of
moral and social duties as well as in their abnega-
tion.[10]

For these various Vedānta theologians, their followers, and the others not
mentioned the world is very much real and has to be reconciled in some way
with the fact that it originates from the pure spiritual nature of Brahman.
Because they also accepted the idea that the world is in some way or another a
transformation of Brahman, they did not resort to a position of the complete
difference between God and creation. Furthermore, in regard to the individual
soul which shares in the spiritual nature of Brahman they had to posit salvation doctrines which respected their substantial unity and individual differences. Most important to us here, they did not resort to saying that these
individual differences and creation as a whole exist simply as illusions of
the souls in bondage.

This observation of mine holds the same for the remainder of Lovejoy's
references to Vedānta.[11] I wish now to summarize one type of Difference-in-
Identity Vedānta theology.

VIJÑĀNABHIKṢU'S NONSEPARATE NONDUALISM

The name Vijñānabhikṣu gave to his position should not be misleading
because he interpreted according to the difference-in-identity model and for-
midably demonstrated the Scriptural, traditional, and sūtra foundation for
it.[12] He resolved the classical problem between the identity set and the difference set of Scriptures into a theology of nonseparation and eternal distinction. Indeed, he gave one of the most discerning reiterations of the principal orientation in Hindu theology. Two features of Bhikṣu's theology will be
discussed here: 1) Brahman as the supporting cause and 2) the relationships
between Brahman and the soul and between Brahman and the world. Much of the
material in this study is from his commentary on *Brahma Sūtras* 1.1.2: "[Brah-
man is that] FROM WHICH THE ORIGIN AND SO FORTH [existence, development,
maturation, deterioration, and destruction] of this [world proceeds]." I
translated Bhikṣu's 40 page commentary on this aphorism in my dissertation.[13]

Vijñānabhikṣu designated Brahman as the supporting cause of this world.
The world has a conscious aspect and an unconscious aspect which become manifest through the material cause. The supporting cause upholds the material

cause according to Bhikṣu's definition: "The supporting cause is that one from which the material cause is not separate and by which the latter, being supported, is transformed into the mode of an effect."[14] Brahman upholds the material cause and anything derived from it simply by being its witness.

Brahman is unmodifiable pure consciousness, but it is also identical with the material cause through a relationship of nonseparation. The nonseparation of effects from their cause applies to an unmodifiable cause while the nonseparation of constituents defines the kind of nonseparation applicable to a modifiable cause. Therefore, Brahman shares a function with its effect, the material cause, and is nonseparate from it.

Vijñanabhikṣu has most often been recognized as a commentator and expositor of the Sāṅkhya and Yoga systems which in their classical forms were difference systems. The general metaphysical scheme of these two schools begins with two first principles, matter and spirit. Matter is the root cause of all things while spirit is the passive witness of matter's unfolding. The emanation process begins when the two first principles come into proximity, and the remaining principles of being unfold from matter in a succinct order of emanations. This metaphysics is implicit to some extent in Bhikṣu's theology.

In his commentary on the *Brahma Sūtras*, Vijñanabhikṣu made it clear that the causal function of matter and spirit is defined through matter which is the material cause; however, he rejected matter's independent causality which is a major feature of atheistic Sāṅkhya. In its place he maintained that the two principles are joined through the efficient causality of Brahman. Hence, matter and spirit are in some sense different from Brahman.

There are several implications in Bhikṣu's understanding of Brahman. In the first place, Brahman is the universal cause, being the basis for material and efficient causality, and this omnifarious causality is another definition of Brahman. Secondly, Brahman is partless in respect to constituent parts in its precausal condition as the supporting cause even though it is "the one which is endowed with all energies latent within itself--such as, matter and spirit."[15] In this state, before the separation of effects, Brahman is indifferent to the distinction between constituent and nonconstituent causes. Also, since the things of experience result from the material cause, Brahman is not directly responsible for evils and imperfections. These are not direct transformations of Brahman. Finally, by the mere fact that Brahman is both the supporting cause and the efficient cause, the term "Brahman" has a general and a specific meaning.

The principal meaning of the term "Brahman" is God in the ultimate sense. When God brings matter and spirit into contact for the manifestation of the world, he is not entirely indentical with the supporting cause, but rather he is the demiurge who is modified by the essential power of Brahman. This is the lower Brahman which is the secondary and more specific use of the term: "Besides, Brahman has a secondary meaning, implied in such terms as eternal will and so on and in majesty conditioned by the energy named his power."[16] The lower Brahman is an effect that is nondistinct from the supporting cause like matter and spirit in the unmanifest condition.

There are two basic relationships which distinguish two levels of Vijñanabhiksu's theology. On one level there is the substantial identity of Brahman and souls, and on a second level Brahman as the supporting cause has a special relationship with the spiritual and material aspects of the world.

The material cause is in some way identical with Brahman the supporting cause, which means that matter and spirit are nonseparate from Brahman. Vijñanabhiksu defined nonseparation in this way: "Nonseparation, like support, is defined as an intrinsic relation and is constituted of total fusion."[17] Nonseparation, therefore, involves an essential identity while separation is a qualitative difference:

> Separation is qualitative difference. Nonseparation can
> be understood as the absence of qualitative difference--
> in spite of the difference between unmanifested quali-
> ties. Still another way of describing nonseparation is as
> an essential relationship or as when something is sup-
> ported.[18]

In the unmanifest state of the world, matter and spirit are constituent energies latent in the essential power of Brahman. In the manifest condition matter, spirit, and time are distinguished and the world takes shape through them. Brahman's universal causality, therefore, is due to its essence being composed of the various energies.

A relationship of nonseparation does not just imply a kind of identity among the entities in relation because it would suffice to state simply that they are identical. In his remarks about the self, Vijñanabhiksu made it clear that the support-supported relation not only implies an essential identity but also an intrinsic difference. When there is substantial identity through a relation of nonseparation, then a relationship of whole and parts is implicit

there too. Hence when one talks about the self, the spiritual nature is the
substance and the various spirits are the parts, or when there is reference to
being, reality is the substance and beings are the parts. Bhikṣu provides
these definitions:

> A part may be defined as the correlative of nonseparation
> in the context of homogeneity; its correspondent is the
> whole. In whatever sense one may wish to describe
> partitioning, in that same sense homogeneity must be
> understood.[19]

The orthodox teaching of Vedānta in regard to Brahman as the supreme self
and the individual soul is the part doctrine, for example, *Brahma Sūtras*
2.3.43: "A part on account of a declaration of difference; furthermore, some
also record [Brahman] to be of the nature of slaves and fishermen." Nonseparation was explicitly taught in those aphorisms too as in 4.2.16, "Nonseparation
according to the statements [of Scripture]," and in 4.4.4, "By nonseparation
because that is seen."

Bhikṣu believed that the part doctrine best explained the identity and
difference between Brahman and souls:

> Therefore the identity and difference between God and
> souls, which is composed of separation and nonseparation,
> is established through the relationship between a whole
> and its parts. Only nonseparation, because it is coinci-
> dent, essential, and eternal, is true at the beginning
> and at the end. Separation, on the other hand, in the
> middle through a limitation of parts is temporary and of
> a purely nominal existence. This is the distinction.[20]

What distinguishes the various difference-in-identity theologians is
their notions of difference, and Vijñānbhikṣu postulated two kinds of difference. In the manifest state of the cosmic process all things become separate
through their various qualities, but this separating difference is only temporary. There is another kind of difference which is eternal and is implicit
in the notion of nonseparation—mutual exclusiveness: "In respect to wind and
its components and fire and its sparks, difference is described as the mutual
exclusivenss between a whole and its components."[21] Bhikṣu went on to say that
the mutual exclusiveness between Brahman and the soul is eternal. Later still,
in his commentary on the *Sāṅkhya Sūtras* 1.151, he defined difference as mutual
exclusiveness without reference to separation: "I, however, think that identity is defined as nonseparation and difference as mutual exclusiveness."[22]

For Vijñānabhikṣu, as well as most other Vedānta theologians, Sāṅkhya
teachers, Yoga masters, sages of the *Upaniṣads*, and the author of the *Bhagavad*

Gītā, the world was very much real and on their hands. They did not resort to illusion but explained things either as resulting from Brahman, which is some kind of differenced unity, or from two first principles, matter and spirit. I hope my point is well-taken: all three possibilities were developed in India. India is a great resource area for our study because under a triple scheme of identity, difference, and difference-in-identity we can find many different possibilities.

CONCLUSION

In the first place, the division which I have proposed here shows the inadequacy of a scheme of "isms," for example, as suggested by B. N. K. Sharma, a well-known authority on Dualist Vedānta: "The sūtras of Bādarāyana have been subjected to a conflicting variety of interpretations representing different shades of *Pantheism, Monism,* and *Theism,* by celebrated commentators like Bhartṛprapañca, Bhāskara, Śaṅkara, Rāmānuja, and Madhva."[23] In such a vision certain theistic Vedānta theologians who formulated difference-in-identity positions would be placed with other theologians who emphasized the absolute difference between creation and the Lord of creation. The division which I propose here would not only distinguish various Vedānta theologians more adequately, but also can be applied to the whole of Indian thought. Difference includes both the theism of Madhva's Dualist Vedānta and the atheistic dualism of Sāṅkhya. Identity encompasses the Nondual Vedānta of Gaudapāda and Śaṅkara and their followers as well as certain schools of Buddhism like Mādhyamiks and Yogācāra. Difference-in-Identity has the largest number of instances ranging from Vijñānabhikṣu's personal dedication to the absolute Brahman to the devotionalism of Caitanya's Ineffable Difference-in-Identity or Abhinvagupta's Trika.

In a thought system which is dominated by the conception of absolute identity between the first principle and the individual, illusion must be introduced at some point to describe both the manifoldness and transformations of the individual, singular, particular things of experience. This is precisely what Śaṅkara does by interpreting the essential power of Brahman, which Vijñānabhikṣu believed was constituted of certain latent energies, to be an illusion making power. Also in Buddhism such ideas as the emptiness of everything or the purely ideational nature of everything are used to direct attention away from the experience of the world to that of *nirvāna.*

Dualism or difference can refer to two basic types of situations: polarity and creative opposition. The former is where there is absolute difference between God and the individual things of experience while with the second kind of difference two first principles are posited and individual things are brought into existence through their creative junction.[24]

The major theme of this study is the difference-in-identity model. I can now put together a list of general characteristics of this paradigm within Vedānta. It should be remembered that, since this is an orientation of reconciliation, there are some features which may be shared with schools under the other two orientations; however, five general features of the Vedānta theologies which I recognize as difference-in-identity positions can be identified.

First of all, identity implies differentiation, and hence difference is a quality of identity. This was clearly formulated by the theologian Bhāskara:

> Difference is a quality of identity. Identity is present
> in the ocean; it is called difference in its waves. Waves
> are not seen in rocks and so forth; they are the ocean's
> energies; and in the relationship of energy and agent are
> observed otherness and nonotherness. This is like in fire
> which has the powers to burn and to brighten .... There-
> fore everything is one and not one; neither eternally
> different nor identical.[25]

Secondly, the aspects of difference and identity coexist as a coincidence of opposites and not as a duality nor as an opposition. Vijñānabhikṣu, it may be recalled, posited that matter and spirit are nonseparate from Brahman, the supporting cause, while remaining mutually distinct. Continuing with the idea of coincidence, the third feature is that the first principle can be viewed in two ways: as cause and as effect. Again to cite Vijñānabhikṣu's way of doing this, Brahman as supporting cause is the cause of Brahman the efficient cause which is seen as the Lord acting in creation. Fourthly, it follows that causality in this orientation is defined in terms of an effect being a transformation of its cause. This is known as the *sat-kārya-vāda* doctrine of Sāṅkhya.

I must digress here for a moment to clear up a possible confusion. Somewhere in each of the difference-in-identity systems the notion of transformation is introduced. Most always this activity is associated with material causality, and it means that the world as a whole is a transformation of the root cause. In the beginning everything pre-exists in the material cause, and through various explanations is made to manifest the world out of itself. For

some of these theologians Brahman was simply the material cause and, therefore, the world in all its material and spiritual aspects is a direct transformation of it. Vijñānabhikṣu, attempting to avoid the problem of an imperfect and evil world being a direct transformation of Brahman, identified Brahman as the supporting cause from which the material cause is nonseparate. It
is then the material cause which is transformed. The clearest explanation of
transformation belonging to Brahman was given by Rāmānuja:

> This is how transformation is explained. The supreme
> Brahman is concentrated goodness, being wholly adverse to
> evil, distinguished from all beings other than itself. It
> is all-knowing, the realizer of all wishes, possessed of
> all its wishes, unlimited and sovereign bliss. Having for
> its body the entire universe of all conscious and uncon-
> scious things, which subserves its cosmic play, it is the
> soul of that body. This universe which is its body sur-
> vives as an extremely subtle unconscious reality known as
> darkness through the successive regression of matter's
> evolutes, the elements, the ego, etc. With this body of
> darkness, now arrived at an extremely subtle form, such
> that it cannot be considered as distinct, then the
> supreme Brahman attains a condition of oneness through
> the thought "may I become the world body constituted of
> the conscious and unconscious beings, distinguished as
> before by name and form," it transforms itself into this
> world body through entering one evolute of matter after
> another. This is the teaching of transformation in all
> the *Upaniṣads*.26

Finally, interpretations within the difference-in-identity orientation
are distinguished primarily through their definitions of difference. Is difference eternal or temporary and is difference intrinsic or extrinsic?
Bhāskara taught that difference is a temporary modification of Brahman since
he employed the term "attribute" to mean an external quality. Vijñānabhikṣu
stated that mutual exclusiveness is eternal, even though separation is temporary, and that there is an intrinsic differentiation within the essential
power of Brahman.

If more attention can be given to the difference-in-identity model as it
was developed in India, then certain interpretive problems of European and
American scholars in regard to their own thought traditions may be avoided. I
believe that this insight is illuminating and liberating. When Lovejoy
examined the conception of the chain of being and its associated ideas, he
discovered that two basic philosophical positions, which he terms "otherworldiness" and "this-worldliness," were never completely separated until

rather late. When he tried to describe the coincidence of otherworldiness and
this-worldliness, he was at a loss for words as the following testifies:

> It is not, indeed, that the otherworldliness of either
> Neoplatonic or Catholic philosophy was in itself less
> extreme in degree than that of the Vedānta or of other
> Indian systems. When the mind of Plotinus, or of
> Augustine, or of the Pseudo-Areopagite, or of John the
> Scot, or even of Thomas Aquinas, is turned solely upon
> that side of his doctrine, he is not less thorough-going
> than the sages of the more mystical Upanishads, or than
> Shankara, in asserting the 'otherness' of the true reali-
> ty and the only genuine good--.... The difference is mere-
> ly that the Occidental doctrine was essentially dual; it
> asserted this, but is also asserted the opposite; the
> second of the two elements was firmly incorporated in its
> substance as much by its Platonistic as by its Jewish
> sources.[27]

We must learn once and for all that there simply are not two possibilities, Monism versus Theism, and a third alternative which is a self-
contradiction. What has been called the "Pseudo-Dionysian" or the "Coincidence
of Opposites" tradition in "Occidental" thought is indeed a justifiable third
position with its own logic, its own definition, and its own sanctity from
being misinterpreted through dualistic or monistic categories. Once the integrity and distinctness of this tradition is respected, then it can be put in a
dialogue context with its Indian counterpart. What can result is not only a
better understanding of our own thought traditions but also the possibility of
higher synthesis.

NOTES

[1] I say that this classification "emerged" during a certain period because there is no one source for it; nor is there a single scholarly account of it. Surendranath Dasgupta's *A History of Indian Philosophy*, 5 vols. (Cambridge: Cambridge University Press, 1922-55; reprint ed., 1968-73), is the best overview of the development even though he does not make the tripartite division explicit.

[2] This is the terminology Ewert Cousins utilizes in his *Bonaventure and the Coincidence of Opposites*, chapter 1, published by Franciscan Herald Press. C. G. Jung in *Mysterium Coniunctionis*, The Collected Works, vol. 14 (Princeton: Princeton University Press, 1963), pp. 457-553, uses the terms "separation," "reunion," and "*unus mundus*." Mircea Eliade in *Patterns in Comparative Religion* (New York: Sheed & Ward, 1958), p. 29, presents several possibilities, one of which is sacred, profane, and hierophany. The specific Indian terms which were used by those who became aware of the similarities and dissimilarities of the various schools are: *bheda* (difference), *abheda* (nondifference or identity) and *bhedābheda* (difference-in-identity).

[3] See for example: J. A. B. van Buitenen, *Rāmānuja's Vedārthasamgrapha*, 36 Deccan College Monograph Series, 16 (Poona: Deccan College, 1956), pp. 209-210 and Vijñānabhiksu, *The Sāmkhya-Pravacana-Bhāsya or Commentary on the Exposition of the Sānkhya Philosophy*, 1.22; ed. Richard Garbe, Harvard Oriental Series, vol. 2 (Cambridge: Harvard University Press, 1943), p. 16.

[4] Arthur O. Lovejoy, *The Great Chain of Being: A Study of the History of an Idea*, the William James Lectures Delivered at Harvard University, 1933 (Cambridge: Harvard University Press, 1936), p. 31.

[5] *Ibid.*, p. 83.

[6] *Ibid.*, p. 25.

[7] *Ibid.*, p. 30.

[8] *Indian Idealism* (Cambridge: Cambridge University Press: 1933; reprint ed., 1962), p. 160.

[9] *A History of Indian Philosophy*, 3:496.

[10] *Ibid.*, 3:471-72.

[11] For example see pp. 42 & 93.

[12] Several Vedānta theologians believed that they were giving the true interpretation of Nondualism meaning that Brahman is a differenced unity. Hence Rāmānuja called his interpretation Qualified Nondualism, and Vallabha called his Pure Nondualism even though, like Vijñānabhiksu, they were presenting some kind of Difference-in-Identity.

[13] John W. Borelli, Jr., "The Theology of Vijñānabhiksu: A Translation of his Commentary on Brahma Sūtras 1.1.2 and an Exposition of his Difference-in-Identity Theology" (Ph. D. dissertation, Fordham University, 1976), pp. 24-75.

[14] Vijñānabhiksu, *Brahmasūtrabhāsyam*, edited by Mujunda Sāstrī, Chowkhamba Sanskrit Series, no. 8 (Benares: Chowkhamba, 1901), p. 32.

[15]*Ibid.*

[16]*Ibid.*, p. 61.

[17]*Ibid.*, p. 33.

[18]*Ibid.*, p. 51.

[19]*Ibid.*

[20]*Ibid.*, p. 61.

[21]*Ibid.*, p. 50.

[22]*The Sāṃkhya-Pravacana-Bhāṣya*, p. 68.

[23]*Lectures on Vedanta*, Extension Lectures Publication Series, 18 (Dharwar: Karnatak University, 1973), p. 17.

[24]Cf. Mircea Eliade, "Prolegomenon to Religious Dualism: Dyads and Polarities," *The Quest: History and Meaning in Religion* (Chicago: U. of Chicago Press, 1969), p. 173.

[25]Bhāskara, *Brahma Sūtra Bhāṣya*, 2.1.18, quoted in Dasgupta, *A History of Indian Philosophy*, 3:6, n. 2.

[26]*Bhagavad Badarayana's Brahma Sutra or Sariraka with Sri Bhashya and its Commentary named Bhashyartha Darpana by Abhinava Desika*, ed. Sri Uttamur I. Viraraghavacharya, 2 parts (Madras: Sreevathsa Press, 1963-64), i. 4. 27, 1:433.

[27]Lovejoy, p. 93.

A SELECTED BIBLIOGRAPHY ON HIERARCHY

As in Lovejoy's great work, *The Great Chain of Being*, each of our chapters contains references to the original and secondary literature. Perhaps we should have followed his example and omitted the following general selections of further sources and commentaries. Our gathering from many diverse fields reinforces Lovejoy's point that there is virtually no limit to the expression of hierarchy; and, we would add, no limit to its exploration in theory and practice of the late twentieth century. Among the bibliographical guides that continue to keep us current we would mention as the most helpful *The Philosopher's Index* of the Philosophy Documentation Center, Bowling Green, Ohio. In addition, there are numerous commercial databases in philosophy and religion, history, literature, fine arts and the sciences. These can be located by consulting the Directory of Online Databases, CUADRA Associates, annual from Santa Monica, California. Among recent writings on the history of hierarchy, the monograph which is the best guide to sources and debates about crucial issues is Edward P. Mahoney, "Metaphysical Foundations of the Hierarchy of Being According to Some Late-Medieval and Renaissance Philosophers" (this study, preeminent of a hundred since Lovejoy's book, is cited below).

We have occasionally added a comment or even a quotation, sometimes chapter number and name or pages when the reason for inclusion might seem obscure or the user might be helped in finding what he or she wants. A relatively complete and annotated bibliography would be the work of a lifetime.

Our thanks for assistance is expressed to Miss Betsey Patterson and the able reference librarians of Emory University, Marie and Eric Nitschke, Mary Ellen Templeton, David Vidor, and to research assistants, Miss Patricia Cook, Miss Anne Owens, Miss Ivia Cofresi and Miss Carolyn Alexander, the latter of Georgia State University.

Mortimer J. Adler, "Hierarchy," commencement address at the College of St. Thomas, St. Paul, Minnesota, c 1940.

_____, "The Hierarchy of Essences," *Review of Metaphysics*, Vol. VI, No. 1, September 1952, pp. 3-30.

_____ and William Gorman, ed., *A Syntopicon of Great Books of the Western World*, Encyclopaedia Britannica, Chicago, 1952, index "Hierarchy and Continuity."

Carlos E. Alchourrón and David Makinson, "Hierarchies of Regulations and Their Logic," in *New Studies in Deontic Logic: Norms, Actions, and the Foundations of Ethics*, Risto Hilpinen, ed., Reidel, Dordrecht, 1981, pp. 125-48.

Angela Ales Bello, "Le Problème de l'Être dans la Phénoménologie de Husserl," in *The Great Chain of Being and Italian Phenomenology*, Reidel, Dordrecht, 1981, pp. 41-50.

Hubert G. Alexander, "Kind and Degree," *The Language and Logic of Philosophy*, University of New Mexico Press, Albuquerque, New Mexico, 1967, revised ed. 1972, pp. 137-47.

Michael J. B. Allen, "Marsilio Ficino on Plato, the Neoplatonists and the Christian Doctrine of the Trinity," *Renaissance Quarterly*, 37, No. 4, Winter 1984, pp. 555-84.

_____, "The Absent Angel in Ficino's Philosophy," *Journal of the History of Ideas*, Vol. 36, April-June 1975, pp. 219-40.

T. F. H. Allen and Thomas B. Starr, *Hierarchy: Perspectives for Ecological Complexity*, The University of Chicago Press, Chicago, 1982.

American Anthropological Association, *Abstracts of the 84th Annual Meeting*, Washington, December 4-8, 1985, "Equality and Hierarchy in Historical Counterpoint," p. 221, and "The Anthropology of Gender Hierarchies," p. 245 and p. 260. In the zeal to correct bias towards hierarchy, the authors of these abstracts adopt a bias toward equality. The critical issue apparently was: Equality between persons is now a great issue of contrast to male superiority over female, etc. Are all hierarchical relationships bad? Are all equal relationships good?

Lorin Anderson, "Charles Bonnet's Taxonomy and Chain of Being," *Journal of the History of Ideas*, Vol. 37, January-March 1976, pp. 45-58.

Ignacio Angelelli, "La Jerarquia de Clases de Johann Caspar Sulzer (1755)," *Cuadernos de Filosofia*, Tucumán, Universidad (Instituto de Filosofia) Vol. 14, January-June 1974, pp. 90-4.

Thomas Aquinas, *Summa Theologiae*, Ia, ii, 3, the argument from degrees, on which there are many commentaries because it seems the most difficult of medieval arguments for moderns to accept.

_____, *On the Truth of the Catholic Faith, Summa Contra Gentiles*, V. J. Bourke and James F. Anderson, tr., Image Books, Doubleday, 4 volumes, Garden City, New York, 1956. On the grades of being including necessity and contingency, so "all grades of being (are) preserved." Bk. III, Pt. I, Ch. 72, p. 242.

Lawrence A. Babb, *The Divine Hierarchy: Popular Hinduism in Central India*, Columbia University Press, New York, 1975, Ch. 7, "Divine Hierarchy: The Pantheon," pp. 215–46.

Kurt Baier, *The Moral Point of View*, Cornell, Ithaca, New York, 1958, "The Hierarchy of Reasons," pp. 304ff.

J. B. Bamborough, *The Little World of Man*, Longmans, Green, London, 1952, pp. 13–20.

Bernard Barber, *Social Stratification*, Harcourt Brace, New York, 1957.

Yehoshua Bar-Hillel, "Theory of Types", *Encyclopedia of Philosophy*, Paul Edwards, ed., Macmillan, New York, 1966, Vol. 8, pp. 168–72.

Ted Bastin, "A General Property of Hierarchies," in C. H. Waddington, *Towards A Theoretical Biology*, Vol. 2, University of Edinburgh Press, Edinburgh; Aldine, Chicago, 1969, pp. 252–65.

C. A. Baylis, "Grading, Values, and Choice," *Mind*, Vol. LXVII, 1958, pp. 485–501.

Morton O. Beckner, "Organismic Biology," *Encyclopedia of Philosophy*, Paul Edwards, ed., Macmillan, New York, 1966. Vol. 5, pp. 549–55.

_____, "Reduction, Hierarchies and Organicism," in *Studies in the Philosophy of Biology*, Theodosius Grigorievich Dobzhansky and Francisco José Ayala, ed., Macmillan, London, 1974, pp. 163–77.

Stafford Beer, *The Heart of Enterprise*, Wiley and Sons, Chichester, 1979, authority and responsibility as "glue" of corporate organization, p. 335.

Y. Belaval, "Leibniz et la Chaîne des Êtres," in *Analecta Husserliana*, Angela Ales Bello, ed., Reidel, Dordrecht, 1981, pp. 59–68.

St. Roberto Francesco Romolo Bellarmino, *Jacob's Ladder. Consisting of fifteen degrees or ascents to the knowledge of God by the consideration of His creatures and attributes*, Printed for Henry Seile, London, 1638. Translation attributed to Henry Isaacson.

There is also a translation of "The Thirteenth Step" (of fifteen) by Peter W. Nash, S.J., in A. C. Pegis, *The Wisdom of Catholicism*, Michael Joseph, London, 1950, pp. 564–78. The Latin of *On the Ascent of the Mind to God* is in V. C. Roberti Bellarmini Politiani, S.J., *Opera Omnia*, L. Vivés, Paris, 1875, Vol. VIII, pp. 295b–303a.

James Benjamin, "On Symbological Hierarchies," *Philosophy and Rhetoric*, Vol. 8, Summer 1975, pp. 165–71.

Henri Bergson, *Creative Evolution*, Arthur Mitchell, tr., Pete A. Y. Gunter, ed., University Press of America, Lanham, Maryland, 1984, "Introduction," and Pete A. Y. Gunter, "Fruitfulness as a Criterion: Philosophy of Science in the Twentieth Century," 6 November 1985, North Texas State University, forthcoming as Regents' Faculty Lecture.

_____, *Two Sources of Morality and Religion*, R. Ashley Audra and Cloudesley Brereton, W. Horsfall Carter, tr. Henry Holt, New York, 1935 (from *Les deux sources de la morale et de la religion*, Paris, several editions and publishers); on two orders: *Hierarchical*, in which the good of whole demands sacrifice of part and *sum-total society* in which the whole comes to the aid of each of its parts.

George Berkeley, *Siris: A Chain of Philosophical Reflections and Inquiries Concerning the Virtues of tar water, and divers other Subjects connected together and arising One from Another*. 2d. ed., W. Innys, Dublin, 1744, in *The Works of George Berkeley, Bishop of Cloyne*, A. A. Luce and T. E. Jessop, ed., Thomas Nelson, Edinburgh, 1953, Vol. V, pp. 1-164.

Ludwig von Bertalanffy, "Levels of Organization," ch. 2 in *Problems of Life*, J. Wiley, New York, 1952.

_____, *Modern Theories of Development; An Introduction to Theoretical Biology*, J. H. Woodger, tr., Oxford University Press, London, 1933.

Ermenegildo Bertola, *Salomon Ibn Gabirol (Avicebron)*, Casa Editrice Dott. Antonio Milani, Padova, 1953.

John Black, *The Dominion of Man: The Search for Ecological Responsibility*, John Black: for the University Press, Edinburgh, 1970. On the God: Man: Nature hierarchy.

H. P. Blok, "Zur altägyptischen Vorstellung der Himmelsleiter," *Acta Orientalia*, Vol. 6, 1927-28, pp. 257-69.

Morton W. Bloomfield, *Piers Plowman as a Fourteenth-century Apocalypse*, Rutgers University Press, New Brunswick, New Jersey, 1961, "horizontal hierarchies (through time) as well as vertical hierarchies (out of time)" thus producing, with the Judeo-Christian stress on time, the concept of itinerarium and progress, pp. 52-5.

David R. Blumenthal, tr., *The Commentary of R. Hōter ben Shelōmō to the Thirteen Principles of Maimonides*, E. J. Brill, Leiden, 1974, 1981.

_____, *Understanding Jewish Mysticism: A Source Reader; The Merkabah Tradition and The Zoharic Tradition*, KTAV Publishing House, New York, 1978, "The Tree of Life and the Tree of the Knowledge of Good and Evil," pp. 143-5.

George Boas, *The Heaven of Invention*, The Johns Hopkins Press, Baltimore, Maryland, 1962, Ch. XI, "The Hierarchy of Values."

_____, "Introduction" to his translation, St. Bonaventura, *The Mind's Road to God (Itinerarium Mentis ad Deum)*, The Liberal Arts Press, New York, 1953, pp. ix-xxi.

_____, *Rationalism in Greek Philosophy*, The Johns Hopkins Press, Baltimore, Maryland, 1961, Ch. IX, "The Final Capitulation," pp. 435-79.

_____, *Some Assumptions of Aristotle*, American Philosophical Society, Philadelphia, 1959.

_____, *Wingless Pegasus: A Handbook for Critics*, The Johns Hopkins Press, Baltimore, Maryland, 1950, p. 90, Ch. VIII and IX, "The Hierarchy of Values," "Factors Influencing the Hierarchy of Values," pp. 136-68.

St. Bonaventure, *The Tree of Life*, Ewert Cousins, tr., Paulist Press, New York, 1978, with *The Soul's Journey into God*, and *The Life of St. Francis*, pp. 117-98.

Daniel J. Boorstin, *The Lost World of Thomas Jefferson*, Henry Holt, New York, 1948, Chapter One, *The Supreme Workman*, pp. 27-56, esp. "Like all Jeffersonian theology, this conception of a chain of beings was at once an expression of personal faith and a description of the material universe. The Jeffersonian insisted that the felt qualities of his universe were not the product of his personal belief; yet his theology had transformed every fact of natural history into a testimony of faith in the Creator." p. 35.

Vernon J. Bourke, "Augustine of Hippo: The Approach of the Soul to God," in *The Spirituality of Western Christendom*, R. Elder, ed., Cistercian Publications, Kalamazoo, Michigan, 1976, pp. 1-12, 189-91.

Irma Brandeis, *The Ladder of Vision*, Chatto and Windus, London, 1960.

J. Bronowski, *The Ascent of Man*, Little Brown, Boston, 1973.

Ch. 1 Lower than the Angels
Ch. 5 Music of the Spheres
Ch. 7 The Majestic Clockwork
Ch. 9 The Order of Creation

On this neglected side of Bronowski's work, see Paul G. Kuntz, "Philosophy as the Discovery of Orders," *Teaching Philosophy*, Vol. 3, No. 1, 1979, pp. 65-81. A further development of the Pythagorean tradition in philosophy, science, religion and the arts, see Paul G. Kuntz, *Bertrand Russell*, Twayne's English Authors Series, G. K. Hall, Boston, 1986; Marion Leathers Kuntz and Paul G. Kuntz, *Harmony and the Pythagorean Tradition* (forthcoming).

Richard Brooks, "The Meaning of 'Real' in Advaita Vedanta," *Philosophy East and West*, October 1969, Vol. XIX, No. 4, pp. 385-98.

H. C. Brown, "A Materialist's View of the Concept of Levels," *Journal of Philosophy*, Vol. 23, 1926, pp. 113-20; see G. P. Conger's reply, "What Are the Criteria of Levels?," *Ibid.*, pp. 589-98.

390

Robert S. Brumbaugh, *The Philosophers of Greece*, George Allen and Unwin, London, 1966, on Plato's doctrine of kinds and levels of reality, using the Divided Line to show the level and kind of reality disclosed by different philosophers and movements of thought.

A. Brunner, *Der echte Gegensatz, die Gestalt und die Seinsstufe des Biologischen, Scholastik: Vierteljahesschrift für Theologie und Philosophie*, 1935, No. 10, pp. 193-228.

Martin Buber, *Ten Rungs: Hasidic Sayings*, Schocken, New York, 1962.

Roger Buck and David L. Hull, "The Logical Structure of the Linnaean Hierarchy," *Systematic Zoology*, Vol. 15, 1966, pp. 97-111.

Mario Bunge, "Conjunction, Succession, Determination and Causation," *Int. Journal of Theoretical Physics*, 1:3, 1968, 299-315.

_____, "On the Connections Among Levels," *Proceedings XIIth International Congress of Philosophy*, Sansoni, Firenze, Vol. VI.

_____, "Hierarchical Structures," in L. L. Whyte, A. G. Wilson, D. Wilson, ed., *Proceedings of the Symposium* held November 18-19, 1968 at Douglas Advanced Research Laboratories, Huntington Beach, California, American Elsevir, New York, 1969, pp. 17-28.

_____, "Levels: A Semantical Preliminary," *Review of Metaphysics*, Vol. XIII, No. 3, March 1960, pp. 396-406.

_____, *Metascientific Queries*, Charles C Thomas, Springfield, Illinois, 1959, Ch. 5, "Do the Levels of Science Reflect the Levels of Being?", pp. 108-123, revision of a paper read at the IV Interamerican Congress of Philosophy, Chile University, July 1956.

_____, *The Myth of Simplicity*, Prentice Hall, Englewood Cliffs, New Jersey, 1963, Ch. 3, "Levels."

_____, "A Philosophical Obstacle to the Rise of New Theories in Microphysics," *Quantum Theory and Beyond*, Ted Bastin, ed., Cambridge University Press, Vol. 71, pp. 263-73.

_____, "Time Asymmetry, Time Reversal, and Irreversibility," *Studium Generale*, Vol. 23, 1970, pp. 562-70.

Tyler Burge, "Frege and the Hierarchy," *Synthèse*, Vol. 40, February 1979, pp. 265-81.

J. M. Burgers, "Causality and Anticipation: Analysis of the concept of anticipation can contribute to the philosophy of biology," *Science*, Vol. 189, 18 July 1975, pp. 194-8 recommends on hierarchy, in which he asserts anticipation from parts of parts to parts to wholes, W. E. Agar, *A Contribution to the Theory of Living Organism*, Melbourne University Press, Carlton, Victoria, 1943.

Donald T. Campbell, "Downward Causation," in *Studies in the Philosophy of Biology*, Theodosius Grigorievich Dobzhansky and Francisco José Ayala, ed., Macmillan, London, 1974, pp. 179-86.

Paul N. Campbell, "Symbological Hierarchy: A Further Word," *Philosophy and Rhetoric*, Vol. 9, Spring 1976, pp. 116-22.

Armand Capocci, *La hiérarchie des Salaires*, Hachette, (Collections les grands problèmes), Paris, 1964.

Maïeul Cappuyns, *Jean Scot Érigène, sa vie, son oeuvre, sa pensée*, Culture et Civilisation, Bruxelles, 1964, le schema des quatre natures, p. 309, et les chapitres sur la processio ou creatio et la reversio ou deificatio.

Douglas Carmichael, *Order and Human Value*, typewritten MS., Indiana University 1954. 262 pp. Mic. 54-1813 University Microfilms, Ann Arbor, Michigan. A development of one theme is "Autonomy and Order," *Journal of Philosophy*, Vol. 55, 1958, pp. 648-55.

Archie B. Carroll, "Business Ethics and the Management Hierarchy," *National Forum*, Vol. 58, Summer 1978, pp. 37-40.

Edwin Casady, "The Neo-Platonic Ladder in Spenser's *Amoretti*," *Renaissance Studies in Honor of Hardin Craig*, Maxwell Baldwin, et al, ed., Stanford University Press, Stanford, California, 1941.

Enrico Cerulli, *Nuove Ricerche sul Libro della Scala e la conoscenza dell'Islam in Occidenta*, Biblioteca Apostolica Vaticana, Città del Vaticano, 1972.

Paolo Cherchi, *Enciclopedismo e politica della riscrittura. Tommaso Garzoni*, Pacini Editore, Pisa, 1980.

Michael Clark, "Degrees of Comparison," *Analysis*, Vol. 44, October 1984, pp. 178-80.

A. Cohen, *The Teachings of Maimonides*, KTAV Publishing, New York, 1968, Ch. II, "Constitution of the Universe," pp. 65-82.

R. G. Collingwood, "The Scale of Forms," *An Essay on Philosophical Method*, Clarendon Press, Oxford, 1933, 1950, Ch. III.

George Perrigo Conger, "The Doctrine of Levels," *Journal of Philosophy*, Vol. 22, 1925, pp. 309-21.

_____, *Epitomization: A Study in Philosophy of the Sciences*, University of Minnesota Library, Minneapolis, 1949.

_____, "A Hypothesis of Realms," *Journal of Philosophy*, Vol. 25, 1928, pp. 205-17.

_____, *Synoptic Naturalism*, University of Minnesota Library, Minnesota, 1960.

_____, "What are the Criteria of Levels?" *Journal of Philosophy*, Vol. 23, 1926, pp. 589-98.

_____, *A World of Epitomizations: A Study in the Philosophy of the Sciences*, Princeton University Press, Princeton, New Jersey, 1931.

Michael Conrad, "Statistical and hierarchical aspects of biological organization," in *Towards a Theoretical Biology*, C. H. Waddington, ed., Vol. 4, Aldine, Chicago, 1972, pp. 189-221.

_____, "The importance of molecular hierarchy in information processing," *Ibid.*, pp. 222-8.

Edward W. Constant, "Communities and Hierarchies: Structure in the Practice of Science and Technology," in *Technological Knowledge*, Rachel Laudan, ed., Reidel, Dordrecht, 1984, pp. 27-46.

Charles Constantin, "The Puritan Ethic and the Dignity of Labor: Hierarchy vs. Equality," *Journal of the History of Ideas*, Vol. 40, October-December 1979, pp. 543-61.

Roger Cook, *The Tree of Life: Symbol of the Centre*, Thames and Hudson, London, 1974.

Henry Corbin, *Avicenna and the Visionary Recital*, Willard R. Trask, tr., Bollingen Series LXVI, Pantheon Books, 1960, passage from one to multiplicity of beings: a necessary mediation pp. 56-7; mystical ladder: "Jacob's Ladder" p. 110.

_____, *Temps cyclique et gnose ismaélinne*, translated as *Cyclical Time and Ismaili Gnosis*, Kegan Paul, London, 1983.

Roger Cornu et Janina Lagneau, compilers, *Hiérarchies et classes sociales*, A. Colin, Paris, 1969.

A. A. Cox and A. Al-Hibri, "Castañeda's Theory of Morality," *Philosophy and Phenomenological Research*, Vol. 38, January 1978, pp. 557-68.

Ewert H. Cousins, *Bonaventure and the Coincidence of Opposites*, Franciscan Herald Press, Chicago, 1978, on Jacob's Ladder among other symbols of cosmic hierarchy and the soul's journey, p. 78.

Ingrid Craemer-Ruegenberg, "The Priority of Soul as Form and Its Proximity to the First Mover," in *Albert the Great: Commemorative Essays*, Francis J. Kovach, ed., University of Oklahoma Press, Norman, 1980.

F. E. Cranz, *An Essay on the Development of Luther's Thought on Justice, Law, and Society*, Harvard University Press, Cambridge, 1959.

John Crossett, "Love in the Western Hierarchy," in *The Concept of Order*, Paul G. Kuntz, ed., University of Washington Press, Seattle, 1968, pp. 219-36.

Dezso Csejtei, "The Levels of Being in Unamuno's Ontology and Its Categorial System," *Magyar Filozof Szemle*, Vol. 2, 1983, pp. 185-226.

Jonathan D. Culler, *On Deconstruction: Theory and Criticism after Structuralism*, Cornell University Press, Ithaca, 1982. Numerous examples are presented of Jacque Derrida's deconstructions of hierarchical oppositions of Western thought.

Walter Clyde Currey, *Milton's Ontology, Cosmology and Physics*, University of Kentucky Press, Lexington, 1957, Ch. 7, "Milton's Scale of Nature," pp. 158-82.

René Daumal, "Payment," in *Parabola, Hierarchy*, Vol. IX, No. 1, Winter 1984, pp. 57-9.

Gustav Davidson, *A Dictionary of Angels including the Fallen Angels*, The Free Press, New York, 1979.

T. J. De Boer, *The History of Philosophy in Islam*, Edward R. Jones, tr., Luzac, London, 1933. Farabi: "We are able to see God better in the regular gradations of beings which proceed from him than in himself." p. 115.

Paul Deutschberger, "Shakespeare on Degree: A Study of Backgrounds," *Shakespeare Association of America Bulletin*, Vol. 17, 1942, pp. 200-06.

H. Dolhagoray, "Hiérarchie," *Dictionnaire de Théologie Catholique*, A. Vacant et E. Mangenot, Letouzey, Paris, 1920, Vol. VI, 2, pp. 2362-82.

Hans Dombois, *Hierarchie: Grund und Grenze einer umstrittenen Struktur*, Herder, Freiburg in Breisgau, 1971.

D. M. Dooling, "The Mythic Dimension," in *Parabola, Hierarchy*, Vol. IX, No. 1, Winter 1984, pp. 41-6.

Myrto Dragona-Manachou, "Posidonius' 'Hierarchy' Between God, Fate and Nature, and Cicero's *De Divinatione*," *Philosophia* (Athens), 1974, Vol. 4, pp. 286-305.

E. S. Drower, "Dana Nuk," retold by Anne Twitty from the Mandaeans of Iraq and Iran, in *Parabola, Hierarchy*, Vol IX, No. 1, Winter 1984, pp. 53-4.

James Drummond, *Philo Judaeus, On the Jewish-Alexandrian Philosophy in its Development and Completion*, Philo Press, Amsterdam, 1969, on Philo's application of the ladder in various ways, pp. 256-69. On the Old Testament background to the analogical interpretation of the angels as *Logoi*, pp. 131-43.

Page DuBois, *Centaurs and Amazons: Women and the Pre-history of the Great Chain of Being*, University of Michigan Press, Ann Arbor, 1982.

Georges Duby, *The Three Orders: Feudal Society Imagined*, Arthur Goldhammer, tr., foreword by Thomas N. Blasson, University of Chicago Press, Chicago, 1980.

Joseph Duchesne (Josephus Quercetanus) *Le grand miroir du monde* .... Deuxième edition reveu ... par l'auteur. A la fin de chaque livre sont de nouveau adjoustées amples annotations et observations sur le texte ... par S.G.S. a Lyon, pour les Heritiers d'Eustache Vignon, 1593.

John Dudley, "La Contemplation humaine selon Aristote," *Revue Philosophique* (Louvain), Vol. 80, August 1982, pp. 387–413.

Pierre Maurice Marie Duhem, *Le Système du Monde: Histoire des Doctrines Cosmoloques de Platon à Copernic*, 5 Vols., A. Hermann, Paris, 1913–17. Also Librarie Scientifique Hermann, 1954–59, 10 Vols.

Robert Eberwein, "Samuel Johnson, George Cheyne, and the 'Cone of Being,'" *Journal of the History of Ideas*, Vol. 36, January–March 1975, pp. 153–8.

Elsa Von Eckartsberg, "Maps of the Mind: the Cartography of Consciousness," in *The Metaphors of Consciousness*, Rolf Von Eckartsberg and Ronald S. Valle ed., Plenum Press, New York, 1981.

Ludwig Edelstein, "The Golden Chain of Homer," in *Studies in Intellectual History*, G. Boas et al, ed., The Johns Hopkins University Press, Baltimore, Maryland, 1953, pp. 58–66.

"Eirionnach," "Aurea Catena Homeri," *Notes and Queries*, 2d Ser., Vol. 3, 1857, pp. 63–5, 81–4, 104–07; Vol. 12, 1861, pp. 161–3, 181–3.

R. Ettinghausen, "Persian Ascension miniatures of the fourteenth century," in Accademia Nazionale dei Lincei, Convegno 'Volta,' *Atti*, XII, Rome, 1957, pp. 360–83.

Majid Fakhry, *A History of Islamic Philosophy*, Columbia University Press, New York, 1970, Ch. III, "Neo-Platonic Elements: The Apocryphal *Theologia Aristotelis* and the *Liber de Causis*," pp. 32–44, and indexed under "Emanation."

Austin Farrer, *The Glass of Vision*, Bampton Lectures for 1948, Dacre Press, Westminster, 1948, "The mind likewise (as the body) is known for what it is by the highest principle in its hierarchic constitution, not by the indefinite multitute of subsidiary elements; by the luminous apex, not by the spreading shadowy base." p. 22, and ff.

James K. Feibleman, *Aesthetics*, Duell, Sloan and Pearce, New York, Ch. XVIII, "The Decline of Literary Chaos," pp. 400–19.

_____, *Foundations of Empiricism*, Martinus Nijhoff, The Hague, 1962.

_____, *Inside the Great Mirror: A Critical Examination of the Philosophy of Russell, Wittgenstein, and their Followers*, Martinus Nijhoff, The Hague, 1958.

_____, *The Institutions of Society*, George Allen and Unwin, London, 1956, "Organization," pp. 159–66, Ch. XVI, "The Leading Institutions," pp. 228f.

_____, "The Integrative Levels in Nature," *Focus on Information and Communication*, Barbara Kyle, ed., ASLIB, London, 1965.

_____, *An Introduction to Peirce's Philosophy: Interpreted as a System*, Harper and Brothers, New York, 1946.

_____, *Ontology*, The Johns Hopkins Press, Baltimore, Maryland, 1951.

_____, *The Revival of Realism: Critical Studies in Contemporary Philosophy*, The University of North Carolina Press, Chapel Hill, North Carolina, 1946, especially Ch. IV, "Lovejoy's Revolt Against Realism," pp. 99-136.

_____, "Theory of Integrative Levels," *The British Journal for the Philosophy of Science*, Vol. V, No. 17, 1954, pp. 59-66.

_____, *The Two-Story World: Selected Writings*, Huntington Cairns, ed., Holt, Rinehart and Winston, New York, 1966, especially Ch. XI, "Culture," "The Social Adaptiveness of Philosophy," and "Culture as Applied Ontology," pp. 268-385.

_____, and Julius W. Friend, "The Structure and Function of Organization," *The Philosophical Review*, Vol. LIV, 1945, pp. 19-44.

J. de Finance, "Les Degrés de l'Être chez Saint Thomas d'Aquin," in Angela Ales Bello, ed., *The Great Chain of Being in Phenomenology*, Reidel, Dordrecht, 1981, pp. 51-7.

John N. Findlay, "The Logic of Mysticism," *Religious Studies*, Vol. 2, No. 2, 1967, pp. 145-62.

_____, "The Myths of Plato," in *Myth, Symbol, and Reality*, Alan Olson, ed., University of Notre Dame Press, Notre Dame, 1980.

_____, "The Three Hypostases of Platonism," *Review of Metaphysics*, Vol. XXVIII, No. 4, June 1975, pp. 660-80.

_____, "Towards a Neo-Neo-Platonism," Ch. XV in *Ascent to the Absolute*, George Allen and Unwin, London, 1970, pp. 248-67. Also Ch. X, "The Logic of Ultimates," pp. 162-83.

Robert Fludd, *Utriusque cosmi maiores scilicit et minoris metaphysica, physica atque technica historia in duo volumina secundum cosmi differentiam divisa*, Aere Johan-Theodori de Bry, Oppenhemii, 1617-21. The engraving shows YHWH connected to man (in the image of the ape of God) through the World Soul, whose right hand is chained to deity above, and holding man on the earth. See *Philosophia Moysaica*, Goudae, 1638, and *Philosophia sacra et vere christiana*, Frankfurti, 1636.

Lewis S. Ford, "The Controversy Between Schelling and Jacobi," *Journal of the History of Philosophy*, Vol. 3, April 1965, pp. 75-90.

Lia Formigari, "Chain of Being," *Dictionary of the History of Ideas*, P. P. Wiener, ed., Scribner's, New York, 1968, 1973, Vol. I, pp. 325-35.

Charles H. Foster, *The Rungless Ladder: Harriet Beecher Stowe and New England Puritanism*, Duke University Press, Durham, North Carolina, 1954, p. ii quotation from *The Minister's Wooing*: "a ladder from human affections to God - with every round knocked out except the highest...."

Michael B. Foster, *Mystery and Philosophy*, SCM Press, London, 1957, Ch. VI, "Hellenic and Biblical Thought-Models," especially p. 90 and notes.

G. A. Foulds, *The Hierarchical Nature of Personal Illness*, Academic Press, New York and London, 1976.

Benjamin Franklin, "An Arabian Tale," *The Works*, Jared Sparks, ed., Hilliard, Gray, and Company, Boston, 1836, Vol. II, pp. 193-4. Also, *The Writings of Benjamin Franklin*, A. H. Smith, ed., Macmillan, New York, 1907, Vol. X, pp. 123-4. "Contemplate ... the scale of beings, from an elephant down to an oyster. Thou seest a gradual diminution of faculties and powers, so small in each step that the difference is scarce perceptable. There is no gap, but the gradation is complete. Men in general do not know, but thou knowest that in ascending from an elephant to the infinitely Great, Good, and Wise, there is also a long gradation of beings, who possess powers and faculties of which thou canst yet have no conception."

J. T. Fraser, "Time as a Hierarchy of Creative Conflicts," *Studium Generale*, Vol. 23, 1970, pp. 597-689.

John W. Gardner, *Excellence: Can We be Equal and Excellent Too?*, Harper, New York, 1961, Ch. XI, "Talent and Leadership" and Ch. XII, "The Idea of Excellence," explore the present possibility of developing Jefferson's ideal of a natural aristocracy, pp. 118-34.

Franciscus Georgius, *De Harmonia mvndi totivs cantica tria*, Venetiis in aedibvs Berardini de Vitalibvs Chalcographi An.D.M.D.XXV.

Etienne Gilson, *Dante and Philosophy*, Sheed and Ward, 1949, Harper Torchbook, New York, 1963. Argues that contrary to Thomas, the hierarchy of dignity (sc. church above state) does not produce as a consequence the hierarchy of jurisdiction (sc. state subjected to authority of church, or emperor to Pope).

John Goheen, *The Problem of Matter and Form in the "De Ente et Essentia" of Thomas Aquinas*, Harvard University Press, Cambridge, 1940. Provides a fine commentary, with particular attention to hierarchy, pp. 88-91, 98-9, 110-21.

M. M. Goldsmith, "Hobbes's 'Mortal God': Is There a Fallacy in Hobbes's Theory of Sovereignty?," *History of Political Thought*, Vol. I, Spring 1980, pp. 33-50.

E. H. Gombrich, "Icones Symbolicae: The Viusal Image in Neo-Platonic Thought," *Journal of the Warburg and Courtauld Institutes*, Vol. 11, 1948, pp. 163-92.

Suzanne Gossett, ed., *Hierarchomachia: or, The Anti-Bishop*, by Bishop Richard Smith (1566-1655), Associated University Presses, Cranbury, New Jersey, 1982.

Moltke S. Gram and Richard M. Martin, "The Perils of Plenitude: Hintikka contra Lovejoy," *Journal of the History of Ideas*, Vol. 41, No. 3, 1980, pp. 497-511.

Robert M. Grant, "Chains of Being in Early Christianity," in *Myths and Symbols: Studies in Honor of Mircea Eliade*, Joseph M. Kitagawa and Charles H. Long, ed., University of Chicago Press, Chicago, 1969, pp. 279-87.

Nicolete (Mary Binyon) Gray, *Jacob's Ladder: A Bible Picture Book from Anglo-Saxon and 12th Century English MSS*, Faber and Faber, London, 1949.

John R. Gregg, *The Language of Taxonomy: An Application of Symbolic Logic to the Study of Classificatory Systems*, Columbia University Press, New York, 1954, Ch. 3, "Hierarchies."

Joshua C. Gregory, "The Newtonian Hierarchic System of Particles," *Archives internationale d'histoire des sciences*, Vol. 33, 1954, pp. 243-7.

Marjorie Grene, "Biology and the Problem of Levels of Reality," *The New Scholasticism*, Vol. XLI, No. 4, Autumn 1967, pp. 427-49.

_____, "Is Biology an Exact Science?," *The Listener*, Vol. LXVIII, No. 1750, 11 October 1962, pp. 558-60 on the inexact ordering of biological stages it is interesting to consult Jean Baptiste Pierre Antoine de Monet de Lamarck, *Recherches sur l'organisation*, 1802, especially Note on Table facing p. 37: "La Progression de gradation n'est nulle part régulière ou proportionelle; mais elle existe dans l'ensemble d'une manière évidente."

Clifford Grobstein, *The Strategy of Life*, W. H. Freeman, San Francisco, 1964, 1965, Ch. 4, "Levels of Organization," pp. 38-52. This is more explicit and full than some other sources, but one needs other sources in ecology; for example, Paul B. Sears, *Where There is Life*, Dell, New York, 1962; and Robert D. Platt and George K. Reid, *Bioscience*, Reinhold Publishing Co., 1967, "Levels of Organization," pp. 4-5, Ch. 8, "The Ecosystem," pp. 172 ff., etc.

Romano Guardini, "Die Lehre von der Gradatio Entium," "Die Hierarchien," Ch. 9, 11, *Systembildende Elemente in der Theologie Bonaventuras, Die Lehre von Lumen Mentis....*, Werner Dettloff: ed., E. J. Brill, Leiden, 1964, pp. 93-183.

G. I. Gurdjeff, "The First Initiation," in *Parabola, Hierarchy*, Vol. IX, No. 1, Winter 1984, pp. 6-7.

Aron Íàkovlevich Gurevich, *Das Weltbild des mittelalterlichen Menschen*, Gabriele Lossuck, tr., C. H. Beck, München, 1982.

Aron David Gurewitsch, *Zur Grundlegung einer Synthese des Daseins*, Rascher Verlag, Zürich und Leipzig, 1935, "Die hierarchische Welt," "Hierarchisches Sein in der Modernen Welt," "Die hierarchische Gedanke in der Philosophie."

Z'ev ben Shimon Halevi, *Tree of Life, Adam and Kabbalistic Tree, Way of Kabbalah*, Rider, London and Samuel Weiser, New York, 1972, also a shortened essay on interpretations of the Sefiroth tree in *Order, Maitroya* 6, pp. 32-42.

Alexander Hamilton, James Madison, John Jay, *The Federalist Papers*, Clinton Rositer, ed., The New American Library, New York, 1961. On a series of courts culminating in the Supreme Court, and all subordinated to the Constitution, pp. 467-8.

Garrett Hardin, "Is Violence Natural?," *Zygon*, Vol. 18, December 1983, pp. 405-14. "Relative peace, which is to everyone's advantage in the long run, is favored by hierarchies. The inevitable changes that history brings about require hierarchies to be changeable. A change in the hierarchy is brought about necessarily by agression."

Douglas Edison Harding, *The Hierarchy of Heaven and Earth; a New Diagram of Man in the Universe*, Faber and Faber, London, 1952.

Charles Hartshorne, "The Cosmic Variables," Ch. VIII, *Beyond Humanism: Essays in the Philosophy of Nature*, University of Nebraska Press, Lincoln, 1968.

Friedrich Hassaurek, *Hierarchie und Aristokratik*, F. Hassaurek, Cincinnati, 1852.

Ronald F. Hathaway, *Hierarchy and the Definition of Order in the 'Letters' of Pseudo-Dionysius: A Study in the Form and Meaning of the Pseudo-Dionysian Writings*, Martinus Nijhoff, The Hague, 1969.

W. H. Hay, "Nicolaus Cusanus: The Structure of His Philosophy," *The Philosophical Review*, Vol. LXI, No. 1, Jan. 1952, pp. 14-25, particularly helpful on the "Principle of the Existence of a Maximum," pp. 22-3.

Charles Hefling, *Jacob's Ladder: Theology and Spirituality of Austin Farrer*, John the Evangelist, Cowley Publications, Cambridge, Massachusetts, 1979.

Thomas Heywood, *The Hierarchie of The Blessed Angells: Their names, orders and offices. The fall of Lucifer with his angells*, Adam Islip, London, 1635.

Jaakko Hintikka, "Gaps in the Great Chain of Being: An Exercise in the Methodology of the History of Ideas," *Proceedings and Addresses of the American Philosophical Association* 1975-76, Vol. XLIX, November 1976, pp. 22-38.

_____, "Kant on the Great Chain of Being or the Eventual Realization of All Possibilities," *Philosophers' Exchange* (Brockport), Vol. 2, 1976, pp. 69-85. See also Simo Knuttila, ed., *Reforging the Great Chain of Being*, Reidel, Dordrecht, 1980, pp. 287-307.

_____, "Leibniz on Plenitude, Relations, and the 'Reign of Law,'" in *Leibniz: A Collection of Critical Essays*, Harry G. Frankfurt, ed., Anchor, Garden City, New York, 1972, also in Simo Knuttila, *op. cit.*, pp. 259-86.

Egbert Höflich, *Hierarchie oder Volkssouveranität? Zum Problem der Antorität der Kirche*, Patmos, Düsseldorf, 1970. Alois Müller antwortet Egbert Höflich.

Robert Hooper, *Right Reason in the English Renaissance*, Harvard University Press, Cambridge, 1962, Ch. III, pp. 46-51, on the influence of the Plotinian development of the Platonic ladder "a ladder in the strictest sense; you reach the higher rungs by leaving the lower ones behind." (C. S. Lewis).

Jan Huizinga, *The Waning of the Middle Ages*, Ch. III, "The Hierarchic Conception of Society," Doubleday Anchor, Garden City, New York, 1954, pp. 56-67.

Edward V. Huntington, *The Continuum and Other Types of Serial Order*, Dover Publications, New York, 1955.

James Hutton, "Spenser's 'Adamantine Chains:' A Cosmological Metaphor," in *Essays on Renaissance Poetry*, Rita Guerlac, ed., Cornell University Press, Ithaca, New York, 1980, pp. 169-91.

Salomon ben Judah Ibn Gabirol (Avicebron), *La Couronne Royale (Kether Malcouth)*, Introduction, traduction et notes de Paul Vuillaud, Editions Dervy, Paris, 1953.

Moshe Idel, "The Magical and Neoplatonic Interpretations of the Kabbalah in the Renaissance," in *Jewish Thought in the Sixteenth Century*, Bernard Dov Cooperman, ed., Harvard University Press, Cambridge, Massachusetts, 1983, pp. 186-242.

Roman Ingarden, *Das literarische Kunstwerk*, Niemeyer, Tübingen, 1960, 1965. *The Literary Work of Art*, tr. and intro. George G. Grabowicz, Northwestern University Press, Evanston, Illinois, 1973.

E. von Ivanka, *Die Hierarchien der Engel und der Kirche*, Einführung von Hugo Ball, tr., Planegg, München, 1955.

Edwin Oliver James, *The Worship of the Sky God*, Athlone Press, London, 1963.

Jan van Ruysbroeck, *De Septem Scalae* (Seven Trappen) *diuini Amoris seu vitae sanctae gradibus*, Bologne, 1538.

Robert Javelet, "Sens et Realité Ultime selon Hugues de Saint-Victor," *Ultimate Reality and Meaning*, Vol. 3, 1980, pp. 84-113.

Soame Jenyns, *A free inquiry into the nature and origin of evil in six letters to _____*, 2d ed., London, printed for R. and J. Dodsley, 1757, microfilm, Micrographics, Charlottesville, Virginia, 1976.

_____, "On the Chain of Universal Being," in *Disquisitions on Several Subjects*, J. Dodsley, London, 1789. Microfiche, Lost Cause Press, Louisville, Kentucky, 1964.

Paul K. Jewett, *Man as Male and Female: A Study in Sexual Relationships from a Theological Point of View*, William B. Eerdmans, Grand Rapids, Michigan, 1975, Ch. III "The Hierarchical View of the Man/Woman Relationship Elaborated and Defended, Thomas Aquinas, Luther and Calvin, Barth," pp.

61-81, "The Rejection of the Hierarchical View of the Man/Woman Relationship," pp. 129ff.

Samuel Johnson, "Review of a Free Enquiry into the Nature and Origin of Evil," *The Works of Samuel Johnson*, Vol. 6, Taboys and Wheeler, Oxford; and W. Pickering, London, 1825, pp. 47-76. Attack on the chain of being used by Soame Jenyns' *Free Enquiry*, 1757.

Hans Jonas, "Spinoza and the Theory of Organism," in *Spinoza: A Collection of Critical Essays*, Marjorie Grene, ed., Anchor Books, Garden City, New York, 1973, pp. 259-78.

W. Tudor Jones, *Contemporary Thought of Germany*, Vol. I, A. A. Knopf, New York, 1931, on Meinong's system of levels pertaining to objects.

Mark D. Jordan, "The Grammar of *Esse*: Re-Reading Thomas on the Transcendentals," *Thomist*, Vol. 44, January 1980, pp. 1-26.

_____, "The Order of Lights: Aquinas on Immateriality as Hierarchy," *Proceedings of the American Catholic Philosophical Association*, Vol. 52, 1978, pp. 112-20.

Philip E. B. Jourdain, *The Philosophy of Mr. Bertrand Russell*, George Allen and Unwin, London, 1918, Ch. XXXIX, "The Hierarchy of Jokes."

Eugene F. Kaelin, "Exposition: Man-the-Creator and the Prototype of Action, A Contemporary Formulation of *The Great Chain of Being*," in Angela Ales Bello, *The Great Chain of Being in Phenomenology*, Reidel, Dordrecht, 1981, pp. 11-37.

Eugene Kamenka and Martin Kygier, *Bureaucracy: The Career of a Concept*, St. Martin's Press, New York, 1979.

Frederick M. Keener, *The Chain of Becoming: The Philosophical Tale, the Novel, and a Neglected Realism of the Enlightenment: Swift, Montesquieu, Voltaire, Johnson, and Austen*, Columbia University Press, New York, 1983.

Frank Kingdon, *Jacob's Ladder: The Days of My Youth*, L. B. Fischer, New York, 1943.

Athanasius Kircher, *Iter exstaticum coeleste ... hac secunda editione praelusionibus & scholiis illustratum, ac schematism necessariis ... excernatum ... expargatum ipso auctore annvente*, a P. Gaspare Schotto ... accessit .... Iter exstaticum terrestre, & synopsis mundi subterranei, Herbipoli: Sumptibus Joh. Andr. Endteri Wolffg. Jun Erdterorum haeredibus, prostat Norimbergae apud eosdan, 1660.

_____, *Itinerarium exstaticum quo mundi opificium, id est, coelestis expansi, siderumque ... compositio et structura ... interlocutoribus Cosmiele et Theodidacto*, typis Vitalis Mascardi, Romae, 1656.

Engelbert Kirschbaum, S.J. et al, *Lexikon der Christlichen Ikonographie*, Herder, Rom, 1970, Vol. 2, pp. 374-5, "Jakobstraum."

Lorraine Kisly, "Focus," in *Parabola, Hierarchy*, Vol. IX, No. 1, Winter 1984, pp. 2-3.

William and Martha Kneale, *The Development of Logic*, Clarendon Press, Oxford, 1962, Ch. XI, Section 2, "Russell's Theory of Logical Types," pp. 657-72.

Simo Knuttila, *Reforging the Great Chain of Being*, D. Reidel, Dordrecht, 1981.

Arthur Koestler, *The Act of Creation*, Hutchinson, London, 1964, "The Concept of Hierarchy," pp. 287-91; "The Ubiquitous Hierarchy," pp. 430-45.

Aurel Kolnai, "The Concept of Hierarchy," *Philosophy*, Vol. XLVI, No. 177, July 1971, pp. 203-21, also in *Ethics, Value, and Reality, Selected Papers of Aurel Kolnai*, Francis Dunlop and Brian Klug, ed., London and Hackett Publishing Co., Indianapolis, 1978, Ch. 8, pp. 165-86.

_____, "Dignity," *Philosophy*, Vol. 51, 1976, pp. 251-71.

Kyriakos M. Kontopodulos, *Knowledge and Determination: The Transition from Hegel to Marx*, B. R. Grüner, Amsterdam, 1980.

Stalislaw Kowalczyk, "El Teocentrismo de la Jerarquia de los Bienes en al Doctrina de San Agustin," *Augustinus*, Vol. 22, July-December 1977, pp. 229-38.

Paul Oskar Kristeller, "Ficino, Marsilio (1433-1499)," *Encyclopedia of Philosophy*, Paul Edwards, ed., Macmillan, New York, 1967, Vol. 6, pp. 196-201.

_____, "Ficino and Pompanazzi on the Place of Man in the Universe," *Renaissance Thought II*, Harper and Row, New York, 1965, Ch. V.

_____, *The Philosophy of Marsilio Ficino*, Virginia Conant, tr., Columbia University Press, New York, 1943, Ch. VI, "Hierarchy of Being," pp. 74-91, etc.

Joseph Wood Krutch, *The Great Chain of Life*, Houghton Mifflin, Boston, 1957; with a new preface by Paul Landacre, 1978.

Marion Leathers Kuntz, *Colloquium of the Seven about Secrets of the Sublime, Jean Bodin*, tr. with Introduction, Annotations, and Critical Readings, Princeton University Press, Princeton, New Jersey, 1975.

SENAMUS: "What then will happen to Plato who, in accordance with the opinion of Homer, represents a golden chain let down by Jupiter from heaven? Must we not grant that the series of natural causes is inviolable and completely unchangeable?"

TORALBA: "In my opinion Homer explains himself sufficiently when he recognized that those *lower gods can be drawn upward by the higher, but the supreme deity cannot be drawn down by the lower.*"

SALOMON: "I think the Homeric *catena* is nothing other than the ladder represented by the nocturnal vision of Jacob the Patriarch; God was at the top of the ladder and angels descended from the top of heaven to the earth and then ascended again to heaven." p. 32.

402

_____, "The Home of Coronaeus in Jean Bodin's *Colloquium Heptaplomeres*: An Example of a Venetian Academy," in *Acta Conventus Neo-Latini Bonovensis*, R. J. Schoeck, ed., University of New York Press, Binghamton, New York, 1985, pp. 277-83.

_____, "Journey as Restitution in the Thought of Guillaume Postel (1510-1581)," *History of European Ideas*, Vol. 1, No. 4., 1981, pp. 315-29.

_____, "Postel and His Idea of Progress and Utopian Reality," *History of European Ideas*, Vol. 6, No. 3, 1985, pp. 311-24.

_____, *Guillaume Postel: Prophet of the Restitution of All Things: His Life and Thought*, Martinus Nijhoff, The Hague, 1981. Part One, *Viator*; Part Two, *Comprehensor*; Part Three, *Congregator*.

Paul Grimley Kuntz, *Alfred North Whitehead*, Twayne Publishers, Boston, 1984, "The Hierarchical Order of Nature," pp. 70-4, Aristotelian and Neo-Platonic gradation, p. 107, p. 137.

_____, "The Analogy of Degrees of Being: A Critique of Cajetan's 'Analogy of Names,'" *New Scholasticism*, Vol. 56, Winter 1982, pp. 51-79.

_____, "Anselm's Ontological Argument in Its Hierarchical Context: Its Relational Logic and Platonic Realism (From 'Is better than' to a Real Best) and Rules of a Coherent 'Onto-Logic'," a lecture at Villanova University, Conference on Patristic, Medieval and Renaissance Philosophy, October 1985.

_____, *The Concept of Order*, The University of Washington Press, Seattle, 1968.

_____, "From Disorder to Order or from Order to Disorder," The Society for the Study of Process Philosophy, Dickinson College, Carlisle, Pennsylvania, December 1976.

_____, "Hierarchy: From Lovejoy's Great Chain of Being to Feibleman's Great Tree of Being," *Studium Generale*, July/August 1971, Vol. 2, pp. 678-87.

_____, "Modes of Order," *The Review of Metaphysics*, Vol. XVI, No. 2, December 1962, pp. 316-45, esp. pp. 343-4.

Jean Baptiste Pierre Antoine de Monet de Lamarck, *Recherches sur l'organisation*, 1802, especially Note on Table facing p. 37: "La Progression de gradation n'est nulle part régulière ou proportionelle: mais elle existe dans l'ensemble d'une manière évidente."

Émile Lasbax, *La Hiérarchie dans l'Univers chez Spinoza*, nouv. ed., J. Vrin, Paris, 1926.

Ervin Laszlo, "Basic Constructs of Systems Philosophy," *Systematics*, Vol. 10, June 1972, pp. 40-53.

403

_____, "The Case for Systems Philosophy," *Metaphilosophy*, Vol. 3, April 1972, pp. 123–41.

M. Guérard des Lauriers, "La hiérarchie métaphysique de l'ordre," *Aquinas*, 1962, pp. 206–29.

Paul F. Lazarsfeld, *Mathematical Thinking in the Social Sciences*, Free Press, Glencoe, Illinois, 1954, Ch. 5 on rank-order.

Keith Lehrer, "The Evaluation of Method: A Hierarchy of Probabilities among Probabilities," in *Science and Ethics*, Rudolph Haller, ed., Rodopi, Amsterdam, 1981, pp. 131–42.

Edmund Leites, "Confucianism in Eighteenth-Century England: Natural Morality and Social Reform," *Philosophy East and West*, Vol. 28, April 1978, pp. 143–59.

Pierre Lévêque, *Aurea catena Homeri: une étude sur l'allégorie greque*, Les Belles Lettres, Paris, 1959.

Herbert Leventhal, *In the Shadow of the Enlightenment: Occultism and Renaissance in Eighteenth-Century America*, New York University Press, New York, 1976, Ch. 8, "The Chain of Being," pp. 219–59.

Denise Levertove, *The Jacob's Ladder, Poems*, A New Directions paperback, 1961.

Jerrold Levinson, "Aesthetic Supervenience," *Southern Journal of Philosophy*, Vol. 22, 1983, pp. 93–110.

Clarence Irving Lewis and Cooper Harold Langford, *Symbolic Logic*, Dover Publications, New York, n.d., Ch. XIII, "The Logical Paradoxes," pp. 438–87.

C. S. Lewis, *A Mind Awake: An Anthology of C. S. Lewis*, Clyde S. Kilby, ed., Geoffrey Bles, London, 1968, "Hierarchy," pp. 52–8.

Martin Lings, "Freedom and Equality," in *Parabola, Hierarchy,*, Vol. IX, No. 1, Winter 1984, pp. 60–7.

C. Linné et I. J. Biberg, *L'Économie de la nature* (1749), in *L'Équilibre de la Nature*, Bernard Jasmin, tr., int. Camille Limoges, Vrin, Paris, 1972.

Roger Lipsey, "Participators of Sacred Things," in *Parabola, Hierarchy*, Vol. IX, No. 1, Winter 1984, pp. 16–21.

John Locke, *Essay concerning Human Understanding*, Peter H. Nidditch, ed., Clarendon Press, Oxford, 1979. Bk. III, VI,§12, "In all the visible corporeal World we see no Chasms, or Gaps," p. 446.

Paul A. Lombardo, "The Great Chain of Being and the Limits to the Machiavellian Cosmos," *Journal of Thought*, Vol. 17, Spring 1982, pp. 37–52.

Arthur O. Lovejoy, "The Argument for Organic Evolution Before the 'Origin of Species,'" *Popular Science Monthly*, December 1909, pp. 499–549.

_____, "The Duality of Thomistic Theology: A Reply to Mr. Veatch," *Philosophy and Phenomenological Research*, 1946-47, Vol. VII, pp. 413-38 (cf. Henry Veatch, "A Note," etc.)

_____, *Essays in the History of Ideas*, George Braziller, New York, 1955, pp. 59, 65-6, 169-71.

_____, "Goldsmith and the Chain of Being," *Journal of the History of Ideas*, Vol. 7, January 1946, pp. 91-8.

_____, *The Great Chain of Being*, Harvard University Press, Cambridge, 1936, Harper and Brothers, New York, 1960, especially Ch. XI, "The Outcome of the History and its Moral," pp. 315-33.

_____, "Necessity and Self Sufficiency in the Thomistic Theology: A Reply to President Pegis," *Philosophy and Phenomenological Research*, 1948-49, Vol. IX, pp. 71-88.

Henri de Lubac, "'Ascent' and 'Descent' in the Work of Teilhard de Chardin," in *Pierre Teilhard de Chardin and Maurice Blondel, Correspondence*, William Whitman, tr., Herder and Herder, 1967, pp. 143-60.

Kenneth G. Lucey, "Scales of Epistemic Appraisal," *Philosophical Studies*, Vol. 29, March 1976, pp. 169-79.

Raymund Lull, *Ars Brevis Illvminati Doctoris Magistri Raymvndi Lulli*, Apud Aegydium Gorbinum, Parisiis, 1578.

J. H. Lupton and J. D. Colet, tr. and ed., *Two Treatises on the Hierarchies of Dionysius*, Translation and Introduction, London, 1869.

Winifred Lynskey, "Goldsmith and the Chain of Being," *Journal of the History of Ideas*, Vol. 6, June 1945, pp. 363-74.

Louis Mackey, "Entreatments of God: Reflections on Aquinas' Five Ways," *Franciscan Studies*, Vol. 37, 1977, pp. 103-19.

Geddes MacGregor, "Up and Down Jacob's Ladder," *The American Theosophist*, special issue, *The Relevancy of Religion*, Vol. 69, No. 5.

T. McAlindon, *Shakespeare and Decorum*, Barnes and Noble, New York, 1974.

Bernard McGinn, *The Golden Chain; A Study in the Theological Anthropology of Isaac of Stella*, Consortium Press, Washington, 1972. Cistercian Studies Series, No. 15.

_____, *Visions of the End. Apocalyptic Traditions in the Middle Ages*, Columbia University Press, New York, 1979.

Ralph McInerny, "*Esse ut Actus Intensivus* in the Writings of Cornelio Fabro," *Proceedings of the American Catholic Philosophical Association*, Vol. 38, 1964, pp. 137-41.

Ernan McMullin, "Compton on the Philosophy of Nature," *Review of Metaphysics*, Vol. 33, Summer 1979, pp. 29-58.

S. de Madariaga, *Anarchy or Hierarchy*, Macmillan, New York, 1937.

Edward P. Mahoney, "Metaphysical Foundations of the Hierarchy of Being According to Some Late-Medieval and Renaissance Philosophers," in *Philosophies of Existence, Ancient and Medieval*, Parviz Morewedge, ed., Fordham University Press, New York, 1982, pp. 165-257. Particularly helpful on a succession of medieval and Renaissance philosophers with the best discussion of the limitation of any spatial metaphor.

Sami N. Makarem, "Isma'ili and Druze Cosmogony in Relation to Plotinus and Aristotle," in *Islamic Theology and Philosophy. Studies in Honor of George F. Hourani*, Michael E. Marmura, ed., State University of New York Press, Albany, 1984, pp. 81-91.

Marvin L. Manheim, *Hierarchical Structure: A Model of Design and Planning Processes*, Massachusetts Institute of Technology Press, Cambridge, 1966.

Karl Mannheim, *Systematic Sociology*, J. S. Enos and W. A. C. Stewart, tr., Rutledge and Kegan Paul, London, 1957. Social Hierarchy: Distance of space and "Mental distance," pp. 47-54.

Dominique O. Mannoni, *Prospero and Caliban: The Psychology of Colonization*, Pamela Powesland, tr., Frederich A. Praeger, New York, 1950, Ch. I, "Dependence and Inferiority."

Lisbeth Mark, *The Book of Hierarchies: A Compendium of Steps, Ranks, Orders, Levels, Classes, Grades, Tiers, Arrays, Degrees, Lines, Divisions, Categories, Precedents, Priorities, and Other Distinctions*, William Morrow, New York, 1984.

F. David Martin, "Architecture and the Aesthetic Appreciation of the Natural Environment," *Journal of Aesthetics and Art Criticism*, Vol. 38, Winter 1979, pp. 189-90.

Abraham H. Maslow, "Basic Needs and Their Hierarchical Arrangement," *Towards A Psychology of Being*, 2nd ed., Van Nostrand Reinhold, New York, 1968, pp. 152-4.

W. Maurer, "Luthers Lehre von den drei Hierarchien und ihr mitteralterlicher Hintergrund," *Philosophische Zeitschrift*, Vol. 147, 1970, Heft 4.

K. R. Maxwell-Hyslop, "The Assyrian 'Tree of Life': A Western Branch?," in *To Illustrate the Monuments: Essays on Archeology Presented to Stuart Piggott*, J. V. S. Megaw, ed., Thames and Hudson, London, 1976, pp. 263-76.

Joseph A. Mazzeo, *Medieval Cultural Tradition in Dante's Comedy*, Cornell University Press, Ithaca, New York, 1960. Argues that "the hierarchies of being, truth, beauty, perfection, indeed of all value, are reduced to a hierarchy of light ..." p. 103.

Karl Menger, "Mensuration and Other Mathematic Connections of Observable Material," Ch. 5 in *Measurement: Definitions and Theories*, C. West Churchman and Philburn Ratoosh, ed., John Wiley and Sons, New York, 1959, esp. pp. 118-20.

Louis J. A. Mercier, "The Primacy of God's Order," *New Scholasticism*, Vol. 20, April 1946, pp. 157-75.

Kathi Meyer-Baer, *Music of the Spheres and the Dance of Death: Studies in Musical Iconology*, Princeton University Press, Princeton, New Jersey, 1970, especially on connection between degrees of angels and the heavenly spheres, pp. 118-20.

G. Michailidès, "Échelle Mystique chrétienne dessinée sur lin," *Jam'iyat al-Athar al-Qibtiyah*, Bulletin, Société d'archéologie Copte, Vol. 11, 1945, pp. 87-94.

Joseph E. Milosh, *The Scale of Perfection and the English Mystical Tradition*, University of Wisconsin Press, Madison, 1966.

Ruth Mohl, *The Three Estates in Medieval and Renaissance Literature*, Columbia University Press, New York, 1933, Ch. VII, "The Philosophy of the Estates of the World," pp. 276-340, followed by Ch. VIII, "The Defections of the Estates of the World."

Noel Molloy, "Hierarchy and Holiness: Aquinas on the Holiness of the Episcopal State," *The Thomist*, Vol. 39, April 1975, pp. 198-252.

George A. Morgan, *What Nietzsche Means*, Harvard University Press, Cambridge, Massachusettes, 1941, "Hierarchy, see Gradation, Rank," in index.

Adam Morton, "Comparatives and Degrees," *Analysis*, Vol. 44, January 1984, pp. 16-20. (Comment by C. J. F. Williams, p. 20.)

Georges Mourelos, *Bergson et les niveaux de la réalité*, Presses Universitaires de France, Paris, 1964.

Roland Mousnier, *Les Hiérarchies sociales de 1450 à nos jours*, Presses Universitaires de France, Paris, 1969.

_____, *Recherches sur la stratification sociale à Paris aux XVIIe et XVIIIe siècles*, A. Pedone, Paris, 1976.

_____, *Social Hierarchies, 1450 to the Present*, Peter Evans, tr., Margaret Clarke, ed., Schocken Books, New York, 1973.

_____, J.-R. Labatut et Y. Durand, *Problèmes de stratification sociales*, Presses Universitaires de France, Paris, 1965.

G. R. G. Mure, "Aristotle: The Scala Naturae," *An Introduction to Hegel*, Oxford University Press, 1940, 1948, pp. 16-27.

Gunnar Myrdal, *An American Dilemma*, Harper and Bros., New York, 1941, "The White Man's Rank Order of Discriminations," lessening in intensity, pp. 60-1.

Ernest Nagel, *The Structure of Science: Problems on the Logic of Scientific Explanation*, Harcourt, Brace and World, New York, 1961, on hierarchical organization in biology, pp. 432-41.

Seyyed Hossein Nasr, *Knowledge and the Sacred*, Crossroads, New York, 1981. Man as *khalifatallah* or viceregent of God in caring for the world and *pontifex*, the bridge between the ideal and the mundane.

Joseph Needham, *Integrative Levels*, Herbert Spencer Lecture, Oxford 1937.

_____, *Order and Life*, Cambridge University Press, 1936, "Hierarchical continuity of the biological order."

William Nicholls, *Jacob's Ladder: the Meaning of Worship*, John Knox Press, Richmond, Virginia, 1958.

William Nisbet, *A Golden Chaine of Time*, Edinburgh, 1650.

Hugh Nissenson, *The Tree of Life*, Harper and Row, New York, 1985.

Kathryn Johnston Noyes, *Jacob's Ladder*, Bobbs-Merrill, Indianapolis, 1965.

Anders Nygren, *Agape and Eros; a Study of the Christian Idea of Love*, A. G. Herbert, tr., Society for Promoting Christian Knowledge, London, 1937-39, pp. 375-7, 440-6, 570-5, 584-608, 616-37.

Robert L. Oldershaw, "Hierarchical Modelling in the Sciences," *Nature and Systems*, Vol. 2, September-December 1980, pp. 189-98.

A. Olding, "Polanyi's Notion of Hierarchy," *Religious Studies*, Vol. 16, March 1980, pp. 97-102.

Dominic J. O'Meara, *Structures hiérarchiques dans la pensée de Plotin*, Philosophia Antiqua, XXVII, E. J. Brill, Leiden, 1975.

_____, ed., *Neoplatonism and Christian Thought*, State University of New York Press, Albany, New York, 1981.

Edward Phillips Oppenheim, *Jacob's Ladder*, Little, Brown, Boston, 1921.

E. F. Osborn, "Pseudo-Dionysius," in *Encyclopedia of Philosophy*, Paul Edwards, ed., Macmillan, New York, 1968, Vol. 6, pp. 510-11.

Lucretia Thatcher (Perry) Osborn, *The Chain of Life*, Scribner's, London, 1925, based on writings of Henry Fairfield Osborn.

Paul Van Ostaijan, "Hiërarchie," *Krities*, Proza I., Gaston Burssew, ed., Antwerpen, Utrecht, 1929, "'Hierarchy' bitterly burlesques the military caste system through the application of segregation by rank in a brothel," E. M. Beekman, *Homeopathy of the Absurd*, Nijhoff, Hague, 1970, p. 53.

Temira Pachmuss, *F. M. Dostoevsky: Dualism and Synthesis of the Human Soul*, Southern Illinois University Press, Carbondale, 1963.

Lauran Paine, *The Hierarchy of Hell*, Hale, London, Hippocrene, New York, 1972, Ch. 17, "The Decline of Hierarchy."

Raimundo Panikkar, "Common Patterns of Eastern and Western Scholasticism," *Diogenes*, Fall 1973, No. 83, pp. 103-13.

Erwin Panofsky, *Gothic Architecture and Scholasticism*, Doubleday, Garden City, New York (also World Publishing, New York, 1973) on the order of a whole into parts by division into book, chapter, section, a style reflecting "a system of logical subordination," pp. 30-2.

_____, *Abbot Suger on the Abbey Church of St. Denis*, Princeton University Press, Princeton, New Jersey, 1946. For criticism of this and other theories, see Paul Frankl, *Gothic Architecture*, Penguin Books, Harmondsworth, Middlesex, 1962, "The Gothic Style and Scholasticism," pp. 260-4.

_____, "Abbot Suger of St. Denis," Ch. 3 in *Meaning in the Visual Arts*, Doubleday Anchor A59, Doubleday, Garden City, New York, 1957, pp. 108-45, especially on the metaphysics of light and the justification of material beauty, pp. 726-33. *Abbot Suger on the Abbey Church of St. Denis*, Princeton University Press, Princeton, New Jersey, 1946.

Robert Ezra Park, *Human Communities, The City and Human Ecology*, The Free Press, Glencoe, Illinois, 1952.

Louis B. Pascoe, S.J., *Jean Genson: Principles of Church Reform*, E. J. Brill, Leiden, 1973.

C. A. Patrides, "Hierarchy and Order," *Dictionary of the History of Ideas*, P. P. Wiener, ed., Scribner's, New York, 1973, 2, pp. 434-9.

_____, *Milton and the Christian Tradition*, Oxford University Press, London, 1966, Ch. III.

_____, "The Numerological Approach to Cosmic Order during the English Renaissance, *Isis*, pp. 391-7.

_____, *The Phoenix and the Ladder: The Rise and Decline of the Christian View of History*, University of California Press, Berkeley, 1964.

_____, "Renaissance Thought on the Celestial Hierarchy: The Decline of a Tradition," *Journal of the History of Ideas*, Vol. 20, 1959, pp. 155-66.

_____, "Renaissance Views on the Unconfused Orders Angellick," *Journal of the History of Ideas*, Vol. 23, April-June 1962, pp. 265-7.

Howard Hunt Pattee, *Hierarchy Theory: the Challenge of Complex Systems*, Braziller, New York, 1973.

_____, "The Problem of Biological Hierarchy," in *Towards a Theoretical Biology*, C. H. Waddington, ed., Vol. 3, Aldine, Chicago, 1970, pp. 117-36.

A. R. Peacocke, "Nature's Hierarchies - 'Things Visible and Invisible,'" in *Creation and the World of Science*, Clarendon Press, Oxford, 1979, pp. 112-46.

Anton C. Pegis, "Autonomy and Necessity: A Rejoinder to Professor Lovejoy," *Philosophy and Phenomenological Research*, 1948-49, Vol. IX, pp. 89-97.

_____, "Four Medieval Ways to God," *Monist*, Vol. 54, July 1970, pp. 317-58.

_____, "*Principale Volitum*: Some Notes on a Supposed Thomistic Contradiction," *Philosophy and Phenomenalistic Research*, 1948-49, Vol. IX, pp. 51-70.

Robert L. Perkins, "Kierkegaard's Critique of the 'Bourgeois State,'" *Inquiry*, Vol. 27, July 1984, pp. 207-18.

John Platt, "Hierarchical Growth," *Science and Public Affairs*, Vol. XXVI, No. 9, November 1970, pp. 2-4, 46-8.

Helmuth Plessner, *Die Stufen des Organischen und der Mensch: Einleitung* in die philosophische Anthropologie, 1. Aufl., Frankfurt am Main; Suhr Kamp, 1981.

Drei Sphaere: Pflanze, Tier, Mensch. "Ein Buch mit dem Titel *Stufen des Organischen* machte sich angesichts solcher Tendenzen biologischer Forschung anachronistischer Sympathien verdächtig. Stufen? Ist der Autor etwa evolutionsfeindlich, wohl gar ein Ahänger idealischer Morphologie. Klingt Stufen nicht nach Hierarchie der Formen Pflanze, Tier, Mensch, für die schon Aristoteles das Modell geliefert hat?" Die Idee von Scheler ist dass Mensch ist Mensch durch seine Beziehung zu Gott. IX-XI

Postel, Guillaume, *Absconditorum a Constitutione mundi clavis* ..., Basel, 1547.

_____, *Astronomicae considerationis breuissima synopsis*, apud Gulielmum Cavellat, Lvtetiae, 1552.

_____, *Compendiaria Grammatices Hebraicae Introdvctio* ..., Martinus Iuuenis, Parisiis, 1552.

_____, *Liber De Cavsis sev de principiis* ..., apud Sebastianum Niuellium, Parisiis, MDLII.

_____, *Musices ex Theorica ad praxim aptatae compendium*, apud Gulielmum Cavellat, Lvtetiae, 1552.

_____, *Tabvla Aeternae Ordinationis Qvaternario constitvto inter svmmae expansionis et coactionis terminos, expositae* ..., s.l., s.d.

_____, *Tabvla Restitvtionis ommivm constitvtionvm natvralivm et svpernatvralium rerum* ..., apud Ioannem Gueullart, Paris, s.d.

_____, *Theoricae Arithmetices compendium* ..., apud Gulielmum Cavellat, Lvtetiae, 1552.

_____, *Vincvlvm mundi* ..., Exemplaria prostant sub ciconiis in vico Iacobaeo, Parisiis, 1552.

Robert Vance Presthus, *The Organizational Society*, A. A. Knopf, New York, 1962. Hierarchy defined as a linear order of society: "The Bureaucratic Model," pp. 30 ff.

_____, *Men at the Top: a Study in Community Power*, Oxford University Press, New York, 1964.

_____, *Elites in the Policy Process Cordon*, Cambridge University Press, Cambridge, 1974.

Karl H. Pribam, "Transcending the Mind/Brain Problem," *Zygon*, Vol. 14, June 1979, pp. 103-24.

F. E. L. Priestley, "'Order, Union, Full Consent of Things!'" *University of Toronto Quarterly*, Vol. XLII, No. 1, Fall, 1972, pp. 1-13.

_____, "Pope and the Great Chain of Being," *Essays in English Literature from the Renaissance to the Victorian Age Presented to A. S. P. Woodhouse*, Miller MacLure and F. W. Watt, ed., University of Toronto Press, Toronto, 1964.

I. Prigogine and G. Nicolis, "Biological Order, Structure and Instabilities," *Quarterly Reviews of Biophysics*, Vol. 4, 1971, pp. 107-48.

Pseudo-Chrysostom, "Sermon VI for Holy Week," translated in Henri de Lubac, S.J., *Catholicism, A Study of Dogma in Relation to the Corporate Destiny of Mankind*, Mentor-Omega, New York, 1964, pp. 279-80; couples the image of the Tree as root metaphor for the cosmos and salvation with the "stairway of Jacob, where angels pass up and down."

J. Roland E. Ramirez, "The Ultimate Why of Evolution," *New Scholasticism*, Vol. 33, October 1959, pp. 446-92.

H. Rausch, "Hierarchie," *Historisches Wörterbuch der Philosophie*, ed. Joachim Ritter, Schwabe, Stuttgart, 1974, Bd. 3, pp. 1123-26. Dr. Rausch traces the theology of Hierarchy from Pseudo-Dionysius to Luther, indicating that this influence can be seen in the commentaries on the Areopogite by Eriugena, Grosseteste, Albertus Magnus, Thomas Aquinas. The secularized concept continued through Hegel (and transferred by Saint-Simon and Comte to society) to exercise great influence. As an ethical and ontological principle of order Rausch cites Fechner, Wundt, Driesch, N. Hartmann, Scheler, Cassirer, Jaspers, K. Mannheim. It is interesting and significant to note the change since R. Eisler, *Wörterbuch der Philosophischen Begriffe*, 3te Aufl., which has no article Hierarchie, Rangordnung, Abstuffung, and refers from Überordnung (logische) to "Subordination: Un-

terordnung eines Begriffes unter einem umfangreicheren; dieser ist dem
subordinierten Begriff superordiniert. Vgl. Sigwart, *Logik*, I, 343 ff."
The only reference to the theological meanings is the briefest reference
to the Arian subordination of Logos to Godhead, "Subordinationismus."

Arnold W. Ravin, "Transformations in Biology," a review of François Jacob, *La
Logique du Vivant*, *Science*, Vol. 172, 23 April 1971, pp. 364-6.

Marjorie Rawlings, *Jacob's Ladder*, University of Miami Press, Coral Gables,
1950; also "Jacob' Ladder," in *When the Wippoorwill-*, Scribner's, New
York, 1940.

Marjorie Reeves, *The Influence of Prophecy in the Later Middle Ages: A Study
of Joachimism*, Clarendon Press, Oxford, 1969. On the influence of Joachim
of Fiora's figure of the Tree of Life, the Jesse Tree, and the Jacob Ladder.

_____ and B. Hirsch-Reich, *The Figurae of Joachim of Fiore*, Oxford, 1970.
On the tree of life as dominant image of Joachim's vision of past and future.

Bernhard Rensch, *Biophilosophy*, C. A. M. Sym, tr., Columbia University Press,
New York, 1971, on "the hierarchical order of elements in organisms," pp.
48-9. Between animate and inanimate are viruses, etc., which have structural features of living matter but lack a metabolism of their own.

Roger E. Reynolds, "'At Sixes and Sevens'--And Eights and Nines: The Sacred
Mathematics of Sacred Orders in the Early Middle Ages," *Speculum* Vol.
LIV, No. 4, October 1979, pp. 669-84.

Richardi a Sancto Victore *Opera Omnia*, Migne, *Patrologia Latina*, Vol. 196,
1855. *Tractatus de Gradibus Charitatis*, 1195-1207, *De Quatuor Gradibus
Violentae Charitatis*, 1207-24.

A. D. Ritchie, *Studies in the History and Methods of the Sciences*, The University Press, Edinburgh, 1958, 'The Great Chain of Being' pp. 96-103, influence on alchemy produced fallacies, which however were necessary to
progress in chemistry.

_____, "George Berkeley's *Siris*: The Philosophy of the Great Chain of Be-
ing and Alchemical Theory," *Proceedings of the British Academy*, Vol. 40,
1954, pp. 41-55.

Fritz-Joachim von Rintelen, *Der Aufstieg im Geiste: von Dionysos zu Apollon*,
2. ed., Metopen-Verlag, Frankfurt, 1968.

_____, "Augustine: The Ascent in Value Towards God," *Augustinian Studies*,
Vol. 2, 1971, pp. 155-78.

James B. Robinson, "The Price of Harmony," in *Parabola, Hierarchy*, Vol IX, No.
1, Winter 1984, pp. 71-8.

Maxime Rodinson, "Dante et l'Islam d'après des travaux récents," *Revue de
l'histoire des religions*, Vol. 140, 1951, pp. 203-35.

Donald W. Rogers, "The Three Patterns of Western Civilization," *Main Currents in Modern Thought*, March-April 1969, Vol. 25, No. 4, pp. 98-109, contrasting hierarchic patterns to atomic-mechanical and organic as to cause, part-whole relation, locus of reality, test-of-truth, genesis, change and time.

Richard Rolle, *The Fire of Love and the Mending of Life*, translated with an Introduction by M. L. del Mastro, Image Books, Doubleday, Garden City, New York, 1981.

Annibale Romei, "Of Universal Proportion," from *The Courtiers Academy*, J. Kepers, tr., 1598, in *The Frame of Order: An Outline of Elizabethan Belief Taken From Treatises of the Late Sixteenth Century*, James Winny, ed., George Allen and Unwin, London, 1957, pp. 197-212.

René Roques, *L'Univers Dionysien, Structure Hiérarchique du Monde selon le Pseudo-Denys*, Aubier, 1954; Cerf, Paris, 1983.

Paul Rorem, "The Place of 'The Mystical Theology' in the Pseudo-Dionysian Corpus," *Dionysius*, Vol. 4, December 1980, pp. 87-97.

Alexander Rosenberg, "Species Notions and the Theoretical Hierarchy of Biology," *Nature and System: Philosophical Studies of Natural and Artificial Systems*, Vol. 2, September-December 1980, pp. 163-72.

James F. Ross, "The Fallacious Bases of Two Theistic Paradoxes," February 1963, mimeographed for APA Western meeting, a formal definition of "metaphysical dependence," close to the medieval concept of reality-levels.

_____, *Philosophical Theology*, Bobbs-Merrill, Indianapolis, 1969, pp. 187-94.

Heribert Rossmann, *Die Hierarchie der Welt; Gestalt und System des Franz von Meyronnes*, O.F.M. mit besonder Berücksichtigung seiner Schopfungslehre, D. Coelde, Werl/Westf., 1972. Franziskanische Forschung, Heft 23. (München thesis, 1968).

William H. Rueckert, *Kenneth Burke and the Drama of Human Relations*, University of Minneapolis Press, Minneapolis, Minnesota, 1963.

Nicholaas A. Rupke, *The Great Chain of History: William Buckland and the English School of Geology (1814-1849)*, Clarendon Press, Oxford, 1983.

Bertrand Russell, *Introduction to Mathematical Philosophy*, George Allen and Unwin, London 1950, pp. 135-7.

_____, *Logic and Knowledge, Essays 1901-1950*, R. C. Marsh, ed., George Allen and Unwin, London, 1956, "Mathematical Logic as Based on the Theory of Types," originally in the *American Journal of Mathematics*, 1908, pp. 59-102, esp., "The Hierarchy of Types," pp. 75-80.

_____, *The Principles of Mathematics*, George Allen and Unwin, London, Seventh Impression, 1956, Appendix B, "The Doctrine of Types," pp. 523-8.

Arich Sachs, "Samuel Johnson and the Cosmic Hierarhcy," *Scripta Hierosolymitana*, Vol. XVII, *Studies in English Language and Literature*, A. Shalvi and A. A. Medilow, ed., Jerusalem, 1966, pp. 137-54.

Jonas Salk, "The Next Evolutionary Step in the Ascent of Man in the Cosmos," *Leonardo*, special issue *Jacob Bronowski: A Retrospective*, Vol. 18, No. 4, 1985, pp. 237-42.

Sven Sandström, *Levels of Unreality: Studies in Structure and Construction in Italian Mural Painting During the Renaissance*, Acta Universitatis Upsaliensis, Uppsala, Almqvist and Wiksell, 1963.

David Sanford, "Degrees of Perfection, Argument for the Existence of God," *Encyclopedia of Philosophy*, Paul Edwards, ed., Macmillan, New York, 1966, Vol. 3, pp. 324-6.

George Santayana, *The Idler and His Works*, Daniel Cory, ed., George Brazeller, New York, 1957. "On Metaphysical Projection by which Existence is referred to the Non-Existent as to its Ground," pp. 116-21, "The Ontological Hierarchy: This hierarchy marks the steps of a spiritual progress."

Gertrude Sartory (Reideck), *Die hierarchische Struktur der Ehe*, K. Zink, München, 1953. Münchener theologische Studien 3. Kanonistische Abteiling, 3. Bd.

Denis Saurat, *Milton et le materialisme chrétien en Angleterre*, Editions Rieder, Paris, 1928, Ch. V, pp. 37-43.

Harold Kistler Schilling, *The New Consciousness in Science and Religion*, United Church Press, Philadelphia, 1973, on absence of lowest and highest level, pp. 110-13.

Jacques Schlanger, *La Philosophie de Salomon Ibn Gabirol*, E. J. Brill, Leiden, 1968.

Richard Schneider, *Eckhart's Doctrine of the Transcendental Perfections in God and Creatures*, Ph.D. dissertation, University of Toronto, 1965, particularly Ch. 10, "The Relation between the Superior and the Inferior."

Rolf Schock, "Classifications and Hierarchies," *Zeitschrift für allegemeine Wissenschaftstheorie*, Vol. 10, 1979, pp. 98-106.

Gershom Scholem, *Major Trends in Jewish Mysticism*, Schocken Books, New York, 1941.

_____, *On the Kabbalah and Its Symbolism*, Ralph Manheim, tr., Schocken Books, New York, 1965.

_____, *The Messianic Idea in Judaism*, Schocken Books, New York, 1974.

E. F. Schumacher, *A Guide for the Perplexed*, Harper and Row, New York, 1979, Perennial Library, 1979.

J. P. Scott, articles "Social hierarchy" and "Cosmology" in *McGraw-Hill Encyclopedia of Science and Technology*, 1960, Vol. 3, pp. 504-05 and Vol. 12, pp. 404-05.

John Duns Scotus, *God and Creatures: The Quodlibetal Questions*, Felix Alluntis and Allan B. Wolter, ed., Princeton University Press, Princeton, 1975, Question 19.17 and 19.26 on hierarchy as dependence relation, e.g. of caused or cause, of imperfect or perfect, of dependent or independent pp. 422-5. See also Father Wolter's commentary on "ontological priority," Duns Scotus, *Philosophical Writings*, Nelson, Edinburgh, 1962, pp. 174-80.

Philibert Secretan, "Edith Stein on the Order and Chain of Being," in *Analecta Husserliana, The Great Chain of Being in Phenomenology*, Angela Ales Bello, ed., Reidel, Dordrecht, 1981, pp. 113-23.

Marie-Rose Séguy, ed., *The Miraculous Journey of Mahomet. Mirâj Nâmeh*, The Scholar Press, London, 1979.

Harlow Shapley, *Of Stars and Men: the Human Response to an Expanding Universe*, Washington Square Press, New York, 1960. Organization clarified from -5 to +9, with no illustration of either bottom or top level of material systems, pp. 22-8.

Fadlou Shehadi, "Theism, Mysticism and Scientific History in Ibn Khaldun," in *Islamic Theology and Philosophy. Studies in Honor of George F. Hourani*, Michael E. Marmura, ed., State University of New York Press, Albany, New York, 1984, pp. 265-79.

Jacqueline Shohet, *Jacob's Ladder*, Roy Publishers, New York, 1951.

Paul N. Siegel, "English Humanism and the New Tudor Aristocracy," *Journal of the History of Ideas*, Vol. 13, October 1952, pp. 450-68.

_____, "The Petrarchan Sonneteers and New-Platonic Love," *Studies in Philology*, 1945, Vol. 42, pp. 164-82.

Paul E. Sigmund, "Hierarchy, Equality, and Consent in Medieval Christian Thought," in *Equality*, *Nomos* IX, Yearbook of the American Society for Political and Legal Philosophy, J. Roland Pennock and John W. Chapman, ed., Atherton Press, New York, 1967, pp. 134-53.

Otto von Simson, *The Gothic Cathedral: Origins of Gothic Architecture and the Medieval Concept of Order*, Bollingen Series XLVIII, Pantheon Books, New York, Second Ed., 1962, Part I, "Gothic Design and the Medieval Concept of Order: 1 Gothic Form, 2 Measure and Light," Part II, 3, "Suger of St. Denis."

Edmund Ware Sinnott, *The Bridge of Life: From Matter to Spirit*, Simon and Schuster, New York, 1966. Although the connotation is going from lowest level, matter, to highest, God, the metaphor is not a ladder but a bridge. Rather than levels, each, matter, life, mind, soul, spirit, the Divine, are footings or abutments, connected to the next by a span of a bridge.

Henryk Skolismowski, "Problems of Rationality in Biology," *Studies in the Philosophy of Biology*, Theodosius G. Dobzhansky and Francisco J. Ayala, ed., Macmillan, London, 1974, pp. 205-25.

J. J. C. Smart, "Benevolence as an Over-riding Attitude," *Australasian Journal of Philosophy*, Vol. 55, August 1977, pp. 127-35.

Ninian Smart, *Doctrine and Argument in Indian Philosophy*, George Allen and Unwin, London, 1964. On synthesis by subordination of lower to higher truth because the higher cannot be contradicted, pp. 100-01, etc.

Huston Smith, *Forgotten Truth: The Primordial Tradition*, Harper and Row, New York, 1976, "a vigorous defense of the Great Chain" in Ch. 3 "The Levels of Reality," and Ch. 4, "The Levels of Selfhood," pp. 34-95.

_____, "Perennial Philosophy, Primordial Tradition," *International Philosophical Quarterly*, Vol. 22, June 1982, pp. 115-32.

Frederick Sontag, *Divine Perfection: Possible Ideas of God*, Harper, New York, 1972.

Oswald Spengler, *The Hour of Decision*, Charles Francis Atkinson, tr., A. A. Knopf, New York, 1934, "Society as order of rank," pp. 88-104.

Adin Steinsaltz, "Becoming Unstable: Hierarchy," in *Parabola, Hierarchy*, Vol. IX, No. 1, Winter 1984, pp. 8-15.

James T. Stewart, "Renaissance Psychology and the Ladder of Love in Castiglione and Spenser," *Journal of English and Germanic Philology*, 1957, Vol. 56, pp. 225-30.

T. L. Sutter, *Hierarchy and Democracy in Australia, 1788-1870: the Formation of Australian Catholicism*, Cambridge University Press, 1965.

Robert Sweeney, "The 'Great Chain of Being' in Scheler's Philosophy," in *Analecta Husserliana, The Great Chain of Being in Phenomenology*, Angela Ales Bello, ed., Reidel, Dordrecht, 1981, pp. 99-112.

Unto Tähtinen, *Indian Traditional Values*, Humanities Press, New Jersey, 1983, Ch. 6, pp. 61-77, and "Hierarchy of Values," pp. 86-90.

A. E. Taylor, *The Faith of a Moralist*, Macmillan, London, 1930, Vol. I, pp. 360-4. A many-levelled whole of various orders superimposed upon each other.

Pierre Teilhard de Chardin, *The Phenomenon of Man*, Harper and Row, New York, 1959, Ch. II, Sec. 3, "The Tree of Life," pp. 122-40.

Irving Thalberg, "Hierarchical Analyses of Unfree Action," *Canadian Journal of Philosophy*, Vol. 8, June 1978, pp. 211-26.

E. M. W. Tillyard, *The Elizabethan World Picture*, Random House, New York, n.d., Ch. 4, "The Chain of Being." etc.

Alexandre Timoni, "Des anges des démons, des esprits et des génies d'après les Musulmans," *Journal Asiatique*, 1856, pp. 147-63.

Stephan Toulmin and June Goodfield, *The Discovery of Time*, Harper Torchbook, Harper, New York, 1965, pp. 50-3, 66-7, 96-7.

Henri Tracol, "The Taste for Things That are True," in *Parabola, Hierarchy*, Vol. IX, No. 1, Winter 1984, pp. 22-5.

Arthur Cheney Train, *Jacob's Ladder*, Scribner's, New York, 1935.

Barbara Howard Traister, *Heavenly Necromancers. The Magician in English Renaissance Drama*, University of Missouri Press, Columbia, 1984.

P. L. Travers, "Tarot Card No. 12: The Hanged Man," in *Parabola, Hierarchy*, Vol. IX, No. 1, Winter 1984, p. 47.

Thure von Uexküll, *Der Mensch und die Natur, Grundzüge einer Naturphilosophie*, Franke, Bern.
Warum verschiedene "Schlichten-" oder "Stufen-" theorien? Auf Grunde des Dualismus kann die psycho-physische Einheit des Menschen nicht gelöst sein. pp 68-9.
"Von der Stufe des Vegetiven Lebens," "Von der Stufe des Sensitiven Lebens," "Von der Stufe des Menschlichen Lebens," pp. 169-247.

Ulpian, "de gradibus cognationium," in *Jurisprudentiae Anteiustinianae quae supersunt*, Ph. Eduardus Hunschka, ed., Teubner, Leipzig, 1886, pp. 627f.

J. O. Urmson, "On Grading," *Logic and Language*, Second Series, Antony Flew, ed., Basil Blackwell, Oxford, 1959, pp. 159-86.

Ulrich Valeske, *Hierarchia Veritatum: theologiegeschichtliche Hintergründe und mögliche Konsegrenzen eines Hinweises im Ökumenismusdekret des II. Vatikanischen Konzils zum zwischenkirchlichen Gespräch, Claudius*, München, 1968.

Jacques Van Luik, *Jacob's Ladder to a Balloon and other poems*, Keith Armstrong, ed., Circle Books, Oxford, 1969.

A. C. Van Melsen, *Science and Technology*, VII, 3, "The Hierarchy of Being," Duquesne University Press, Pittsburgh, 1961, pp. 146-70.

Gertrude Wyckoff Van Pelt, M.D., *Hierarchies: The Cosmic Ladder of Life*, Point Loma Publications, San Diego, 1975.

Julio Cesare Vanini, *Amphitheatrum aeternae providentiae divino-magicum ...*, Lyon, de Harsy, 1615.

Cesare Vasoli, *Immagini umanistiche*, Morano Editore, Napoli, 1983.

Henry Veatch, "A Note on the Metaphysical Grounds for Freedom, With Special Reference to Professor Lovejoy's Thesis in 'The Great Chain of Being,'" *Philosophy and Phenomenological Research*, 1946-47, Vol. VII, pp. 391-412. Cf. Arthur O. Lovejoy, "The Duality," etc.

G. de Vaucouleurs, "The Case for a Hierarchical Cosmology," *Science*, Vol. 167, No. 3922, 27 February 1970, pp. 1203-13.

Gregory Vlastos, "Slavery in Plato's Thought," *The Philosophical Review*, Vol. L, No. 3, May 1941, pp. 239-304.

_____, "Degrees of Reality in Plato," *New Essays on Plato and Aristotle*, R. Bambrough, ed., London and New York, 1965, pp. 1-19.

Voltaire, *Dictionnaire Philosophique*, Raymond Naves, ed., Garnier Frères, Paris, 1936, pp. 141-4.

C. H. Waddington, *Towards a Theoretical Biology*, Vol. 1-4, University of Edinburgh, Edinburgh, and Aldine, Chicago, 1968-72.

Daniel Pickering Walker, *Spiritual and demonic Magic from Ficino to Campanella*, London, Warburg Institute, University of London, 1958, *Warburg Institute Studies*, Vol. V.

C. C. J. Webb, *History of Philosophy*, Oxford University Press, London, 1956, on the problem of Judaism and Neoplatonism, how to bridge between God and man. The setting in which it makes sense for Augustine to say that the Platonists had everything, the "light and life of man:" but not the ... "Word ... made flesh (who) dwelt among us." (*Confessions*, VII, c. 9), pp. 76-88.

Anders Wedberg, "How Carnap Built the World in 1928," *Synthèse*, Vol. 25, April 1973, pp. 337-71.

Paul A. Weiss, *Hierarchically Organized Systems in Theory and Practice*, with contributions by H. K. Buechner et al., Hafner, New York, 1971.

Albert N. Wells, *Pascal's Recovery of Man's Wholeness*, John Knox Press, Richmond, 1965, Ch. I, "A Principle of Order," pp. 23-37; rank ordering of body: mind: chartiy; without continuity.

W. H. Werkmeister, "Kant, Nicolai Hartmann, and the Great Chain of Being," in *Analecta Husserliana*, Angela Ales Bello, ed., Reidel, Dordrecht, 1981, pp. 69-97.

_____, "Problems of Value Theory," *Philosophy and Phenomenological Research*, Vol. 12, June 1952, pp. 495-512.

John Wesley, *A Survey of the Wisdom of God in the Creation, or A Compendium of Natural Philosophy*, 3rd ed., J. Fry, London, 1777, Vol. IV, Ch. II, "Of the relative Perfection of Beings," pp. 70-4; "General View of the gradual progression of Beings," Ch. III, pp. 75-102; "Continuation of the gradual Progression of Beings," pp. 103-14.

Jan Willem van de Wetering, "Master : Disciple or how to beg for problems," in *Parabola, Hierarchy*, Vol. IX, No. 1, Winter 1984, pp. 26-32.

Lancelot Law Whyte, Albert G. Wilson, *Hierarchical Structures*, Donna Wilson, ed., American Elsevir, 1969.

Philip P. Wiener, "Towards Commemorating the Centenary of Arthur O. Lovejoy's Birthday (October 10, 1873)," *Journal of the History of Ideas*, Vol. XXXIV, No. 4, October-December 1973, pp. 591-8.

Patry Williams (ps. for Marguerite Patry and Dorothy Frances Williams), *Jacob's Ladder*, Hurst and Blackett, London, 1929.

Daniel J. Wilson, "Arthur O. Lovejoy and the Moral of *The Great Chain of Being*," *Journal of the History of Ideas*, Vol. 41, April-June 1980, pp. 249-65.

Thomas Wilson, *Jacob's Ladder, or A Short Treatise laying forth distinctly the severall degrees of God's eternall purpose, whereby His grace descends upon the elect, and the elect ascend to the predestinate glory....*, W. Hall for N. Butler, London, 1611.

Colwyn Williamson and Stuart Brown, "The Social Order and the Natural Order," *The Aristotelian Society*, Supplementary Volume LII, Compton Press, Tisbury, Wilts, 1978, pp. 109-41.

James Winny, ed., *The Frame of Order*, George Allen and Unwin, London, 1957.

Ryszard Wiśnowski, "The Hierarchy of Goods in the Ethics of Wladyslaw Tatarkiewicz," *Etyka*, 1978, pp. 131-46.

Emil Wolff, *Die goldene Kette: Die Aurea Catena Homeri in der englischen Literatur van Chaucer bis Wordsworth*, Hansischer Gildenverlag, Hamburg, 1947.

Karol Wojtyta, Pope John Paul II, "The Degrees of Being from the Point of View of Phenomenology of Action," in Angela Ales Bello, ed., *The Great Chain of Being in Phenomenology*, Reidel, Dordrecht, 1981, pp. 125-30.

Frances A. Yates, *The Art of Memory*, The University of Chicago Press, Chicago, 1974.

_____, *Astraea. The Imperial Theme in the Sixteenth Century*, Routledge and Kegan Paul, London, 1975.

_____, *Lull and Bruno. Collective Essays*, Routledge and Kegan Paul, London, 1982.

Philip Zaleski, "The Flattened Cosmos," in *Parabola, Hierarchy*, Vol. IX, No. 1, Winter 1984, pp. 54-7.

426

430

Marion Leathers Kuntz is Fuller E. Callaway Distinguished Professor at Georgia State University, Atlanta, and also Regents' and Research Professor. She is known in Europe and America for her work in Renaissance studies. In 1982 she organized an international congress held at the Fondazione Giorgio Cini, in honor of the fourth centenary of the death of Guillaume Postel and is the editor of the soon to be published *Atti* of this Congress. She is the author of *Colloquium of the Seven About Secrets of the Sublime* of Jean Bodin, the first complete translation of this important sixteenth-century Latin text, and *Guillaume Postel: Prophet of the Restitution of All Things*, and also numerous articles on Renaissance and classical topics.

Paul Grimley Kuntz, Professor Emeritus of Philosophy, Emory University, is known for his studies of order, including *The Concept of Order*, *Lotze's System of Metaphysics*, *Alfred North Whitehead*, and *Bertrand Russell*. His articles, about a hundred in number, have been in American philosophy and modern philosophy generally, medieval philosophy, aesthetics, and in such recently discovered areas as philosophy of sport.

Richard H. Schlagel

FROM MYTH TO THE MODERN MIND
A Study of the Origins and the Growth of Scientific Thought
Volume I: Animism to Archimedes

American University Studies: Series V (Philosophy), Vol. 12
ISBN 0-8204-0219-2   281 pp.   hardback   US $ 30,00

Recommended price - alterations reserved

Written before the collapse of the research program of the logical positivists and the resurgent interest in the development of scientific thought as exemplified in analyses of actual historical transitions, this book is unique in undertaking to elucidate the *cognitive developments and their causes* underlying the history of science. Beginning with a description of forms of primitive mentality, as exemplified historically in the earlier animistic, mythopoetic, and theogonic traditions, the present volume identifies the transformations in the *thought processes* inherent in the emergence and the growth of scientific rationalism from the Presocraties through Plato and Aristotle to Archimedes, the culminating scientific figure in the ancient world.

Contents: The purpose of the present volume is to contrast scientific rationalism with the earlier animistic, mythopoetic, and theogonic traditions, tracing the origins and the growth of scientific thought in the works of the Presocratics, Plato and Aristotle, to Archimedes.

PETER LANG PUBLISHING, INC.
62 West 45th Street
USA - New York, NY 10036